LU "Children are Sunday Sunday"

P338 - list of all her medical problems also health
P347 also health
P357 health
P358

Nov/Dec
Sim cally -
answered about
people today -
letters - got email -
can't retrieve penicillis -
email how would aus
be retrieved.

√ Lippia — es
— all
to
never done

Philologist ? LU
Pedagogy

Dorothy Day LU
2015 mentioned by Pope

Syphilis
waxerma
gonorrhea

LU A.J. Liebling
"too many minor characters"
ausculptim of me
of her stories
felt that way about
book

Jean Stafford

Jean Stafford

A BIOGRAPHY

BY

DAVID ROBERTS

Chatto & Windus
LONDON

Published in 1988 by
Chatto & Windus Limited
30 Bedford Square
London WC1B 3SG

A CIP catalogue record for this book is available from the British Library.

ISBN 0 7011 3010 5

The author is grateful for permission to include the following previously copyrighted material:

Excerpts from "An Influx of Poets" by Jean Stafford. Copyright © 1978 by Jean Stafford Liebling. First
published in *The New Yorker*. Reprinted by permission of the Estate of Jean Stafford Liebling and *The New
Yorker*.

Excerpts from "Unwanted", "Jean Stafford, a Letter", and "Louisiana State University in 1940" from
Day by Day by Robert Lowell. Copyright © 1975, 1976, 1977 by Robert Lowell. Reprinted by permission
of Farrar, Straus & Giroux, Inc.

Excerpt from "To Delmore Schwartz" from *Life Studies* by Robert Lowell. Copyright © 1956, 1959 by
Robert Lowell. Reprinted by permission of Farrar, Straus & Giroux, Inc., and Faber and Faber, Limited,
Publishers.

Excerpts from the unpublished letters of Robert Lowell and Charlotte Lowell are reprinted with the
permission of the Lowell Estate. Copyright © 1988 by Caroline Lowell, Harriet Lowell, and Sheridan
Lowell.

Eight lines from "Her Dead Brother" from *The Mills of the Kavanaughs* by Robert Lowell. Copyright ©
1947, 1975 by Robert Lowell. Reprinted by permission of Harcourt Brace Jovanovich, Inc., and Faber and
Faber, Limited, Publishers.

Excerpts from letters written by employees of Harcourt Brace Jovanovich, Inc. are reprinted by permission of the publisher.

With love, to my parents,
Walter and Janet Roberts,
for the verities of Bluebell Avenue

Contents

Preface

I FIRST READ Jean Stafford's work in 1975, in conjunction with a visit to Damariscotta Mills, the exquisite town in Maine to which Stafford had moved thirty years earlier at the age of thirty, newly rich from her writing, and where she was planning to be happy for the rest of her life. Her stay there lasted a year; her happiness, even less.

That encounter with Stafford's two short stories set in Maine, "A Country Love Story" and "Polite Conversation," introduced me to a writer whose command of English prose — and of the human heart — left me dumb with admiration. Visiting the scene of an author's life, however, can be a naively literal business. A blustery November trudge I once took along Cape Cod's outer coast served, for me, only to tack a footnote to Henry David Thoreau's sly transcendentalisms; on a sunny day in April the woods behind Robert Frost's farmhouse in Derry, New Hampshire, seemed too genial to mirror the poet's dark vision. And from her upstairs bedroom in Amherst, Massachusetts, Emily Dickinson has wholly vanished.

Yet in Damariscotta Mills, Stafford's yearning for a brave new life, crossed with the rueful self-knowledge that prevented it, sprang upon me in the most visceral way as I walked past the places in her stories: the alewife weirs, the lily-thick lake, the sharp brick Catholic church with its graveyard, the handsome clapboard house she had bought with her unexpected earnings. I wanted to know more about this enigmatic, thwarted writer. I wanted to read everything she had written.

It was odd that I had never read Stafford before, for she had lived from age ten to age twenty-one in Boulder, Colorado, the town in which I had grown up. In part because of her caustic ambivalence toward the West, the best writer ever to come out of Colorado is not honored in her own land. During the 1950s, when I was an adolescent, my parents subscribed to *The New Yorker,* which at the time was publishing Stafford's mordant stories about her youth in a thinly disguised Boulder. Yet my parents do not remember reading those stories — and have, in fact, no recollection of hearing Stafford's name at the cocktail parties hosted by locals who had gone to high school with her. It was not until I, like Stafford, had moved East for good that I ever heard of her.

In 1983 I wrote an article about Stafford for the *Boston Globe.* In turn, my research nudged me toward the prospect of attempting a biography. I had browsed through her papers in the Norlin Library at the University of Colorado, where I was delighted to find that even her ephemeral writings were masterly and unique. I had developed something like a "crush" on Jean Stafford, who had died four years earlier and whom I had never met. Some photographs that documented her icy beauty as a young woman no doubt contributed to my attachment.

Most biographers, I suspect, begin in infatuation; this is perhaps a good thing, for passion can carry one through the mountainous frustrations and disappointments that inevitably attend one's toil. By the time my own labors were coming to an end, I had, like so many of the friends of her last two decades, reached a state of loyal but bemused irritation at the difficult person Stafford eventually became, at the transparent excuses she made for not writing. I like to think that I never lapsed into the hostile possessiveness that some biographers who live too long with their subjects seem to adopt. As to her prose, I end as I began —with the strongest admiration for her technique and her vision, and with sadness that she could not finish what she promised the world.

Much of the time while I was researching and writing, Jean Stafford was looking over my shoulder, usually with a raised eyebrow. It is harrowing to try to probe the soul of so profoundly self-aware a person as Stafford. Constructing an explanation from one's meager collection of facts — this is the impossible task of the biographer. Of course all "lives" are fictions, but as many biographers have pointed out, unlike novelists, we are not free to invent our details.

To do justice to the ambiguity of those details — to confess one's hesitations, to entertain thoughts of the myriad other ways those quiddities could be glued together — is half of the biographer's daunting mandate. The other half is not to surrender to that ambiguity — not to mire oneself in detail, but rather to craft a narrative that comprehends it.

It is no good, at the end, to glance back over one's shoulder — in my case, to look Stafford in the face and imagine her eyebrow lowered to benign indifference. The truest biography is not likely to please its subject. My fondest fantasy is that those who knew Jean Stafford best — such friends as Robert Hightower and Eve Auchincloss — might apprehend my version of the life and murmur, "Yes, that's plausible, that's something like the Jean I knew." And that all the others to whom Stafford comes as a stranger might put down my book and say, "What an interesting woman. I wish I'd known her."

Jean Stafford

A BIOGRAPHY

Introduction

M OST BRILLIANT of the new fiction writers," *Life* magazine called Jean Stafford in 1947. Placing her in an elite that included Truman Capote and Gore Vidal, *Life* declared that "Stafford is the only one of this group of literary psychologists who makes finished art of her material."

At thirty-one, Stafford had just published her second novel, *The Mountain Lion,* to almost universal acclaim. Three years earlier she had seen her first book, an ambitious novel called *Boston Adventure,* become a best-seller: at one point there were nearly four hundred thousand copies in print. As *Life* was hailing her talent, she had just begun sending short stories to *The New Yorker,* which was proud to publish her. Critics compared Stafford's prose to that of Proust, James, and Austen.

The young novelist had grown up in California and Colorado. Raised in a family beset by poverty, Stafford had blazed her way through school, earning both a B.A. and an M.A. in four years at the University of Colorado. Upon graduating she had fled the West and her family for good. Among bohemian cohorts in Germany, Boston, and New York, her soul selected the society she had longed for throughout an unhappy childhood.

Tall, blond, thin, shy, and cerebral, Stafford had been a misfit in high school and college. On the East Coast, her austere beauty combined with her cutting wit to create a *personnage formidable.* At the age of twenty-four Stafford had married a handsome and self-confident young poet whose Boston Brahmin lineage could

not have been more different from her own. They had published
their first books in the same year, but while Stafford's had turned
her into a celebrity, her husband's had made only a small splash
in the literary magazines. With the earnings from her best-seller
Stafford bought a house in Maine in which the two writers could
hole up and produce masterpieces. It would be a while yet before
Robert Lowell would become as famous as his wife.

At the very moment, however, when she ought to have been
basking in her achievement — her picture in *Life,* her praises on
the lips of such critics as Howard Mumford Jones and Alfred
Kazin — Stafford was recovering from a mental breakdown and
a long, bitterly lonely stay in a psychiatric hospital. Her marriage
to Lowell was finished; the brilliant poet had proved in domestic
life to be a spoiled bully. At the end of their troubled year in
Maine, Lowell had begun an affair with one of their last summer
guests. Devastated, Stafford fled to New York City, then committed herself to Payne Whitney.

Stafford would live for twenty-seven years after the publication of her third novel, *The Catherine Wheel,* in 1952, yet she
failed even to come close to completing another. She won the
Pultizer Prize in 1970 for her *Collected Stories,* but by then her
knack for short fiction had been effectively dormant for a decade.
She survived by turning out book reviews, essays, and cranky
polemics. Her nonfiction prose from the 1960s and 1970s includes pieces that are among the best journalism written during
those decades; indeed Stafford seldom wrote even a personal note
that is not in some way memorable. Nonetheless it is hard not
to see the ephemeral articles of these years as a calculated avoidance of the greater demands of fiction.

The causes of Stafford's decline are several and elusive. For all
the excuses she loved to make, at the deepest level she knew that
she had no one to blame but herself; yet in some sense she was
powerless before the tangled imperatives of her own nature. In
any event, the novelist who had leapt so spectacularly onto the
stage in the 1940s and who had seemed possessed of limitless
promise was starting, by the 1970s, to be relegated to a defunct
generation. Despite the Pulitzer, her fame faded drastically.

By the mid-1980s, however, Stafford was riding the crest of a
revival. Legions of readers are now discovering her for the first
time, marveling anew at her humor, her narrative power, her

ironic verve, her disdain for all things shabby and chic — and at the perfect sentences she worked so hard to construct. What Robert Fitzgerald wrote about *The Mountain Lion* is true of all her best work: "Though you read it with amusement, you will feel it aching in you like a tooth for days."

I

The Lippia Lawn

JOHN STAFFORD had promised the children a big surprise when they got home. In the family Model T, it took the better part of a day to drive the eighteen miles east from Grandmother Stafford's house in Los Angeles to the walnut ranch in Covina. Despite a vacation full of diversions, the children had missed their mother, who had stayed at home. Now, as the Ford bounced along the dusty two-lane road, they dreamed away the miles in a reverie of anticipation. Mary Lee, who was seven, longed for finery: perhaps a diamond lavaliere or a blue velvet dress. Marjorie, at five, hoped for a Shetland pony, or a whole cheese, or a bisque baby doll, or a year's supply of chewing gum. Four-year-old Dick had a single passionate wish: a new dog to replace the family's yellow hound, which had been run over by a car.

When they got home, the children discovered their mother in bed, attended by a nurse. The girls burst into tears and rushed to embrace her. In the nurse's arms, wrapped in a blanket, lay the surprise: a week-old baby, crying and wriggling. Jean Wilson Stafford had been born on July 1, 1915.

The girls were instantly delighted, but Dick remained glum. John Stafford said, "Dick, don't you like your new little sister?" "She's all right, I guess," Dick answered, "but I wish she'd been a dog."

"I still wish it!" Dick would yell throughout Jean's childhood, whenever the two had a quarrel. (Dick soon got his dog, however: a black and white shepherd collie the children named Rover.)

The children actually believed that a stork had brought the baby, since they had managed not to notice Ethel Stafford's pregnancy during the spring of 1915. As Marjorie would recall seventy years later, "Mother wasn't slim, anyway." It was a squeamish family: "We were so shy and unworldly that we considered the words 'body' and 'nervous' to be embarrassing obscenities. . . ."

The baby had blond hair, blue eyes, and a dimple high on one cheek. Her mother dressed her in blue smocks to match her eyes. Jean's sisters thought her "pretty" and "enchanting"; as soon as she could walk, they took her to their school in West Covina to show her off to the other kids.

Three years before Jean's birth the Staffords had moved to California from the northwest corner of Missouri — one family among a throng of midwesterners whose rush to the Los Angeles area constituted one of the greatest internal migrations in United States history. It was John Stafford's fancy to play the gentleman farmer, harvesting English walnuts on a ten-acre ranch. Earlier in life he had been a telephone-company employee and a newspaper reporter; he was now a writer of western fiction who aspired to serious prose. Having inherited a fortune from his cattleman father, Stafford bought a plot of land in rural Covina, some twenty miles east of Los Angeles, and had an eight-room house built to order. With the construction barely under way, he planted seedling walnut trees in the fields out back.

Once built, the Stafford residence made a local splash: neighbors called it the Big House. Its proud proprietor put a great deal of work into landscaping the yard. The house, set well back from Lark Ellen Avenue, was approached by a long, curving driveway bordered with chrysanthemums, poppies, gladiolus, cannas, and roses. English ivy soon clung to the fireplace chimney. On the south side of the house, John Stafford planted a circular lawn of lippia, a close-growing ground cover. In its center stood an umbrella tree, the haunt of scores of hummingbirds. The back of the house was guarded by a geranium hedge. Along the street that fronted the property, Stafford planted a row of palm trees.

As satellites to the Big House, Stafford built an auxiliary solar water heater, a tank house, a barn occupied by a horse named Dolly and a cow named Bossy, a cement water box for irrigation, a garage, and a playhouse thatched with palm fronds for the children. Next door was an orange grove, from which the young Staffords stole fruit. A quarter of a mile north of the house lay the "Wash," a dry creek bed in which the children gathered colored stones and, under the road bridge, played Troll. So rural was Covina in 1912 that the family often heard coyotes howling at night, or saw them trotting single-file though the orange groves.

John Stafford's ten acres amounted to a small-to-medium-sized walnut ranch. In September and November he harvested his crop. Hitching Dolly to a plow, he harrowed the ground beneath his trees and then ran a drag over it, leaving a soft, smooth surface on which the walnuts would fall of their own accord. Recalcitrant fruit was knocked loose with long, hooked poles. The walnuts were washed and then laid out in drying trays spread in the sunlight between the garage and the house. Compared to the kind of labor Stafford had been used to in Missouri, walnut farming was easy.

For Mary Lee, Marjorie, and Dick, the ranch at once became a halcyon playground. They converted their father's glass solar panels into slides; in the water box they played hide-and-seek and Bear; they hid from their mother's scoldings in a loft in the tank house that could be reached only by a ladder. In the hedge they hollowed out a "Geranium Cave" that served as a general store, pirates' lair, enchanted castle, and Conestoga wagon. They sneaked up on hummingbirds in the umbrella tree, only to have their bare feet stung by the bees that lurked in the tiny blossoms of the lippia.

In her turn Jean discovered the joys of yard and neighborhood. She sat under the umbrella tree, waiting with her hands clasped for her father's four-o'clocks to open each afternoon. She ate fallen figs, smearing her face and clothes with the purple juice. In pockets of bark in the palm trees, she hid her treasures: stones from the Wash, peach and plum pits, sand dollars and abalone shells from the beach. In the afternoons she stood in the yard and watched for her siblings to come home from school laden with presents of stolen paper clips and rubber bands.

Despite the bee stings, Jean loved the lippia, the memory of which came in adulthood to symbolize for her a lost paradise. In a speech almost sixty years later she claimed, "Our ground-covering was a lippia lawn, something I have never seen since, and it was only a few months ago that I even found the name of it in a garden encyclopedia though I spent a lifetime looking it up in every horticultural lexicon I chanced upon."

The Wash was redolent of mystery and magical power. The

children treated the colored stones they gathered there like dolls, inventing families among them, and tried to take them home during rainstorms. One year a flash flood came down the Wash, and a couple living on the far bank was swept away and drowned. Another couple, named Hedges, made a desperate ride on horse-back — Mrs. Hedges in the nude, her long hair flying — to the safety of the Big House, where Ethel Stafford put on tea and potato soup and got out blankets and smelling salts.

The Stafford house at 831 Lark Ellen Avenue still stands today, in the middle-class suburb that Covina has become, a short and smoggy jaunt on the freeway east of downtown Los Angeles. More recent dwellings crowd it on three sides, and the Big House is no longer remarkable for its size. There is no trace of the lippia lawn, and the walnut trees and the orange grove are gone, but John Stafford's palms now tower more than sixty feet above the paved avenue. The Wash has been tamed: today it is a concrete canal lined with chain-link fences to keep kids out. The coyotes, of course, have long since vanished.

The Stafford household was a literate one. In the evening their father read to the children from Mark Twain, Robert Louis Stevenson, or his own cowboy tales in manuscript. Their mother read them Hans Christian Andersen, the milder tales from the Brothers Grimm, Charles Dickens, or James Whitcomb Riley; sometimes she told stories of her girlhood in Missouri, which seemed to the children "to be one long and joyous hayride or bobsled race after another." The bookshelves held "a vast assortment of children's books" as well as works by Shakespeare, Balzac, and Voltaire. In the den was a set of the *Encyclopaedia Britannica*. The children made a litany out of the abbreviations on the bindings, chanting to each other, "A to And," "And to Aus," "Aus to Bis," "Bis to Cal," and so on. (Fifty years later Jean and Marjorie would recite the litany to each other over the telephone late at night.)

"We all became bookworms," remembers Marjorie. From an early age both Mary Lee and Jean planned to become writers. Marjorie, on the other hand, wanted to be an artist. Inclined toward the musical, John Stafford played the Victrola incessantly or whistled "La Paloma," even though "None of us [children] could carry the simplest tune."

The children spent much of their spare time outdoors, playing tag and Bear, staging footraces, and sharing a family bicycle. Mary

Lee and Marjorie invented a game called Boy in which, under the names Frank and Alfred, they pursued manly adventures. When this sport paled, they acted out another charade as the genteel English ladies Grace (a romantic novelist) and Eleanor (a portrait painter). Dick and Jean, forbidden to participate, turned instead to their imaginary friends. Dick's was named John Greenleaf; Jean's, Rose Mary Pickford.

According to a Los Angeles cousin, the three older Stafford children formed a "closed corporation" that excluded Jean. "They were always going into huddles. They would go off and discuss things, never telling their parents. Jean was always trying to join in. She followed them to school. But she was always an outsider."

Mary Lee and Marjorie had a penchant for playing "teasing games" on their baby sister.

> We told Jean what a tiny scrap of humanity she had been as a newborn. We assured her that she had been no larger than a can of talcum powder with a head the size of an orange. . . . Mary Lee additionally teased Jean about her non-existent fatness which Mary Lee made sound worse by calling it "avoirdupois" and "adiposity." She offered to help Jean overcome this fabricated unpleasantness by sending away for rubber underwear, a reducing balm by the name of "Marmola" and exercise records to play on the Victrola.

In Marjorie's view this teasing was gentle and good-natured, but it would have a lasting traumatic effect on Jean.

Marjorie's recollections of Jean as a young girl include some intriguing touches. She was not a whiner or complainer; instead "she usually waited to voice protests until she had thought of something incisive and withering to say." Jean's room was usually messy, like her sisters', until she abruptly went on one of her obsessive cleaning binges — a habit that would last throughout her life. She bit her thumbs. She was terrified of snakes. And riding in a car so frightened her that she often hid on the floor of the backseat. It is perhaps not surprising that as an adult Jean never learned to drive.

Jean Stafford's ancestry was Irish and Scottish. Both her grandfathers died before she was born, but she grew up with a clear grasp of the different styles and values embodied by the two sides of her family. On her father's side, the Staffords were adventurers and wanderers, mavericks and self-made men and women, liberal-minded and with an intellectual bent. On her mother's side, the McKillops stood for small-town propriety and were incurious and devout, measuring success by social standing and taste by the furnishings of the home.

Richard Stafford, Jean's father's father, had fled Ireland when he was about eighteen to make a new life in America. He drifted to the Midwest, where he became a prosperous cattleman with ranches in both Missouri and Texas. Jean grew up on stories of her grandfather's adventures in the Wild West. "One night," as she would later recall the family legend, "Jesse James had ridden up to Grandpa's Missouri place, his lieutenants on their fine horses beside him, and had asked him for lodging for the night. 'Mr. Stafford,' he said, 'me and my boys are tired and we got to rest. If you hain't got a bed, you can hang me from a nail.' "

Richard Stafford married a forceful, independent woman named Phoebe Anne Wilson, who long outlived him. (From her, Jean derived her middle name.) In 1874, on the Missouri farm, she gave birth to John Stafford. After her husband died in 1899, Phoebe Anne moved to Los Angeles. She had already written a newspaper column; in California she lobbied strenuously for women's suffrage and joined the Women's Christian Temperance Union. She wrote articles on temperance, corresponded with leading feminists, and went on the road to make speeches. Late in life she also became a Christian Scientist, but she repudiated the religion before her death.

The McKillops, on Jean's mother's side, hailed from the Isle of Arran, off the southwest coast of Scotland. Malcolm McKillop, Jean's grandfather, was born in Quebec; he taught school in Vermont, passed the Illinois bar, and ended up as a stuffy Republican lawyer in Rock Port, Missouri. He married a distant cousin in Illinois; in 1876 she gave birth to Ethel McKillop, Jean's mother.

Richard Stafford's three brothers had, like him, fled to the corners of the globe to make their fortunes. In contrast, the McKillops had clanned together. They were all Scottish Presbyterians of a devout sternness that verged on fanaticism; supposedly they could read and speak Gaelic. Malcolm's two brothers and his sister never married. Instead the trio came to rest in San Diego, where all three lived in a single house.

John Stafford spent his childhood on the farm in London, Missouri, where he learned to shoot and ride and to round up cattle. Although deeply imbued with the outdoor life, when he left home to go to college it was with intellectual ambitions. He attended the now-defunct Amity College, only a few miles away in College Springs, Iowa, where he majored in classics and graduated cum laude. Family legend has it that he was later offered "the classics chair" at the tiny college. A studio portrait from Stafford's student days suggests an aristocratic dandy: you would never guess that this young man had handled a plow or fired a rifle.

After college Stafford returned to the outdoor life, punching cows on his father's ranch in the Texas panhandle and prospecting in Colorado with a college classmate. His goal, however, was to be a writer, so he enrolled in journalism school at the University of Missouri. At some point he worked as a reporter for the *Chicago Sun,* and perhaps also for a newspaper in New York City.

When Richard Stafford died in 1899, he left his son at least thirty thousand dollars in cash — a huge inheritance for a twenty-five-year-old at the turn of the century. Eventually John Stafford bought land in southern California and Arizona, but at first he stayed in London, helping his mother run the farm.

It may have been during this time that John Stafford met Ethel McKillop. Rock Port, where she was raised, was only six miles from Tarkio, where John had worked for the telephone company. Two years younger than John, Ethel had grown up in a literate, if conventional, household. She took elocution lessons, memorized Tennyson and Whittier, and kept a memory book. In school she got high marks in deportment and rhetoric, poor ones in mathematics. She wrote love letters in the stylized language of flowers and was lauded by a teacher for an essay in which she deplored the use of slang as leading to swearing, and thence to drinking and gambling. After high school Ethel went to the Presbyterian-affiliated Tarkio College for two years, after which she became a schoolteacher, first in Rock Port and then in Salida, a town in the Arkansas Valley of the Colorado Rockies.

In 1907 Ethel McKillop married John Stafford. She was thirty-one years old, he thirty-three. They honeymooned in Mexico and southern California and aboard a steamer from San Francisco to Vancouver. As they reentered the United States from Mexico,

Stafford convinced his bride that she must smuggle through customs the weavings they had bought in border towns. He helped her wrap the cumbersome treasures around her waist and hide them under her skirt. Ethel trembled and blushed her way through the ordeal, only to have her husband reveal that the whole thing was a practical joke, the booty being well within import allowances.

The couple settled down in Tarkio to raise a family. In the spring of 1908 their first child, Mary Lee, was born. She was followed by Marjorie the next year, and by Dick in 1911. John Stafford served in the Missouri national guard from 1908 to 1910; it was around this time that he decided to pursue his star as a writer of western fiction. In 1910 a New York publisher, Dodge & Company, brought out his first novel, *When Cattle Kingdom Fell*. It is a conventional western in the Zane Grey mold, smoothly written, if riddled with stereotypes and clichés. Here is its opening paragraph:

> The last circle had been ridden, the last calf branded and turned loose, the last stray cut and driven into the big corral at the headquarters. The round-up of the *Double K* was finished. Now, at about three o'clock of this afternoon of June 23, in the year of grace, 1883, on the dusty branding ground where a little while before they had been roping and tussling calves, forty wide-hatted, high-heeled, gauntleted and armed men lolled in their saddles waiting cowboy fashion for the boss to give his orders.

No doubt John Stafford looked on the publication of his novel as the start of an illustrious career, but in fact it was to be the high-water mark of his life in print.

At the time of Jean Stafford's birth in 1915, her father was forty-one years old, her mother thirty-nine. Ethel Stafford's chief project was her home. She gathered wildflowers from the fields to decorate the tables and windowsills and made preserves and jam from the apples, peaches, apricots, grapes, and berries that grew on the farm. She hung oil paintings of roses and sunsets that had been executed by her sister in Missouri. Unlike her daughters, Ethel was a demon for cleanliness. At the end of each day she would tot up the "accomplishments" of her previous twelve hours of homemaking. An excellent cook, she inflicted routinely hearty meals on her family.

Her niece Lois remembers Ethel as a rosy-cheeked woman with pretty blue eyes, "the most pleasant person" she had ever known. According to Jean's sister Marjorie, "Mother herself always looked fresh and pretty with a minimum of primping. She had a fresh complexion with clear blue eyes and an expression of innocence and wholesomeness. She was as good and as pure as she appeared to be too." In the less infatuated memory of a junior-high-school friend of Jean's, Mrs. Stafford was "big, bountiful, bulbous, optimistic. . . . Smile, good news, nothing but optimism, which made Jean upset. Her mother could only see the bright side of everything. . . . [She] would just barge out and embrace me, and say, 'You want a peanut-butter sandwich?' She was always offering food."

In a photograph taken perhaps when she was in her midthirties, Ethel Stafford has a bland, matronly look. Her hair is swept up in a pompadour; she has a thick neck and a shallow chin, round cheeks and a pug nose. Her mouth is set in a prim, emotionless line. Despite the ambition of the pompadour, the face in the photo bespeaks a homespun woman, preoccupied with the domestic life.

When a neighboring couple visited, Ethel would confer with the wife about recipes and patterns. The men would talk about crops, prices, and irrigation. One regular visitor always brought along his Ford joke book (a favorite publication of the day) to tease John Stafford about his Model T. Although he "thought fancy cars ridiculous," Stafford soon replaced the Model T with a more prestigious black Reo.

By the time Jean was born, it had been five years since the publication of *When Cattle Kingdom Fell*. John Stafford continued to sell western stories to the pulp magazines, writing under the pseudonyms Jack Wonder, O. B. Miles, and Ben Delight. Typing frenetically in an upstairs study, he also composed brief, opinionated essays — which he called "shorts" and "squibs" — for the slick magazines, and fired them off indefatigably to one rejecting editor after another. The income from his writing was meager at best, but for a gentleman farmer, profit was of little importance. He regularly read his compositions aloud to his children, who would always "try to avoid being the listener."

John Stafford was thought courteous and chivalric in his social dealings. Marjorie recalls, "He quoted long passages from Greek and Roman writers in the original. He was, as our cousin Lois often said, a walking encyclopedia. His mind was an orderly and vast storehouse of information on almost any subject one could think of." Stafford remained, at the same time, a devotee of guns and hunting, and even slept with a "six-shooter" under his pillow every night. It was a disappointment to him that Dick showed little interest in shooting.

The Stafford children were disciplined with a switch applied to their bare legs — more often by Ethel than by John. According to Marjorie, all three sisters were lifelong hypochondriacs; their mother bore illness stoically, but when their father got sick, he "would become desperately ill, in abject shame and misery." John Stafford was "sort of anti-doctor," perhaps because of his mother's flirtation with Christian Science. The Staffords relied on a small cache of bromides, including arnica and bichloride of mercury, to treat all ailments. Ethel "believed in the daily bowel movement," and dosed her children with Castoria and syrup of figs. The children did not see a dentist very often. As an adult Jean would recall with fury her father's "egomaniacal hatred of doctors" and the fact that he had once treated a blister on her finger by lancing it daily with a dull needle.

Once, when Jean was about six, her father gave her a haircut. Using a bathing cap as a guide, he had crudely lopped off the long blond locks from one side of her head when Jean suddenly tore off the cap and fled. She refused to let him finish the job and went around for weeks with one side short, the other long.

Perhaps in a kindred rebellion against her mother's lavish meals, from early childhood Jean was, to use her own phrase, a "problem feeder." She particularly hated string beans, pears, dates, honey, and her mother's prized jams and jellies. Ethel's response was to shovel "triple rations" onto Jean's plate and force her to eat. The only foods she really liked, Jean would later say, were raw potatoes and cabbage cores.

Even though there were vacant rooms upstairs, Dick and Jean shared a bedroom in the Big House. Four years older than Jean, Dick resented her efforts to tag along after him. Teased and excluded by her sisters, she tried to form a special bond with her brother despite his efforts to discourage her. In a blurry photo-

graph from their childhood, Dick and Jean ride the family bicycle. He pedals confidently forward while she, in a shapeless smock,
holds on to his waist and giggles with pleasure and fright. Decades after the photo was taken, Marjorie sent Jean a copy of it.
In 1974 Jean wrote her sister, "I have it on my bulletin board and
sometimes when my eye falls on it, I go rather funny in the head
at the spectacle of such joy."

In 1921, after nine years in Covina, John Stafford decided to
sell the walnut ranch. According to Marjorie, her father had simply tired of the walnut-raising life; his immediate plan was to
play the stock market. The family moved to San Diego so he
could be near an exchange. For the last and most sorrowful time,
the children intoned their parting *ave,* which they recited whenever they left the ranch for more than a day: "Good-bye, House;
Good-bye, Garage; Good-bye, Tankhouse; Good-bye, Water-
box."

In San Diego the family rented a white stucco house that, in
Jean's memory, was so close to the Balboa Park zoo that she
could hear the lions roaring. There were new entertainments to
replace those of Covina — fishing expeditions on the waterfront;
trips to the zoo, where Rover's frenzied barking at the deer earned
the dog his banishment; softball games in the street with a neighbor who wrote about sports for a San Diego paper; drives to
Coronado to hear outdoor band concerts; a cruise in a glass-
bottomed boat, during which everyone got seasick.

Before an audience of family and neighbors, the children put
on a melodrama written by Mary Lee. The playwright herself
took the part of an evil gypsy king who kidnapped an innocent
child (Jean), the daughter of a wealthy couple (Marjorie and Dick).
Rover was a gypsy horse. In the end Jean was restored to her
parents and Mary Lee stabbed herself to death with her father's
sheathed hunting knife, while a chorus consisting of Dick and
Marjorie chanted, "Good riddance to bad rubbish, good riddance
to bad rubbish."

Jean started kindergarten in San Diego. She later claimed to
have only three memories of that year's schooling:

A brawny girl in the second grade conned me into giving her a
nickel I had been saving for a small blue bathtub I had seen in the
ten cent store — I think she offered to bean me with an Indian

Club if I didn't; I made a dress out of paper and was applauded by my teacher and laughed at silly by my older sisters. And I learned Braille. Later on, my elders, who meant well, told me I had probably been introduced to the rudiments of arithmetic on an abacus. But I said I learned Braille when I was five years old and I say so now.

In San Diego the Stafford children got to know their McKillop great-uncles and great-aunt, the stern trio of celibate Scottish Presbyterians who lived together. During regular Sunday-evening prayer meetings at the McKillop house, Great-uncle Duncan, the eldest, would deliver a short sermon and then quiz the young children about the text of the one they had heard in church that morning. Only after this ordeal were refreshments served — invariably soggy cake doughnuts, peppermint sticks, and milk. In Marjorie's recollection, her great-aunt and great-uncles were "very Scottish, very God-fearing and full of dry humor." Jean, however, would recall the prayer meetings with terror and contempt.

The three unmarried siblings were also strict teetotalers. In family memory, their brother Malcolm McKillop (Jean's grandfather), who had died in the 1890s, was gilded as a saint of civic virtue. It was thus a shock for Jean to learn when she was in her twenties that the revered Missouri lawyer had actually been an alcoholic whose habit the family had for decades done its best to conceal.

The children had attended Presbyterian Sunday school in Covina, in spite of the fact that their parents did not go to church. At the age of five, Jean considered herself a devout Presbyterian, even though, unlike her older siblings, she had already ceased to believe in Santa Claus.

One Christmas, when she was four or five, Jean was singled out by Grandma Stafford as the only child to receive a gift. She was overjoyed to get a "charming" little bag. By afternoon, however, she had managed to lose the present, and she never found it again. More than fifty years later Jean would say that ever since then Christmas had been associated in her mind with a desolate sense of loss, and that she had found herself at different times looking for the bag in Germany, Louisiana, Maine, Tennessee, and Boston.

Investing the cash he had earned from the sale of the walnut ranch, John Stafford hoped to double or triple his money on the stock market. Instead, in a catastrophically short time, he lost it all. Deeply shamed, he borrowed money from his mother. One day he announced to the children that the family was going to move to Colorado. He tried to present the upcoming journey as a bold adventure, but his wife knew that it signified a flight from his own humiliation. For the rest of her childhood — and in a sense for the rest of her life — Jean Stafford would never again know a day free of the fear of poverty and of social inferiority.

II

Disenchantment

IN JULY 1921 the Staffords headed east out of Los Angeles in their stately black Reo. For the drive they wore khaki traveling outfits and "explorers'" boots. Planning to camp along the way, they had loaded the car with army cots, tents, blankets, groceries, and a stove.

The journey lasted more than a month. From Los Angeles the Reo chugged east across the Mojave Desert, through Arizona with stops at the Grand Canyon, the Painted Desert, and the Petrified Forest, across New Mexico via Santa Fe, and finally into southern Colorado. In Marjorie's memory sixty years later, the drive was perhaps the most exciting adventure of her youth, yet it was also "fraught with dirt, dust, discomfort, and uncertainty."

Before they crossed the Mojave, John Stafford filled canvas canteens with drinking water and hung them from the Reo's bumpers. In the tourist camps, drivers swapped bulletins on road conditions ahead. A spirit of shared adversity reigned: men organized impromptu horseshoe-pitching tournaments and softball games, and there were marshmallow roasts and campfire sings accompanied by ukeleles and harmonicas.

In Arizona and New Mexico the children were both repelled and intrigued by the Navajos. In Covina they had lived in casual proximity to Japanese farmers, but the Indian reservations gave them a new comprehension of ethnic discrimination. According to Marjorie, "Their miserable little dwellings depressed us and made us indignant. . . . Our indignation was roused by our father's comments re the 'damned government and Bureau of Indian Affairs.' "

Nine years later Jean would write an essay called "Disenchantment" about the drive to Colorado. The tone and diction of the piece are those of a precocious fifteen-year-old trying to sound worldly, but the perceptions must have been Jean's at six. The essay hinges satirically on the children's expectations of Colorado, "that land of adventure, that storied country where life and death hung in the balance, where college professors wore chaps, and where barbers were unnecessary because of the abundance of Indians who scalped you gratis." The young protagonist scorns Mexicans and Anglos alike. The former "were all stupid oxen and worshipped the Reo as if it were an omnipotent Zeus"; the latter included "red-faced men who lied chronically about having read Faust and Shakespeare." The "greasy-faced Indians" who met the Stafford girls coveted their "mustard colored stockings."

It is the arrival that supplies the disenchantment of the title: "Colorado was just as uninteresting as California and more spread out in [sic] it." The children, says the narrator, have been tricked by Tom Mix and Zane Grey. One of the girls writes in her journal, " 'We have got ourselves rooked. There aren't any Indians or any guns or anything. And they've even got schools way out here.' "

John Stafford told his children that the main reason for the move was that the changing seasons in Colorado would improve their health. Ethel had fond memories of her brief teaching stint in Salida; John, of his prospecting days in the state. But Stafford's real reason for choosing Colorado may have been that the family knew no one there. The Rockies promised a refuge from his shame at having squandered a fortune.

For if their journey to Covina in 1912 had found the Staffords in the midst of a great popular migration, the move nine years later went very much against the grain. By the 1920s Colorado was a depressed region. All the mining bonanzas on which the state had built its very existence had fizzled out, and the end of World War I had devastated the wheat growers and cattlemen on the eastern plains. During the first two decades of the twentieth century, Colorado's population had increased by 74 percent; during the 1920s and 1930s it leveled off. For the first time ever, more people moved out of the state than moved in.

Ironically, the vast plurality of settlers who left Colorado in the
1920s flocked to Los Angeles.

With the economic decline came a political and cultural turn to
the extreme right. In 1921, as the Staffords crossed the New
Mexico border in their Reo, the Ku Klux Klan was gaining its
first toehold in Colorado. The movement found fertile ground
in the state, which soon became the western bastion of an Invisible Empire that claimed two million members nationwide. In
1924 men who openly belonged to the KKK were elected as the
state's governor and to a majority of the seats in both houses of
the state legislature.

The Staffords made their first Colorado home in Pueblo. The
children instantly hated the town. "It was an ugly, smoky-
looking place, hot and uncomfortable," recalls Marjorie. "We said
if this was healthful Colorado we would take monotonous un-
healthful California any old day." The town must have looked
particularly dreary in August 1921, for only two months before,
the Arkansas had topped its banks in the worst flood in the state's
history, drowning a hundred people and doing sixteen million
dollars' worth of damage. In Pueblo Dick and Marjorie went to
grammar school in an ugly redbrick building, where they had to
unlearn their California penmanship and adhere to the Palmer
Method. They hated the school at least as much as the town.
To their delight, only a few months after they arrived, John
Stafford packed his family in the Reo and moved to Colorado
Springs.

Unlike Pueblo, a grimy town of steel and iron, Colorado Springs
had developed as a tourist spa — the first true resort established
west of Chicago. Here the children approved of "the widest and
cleanest streets we had ever seen and all sorts of interesting shops
and stores." In a neighborhood called Ivywild, the Staffords rented
a house from a spiritualist landlady who had séances in which
she communicated with her dead husband. Here Jean started first
grade at the same school Marjorie and Dick attended. Mary Lee,
now thirteen, went downtown to high school.

During the winter of 1922 the whole family came down with
influenza. For the first time Ethel was unable to take care of her
children. John hired a domineering practical nurse who took over
the house, scolding the children for wasting toilet paper and
tricking them into submitting to enemas by promising them re-

freshing "internal baths." Almost forty years later Jean would
revive this terrifying and exotic figure in a short story built around
her domestic tyranny.

After about two years in Ivywild, the Staffords moved once
more, to outlying Stratton Park, a kind of "people's park" designed by an eccentric turn-of-the-century philanthropist. By the
1920s the park lay in decrepitude, with the land gradually being
taken over by low-cost housing. To the Stafford children it was
nonetheless a fascinating place. They played on the swings, the
teeter-totter, and "an enormous rocking device with seats for half
a dozen people." They roller-skated at a pavilion to recordings
of "Valencia" and "Ramona." They listened in silent scorn to
the hellfire sermons of traveling evangelists.

Stratton Park had become a turberculosis colony, filled with
gimcrack cottages with screened-in sleeping porches. As the Stafford children played outdoors, they were constantly aware of
people coughing and slipping furtively past, cheeks livid with the
telltale tubercular flush. Many of their playmates' parents had TB,
and there were deaths almost daily.

Jean was deeply interested in these neighborhood freaks, the
"walkers" and "lungers," as they were called. She would return
to them repeatedly in her mature fiction, sometimes in the guise
of a protagonist who fears or even wishes she had tuberculosis.

During these years of relative poverty, John Stafford plugged
away at his writing. It would have seemed logical that with a
wife and four children to support, he might feel some responsibility to take a job. Instead he got by on the money his mother
kept lending him; to his wife he explained that "he had to be a
writer, and he didn't want to work for anybody else." He was
cranking out western stories, but his sales were minimal. As
Marjorie recalls, "Every time he sold one of his stories we had
beefsteak for dinner." Ethel bore his decision without complaint,
but her disposition lost its cheerful complacency; she worried from
one season to the next and fell into lasting depressions.

Her husband, it was clear, was becoming a bit of a crank. A
malevolent streak in his temperament came to the fore as he inveighed against such distant figures of authority as American
presidents and editors who rejected his work. He paid less and
less attention to his dress and chewed tobacco constantly. "The
worst of it," remembers Marjorie, "was that when we were

riding in the Reo, which was an open car, and he had to spit, it
would blow right back on the passengers."

During the Stratton Park years, Mary Lee finished high school.
A diligent student who got good grades and had retained her
interest in literature, she had grown to be a great beauty. Years
before, in San Diego, she had dismissed Marjorie and Dick as
"uncouth." In high school, Marjorie says, she "began to wear a
great deal of very white face powder and to be much embarrassed by the rest of the family. She quit going on our ritual
Sunday drives in the Reo and if Mother asked her to return
something as coarse and pleb[e]ian as a wash tub to the neighbors
she waited until after dark."

Marjorie lacked her older sister's looks. She continued to fancy
herself a painter, taking as many art classes as she could. The
principal of the Staffords' school and his wife had written a
Christmas play called *The Littlest Wise Man,* which students presented annually for the community. For several years running
Mary Lee landed the star role of "the beckoning angel." Marjorie
only made the corps of lesser angels.

Dick, three years younger than Mary Lee and a year and a half
Marjorie's junior, was fast becoming an outdoorsman. Several
times he completed the long hike up Pikes Peak, coming home
with blisters and sunburn. He also learned how to trap skunks
on the slopes of the mountain. He brought home the pelts and
hung them out to dry beside the house, much to his sisters' dismay.

Jean spent the years between the ages of six and ten in Colorado Springs. She would later maintain that she had wanted to
be a writer ever since she had learned the alphabet. From the
time she could first read, she made it a habit to pore through the
dictionary. At six she wrote her first poem, called "Gravel":

> Gravel, gravel on the ground
> Lying there so safe and sound,
> Why is it you look so dead?
> Is it because you have no head?

(The poem finds its way verbatim into *The Mountain Lion,* as
Molly Fawcett's creation.)

By the age of eight Jean was manufacturing western stories
just like her father. Her heroes, modeled on General Custer and
Wild Bill Hickok, were, as she reminisced decades later, "daring,

dashing, tall in the saddle and easy on the eye. . . . To a man, they had steely-blue eyes to match the barrels of their Colt .45s." She also wrote a long tale about kidnapping, which she called "The Unsuccessful Amateur." All of her protagonists were men.

Still, writing was not her sole ambition. Until she was about thirteen, she wanted to be a dancer.

> I was a whiz at cartwheels, a degree less accomplished at hand-springs and I could do a sensational backbend — the fact that I couldn't get up didn't seem important to me because I was sure I could learn that with proper instruction. My toe-dancing which, of course, was essential to the act, left a good deal to be desired but I blamed (blame) that on the fact that I never had any toe-dancing slippers and had to make do with my brother's basketball shoes, stuffed with socks in the toes.

Like Mary Lee, Jean at ten was offended by uncouthness in her siblings. Greasy hair, dirty fingernails, and sloppy clothing earned Jean's contempt, but her sharpest scorn was reserved for those occasions when she caught Marjorie mispronouncing a word.

More than twenty years later, in the midst of a deep personal crisis, Jean looked back at her youth and saw "an angry, wounded child."

> I had mutilated myself constantly when I was a little girl in order to gain pity and love. My father was too cold and awkward to give me affection; my brother soon resented me because I tagged along everywhere; my mother was too busy; my sisters found me too young; is it any wonder that I wanted to marry Laddy [the family dog, Rover's successor]?

In another retrospective remark, embedded in an angry letter written to Marjorie sometime during the 1960s, Jean claimed, "The Stafford-McKillop predilection for complaint, for perpetually blaming others for their misfortunes and even for the *accidents* that befall them[,] is one of the many reasons that for all practical purposes I left home when I was 7."

Although it seems not to have been abundantly apparent to her siblings or her parents, at ten Jean Stafford was already seriously alienated from her family. The detectable causes — her sisters' cruel teasing, her brother's indifference, her father's egocentric delusions, the sudden onset of poverty after six years of affluence — do not on the surface of things account for the depth of that alienation. It is remarkable that Mary Lee, Marjorie, and Dick seem never to have expressed even a hint of a comparable estrangement. Less remarkable, though far more significant, is the fact that by the age of ten Jean had linked the idea of becoming a writer with the promise of an escape from home.

In 1925 Mary Lee graduated from high school and won a scholarship to the University of Colorado in Boulder. Rather than suffer her departure, John and Ethel decided to transplant the whole family to Boulder. They rationalized the move as fiscal common sense: if Mary Lee could live at home, the family could afford the cost of her attending college. But the Staffords' fourth change of residence in four years signified a curious shift in the family dynamics. The patriarch who in 1912 had spirited his progeny west to golden California and a new life had become, by 1925, a clinging parent who preferred tagging after his oldest child to letting her graduate from the family.

Meanwhile, Ethel's uncle Duncan McKillop had died, leaving her some money. Her genteel fantasies undimmed by four years of scraping by, Ethel laid plans to turn their new home into an English-style tea shop. It soon became clear, however, that this was not the sort of enterprise the citizens of Boulder were clamoring for; the tea shop never opened.

The small town to which the Staffords moved in the summer of 1925, and in which Jean would spend eleven profoundly formative years, was a far cry from the trendy place Boulder has since become; at that time it was a smug, sleepy hamlet with a core of Bible-belt conservatism. Spawned as a gold-rush camp in 1858, it never saw a real boom. After its wide-open early years (in 1883 Boulder had twenty-eight saloons and a thriving red-light district), the town turned proper and conservative. The citizens voted dry in 1907; it would take fifteen referenda and be another sixty years before a glass of wine could again be purchased within the city limits.

Old Main, the first university building, was erected in 1875; for some time it stood in stark isolation atop the otherwise uninhabited University Hill. Two years later the University of Colorado opened its doors to an initial class of forty-four students.

In 1920 Boulder's population was 11,006, not including some twenty-one hundred university students. Like Colorado as a whole, the town grew hardly at all during the next two decades. By the time the Staffords arrived in 1925, Boulder had become a stronghold of the movement that was already entrenched in the state's government. A verse published that year in a Boulder paper summarized the Ku Klux Klan's case against Catholics:

> *I would rather be a Klansman*
> *in a robe of snowy white,*
> *Than to be a Catholic Priest*
> *in a robe as black as night;*
> *For a Klansman is AMERICAN*
> *and AMERICA is his home,*
> *But a priest owes his allegiance*
> *to a Dago Pope in Rome.*

The Klansmen held a night parade, marching down Pearl Street in white sheets; they burned a fifty-foot cross on Flagstaff Mountain above town, tried to get the university to fire Jews and Catholics on its faculty, sponsored a bill to bar the use of wine as a sacrament, and agitated for the deportation of "insane, feeble-minded and diseased undesirable aliens."

In the 1920s Boulder also had its outcast minorities. A small population of blacks was confined to a slum on Goss and Water streets. Their numbers had actually dwindled since the mining days, thanks to prejudice: the men could find jobs only outside Boulder, the boys were not allowed to play high-school sports, and even black university students were forbidden to live near campus or participate in recreational activities. Like Colorado Springs, with its Stratton Park, Boulder contained a tuberculosis colony, with a monumental sanatorium on Mapleton Hill. Since many of the tuberculars were well-to-do émigrés from the South, the town's blacks felt an intensification of prejudice as the colony grew in size.

There was plenty of poverty in Boulder in 1925. A collection of squalid shacks near the mouth of Boulder Canyon was nicknamed the Jungle. Its denizens lived like hobos, begging door-to-door and cadging odd jobs. One longtime Boulder resident swears that their number included a band of gypsies. The most notorious inmate of the Jungle was "Em Bugtown," a disturbed woman who made the rounds barefoot, dressed in an old wrapper. As a girl, Jean Stafford had a deep fascination with these down-on-their-luck pariahs. She made adventurous forays into their midst, and though Boulder history books consign them to oblivion, with scarcely a word recording their passage, she would write memorably about them. In her fiction she did not even change Em Bugtown's name.

During the 1950s Stafford wrote seven of her best short stories, about a young girl in Boulder. In these tales Boulder is called Adams, and the protagonist, who ranges in age from about eight to thirteen, is usually named Emily Vanderpool. There are seven slightly different personae among these deft stories, but all seven bear an unmistakable resemblance to the young Jean Stafford.

On the evidence of the geographical detail given in these stories, we can identify some of the Boulder landmarks that the curious, rebellious ten-year-old began to explore in 1925. Her haunts included the bandstand in its "dreary" Central Park, the "high school shaped like a loaf of bread" (Boulder "Prep," torn down in 1939), the "mongrel and multitudinous churches," the handsome Boulderado Hotel (which Stafford called the Goldmoor), the train depot, the tourist camp near the Jungle at the mouth of Boulder Canyon, the town dump, and even the visitors' waiting room outside the jail in the basement of the county courthouse. She shopped in the two dime stores on Pearl Street, Kress's and Woolworth's, and drank Cokes in the drugstores, Jones and Public, on the same street.

The Staffords' first Boulder residence was on Arapahoe Street, one of the cheapest parts of town to live in, not far from either the Jungle or the black district. It was here that Ethel's dream of the English tea shop dissolved: in Marjorie's delicate phrasing, "The street itself was not one where the sort of foot traffic needed for success was in evidence."

Jean went to University Hill School ("Uni Hill"), which was housed in a grand, three-story stone building with large windows, high-ceilinged classrooms, broad staircases, and varnished wooden floors. As she walked to school, Jean skirted the lovely university campus. Most of the buildings were made of pink flagstone (flat blocks of sandstone quarried from nearby Green Mountain); the architectural style was derived from Renaissance Italian hill towns, with ornamental cupolas and scalloped red roofing tiles.

Here was the all but inconceivable world to which Mary Lee had gained admission. Sometimes on her way home from school

Jean would detour through the campus, stepping along sidewalks that bisected sweeping lawns, skirting tall pines and spruces, gazing with longing at Old Main and Macky Auditorium and the theater building or sneaking across the footbridge over the lily-pad pond called Varsity Lake (off-limits to freshmen). Crossing the campus always infused her with the clandestine thrill of trespass.

Jean's fantasies of college life stood in stark contrast to her experience at Uni Hill, where she felt the scorn of a gifted child for the "stupid things" her classmates did; not surprisingly, she came to regard herself as unpopular. She walked home from school with special friends, but rather than inviting them to her home, she stood with them on the corner near her house, awkwardly prolonging the chat. Howard Higman, who became one of Jean's closest Boulder friends, has a vivid memory of first seeing the ten-year-old girl as she walked home from Uni Hill, "wearing her father's sword [a Civil War saber] fastened to her waist in a scabbard. It was so long it dragged on the sidewalk."

Jean's solitary rambles about Boulder began to elaborate for her a secret life. One of her deepest secrets was the fact that by junior high school she had started to take formal instruction in Catholicism from a Boulder priest. It seems unlikely that anyone in the family knew about this program. Given the Klan's attack on that religion and Boulder's bedrock fundamentalism, it may be that the appeal for Jean of a clandestine Catholicism lay in its very illicitness. In a fictionalized but highly autobiographical version of this period, Jean's ten-year-old protagonist furtively reads the Bible and methodically shops for a religion among the churches of her town. When her father catches her exiting from an Episcopal church, he marches her home, takes her down to the basement, and whips her with his belt.

From her earliest years Jean always seemed to think of herself as physically unattractive, even ugly. "We all thought she was beautiful," says Marjorie, while acknowledging Jean's poor self-image. "I think she was embarrassed by her hands . . . her hands were kind of big, and she used to tell me her fingers looked like Idaho potatoes." Jean bit her thumbs and thumbnails so compulsively that the skin stayed constantly bloody. "This embarrassed her," recalls Marjorie, "but she was so nervous she felt compelled to savagely attack herself."

In a photograph taken when she was sixteen, Jean smiles as she squarely faces the camera. Her hair is combed close to her skull, sideways in either direction from a prominent part at the top of her head. She wears a dark dress fringed in crepe, like a graduation gown, and a shiny cloth collar tight around her neck. She looks prim and innocent, in an Emily Dickinson–ish way, but she is evidently a pretty, perhaps even beautiful, girl. Her eyes are misted over, under brows that arch quizzically at the corners; her smile is La Giocanda's.

An earlier photograph, taken by John Stafford when Jean was twelve or thirteen, is more surprising. In it Jean is dressed as a foppish young man. She wears a light suit of her father's, with the pants legs dragging on the floor and the bottom of the jacket reaching almost to her knees, and a round top hat tilted jauntily back. Her hair is tucked completely under the hat, like a man's. All six buttons of the vest are fastened, over a dress shirt and cravat. The young "man" leans on her father's blackthorn walking stick. Despite the comic misproportions of the clothing, there is an eerily prepossessing air about the cocksure dandy Jean impersonates. Just as in her earliest stories she habitually chose adult male protagonists, so she looks comfortable pretending to be a man.

Jean had surprised her father in this getup as he sat downstairs working on a manuscript. The disguise was so good, wrote John Stafford nearly a quarter of a century later,

> that for a fleeting instant it was given to me to believe or at least
> to hope that I was being honored by the very personable agent of
> some hopeful editor who had heard of me but who had never seen
> any of my stuff. When I came out of my trance I took the picture
> of her and we were both hilariously proud of it for a long time.
> But in time her enthusiasm for it weakened while mine increased.

By 1928 the Staffords had moved to a redbrick house on top of University Hill. Its address was 1112 University Avenue — a choice location, for the house stood on the very edge of the Hill, with a lordly view north across one of the broadest streets in Boulder. Next door on the east side stood the Kappa Kappa Gamma house, then, as now, one of the two or three most desirable sororities on campus. The family's shaky finances at last drove Ethel Stafford to action. She began to rent out the top floor of her house to student lodgers, and to serve meals to them downstairs. As a consequence, Jean and Marjorie had to share a bedroom, and for at least part of the time they slept together on an army cot on the front porch. The children canvassed Boulder for odd jobs — baby-sitting, dishwashing, working in a print shop — to help pay their school expenses.

The propinquity of the sorority was later to work a cruel humiliation on Jean, when she was in college and had to wait on table for Kappa girls — classmates who pretended not to know her — who lodged at the Stafford house as if it were a sorority annex. Today the house at 1112 University, where Jean spent most of her adolescence, no longer stands. In its place is an asphalt-covered parking lot for the Kappa Kappa Gamma girls.

The house was perpetually cold because the furnace worked poorly, belching forth smelly fumes, and because John Stafford often forgot to stoke it. The walls were lined with books. A stuffed deer's head stared down on the inhabitants. On the floor lay an Olson rug — a patchwork of rags Ethel had sent away to be made into a carpet. The family still had its entertainments: Marjorie, Dick, Jean, and their mother played a word game together, the point of which was to guess the names of friends or famous people from homonymic riddles. Thus Hazel Walton was "Nut-bearing tree, Barrier Two Thousand Pounds," and Marie Parent was "French Mary Progenitor." Mary Lee, however, had become absent and aloof now that she was in college, and Dick's love of the outdoors kept him at his own distance.

In the Big House in Covina John Stafford's sanctum had been a spare upstairs bedroom. On University Avenue in Boulder he descended to the basement, where he sat on an old automobile seat, facing a typewriter propped on top of an apple crate. He often wrote wearing only trousers, suspenders, and an undershirt. As an economy measure he sent away for cut-rate tobacco to smoke in his pipe. It arrived, to his dismay, in the form of huge yellow-brown leaves, which he had to crumble and stuff into the pipe; the residue was almost impossible to light. He also chewed tobacco in the basement, spitting into a coal hod.

As he worked, he talked out loud to himself. In a fictional rendering of John Stafford's subterranean ritual, Jean's protagonist overhears her father talking to ancestral photos on the walls: " 'Cave Canem, old Horsefeathers, there's going to be the devil to pay and no pitch hot,' and this promise was followed by a

spasm of glottal laughter. . . ." (Marjorie verifies that this vignette has the ring of truth.)

John Stafford had no friends in Boulder. Increasingly misanthropic and reclusive, he worked long hours in his lair, rehears-
ing on the typed page his grievances against the world. "My
father . . . cursed the stock exchange where he had lost his
money," Jean later reminisced,

> and cursed the editors who would not buy his stories. My father
> believed . . . that his failure could be attributed to the degeneracy
> of the modern world. . . . My father, a small poor friendless man,
> believed he cut quite a figure in the world.
>
> For fifteen years he sat before the typewriter, filling page after
> page. . . . We [children] bought our father postage and paper; my
> mother spared his feelings; we believed he was an artist. . . . One
> time when he had decided to make a sacrifice to us and was about
> to take a job on a newspaper whose policy offended his moral
> being, he became mysteriously ill.

Marjorie says that Jean began writing stories in junior high
school. Jean herself claimed that she wrote western stories at eight
and her first "novel" — a twelve-page thriller set in the British
Museum — in seventh grade. She had her own typewriter at the
age of eleven. Her first efforts were typed all in capitals; she filled
in the punctuation later, by hand, with colored pencils. The few
manuscripts of Stafford's juvenilia that have survived are difficult
to date, but some of the prose seems immature enough to have
been written when Jean was eleven or twelve. These quite short
stories and fragments, all typewritten, fall into two categories:
romance and satire.

Some of the first sort are entirely fanciful, sagas of imagined
lives that take place far from University Avenue. One, called
"Along the Border," is in the pulp-western vein her father was
mining. It opens, "One sweltering day, I was riding over a faint
desert trail to a remote little town called Columbine. The relentless sun sent painful rays down my back. I had ridden all day but
I seemed to get nowhere. . . ." Jean attempts the vernacular: a
very big woman on a donkey says her husband " 'up an' died on
me nigh week gone yistaday' "; a "theif [sic]" says, " 'Don't git
uppish or I'll treat y' ter a hunk o' lead in yer breathin' apparatus.' "

Another manuscript, called "Miss Lucy," identifies itself as the product of a ninth-grade class at Uni Hill, its author "Age-13." Although it is written from a male point of view, the story focuses on Lucy, who sounds like a persona for Jean: "Miss Lucy is the most wildly imaginative of all our imaginative family. She always is or has a new character and she keeps us in gales of laughter from dawn to night." Lucy occupies herself by inventing roles and intrigues. One of her suitors is a Lord Garnsborough, who says, " 'I've been in London — wretched bore. I was up there on business and while I was there I decided to change my clothiers. Ran all over London trying to find decent outfitters. Who is your hatter?' "

Marjorie remembers a story by Jean about a rejected damsel who, dressed in black and gray, commits suicide by jumping into a pond in winter. The last that is seen of her is a gray chiffon scarf floating on the water's surface. In Marjorie's account of Jean's fictional method, "She could take some experience — her own or some other family member's [—] and by adding bits and pieces here and subtracting things there and putting it all down in her own style she created things which I found delightful." Jean usually read her stories aloud to the family, Marjorie recalls:

> I particularly remember one about a family which bore some resemblance to the Stafford family. It was certainly not flattering and it made fun of the mother for being more interested in the prices of pot roast and toilet paper than in current events or English literature, and none of the other family members came off any better.

Indeed. In this second kind of story, Jean discovered the satirical. Three surviving manuscripts adumbrate an emotionally detached view of the "Smith" family, once again unmistakably Jean's own. In "Smith Saga," Charles, the third-youngest child and only son, a "serious and unimaginative boy,"

> had been disappointed when his youngest sister was born. Mr. Smith had said there was going to be a surprise and Charles had been expecting a dog all along. He had never quite gotten over his first disenchantment. He had felt cheated when he saw the squawling baby that should have been an airedale, but after the first pangs of disillusion had gone, he had enjoyed his unhappiness

and secretly compared himself to the martyrs in "Foxs' [*sic*] Book of Martyrs."

The narrator's father, Mr. Smith,

> was an unassuming author who was still so optimistic as to be-
> lieve that editors did not lack the milk of human kindness. He
> spent most of the time in the seclusion of his basement sanctum
> pounding out "shorts" and "squibs" on an ancient Remington.
> At various intervals checks for stories came in long envelopes and
> the Smith family, on occasions like this, celebrated with beefsteak
> and bananas and considered the advisability of paying the light
> bill. Mr. Smith was always surprised and flattered when he re-
> ceived a check. He would chew a match thoughtfully and say "May
> Plutus be praised." He was never quite sure about his classical
> references but since the rest didn't know the difference he could
> consult Bullfinch [*sic*] before he said anything else. . . .

It is hard to imagine even the teenage Jean Stafford having the
nerve to read such a story out loud to her own family. Yet Marjorie recalls the fictions Jean recited as "awfully funny and full of
wry observation," and she often boasted to her friends about her
talented younger sister. It is possible, of course, that the surviving manuscripts are ones that Jean did not read out loud.

Another untitled story about the Smith family has Ursula, the
youngest girl, putting on her brother's discarded Boy Scout shirt.
He demands that she remove the "Be Prepared" insignia "because he said it was disloyal." (In *The Mountain Lion* the incident
is revived: the brother sneers, " 'Having that on a girl is like
dragging the American flag in the dirt.' ") Ursula is a forlorn,
rejected waif. She asks her brother to go hiking with her, but he
makes excuses since he abhors wasting time with "a darn fool
girl." She turns to her sister, asking her to walk with her up onto
the mesa, where they can eat cheese and crackers and pretend
they're "the little Swiss twins." The sister refuses. In the end
Ursula hikes to the mesa alone, where she sits under a tree and
talks to herself, bragging about killing birds with stones.

In a third Smith family story (also untitled), the son, Charles, is
deeply disappointed when Ursula — an ugly, "silly red baby" — is
born. He stands over her crib saying, " 'I hate you.' " But when,
at age two, Ursula utters her first word — *Charles* — the boy

undergoes "the most thrilling spiritual transformation," lifts the baby out of the crib, and kisses her.

In the same story Mr. Smith, writer of "shorts" and "squibs" on the ancient Remington in the basement, confides in his son: " 'If I should live over again . . . I should get me a wife whose tongue was cut out; provided, of course, that she couldn't talk with her hands.' "

In later life Jean insisted that she had met Robert Frost — "the first writer I ever saw" — in Boulder during the late 1920s. In one version of this recollection, Jean, age twelve, was a waitress in a lodge in Boulder Canyon where Frost ate lunch one day; in another (probably more apocryphal) version Frost came to the Stafford house for dinner when Jean was fourteen. In both tellings Jean is so nervous that she nicks her finger with a knife, and a few drops of her blood spill into the glass of milk that she serves the great poet. "For weeks I was rapturous that MY blood was coursing through Robert Frost's veins." Frost indeed visited Boulder often during the 1930s, giving talks at the summer writers' conferences. He first went there in the fall of 1931, so Jean must actually have been at least sixteen when (and if) she served the poet the adulterated glass of milk.

One summer when Jean was about twelve, her father rented a cabin in the town of Eldora, some twenty miles west of Boulder in the mountains. The plan was for the two writers to spend several months in seclusion from the rest of the family, producing great works. A few years later, still an adolescent, Jean wrote a story about the Eldora summer, called "Fame Is Sweet to the Foolish Man." "Since Christmas," her protagonist ruminates, "my father and I had planned the novels and dramas we would write during those glorious months. . . ." The authors pack two typewriters in the car and leave Boulder "with promises to our family that before August was over we would have gained national recognition for our outstanding work in the literary field. . . ."

Instead the father and daughter are distracted by fly-fishing, by a hike to the Arapaho Glacier, by chess and conversation: they discuss "psychology, modern art and subways." But neither gets much writing done, and the narrator ruefully concludes:

So I gave up, abandoning all hopes of ever becoming a second George Eliot. . . .

What fools we had been! Here we had accomplished nothing. We had been painfully blistered by the sun and our brains had become rusty with idleness.

On the relatively thin evidence of these few surviving examples of Jean's earliest writing, we can judge that her teenage prose was precocious but not brilliant. Her teachers seem to have recognized a bright student but to have had no inkling that this shy, sardonic girl would become the best writer any of them would ever teach. After she won a statewide essay contest at fifteen for "Disenchantment" — the memoir about the drive from California to Colorado — the local papers gave her only the sort of attention one of her classmates might have garnered for winning a prize at a state fair.

Yet the interest of these juvenile fragments far exceeds their merits as fiction. It is clear that by a very early age Jean had turned to writing not only as an escape from her family, friends, and neighborhood — whence the fantasies of cowboys and London dilettantes — but also as a way of coming to terms with the hurt that growing up as the youngest Stafford had inflicted upon her. The several versions of Dick's reaction to Jean's birth illustrate this struggle. For the other Staffords, Dick's wishing the surprise waiting at home had been a dog instead of a baby was merely a funny family yarn. To Jean it was a document of trauma. Sixty years later Marjorie would commence a memoir about Jean with an elaborate retelling of the story, and there is nothing in her tone that even hints at a suspicion of lasting psychological harm. As an adolescent, however, Jean was already wrestling with the family joke, recognizing its humor, trying out a happier ending in Charles's "thrilling spiritual transformation" even as she placed herself empathically in her brother's head while he stared down at the "silly red baby" she had been to him.

Similarly, Marjorie would go through adulthood with an uncomplicated memory of John Stafford as a "walking encyclopedia" effortlessly quoting long passages from Roman and Greek authors "in the original," while Jean, still in high school, saw her father bluffing his way through uncertain classical allusions, cribbing from Bulfinch.

What granted her such distance, such clarity of vision? What allowed her, in her own phrase, to leave home at the age of seven?

The ultimate sources of her alienation lie hidden in unrecorded events. But there is a striking tension at work in these bits and pieces of Stafford juvenilia. Like her father, Jean was tempted to flee the dreary quotidian by riding the written word to realms of enchantment — the Wild West, the gothic forest, foppish and lordly London. Her imitations of the genre fictions of the day, including her father's vein of cowboy romance, may have been utterly sincere; yet it is hard not to hear a hint of parody in them already, in the drawl of the woman on the donkey, the affectations of Lord Garnsborough.

The other pieces, in which she writes about the Smith family, point toward the mature Stafford. It is extraordinary that by the time she was fifteen, this young author had not only discovered irony as a prose technique but had mastered it sufficiently that she could employ it to make sense of some of her own most disturbing experiences. In pursuing irony, she made a vital choice as a writer. She rejected the easy seductions of enchantment and turned instead to its opposite. For the most interesting of these early pieces could all bear the title of her prize essay; it was disenchantment, not enchantment, that would become perhaps the central theme of Jean Stafford's work.

III

Prep

In the fall of 1929 Jean entered high school. "Prep" was a dilapidated, gloomy, brick and stone building that stood at Seventeenth and Pearl streets, on the east end of Boulder's downtown business district and only a few blocks from its impoverished black neighborhood. Although Jean was now in tenth grade, she was only fourteen years old, having skipped a grade at some point, perhaps while the family was living in Colorado Springs. Thus she was a year younger than most of her classmates.

As she had been at Uni Hill, she remained a solitary person with few friends. One of them, Jane Fitz-Randolph, would become a professional writer herself while continuing to live in Boulder. As she recalls,

> [Jean] was one year ahead of me. She looked like a boy with a dress on. She had a very boyish figure, and she had her hair cut like a boy. . . . She had an interesting voice — warm and deep. She had a lot of enthusiasm, but she was also terribly shy. She was, I'm sure, very embarrassed about her family, the fact that her father — not that he was a writer, but that he was not a good writer.
>
> She was a very private person. She always had this enormous vocabulary. She was always terribly smart in school. . . . She was definitely a loner. I don't know anybody who ever went into her home.

Fitz-Randolph and Stafford often walked to school together. But, Fitz-Randolph remembers,

[Jean] never discussed anything personal. She talked about objective things. We didn't even gossip, though I realized later that she was intensely interested in other people and what made them tick. And I think she thought, Why am I not like them? She felt her outsideness always. . . .

She always had a chip on her shoulder. She made people uncomfortable. You never knew what she was going to say. She was pretty negative, and seemed to be utterly humorless except for caustic remarks.

Another high-school friend remembers Jean's looks as unusual rather than beautiful: "She had an *interesting* face, with high cheekbones and a somewhat snubby nose." Howard Higman, who had known her since grade school, thought Jean had a Garbo look: "Her head would be held high and back. . . . She had a serenity, an internal sense of self-worth, with a slight touch of scorn in her smile and in her speech. She spoke very slowly, in a put-down sort of way."

In high school Jean had great difficulty with algebra and plane geometry, and she studied as little science as possible. Hating physical education, she "weaseled out" of gym classes. On the other hand, she did well in Latin, which she began in seventh grade, and eventually became proficient enough to read Virgil and Livy. While still at Uni Hill, Jean made up a kind of speech of her own, using Latin words for English ones:

> "*Cur* do you not have a hippocampus in your *pisces* olla?" I would ask of somebody who had invited me to his house after school for a raw potato sandwich and a look at his new guppies. I would not be asked again. When my mother and a visiting aunt were about to anatomize the character of a cousin whose problem was D-R-I-N-K, and I was told to go upstairs to do my homework, I would smirk and mince and say, "*Certe,* I ken that little ewers have big *aures.*"

In later life Jean would credit Latin with teaching her far more about English grammar than she ever learned in English classes.

In tenth grade Jean wrote an essay for a school contest, which she entered under the "Declamation" category. The essay, whose text and title seem not to have survived, won first prize at Prep and second in the state. The following year "Disenchantment" won first prize statewide.

At Prep Jean joined a group of about six girls who called
themselves the Scribblers' Club. They met once a month to read
their poetry, sketches, and short stories to each other. Fitz-
Randolph, a fellow Scribbler, remembers Jean as a very good
writer even in high school, but a poor critic of others' works.

> She always wrote about kind of bizarre things. The rest of us felt
> that she was far more worldly or knowledgeable about what went
> on elsewhere [than we were]. She was sophisticated for her age.
> But I think in large part that was a defense. . . .
>   She just had a rapier attack on people and things she didn't ap-
> prove of. . . . She certainly had an ability to tell people off when
> she felt like it. She said things to teachers that the rest of us wouldn't
> have dreamed of saying.

In tenth grade Jean submitted several articles to the *Prep Owl,*
the student newspaper. The editor, Goodrich Walton, thought
the pieces "great" and quickly made her features editor. In the
spring of 1931, near the end of her eleventh-grade year, Jean wrote
an anonymous polemic for the "Vox Populi" column of the *Owl.*
A scornful attack on the privileged elite that dominated the school's
social life, it caused a huge furor. As Howard Higman recalls,
"The whole school was in a rage — the fast crowd, that is — at
this terrible attack on them as persons. For days, people wrote
rejoinders, and tr[ied] to find out who wrote it, and they kind of
knew Jean did."

In its pseudo-sophistication, its studiedly blasé tone, the essay
betrays not only Jean's longings and pretensions but the anguish
that being an outsider had caused this shy, proud fifteen-year-
old. It gives a more vivid sense of the angry, disaffected idealist
Jean had become than do the recollections of her friends. And in
an uncanny way the piece anticipates the ambivalent vexation at
social inequality and the hypocrisies of class that would inform
the novels and short stories of Stafford's maturity.

> It seems to me that people of such immature judgment and utter
> lack of experience as high school students take things a little too
> much for granted when they divide themselves into classes al-
> though I believe the popular expression is "gangs." For two years
> I have watched several of these, and have arrived at the end of
> every period of contemplation that there is just about one individ-
> ual in the whole school that being the janitor.

I was in a gang once for two weeks and I caused so much disturbance and distressed the young hypocrite[s] so much with my
candor that I was promptly ostracised, and I laughed for five weeks
steadily with genuine mirth. . . .

I am a democrat of the most radical species. Of course I am not
acquainted with aristocracy (thank the powers that be!) and so
perhaps I am unjust. I would appreciate a prolonged torture for
any one who discriminates to the point of insult and utter rude-
ness in the question of race. There are a good number of Negroes
whose company I would prefer to that of any one so lacking in-
dividuality and courage and incidentally, honesty, that he belongs
to a "gang." Next year all those girls of whom I have spoken,
will attend universities. "It's being done, you know," and of course
deviation from that which is correct would be lacking in shrewd-
ness. I'm strong for university education for women, but not for
women like these, because they don't want education. They're
going to make a sorority, to probably flunk out of school to give
their lives a collegiate air, and to return, fine and finished young
Americans. . . . Colleges and universities are cram[m]ed to the
gates with sweet "young things" and "good eggs" and "grand
boys" who are utterly brainless and all of whom ought to be serving apprenticeships in onion-stinking kitchens and blacksmith shops,
in order to knock some of the nonsense out of them.

Jean felt more comfortable on her solitary prowls about Boulder than she did at Prep. Long before tenth grade she had formed
the habit of taking after-school hikes by herself to the mesa
southwest of town. There, on top, she would sit until sunset,
indulging in a favorite fantasy. The mesa became her private island, alternately a tropical paradise (with palm trees, a monkey,
and "the footprints of my own Friday") and the Isle of Arran,
from which her McKillop ancestors had come. The deep satisfaction of these daydreams came from pretending to occupy a place
in which "I was sufficient unto myself and free and masterful and
familiar with every inch of my domain. . . ." Once a group of
kindergartners, out looking for pasqueflowers in the spring, in-
truded upon Jean's solitude. She scared them off by telling them
she had pinkeye.

Later in life Stafford became an increasingly indoor soul, all
but oblivious to nature beyond the confines of her yard and garden. But as a girl she responded viscerally to the outdoors. The

dramatic scenery of Boulder awed but at the same time intimidated her. The cozy island in her head was in part a deliberate
evasion of "a titanic landscape, of mountains that stretched —
peak and chasm and hummock of purple rock — miles beyond
vision. . . ." Unlike her brother, Dick, Jean never became an
explorer. Her after-school hikes were at most a mile or two long,
and their aim was rumination, not exercise or discovery.

She continued to be fascinated by the down-and-out of Boulder, whose numbers grew as the Depression deepened. Often
Jean visited the little square on Pearl Street surrounding the county
courthouse, or Central Park on Broadway, where unemployed
men sat on benches all day long. Thirty years later she recalled
them vividly.

> Sometimes these able men, disabled by inaction, held bitter sym-
> posia to discover why their decent lives had become ignominious;
> shouting and gesticulating, they inveighed against the Govern-
> ment, berated Wall Street, denounced the vile, mysterious forces
> that had closed mines and mills and put an end to building, and
> had subjected them and their blameless families to the indignities
> of the soup kitchen. For the most part, though, their travail was
> silent; hour after terrible hour, they sat dumbly staring into sunny
> space, killing time that died hard.

In her early stories Jean hints at an analogy between these dis-
heartened anchorites and her own father — though instead of a
wire bench under the courthouse elms, John Stafford chose as his
perch an old automobile seat in the basement.

In 1929, three months before Jean entered high school, Mary
Lee graduated from the university with a degree in English. Unlike Jean, with her withering contempt for the in-crowd, Mary
Lee had sought out society, pledging and then being initiated
into the Delta Zeta sorority. It was not one of the university's
more exclusive sisterhoods, but after all, Mary Lee's mother ran
a boardinghouse. On graduating, instead of trying to become a
writer (the career she had planned when she was a child), Mary
Lee decided to teach school. Her first job was as an instructor of
high-school English in Hayden, a small town in northwest Colorado. She quickly married a tall, ruggedly good-looking local
youth named Harry Frichtel, who became a rancher. Mary Lee
spent the rest of her life in Hayden.

By the fall of 1929 Marjorie was a senior at the University of Colorado, still living at home, apparently still sharing a room with Jean. She had followed Mary Lee's lead and pledged Delta Zeta, but she never went beyond "rush." "I wasn't interested after I'd cleaned a few bathrooms," Marjorie recalls. In 1930 she graduated as an art major, and a year later she got a job teaching art on an Indian reservation in Tahlequah, Oklahoma. From the start Marjorie sent a portion of her income home to subsidize her parents and Jean.

Dick had left home to attend Colorado A&M (now Colorado State University) in Fort Collins. In Boulder, just as in Colorado Springs, he had spent much of his free time taking long solo hikes into the mountains. Far from emulating his father's love of guns and hunting, Dick was temperamentally a pacifist. At Colorado A&M he majored in botany, taking summer jobs on fire lines and as a fire lookout. After college he joined the forest service.

The Depression had only made the Staffords' financial outlook more precarious. During one period when John Stafford was ill, Ethel's worries about money plunged her into new depths of despair. John's relationship with his mother in Los Angeles had been strained by his continued dependence on her cash. At one point his mother wrote and exhorted him to take Marjorie and Dick out of college and put them to work; as her grandmother's favorite, Mary Lee could be allowed to go ahead and finish her studies. Eventually Grandma Stafford cut off her funding altogether, and this caused "some unpleasantness" between mother and son.

Ethel also worried about her children's health. In a 1975 essay Jean half bragged that in Boulder "I had the longest list of contagious diseases on record at the board of health and singlehandedly started a prominent scarlet fever epidemic. . . ." Yet in a medical history she gave to her doctor in 1963, Jean listed measles at eight (in fact, she was six) and diphtheria at ten as the only illnesses of her first eighteen years; there is no mention of scarlet fever.

Since early childhood Jean had rebelled against her mother's tyranny of feeding. Ethel believed anyone who was ill should invariably be served beefsteak with hot buttered toast and tea or cocoa. Within the family, she was the one who refused to get sick, who rushed to tend husband and children when they were ailing. Whenever Marjorie became ill, for the rest of her life, she longed for the "comforting and reassuring" presence of her mother. Jean's response was exactly the opposite: when ill, she could not bear commiserating attention from her family, and even after leaving home, Marjorie claims, "She always said she preferred to lick her wounds in solitude like some of the lower animals."

Howard Higman offers a vignette illustrating Jean's relationship with this fussy and intruding mother.

> I went down to see her one time and her mother said, "Well, Jean's feeling pouty, she's locked herself in her room, but I'll get her out. She just loves fried bananas." So her mother fried a bunch of bananas in a frying pan and set them on the floor outside Jean's door, thinking the odor would go under the door and Jean would not be able to not unlock it. I don't think she did unlock the door.

During summers in high school and college, all three Stafford sisters worked at a dude ranch near Ward, in the mountains west of Boulder. At Lodge of Pines, first Mary Lee, then Marjorie, then Jean worked as waitress and maid for twenty-five dollars a month plus tips (usually another twenty-five dollars monthly). They lived in a converted chicken house infested with pack rats and chipmunks; their board consisted of leftovers from the paying guests' meals. Marjorie remembers regularly violating the after-dark curfew by sneaking off to dances in Ward or having boys drive her down Left Hand Canyon to Boulder. Though frequently homesick, the girls stuck out their jobs so they would be able to afford new clothes for the fall.

In high school Jean grew tall and thin. At seventeen she stood about five foot seven — an inch taller than her father — and weighed 120 pounds. The plain cotton dresses she wore did nothing to advertise her looks. Her shyness and her aloof bearing kept boys at a distance, and indeed she did little to encourage their attentions.

During the whole span of her junior-high and high-school years, Jean seems to have had only two male companions who approached the status of boyfriend. One was Howard Higman, who had first noticed Jean when she was dragging her father's saber along the sidewalk on her way to Uni Hill. Higman was a year younger than Jean. Born in Boulder, he eventually became a flamboyant and popular professor of sociology at the University

of Colorado, and the founder of its renowned World Affairs
Conference.

By the time Jean was in ninth grade and Howard was in eighth,
they had been drawn together by a common aversion to their
classmates. "We thought of each other as some kind of kindred
spirits," says Higman, "against all the folderol of the athletic
contests and the cheerleaders and all that sort of thing. We were
self-styled intellectuals."

Since the age of eleven Higman had had his own basement
apartment in his parents' house, with a separate entrance. With a
small group of like-minded friends, including Jean, he started a
"Voltaire Society Club."

> We had a dinner party in my house. . . . Bob McCammon went
> out and shot pigeons. We cleaned them and cooked them and called
> them roast squab. We had fake champagne, by putting catawba
> grape juice and soda water and grain alcohol [together], and the
> women all wore formals, and one earring, and we had this long
> table made out of a door on boxes, with a tablecloth to the ground
> and candles, and the dinner was served at midnight. . . .
>
> We [also] sat around in the afternoon and did book reviews. We
> tried to buy every Modern Library book — they were new then.
> We'd have book reviews, and drink tea, and eat cakes. . . .
>
> It was in this apartment where Jean and I would be reading
> *Strange Interlude*. We'd lie on the bed and read *Strange Interlude*.
> She was in the group, but with one foot outside.

Higman remembers Jean as a "loner." "You could almost say
she was a pre-hippie hippie — the only one in town. She affected
dirty fingernails, in contempt with the idea of manicuring, cos-
metics. She took big steps when she walked."

As Higman entered high school, however, he found himself
drawn to the "fast" crowd, with their pep rallies and social whirl.
Yet he tried not to alienate Jean with his newly divided loyalties.

> In effect, I was trying to court Jean greedily all through high school,
> and at the same time maintain membership in the group she hated.
> . . . [The fast crowd] went in in a big way for sexual stuff. Neck-
> ing and petting. Jean wasn't interested in any of that. . . .
>
> With me . . . it wasn't really a sexual thing, it was more — I
> mean, we didn't kiss each other. We read stuff, and we went to

things. Actually, we toyed with the idea of becoming lovers, but we never were, really. She had a fabulous ring. It was an enormous brown cameo about an inch by three quarters of an inch, and it was gold and had a band [that circled the finger several times]. She would give that ring to her favorite person. The guys that wanted her would get to wear that ring. I had it longer than anybody else. And then she took it back. She didn't give it to you, she loaned it to you.

Jean's other "boyfriend" was Goodrich Walton, the editor of the *Prep Owl.* He was two years older than she. From her own copy of the 1930 *Odaroloc,* the high-school yearbook, she cut out Walton's photo. If this indicates a romantic interest, it must have begun when Jean was in tenth grade, the year she first gave Walton her articles and ascended to the post of features editor.

Walton's retrospective description of Jean is not very flattering, but it may be colored by a postcollege estrangement between the two. "She was an intellectual, and she was unattractive. Very plain. She and I were both kidded because we talked so slowly. She was not attractive to men, and she was not attracted by them." Jean had long, light-brown, almost blond hair, Walton recalls, and wore plain dresses.

> She didn't try to be seductive at all. Jean was not affected by styles. She was negativistic because boys never paid any attention to her. . . . [She was] slender, with kind of heavy legs, heavier than the rest of her. She was flat-chested, and tits were real important then.

Walton, who was himself sexually experienced at seventeen, says that "When Jean was in high school she did not date. She didn't have dates like the rest of us did where you went up on Flagstaff [Mountain] and screwed in the back of the car or wherever. She was not that kind of person." Yet in other ways she was experimental. On the second floor of Jones Drug and in the back of Public Drug, Prep students drank Cokes, smoked cigarettes, and danced to records played on a phonograph. Some brought their own bootleg alcohol to mix with setups provided by the drugstores. Walton has no memory of Stafford smoking cigarettes or drinking, but he says that she had developed her own "kick." "She'd swipe ether out of the chemistry lab at the high school, a little vial of it, and we'd go up to the Public Drug

and sit in one of the back booths and she'd put it in a handkerchief and sniff it and get higher 'n a kite."

What drew Walton and Stafford together was intellectual kin-
ship. They went on hikes up Bluebell Canyon together, on the
same paths that a few years earlier Jean had taken to the mesa of
her island fantasies. They sat under the trees and talked. They
partook of the Colorado tradition of "steak fries," backwoods
picnics where usually only hamburgers were served. Once they
both attended a class party at Blanchard's Lodge, a fancy restaurant a few miles up Boulder Canyon. Jean and Goodrich "ended
up by ourselves talking about religion in the balcony. We were
sober." Her secret junior-high instruction in Catholicism not-
withstanding, Jean was an emphatic, even an antireligious, athe-
ist in high school, Walton insists.

They did not go to school dances together, but they often
stopped in at one of the drugstores for a Coke. "My God," Walton reminisces, "you could have a date with a girl and just spend
ten cents." They frequently talked about writing. "I don't remember kissing Jean the way — you know, you might kiss her
on the cheek. She and I exchanged rings when I was a senior."

In the spring of Jean's final year in high school, a boy in Manitou Springs, Colorado, conducted a brief courtship of her by
letter. He had come across a story or essay of Jean's that had been
published in a magazine (perhaps *Scholastic,* the piece possibly
being Jean's prizewinning "Disenchantment") along with her
picture. Three letters from this stranger are among the relatively
few memorabilia from high school that Jean kept for the rest of
her life, and though her side of the correspondence has vanished,
his jaunty letters give an indication of how she dealt with his
flirtations.

In his first letter, the Manitou Springs high-school student says
that Jean's picture and story intrigued him, and he goes on to
declare, "I have visited most every state in the union and believe
it or not you are the best featured, all around good looking girl
that I have ever seen. . . ." The boy mentions that he is a basketball player. By the end of the first letter he is addressing Jean
as "dear."

His second letter is dated June 9, 1932, which must have been
within a week or two of Jean's graduation from Prep. "You should
not start telling me about your 'figure,' " he complains, "you're

O.K. I know, I can tell from your picture. And another thing, you kinda discouraged me when you said I was wrong, when I said you were a sweet girl." He proposes "going with" her: "I sincerely would like to go with you instead of so called 'dance hawks,' and 'night birds.'

"You say, you don't know how to cook, sew or raise *babies,*" the amorous swain continues, "well why not? . . . I'm sure glad to know that you like your new home. I'm sorry to know that you must work so hard." The letter goes on to reveal that Jean, in her reply, had sent him another photo of herself.

The third epistle opens,

> Now listen! Jean, don't you tell me that I am wrong when I say you are good looking. . . .
>   You say you weigh 120 pounds, well dear, that's the way I'd like you to be, but I can't figure out what you mean when you say "a form that *won't cover* broad shoulders and narrow hips."

The boy signs himself "a future lover." There is no indication that the teenage Lothario ever managed to meet Jean Stafford.

The new home alluded to was farther west on University Avenue, at number 631. The Staffords' 1932 move represented a minor social retreat, for the one-story clapboard dwelling on the north side of the broad avenue was not as spacious or as grand as the brick house at 1112. As if to acknowledge Jean's passage from high school to college, her parents allowed her to live in a completely separate bedroom with its own entrance, which stood slightly behind the main house. By 1932, of course, Jean was the only Stafford child still living at home.

Goodrich Walton visited Jean regularly at her "cabin" late at night, a practice he says John Stafford did nothing to chaperone. At the time, Walton recalls, Jean was not getting along with her parents.

> I would go by her place after I'd had another date, and had taken the other date home, and Jean and I would sit there in that little cabin with a fire in the stove and talk for two or three hours. She was interested in writing, and I'd read what she had written and tell her what I thought of it.

Taken as a whole, the documentary evidence about Jean Stafford's family suggests that it was a mildly eccentric ménage. But it is hard to find in those quirks and interactions the sources of

Jean's profound and lasting antipathy toward all the members of her family except Dick — an antipathy complicated by her need, with respect to Marjorie and Mary Lee, both to keep open the lines of communication for the rest of her life and, at the same time, to choose up sides in a tireless reenactment of the past, as if she were fighting the psychic battles of childhood over and over again.

John Stafford's most potent aberration was his abdication from the responsibility of making a living, but there is no evidence that his wife or any of his children ever told him that he ought to climb out of his basement "yarn factory" and get a real job. All the Staffords seem to have colluded in the premise that the author of *When Cattle Kingdom Fell* was a serious writer who should put his craft ahead of the sordid quest for the dollar.

A case can be made — Marjorie in fact makes it — that at least John Stafford ensured, in the middle of the Depression, that all four of his children could attend and graduate from college. To be sure, the children had to win scholarships and waivers of tuition and had to work menial jobs in their spare time and through every vacation in order to pay for their higher education. But John Stafford resisted his mother's demand that he take Marjorie and Dick (and by implication Jean, once she was old enough) out of college and put them to work to support the family.

Ethel Stafford may have been mindlessly conventional and domestic, the mother who cared more about the price of pot roast than about current events. Yet she never stinted in her loyalty to her kin, even when it dictated the humiliation of having to make beds and cook meals for spoiled sorority girls. There may have been a claustrophobic closeness within the family, exemplified by everyone's picking up and moving to Boulder to follow Mary Lee to the university. But once they had graduated, all four offspring left home, found jobs, and got married. The two older daughters became teachers; Dick, a forest ranger. Jean herself would first make a living as a teacher.

The psychology of any family, however, is opaque from the outside. Howard Higman's and Goodrich Walton's brief reconnaissances inside 1112 and 631 University Avenue cannot be relied upon to decipher the psychic furniture at hand. Had Jean Stafford never become a writer, her family would have passed into oblivion unprobed.

From the documentary evidence alone, Jean emerges as a

haughty, difficult, mordantly critical yet romantic girl. The deeper questions, though, go unanswered. What lay beneath her shy prudery? What fueled her disaffection from her peers, her contempt for everything "bourgeois" (a favorite adjective of her teenage disdain)? Did she take refuge in intellectual superiority merely because she could not compete in terms of clothing and makeup? Where did her anger and sorrow come from, and from where, beyond invidious emulation of her father, her steadfast determination to be a writer?

In 1941, when she was twenty-six, Jean wrote a long story about her college years that she soon decided was "a complete failure." Six years later she returned to the story, determined to convert it into a full-fledged novel. She worked on this project for three and a half years before abandoning it; in the process, she later said, "I accumulated 25 pounds of manuscript and destroyed an equal amount." Although the embryonic novel focused on her years in college, Stafford used scenes from childhood and, more elaborately, high school as crucial background.

The reason that the novel, too, failed, she would later ruefully conclude, was that she had written "directly out of experience, adding only a few camouflaging details and subtracting very little. . . . I was everywhere hampered by the conviction that I must not alter the facts, that I must tell the truth, and nothing but the truth and the *whole* truth, that every act must come in its proper chronological order. . . ." Having come to this realization of the novel's fatal flaw one day in December 1950, "I burned [the manuscript] up, leaving not a word of it behind."

Even this account of "Truth and the Novelist" is not strictly truthful, for Stafford did not burn her novel in its entirety. Among the papers she left behind at her death are hundreds of pages of the autobiographical manuscript, in folders and boxes under the provisional title "In the Snowfall." The surviving pages do not add up to anything like twenty-five pounds of paper, but enough exists to give a very clear idea of what the novel might have been.

It would be naive to take "In the Snowfall" as pure nonfiction. At the same time, the manuscript represents by far the most autobiographical piece of fiction its author ever wrote. Joyce Bartholomew, the protagonist, is an extremely close alter ego to the Jean Stafford of ages fourteen through twenty-one.

Joyce's solitary walks are meditative excursions along the paths of her inner life. In the novel we can hear what she is thinking. All the children in Adams, Joyce reflects, ventured into the mountains in search of secret play: "The offices of their detective agencies and the headquarters of their outlaws were set up under the overhang of cliffs; they sinned in caves. . . ." For Joyce, the mountains are a hiding place.

> There were enclosures where she was as safe from the whole world as in a locked room; glades within the lodgepole pine forests where she could lie, and did, full-length on pink-brown needles and hear nothing at all but the patient voice of lamentation in the branches of the trees. . . .
>
> Here she had nursed the heart that boys had broken and at those moments when the pain receded temporarily had thought, "Somewhere yonder is London and that's where I'll go when I'm grown up," for she looked on London as a place where no one ever hurt another. . . .
>
> Within this glade, she had written poems, under that yellow pine she had stood declaiming Cicero's oration against Cataline, beside the creek just yonder she had dreamed of marriage and children, upon that mesa she had, not denying it, desired her father's death.

In her room at home Joyce plays solitaire against a rich imaginary opponent, composes unrhymed poems, draws "crabbed and geometrically perfect avenues of trees," writes her name over and over again in a notebook along with lists of books read and movies seen, lies on her bed dreaming of becoming an actress or a Ph.D., and keeps a journal in which she puts down "all her venomous hostility to her family, to Adams, to all people who were richer than she and who were popular and who knew how to dance."

There is a tart, satiric vignette of Joyce's mother as "an acquisitive landlady, lying in wait to pounce" on prospective roomers as she sits on a porch swing shelling peas, darning socks, and cutting old tablecloths into napkins. But a much deeper disturbance attends Joyce's thoughts about her father. On a walk behind the tuberculosis sanatorium, Joyce talks to herself:

> "I cannot love them, and I have never loved them," she said aloud.
> . . . Her friendships died, sometimes in a quarrel over a trifle,

sometimes simply through her own boredom or hidden envy; her
flirtations with boys came to nothing; she had never missed her
sister Amy since she went away three years ago and had not cared
that Amy never came back to visit. . . .

"I have never had any fun in life and it is *his* fault." . . .

"The fact is," she said practically, "the fact is that when all is
said and done I really hate my father."

"In the Snowfall" suggests that Jean's lofty disdain for boys
and dating concealed a despairing failure of nerve. At an age at
which Joyce and Amy still share a bedroom and, in the summer,
sleep on the same davenport on the porch, they flee the house
nightly to walk through the neighborhood together, invariably
seeking out the fraternity houses and the couples in parked cars.
It seems as if they can "smell the smells of good grooming and
see, through the pitch blackness, the badges of aristocracy." In
the summer Joyce and Amy stay out very late, drinking Cokes
in a café on the Hill.

> When at last they did go home, they could not sleep until all the
> roomers came in; they rustled and jerked on the davenport, dis-
> turbed by the silence of the upper floor and vexed by the deep
> breathing and the slumbrous mutters of their parents who slept in
> the room beyond. And then, when the cars began to steal up qui-
> etly to the parking and the soft good-nights began and there was
> kissing just beyond the front door, they were as lithe and mean as
> weasels, burying their heads under their pillows where they hissed
> and cursed and hated the world.

Yet Joyce soon begins to disapprove of Amy's efforts to catch
up with the world of frat boys and parked cars. At the dude
ranch in the mountains where both sisters work during the summer, Amy starts to take what Joyce calls "shortcuts" — dancing,
skinny-dipping at night, drinking home brew. Joyce swears never
to follow her older sister's lead, and prays to herself, " 'I will be
a nun or a Ph.D.' " (In verification of this fictional portrait, Marjorie, on whom the character of Amy is modeled, admits, "Yes,
I think [Jean] felt that way about me.")

"In the Snowfall" contains no character who clearly corresponds to Howard Higman or Goodrich Walton. Joyce goes out
on awkward dates and talks at length about boys with a more

worldly friend named Alice, who says, " 'You scare them all away, Jo. . . . If you want a boy-friend, don't use those big words and stop talking about Shakespeare or whatever.' " The Jean who blasted the "gangs" of popular girls in the *Prep Owl* is ironically mirrored in Joyce, who ponders "the pretty, stupid girls whose popularity, even though it was theirs through bad reputations, had made her sick with envy."

A few boys aggressively court Joyce.

> Once in high-school, she had been shocked by a boy who was an excellent Latin student and who had taken her to drink a coca cola at the Palace drug store and there in a dark booth, sitting on the same side with her, he had crudely put his hand inside her jacket. She had felt shamed and smirched, fearful that his gesture, which her sharp withdrawal had made much worse as if he had torn off her dress, had been observed by others in the adjoining booths and after her rout, she had reproached him in a soft, sarcastically patient voice, reproached him less for taking liberties than for his failure to "live up" to the lofty decorum she had endowed with him [*sic*] because of his brilliant translations in the Vergil class. She never forgot any particular of that scene: the booths were on a mezzanine and it was always twilight up there. . . .

Alice later goes steady with the same boy for about three weeks, prompting Joyce to wonder if her friend is a virgin and "if she knew some way to make them stop those frightening onslaughts without offending them."

These scenes from "In the Snowfall," together with Stafford's admission that the novel was written "directly out of experience," may fill in the picture of her high-school years. They hint at a socially insecure girl who longed quite normally for flirtation and romance but became flustered by the normal passes made by the boys she went out with. Pride forced her to cover her confusion with a smokescreen of haughty propriety, which served its purpose and kept the mystery of sex temporarily at bay. Yet the bookish loner who walked through the halls at Prep feigning indifference to the "gangs" and the boosters' club and the backseat necking up on Flagstaff may have been a secret voyeur, passionately curious about the cliques she felt excluded from.

"In the Snowfall" conjures tellingly with the Stafford family. The novel reduces the number of children to two, Amy and Joyce, who correspond to Marjorie and Jean. This may be only artistic simplification, to give focus to the dynamics of the Bartholomew household. Yet by the time Jean started high school in 1929, Mary Lee had left home for Hayden, and Dick was fifty miles away, in Fort Collins; Marjorie, meanwhile, still shared Jean's bedroom and, in the summer, Jean's bed. The novel further suggests that complex as Jean's reaction to her whole family may have been, her most intense feelings were reserved for her father.

Thus Joyce's mother, newly moved to Adams, is handled with satiric detachment: "She was afraid of the coyotes that howled at dawn and she suffered sorely from mountain sickness; she missed her friends in the Sorosis Club, and she was additionally distressed that there was no United Presbyterian Manse at which to call. . . ."

The father of "In the Snowfall," however, is never reduced to ironic cameo, and one of the two or three binding tensions at work throughout the novel is Joyce's tortured identification with Fulke Bartholomew. Among the pages that Stafford did not burn in 1950 are several that seem to constitute an extended preliminary note from the author to herself — almost a plan for the novel — and that summarize this relationship. In this form the pages suggest an autobiographical application even more immediate than that of the dramatized scenes of the narrative. It is easy to interpret the paragraphs as Jean's analysis of her feelings at seventeen about John Stafford.

> In the beginning of her life, Joyce adores her father much as her mother does and imitates him so that she acquires many of his useless and ill-natured attitudes, the habit, chiefly, of taking the other side of any argument for the keen pleasure of indulging her anger at an imaginary injustice. . . . Because he often voices to her his disappointment that she was not a son, she does what she can to compensate for this and wears her hair cut short like a boy's and, except when she is in school, dresses in blue-jeans and boys' shirts. . . . It never occurs to her that she will not be a writer and only occasionally does it occur to her, depressingly, that she is going to grow into a woman, not a man.
>
> By now, though, Joyce hates him and she is resentfully embarrassed by his infantile assumption that the same relationship exists between them that did when she was a little girl. . . . The very

sight of him (he chews tobacco constantly, he seldom shaves, he is always dirty and as shabby as a hobo) is intolerable to her and she avoids him as much as possible but in doing so is guilt-stricken because she pities him and fears that he is lonely and that he believes she has wilfully disappointed him. Sometimes, indeed, her guilt grows so intense that on an impulse, she leaves her studies and goes down to his room in the cellar and with great enthusiasm asks him how his book is coming along; this is always a terrible mistake for he turns the whole weight of his madness upon her and pinions her so that she is obliged to stay with him for hours, listening to him read (and laugh as he reads) chapters and chapters of his crazy book, hearing his unintelligible expostulations, watching him spit. It is the more awful because he makes her feel — and does so with a sort of mutilated gallantry — that no one understands him except herself. This is the closest he ever comes to tenderness. . . .

She longs with physical hunger for money to buy pretty clothes and then she is stricken with remorse, feels that she . . . has been disloyal to her father who, being a man of integrity, will not sacrifice himself to a job but continues, year after year, to write his book. . . . She is persuaded that only with wealth can there be peace of mind and that it is only amongst the poor that are to be found quarreling, hatred, misanthropy and violence, and yet she believes — because her father taught her this in her basinette — that only this very turbulence and misery can produce things of value, that the intellectual can thrive only in want. . . .

Perhaps this is merely the skillful memorandum of a novelist shaping a fictional character. On the other hand, the long note may be the most coherent statement Stafford ever set to paper about her father's impact upon her.

The "crazy book" was no mere invention. Sometime in the 1920s John Stafford started writing what he himself regarded as his magnum opus. It was to be a huge book analyzing the whole of the American government's fiscal system — in particular the national debt. No one else had understood this matter properly; Stafford would set the world straight. For forty years he worked on the book. Near the end of his long life he published, at his own expense, a small, innocuous pamphlet — the only extant product of his four decades' labor. It seems very likely, given its choice of subject, that John Stafford's obsessive toil had its psychological genesis in the 1921 trauma of his losing his fortune in the stock market.

Jean's father may well have been entering, by the late 1920s, a kind of madness. In the unpublished pages of "In the Snowfall," the reclusive patriarch has passed beyond the bounds of mere eccentricity:

> Now and again, he appeared on the streets of our town barefooted, a pair of overalls rolled halfway up his legs, two days of beard on his face. A crazy, misanthropic mood went with this guise and he would lope down alleys muttering to himself, or he would sit unmoving on an iron bench near the statue of Lincoln in the park, chewing tobacco and spitting as if he spat out lethal venom.

And:

> He spent a working day of seven hours, from five until noon, in a room in the basement of the house on Benedict Street, delivering orations to the four green walls where hung the portraits of his enemies, his mother, his father, his brothers and sisters. . . . He spoke in a low monotone and no one in the house heard him except Joyce who woke each morning when he began. . . . He had been doing it for nine years, delivering this quiet, wild pastiche of learning and approximation to the helpless victims on the walls. . . . He chewed tobacco as he preached and paused to spit into a coal hod and afterward to clap his hands together and then rub them, cracking his knuckles, and grin and address his company, whom he called "The Conquistadors[,]" once again in shameless expletives.

The title of the novel is elucidated in one of Joyce's reflections:

> She had for the snow a love like a love of a person, a person unimaginably good and tender; as a child, she had never remembered, from one autumn to the next[,] how cold it was so always, when the first flakes flew, she had run out in her bare feet expecting it to be soft as a cat; she screamed with surprise and delight and ran back into the house to lie on the floor in the hall, laughing hysterically. There was nothing at all in the natural world that moved her so much as snow and nothing in any aspect of the

world that so much consoled her, that imparted to her such a
sense of well-being and of hope that in some year of her life, in a
snowfall, she would discover her life.

The scene may be fictional, but the sentiments are not. Marjorie
reports, "[Jean] used to always say that she'd been deprived because she'd never known snow as a little child."
In the unfinished novel there is a terrifying scene from early
childhood, recollected by the seventeen-year-old Joyce:

> Long before they came to Adams, she and Amy had run one
> afternoon, stark naked into the snow that had begun to fall lightly
> and warmly; they had run around the house, laughing and aware
> of nothing but their enchanted bodies fondled by the flakes and
> stars and when they came to the windows of their father's study
> . . . they stopped and cried out, "Look at me, Daddy! Look at
> *me!*" Immediately the brown velours curtains parted and their fa-
> ther stood between them like an actor on the stage; he was petri-
> fied like a skeleton [and] as long and thin as a gibbet. At first he
> did not look at them but at the holly tree beyond them as if he
> were still deliberating a choice of words, but slowly his gaze (that
> gaze! How it had run a child through like the thinnest, sharpest
> blade! It came burning, boring, needle-fine through his eyes so
> black the pupils did not show: blue hair grew around their sockets
> like a lemur) his gaze apprehended them, arrested them so that
> after he had disappeared from the window, on his way to come
> and whip them, they stood stockstill, unable to console each other,
> trembling with the cold which until now they had not noticed.

When this passage was read aloud to Marjorie, she laughed and
said no such incident had ever occurred in the Stafford family.
Indeed there cannot have been many snowstorms in the Covina
or San Diego of Jean's first five years. Marjorie further says that
her father's physical violence never exceeded light applications of
the switch. Yet as an oedipal nightmare the scene has a vivid
reality that transcends the circumstantial. Perhaps the truest arti-
fact of Jean's intense relationship with her father lies in this imagined, rather than literally autobiographical, scene.
A kindred episode in "In the Snowfall" takes place when Joyce
is twelve. One night Amy comes home drunk.

Joyce was plucked rudely from her sleep by the sound of Amy's screams and she ran downstairs, barefoot. They were in the basement, in her father's study. In the green-calsomined room with the dawn coming like a sickness through the windows covered with grasshopper's tobacco spit, her sister lay stark naked and her father knelt, beating her with his driving gloves. He must have struck her thirty times while Joyce and her mother watched, dumb, and rooted to the spot. Fulke laughed each time Amy screamed and time and again called her a whore. At that moment, Joyce wished that it were she who lay there, suffering that monstrous indignity and that awful pain so that with no more guilt she could fully hate him.

(In the process of interviewing Marjorie, this writer asked her if there had ever been an occasion in her adolescence when she had come home drunk and was punished by her father. Marjorie said, "That did happen once, but I don't think I care to go into it." During the course of a lengthy interview over two days, this was the only time Marjorie seemed to be seriously upset and embarrassed.)

A passage from "In the Snowfall" takes Joyce's wish to be the victim of her father's violence to its utmost logical extreme: "She wanted him to kill her, for she felt that only through dying and only through a death that he himself had instigated would she ever be free of this sickness of the heart that sometimes crept into her flesh so that she could not eat and could not rest."

IV

Barbarian

As Jean Stafford entered the freshman class at the University of Colorado in the fall of 1932, the Depression had reached its nadir. The university suffered accordingly. Enrollment was down from the previous year's total of 3,310 students. Despite this fact, classrooms and dorms remained overcrowded, and the faculty grudgingly accepted salary cuts of as much as 18 percent.

Still, a bright student had many reasons to be excited about CU. An Honors Program begun in 1930 freed those who qualified from routine class attendance while pushing them scholastically with a general reading list and comprehensive exams. The faculty included a number of scholars with national reputations and as a whole was significantly more liberal than any other body of intellectuals in Colorado. In 1930 the university also started a summer writers' conference. By the mid-1930s, under the leadership of the poet Edward Davison, the conference had become an illustrious event, bringing to Boulder such writers as Thomas Wolfe, Robert Frost, Sherwood Anderson, Robert Penn Warren, John Crowe Ransom, John Peale Bishop, Bernard De Voto, Howard Mumford Jones, and Ford Madox Ford.

Tuition, books, and fees for a year came to only one hundred dollars. Stafford, however, received a scholarship "waiver of fees" that excused her from the sixty-six-dollar tuition charge. She bought books with the money she had saved working summers at Lodge of Pines, and she took student jobs on campus every term. For the first two years of college she continued to live at home at 631 University Avenue.

Student life at CU centered around the distinction between "Greeks," or members of fraternities and sororities, and "Barbarians," the unwashed remnant who were too poor to join, too socially undesirable to be accepted, or too contemptuous of Greek life to apply. Unlike her sisters, who had both pledged Delta Zeta, Jean never went near sorority rush.

The CU football team was a leading power, first in the Rocky Mountain Conference and then in the Big Seven. Nothing roused students to a greater fervor than Homecoming Week or the migration by bus, train, and auto to Salt Lake City for the big game against CU's arch-rival, Utah. The campus god of the era was Byron "Whizzer" White (now an associate justice of the United States Supreme Court), CU's first all-American and the national scoring leader in 1937.

The favorite student hangouts were Somers Sunken Garden, a café and beer hall known far and wide as the Sink, and a second-floor dance parlor called Varsity Hall. Up Boulder Canyon, couples flocked to Cañon Park to dance to the Pete Smythe Orchestra. CU had its endemic slang: girls were known as "heifers" and "fluffs"; drink was "giggle water" or "soup"; exams were "crimes against nature"; and courting might be referred to as "tangling" or "yum-yumming." According to a self-styled expert in the student newspaper,

> You must have one of the three following assets to be a successful wooer —
> 1. A good car.
> 2. Have access to a federal reserve bank.
> 3. A smooth line and a polished necking technique.

Such was the setting into which Stafford stepped in the fall of 1932, torn between her envy of the nonchalant world of "woo pitching" and her isolating disdain for a campus on which a majority of the coeds admitted that their main agenda in college was landing a husband. From her first weeks Jean was an intense scholar. She would later look back with affectionate irony on the "gawky, wobbly, sloppy student" she had been, "restless, plunging into work, into getting honors because . . . I could not express myself in the way I really wanted to, with friends, by going to dances, by learning to *do* things."

At CU Stafford was "vociferously contemptuous" of sports, resenting the mandatory fee she had to pay for a student athletic ticket. Only "after many humiliating failures" did she manage to gather enough physical-education credits to graduate at the end of her four years. One of the student jobs she took was working as a "shower checker" — handing out towels after gym class and marking off names to make sure each girl took her shower — for twenty-five cents an hour.

Stafford unhesitatingly chose English literature as her major. She was also enthusiastic about Latin and philosophy, and a course in the history of science made her "mad with excitement." She took a writing class under the stern John McLucas, who recognized Stafford's talent as a writer but found her an indifferent critic of her peers' work. One of her favorite teachers was George Reynolds, an Elizabethan scholar and head of the department of English literature.

The two professors who had the greatest influence on Stafford were Joseph Cohen and Irene McKeehan. Cohen was a short, slight, fierce-looking man with a bristly mustache. A Marxist professor of philosophy, he was famous on campus for his inspiring, provocative classes. In a course taught by Cohen on the interrelationship between philosophy and literature, Stafford discovered psychology. This spark led to a lifelong interest in Freud, psychoanalysis, and the unconscious, which in turn would inform and deepen her writing. Cohen also apparently "pursued" his bright, attractive student outside the classroom, but there is no evidence that anything came of his infatuation.

Irene McKeehan taught English literature. In the memory of the poet and editor Peter Davison, whose father was in the same department, "Miss McKeehan was very much the English teacher, very much correct, scrupulous, perfectly spoken. She also had a lot of heart." According to Jean's close friend Howard Higman, McKeehan was "exactly the opposite of Jean's mother." To Stafford, who first encountered her in a class called "The Victorian Age," the tiny, severely dressed teacher seemed at once intimidating and marvelous. In a memoir written at a distance of forty-three years, Stafford recalled her mentor:

She came into the room precisely at the last stroke of the bell in Old Main and nodded at her full complement of students, and she put her pocketbook down on the desk squarely in front of her.

She cast her blue eyes over us, said "Good morning," and from her pocketbook took out the roll-call; she exchanged her distance glasses for her reading glasses, and, having made sure no one was missing — no one ever was except for a provable alibi such as an acute attack of appendicitis or a leg broken on the ice on the way to the campus — she switched spectacles again, and for the next fifty minutes, she told us the most remarkable, the most breath-taking, the most peculiar and heart-breaking and thought-provoking, the wretchedest, the most admirable things about Carlyle and Matthew Arnold, George Eliot and the Brownings.

Jean went on to take Middle English and Anglo-Saxon from McKeehan, who directed her in a precocious master's thesis. The teacher also had much to do with Stafford's choosing to make her living as a writer.

CU provoked in Stafford the most contradictory emotions. On the one hand she felt "destitute and friendless and unhappy" and was "mad at the world, terribly gloomy"; on the other, "in some more sagacious part of my mind, [I was] perpetually thrilled." By her junior year, as an honors student, she could skip classes whenever she wanted. A former schoolmate has the recollection — an odd one in view of Stafford's loyalty to her best teachers — that Jean went to almost no classes at all, having mastered the course material in the first three or four weeks of each term.

Peter Davison was a boy of seven when Stafford first came to his home as a student in his father's seminar. He was well aware of her reputation as the most brilliant of his father's students, and he was struck by the "remarkably pretty" college girl with freckles and a perpetual cigarette. Two years later Edward Davison would give Stafford a summer job as secretary to the writers' conference. As early as 1935, however, the talented student began, thanks to the conference, to make the timid acquaintance of such deities as Robert Penn Warren and John Crowe Ransom.

Stafford would later assert, somewhat misleadingly, that she had been "a secret writer" in college. Besides the stories she was quite publicly penning in John McLucas's class, as early as her freshman year she was writing experimental plays in another course. An old theater program identifies a work of that freshman year: " 'Wind through the Cottonwood Trees,' a play of death, by Jean Wilson Stafford."

Goodrich Walton, Jean's high-school boyfriend, remembers

reading long sections of a novel she wrote while at CU. "It was a hard-hitting thing with profanity and obscenity that were not allowed in books at that time," says Walton. "I'm absolutely sure it was the first full-length kind of writing she did." Walton further insists that Stafford submitted this novel to several American publishers and, in 1936, to a publisher in London who nearly accepted it.

It seems likely that Stafford wrote a good deal of fiction during college; she may even have been prolific. Perhaps the works of this era were part of the twenty-five-pound loads of manuscript she later bragged about carting to the incinerator. As far as we can tell, not a single piece of Stafford's fiction survives from all of her four years at CU, nor from the first year after her graduation. Fragmentary though the remains are, we actually have more of Stafford's juvenilia and high-school writing than we do of the work of her eighteenth through her twenty-third years. The span from 1932 to 1937, so crucial to her development as a writer, thus stands as a lacuna in the record of her creative process.

Stafford seems to have destroyed even her CU term papers. Her M.A. thesis, titled "Profane and Divine Love in English Literature of the Thirteenth Century," which she finished in the spring of 1936, is a ninety-six-page academic exercise whose stated purpose is "to show how the French ideas of love-service were taken into English literature in the first forms in the thirteenth century." As the product of a twenty-year-old, the thesis is an extraordinary performance, both in its confident grasp of early Middle English poetry and in its lucid, straightforward prose. But there is nothing in the slightest bit personal or speculative in it, and it has less of the stamp of Stafford's mature fiction than do the short stories she was writing at twelve.

Both Goodrich Walton and Howard Higman attended CU, but Jean's attachment to her two platonic boyfriends from high school dwindled. Says Higman, "She gave me up because I joined a fraternity." Early in Stafford's CU career, however, Higman persuaded her to model for a life mask made of plaster. She lay supine while Higman waxed her face with petroleum jelly. Then he put ice-cream-soda straws in her nostrils so she could breathe. Next Higman dripped plaster onto her face, waited for it to harden, and then dripped on another layer. When the mask was thick enough, he allowed her to pull it off.

The mask still exists, an eerie facsimile of Stafford's physiog-

nomy at seventeen. To make the cast look more human, Higman
painted the lips with lipstick and penciled in thin black lines for
eyebrows and eyelashes. The effect is somewhat garish, a pale,
blank countenance tarted up with makeup that Jean would never
have worn. Yet the plaster captures something of her proud disdain: her eyes are closed with a theatrical serenity; her mouth
turns down in a moue of scorn. The mask gives a vivid glimpse
of Jean's profile, with her thin, patrician nose, her flat, almost
browless forehead, her roundish chin and pouting lips.

In college Stafford remained as evasive about her family as she
had been in high school. A friend who sometimes walked her
home recalls, "We'd near her place when suddenly she'd find
some pretext for running off — there must've been some de-
formity in the family she didn't want anyone to see." Several
men were intrigued from afar by Stafford and decades later remembered their impressions — of the "deadly serious gal with
the occasional far-away look," as one put it, "the . . . soft voice,
the little wisp of smile that always faded back into seriousness."

Mary Moore, a classmate of Stafford's, remembers her as indifferent to the clothes she wore but "terribly smart. She seemed
to have some kind of witticism to offer about almost anything
that came up in the conversation." Moore was one of the few
friends who was invited into the Stafford house.

Jean may have cared more about her appearance — and about
conventional standards — than her friend thought. Even though
her vision was twenty-twenty, she wore a pair of Oxford glasses
because they were in fashion at CU. In general, though, she accepted her status as a Barbarian. By her junior year Stafford had
begun to hang out regularly not in the parlor of some sorority
house but at a second-floor sandwich and beer place on the Hill,
where a group that styled itself "the intelligentsia" met about
once a week. The literature she was studying in her classes ended
with the Victorians, but in the dim mezzanine of the café she and
her fellow thinkers and would-be writers read Mann and Proust
and Joyce, Wolfe and Faulkner and Hemingway, Auden and Eliot
and Pound. They read out loud from their favorite books and
occasionally, fueled by 3.2-percent beer, got up the nerve to read
from their own works-in-progress.

One member of the group, older and more worldly as a veteran of the Merchant Marine, had smuggled into the country an

unexpurgated version of *Lady Chatterly's Lover,* which he rented to others for $1.50 a day. Politically the group was vaguely leftist, and sometimes its members took in a meeting of the Young Communist League. But it was literature, not politics, that impassioned them. Stafford found herself "moonstruck by the world of modern writing that had opened up before me."

It was in college that Jean began to drink, no doubt without the knowledge of her teetotaling mother. Besides the 3.2 beer that had become legal after April 1933, bathtub gin made from grain alcohol bootlegged out of Denver was readily available. It is hard to picture her in this vignette, but in 1960 Stafford claimed that during college

> we ascended peaks in blizzards, and when we were at the top and still had the downward path to go, we disengaged ourselves from any sort of reality by drinking rotgut (slang is an accurate language) that we had bought from a bootlegger at the edge of town, who kept his bottles of filmy booze under a manure pile to outwit the Feds.

Boys with cars organized expeditions to abandoned mining cabins where "[we] held indoor beefsteak fries and drank up a storm. . . . We bought Dago red by the demijohn and our bright blue mouths puckered as if we had eaten green persimmons. . . . We drank sloe gin mixed with Coca-Cola and rum combined with cream soda pop. On Sundays we were awfully sick."

The girl who in high school had swiped ether from the chem lab to sniff in the back of a drugstore was, in college, willing to volunteer as a paid hypnotic subject for the psychology department. According to Goodrich Walton, the professor in charge told Stafford that she was the most suggestible subject he had ever had. She showed Walton a cigarette burn on the back of her hand, which she said had been inflicted under hypnosis without her feeling a thing.

As she immersed herself in this new bohemianism, Stafford was inexorably drifting away from her family. By now she saw relatively little of her siblings, with Dick in Oregon, Mary Lee on the ranch in western Colorado, and Marjorie teaching in Oklahoma. One summer Jean and Marjorie took a bus trip back to the Tahlequah reservation where Marjorie taught, going via Carlsbad Caverns, El Paso, and Juárez in Mexico. In Marjorie's memory, the trip was fraught with minor horrors — a worm in a Milky Way candy bar, bats in the caverns. Jean was, however, interested in the Cherokee orphans her sister taught, and beguiled by some of their names: Calvin Dreadfulwater, Rock Backward, Lucinda Hornet, Harold Curlychief, and the like. She later wrote several stories about these outcasts.

By her junior year Jean had managed to move out of her parents' house. The chronology of this escape, and thus its official rationale, is murky. Stafford later wrote that she took a room in a boardinghouse (at 1001 Tenth Street, about eight blocks from home) because her parents moved to Denver, but in actuality her parents stayed on at 631 University for at least a year and maybe two after Jean left the household. Whatever the pretext, the move was a vital step in her psychological disentanglement from her family. In her new digs Jean got a free room in exchange for making beds and cleaning the upstairs, and she made pocket money by cleaning the downstairs as well.

She also earned cash by working in the university bookstore and print shop, by typing theses for graduate students, and by ghostwriting term papers for undergrads. Another job, which Stafford took in part because at seventy-five cents an hour it was the highest-paid on campus, earned her a certain notoriety: she posed nude for life-drawing classes in the art department. In an underheated tower room of Macky Auditorium, for three hours in a row two mornings a week, she stood on one foot or lay half reclining while students painted her in oils or sketched her in charcoal. Jean's friend Mary Moore recalls the campus attitude toward such exhibitionism: "You were not a nice girl in 1935 if you did that. . . . My peers scolded me because I was friendly with her."

In view of Stafford's bashfulness, and her shock at boys' sexual advances in high school, nothing seems more improbable than that she would have taken off her clothes to pose in front of her classmates — even for seventy-five cents an hour. Yet on an overnight visit to Stafford's house at 631 University, Moore saw mounted on Jean's bedroom wall a charcoal sketch of her own nude torso, executed by a student in the drawing class. Another member of the class was Howard Higman, who had never dared to kiss Jean; now he found himself, in the chilly tower room, contemplating her naked body as she stared out the window over the heads of her appraisers.

Mary Moore thinks Stafford may have posed partly because "it amused her to shock people. Had she grown up in the 1960s, I'm sure she would have been a hellcat, because she would have had so much encouragement from her peers. But at that time her peers were busy putting her down." Jane Fitz-Randolph echoes that view: "Jean Stafford was a nobody. She was kind of freaky and far-out." But the sort of shock Stafford and her bohemian set managed to produce at CU counted for little, says Fitz-Randolph, compared to the scandal of the Delta Gamma girls who went to the Kentucky Derby during finals week.

Higman's fairly skillful charcoal sketches from 1935–1936 reveal Stafford's body as beautifully proportioned, with a flat, almost concave stomach, broad but angular hips, high, rounded breasts (contradicting Goodrich Walton's description of Jean as "flat-chested"), and square, well-defined shoulders. In Higman's best drawing, a side torso view, Jean's large hands rest with an eerie, disembodied grace on her left shoulder and left hip.

In the spring of her junior year Stafford met a young couple named Paul and Dorothy Thompson, who would become her friends for life. Dorothy first became aware of Jean when, as a graduate student, she read Jean's essay on James Joyce. "She was way beyond any other student," recalls Dorothy; "Her talent was unmistakable." The Thompsons lived across the street from the rooming house into which Stafford had moved. Having heard that Jean had fainted in life class "because she hadn't been eating breakfast," the Thompsons began inviting her to drop over for a proper morning meal every Saturday and Sunday. Sometimes these visits lasted well into the evening.

"Jean said the ones who painted her in life class, what they especially liked was a sort of lavender tone to her skin," says Dorothy Thompson. "She was very blond. Slender, not tall, really a beautiful girl. Her voice was slow and husky. She used to say she had the voice of an undertaker. She had rough, chapped hands." Adds Paul Thompson, who became a CU professor, "She was one of the funniest people I ever knew. She would get me laughing so hard I'd cry." Although only a few years older than she, the Thompsons adopted Stafford as if she were an orphaned child. Loyal to them throughout her life, she recognized their self-appointed role as her guardians, nicknaming them Daddy Paul and Mama Dorothy.

If throughout her childhood and adolescence Stafford had

fantasized about having a worldly sophistication, at CU she acted upon that desire. In college she began smoking as well as drinking — at first perhaps only the odd cigarette furtively consumed in the rest room of a campus building. And the intellectualized, platonic "dates" of high school slowly gave way to more amorous liaisons. To be sure, Stafford's first instinct when men showed an interest in her was always to recede into aloofness. There was an eccentric Russian in one of her English classes who courted her relentlessly. An older student who habitually wore a cape and hat and carried a cane, he would leave poems translated from the Russian hanging from her doorknob at 631 University. Jean ignored him.

Mary Moore recalls Stafford's account of an evening she spent with two teachers from the law school.

> She told me that she went out with both of them one night. It's possible that she went out with one of them, and they found the other during the course of the evening. But anyway, they got into a fight about who was going to take her home, because whoever took her home was going to get to kiss her goodnight. They got into a fight, and she just took herself home. She just walked off and left them.

Stafford developed something of a crush on one of her fellow members of the sandwich-and-beer-hall "intelligentsia," a man named Edward J. ("Joe") Chay. Egged on by a woman friend who tipped him off to Stafford's well-hidden infatuation, Chay got up the nerve to put his arms around Jean and kiss her on the street one afternoon in 1934. "What surprised me most," he recalls, "was how very fragile she was." Amplifying that intuition, Chay says, "Her single most significant characteristic was her complete fragility. You had to be very careful not to upset her — not in a frivolous way, but in a serious way that would ultimately harm her very deeply."

Another classmate who was much taken with Stafford was Robert Hightower; like the Thompsons, he would become her lifelong friend. A disgruntled chemistry major who was turning his back on premed studies, Hightower met Stafford in 1934 at a meeting of some campus group, perhaps the German club. She was sitting behind him; they struck up a conversation.

I think she told me that she had written a novel. I was impressed
but wouldn't let on. James Joyce's *Ulysses* came up. [The book
had just become available in the United States.] She had read it,
and I had read it. She wanted to know if I knew what the "Agenbite of Inwit" was. I didn't, but she did. And I was again impressed by that. . . .

I think we spent maybe fifteen minutes sparring and showing
off. I was intrigued, and would very much like to have seen more
of her.

The two Joyceans later became good friends, although Stafford
showed no interest in having the relationship turn romantic. It is
thanks to Hightower that we have the only objective testimony,
sketchy though it may be, about how Stafford lost her virginity.
The "unfortunate seduction" had happened sometime before she
met Hightower. It was, in Jean's own parlance at the time, a
"one-night stand." Hightower thinks her lover must have been
a fraternity boy. "She was bitter about it," he remembers. "She
felt she'd been a sucker. [But] she certainly didn't brood over it."

Hightower's second meeting with Stafford occurred at a party
in the summer of 1935. The core of the gathering was a homosexual group known, apparently without opprobrium, as the "fairy
literati." In a basement apartment where there was lots to drink,
Hightower spotted Stafford and tried to talk to her. Another guest
was Lawrence Fairchild, a premed student who had been Hightower's roommate and whom he "disliked violently, having lived
with him for a year."

He was also interested in Jean. Well, in the course of the evening,
another girl made passes at me and distracted me, and, involved
with her, I let Fairchild appropriate Jean. And I was very sorry
about that, because they became lovers and I didn't see any more
of Jean [for a while].

Fairchild, who died in the 1950s, eventually became a Colorado doctor. His affair with Stafford continued through the fall
of 1936, her senior year. By February the Thompsons understood her to be engaged to him. Hightower, who admits, "I think
Fairchild was her first love, really," was aghast at her choice.

I don't think I'm doing him a gross injustice by saying . . . Jean
deserved better. My theory was [that] my trouble with Jean was

that I wasn't sufficiently domineering. I didn't inflict myself on
her, and Fairchild certainly had no inhibitions in that direction.
. . . He was almost brutally possessive and overbearing.

The picture of Jean Stafford's college years that emerges from
the documentary evidence is largely an external one. Because she
preserved none of her imaginative writing from the CU period,
and because virtually none of her letters survive, if we are to gain
an inkling of what went on inside the mind and heart of this
enigmatic "coed" we must rely mainly on the somewhat breezy
memoirs of her adulthood, which boast vaguely about peaks ascended in blizzards, beefsteak fries in the mining ruins, and
demijohns of Dago red.

The only source that may give us deeper internal clues to Stafford's CU years is once again "In the Snowfall," the unfinished
novel she began more than a decade later, which she finally rejected because it was written "directly out of experience." The
pages of the novel have an uncanny congruence with events recorded independently by friends such as Hightower and in Stafford's own retrospective essays.

"In the Snowfall" opens on the day the seventeen-year-old Joyce
Bartholomew begins her freshman year of college in Adams,
Colorado. She has been longing for this day ever since her family
moved to town. During the dreary years through which she has
waited, she has become acquainted with the university campus,
"which, maddeningly, one could see and touch and lie in on the
bee-filled grass, skate through, skip through, play run-sheep-run
in on the marine blue nights of spring, but where, withal, one
did not belong because one was still a beastly child."

Now, in the "most auspicious autumn of her life," Joyce is
rapturous at starting college: "Culture was a word that inhabited
her like a truth or a fragrance; it was the agent, she believed, that
could put in quarantine people like her parents." During that first
fall, whenever she is on campus Joyce feels a "transport that was
almost intolerable." Yet despair reclaims her nightly as she re-
enters her parents' house.

There are characters in the novel who plainly correspond to
Jean's two favorite teachers, Irene McKeehan and Joseph Cohen.
The fictional version adds little to our understanding of the for-
mer. The Cohen figure, however, who is called Dr. Rosen, makes

passes at Joyce when she is alone with him in the classroom. She
eludes his clutches but reflects in solitude, "Dr. Rosen, my philosophy teacher, was the first Jew I had ever seen up close. . . .
I was infatuated with several of my professors, but most of all
with him."

The infatuation leads Joyce to the odd practice of spying at
night through the front window of Dr. Rosen's home, where she
sees him playing Chopin on the piano, his children cavorting on
the floor beside him. "He was an ugly man," Joyce ruminates,
"but his face was full of cleverness." The description and location of Dr. Rosen's house correspond exactly to those of Joseph
Cohen's home in Boulder. Perhaps Jean actually peeked through
Cohen's windows, and perhaps she felt a reciprocal attraction that
Cohen never suspected.

"In the Snowfall" offers other vignettes that reinforce the notion of a voyeuristic protagonist. When Joyce first visits Eddie's
Oasis, the fictional counterpart of the café where the "intelligentsia" hung out, she habitually smokes a cigarette and hides
behind a ponderous book. Yet her private wish is that some boy
will stop and speak to her, and the book is a screen from behind
which she seizes upon every bit of gossip and flirtation at the
neighboring tables.

Just as Goodrich Walton remembers John Stafford as an un-
interfering parent who let Jean see male visitors late at night in
her "cabin," in some respects the father in "In the Snowfall" is
oblivious to his daughter's behavior:

> Even if he knew of it, he would not care about her posing in a
> mixed class; now he would not care if she walked through the
> streets at midday in a birthday suit with a sign on her saying that
> she was his daughter, for he had given her up long ago with the
> rest of the human race, had washed his hands of her, as he told
> her perhaps half a dozen times a week.

When Joyce begins to have dates in college, however, Fulke Bartholomew insists that the boys bring her home before nine-thirty,
"when he, my father, was still up and could see through the
window that I was not being kissed."

Joyce is befriended by a classmate in Dr. Rosen's course, Luke
Corelli. The two spend many hours together at Eddie's Oasis. In
the novel Corelli is twenty-five years old, a veteran of the Italian

navy; he is huge, with dark curly hair and "a way of moving about like a bear which is conscious of being a bear." Despite the fact that Joyce finds him unattractive, in her view Corelli has "that rather repulsive excessive masculinity that acts like an aphrodisiac on a girl who is too green to know that a man who has no womanliness in him will be no good to a woman." She is excited by Corelli's intelligence and thinks she is falling in love.

Corelli is based in large part on Joe Chay, the schoolmate who got up the nerve to kiss Jean on the street one day in 1934. In the novel, as in Stafford's life, the relationship never goes beyond friendship. Joyce keeps Corelli at a distance, as she had the high-school boys who were interested in her, by insisting on a strictly intellectual interchange. In a nostalgic letter she wrote to his sister in 1974, forty years after she met Chay, Stafford claimed that her friendship with Paul and Dorothy Thompson had "helped me over the heartbreak of Joe Chay's never so much as giving me a peck on the cheek." Apparently she had forgotten the sudden embrace on the street. In a PS to the letter she adds, "How could Joe Chay have been so cold-hearted? All I wanted in the world was to cook his meals and wash his clothes and speak only when he spoke to me!"

In the novel, when boys call to ask Joyce out on dates, "she refused coldly, with high rhetoric." Her hunger for romance is outweighed by the humiliation of knowing that in their eyes she is a townie, a "Barbarian."

> For the boys who called her did not want to cultivate her in the public way, not at the movies nor at Rainbow's End nor at Martha's College Vineyard, but in some second-hand Model A roadster parked behind some pitch-black gully at the hind end of some mountain with no houses and with bad roads.

"In the Snowfall" may be written "directly out of experience," but although Stafford scrutinizes some of the cardinal events of her college years in it, she virtually ignores others. In particular, there is no correlative in the novel to Jean's extended affair with Lawrence Fairchild, the premed student to whom she may have been engaged. Instead the smooth seducer who took Stafford's virginity in a one-night stand gets major treatment.

Late one Saturday night a boy who refuses to identify himself calls to ask Joyce out. Knowing that the caller must have "been 'stood up' or had carelessly failed to provide for himself," she refuses. In response to Joyce's rebuff, the voice says,

> "They told me it would be like that, but I didn't believe them."
> She was pleased to have a reputation for unavailability and she asked, "Who said so?"
> And the voice replied, "Oh, you know. The boys, the boys at the Lodge."

Joyce understands the nickname as shorthand for the "Chi Psi" fraternity. Eventually she deduces that "a handsome and already soft tweed-smelling boy" who regularly sits on her left in her philosophy class is the anonymous caller. And much later, after it is too late, she learns that one of the caller's "brothers" had bragged, immediately after Joyce's rebuff, that he would make a sexual conquest of this haughty virgin "if it was the last thing on earth he did."

In the various drafts of "In the Snowfall" there are several versions of how Joyce gets to know this young Don Juan, whose name is Bernard Allen. In each of them, however, he courts her with flattery and promises, takes her out, and then goes weeks without calling. She sees him with other girls but naively ignores the evidence of his philandering. Finally, on the fateful night, he picks her up in his blue roadster and drives her to Rainbow's End, an amusement park–cum–dance pavilion in the mountains (based largely on Eldorado Springs, a resort south of Boulder).

Bernard Allen holds Joyce's hand and says how much he has missed her. She wonders why he hasn't called. He promises to explain later but never does. He is astonished that she has never before been to Rainbow's End. He drinks heavily; she stays sober. As he gets more drunk, he outlines a romantic future for the two of them. Since he is rich, she can quit her job posing for the life-drawing class. He will buy her new clothes and an engagement ring. They will marry at the end of the spring term and go abroad for their honeymoon. The next year he will study at Harvard; if she wants, she can go to Radcliffe. Dazzled and confused, she goes back to his apartment with him.

In the whole body of Jean Stafford's surviving work, both published and unpublished, there is a virtually complete lack of scenes dealing with sex. Characters may kiss, but they never go further. That sex ever takes place between men and women is implied in Stafford's fiction only indirectly, and usually in terms that freight the liaisons with archness and irony. To put it bluntly, Stafford either could not or would not write about sex, and even getting near the matter seemed to make her uncomfortable.

The account, then, of Joyce's one-night stand with Bernard Allen — which corresponds to Jean's own loss of virginity — is the closest thing in all of Stafford's surviving fiction to a direct treatment of sex. Even in this instance, the author seems to have been unwilling to face it head-on. The long scene that begins with Bernard Allen picking up Joyce in his blue car ends abruptly with the couple leaving Rainbow's End to go back to Bernard's apartment. The subsequent scene begins just as abruptly, with Joyce at home in her own bed in the early hours of the next morning:

> She could not sleep. She writhed between her tangled sheets and tried to find a daydream to rescue her from all this terror and disgust, and could not, could only remember . . . Bernard, naked, crossing the darkened sitting room of his basement apartment, coming toward her, smiling. It had not been a smile at all, it had been a grin, a leer; in the dimness, he had had the face of a deathshead.

This bleak passage has the air of tragedy: a girl's introduction to the supposedly blissful act of sex turns into a hallucinatory pageant of assault. (When Joyce finally falls asleep, she has a nightmare about a huge black dog, an insane hired man carrying a gun and several dead birds, and some cryptic notes left for her in her father's study, which is in a rectory.)

Joyce's troubled sleep is interrupted at dawn. The long dramatic scene that ensues is as explicit as the sexual scene was oblique.

> She woke to the sound of someone coming up the stairs. It was the half light just before sunrise, the coldest, hollowest light in all the day. . . . She waited, frozen and burned alive as the footsteps slowly came down the corridor which opened with a squeal. Her father stood barefoot in his night-shirt holding a letter in his hand. He paused before he closed the door behind him and approached her bed; in the pause he rolled his eyes around a few times, his habit when he was about to deal out a punishment. Joyce watched him fascinated.

"This was put under the front door of my house about three minutes ago," he whispered and he held out the letter, addressed to her.

She read, "After this, don't believe everything you hear the first time you hear it and don't go to bed with a man the first time he asks you to. I wanted you to know right away that I handed you a line so that you wouldn't try to communicate with me. B."

Before she had finished reading it and before she had taken in its finality, delivered so quixotically, her father flung the bed-clothes off and seized her shoulder with his hard, huge hand. "Downstairs," he ordered and when she shrank away, he grasped her the more sternly and with his other hand, pulled at her arm. The smell of him and the sight of his thin, hairy legs beneath the short skirt of his dirty night-shirt, the look of the greenish stubble on his chin sickened her as if she were looking on something ta-boo. As she got up and followed him, she thought with panic of her dream of the madman and how this tall madman going bare-foot down the cold hall had brought her a note almost as strange as those in the rectory.

Her mother, with her hair in pigtails, stood in her nightdress in the study, waiting for them, and Joyce observed her sagging breasts under the thin cotton and with revulsion looked at her fat feet stuck into a pair of purple satin mules, discarded by a roomer. Fulke's belt was ready on his writing table. It lay there with all his other weapons, his quill pens, his indelible pencils, his re-volver.

"Pull up her shift, Violet," he said and her mother lifted Joyce's pajama top over her head and whispered, "Turn toward me." She crossed her arms over her breasts so that no one could see them in this sordid light streaming sickly through the fly-blown win-dows. No one! What was this passion to undress her? . . .

She heard her father pick up the belt; she heard the normal milkman coming down the alley, the bottles rattling in his horse-drawn wagon. Her mother said, "Don't over-exert, Fulke."

He beat her twenty times and each blow was as strong as the one that had come before. At first he took his time and at his faithful wife's injunction paused between the lashes. Once, he spat. But then, in his excitement, he could not stop for anything. They came in a mass like a wildfire and he snorted with his passion. Aflame, she was conscious of nothing but this vehement pain and

in the brief ebbings of it, of the knowledge that there would be
no one to comfort her afterward.

The moment he finished, her mother quickly threw the pajama
top around her shoulders and the cloth stung intolerably. She turned
to face her father who stood arms akimbo, the belt still dangling
by its buckle from the little finger of his right hand. He was out
of breath and his half-smiling lips were wet. A long lock of hair
had fallen down and lay on his high forehead between his feral
eyes. "Go to your room," he said, "and stay there until I release
you. This is not all: we will get to the bottom of these fornications."

Robert Hightower, who eventually came to know Stafford better
than anyone else from her CU years, believes that the letter slipped
under the front door by Bernard Allen is Jean's fictional invention, a dramatization of the shame she felt over her one-night
stand. The vividly detailed scene in which Joyce is beaten by her
father may also be purely imaginary, but this is a cloudier question.

If the cruel, gloating letter written by Bernard Allen represents
novelistic poetic justice for Stafford's having been a "sucker" for
a frat-boy Don Juan, then it is tempting to conclude that the
beating scene is similarly invented to dramatize Jean's relationship with her father. If Goodrich Walton's testimony is accurate,
and John Stafford really did let Jean date whom and as she pleased,
then the beating scene may be psychologically — but not fac-
tually — autobiographical. It may embody not only Stafford's need
for self-punishment as a response to the real "Bernard Allen" but
also a sexually charged tension between her and her father. The
kindred scene in "In the Snowfall" — in which the young Joyce
watches her father beat her naked sister, Amy, for coming home
drunk, and wishes she were receiving the beating instead — seems
to reinforce this surmise.

On the other hand, the scene may actually have taken place.
Jean's sister Marjorie insists that John Stafford never beat his children with anything more than a light switch, yet her reticence
and apparent embarrassment when she was asked if she had ever
been punished for coming home drunk may argue for autobiographical verisimilitude in the "Bernard Allen" case as well. In
later life Jean sometimes referred to her father as a violent man
"in every way."

During her last two years at CU, however, Stafford became involved in a series of events that climaxed in the most important and disturbing turn her life had taken up to that point — and which eleven years later would provoke her to write "In the Snowfall." At the center of these events was an intense, gifted student at the CU law school. Her name was Lucy Cooke.

V

Lucy

B ORN IN DAVENPORT, IOWA, in 1912, Lucy McKee was three years older than Jean Stafford. Her father made a comfortable living working for an investment company, and Lucy's childhood was as privileged as Jean's was penurious. By temperament rebellious and experimental, from an early age Lucy burned her candle at both ends. She was expelled from Northwestern University in her second year for disciplinary reasons that had to do with her sexual adventures.

Around 1931 she went to the University of Colorado. Her indulgent parents sent her an allowance of at least $150 a month, and she felt secure in the knowledge that she could always ask for more. In the summer of 1932, with two girlfriends from Colorado, she crisscrossed Europe. The diary from her Grand Tour limits itself to brief, telegraphic entries, mostly concerning boys and parties; in its pages its author seems a bedazzled and superficial ingenue.

Yet for all her hedonism Lucy McKee was an exceptionally bright and strong-willed young woman. She wanted to be a writer, belonged to a playwriting circle at CU, and wrote a novel while still in college. Though disinclined to study, she breezed through courses whenever she put her mind to the task.

Petite and lithe, she brushed her wavy red hair well back from her face, emphasizing her remarkably high forehead. Her chin was pointed, her features sharp and intellectual. "I don't think you'd call her pretty," recalls a male college friend who knew her well. In Stafford's retrospective vignette, Lucy could contract her skinny little body into a pigmy's size and it [was] capable of any distortion. When she studied, she crouched before a table with her heels on the chair and her queer toes clinging to the edge of it, her hands locked behind her head and hidden under her fine, fluffy hair. She was left-handed and when she wrote, she twisted about in such a way that her paper was almost upside down. . . .

There was, adds Stafford, "a certain meanness in her face, a narrow canniness in her amber eyes and a starched pallor on her thin lips."

One of Lucy's avocations was horseback riding. There were no facilities for the sport at CU, so she joined the Sunset Ranch Academy east of Boulder. Late one afternoon at the ranch, she caught sight of a tall, good-looking youth riding alone back and forth across the turf, vigorously practicing polo shots (the academy fielded a team). As the rider led his horse to the stable after his workout, Lucy, with her characteristic boldness, accosted him: "Hi. Got a light?"

The young man pulled out a lighter and held it to her cigarette. As darkness gathered, the two leaned against the fence and chatted. The man's name was Andrew Cooke; like Lucy he was twenty years old, a CU student, and a native midwesterner. He wore wire-rimmed glasses, but his lean, raw-boned grace and boyish cowlick bespoke an adventurous, outdoor life.

As they were on the verge of parting, Lucy ventured that she would like to drop by and say hello sometime. Andrew took the hint and asked, "Want to stop over and have a drink?" The new acquaintances drove back to his apartment, had several drinks, and went to bed together. The mutual attraction survived the night; soon Andrew and Lucy were inseparable.

Andrew Cooke had grown up in Illinois. Both of his parents died before he was five, and he was raised by an aunt who headed the Waukegan High School English department. Andrew's father had been an exemplary student who had become a prosperous lawyer. When Andrew proved to be a negligent pupil and got kicked off the track team for smoking a cigar, he found himself scorned as the black sheep of the family.

His aunt shipped him off to the elite, private Lake Forest Academy, where his father had been the top student in his class. The truant son "worked like a dog," returned to Waukegan to graduate, and headed west to enter the University of Colorado in midyear.

Once again the lure of a good time interfered with Andrew's scholarship. He moved into the Phi Delta Theta house (his father's fraternity at Northwestern) but left because he wasn't allowed to brew his own beer there. He took an apartment on the Hill with a friend named Donald Hays, who, as Cooke's upperclass adviser, was supposed to keep him out of trouble. With a trust-fund income of $150 a month, Andrew never needed to work at a job to pay for college. His life with Hays passed in a blur of drink and card playing. The roommates had so much trouble getting up in the morning that they placed a Big Ben alarm clock atop a washtub to amplify its morning Klaxon.

By the end of his second semester Andrew was flunking three of his five courses and barely getting by in the other two. The freshman dean gave him a reprieve on the condition that he and Hays stop rooming together. Cooke moved to a new apartment that had more room for visitors and for his beloved bridge games.

It became clear to Andrew on their first night together that the aggressive, red-haired girl he had picked up at the riding academy was far more experienced sexually than he was. Lucy began candidly to detail the exploits of her past, but he was reluctant to listen. "I just didn't care to have my nose rubbed in it," reflects Cooke today. Within three days of their first meeting Lucy announced that she was going to a doctor to get fitted for a diaphragm.

Lucy began to spend the night with Andrew on a regular basis, scandalizing the landlady of the rooming house she lived in, only a couple of blocks from Jean Stafford's home on University Avenue. Sometimes, in Andrew's presence, Lucy would get together with her friends from the Europe trip to reminisce. "I said I just didn't care to hear about it," he recalls. "But I knew there [had been] considerable sexual activity and drinking and carousing."

Andrew's squeamishness had little to do with propriety; he had fallen in love with Lucy and was jealous of the shadowy lovers of her past. In some ways theirs was an odd match. Andrew turned a bored ear to the literary talk that sustained Lucy, and he was daunted by her willful self-assurance. "Lucy was a very hypnotic, leader-type person," he says. "She could boss anybody around."

Yet in other respects the two fit well together. An instinctive bohemianism drew them to each other, though Andrew never thought of their life in such terms. Both were used to living well, without worries about money; both flaunted their self-indulgence in drink and gay parties and spontaneous larks. Neither cared what the rest of the campus thought.

For her part Lucy seemed smitten as well. Within a few months she asked Andrew to marry her. He recalls his response: " 'Gosh,' I said, 'I'm not even through school yet, I can't get married. I don't have a job. Besides, I'm not twenty-one years old yet.' " She waved aside his objections. If they pooled their allowances, she said, they could easily live on the three hundred dollars a month. She could get more money if they needed it. Early in 1933, half as a joke, they drove to Fort Collins and applied for a marriage license. One day shortly after that, Donald Hays picked Andrew up; Lucy was in the car with him. They set out on a drive without telling Andrew where they were headed. He demanded an explanation. At last Lucy said, "We're going to get married." They found a judge somewhere south of Denver and solemnized the vows.

Lucy, however, kept the marriage a secret from her parents, as her husband did from his aunt. On July 1, 1933, the day Andrew turned twenty-one (Lucy had reached her majority two weeks earlier), the couple held a big family wedding in Waterloo, Iowa, where her parents had moved. "We'd been married for six months," says Cooke, "but we never told them."

Back in Boulder, the Cookes moved into a comfortable house on Columbine Avenue, near the southern edge of town. Their blithe style of living had not prevented either Andrew or Lucy from graduating. Donald Hays, a few years Andrew's elder, had gone on to the CU law school, to whose ranks he promptly managed to recruit his friend, despite Andrew's initial reluctance to train for the same profession his father had plied. Lucy, perhaps out of idle curiosity, entered the law school as well. She was the only woman in a student body of ninety-nine. She may also have been its smartest member, able to pull straight A's with only a halfhearted effort. By her senior year, in an irony she must have found delicious, she had been chosen judge of the student disciplinary court, charged with handing out sentences to freshmen who violated school traditions.

In a town as conservative as Boulder was in the 1930s, amid a

student body as provincial and conventional as CU's, the couple
became a cynosure. The novelty of a marriage between students
was rare enough; in addition, the Cookes were rich, conspicuously dedicated to pleasure, and yet academically successful.

The house on Columbine Avenue soon became a genuine salon, the likes of which had perhaps not been seen at CU before.
Donald Hays was a pivotal figure. Andrew's former "adviser"
had acquired an old mining cabin at El Vado, up the Big
Thompson Canyon north of Boulder. Hays and Cooke set to
work fixing it up, commuting every day after school in Andrew's Model A.

The cabin had no windows or doors. One evening, after hearty
libations, Donald, Andrew, and Lucy drove to a deserted house
in Boulder, stole eight or ten doors and as many windows, and
carted them up to El Vado. They lifted a stove from an abandoned mine. Box springs propped up on bricks served as beds,
and they hung a steel cable as a nocturnal handrail to the distant
outhouse.

The cabin became a sybaritic retreat, "way off where we felt
free from prying eyes." Lucy had become friendly with a coed
by the ambitious name of Dorothy Regina Theresa Convalinka
Grabill, a kindred spirit who had the distinction of having been
kicked out of a CU sorority. The Cookes pushed Donald and
Dorothy together, and soon they were having an affair. On Sunday mornings Dorothy had to be driven all the way down to
Boulder so she could go to confession. "She'd tell the priest that
she'd try not to sleep with Donald any more," says Cooke. Then
the foursome would pile into the car and race back to their
mountain love nest.

In the basement of the house on Columbine Avenue Andrew
built an eighteen-foot bar. He made his own beer and returned
from trips to Illinois with gallon jugs of 98 proof grain alcohol.
Mixing it with distilled water and juniper drops bought in the
local drugstore, he filled pint bottles with bathtub gin.

The Cookes played host to a more or less continuous party.
From Denver came Helen Bonfils, daughter of one of the state's
leading families, and another woman who was a fellow veteran
of Lucy's bacchanal in Europe. A classmate of the Cookes' regularly used Andrew and Lucy's bedroom for his trysts with this
woman; months later, cleaning the attic, Andrew came upon an

abundance of used condoms tossed on the floor. Helen Bonfils brought along a male homosexual writer from Denver. He spent one night passed out on the lower bunk of a double bed while Andrew slept in the upper. In the morning he said to his host, "I hope I didn't make any passes at you." Lucy had two lesbian acquaintances, one a beautiful equestrienne.

A physical casualness was de rigueur at the Cookes'. Says Andrew, "We didn't hesitate to go into the bathroom when someone else was taking a bath. If you wanted to come in and pee, so what?" For the members of her salon Lucy took it as her role, in Andrew's phrase, "to stimulate a sex life."

It is not clear at what point Jean Stafford met Andrew and Lucy Cooke. There is no doubt that she was acutely aware of their wild reputation long before she actually met them. It may be that, as a reading of "In the Snowfall" suggests, Lucy McKee first came into Stafford's consciousness when she overheard landlady gossip between her mother and Lucy's overseer.

At any rate, by her junior year in college, and perhaps earlier, Jean had become friends with Lucy. In "In the Snowfall," a male friend takes the character based on Jean along to one of the infamous parties, where the Lucy character discovers in her a new protégée. Their actual first meeting, however, took place after Jean's rueful one-night stand with the fraternity boy. Robert Hightower remembers, "She said when she first talked to Lucy, Lucy had given her an account of her love life, and Jean immediately had to start inventing because she didn't have anything to match it with, beyond this one unfortunate seduction."

Stafford became a regular at the Cookes' parties, though she held herself back from most of the excesses perpetrated on Columbine Avenue. As a fellow writer, Lucy seized upon Jean's talent and intelligence. She lent or gave Jean the diary she had kept on her trip to Europe. Andrew escaped the literary discussions that the women relished, but he remembers making fun of Jean's "ostentatious vocabulary." At some point Jean effectively moved in with Andrew and Lucy, no doubt keeping her apartment on Tenth Street for appearance' sake.

Donald Hays had moved in as well. Jean and Donald had separate bedrooms. The Cookes were content to pay the bills for all four roommates; Hays may have contributed to the cookie-jar kitty for groceries, but Stafford was not expected to. The

standing joke was that Hays was the Cookes' butler, Stafford
their live-in maid. Donald occasionally went so far as to lay a
white towel over his left forearm when he answered the doorbell.

Lucy, meanwhile, believed that she had picked up the knack
of hypnotism. Her regular party trick was to demonstrate it on
Jean, who had previously been hypnotized by a psychology professor. In a trance, Jean would hold out her hand so Lucy could
stick a darning needle through the crotch of skin between thumb
and forefinger. She never flinched.

Among the four housemates and Dorothy Grabill, dishabille
was the norm. Cooke says, "In fact, we were a semi–nudist colony. I never saw Jean wandering around the house with no clothes
on, but the rest of us did. Dorothy and Lucy and I wouldn't
hesitate to walk into the living room stark naked and sit down
and talk for a while."

Since Jean seemed to have no current boyfriend, Lucy set to
work to find one for her. The sexual tension hovering over the
Cooke ménage seemed as unavoidable as the exhalations of home
brew and bathtub gin. Reminisces Cooke, "Dorothy Regina
Theresa Convalinka Grabill had the most gorgeous bosoms of
any female I've seen in my life. And she used to be proud of
them, whether or not she was taking a bath, and sometimes we
would watch."

It was characteristic of Stafford that no matter how deeply she
immersed herself in this new, thrilling *vie bohème,* she kept it
rigidly separate from her other worlds. With the exception of
Robert Hightower, none of her other friends had much knowledge of Jean's ties to Andrew and Lucy. Howard Higman explains, "It was an invasion of our relationship that she had that
thing going. . . . I think I was probably jealous of them." Dorothy and Paul Thompson, Goodrich Walton, Joe Chay, Mary
Moore, Jane Fitz-Randolph, and others knew little of the Cookes
besides the latest campus gossip. Even Hightower, to whom
Stafford later confessed so much, never met or even saw Lucy
Cooke.

At the same time, Andrew and Lucy had little knowledge of
Stafford's outside life. Understandably, Jean did not invite them
to meet her family, but neither did she introduce them to her
friends: Andrew never even heard of Robert Hightower, or of
Lawrence Fairchild, the lover Jean took while she was still living

with the Cookes. Before Fairchild, however, Lucy succeeded in persuading Donald Hays and Jean to go to bed together — "not often, but on a kind of experimental basis." Dorothy Grabill (whom Hays later married) was unhappy with Jean's accessibility to her lover, but despite the sex, Donald and Jean never really hit it off.

One day Andrew came up with the idea of wine enemas, on the theory that the large intestine would absorb the alcohol. "We were just curious," he says today, "to see what it would be like. We kind of all stood around [taking turns]." Cooke's memory is hazy as to whether Stafford actually participated in the ritual, but he says she was definitely present. "We wondered whether you could get drunk," he says. "It was rather disappointing. So finally we put the enema bag away, went out in the kitchen, and sat drinking through the mouth again."

Four years later Stafford confided to Anne White, who was briefly her roommate in Concord, Massachusetts, that in addition to having taken wine enemas with Andrew and Lucy, she had also separately had sex with each of them. According to White, Stafford said that "this was an initiation for her. . . . She said she didn't really enjoy it, but it was 'experience.' " The testimony must be taken with a grain of salt. By White's own account, she was a naive young woman at the time, and it may have pleased Stafford to shock her. "When she talked about it, she almost made herself into a Brontë heroine, someone who has things done to her. And [she said] that it was her innocence and youth that appealed to them."

Andrew Cooke insists, "I don't know anything about Lucy, but I never had sex with Jean in my life. Frankly, I had a slight feeling it would have been incestuous. . . . It's even conceivable Jean wouldn't have minded having sex with me. I was not sexually attracted to her. She was somewhat peasant stock. She had thick ankles — we sat around the house, and her ankles were bigger around than mine. Her wrists were bigger around than mine."

Whether Lucy and Jean went to bed together is uncertain. According to one member of her salon, Lucy was widely thought to be lesbian. Robert Hightower remembers, "Jean said at one time that Lucy was, well, if not lesbian, at least interested in Jean as more than a friend." Andrew himself remarks, "Had Lucy

decided she wanted to have a lesbian affair with Jean, Jean would
have participated, just because she would do anything Lucy wanted
her to do. Lucy had this obsession with sex."

Whatever its amorous content, the relationship between Jean
and Lucy deepened steadily, and an intimacy developed between
the women that necessarily excluded Andrew. In the fall of 1935
Stafford began her senior year at CU, as the Cookes did their
last year of law school. Gradually Lucy's spirits darkened, and
the parties seemed to lose much of their gaiety. The landlord had
thrown the Cookes out of the Columbine Avenue house because
of excessive drinking. Jean, Andrew, and Lucy moved their
ménage to a house on Ninth Street. Often Jean and Lucy sat at
the table talking about suicide. Lucy's brother had been killed in
a mysterious hunting accident; to Andrew she barely hinted at
this past tragedy, but she may have confided more in Jean. Andrew tended to dismiss the women's "morbid" discussions just
as he did their literary ones.

Lucy's health, which had never been good, deteriorated that
fall. She developed ovarian cysts that had to be removed. Shortly
thereafter, because of what she called a tipped uterus (she only
vaguely specified her troubles to Andrew), she had to have stitches
taken in her abdomen. An abscess developed, with pronounced
swelling; her doctor punctured it, releasing a great deal of pus.

Around this time Lucy encouraged Andrew to have an extramarital affair. "I began thinking, maybe her sex life with me was
getting to be old stuff," he reflects. "I wasn't sure. I never knew."
Nor did Andrew know whether Lucy was having affairs of her
own. One evening she left her husband a note saying she wouldn't
be having dinner at home, and disappeared for hours. "I was
disturbed. I thought she'd probably gone off somewhere."

On Saturday, November 9, 1935, Lucy drove to Denver in the
morning to see her doctor. Andrew expected her to get back in
the early afternoon. Waiting for her in the house on Ninth Street,
Andrew and Jean talked about Lucy. As Andrew remembers it,

> I guess maybe I was a little nervous about what she had been up
> to in Denver. I thought, what the hell is she doing, going down
> there and visiting a boyfriend or something? . . . During the course
> of this, I began saying [to Jean], "You know, we live kind of a
> wild existence here. I think that maybe somewhere along the line
> we could live a more conventional type of existence."

Lucy did not get home until 7:30 P.M.

> She came in, and I asked her something about what she'd been doing, and she gave me an evasive answer. I was maybe a little sharp with her. We were sitting around the table, and she had a drink, and all of a sudden she took the drink and threw it in my face. She jumped up from the table and ran into the side bedroom.
>
> For some reason or other, I must have sensed — I knew we had a pistol in the top drawer. I leapt up and chased after her. I was about five feet behind her. Jean was five steps behind me. And she raced out of the room and into the living room and "Bang!"

Lucy had raised the .25-caliber revolver in her left hand and, without hesitation, shot herself in the left temple. The bullet tore downward through her head, remaining lodged inside. She collapsed on the living-room floor.

Within minutes two doctors and a downstairs lodger arrived, followed by the police. In his grief Andrew took another gun from the closet and threatened to shoot himself. Several of the newly arrived men fought him for the gun and took it away from him. Looking back on that moment fifty years later, Cooke says, "I never would have shot myself. That was strictly grandstand stuff. I've thought about that many times, and I was ashamed at what I'd done, it was so insincere."

With Jean at her side, Lucy was taken to the Boulder Community Hospital, where she died at 10:00 P.M. The police locked Andrew up overnight. "The jail was as good a place for me as any because I was terribly upset," he says. "They put me in a comfortable cell with a good bed in it. I just sat there all night long in absolute shock."

In the write-up of Lucy's suicide in the *Boulder Daily Camera* of November 11, 1935, there are minor discrepancies with Andrew's account. The newspaper report has Lucy returning from Denver by bus, not by car; it places the deed in the bathroom, not the living room; and it claims that at the moment Lucy pulled the trigger, Jean was phoning a physician "because she and Mr. Cooke were alarmed over Mrs. Cooke's hysterical condition which verged on mental collapse." It has Lucy leaving the house after a quarrel and returning an hour later in a distraught state. The *Camera* concludes, "Friends attribute Mrs. Cooke's act to ill health rather than the quarrel, which they said was over a minor matter."

For a while the police interrogated Stafford, trying to get her to admit that she had been having an affair with Andrew that had driven Lucy to suicide; eventually they abandoned this soap-opera suspicion. To this day Cooke remains puzzled as to why his wife took her life. "Dissatisfaction in all kinds of things" is his stab at an answer. Certainly Lucy's poor health contributed to her despondency; Cooke is vexed now that he never thought to talk to Lucy's doctor in Denver and find out what had happened in his office that ominous Saturday. "It was obvious," he says, "that her physical examination with the doctor had done something to her."

On November 12 Lucy was buried in Green Mountain Cemetery in Boulder. Her parents came from Iowa for the funeral. With the suicide growing into a scandal all over town, Andrew dropped out of law school and returned to Illinois. In the summer of 1936 he came back to Boulder, where he saw Jean often. "She and I were a great comfort to each other," he says. "I could rush into her arms, and vice versa, and we would both cry and hold each other with brotherly affection."

In 1937 Cooke graduated from the CU law school; the dean congratulated him on his courage in doing so. Four years later he remarried and then settled into law practice in Battle Creek, Michigan, where he has lived ever since. After 1941 his contact with Stafford dwindled to an occasional Christmas card. He never saw her again.

Stafford never talked to her family about the tragedy. There is thus only one possible source for a deeper understanding of the complex affinity that developed between Jean and Lucy, that source being, of course, "In the Snowfall." Indeed, the hundreds of manuscript pages of the unfinished novel make it clear that the relationship between the two students was meant to dictate the book's very structure, with the suicide as the climax.

In 1946, writing to Joe Chay, her fellow crony in the CU "intelligentsia," Stafford said,

> Yes, you are right about Andrew; he was Lucy's husband. And Lucy, of course, is the one who killed herself, but one particular is wrong: you say "for no reason which anyone could fathom." After almost eleven years, I think I understand it now. It has lain in my consciousness without ever departing although it has sometimes blessedly submerged itself. I am almost ready to write about it, although I have really written about nothing else ever.

Four months earlier, on the tenth anniversary of Lucy's death, Jean had sat down and written a one-page note to herself — a sketch for the novel she was just beginning to plan. In it she reviews the conventional explanations for Lucy's violent act:

> At the time it seemed to everyone that the reasons for her suicide were perfectly clear and, though deplorable, not difficult to understand. She had always, in all company, had an indiscreet tongue and very much was known of her in the college and in the town. She was, they said, unbalanced with drink; her marriage, entered into quickly and probably drunkenly, had gained her no reward for her husband was less brilliant than she and was less rich and had neither her wit nor her vitality; she was, despite her extrovertive ways, introspective; she was a prodigy and her brilliance had consumed her. The town was shocked, absorbed, delighted and for days talked of little else.

(It seems surprising that this list of reasons fails to mention Lucy's ill health.)

Now, in 1945, wrote Stafford, "I revise my judgment. I have reached, so far as it is possible for the human mind to do, the knowledge of why she killed herself and I will never know further." The decade of struggling with Lucy's ghost had unearthed in Stafford a rage she had never known while Lucy was alive. In another letter to Chay she claimed, "I daresay I have been unhappy all my life but I was never so wretched before I knew that awful girl and her terrifying modus vivendi and her limp, disreputable entourage." "In the Snowfall," then, was to be not only a coming-to-grips with Lucy but also a purgation of her. The one-page sketch for the novel announces, "I desire to defecate this memory from my spirit; for ten years it has run in my blood as black as a squid's ink."

In the novel Joyce Bartholomew, Jean's alter ego, first learns about Maisie Maxwell when she eavesdrops on the neighboring landlady's appraisal of her new roomer: "A very refined looking girl, I must say." Soon afterward, Joyce sees Maisie dashing around town in her yellow roadster, which she drives "fast and cleverly." (Lucy in fact drove a yellow Plymouth coupe.) There are always boys around her. Joyce envies Maisie's fine clothes, her money, and the fact that she has been to Europe. She is, it seems, the richest student at the university, as well as "the most sought-after girl in Adams."

Joyce's feeling that she is inferior to the "fast," socially adept coeds at the university finds a heartsick focus.

> Shining above them all, above all the bright young people, was Maisie Maxwell whose name she heard everywhere. "Did you hear what Maisie said to Dunny McKenzie when he wanted to pin her?" "It was a good party but only because Maisie was there." "Maisie's a scream," "Maisie's tops," "Maisie dances like something out of this world."

The girl in the yellow roadster is not just popular; she is also a freshman whiz at the law school. Joyce fancies Maisie "a union of Miss Martindale and of the most trifling Pi Phi." (Miss Martindale is based on Irene McKeehan, the spinsterly professor whose teaching so captivated Stafford.)

"In the Snowfall" may be directly autobiographical, but in one important twist of the plot Stafford invents a coincidence that seems too neat to have been historically accurate. Immediately after Bernard Allen, the callous fraternity boy, takes Joyce's virginity and then mockingly dumps her, Maisie Maxwell seduces Bernard. Maisie in turn drops him, and — evidently in response — he takes his own life by lying on the railroad tracks east of town and letting a train run over him.

There is no evidence that this stock denouement of Victorian melodrama corresponds to any actual suicide of a CU student in the early 1930s. "That's invented, of course," says Robert Hightower of the plot device. "That's the way [Jean] would like to have disposed of him." Whether or not the real "Bernard Allen" committed suicide, it just might be true that the blithe seducer who took Jean's virginity was in turn one of Lucy McKee's casual conquests. It seems more likely, however — and, if true, psychologically more revealing — that Stafford devised the Maisie-Bernard liaison to dramatize the thralldom she felt under Lucy's power.

By this point in the novel Joyce is attuned to every scrap of campus gossip about Maisie. With other law students, Maisie shares a "ramshackle cabin" in the mountains: "It was Maisie's custom, with every current beau, to ride horseback up to the cabin on the first night of the full moon; usually she chucked them after that." A fraternity boy tells Joyce, " 'She can drink anyone under the table, and she can lift any pin she wants and she's got enough money to buy half the state.' "

Only a few months after Bernard Allen's death, Maisie marries a fellow law student named Cecil Perrine. He is described as her intellectual inferior, a transfer student from a midwestern college who walks with "a neanderthal carriage in his arms and shoulders and his dark, curly head . . . outthrust like an inquisitive turtle's." In the town's eyes the marriage only makes Maisie more intriguing, as the Perrines flaunt their high style:

> They had rented a house on the outskirts of town at the base of the foothills and it was said that they had fitted up a bar in the basement where, on Fridays and Saturdays, they had drinking parties of surpassing sophistication. Another law student, by the name of Arthur Goodenough, lived with them in an omnibus role which included various kinds of servitude: he was their butler and their bartender and their secretary and tutor to Cecil. . . . On week-ends, Arthur's girl came on from the city and it was believed, in a mixture of pleasure and horror, that they slept together after those wonderful drunken evenings when the bar and the living room were strewn with the bodies of law students and their girls who had passed out.

Joyce hears further gossip — that "a week ago, [Arthur's girl] had had such a bad hangover that the doctor had had to come and give her a hypodermic, that Cecil and Maisie smoked marijuana, that Maisie had had an affair with Arthur Goodenough before her marriage, and that none of them wore any clothes around the house."

As she did with her philosophy professor, Joyce starts spying on the Perrines' house. From a nearby hiding place she hears Arthur arrive from a shopping expedition: " 'Cheerio! I say, old bean, here I am with the grog.' " Then Joyce hears "Maisie's light, metallic rejoinder in which she urged him to hurry up, she was perishing of thirst, she needed a quickie. . . . Sometimes Joyce could all but taste the whiskey . . . in the glass which she imagined Maisie held."

A strong ambivalence about Maisie creeps over Joyce's spirit. "Her own identity left her, for she had not this same existence in Maisie's mind and thus, in order to make certain of her being to herself, she had to see herself, at some future, but actual time, beside Maisie and in a breathless trance. . . . She did not want to *know* Maisie but wanted to *be* her; it was a suicidal thought and she shuddered." Joyce makes it her goal to force Maisie to think about her. But she also hates Maisie "because my being like her was so impossible."

At last Joyce is taken to one of the Perrines' parties, where Maisie shows an immediate interest in her. Joyce has never tasted alcohol before that night; it seems unlikely that this would have been true of Jean, but it may well be that she had never drunk seriously before she came under Lucy's spell. In view of Stafford's lifelong dependence on alcohol, it is interesting to see how she captures Joyce's first experience of its seductions:

> Probably the process was gradual but it seemed to her that very suddenly and with no warning at all she was drunk. The sensation was wholly novel and delightful. It was an awakening to a new surrounding: the light altered, the room expanded, the faces were familiar and her host and hostess acquired a hospitality of which she was the principal beneficiary. But the awakening was combined with a delicious bodily drowsiness and though to her eyes the barroom seemed large, to her physical being it contracted its spaciousness into a small, snug nest. . . . Maisie . . . cried, "You see, everybody, it's what I've been telling you. She's a natural."

Maisie takes Joyce upstairs to trade life stories with her.

> She was without shame and without doubt as she recounted her interminable list of affairs, consummated in the dormitories of fraternities and on the shores of Lake Michigan and in the drawing rooms of trains, on country-club golf links and at dude ranches and in fashionable hotels, tourist camps, mountain cabins, boarding houses, automobiles and yachts, after picnics and cocktail parties and swimming parties and skiing excursions and horse back rides and dances and movies and final examinations in Fourth Year French.

To Joyce Maisie reveals a short-lived secret marriage at seventeen to a Chicago gangster; her subsequent promiscuity at a Chicago university, leading to a case of gonorrhea that got her expelled; the fact that she "had stretched herself across the tracks of the Illinois Central but had been found"; and the details of her sex-filled tour of Europe.

The story about Maisie lying on tracks of the Illinois Central sounds as fictional as Bernard Allen's similar demise. But perhaps the rest of this recitation of debauchery bears some resemblance to what Lucy actually told Jean. It may suggest those details of Lucy's past that Andrew never wanted to know about.

Now, in the upstairs séance, comes Joyce's turn. In a panic at the poverty of her own experience with men, Joyce makes up a bizarre tale about an all-but-consummated romance with the Catholic priest who had instructed her in high school. Maisie swallows the lie. " 'Well,' she said. 'That's really exceptional. I mean you're a nine day wonder. Now this Father Whosis, do you think he would come to a party here?' " Joyce gasps and protests, but Maisie proposes that she visit the cleric. " 'I've always wanted to have an affair with a priest or a monk. A monk would be even better.' "

Joyce is fascinated by Maisie's appearance up close. She discerns that Maisie is actually plain, with "an old person's thinness." Her chin is pointed, and the green paste she uses on her eyes gives her, in certain lights, "a serpent's watchful look." Her skin is beset by rashes and distempers:

> When she was really old, I thought, she would shrink and wrinkle like a raisin, but even the sticky moisture of the raisin's core would not be there; she would be arid inside and out like a dead tree. And as I looked at her, it was not hard for me to imagine her face folded into countless furrows, her eyes settled deeply into her skull, her lips and her hands fretful with tremors and knobbed with rheumatism. Still, deplorable as she was, she was provocative; repulsive as she was going to be in time, there was an imponderable in Maisie's being that made her the most attractive person I had ever known.

Racked by a hangover, Joyce wakes up the morning after the party full of remorse. Briefly she vows to have nothing more to do with Maisie. Yet as the days pass she finds herself longing for a phone call from her. Too proud to make the first move, she waits through six days of torture before Maisie calls.

The second party is just like the first. Gradually, during the months that follow, Joyce goes from the status of "Maisie's discovery" to that of "Maisie's best friend." The worldly older girl teaches her protégée how to fix her hair, how to paint her fingernails, how to smoke, how to walk. She buys her a scarf and a sweater and a pair of gloves, but Joyce takes the latter gift as a criticism of her rough, chapped hands. Maisie is impressed, however, by Joyce's literacy. "It amused Maisie to point out what a rare combination [Joyce] was of the blue-stocking and the Bohemian. 'It's a rare whore,' she said, 'who can read Latin.' "

At parties in the mountain cabin, Maisie demonstrates her hypnotizing skills with Joyce as her subject; the proof is the darning needle stuck through the skin between Joyce's thumb and forefinger. But Joyce only pretends to be hypnotized, bearing the "monstrous" pain without a flicker of emotion showing on her entranced face.

Maisie's reckless hedonism awes her disciple. Her heroic drinking is juxtaposed by violent, hung-over tantrums. To defy what she calls Victorianism, she tries to push her friends into bed together. Maisie cultivates the homosexual community, smokes marijuana, inhales ether, and gives herself wine enemas. She tells Joyce of her desire to spend a weekend in a whorehouse. When Joyce describes the beating her father had given her after discovering Bernard Allen's note, Maisie coolly says, " 'What would he take to do it to me?' " "She voraciously reads everything she can on sexual aberration and she begins a novel in which the protagonist, a medical student, is in love with the corpse of a Negro girl." (After Lucy's death, Andrew Cooke kept the manuscript of the novel she had written. When he remarried in 1941, he burned the manuscript. "I didn't think it was very good," he says.)

The insouciance of Maisie's abandon makes Joyce feel that "her own chastity, far from being a virtue, was no more than a proof that she is unattractive and lifeless." She begins to imitate Maisie simply to earn her approval: " 'She allowed me to indulge myself in my freakishness until I really did become a freak.' " When Maisie disapproves, " 'I would seem to hit the bottom of despair and for days I would wish to kill myself. . . .' " Maisie shows Joyce the diary from her continental fling, inspiring her with "an almost frantic craving to go to Europe in the same way, to acquire, overnight, the same *savoir faire*. . . ."

Yet the signs are unmistakable that Maisie is burning herself out. Joyce sees and shares her friend's "dread of loneliness and age and illness so that, while the desire is ebbing, there is the necessity to keep on at top-speed." Maisie begins to drink before breakfast. She has a pair of affairs and encourages her husband to do the same. Then she falls ill "with some disease that is never named but one which requires an operation of some delicacy." During her slow convalescence, there are no parties. When Maisie tries to resume them, she finds that "her parties are a thing of the past, that her retainers have all betrayed her, that they go on Saturdays to other parties to which she is not invited. . . . Then there is a desperate and pathetic period when she believes she is pregnant and she has a party to announce that fact." But she is not pregnant. In despair Maisie runs away to Mexico and stays for three weeks.

More and more during these gloomy months, Joyce and Maisie spend long periods alone together. One day, as the two women sit studying in the pine woods near the mountain cabin, Maisie confesses that she has become bored with Cecil. His intellectual mediocrity and servility gall her; she no longer respects him.

> "If I could leave him," she said, "I would and could go on for years this way being Miss Popularity. It's not too bad a life as long as the gin holds out. But I feel about him the way I would feel about a child crossing a street in front of a truck. He wouldn't know what to do without me."

Nevertheless Maisie unveils a plan. Laying aside her book, she says to Joyce,

> "If I went away for a year, he'd get used to not having me around. A year will take care of anything."
> "And while you were gone, he'd get stuck on me? Is that the way I'm going to help you?"
> Maisie laughed. "Keep your shirt on. You're going with me."

Joyce stares at her friend in astonishment, "for this was what a dreaming boy, in love, said to his girl, not what one girl said to another." But Maisie's power coincides with Joyce's reveries of Europe: within moments she has consented to the plan. It becomes the women's rapturous secret.

The possibility that Lucy planned to run away to Europe with Jean was one that Andrew never entertained. Fifty years later, however, when apprised of this turn in Stafford's unpublished novel, he says, "I'm not surprised. [Lucy] always was an escapist. I wouldn't be surprised if she came in sometime and told me,

'Andrew, Jean and I are going off to Europe, to have some fun again.' . . . I think that's plausible. But Jean never told me anything of the sort."

Nor is it farfetched to believe that had Lucy hatched such a scheme, Jean might have agreed to it. Since childhood she had fantasized about London, Scotland, and Europe as places to which she might flee from the tedium of home and family. And despite Lucy's death, Stafford did in fact spend the following year in Europe.

In the novel, even as Joyce enters her secret pact with Maisie, she begins to betray it. Unbeknownst to Maisie, she starts an affair with an "upright and sentimental medical student" named Harry Phelan; soon she becomes engaged to him. Phelan obviously corresponds to Lawrence Fairchild, to whom some of Jean's friends understood her to be engaged by early 1936, and of whose existence Andrew (and perhaps Lucy) never learned.

It is hard to deduce from the pages Stafford left among her papers just how close "In the Snowfall" came to being finished. The various drafts, which often overlap, do not quite add up to a continuous narrative. But even given the disarray of the manuscript at Stafford's death, it would not be difficult for a skillful editor to stitch together about 90 percent of a novel. The least well realized episodes, unfortunately, are those that surround Maisie's suicide. Here Stafford wrote mainly schemata, in the form of extended notes outlining the scenes she intended to write, with fragments fleshed out in full narrative style. Thus, in one scene,

> There is a final party at which she announces that she is, after all, not pregnant and she tells everyone that she has "taken a new lover and a new kind of love," and moving to Joyce, she kisses her on the lips until Joyce pushes her away and in the gesture notices how dry and light like straw she was. The guests are speechless. "Well," she cries, "Well, what the hell? What the Jesus Christ? What the goddam awful hell?" Someone says, "She's crazy," and does not say it carelessly. Uneasily they all leave and Maisie and Cecil and Joyce are left in the lonely bar.

Andrew Cooke insists that nothing resembling this scene ever took place. Nor did Lucy ever hold a party either to announce or to deny that she was pregnant. Still, Andrew wonders whether she might have mistaken the swelling in her abdomen, caused by the abscess, for a sign of pregnancy, and confided this to Jean.

In the novel, Joyce reacts to Maisie's pass with a well-hidden revulsion.

> Joyce thinks, "There is only one escape for her and that is death. I do not care about her escape, though, but only about my own. . . . She has killed everything in me, even the energy for revenge. . . . She has corrupted even my hate and I am nostalgic for those days, unhappy as they were, when I did not know her."

(The intensity of this reaction may argue that Jean never had an affair with Lucy; alternatively, its very vehemence may suggest that Stafford was covering up the truth of an affair.)

The following day is the fatal one. In one draft Stafford dramatizes that November Saturday at considerable length. While Maisie is off in the city for the day, Joyce and Cecil talk about her. Cecil is distraught about her behavior; Joyce dismisses the lesbian pass as Maisie's "fad for the evening." The two of them resolve to confront Maisie and demand that she mend her profligate ways.

When Maisie returns, she is extremely upset and distracted. The planned confrontation deteriorates into a name-calling fight between Cecil and Maisie. Maisie lays her trump card on the table, laughing at her husband as she says, " 'You're an ass. Joyce, tell him what we're going to do next year.' "

There is a long moment of terror for Joyce as both Maisie and Cecil stare at her. She weathers it in silence. Maisie gets up from the table and leaves the living room. A moment later Cecil looks for her, but he finds only a note indicating that she has left the house and will return later.

Cecil and Joyce drink on into the evening. Both have an eerie sense that the house is not empty. Stafford embellishes the scene with gothic atmospherics — a wild wind, heavy rain, a clattering pan, a spooked cat. Cecil initiates a discussion of suicide. He proposes that, if Maisie does not promise to change, he and Joyce enact a suicide pact that very evening, by driving to an abandoned mountain road and shooting themselves with his Luger. Joyce envisions the scene vividly, hovers in indecision, and then consents to Cecil's plan. "Joyce agrees through pity, through the suddenly acquired belief that she, too, has no further reason to be alive; she agrees because she is drunk, because it was her habit to agree to everything proposed in this house; but chiefly she agrees because she abruptly and passionately craves excitement."

And here the scene breaks off. Although there are, among the pages of "In the Snowfall," summary scenes that deal with the aftermath of Maisie's suicide, the suicide itself goes undescribed. Just as Stafford, grappling with the one-night stand in which she had lost her virginity, could only write around the edges of the traumatic act of sex, perhaps when it came to setting down the even more disturbing moment when her best friend shot herself before her eyes, she could not face the deed in print. This failure, as much as any other dissatisfactions with what she had written, may explain why Stafford did not finish "In the Snowfall."

In many respects the novelistic details of the prologue to the suicide corroborate Andrew Cooke's memory of it — Lucy's trip to Denver, his attempt to force a moral reform, the drinking at the living-room table, the quarrel — yet on other points Stafford's fictional version contradicts Cooke's recollection. Lucy's leaving the house and then returning to shoot herself (reported, oddly enough, in the *Boulder Daily Camera* news account) is one such contradiction. Further, Cooke insists that there was not even a hint of a suicide pact between himself and Stafford; he says there was constant talk of suicide among the trio but he never took it seriously.

There may, however, be a sense in which Stafford's novel tells an autobiographical truth more significant than any circumstantial veracity. Whether or not Jean and Lucy ever slept together, it seems undeniable that they developed a passionate rapport, even a merging of identities, the depth of which outsiders, including Andrew, can only have guessed at. This rapport, based at first on a simple mentor-acolyte relationship, grew to become an intense, murkily erotic symbiosis.

Thus in "In the Snowfall," Joyce suspects that even as she puts the gun to her head, Maisie does not really intend to kill herself. As Joyce ruminates: "It is not her own death she desires but the death of her husband and of Joyce[,] who[m], while she seems to be rejected by them, she has actually rejected. . . ." Only days before the suicide, Joyce had come to recognize that she longed for Maisie's death. Afterward, she struggles with her guilt.

"If Maisie had lived," I thought, but there was no logical conclusion to the clause. . . . If she had lived, I would not have . . .

for the mischief of the night she died had prohibited life for one of us; that it happened to be Maisie who shot herself, not I, was little more than luck for me, for the odds were equal and the stakes were the same.

The tortured give-and-take of this extraordinary bond sounds like what psychologists call a folie à deux. If such was indeed the case between Lucy and Jean, and this is not merely Stafford's novelistic embroidery, it may help account for the well of anger she uncovered in herself ten years later as she began to write about Lucy, and for the apparent hyperbole of her remark to Joe Chay in 1946: "I am almost ready to write about it, although I have really written about nothing else ever."

In the novel Joyce grieves like a lover after Maisie's death. "She begins to suffer from insomnia and if she sleeps at all, she dreams constantly and constantly of Maisie. She is driven, as if by an addiction, to loitering about the house where Maisie lived and she cannot attend her studies nor eat her food nor hear anything that is said to her."

Yet Joyce's valediction as Maisie is lowered into the grave is a black one. She thinks:

> The only thing spectacular about her life was the end of it and the only thing spectacular about the end of it was this, her mother's piercing scream as the first shovelful of dirt fell on the coffin. All the rest of it — the solemn students of law, the pinched, Dickensian undertaker with his nut-brown toupee, and the traditional flowers, and the traditional Cadillacs that had brought us all in our Sunday-best sorrow — testified to the enormous unimportance of her treacheries, the hopeless and helpless and pathetic lifelong infidelity to the real world, the slow and steady eating away of her poor, ungifted heart. There were no trees where she was buried and the weeds began a little way from her grave. It all looked utterly final and yet, at least to me, it was not over yet: in me, the death had only just begun.

VI

Innocent Abroad

IT WOULD HAVE BEEN understandable had Jean, like Andrew, dropped out of college and fled Boulder in the wake of the scandal over Lucy's suicide. Instead she stayed put and finished her senior year. Her performance in the months following the tragedy was little short of heroic.

One can imagine, for instance, the courage it must have taken for Stafford to continue posing nude for the art classes in the tower room of Macky Auditorium. Most of the campus was already quick to censure any girl who took that notorious job; now every pair of eyes glancing up from a sketchpad added the image of Jean's nakedness to the lurid fantasies of a doomed triangle, which had become town gossip.

In the library Stafford still labored away at her thesis on thirteenth-century poetry. At year's end she turned in, on time, a skillful treatise whose measured prose bears no hint of the strain its author was under. The thesis won her not only honors but simultaneous B.A. and M.A. degrees. She was one of a very few students in CU history to accomplish this feat in only four years.

In April 1936 the theater department performed a one-act play by Stafford that had won first prize in a university contest. *Tomorrow in Vienna* is a melodramatic recreation of Beethoven's deathbed agonies. The only surviving creative work from Stafford's college years, it gives little indication of her promise. The characters speak in romantic platitudes. Thus the doctor inveighs, "Artists are great fools. They starve their bodies to nurture their minds. . . ." Beethoven's nineteen-year-old nephew soliloquizes, "You search the four corners of the earth for love and warmth, and your soul yells out in anguish. But the world is hostile eternally, even to those who make the most beautiful things. Pretty rotten, isn't it?"

As winter rounded into spring, Jean's health seemed to deteriorate. The Thompsons began to take her in and feed her on weekends. In March Jean had to have a tonsillectomy, and in May she suffered appendicitis attacks. These ailments signaled the inception of a lifelong, nearly uninterrupted gauntlet of health problems. Many of these would be the result of Stafford's own habits — smoking, drinking, and poor eating — but most were beyond her control. Years later her sister Marjorie would look back and moralize, "I don't remember Jean ever complaining of not feeling well until she left home after graduating from college. Of course she more than made up for lost time once she was away from Mother's sensible and concerned nursing. . . ."

Late in the summer of 1935 Jean had met Larry Fairchild, the premed student who became her lover and whose existence (if we can trust "In the Snowfall") she kept a secret from Lucy. Stafford told Robert Hightower, Fairchild's ex-roommate, that Fairchild had first made an impression on her, as he drove her home from a party, "by banging a whiskey bottle on the car seat, trying to hypnotize her, and talking a lot of theosophy." Later she confessed that Fairchild appealed to her because " 'he takes charge.' "

In January 1936 the premed student graduated from CU and went home to Pennsylvania. Stafford traded letters with him through the spring and let some of her friends know she was engaged to him. Meanwhile, though, she started to spend time with Hightower. "Jean was at loose ends," he recalls, "and we soon found ourselves very congenial indeed." At a drugstore outside Boulder they bought cheap fortified wines by the gallon. "We had many happy alcoholic evenings." Hightower had a Japanese girlfriend, however, and Stafford was faithful to Fairchild; the friendship remained platonic.

In the aftermath of the suicide Jean had befriended Lucy's parents. At some point she revealed to them that she had planned to go to Europe with Lucy; remarkably enough, the McKees agreed to lend her the money to realize her hopes.

In the spring Stafford saw a notice on a CU bulletin board offering scholarships for American students to the University of Heidelberg. She applied and was promptly accepted. Suddenly the daydreams she had nursed on her solitary twelve-year-old hikes up the mesa, dreams in which she saw herself transformed by the sophisticated whirl of Europe, promised to become real. Spurred by Irene McKeehan's class in Anglo-Saxon and by the work she was doing on her thesis, Stafford had conceived the ambition of becoming a philologist. At Heidelberg she would study with the internationally renowned Anglo-Saxon scholar Johannes Hoops.

Hightower longed for the continent also. His best friend, Robert Berueffy, flunked out of medical school in the spring and instantly took off for Paris. "My one wish in life was to join him," says Hightower, "because we were really romantic escapists and we wanted to get away from Boulder most of all, from America just about as badly. I thought I wanted to write, and Berueffy was a composer, and we were going to be artists."

Stafford told Hightower that he ought to apply for a Heidelberg scholarship: as she jauntily put it, " 'They're handing them out free.' " He took the hint and was also accepted. As summer neared, the two friends planned their year in Germany together. It was something of a secret. Even afterward, Jean's family never learned that she had shared her year abroad with a Boulder friend of the opposite sex.

In June Stafford graduated from CU. Her parents came from Denver for the ceremony, as did Marjorie from her job in Oklahoma and Mary Lee from the ranch on the western slope. Dick, who had settled in the Northwest and was working as an assistant forest ranger, could not attend.

Within the family it was taken for granted that John Stafford would continue to pursue his elusive star as a writer while his wife supported the couple with demeaning jobs. At the age of sixty-two, he now had poor health to add to his excuses for not getting a job. During a summer visit with Mary Lee on the ranch, he had suffered a ruptured appendix and had nearly died in the hospital in Hayden, Colorado. According to Marjorie, the ordeal left him with a large abscess on his rib cage that drained constantly. For years he looked pale and suffered from exhaustion.

Mary Lee, happily wed to her rancher husband, still taught

school in Hayden. At the end of 1936 Marjorie married and left the Oklahoma Indian reservation where she had been teaching. Her marriage quickly failed, however, and in 1938 she landed in Oswego, Oregon, with a newborn child to care for. Dick had already settled in Oswego, where he worked as a timber cruiser.

A decade earlier John and Ethel Stafford had transplanted the whole family to Boulder so they could keep Mary Lee in the household while she went to college. Around 1937 the parents moved from Denver to Oswego, traipsing after Dick. For a while son, mother, and father lived under a single roof, with the added companionship of Aunt Ella, Ethel's maiden sister from Rock Port, Missouri.

The Staffords still suffered from poverty. Recovered at last from his abscess, John Stafford relented in his authorial obsession and briefly took a job as a carpenter in the Portland shipyards. According to Marjorie, during the first years after Jean graduated from college, she often wrote her parents saying she had neither food nor money. Ethel Stafford "would subtract dollar bills from her limited household budget and send them to Jean with admonitions to eat properly and to buy a steak. . . ." Jean wrote thanking her mother for the cash but deliberately piqued Ethel's teetotalism by describing how she had cooked her steak in wine.

Stafford stayed in Boulder the summer after her graduation so she could attend the CU writers' conference. With the advent of Edward Davison as its director in 1935, the conference had gone big-time, gaining an immediate reputation as one of the best summer draws in America for famous writers. That same year the conference had Robert Frost and Robert Penn Warren as lecturers, Whit Burnett and Martha Foley of *Story* magazine leading workshops, and — as a last-minute replacement for Bernard De Voto — Thomas Wolfe (whose second novel, *Of Time and the River,* had recently appeared) as a popular and enthusiastic guest. Wolfe sat in on Davison's poetry class, drank hard and showed off at parties, attended a barbecue on Flagstaff Mountain, and later recommended the work of several conference students to his editor, Maxwell Perkins.

In 1935 Stafford had been a timid undergraduate, loitering on the fringes of the summer scene. By the following year she was a little more confident of her talents. Warren was back at the conference, as was Foley, who read Jean's writing in a workshop. Many years later Foley would recall having been alerted in advance "by excited professors there that a girl on the campus was writing remarkable stories." In 1936 she took a special interest in the precocious Coloradan; she was probably the first important editor or writer to notice Stafford. Foley stayed in touch with her student during the following year, when Jean was abroad.

At the beginning of September, two months after Stafford's twenty-first birthday, Andrew Cooke drove her to New York City. It was the first time she had ever been east of Missouri. Cooke saw her off when she boarded the ocean liner that would take her across the Atlantic.

"The boat trip was sort of fun but I got bored to death before it was over . . . ," wrote Jean to Mary Lee upon her arrival in Germany. Her ship docked at Cuxhaven, the seaport for Hamburg, on September 18, 1936. Hightower had already been in Germany for three months, having taken a summer job in Berlin, where he had also attended Hitler's Olympics. By September he was staying with a friend in Schweidnitz, a Silesian town in eastern Germany (now part of Poland). Stafford had sent Hightower a telegram begging him to meet her in Hamburg. "Damn it," he recalls, "I was a long way from north Germany at the time. And also a long way from Heidelberg." Instead he sent her a letter spelling out, as one might for a child, every step she must follow to get herself from Cuxhaven to Hamburg to Heidelberg. Thus: "Turn right and across an alley is the office of the HambAmLinie. Go upstairs. They speak English there. . . . Make them write down when you leave and when you arrive and when and where you change trains (umsteigen)." Hightower promised to meet her soon in Heidelberg.

It was Hightower's plan for the two of them to take a room together "for a week or so until we find a permanent dwelling." For the sake of prudish landlords, Stafford was to pretend to be his half-sister. Later, he hoped, his friend Robert Berueffy would come from Paris to join them. Eager and protective, Hightower got to Heidelberg the day before he expected Stafford. She had already arrived, however, and the two friends ran into each other on the street.

They soon found lodging in the house of an elderly, often tipsy schoolteacher, a woman who spoke not a word of English. Jean insisted on separate rooms. There was no bathtub in the house

(Stafford had to walk to a hotel a mile away and pay to take a bath); in her room, only a cold-water tap and no heat.

Stafford had carefully prepared for her year in Germany. She had had stationery printed with the heading, "jean wilson stafford/ heidelberg, germany." She had taken German courses at CU, but a gloomy premonition came true. As she described her arrival to Mary Lee,

> When I saw land I nearly wept for joy except that I was quite nervous about the language, and it was just as I feared. I couldn't understand a word. Everything was run together and I hadn't the vaguest notion what the score was. The idea here seems to be that when you can't make a foreigner understand you shout louder and faster until the foreigner is completely bewildered, cowed, and miserably nostalgic.

Nineteen years later Stafford wrote a funny story, called "Maggie Meriwether's Rich Experience," about a young woman who thinks she has mastered French in school; upon her arrival in Paris, to her dismay, she finds herself unable to utter a word. In 1936, however, such a mortification was no joke. Jean had left the United States planning to write breezy letters home full of cavalier accounts of her exploits abroad. Instead she was so wretched and homesick that she did not even try to camouflage the fact in her letters. "I wish I had never heard of Heidelberg," she wrote Andrew Cooke, "though the town itself is quite lovely."

Indeed it was, and is. The ancient city lies snug on the left bank of the Neckar River, where it leaves the limestone foothills of the Odenwald to meander toward the Rhine. Just north of town stands the Heiligenberg, topped by the ruins of a ninth-century basilica; opposite, to the south, looms the deep-wooded Königstuhl. The town is laid out to delight the eye. Beneath the balconies of the famous ruined castle, the heart of old Heidelberg unfolds, a dense jumble of Gothic spires and baroque houses, hazy in the setting sun. North of the river, across the lower slopes of the Heiligenberg, climbs the splendid promenade of the Philosophenweg, where for centuries contemplatives have strolled.

The university, founded in 1386 by the elector Ruprecht III, is the oldest in Germany. By the 1930s it had a long tradition of welcoming foreign matriculators, and the town itself was one of the favorite German stops for American tourists.

At the end of June 1936, only a little more than two months before Stafford's arrival, the university celebrated its 550th anniversary. Letters were sent to many foreign universities, inviting their representatives to participate in the festivities. In England this request provoked a storm of controversy, for the Nazi persecution of the Jews was in full swing, and the German universities were playing a leading role. By February 1936, of the seven thousand faculty members in German universities and other seats of higher learning, thirteen hundred had been fired or forced to resign. The victims included not only Jews but pacifists, socialists, and liberals. Their careers ruined, seven hundred of these scholars fled Germany; a number of others committed suicide. Of the 189 members of the Heidelberg faculty, forty-seven were dismissed.

Several leading English universities declined the invitation to Heidelberg's anniversary. No comparable debate was sparked in America, though, and indeed there is no evidence that Stafford was even aware of the Heidelberg imbroglio. Along with her friends in the CU "intelligentsia," she may have sat in on a few meetings of the Young Communist League, but at the age of twenty-one she could only be categorized as politically naive. (One wonders, for instance, whether Joseph Cohen, the Jewish Marxist philosophy professor who had so deeply influenced Jean, did not deplore her very decision to go to Heidelberg.)

There was, however, no ignoring the Nazi presence. Hightower must have regaled Stafford with vivid accounts of the Olympic Games, where Jesse Owens had triumphed over Aryan theory. The classes Jean attended at Heidelberg opened with the obligatory salute "Heil Hitler!" She mouthed the phrase along with her Teutonic classmates. She wrote Cooke, "The educational system seems to be that you go to two or three lectures the first week of the semester and then sit down and drink beer until the summer vacation when you study. . . . All the students have duelling scars on their cheeks and for the most part they are just about like American boys."

Hightower had hopes of becoming Stafford's lover, but she did not respond to his hints. A tall, thin youth, he sported a neat mustache; his voice was oddly high-pitched. By temperament he was gentle, curious, considerate, empathic — at the opposite end of the spectrum from the domineering Larry Fairchild. Intellectually Hightower made a nearly perfect match for Jean, but she was not yet disposed to see him in a romantic light.

After about a month of living in the same house with Stafford, Hightower was asked to leave by the landlady's son. The pretext was that he was "unsociable," since he did not try to engage the lonely mistress of the house in conversation. With more training in the language and a three-month head start on Jean, Hightower got along much more easily in German than she did, but he still felt clumsy speaking it.

At the beginning of November Stafford changed her residence. A little more than a mile east of town, on the right bank of the Neckar, she found the Hotel Haarlass, where the rooms were cheap because winter was the off-season. Hightower moved into another room in the hotel. The two students spent many hours studying in the café on the veranda under the gaze of waiters in alpaca jackets; they drank local wines and German beer and dined on the house specialty, *Schwedenplatte,* a cold antipasto built around eels from the river. Once again their rooms were unheated, but they discovered an empty chamber in the hotel that was relatively warm. Here they worked on their writing, reading aloud to each other and stuffing themselves with *Berliner* (jelly doughnuts).

Stafford's room looked east, away from Heidelberg, directly onto the fields of the twelfth-century Neuburg Abbey. She grew fond of watching the Benedictine monks, in sandals, cassocks, and aprons, sowing winter wheat or hurrying to their vespers. The Haarlass — "Haircut" — was so named because centuries earlier it had been the place where the monks had had their heads shaved.

Jean's homesickness steadily evaporated as she discovered the intimate delights of Heidelberg. She browsed in the bookstalls nested between the buttresses of the Heilig-Geist-Kirche, where Ruprecht III, the founder of the university, was entombed. She searched hungrily through bins in the open-air Marktplatz for fresh fruit, a great rarity in 1936. When she could splurge, she passed beneath the splendid Renaissance facade topped with the statue of Saint George and dined in the cozy Ritterhalle. She prowled with the tourists through the castle and was amused by its Great Tun, a vat built to hold forty-nine thousand gallons of wine. Riding the funicular up the slopes of the Königstuhl, she stopped at the Molkenkur Café for a matchless view of the town and a therapeutic cup of whey.

On long walks along the Philosophenweg she communed with herself. There were outings to nearby towns: to Schwetzingen to stroll through the palace gardens; to Mannheim for opera; to Speyer to see the famous cathedral; to Neckargemund by electric tram to drink Greek wine. Stafford's favorite hangouts were the bars and cafés of the old town, especially the Café Sö, the Kolpinghaus (where she tended to get "a body drunk without a mind drunk"), and the American bar at the Europäischer Hof, Heidelberg's ritziest hotel.

Daily, on her way to the university, she walked along the Hauptstrasse, the town's central artery, as blue trolleys clanged by. She sat bundled up over her textbooks in the unheated university library, and often ate at Mensa, the "barnlike" student cafeteria, where for sixty pfennigs she could buy a meal that "was cooked to pallor and flaccidity and then was seasoned with unheard-of condiments."

Gradually, too, she came into political awareness. By the end of October she was analyzing European tensions in a letter to Andrew Cooke. "I may be imagining this," she wrote, "but it seems to me that there are daily more and more troops arriving here." She was shocked by the signs put up around town that read, "The Jews are our misfortune!" In cafés she argued about the looming Spanish civil war; one of her acquaintances was a Spaniard who soon left to fight for Franco. She criticized Germany in letters to her family, who worried that her witticisms would land her under house arrest.

The actual nature of Stafford's first response to Nazism is not easy to pin down. The months in Heidelberg profoundly stirred her imagination; she later used them as the basis for five published short stories and a novella, at least two versions of an unpublished novel, and the beginnings of several incomplete stories. In 1949 she returned to Heidelberg for *The New Yorker* to write an essay on her postwar impressions. Like many another American who had visited Germany in the 1930s, Stafford was all too willing, after the war had revealed the full horror of the Third Reich, to credit herself retrospectively with foresight.

But even after the fact, Stafford did occasionally confess to an initial confusion and ambivalence about Nazism. In a lecture she gave at Columbia University in 1969, she recalled a huge parade of storm troopers that she had seen in Nuremberg, the soldiers singing "Deutschland Über Alles" and the Horst Wessel song as they marched by.

> I was swept along on a tidal wave of this well-organized collective conniption fit; my cortex ceased to be in charge and the optic thalamus took over. If a recruiter had come by and asked me to pledge myself for the rest of my life to the NSDAP, in all likelihood I would have done so.

One of the versions of her Heidelberg novel, which she wrote within a year or two of her return from Germany, hinges on its Staffordlike protagonist's getting so caught up in the Aryan fervor that she becomes a secret Nazi. Goodrich Walton swears, "She was a Nazi in her head for a while after she was at Heidelberg. . . . Jean and I had our falling-out over the stuff Hitler was doing in Germany when she came back. She thought Hitler was doing a wonderful thing." Hightower, however, derides Walton's claim as utterly untrue.

Upon her graduation from CU Stafford had fully intended to pursue a career as a philologist. She planned to follow her year of Heidelberg language study by applying to graduate school at Harvard. Johannes Hoops seemed an ideal mentor; seventy-one years old in the fall of 1936, he was famous in academic circles for his commentary on *Beowulf*. But things failed to work out as Stafford had hoped. According to Hightower,

> Hoops was delighted with Jean. Here was this pretty American girl, a serious student. He announced one day that he was having his seminar over to his house for the evening. . . .
>
> The seminar assembled and they waited and waited, and Jean didn't come. So finally he brought out the wine without Jean. Jean had something else to do — it didn't occur to her to go. But from then on Hoops was hostile in class. He never called on her. He ignored her. And so she stopped going.

Hightower himself was supposed to be studying Chinese, but there were no courses in that language at Heidelberg. Soon he too stopped attending his classes, though he continued to swap language lessons with a Japanese student. In the warm empty room at the Haarlass, Hightower and Stafford spent their mornings and afternoons working on their novels.

Hightower has only the dimmest recollection of what Stafford was writing at the time. One of her efforts was a long poem, of which his only memory is that a plum figured centrally in it. She was working mainly on a novel, which he thinks may have been about Boulder. In various letters written during 1936 and 1937, Jean alludes to "my new novel," distinguishing it from a previous, apparently completed work. In one instance she refers to characters based on Andrew and Lucy. These hints suggest that Stafford had written a novel while still at CU; it may have been the "hard-hitting thing with profanity and obscenity" that Goodrich Walton recalled. Perhaps the "new novel" she worked on at Heidelberg was her first attempt to grapple with the events that had led up to Lucy's suicide.

Hightower remembers that Stafford also wrote daily in a journal, which she kept in large, bound notebooks; her diary habit had begun in Boulder and would continue at least through 1939. She transferred, as he recalls, large sections of writing from her journal to the novel-in-progress. "It was a literary workbook," he says, "as well as a record of what went on and what she thought and felt." Often she read him excerpts. These notebooks, unfortunately, have vanished.

In the fall Robert Berueffy, Hightower's best friend, had moved from Paris to Brussels. Instead of coming to Heidelberg, he wrote Hightower to ask for his help with a get-rich-quick scheme he had devised. At the beginning of December, no longer invested in the academic life at Heidelberg, Hightower left to join his friend in Brussels.

> One reason that I was anxious to leave Heidelberg was that I tried to make love to Jean, and she wasn't having it. I felt it was too painful.
> There was one episode that settled my resolve. I was looking out the window one morning, and a taxi came up. Jean got out, paid the driver, and came in. I didn't know where she'd been spending the night, but I felt it was time for me to get out.

Berueffy's wacky scheme involved collecting used "hypo," the sodium thiosulfate solvent photographers employ as a fixing agent, and extracting silver from it. As soon as Hightower joined his friend in Brussels, he, too, plunged into the project. In the end both men squandered months of effort and sizable sums of money on the alchemy, and never produced a nickel's worth of silver.

The identity of Jean's Heidelberg lover (or lovers) remains a mystery. Sometime after 1945 Stafford told her good friend Frank Parker that she had had a passionate love affair in Heidelberg with a German aviator who was later killed in the Spanish civil war. In both Heidelberg novel attempts, and in the published novella "A Winter's Tale" (which was largely resurrected from one of the earlier, abandoned novels), this lover is developed in some detail. He is called either Max or Rheinhard Rössler. Although the details vary from one version to another, in all three he is a Nazi pilot whom the protagonist first meets in a beer hall. While still in Heidelberg she learns that he has been killed, not in Spain but on maneuvers in Karlsruhe as he is preparing to go to Spain.

The plausibility of this character's having been based on a real person is slightly enhanced by a note left among Stafford's papers, which seems to be a preliminary list of characters for one of her German novels. The list includes "Berueffy" and other autobiographical references with the real names undisguised. "Rössler" also appears on the list. This may suggest that the aviator existed and, just conceivably, that Rössler was his real surname.

On the other hand, Hightower knew nothing of a German aviator, and he says, "I can almost guarantee it's fiction. I saw her every day at that time. I think it's unlikely. . . . We were both liars by profession. You told stories that gave a creative twist to things." One bone of contention between Hightower and Stafford in Heidelberg concerned each other's choice of company. Hightower avoided other Americans "like the plague," while Jean sought them out.

In December Stafford began to be sick much of the time. Jokingly, she alluded in letters to dysentery, tuberculosis, and tapeworm; in fact, she often ran a fever and vomited. Around the first of the year Hightower returned to Heidelberg. He stayed at the Haarlass for about a month; Berueffy joined him for part of the time before heading once more for Paris. The days during which the three friends sat in the hotel writing, smoking, drinking, and talking were some of the happiest of the year for Jean.

Stafford was still not interested in having an affair with

Hightower, however, so he left for Paris in the beginning of February to share lodgings with Berueffy. The two men found an apartment on Rue Primatrice, an obscure lane just off the Place d'Italie where crippled beggars and street singers seemed to congregate. There Hightower struggled with his intractable novel while Berueffy, who had found a piano, composed popular songs and doggedly practiced Chopin.

The steady, rich correspondence between Hightower and Stafford developed its own highly stylized idiom. In keeping with the bohemian fashion of the day, the three artistes addressed each other in person only by last name. For the salutations and signatures of their letters, the object was to be absurd, inventive, and allusive. Jean calls Robert "Ruprecht" (after the founder of the university); the two Roberts together are addressed as "Gents," "Boys," "Buck + Stephen" (after Joyce), and "Pound + Stravinsky." She signs herself "Mary Baker Eddy," "Thomas Wolfe," "Florence Nightgown," and "Always Krank" (*krank* being German for "sick"). Hightower, on the other hand, writes to "Electra," "Clymenestra [*sic*]," and "Iseult," while he signs himself "albert roi de belgique," "Karl Marx," "Zarathustra," and "Atta Troll." As slapdash as these pseudonyms sound, they hint at the images and ambitions around which the friendship pivoted.

More consistently, Hightower and Stafford adopted a homespun American vernacular for their letters. Thus (he to her), "You wuz right. Dont do wot i said wotever you dont do"; and (she to him), "There isn't anything else to write so I will hang my close on this line and hit the hay." According to Hightower, this discourse began as a private joke between Berueffy and himself; they took on the roles of rustic bumpkins, partly in the spirit of Ezra Pound. Stafford soon joined in the game. In their pastoral fantasy Berueffy became "Bro" or "Brother," Stafford "Sis" or "Sister," and Hightower "Ma." As Hightower explains the family, "I was frugal and abstemious to a certain extent, and they thought naught for the morrow. If we had a little money, they liked to get some wine and get drunk, and I felt we should keep it for food." In her letters Jean gave herself the persona of "Bessie Barnstable" — "a milkmaid, a country girl, not very clean, not very well behaved."

Hightower and Berueffy entreated Stafford to join them in Paris.

In the meantime, however, she had received a letter from Lucy Cooke's parents. "The score is," she wrote Hightower, "Mrs. McKee says I'd jolly well better get a job for next year and I've gotta go back to Am[erica]." No doubt her money was running out, and she may have unwisely asked the McKees for a further loan. Facing the inevitable, Jean determined to make a quick trip to Munich and Italy before she had to turn her back on Europe.

In late February she left Heidelberg, passed through Munich and the Austrian Tirol, and entered Italy by the Brenner Pass. Trying to fit as much experience as she could into a short time, she followed a standard tourist itinerary — Florence, Venice, Rome, and Naples. In Italy she lost her passport, but luckily it was mailed back to her. In a rambling poem about her travels, she summed up March 1937: "I was in Italy five weeks and I didn't say a word."

Realizing that her year abroad was coming to an end, Stafford had written her beloved CU teacher Irene McKeehan, asking for a recommendation for a Harvard fellowship. To Jean's chagrin, McKeehan refused, saying that she thought her former student lacked the makings of a scholar. " 'Why don't you get married?' " her mentor advised; " 'Or, better, why don't you write?' "

In 1976 Stafford would claim, with considerable hyperbole, "For thirty years now I have been earning my living as a writer, largely because of Miss McKeehan's blunt demolition of an impossibly silly daydream." Despite this overstatement, the "astringent honesty" of her teacher's advice, along with the embarrassing difficulty she had had in assimilating German, did have a great deal to do with Stafford's abandoning her philological ambitions.

On April 5, after her return from Italy, Jean left Germany for good. Her reunion with Hightower and Berueffy in Paris was brief but joyous. The "boys" took Jean on a day's outing to Fontainebleau. On April 8 they put her on a train at the Gare du Nord and said goodbye.

As soon as she had parted from her friends, Stafford began to dread her arrival in the United States. On April 10 she sailed from Southampton on the SS *Hansa*. The ship was full of Jews fleeing Germany. She arrived in New York harbor on April 17 and went to stay with some friends from Colorado who lived in Brooklyn. At once she sank into a deep depression. In letters to Berueffy and Hightower she vowed to return as soon as

possible: "I have realized suddenly to my horror that I'm an artist + have to be with my fellow beings."

Everything American appalled her. She derided the provinciality of her hosts: "These *horrible* people I stay with have back
copies of the *Colorado Alumnus* to read aloud to me — all about
how Harold Bumpkin is teaching Spanish, English, History, algebra + coaching basketball at Eads, Colo." Her return had jolted
her back into her own history: "I *can't* stay in America next year
unless I completely repudiate the whole past and live in some
foreign quarter."

Hightower fed her dissatisfaction, recounting how, when bicycling through the Paris streets, he had spotted James Joyce and
then loitered in awe, watching the great man for half an hour. In
their letters the three soulmates traded vague promises about
homesteading together on a farm in Oklahoma. Hightower and
Berueffy, however, also had plans to go to China; when these
fell through, the two friends stayed on in Paris through August
1937. Trying to tease Jean out of her despair, Hightower wrote,
"I tell you if we all hang on for 20 more yrs we will all be famous. And it's the next 2 that are impt."

The year abroad had given Stafford a new perspective on her
Boulder entanglements. She confided to Hightower that she had
lost all interest in Fairchild. "I consider with stark horror," she
wrote, "how I might have married Larry." The Cooke entourage no longer seemed glamorous. Donald Hays and Dorothy
Grabill, who had married, were now "Donald and Dorothy
Babbit."

More significantly, Jean felt a dawning astonishment at the fact
that she had so idealized Lucy.

> My grief for her was as hypocritical as most grief is, and it was
> merely the horror and the strangeness of that night that appealed
> to me so. . . . Her brain was only approximately the brain I wanted
> to know. What I have done all my life is substitute. I substituted
> Lucy's mind for the one I was really looking for which was yours,
> Ruprecht, and probably Berueffy's too though I don't know his
> very well.

One night in Brooklyn, however, Jean had a nightmare. In it she
heard horrible screams, but Hightower told her not to worry —
"it was just Lucy having the bullet taken out."

Having given up her plans for graduate school at Harvard, Stafford had applied for jobs teaching English. A college in Illinois, another in Oregon, yet another in Puerto Rico, Grinnell in Iowa, and the University of Montana all turned her down. She wrote the "boys" ruefully, "I have four prospects of jobs — one at $660 per year. They are at Pullman, Washington; Crete, Nebraska; Baldwin, Kansas; Jenkintown, Pa. Which do you choose? Any one of those addresses wd. certainly give me prestige."

One reward awaited Stafford in Brooklyn. While Jean was in Europe, Edward Davison had talked to Whit Burnett at *Story* magazine. Burnett had apparently found some of Jean's fiction promising, for he had asked Davison to tell her that "he was 'disposed to consider my next work as probably publishable.' " At the end of April she had lunch in New York with Burnett and Martha Foley. This couple had started *Story* in Vienna in 1932 and then moved the magazine to New York the following year. Almost immediately *Story* had gained a reputation as one of the best outlets in the country for serious fiction. Burnett had also launched Story Press, a book-publishing house affiliated with Harper and Brothers.

The meeting was the most auspicious turn yet in Stafford's career as a writer. During lunch Foley echoed her husband's praise and asked Jean if she might look at excerpts from her Heidelberg journal with a view toward publishing them. Fired with new enthusiasm, Stafford speculated in a letter to Hightower that perhaps she could survive and write in Manhattan after all.

Stafford's stay in Brooklyn was intended to be a brief one, but in late April she became seriously ill. She had been sick off and on since December, with recurring high temperatures and intestinal upsets. All through her trip to Italy and during her stay in Paris she had felt feverish. Now, however, her temperature climbed above 103 degrees, and a worried doctor admitted her to Brooklyn Hospital.

During two hospital stays of some ten days each, Stafford developed a bewildering series of symptoms. Her stomach ached so much that she could not touch the skin on her abdomen. Her temperature peaked at 103.8 degrees. She had, as she put it, "the curse" for thirty-three days in a row. A throat and mouth infection that she had had for months got worse. Her gums became infected. She was unable to eat and had trouble keeping even water down. Her joints began to ache, as well as her back. She developed a pelvic abscess. As her condition deteriorated, she felt "on fire with pain."

The doctors were mystified. They gave her enemas and mineral oil, tested for trichinosis, wondered about scurvy, dysentery, and gall bladder or kidney problems. Stafford grew exasperated and despondent and felt she was on the verge of a nervous breakdown.

Finally her ailment was diagnosed. A bit euphemistically, she delivered the verdict to Hightower and Berueffy:

> It's *female trouble* which heretofore has always been good for a laugh. My uterus is turned over, pressing against the intestine. I have an intestinal infection. I have ovarian cysts. It will be months before I have recovered and until then I've got to be a bloody invalid of the E. B. Browning variety. . . .
>
> The pain is intolerable and unless I constantly see doctors, constantly stay on a diet and stay in bed most of the time I'll have to have an operation — which I simply couldn't face. . . . This is one of the things that contributed to Lucy's suicide.

This somewhat misleading account was not the whole truth. Even further from the truth was the explanation Jean offered her other friends and her family — that her ailment had turned out to be malnutrition, originally misdiagnosed as trichinosis.

Three years later, in 1940, Stafford gave Hightower a more humiliating explanation, in the strictest of confidence.

> She said, "Have you ever had gonorrhea?" "No." "Well," she said, "I have." Then she told me — she gave me one account of how and where, then almost in the next breath revised it. And I think the revision is true.
>
> The first one was, "Well, I told you about that handsome Italian that followed me when I was in Italy . . . no, that wasn't it, it was in Heidelberg."
>
> [I remembered] that morning I had seen her come back in the taxi. . . . It had been an American, she said, a baseball player . . . she had met someplace, I suppose at the German equivalent of a bar. . . .
>
> When she told me, she hadn't told anyone else.

Nor, it seems very likely, did Stafford ever tell anyone else — not even any of her three husbands. To the doctor who, after 1963, became the most trusted personal physician of her life, she never hinted at this secret illness.

What an American baseball player might have been doing in Heidelberg in November 1936 is hard to imagine. Yet such a character seems consistent with Stafford's penchant for hanging out at American haunts like the bar at the Europäischer Hof. Her dashing Nazi aviator's going off to perish in the Spanish civil war sounds like a romantic fiction, akin to Bernard Allen's laying himself on the tracks in "In the Snowfall." Perhaps in both cases the tawdry reality, joined to the traumatic result — a slick frat boy stealing her virginity, an American tourist giving her gonorrhea — seemed to Stafford so degrading that to be able to write about these predators at all she had not only to camouflage their identities but also to kill them off with tragic denouements.

Even Stafford's later confession to Hightower may not tell the whole story. Many of the symptoms she reported to her friend are indeed compatible with gonorrhea: pelvic and intestinal distress, ovarian cysts, nausea and vomiting, aching joints. So is the doctors' suggestion, after they discovered what was wrong, that she have an operation. But other symptoms do not fit so well. Stafford's "trench mouth" (as she called it) and infected gums; her very high, intermittent fevers; the delay of six months in the full-blown appearance of the disease; and the doctors' difficulty in diagnosing what was wrong — all of these signs are more characteristic of secondary syphilis, one of whose fiendish traits is that it can mimic dozens of other diseases. Most suggestively, after the diagnosis Jean was put on a treatment regimen of arsenic compounds. Since 1907 these drugs had been used to combat syphilis; they were not prescribed for gonorrhea.

It is entirely possible that Stafford's Heidelberg fling infected her with both gonorrhea and syphilis. The consequences of these diseases, in an age before penicillin was widely available, could be dire. If gonorrhea spread to the fallopian tubes (often indicated by fever, nausea, vomiting, and abdominal pain), it could easily cause sterility. The arsenic compounds did not offer a permanent cure for secondary syphilis; they worked only as long as the treatment was in effect. Once the patient stopped taking the medicine, the disease could break out again at any time during the rest of her life. It could even develop into fatal tertiary syphilis. Moreover, without the intervention of a cure, a female syphilis carrier ran the risk of infecting not only any future sexual partner she took but also any offspring she bore.

During the time of her hospital stay and the months following, Stafford wrote unhappy letters to Hightower in which she conjured with thoughts of suicide. As she had in Boulder with Lucy and Andrew, in Heidelberg Jean had often talked about suicide with her friend. Like Andrew, Hightower was not inclined to take it seriously.

Yet in the late spring of 1937, despite the bright new prospects greeting her as a writer, despite the excitement of Europe and New York, Stafford may well have confronted the stigma of her venereal disease with genuinely suicidal despair.

Reflecting on his long, intimate knowledge of Stafford's life, Hightower says, "Wherever Jean was, things happened. And there was excitement always. But Jean usually got the shitty end of the stick."

VII

The Grooming Clinic

BURDENED with the distressing diagnosis of her illness, Stafford left Brooklyn in June 1937 and took the train to Colorado. Her passage across the Midwest reinforced her despondency at being back in the United States. She made a brief stop in Boulder, where she saw Larry Fairchild, her lover of the previous year. "He just about made me vomit," she wrote Hightower.

> Goddam if his white collie didn[']t die so he bought a new bitch —
> and in those very words. He is a medical student all right — greatest
> stuff on earth, lives in the palm of your hand, to hell with art,
> m.d.'s the only people who know the score. . . . Can you *imagine*
> I wanted to marry him once?

She ordered Fairchild to return her letters and a portrait she had given him, which had been executed by a student in the life-drawing class. In response he wrote an awkwardly pompous but earnest letter begging that they might remain friends. Jean copied the letter and sent it on to Hightower and Berueffy, appending her own derisive commentary.

Her venomous mood persisted as she traveled to Hayden to stay with Mary Lee and her husband on the cattle ranch. From Oregon her mother had written her an affectionate letter, addressed "Dear Pigeon" and full of such homely lines as "I hustled up dinner and then since it was beastly hot we took off most of our clothes and just loafed around." Jean transcribed the letter, underlined what she considered the more egregious Americanisms, and mailed it to her friends in Paris, moralizing, "Well, all I can say is, it shore is a pity that Pa ever got hitched up with those fat McKillop girls." She also started keeping a notebook of her mother's clichés.

The job rejections accumulated. Not only was Stafford under pressure to return the McKees' loan, but she now felt it her duty to help support her own parents. As soon as they had taken their first jobs, all three of her siblings had begun sending home part of their meager incomes to aid their father in his dogged evasion of gainful employment. Now it was Jean's turn.

Her health was not improving. "Last night my mouth bled about a pint, and it is full of pus all the time," she wrote her Paris cronies. She went to a dentist who claimed that "the disease was in every piece of gum in my head," and to a doctor, who suspected another pelvic abscess. Teasing nonchalantly at what may have been the truth as a way of deflecting any suspicion, she wrote Berueffy and Hightower about her "trench mouth": "They have to treat it in the same way as they do syphilis." Thus a week or two later she could jest, "I have started the treatments for my syphilis. . . ."

At the end of July Stafford returned to Boulder for the writers' conference. Edward Davison had given her a job as a kind of secretary-cum-hostess, and she planned to get the most out of her contact with the visiting luminaries. She brought with her a short story, eight poems, twenty pages of journal excerpts from Heidelberg, and 105 pages of the novel she had worked on in Germany.

The gathering of writers in 1937 was illustrious in the extreme. And Davison treated Jean as no mere secretary. Even before the conference began, he gave Stafford's novel to Ford Madox Ford, her poetry to John Crowe Ransom and Howard Mumford Jones, and her short story and journal excerpts to Whit Burnett. In Boulder Stafford also hoped to make the acquaintance of Sherwood Anderson, and she succeeded in persuading the poet John Peale Bishop and the novelist Evelyn Scott to read her writing. She was no longer a conference hanger-on, as she had been in 1935, but rather the director's chief deputy and pet prodigy.

The most renowned of the guests was Ford, who, at sixty-three and in poor health, had only two more years to live. The famous novelist found his Boulder accommodations uncomfortable, so the Davisons invited him to stay at their house. Peter

Davison, who was only nine at the time, vividly remembers Ford's arrival. "He was wheezy and red-faced, with a funny little mustache, and he had a huge gouty foot. . . . I can see him hobbling up the front walk on [his mistress] Janice Biala's arm, with a cane, and his foot swathed in bandages."

The highlight of each year's conference was a public lecture by its principal attraction. In 1935 a very nervous Thomas Wolfe had enthralled the crowd by reading an essay that grew into *The Story of a Novel*. In 1937 Ford outranked even Sherwood Anderson as a celebrity. His lecture was to become every bit as legendary in Boulder annals as Wolfe's, but for the opposite reason.

On August 3, before an audience of 650 people in the university theater, Ford announced that he would give an intimate account of his long collaboration with Józef Korzeniowski; very few of the listeners recognized Joseph Conrad's given name. Because of his health, Ford lectured sitting down. Edward Davison had provided a microphone. Ford leaned into it and asked, "Can everybody hear me?" The audience chorused assent, "at which point," recalls Peter Davison, "he buried his head in the manuscript and never lifted it again, and went on for an hour and a half. Nobody could hear anything he said." The audience, initially polite, gradually slipped out of the auditorium. By the end of the lecture only a handful of admirers remained.

Stafford was in the thick of all the conference doings. As the colloquy drew to a close, she wrote Hightower and Berueffy her good news. The mannered telegraphese of her letter — an uncharacteristic prose for Stafford — betrays the self-conscious elation she felt at her mentors' approval.

Saw Bishop. Said I was best. Not surprised after spending morning idly contemplating 60 fat female rumps in the W.C. chambers. Said I had an eminent nerve writing s[tream] of c[onsciousness] + thereby putting myself up to compete with biggest boys meaning Joyce. Said I cd. however make the grade. Was *v.* encouraging. Evelyn Scott who read journal + short story said hell, gal, you ain't serving an apprenticeship, you're graduate professional. Said if I can get away from the academic will become great writer. . . . Said I was most unusual for age had ever seen. Have not embellished. Am not embarrassed. Know now for sure I'm good — like hell.

In addition to these other encouragements, Howard Mumford Jones took Stafford's journal excerpts back to Boston to show a friend at the Atlantic Monthly Press, Whit Burnett took her story and several poems for consideration for *Story,* and Ford himself "said one day mine will be a great name in literature." The happiest moment of the conference for Stafford came one evening at a dinner party hosted by Burnett:

> That was the night that Evelyn Scott said let's ask the poet in our midst, we will be hearing from Jean Stafford in ten years and we will be talking about her on occasions like this, and Ransom said, yes, she is unique, and Davison sat there pleased as punch, not saying anything, just pleased because he thought of me first.

Tagging along with Ford everywhere he went at the writers' conference was a twenty-year-old Harvard dropout and native Bostonian named Robert Lowell. Ford had met this intense would-be poet at a party in Boston the previous spring. Seizing upon the great writer's scraps of encouragement, Lowell had appointed himself Ford's disciple and had followed the novelist around the country for four months. In Boulder, once Ford and Janice Biala had been installed in the Davisons' house, Lowell showed up regularly, trying to crash their nightly get-togethers with Bishop, Ransom, and Anderson. According to Peter Davison,

> One Saturday evening when he rang the bell my mother said, "I'm sorry, Mr. Lowell, you can't come in. I don't like your manners." He went away but retaliated, I'm told, by standing on our lawn, swaying slightly, the next morning, and urinating, while the churchgoers of Boulder passed by.

It was almost certainly at the Davisons' house that Jean Stafford met Robert Lowell. Of this encounter, which was to prove so fateful for both, nothing is recorded. It seems that at first Lowell was far more smitten with Stafford than she was with him. As one friend recalls Lowell's own account, "he chased her around" in Boulder; then, through the subsequent months, by mail, he "wooed her something fierce."

Tall, darkly handsome, and athletic-looking, with immense energy and intelligence, Lowell was the somewhat spoiled only child of a Marlborough Street couple who dangled from a slightly déclassé branch of the famous tree of Boston Lowells. After St.

Mark's School and a year at Harvard, Robert had declared his intention of marrying the cousin of one of his best friends. But Anne Dick was six years older than he, and the Lowells regarded her as their son's social inferior; they scheduled a meeting with Anne's father, at which they scolded him for allowing his daughter to visit Robert unchaperoned in his Harvard room.

The climax of this debacle was a fight in which Robert knocked his father to the floor and stormed out of the house. Mrs. Lowell briefly considered having her son committed to an institution. Robert eventually apologized to his father, but he kept up a secret engagement to Anne Dick.

His parents wanted to separate Lowell from his fiancée, and they knew he loathed Harvard. Thus they arranged to introduce him to Ford Madox Ford, in the deliberate hope that if their son apprenticed himself to a "real writer" and left Boston, the various tensions could be resolved. When Lowell met him in Boston, Ford was on his way to Tennessee to visit his old friend the poet Allen Tate.

One day in April 1937 Lowell drove up to Tate's country house in Tennessee, signaling his arrival by knocking over Tate's mailbox. At "Benfolly," Ford and Janice Biala had settled in with Tate and his wife, the novelist Caroline Gordon; all three writers were pounding away at books. The upstart twenty-year-old "offered [him]self as a guest." By way of refusing, Tate said there was no more room at Benfolly unless the newcomer were to pitch a tent on the lawn. Lowell took him at his word, bought a Sears Roebuck umbrella tent, and homesteaded in Tate's front yard for three months. Besides absorbing lessons from his captive idols and turning out "grimly unromantic poems," Lowell sat in on John Crowe Ransom's classes at nearby Vanderbilt University.

In July Lowell squeezed into a car with Ford, Biala, Tate, and Gordon as they drove to a writers' conference at Olivet College in Michigan. After Olivet Lowell took the train to the writers' conference in Colorado, where he met Jean Stafford. Once the Boulder session was over he followed Ford back to Olivet, where the latter was to teach through the fall term. For the month of August Lowell served as Ford's personal secretary.

By now Lowell had lost all interest in Anne Dick. In September 1937 he transferred to Kenyon College to follow Ransom, who had accepted a teaching job there. Lowell's first Kenyon roommate was Randall Jarrell, his second was Peter Taylor, and a close neighbor was Robie Macauley — all three budding writers who worshiped at Ransom's knee. To his new friends that fall, Lowell talked often about the girl he had met in Boulder.

For Stafford the three weeks of the writers' conference had been fruitful beyond her dreams. To be in Boulder again, however, was to stagger under the weight of her past. "Well, i am now back in the cesspool," she had written the "boys" after arriving for the conference, "and i swear by god this is the last time." Just when her search for a job was beginning to seem hopeless, she landed a position at Stephens College in Missouri. The salary was a hundred dollars a month plus room and board.

Hightower was still in Europe. He had spent a summer month bicycling through Denmark, thus indulging in a vigorous pastime that would become his lifelong passion. But his dreams — of China, of a farm in Oklahoma, of a fortune made mining "hypo" — had succumbed to practicality: he had been accepted as a graduate student in Far Eastern languages at Harvard. At the beginning of September he sailed to New York and then went straight to Cambridge, getting there on almost the same day that Stafford arrived in Columbia, Missouri.

Two months previously, Jean had turned twenty-two. Although she would suffer brief failures of nerve during the next few years, from the summer of 1937 on she never seriously wanted to be anything but a writer. If the combination of her language problems in Germany and Irene McKeehan's discouragement had not sufficed to turn Stafford away from the life of a scholar, in Boulder her old English professor George Reynolds had told her that "he wd. not advise my getting a PhD ever. . . . I suspect that he means I haven't got the footnote mind."

At Stephens Jean embarked on the first full-time job of her life. She never pretended that teaching English was her true ambition, but she knew that many of her writers'-conference heroes, from John Crowe Ransom to Howard Mumford Jones and even Ford Madox Ford, used teaching jobs as platforms from which to launch their belles lettres.

Before September 1937 Stafford had never taught a single class. She was predictably nervous as she faced her students for the first time, and in fact the session went badly. "I just had my first class," she wrote Hightower in dismay, "and o you just can't imagine how a[w]ful it is. They didn't laugh at one of my pearls and they all hate me and I was so damned scared that I didn't say anything I intended to and in general I wished I was dead. I wanta be a novelist."

Things would get worse. Jean knew very little about Stephens College for Girls before she got to Columbia. The irony of her first appointment is that even in the most Aldous Huxley–ish stretches of her imagination she could hardly have devised an institution of learning more inimical to her spirit.

Stephens had been rescued from bankruptcy in 1912 by a new president, James Madison Wood, who turned a Baptist women's institution into an expensive two-year junior college, building it a national reputation for "progressive education." By the time of Stafford's arrival in 1937 Wood was a gray-haired demigod in the twenty-sixth year of his reign. His nickname was Daddy, and his favorite pastime was entertaining select groups of "Susies," or Stephens girls, at "luncheons" in the college-owned country club.

A disciple of John Dewey, Wood had made the mandate of his college "learning by doing rather than by merely memorizing." The curriculum was practical in the extreme, for "the object of education is to enable men and women to make more easily those life adjustments that are essential to well ordered and satisfactory living."

By the 1930s Stephens had become an economic success. Twelve hundred students filled its two classes, with 120 faculty members attending to their needs. The school's unusual pedagogy had won widespread notice in newspapers and magazines, and the college appealed to the well-heeled parents of would-be sorority girls. Yet Stephens's pretensions to academic quality only camouflaged the fact that it was really a finishing school.

Stafford saw through those pretensions from her first day on campus. "Not even my salary can atone for these tortures," she wrote Hightower.

I do not approve of progressive education (one of my advisees wanted to take "The Selection and Preparation of Foods" as her laboratory science. . . .)
When I went to school I studied Latin, Plane Geometry, Gothic,

Anglo-Saxon, Chemistry, Botany, Long Division, and Verbs, and
I can't see that it hurt me.

"Do you know," she regaled Hightower, "that somebody said
to me the other day, why don't you go to the Grooming Clinic,
Miss Stafford? You might pick up a few pointers."

Her friend in Cambridge may have thought she was exaggerating, as was her wont, for satiric effect. But Stephens College
in 1937 was actually a living parody of progressive educational
theory — Deweyism gone mad and soft. Daddy Wood's school
explicitly disavowed any aim of liberating the young minds of
its students from the provinciality of their upbringing; instead,
"the College freely subscribes to the parents' objectives, which
are fundamentally sound."

The curriculum included such courses as "Scientific Eating,"
"Filing and Secretarial Techniques," "Commercial Buying,"
"Home Management," "Principles of Dress," "Principles of Interior Decoration," "Posture," "Marriage and the Family," "Golf"
(at the college's 170-acre country club), "Horseback Riding," "Tap
Dancing," and "Playgrounds." Girls could major in "Kindergarten and Pre-Nursery," "Pre-Commerce," or "The Home-Makers
Course." Grades were tabulated not only on the basis of class-
work but on a steady surveillance of each student's day-and-night
performance in such areas as "initiative," "self-discipline," and
"balancing of class and extra-class time."

Stafford's appointment was as an instructor in the Communications department. This gathering of thirteen teachers was part
of the Division of Skills and Techniques, along with the staffs of
Tap Dancing and Office Practice. The five sections of English
composition that Stafford taught had no links to the Division of
Humanities, and indeed bringing literature into the course at all
was frowned upon. What Communications was supposed to be
about had been succinctly codified in a college position paper:
"(1) letter writing, (2) conversation, (3) group discussion, (4)
making a speech, (5) giving reports of experience, (6) giving directions or explanations, and (7) storytelling."

The Voice Clinic, a bellwether of the Communications department, had as its raison d'être the notion that "a pleasing voice is
a desirable characteristic of women." There really was a Grooming Clinic. The college had also devised what it called the Siesta.

No classes were scheduled between one and two o'clock each afternoon, so the girls could take after-lunch naps. "Roommates are not supposed to chat, nor are students expected to study. . . ."

Two weeks into the fall semester, Stafford was already thoroughly disenchanted. "My advisees are loathesome little bitches who are homesick and have rumps like a kitchen stove," she wrote Hightower. "They want to take English comp at ten instead of eight and zoology instead of chemistry and riding instead of mathematics, etc." Daddy Wood was "a lecherous old fool who goes around with about eight virgins squeezing his arms, legs, ears, nose, Rolandic fissures. . . ."

Her students' term papers drove her to waspish irony. One of the girls, she wrote Hightower, "is going to write on the orient, do you think that is too broad Miss Stafford." In December she wrote, "I have to get out 215 grades and I don't even know who my students are yet." She related the titles of some of the papers: "The History of Corsets, The Life of Apollo, Literature, The History of Buttons, Prostitution as a Career." Stafford planned a subversive course for the spring term: "It is going to be a survey of english literature (alias Eng. Comp.) but nobody knows what we do here so that you can do anything you damned well please."

Despite her contempt for the rich girls she taught, she claimed that she had become a popular instructor. Once they found out that she was writing a novel, some of Stafford's students asked her to autograph copies for them to give away as Christmas presents.

At first Stafford had been appalled at the number of dinner parties and school functions she had to attend. But by November she had learned to hide her disdain for Stephens social life: "I have begun being politic and hypocritical and I go to dinner at the faculty members' houses and I say isn't this weather just comic and I go to formal dinners at the dormitory and I am respectable and dull and bored. . . ."

Stafford felt as much contempt for her colleagues as she did for her students. One English teacher, she told Hightower, used *Reader's Digest* as a text in his classes. Another figure of fun was "the head of the English Department [i.e., Division of Skills and Techniques]. . . . He is a man of sixty and is married to a woman of twenty-three, a former student. They make me vomit-sick." To her mordant delight she had come across an anthology of verse that contained a poem written by the man, called "Baby Wisdom." This is its first stanza:

> *Baby, dear, tell me true:*
> *Would you laugh and kick and coo,*
> *Would you dimple as you do*
>   *If you knew*
> *What the world we've brought you to*
> *Would in its turn bring to you?*
>   *Would you — if you knew,*
>   *Baby dear?*

Another colleague of Stafford's in the Communications department was Bill Mock, a friend of Dorothy and Paul Thompson, who had commended him to Jean. Mock had graduated from Dartmouth in 1934 and earned an M.A. at Northwestern two years later. He had begun teaching at Stephens at the same time as Jean, and he stayed on after her departure. Eventually he became an ambulance driver in the French army and then a policeman in Ormond Beach, Florida. Jean described him in a letter to Hightower as "not so bad," with a Paul Thompson–ish wit.

> He is furthermore rich and has a car and drinks whiskey and has some friends who are drunken cigarette salesmen who have an apt and we can get away from the Stephens spirit occasionally. He is fat and short and black and has a mustache and athlete's foot. He bounces.

According to Stafford, Mock fell passionately in love with her almost at once. By December he had let her know that he was determined to marry her. Although she never took him seriously as a suitor, Jean found him a kindred outsider in the brave new world of Stephens and recognized that his car and cash could buy her momentary escapes.

With Mock she went to St. Louis for the opera and slummed in the "dives" on the Mississippi waterfront. She described one Saturday-night adventure:

> There wuz a couple of dames along in our party with a Camels salesman + a Philip Morris salesman + they wuz shocked + wuz collitch girls. There was 1 joint that is called the Rock House and it's pretty grim. You go upstairs and at first it's dark as a pocket + then you see an orchestra + then some tables with people and

then some nigger whores singing real low to the customers. Well, the Scotch tastes like 1930, American made, but by the time you leave you don't care because you realize that there are Other Things besides liquor, and 1 of them is this: you put a quarter on the edge of the table and one of these nigger babes sings a song to you, something pretty vilely ambiguous and then she starts hitching herself around, raising her skirt + finally picks up the quarter without using her hands. They can even do it with change — two dimes and a nickel.

Stafford's health remained poor throughout her year at Stephens. In the fall she complained to Hightower about a bad cold that made her feel as though "my chest has pancake batter in it" and "my brains are writhing in a bed of phlegm." She also suffered from severe headaches and an intestinal flu that made her miss classes. By February she was grumbling about her doctor and dentist bills. "Now I have got a sore throat and a stiff neck, obvious signs of spinal meningitis. My viscera feel bad too because my schwester [sister] sent me an electric percolator and all I do now is sit on my rump and drink coffee." She had also developed a rash on the left side of her face, which she jokingly attributed to measles.

Despite Bill Mock's zealous pursuit, during her year at Stephens Jean saved her deepest thoughts for Hightower, half a continent away in a Spartan Cambridge boardinghouse room. The correspondence between the two friends, which had begun when Hightower had first left Heidelberg for Brussels, grew through the fall of 1937 until theirs became the most important relationship in either one's life.

At first Stafford and Hightower wrote to each other only every week or so, but by midyear they were sending letters at least every other day. Hightower was also having an unhappy year. He felt deeply ambivalent about studying Chinese and Japanese; beset with poverty, he worked as a hash cook in the boardinghouse to make enough money to buy beer; he had no luck finding girlfriends; and he found the weather in Cambridge intolerable and the students at Harvard callow and smug.

One of the linchpins of the correspondence was an extended commentary about books, in the spirit of the very first exchange the two had shared back in Boulder, when they had bandied obscure allusions from *Ulysses*. The letters from this time document

Stafford's taste in modern writers during her twenty-third year. James Joyce remained her paragon, and she kept up a running joke that Thomas Wolfe was stealing her ideas. She voiced her horror that *Gone with the Wind* had won the Pulitzer Prize; its success, just when Jean returned from Germany, seemed to her to epitomize all that was wrong with America. At first she admired Santayana's *The Last Puritan,* but by the time she finished the novel she was ready to dismiss it: "His characters speak like a Platonic symposium and they are all abstractions."

Hightower was a prodigious reader. While he neglected his Japanese and Chinese texts, he devoured Western literature, buying cheap used books and borrowing (and occasionally stealing) volumes from Widener Library. At one point in the spring of 1938 he calculated that he had read ninety-six books since the first of January, taking two days per book on the average but reading as many as fifteen at once.

In their letters Stafford and Hightower weighed Hemingway's merits, agreed on Joyce's superiority to Somerset Maugham, and argued over which of them had first discovered Gerard Manley Hopkins. Hightower promised to buy Jean Proust for Christmas, thinking that she might acquire a taste for the French writer — a hunch, as it would turn out, that was a colossal underestimation.

As intellectual as these letters often were, they also served to develop the timid overtures of a romance. Hightower seized upon Stafford's unhappiness and her frequent expressions of the need to see him again. As early as September he offered a tongue-in-cheek proposal of marriage. She teased back, taking him to task for his Japanese girlfriend in Colorado, who was still pursuing him from a distance. In October Jean confessed, "I won't never be happy as long as I ain't nigh you and . . . I don't want you to be in love with me but I'd kill you in cold blood if you was in love with anybody else. I want to be in love with you myself and maybe I am i don't know."

Yet during these same months Stafford was also fielding Robert Lowell's attentions, which came to her by mail from Kenyon College in Ohio. She never hinted at this other relationship in her letters to Cambridge; indeed it would be almost a year before Hightower even knew that Lowell existed.

In later years Stafford destroyed all but one of the letters Lowell had ever written her, and Lowell himself kept her letters only after 1946. Thus it is impossible to reconstruct in any detail the course of their early courtship. It is clear, however, that between August 1937 and September 1938 Lowell had no more idea of Hightower's existence than Hightower had of his.

In his lonely room in Cambridge the disgruntled grad student plotted ways of getting together with the woman he longed for, whom he had not seen since he put her on the train at the Gare du Nord the previous April. He begged Jean to come to Boston at Christmas. He laid plans for them to spend a summer together out West or in Paris. And he wanted to know just what was going on with this fellow Bill Mock.

At the beginning of that fall term a kind of locker-room cynicism on the subject of lovers had prevailed in their letters. Hightower coolly appraised his chances of "getting laid" by a Radcliffe girl. Stafford bragged sardonically that Mock had proposed marriage; she added that "he is fat and a lot shorter than me maybe a foot but he's got dough."

Mock, however, was entirely serious about marriage. He gave Stafford a 1927 Paris edition of *Ulysses,* took her to hear Kirsten Flagstad in St. Louis, and invited her to his parents' home in Chicago for Christmas. When Jean accepted the invitation, Hightower was hurt and suspicious.

Stafford treated the Christmas trip as a lark, regarding it opportunistically — one of her primary incentives for going to Chicago, in fact, was to attend the annual meeting of the Modern Language Association, where she could not only hunt for a better job but see John Crowe Ransom and Howard Mumford Jones again. After her stay in Mock's "swell dive" in Evanston, she wrote Hightower, trying to allay his jealousy, "I told you it was all free and I didn't get involved. He don't like me as good as he did."

The MLA meetings were splendid. "I drank three rye and sodas with John Crowe Ransom in the bar at the Drake and we talked about how good I was and how maybe I wd get to talk to All[e]n Tate next year." Stafford was encouraged to pursue job possibilities at Vanderbilt and the University of North Carolina at Greensboro. She confided her teaching miseries to Howard Mumford Jones, who told her that "the only thing to do about Stephens is to write a novel about it."

All through the fall Stafford had anxiously awaited responses from the East Coast publishers her summer mentors had helped her approach. In her first week at Stephens she had had extremely encouraging news from Jones, who had taken her Heidelberg journal excerpts to the *Atlantic Monthly*. She transcribed Jones's missive in a letter to Hightower:

> I had lunch with Ted Weeks late in August, when he seemed to be much impressed with your diary, but said that, to check his own judgment, he was going to have it read by one or two of the staff members . . . [Stafford's ellipses] If the Atlantic doesn't take it, I think the Nation, Scribners' or Harper's probably would.

Jones also mentioned the journal to an acquaintance at Henry Holt and Company, who promptly wrote Stafford to ask if Holt could consider it for book publication. She had additional leads at Alfred A. Knopf and Houghton Mifflin.

Stafford was working madly on a new novel while she taught at Stephens. By mid-November she had eighty-five thousand words on paper. She finished the novel in December and submitted it to the Atlantic Monthly Press, which was running a contest that offered the remarkable first prize of ten thousand dollars. She sent a new short story to Whit Burnett at *Story*. Burnett had aroused interest at Harper and Brothers, the book publisher, and Jean sent her new novel there, worrying about simultaneously submitting it to the Atlantic Monthly Press. Evelyn Scott, meanwhile, had promised to do all she could at Scribner's. For a few weeks Stafford entertained giddy thoughts of having to choose among several publishers, all vying for her works.

Nothing tangible came of any of these hopes. Weeks, at Atlantic, turned down the diary but was happy to look at the new novel. Holt passed on both the journal and the "old" Heidelberg novel, as Harper did on the new one. Burnett did not like the short story; it was little comfort to Stafford that he wrote her, "You are one of the most brilliant people I have ever read," for he went on to add that her new novel was "unpublishable." After months of agonized waiting Stafford learned that she had mailed her manuscript to Atlantic too late to meet the deadline for the ten-thousand-dollar contest. Daunted but game, she sent the book to Vanguard Press, Farrar and Rinehart, and Random House; eventually it came back from all three publishers.

In one odd sense it was almost a relief for Stafford not to be published. Her father had bitterly endured years of having virtually every article he tried to place be rejected. In October, writing his daughter about sending off a piece to *Harper's,* he added pathetically, "Eventually of course the manuscript will come back and I will start at the beginning again. What a case history of dead from the neck up!" Jean confided in Hightower, "I don't even want to sell anything as long as he's alive."

Stafford overcame this reluctance, however, and during the spring of 1938 she pinned her hopes on winning a Houghton Mifflin literary fellowship. The prize was only a thousand dollars and publication, but the latter seemed abundant reward. Edward Davison, Evelyn Scott, Howard Mumford Jones, and Ford Madox Ford agreed to write letters of sponsorship. By May, when the winners were supposed to be announced, Stafford had grown frantic with the wait. Despairing of a direct answer from the press, she developed a ritual of leafing deliberately through each day's *New York Times* in the Stephens faculty lounge, saving for last a glance at the "Book Notes" column, where she dreaded seeing a rival proclaimed the winner. Finally, in late June, Houghton Mifflin informed her that while she had not won, her novel had been one of a handful of finalists. "I'm sick at heart," she wrote Hightower.

By the spring of 1938 Stafford had written a great deal of fiction. It is no easy matter, however, to deduce the nature of the works of her early adulthood, as it seems likely that she subsequently destroyed almost everything she had written between high school and 1938. In a letter she wrote to Hightower in March 1938, Stafford says, "Thus far my books have been 1935, 1936, 1937. One a year. Not so bad. Very poor books to be sure."

From fragmentary references here and there, it is possible to construct a very tentative schema:

1935 book: written in Boulder; subject unknown, but presumably autobiographical; perhaps the "hard-hitting thing with profanity and obscenity" of Goodrich Walton's recollection; sent by Edward Davison to Whit Burnett, who admired it.

1936 book: written in Heidelberg from fall 1936 through spring 1937; subject at least partly Boulder and Lucy Cooke; 105 pages of manuscript shown to her mentors at 1937 writers' conference;

criticized by John Peale Bishop for its stream-of-consciousness imitation of Joyce; rejected by Holt.

1937 book: written at Stephens College from September to December 1937; subject both Germany and Boulder (Lucy); tentatively titled "Which No Vicissitude"; rejected by Atlantic, Harper, Houghton Mifflin, Vanguard, Farrar and Rinehart, and Random House; called "unpublishable" by Whit Burnett and too "experimental" by Random House.

A few pieces of the 1937 book have survived because Stafford sent them to Hightower; a one-page prologue, a two-page interior monologue, and a three-page epilogue. They make it clear that the narrative framework of the novel was based on the triangle among Lucy, Andrew, and Jean, and that at this point Stafford was stylistically very much influenced by Thomas Wolfe. They also, perhaps, give some indication of what Burnett meant by "unpublishable" and Random House by "experimental." From the prologue:

Which of the three of us has died? What ghost, followed only by the night, seen only by it, has gone into the valley of the shadow of death? I, Ishtar, gathered a handful of white flowers and cast them on the unmarked grave. Like a great wind she moved among her tombs, she locked the gates behind her and she lost the keys.

From the interior monologue:

A word was there: Dharma. The Rupa goes, the Atma is approached. Mephisto goes with all his ghosts, and the wind plays the broad-leaved catalpa. And the sound of stirring fabrics, the stuff of a man's clothes and a woman's clothes has no meaning but this: hurry, hurry, hurry, for the sake of God! . . . Mephisto has a voice most mesmerizing: ohhh, ohhh, the wind and the flowers and the moon and the moments are short to the grave.

22 caliber pistol, pearl-handled: Dharma.

The writing here is so pretentious and affected that it is hard to fathom why, if these pages are representative, Stafford's novel impressed as many professional readers as it did.

The spring term at Stephens seemed from the first days onward a tedious ordeal to Stafford. As early as mid-February she vowed, "I ainta gonna come back here next year no matter what." She still felt "the most paralyzing dread" each time she entered her classroom, even though she had "complete and unreasonable contempt" for her students. By late February Stafford could say, "I have not looked forward to the end of a school year so much since I was in grammar school." Yet she dutifully kept up her social obligations, going to student dance recitals, administrative teas, and faculty dinner parties.

She had turned so sour in the classroom that she was no longer a popular teacher. To Hightower she described herself as "actively hated by 30 people" at a time. In turn, she said, "i hate the bitches more and more," and "they bore and annoy me because they are stupid." Expanding on the rumor that students sometimes entertained boyfriends from the University of Missouri overnight in their rooms, she called Stephens "the biggest Whore House west of the Mississippi."

Nothing had come of her inquiries at Vanderbilt and Greensboro, however, and as the Stephens reappointments committee met in mid-March, Stafford admitted to Hightower that she would probably "not have the guts to resign" if she was asked back. More and more she turned to her friend for solace. In Cambridge he was reluctantly adjusting to a scholarly life. Harvard gave him a thousand-dollar fellowship for the next year; despite the distractions of modern literature he had become, to his great bafflement, the star grad student of his department.

Jean wrote in March, "i want to see you. not that you can do anything. but you ain't a underaged debutante. you don't wear fingernail polish." In her journal she mused,

> Sometimes the hardest thing is that I do not love a man. In such a town as this you are constantly aware of youth, loving. . . . You recall darkness and coolness and young men beside you, and you wonder if it will ever happen again and you know damned well it won't because you ask of a man a brain as well as a body and when you get the brain you want to twist it and you ignore the body and you give them nothing. . . . I won't ever marry anyone now and my desire to love someone is desperately futile because I have destroyed everything in my soul. I will not because of Ruprecht and I cannot marry him because he would be unhappier with me than he is without me.

As proof of her feelings, she later copied out this passage and sent it to Hightower.

Unable to ignore Stafford's declarations, Hightower pressed

her in earnest to spend at least part of the summer with him. He was planning to go home to Salida, Colorado — the town where Ethel Stafford had once taught school — to work for his father, rebuilding houses. The family had decided to buy a new car, and he was to pick it up in Detroit. Stafford was too harried to plan her summer yet, but she felt a strong obligation to visit her own family in Oregon. Hightower offered to pick her up anywhere she liked, from Cambridge to Chicago, so that they might drive west together.

The multiple rejections of her novel plunged Stafford into temporary despair. "I guess I'm not half as good as I think I am," she wrote her friend. "I guess I am not a writer after all, or at least not a writer that will get published. . . . I think with horror what my father must have been going through for thirty years." When this mood lightened, though, she faced her métier with renewed determination. "I have been working on this writing habit ever since Martha Foley discovered my unpublishable genius. You've got to get a *habit* just like cigarettes + beer."

In March she had a minor triumph. *American Prefaces,* a well-regarded literary monthly out of the University of Iowa, accepted a short story called "Meridian." "I am in print at last," she bragged to Hightower. (As it turned out, however, the journal never published the story.) At about the same time, Stafford heeded Howard Mumford Jones's advice and began a novel about Stephens College. It became her private act of revenge. By the end of the spring term she had a plan for the book and the first chapter completed.

One day on campus the night watchman tried to commit suicide. The incident deeply shook Stafford.

> He shot himself three times with a 32 in the head and he is conscious now and may live. He shot himself in the front of the head and the bullets pushed his eyeballs out. They are sticking out from their sockets. None of the bullets hit the brain, so if he lives he will be sane but blind. When I heard about it I got sick at the stomach and my hands got cold. I couldn't talk to my classes so I had them write class themes. . . . I liked him about the best of any of the college employees. I hope to God he dies.

Obviously the event had reanimated Jean's feelings about Lucy's suicide. The watchman survived, with the bullets still lodged in his skull.

No matter how many polite teas Stafford attended, she had a hard time disguising her alienation from the "Stephens spirit." Her mass flunkings of students and her attempts to drag good books into her English comp class had earned criticism from some administrators. In March she got a notice in the mail about a job opening at DePauw University. She took this as a sign that Stephens was having her "subtly fired," for rumor had it that when the college did not wish to reappoint, it wrote the teacher's employment agency to request that another job be arranged for the luckless pariah. Stafford fully expected not to be asked back.

In later years she told colorful stories about getting fired from Stephens. In one version she was "frequently summoned . . . to a dean's office for hurting students' feelings by asking them to come to class in something other than their sleeping pajamas and to refrain from knitting while I was demonstrating subjunctives on the blackboard." In another she got the ax for "having ordered outside reading matter that included Hardy, Flaubert." In a third version she held, on campus, a public burning of the *Reader's Digest* to protest its assignment as a text in English composition.

The true story was just as outlandish but far more humiliating. The natural course for the college in Stafford's case would have been simply to decide against reappointment. The usual regrets and wishes that she might find her niche elsewhere could have been politely tendered. For some all but unfathomable reason, however, the administration chose instead to confront Stafford.

On about April 18 Roy Ivan Johnson, the head of the Division of Skills and Techniques (and the author of the poem "Baby Wisdom"), called Jean into his office. He told her that the Committee on Instruction (a kind of Star Chamber within the Stephens administration) had raised a "serious question" about whether her health was interfering with her teaching. Jean had missed classes now and again, but she was surprised to be challenged thus. She said that she had had scurvy the previous summer but was now all right.

Johnson persisted: "A rumor has spread that you have a contagious disease."

Stafford admitted to having had angina, of which she was now also cured. (There is no evidence that she ever had either disease.)

Johnson went on to complain of Stafford's "literary rather than expository" approach to English comp, of her obvious discontent, and of her having talked over the heads of her students all year. Perhaps she would be happier writing instead of teaching. In any event, if she wished to stay on at Stephens she would be required to submit to a Wassermann test administered by the college physician. Although Johnson had not uttered the word, he was accusing his twenty-two-year-old instructor of having syphilis.

Stafford walked out of Johnson's office numb with incredulity. Then she felt "sick, deathly sick, and scared, more sick and scared than mad, and I kept saying it isn't happening to me." Only after reflecting for a while did she become aware of a violent anger.

As repugnant as the inquisition was, the specificity of Johnson's attack raises the question of how the Stephens authorities had divined Stafford's medical secret. There are various possibilities. One is that Stafford had confided the facts about her venereal disease to a friend at Stephens. This seems entirely improbable, however; it was another two years before she even told Hightower the partial truth, and no one at Stephens had gained from her a fraction of the trust she was already showing in him in early 1938.

A second possibility is that the authorities simply guessed what her ailment was from the symptoms she could not hide: her missed classes, her intestinal upsets and headaches, the rash on her face. This too seems a bit farfetched, and certainly Stafford's behavior at Stephens could have led no one to think her promiscuous.

A third possibility is that Stafford had been treated for syphilis by a doctor either at Stephens or in Columbia (which was then a small town numbering eighteen thousand citizens), and that the doctor had violated confidentiality either by gossiping about her case or by going directly to the college administrators with his knowledge.

Unable to sleep because of "hatreds that give me headaches," Stafford decided to fight back. She wrote Hightower in savage indignation, detailing the showdown in Johnson's office and speculating that a particular colleague, the man who used *Reader's Digest* as a text in his classroom and whom she described as a "dirty, snivelling little pipsqueak," had "manufactured this dirty lie" because he wanted her fired. She contemplated hiring Andrew Cooke, fresh out of CU law school, to come to Missouri to "sue for slander and get this infamous place smeared all over the newspapers." She pondered denouncing the Committee on Instruction in a faculty meeting. She also wrote to Evelyn Scott, telling her the whole story.

By revealing the sordid contretemps to Hightower and Scott, Stafford may of course have been inviting them to suspect the truth about her venereal disease. Perhaps her action betrays an unconscious wish to confess; yet in their loyalty, neither Scott nor Hightower believed Johnson's implicit accusation at all. Hightower counseled avoiding a scene. Scott, though twenty-two years older than Stafford, was no bluestocking, having eloped to Brazil at twenty and later lived hard and fast in Greenwich Village. She took up Stafford's indignation as if it were her own, wrote a letter to Daddy Wood threatening to publicize the scandal, and even enlisted her son (who was in his early twenties) to write a similar letter, in which he promised to kick the president's "behind."

In the end — if Stafford's account can be trusted — the authorities backed down. She may have tried unsuccessfully to persuade a lawyer to file suit, for a letter from Scott to Stafford reads, "Lawyers have an awful way of being right. It's just too bad you are to be deprived of revenge." Scott added maternally, "Yes, my child, you'll 'get over it' but in another sense you won[']t and shouldn[']t, and in that sense books will profit."

There was no Wassermann test, but neither was there a contract for the following year. Stafford's distress as she crawled through the last five weeks of the term can only be imagined. One Saturday night she wandered into a Catholic church in Columbia, intending to go to confession and take communion. "I told my rosary through once. All that happened was that my knees got sore. I was just dead. Nothing happened at all." She left without confessing, walked home in the rain, and "wanted to die more than I have ever wanted to before."

The spring term ended on May 31. Stafford packed her belongings, sent her books to her parents' house in Oregon, and went to Chicago for a brief stay with Bill Mock's family. From there she traveled to New York to see Evelyn Scott and Whit Burnett. She had very little money, an unpublishable novel, and no prospect of a job.

On June 12 Stafford traveled to Albany, New York. Last-minute notes from Hightower had confirmed the logistics of a reunion. That evening she met the train from Boston at the Albany depot. Hightower was on board, waiting for her. It was the first time in fourteen months that these closest of friends — and, Hightower hoped, soon-to-be lovers — had seen each other.

VIII

Runaway

WAITING IN THE JUNE NIGHT for Hightower's train, Stafford had felt both excitement and an anxiety akin to that she had known two years earlier on her arrival in Heidelberg. Now, as the reunited friends settled into their seats and the train sped west through the darkness, it was excitement that prevailed.

The next morning, in Detroit, Hightower picked up the new Buick that his father had paid for. The couple drove onward to Battle Creek, where the family of a high-school friend of Hightower's lived. They spent the night there, in separate bedrooms. On the following day, at a leisurely pace, they drove across the corner of Indiana into Illinois and pulled up for the night in front of a string of tourist cabins in Geneseo.

For three years Hightower had longed for the event that now seemed imminent. He went to the office and rented a room, then returned to the car. But Stafford balked. She was adamant: he must go back to the office and rent a separate room for her. Embarrassed, hurt, and angry, he complied.

Their first night alone together in a year and a half deteriorated into a bitter quarrel. Hightower recited the litany of all his grievances against her from Heidelberg on. Stafford insisted that the ghosts of their former lovers — Fairchild and the Japanese girl — stood between them. In his anger and disappointment Hightower suggested that Jean take a bus the rest of the way to Colorado, while he drove the Buick there alone.

At last they went to bed in their separate rooms. Hightower

could not sleep. He lay cursing softly to himself, rolling little folds of bedsheet between his fingers. In the morning Stafford tried to patch things up. Hightower's wrath diminished, and instead of putting her on the bus he drove on toward Colorado with her beside him in the front seat of the Buick.

"And by the time we got to Salida," Hightower remembers almost fifty years later, "she decided she was in love with me after all." Jean spent only six days in Hightower's hometown; she stayed in a neighbor's house, where his parents had arranged for her to have a room. By now the young couple seemed so visibly infatuated with each other that it was assumed they were engaged.

Stafford and Hightower put in their obligatory hours socializing with his parents and friends, but the days were fraught with their urgency to slip off and be alone together. On the first evening, in a dark room, Jean groped for and found Hightower's hand. All night, in her bed alone, she "kept waking up and wondering . . . if you could ever possibly be happy with me. . . ."

One day the friends were driving slowly along a backcountry logging road. Suddenly a mountain lion leapt across the road, pounced on something — a rabbit, perhaps — and then vanished into the trees. The startling moment (even then, mountain lions were exceedingly rare and furtive) became for both of them an emblem of their happiness during Jean's short stay in Salida. Seven years later Stafford would transform this private icon into the central symbol of her second published novel.

In Salida, for the first time, Stafford seemed to become acutely aware of her friend's physical reality. After she left, the memory of certain details filled her daydreams: the way Hightower held his right wrist as he drove; how small his hands really were, compared to her own (which she had always deplored as too large and rough-skinned); the way he cradled the back of her head in the palm of his hand. At the end of the Salida visit Jean finally allowed her friend to kiss her.

In their euphoria Stafford and Hightower agreed to be engaged. She told him, "I won't sleep with you until we're married." In letters she wrote him shortly after the visit, she claimed that she had loved him even in Heidelberg but had not been able to let him touch her. She blamed the impasse in Geneseo on a remark he had made as they were riding the train west from

Albany; if they got married, he had blurted out in his ebullience, he could get more money from Harvard. The excitement she had been feeling for hours had vanished in an instant's sharp dismay.

"If I had slept with you in Geneseo," she later wrote,

> . . . it would have been an affair and it would have been hateful because I wasn't in love with you then. But after we got to Salida and it was necessary to hide from Nellie and Pa [Hightower's stepmother and father] and to think up those pitiful excuses to be alone, then it became an adventure and that's the only way it could have been.

In her rationalized evasion, Stafford was dissembling. Despite her veiled allusions to the truth over the previous year, Hightower had no suspicion of the venereal disease or diseases Jean had contracted in Heidelberg. She had almost certainly gone eighteen months without sleeping with anyone, and as her journal entry in the spring had made clear, she had wondered if she would ever again know the intimacy of sexual love. The distinction between an "affair" and an "adventure" meant less to Stafford, one must surmise, than the fear that she might infect anyone she made love to with a potentially deadly disease.

At the end of the too-brief idyll in Salida, Hightower put Stafford on the train for Denver. She made a quick trip to Boulder to see Edward Davison and Paul and Dorothy Thompson. As always, returning to the town of her high-school and college years brought out the most cheerless side of Jean. The Thompsons remained loyal friends for the rest of her life, but now Stafford wrote Hightower: "Paul is getting fat. The baby is hideous as all babies are. They are the Great American Family." Davison told her that "I hadn't written anything yet."

From Denver Stafford took the train to Oregon, planning to spend much of the summer in Oswego (today Lake Oswego, a Portland suburb). Room was made for her in the house already inhabited by Dick, her parents, and her aunt Ella. The visit was in large part a dutiful one, but it was also motivated by the fact that Stafford could hole up rent-free in Oswego and write while she cast about for a job and a future.

In Hightower's recollection, the romantic intensity of those six days in Salida "didn't survive many weeks of her absence. There was too much that had gone on before." His own letters, however, tend to belie this summary. Throughout the summer of 1938 he wrote as if still clinging to the hope of eventually sharing his life with Stafford; his phrases mingled insecurity with lovesick gratitude.

Stafford had not seen her parents in almost two years. In the interval she had been to Germany, Italy, and Paris; she had met famous writers, many of whom had praised her work; she had lunched with editors in New York; and she had taught college English for a year. Even so, the first thing her father said to her as he picked her up at the train station was, according to Jean, " 'I will have you in diamonds pretty soon.' " It was John Stafford's conceit that he was about to get rich by selling his revolutionary book on the national debt. Her parents were "still quarrelling endlessly," she reported to Hightower.

> There is nothing to talk about. They have not asked me about Germany. Not about Columbia. Not about you. They have told me the prices of large strawberries in Portland and about their feet and their teeth and their circulating library. Mother was crushed that I had not looked up anyone in Salida [where she had once taught school].

Ethel Stafford seemed to her daughter every bit as vapid as she had remembered her. "Mother has no emotions at all," Jean wrote. "She said she used to have a *lovely* time in Salida with so much social life. Why every week some parent or other invited the girls to dinner and my, such *lovely* dinners." When Jean retreated to her writing, her mother tried to roust her out: " 'You're just like your Dad[,] always typing. Come on out and *visit*.' "

By the end of a month and a half in Oregon Jean hated her mother's maiden sister. "Aunt Ella is a *dreadful McKillop* girl who is illiterate (so Dad and I must not talk about the *Book of Job* at the table), who gets no mail (so we must not be seen reading a letter because she is so sensitive) and for whom Mother has developed a persecution complex." Jean concluded that Ella's meddlesome presence in the house was at the root of her parents' marital difficulties.

At first Stafford felt sympathy for her father, who seemed out of his element in the overwooded landscape of the Northwest. With him she could talk about H. L. Mencken and Chinese phi-

losophy. She described the frail, 117-pound, sixty-four-year-old
man to Hightower:

> He sits in the corner of the couch with his legs drawn up and he
> looks like a dwarf. He is a combination of the oldest man in the
> world and the youngest child. I am sick to death to look at him
> and to know what hell he has lived with this dreadful woman.
> . . . My only hope is that he will die pretty soon.

Another source of Jean's resentment of her mother was the
snobbish ancestral fiction that Mrs. Stafford insisted on maintain-
ing. On one wall in Oswego hung a portrait of Grandfather
McKillop.

> Of course my grandfather Stafford is never mentioned in the house
> because he didn't go to college and he was a cattle man. Grandpa
> McKillop was a collitch professor at the univ. of Vermont [ac-
> tually, the head of a small secondary academy] and oh such a fine
> dear man he was and looked exactly like A. L. Tennyson. . . .

Later in the summer Jean heard her father's version of the ancestral myth:

> He said Grandfather McKillop was not only the worst drunkard
> in Missouri but he was also a seducer of barmaids and milliners,
> and all these years he has watched her hold up that smug, bald
> headed, dipsomaniacal Victorian Scot to us as what Castiglione
> had in mind when he wrote *The Courtier*.

Jean only pitied her father in his hapless efforts to publish. One
day he received a rejection slip for an article on farm production
that he had sent to a magazine called *The Country Gentleman*. Jean
heard him laughing bitterly to himself in the next room. His
response, she told Hightower, was that " 'trying to please an
editor these days is like trying to put a shot gun barrel on a fish
hook.' . . . The blame, of course, rests entirely with the editors
who do not know what they want, who are afraid to print the
truth, who are hypocrites, etc."

In her letters to Hightower Jean admitted that she was using
her family to "gather material" for her writing. But her father's
misanthropy began to frighten her. One day, as he was describing to Jean the corruption in Thomas Jefferson's administration,
he went into a kind of convulsion. By August she had decided

he was "psychopathic. He hasn't said a word for days — just laughs to himself at things he thinks about."

In Oregon Stafford was able to write daily. She completed an article about Stephens that she called "A Manicure with Your Diploma," and sent it to the *Atlantic Monthly*. The piece was turned down as too similar to several other recent essays, but the note from Joseph Barber, the editor who rejected it, was encouraging: "Your article about Stephens College certainly made us all sit up and take notice. It is appalling that such conditions exist. . . ."

Within ten days of her arrival in Oswego, Stafford had started her Stephens novel anew. Her determination was to treat the college comically, aiming for broad satire. The writing came easily; on some days Jean produced as many as four thousand words, and in two months she had sixty thousand, or the bulk of the novel, on paper. In the fall, capitalizing on Barber's friendly rejection note and Howard Mumford Jones's support from the previous year, she submitted the new novel to the Atlantic Monthly Press.

Meanwhile, during the early part of the summer she plugged listlessly away, through an agency in Portland, at finding a teaching job for the fall term. Vague leads in Kansas and Florida came to naught. In case nothing else materialized, she hatched a scheme to go to the University of Iowa and work toward a Ph.D. in writing. The editor of *American Prefaces* had promised to recommend her for a fellowship.

After Salida Stafford's letters were at first markedly cooler than Hightower's. While he wrote unguardedly about his memory of her embraces and his fear that she would fall in love with someone else, she filled her pages with news about her writing and tidbits of Stafford family life. Yet she closed one letter, "I love you, darling," and in the next confided "how I relive every minute of those last days." No longer did they address each other as "Ma," "Bessie," or "Ruprecht": for the first time they were merely "Jean" and "Robert."

Stafford had kept up her correspondence with Evelyn Scott, and to this mentor she confessed that she was planning to marry Hightower. Scott responded, "I think it is the most perfect thing that could happen," but in another letter she warned against the problem of two "artists" marrying. Perhaps Stafford expressed doubts to her that she could not admit to Hightower, for in this second letter Scott cryptically wrote, "Oh, don't marry your man if it is as you describe, for heaven's sake. The enslavement of someone (you) by pity (what it would amount to) represents such a lurid mutually degrading bond. . . ."

The summer-long romance by mail was an exercise in ambivalence for Stafford. She denigrated her affair with Fairchild as "entirely physical," yet was afraid Hightower would compare her to his Japanese girlfriend: "Whenever I remembered the superiority of her body, I was ashamed of my own." She voiced her fears about the "bourgeois respectability" marriage might dictate: "Ten years from now we would have taken up bridge and gardening and probably we would be drinking heavily and trying to forget whatever we could. . . . And eventually we would be Mother and Dad." She was not seduced by Hightower's fantasy of retiring to a farm: "I would be ridiculous. I would probably also be pregnant, and I am not interested at all."

In August Hightower was still writing seriously about marriage. Without telling Stafford, however, he had started a casual affair with a Salida music teacher. Still disaffected with Harvard, he was nonetheless resigned to returning in the fall. Anticipating a future as a professor of Far Eastern languages, he begged Stafford to save him from that fate. (Eventually Hightower became just such a professor, spending a long, gratifying career at Harvard.)

He had lobbied all summer for a few more weeks with her in Colorado. Stafford held out vague promises of a liaison at Mary Lee's ranch in Hayden in early September. As August slipped by she vacillated maddeningly. "Come marry me," she wrote half flippantly at the end of August. Hightower's private defense was a wary exasperation.

In July Stafford had been offered an assistantship at Iowa. She hoped for a half-time teaching job on top of the waiver of tuition. In the end she was offered only a quarter-time position, teaching two sections of a course for a salary of twenty-five dollars a month (a mere fourth of what she had earned at Stephens). Realizing that Iowa was her only choice, she confessed her insecurities to Hightower: "I am terrified of (1) the course I have to teach (2) the poverty I will live in (3) the language exams (4) the prelims." Although it was little more than two years since she had written her M.A. thesis on thirteenth-century poetry, she claimed she could no longer read a word of Anglo–Saxon or Middle English; her knowledge of the Middle Ages, she said, was a "hodgepodge in a vacuum." The course she was to teach had a reading list that ranged from Froissart to Sinclair Lewis. At the end of the summer, in a panic, she started rereading Chaucer, *Beowulf,* and the Bible.

Controlling every detail of the logistics, Stafford allowed her putative fiancé to meet her at the ranch in Hayden on September 7 for a handful of days. As Hightower recalls, "Our first moment alone, she said, 'Now there's no point in our pretending to be in love any more.' And I said, 'Thank God, no, there isn't.' . . . I guess [Jean's remark] wasn't a statement, it was a question. But I took it as a statement."

Hightower told her about his affair with the music teacher. And for the first time, she told him about Robert Lowell — a "guy" she had met at the 1937 writers' conference, who had been writing to her and who "seemed interesting." Once again the pair rehearsed their resentments from the past two years, with Hightower throwing in the night in Geneseo for good measure. "She was reproachful and unhappy, and I felt bad, guilty," says Hightower. Once more, only when Hightower was preparing to leave did Stafford thaw: "So as we parted, it was again patched up, and we would get married." During the three-day bus ride to Cambridge, Hightower tortured himself with doubts: "I was not at all sure I had done the right thing at any time."

Face to face with her all-but-lover, Stafford had been unable to give voice to her deepest feelings. Characteristically, she saved them for her first letter to him after their meeting. She recalled how, when Hightower had first gotten off the bus at Hayden,

> I was sick with joy (and so I was a complete cold potato) and how every night you were here I hoped you would come into my room and how after you told me about the music teacher I wanted to die and that was the reason I said I should never see you again. . . . That day we sat on the hay rack and you said she was the sort of woman you needed because she would darn your socks I wanted to tell you how all summer long in Oregon I had day-dreamed about just that and how I had wanted to be so efficient that you wouldn't even be aware of my doing anything.

By that fourth week in September, however, Hightower and Stafford were once again separated by half a continent, he in Cambridge, she in Iowa City. The Iowa writing program was a far cry from the finishing school in Missouri. Stafford no longer felt contemptuous of her colleagues — only intimidated by them. She was, nonetheless, at least as unhappy as she had been the previous year. "College is *awful*," she told Hightower in her first letter from Iowa. "I am not going to pretend any longer that it isn't."

"I am not smart enough for this place," Stafford complained a week later. "My colleagues are all intense, erudite young men with PhD's who make jokes about Gothic jan stem verbs at which I cannot very well laugh." She had rented a lonely room in a house near campus, where the lighting was poor and she lacked a desk. The pinch of poverty caused her to go whole days without eating. If there had been any doubt in her mind, her composition classes reminded her that "I hate teaching."

At Iowa, however, Stafford befriended the editor of *American Prefaces,* who had accepted one of her short stories the previous spring (the piece was never published). In October the editor took another story; "And Lots of Solid Color" appeared in November 1939. Little more than a vignette based on the summer in Oswego, the story was Stafford's first piece of mature fiction to reach print.

With her Stephens fable off at the Atlantic Monthly Press, Stafford gamely started yet another novel — no less than her fifth major effort by the age of twenty-three. At last the verdict came from Boston. It was not the acceptance Stafford had desperately hoped for, but it was the most encouraging rejection she had ever received. The editors at the press had a firm belief that her next novel would be publishable, and they wanted to work closely with her in shaping it.

One of these editors, Archie Ogden, had read the Stephens College novel with great care. To his colleagues he reported that Stafford had written "a perfectly good book." He went on to praise her stylistic virtues: "Here is a young author who can handle the English language as a skilled carpenter handles a chisel. . . . A situation is summed up in a line of conversation; a character delineated by one fatuous remark that tells the whole story." But Ogden recommended against publication, for two pragmatic reasons: first, the picture of Stephens was so "thinly-veiled" that the book might well be libelous; and, second, "We know too well the difficulty of selling novels based on college faculty life in a small town."

The manuscript of the Stephens novel is the first long work of Stafford's that has survived. Any tale conceived in part as an act of revenge runs the inevitable risk of sacrificing art to vendetta. Much of what is worst in the Stephens novel comes from the crudeness of Stafford's satire. The president, nicknamed Poppy, is a "hill-billy" who never reads books — "had never, in fact, been caught in the act of looking at one." He garners anecdotes for his convocation speech from the pages of *Reader's Digest*. Sixty-three years old, he falls buffoonishly in love with a brainless student who flirts in a Texas drawl, and he whisks her off on private trips to New York.

The hopelessly bland Dean Lambert Sullivan is nicknamed Lambie Pie. The chairman of the Humanities Division gives his teachers a pep talk at the country club, exhorting them, " 'Foremost on your mind must always be that you are training these girls to be wives and mothers and not professional women. Our setup has been recently renamed "Consumer Education." By this we mean that the student is a consumer, the teacher is the salesman.' "

Occasionally Stafford's ear for the inanities of Stephens life serves her well, but the credibility of the story is seriously undercut by her reduction of deans and professors to shallow caricatures. As Archie Ogden observed, it makes little difference that Stephens was really like this. (There was indeed an Institute of Consumer Education at the college.)

Stafford's protagonist is a young, naive teacher of German descent, Gretchen Marburg. The name (and the character) intriguingly foreshadows Sonia Marburg of *Boston Adventure*. As had Jean, Gretchen gets stage fright in front of the students in her first classes: "At times she looked up and saw them motionless, looking at her, staring at her straggling hair, her unpressed skirt, her thick ankles. . . ." Gretchen survives that anxiety and comes to despise her students, earning a stern reprimand from the department chairman for teaching Matthew Arnold in a class — " 'material,' " he scolds, " 'diametrically opposed to the principles of the college.' "

The influence of Thomas Wolfe (who died in September 1938, just as Stafford was finishing the novel) still looms large, concentrated in those passages where Stafford strives for lyrical power:

> Come then and say, when we were young, she lived in this house near the foothills where morning glories half hid the windows and when it rained the blossoms sucked the drops into their dark wombthroats? Where has she gone? We stole flowers from new graves to throw on the doorstep of the young virgin, but now she is dead and over her house hangs crape. Ah, we have come too late to sing under the window the lovely song for the quick. . . .

Stafford's ambition in this book is self-evident: she was undertaking a full-fledged novel of manners, with dozens of characters and subplots. At times Stafford's authorial voice attempts ironic omniscience in the manner of Thackeray or Austen, yet on the basis of the pages that she preserved, it is hard to see many signs of the talent Ogden praised — her ability to wield language "as a skilled carpenter handles a chisel." The encouragement given her by the staff of Atlantic Monthly Press was both generous and speculative, the shrewd judgment of good editors who saw the promise of an important writer behind the affectations of youthful overreaching.

In June, after Stafford had parted from Hightower in Salida, her first letters had been cool while his waxed ardent; now, in September, after their meeting at the ranch, the situation was reversed. Hightower kept his guard up, while Stafford lowered hers more recklessly than she ever had before. Only a day or two after he had left Hayden, she wrote, "I am so ecstatically happy at remembering the feelings I had every time you touched me that now even the pain of that hateful music teacher (oh I knew she was petite and neat and beautiful oh dear God I hate her hate hate hate her) is tolerable because it is so intense it is almost pleasure."

Ten days later she pleaded, "And how am I to sleep so long alone when I am in love with you?" When Hightower did not respond in kind, she opened her next epistle frostily, "Your remarkably impersonal letter just arrived and I hasten to ask where do we stand. . . ." Yet within two paragraphs she was making a surprising proposition.

The suggestion I would like to make is that we live together right now. I don't know how. I go over everything in my mind, how I am only 23 and seem to be at the end of my life, how I cannot live very well without you and how, if I do not live with you pretty soon, I will turn to prostitution (which would be lots better than teaching) or kill myself. Couldn't we get a job maybe? Couldn't you find a job for me in Boston?

Hightower's answer was born of past disappointments. He argued that Jean attributed qualities to him — including a contempt for domestic life — that he did not possess. He was still "implacably jealous" of Fairchild. He felt obligations of his own to the music teacher. He insisted that Jean not come to Cambridge, that in fact it must be at least eight months before they could see each other again.

It would have been characteristic for Stafford to react to this rebuff with aloof sarcasm and a show of independence. Her need, however, had become too great. On October 3 she sent Hightower a remarkable letter:

I have examined the other women in the Eng. department (darling, you can't let that happen to me!) and I have found that I am superior to them only in one way — physically. I am built for bed, not for a classroom. . . .

[In Salida] in the dark I finally found your hand. And when I touched you then, it meant, I love you, I am a woman loving you. You didn't know though. . . . I can still feel [the touch of your hand] and I can feel your kissing me, your body tense against me, my breast against yours. . . .

I have wanted domesticity. I have wanted to be your wife and not much more. I have wanted to bear a child for you. I have wanted you to be sick so that I could nurse you, could rub your legs and back with alcohol, could delicately kiss your forehead and your hands. I have wanted to be consumed in your body. . . . I know I am a woman. Never so much before have I been one. I look at myself, undressed, in the mirror and I desire your eyes to be upon me. . . .

Robert, a woman romantically in love with you, vibrant at the memory of touching you, aching to know the touch again, to know at last (so many years of love and hate! So many wasted years! I deserve none of it!) the full articulation of passionate love.

It was as if the sexual starvation of the past two years had pushed Stafford over the brink. The outpouring of sensual feeling in the letter, so unlike the platonic idealizing with which she was wont to address Hightower, seems entirely genuine, as does the complaint about her deprivation ("I deserve none of it!"), which once more may come close to being a confession of her illness. The letter also breathes ecstatic physical anticipation. Perhaps by October 1938 Stafford had reason to believe that her venereal disease was cured, that at last it might be safe to have sex again.

The series of letters culminating in this one had their impact. As Hightower recalls, "I was helpless against them." He dreamed constantly about Stafford; one day he thought he saw her on a Cambridge street. The music teacher had sent Hightower letters from Salida, and the effect was to disillusion him: "Oh, God, she couldn't write. She was hopeless. I was lost." Writing to Stafford, he confessed that he had discovered he was in love with her after all, and revised his injunction: "Darling, if there is any way for you to come here, you must come at once." He urged that they marry immediately.

For Stafford to come to Cambridge, though, presented serious problems. Hightower had already rented a small apartment and committed himself to a lease. There was not enough room for Jean to live there with him, but he could never afford an additional apartment. And Stafford was virtually broke. Nonetheless, in mid-October Hightower began to look for a job for her and to shop for a larger apartment.

Before he could report any progress, however, Stafford assumed, because she had not heard from him for a few days, that he was rejecting her. In a bitter yet teasing letter, she wrote,

> No, I won't come now. We will never be impetuous, you and I, we will go on making Lists and Plans. Goddammit, *why* did it [the music teacher] happen this summer? But I am not asking you to be faithful to an ideal. I am asking you to receive a gift which I have: secret laughter, secret memory, thighs and lips and breasts and hands, friendship come to such a perfect consummation.

There was another reason for Stafford's unhappiness in Iowa, besides her missing Hightower and having to endure the rigors of the graduate program. The McKees, Lucy's parents, had come from Waterloo to visit Jean several times, and they had begun to demand that she repay the loan that had smoothed her way to Heidelberg. On top of this harassment, Stafford found herself unable to make any progress on her new novel.

Now that his reserve had given way, Hightower hastened to reassure Jean. His affair with the music teacher was over and done with. He had a chance to rent an apartment for six months at fifty dollars a month. She would have to work, but they might just scrape by: "We will live on what we have and worry when we have no more." As October dwindled, Stafford sent short notes begging him to let her come. Finally Hightower arranged to borrow enough money to rent the new apartment. "Come now if you can bring 20$," he wrote.

In accordance with her maddening pattern, Stafford wrote back that she didn't have twenty dollars, that she was feeling better about Iowa because the chairman had let her drop her course work, and that she had started her novel again. Only three days later, however, she was again making plans for her escape.

At the age of twenty-three, Lucy Cooke had shot herself on November 9, 1935. On November 8, 1936, Stafford had stopped going to classes in Heidelberg; the date was firm in her mind almost two years later. She may well have had a sense, early each November, of reliving a cathartic loss. Herself now twenty-three, on about November 4, 1938, Stafford boarded a Greyhound bus in the middle of the night and fled eastward. She left a note only for her landlady, saying that she "was tired of being a genteel pauper" but giving no hint of where she was headed.

Stafford changed buses in Chicago and again in Cleveland. In her last letter, she had told Hightower that she planned to stop in New York to see Robert Berueffy, but that he should expect her in Cambridge late on November 6.

The night of the sixth passed with no word from Jean. Hightower waited in vain through the seventh. Finally, on the afternoon of the eighth, he received a telegram: "ARRIVE 1105 PM TODAY MISSED BUSSES UND SO WEITER [AND SO FORTH] — JEAN."

That evening Hightower picked Stafford up at the Greyhound station in Boston. They went back to the new apartment he had rented. After all she had said in her letters during the past two months, there could be no more postponing sexual intimacy. Yet as Stafford got into bed she said, "Now, I must tell you, I'm frigid."

They made love. Hightower was deeply upset. Jean's declaration had been "terribly shocking to me, but I respected it. . . . She meant that she had no sexual desire. And this seemed to me utterly devastating. It disqualified her as an object. I couldn't impose myself on her." After this first and only act of love-making, Hightower did not importune her further.

For about a month Stafford and Hightower shared the apartment. He went to classes; she stayed at home and wrote. Each evening they got into bed together but spent the night without touching. For Hightower the ritual was like some "ancient Chinese torture."

On November 20 a telegram arrived for "Miss Jean Stafford," with directions to deliver "care Hightower." The curt message read, "ARRIVING TOMORROW MORNING TELEGRAPHIC RESTRAINT FORBIDS OBJURGATION." It was signed "CAL" — the nickname Robert Lowell had gone by since prep school, a blend of Caliban and Caligula.

In this abrupt way Hightower learned that the "interesting guy" whom Stafford had vaguely mentioned at the ranch was a very real rival. Pressing her, Hightower now learned why Stafford had arrived in Cambridge two days late. In Cleveland she had stopped not merely to change buses but also to meet Lowell in a prearranged liaison. He had traveled the hundred miles from Kenyon College to see her. She had spent the night with him, and Hightower was convinced that they had made love.

On the same day that Lowell's telegram arrived, Stafford got another wire: "LOWEL [sic] ARRIVING AT HIGHTOWERS SAID YOU LEFT TWO DAYS AGO — UNSIGNED." Hightower and Stafford realized that this was an attempt by Berueffy to tip them off that Lowell was hot on Jean's trail. In Hightower's retrospective interpretation, by "telegraphic restraint precludes objurgation," Lowell meant something like, " 'I would tell you what kind of double-crossing bitch you are, if I weren't writing a telegram.' " Trying to reconstruct the series of events that led up to the telegram, Hightower conjectures that Stafford wrote Lowell from Iowa, telling him of her trip east and offering to stop in Cleveland for a drink. The meeting stretched into a night together. Lowell wanted to see her again, but she had vanished. Two weeks later, freed from Kenyon for Thanksgiving vacation, Lowell tried to track her down. Perhaps Stafford had mentioned stopping to see Berueffy; somehow Lowell managed to locate him, and he relinquished Hightower's address.

In the fall of 1938 Lowell had begun rooming with Peter Taylor at Kenyon. At Thanksgiving the pair drove to New York in a borrowed car. Taylor had a girlfriend in the city, a painter, and Lowell thought Stafford was there. Their quest — with many details invented — is dramatized in Taylor's wonderful short story "1939," in which Jean, alias Carol Crawford, is the "glorious, talented girl with long flaxen hair" who is on the verge of becoming a major writer.

Taylor recalls Lowell's urgent attempt to find Stafford: "He was really pursuing her, trying to win her." In New York, however, the trail went cold. Before the drive, Taylor had enlisted a friend in the city to hunt down the elusive quarry; telegrams were fired off asking, "Have you found Jean Stafford?" At last Berueffy provided the clue.

Lowell arrived in Cambridge. Stafford, who was extremely anxious to prevent his knowing that she was living with Hightower, arranged to meet Lowell elsewhere. She told Hightower that she was terrified of the tall, angry young poet. On November 23 she left a note for Hightower: "Darling he called again so I left without doing anything to the house. I'll be back as soon as possible. I am *scared*." The note goes on to urge that Hightower arrange to have a mutual acquaintance, posing as a friend of Jean's from New York, stage an "accidental" meeting with Jean at a nearby drugstore, "so that I can get away from him [Lowell]."

Stafford weathered the Thanksgiving vacation, and Lowell, still in the dark about Hightower, took the train back to Kenyon with Taylor. The two roommates were an odd pair — Taylor a southerner, Lowell a Boston Brahmin; the one a prose writer, the other a poet; and, in Taylor's words, "I was rather neat, and Lowell was the messiest human being that ever lived." Taylor's tryst had not gone well, either. "You see," he recalls, "Lowell hadn't really won Jean. He went meaning to. I don't know how much he even saw Jean in Boston. . . . We both felt rejected, that's why we were so unhappy on the train. We were sort of sick of each other."

The testiness finally erupted in a physical brawl, detailed in "1939." An ineffectual half hour's worth of shoves and blocks ended with the conductor glaring the college boys into submission. By the time they got back to Kenyon Lowell and Taylor were fast friends again.

The deceit Stafford had practiced on both Lowell and Hightower was not at all characteristic of her. Nor was it her penchant to have two lovers at once. The only other time in her life when she may have entered such a tangle was during the month or two when she had started sleeping with Fairchild but had also possibly assented to run away to Europe with Lucy. What *was* characteristic of Stafford, however, was her knack for keeping one set of friends entirely unaware of the existence of another, as she had done in Boulder.

She seems to have felt guilty enough in November 1938 to write the truth to Evelyn Scott, her novelist mentor. On November 12 — after Jean's escape from Iowa but before Lowell's descent upon Cambridge — Scott wrote Stafford a long, sympathetic letter. Stafford had apparently proposed bringing Hightower to stay at Scott's apartment in New York (to avoid Lowell?). And she had wondered whether her flight from Iowa and her "double ménage" with Lowell and Hightower were "pathological." Scott hastened to reassure her that only the prosaic-minded could find fault with what she was doing, that "You are defying the stars and challenging the moon, and that is beyond all poetry and art."

Hightower had been furious and dismayed at the advent of Lowell: "I would have done him in if I could have gotten the opportunity." Now he harbored the suspicion that Jean's "frigidity" was a convenient fiction. It was more than a year later that Jean finally admitted to him that she had contracted gonorrhea. Only after that confession did his memory revive an odd exchange that had taken place on their first night in bed together, just after they made love:

She asked something about the danger of pregnancy, and I said, "Oh, you couldn't be pregnant." "How do you know?" she said. And I said, "Well, it's obvious." "But I have to know." She was very insistent, desperate almost. I realized later that she wanted to know if I knew.

Hightower interprets Stafford's persistent questioning as an indication that she knew, or believed, that her venereal disease had rendered her sterile. For the sake of appearances, she pretended to worry about pregnancy. When he dismissed the possibility, she grew frantic with the fear that he had guessed her shameful secret.

If Stafford had indeed become sterile from the gonorrhea spreading to her fallopian tubes, or even if she only believed she had, she apparently never told anyone. For another fourteen years she would insist that she still hoped to have children.

Stafford had freely admitted to Hightower that an added attraction of Boston was its abundance of publishing houses, in particular the Atlantic Monthly Press. On December 1 she was invited to lunch with Archie Ogden and his fellow editors at the Atlantic offices at 8 Arlington Street. To Stafford's joy, the press offered her $250 as an option on her next novel, the bulk of which she was to deliver by June 1, 1939.

Unless *American Prefaces* had paid her some pittance for "And Lots of Solid Color," this was the first time Stafford had earned any money from her writing. And $250 seemed a pot of gold: ten months' salary at the rate she had been paid at Iowa.

Under the pressure of recent events, Hightower had reached the point of feeling, "Jesus Christ, I can't stand this any longer." When the option money came through, it allowed Stafford to move out of the apartment. Her departure was a relief for Hightower, who helped her look for a new place to live in Concord, about fifteen miles away. She took a room on Monument Street, just off the small green at the town center. She began sending Hightower ten dollars a month to help pay off the loan he had taken to rent the apartment in which they had tried to live together.

Stafford felt sad in Concord, but she was writing steadily. She and Hightower kept up a certain intimacy. They had developed affectionate nicknames out of A. A. Milne: he was Pooh, she Honey. She took the bus in to Boston for brief rendezvous. In mid-December she wrote, "I am very lonely + I wish I were sick so that I could come home. I love you the most and I think I can work better with you. . . ."

Before she transferred her belongings to her new quarters, Hightower had asked if he might type out copies of the letters he had sent her over the previous two years. (It is thanks to this effort that both sides of their remarkable correspondence have survived.) He had also — without her permission — read parts of Stafford's diaries. He had not been entirely surprised to find a considerable discrepancy between the diary and her letters. During the same weeks that she had been writing him passionately of her love, the diary scarcely mentioned his name. "When Jean wrote," Hightower says today, "I don't think she deliberately falsified. It was like a conversation. She made it *good,* as an actor might put himself into a role, and actually be the role as he was playing it."

One of the ostensible reasons for Jean's moving to Concord was to hide once more from Lowell. From the start, Stafford had sensed her suitor's potential for violence. During Lowell's Thanksgiving visit she had told Hightower that "she was physically afraid of him, and afraid of what he'd do to me." Now Jean made plans to spend the Christmas holidays with Hightower.

Yet at the same time Stafford must have been prolonging her double ménage. Back home in Boston for the holidays, Lowell had no trouble locating her in Concord. A few days before Christmas he borrowed his father's car and took her out on a date. A poor driver under the best of circumstances, that evening Lowell had a good deal to drink. As he drove her through west Cambridge on the way to Concord, he took the wrong turn at a fork in the road, entering a dead-end lane, and ran head-on into a wall. Lowell was unhurt, but Stafford's head smashed into the windshield, crushing her nose and fracturing her skull.

IX

"6:05 It's Done"

STAFFORD TOOK THE BRUNT of the impact on her face. Her nose was smashed into many pieces, and one of her cheekbones was fractured; she also had bones broken in the back of her head. Someone summoned a taxi, which took her to nearby Mount Auburn Hospital. The driver later reported that when he arrived at the scene, Stafford was hysterical.

Lowell's behavior after the accident is difficult to determine. No police records survive, and the testimony of the single eyewitness is lost to history. It is entirely possible that Lowell ran away from the wreck, leaving Stafford to fend for herself. At least three independent sources (who would have had the story from Stafford) suggest as much; one of them states that Lowell only showed up at the hospital days later, bearing a propitiatory gift. On the other hand, the cabdriver testified that when he got there, Lowell was drunk. Lowell was eventually fined fifty dollars in the Cambridge district court for operating a motor vehicle under the influence of alcohol, and twenty-five dollars for operating to endanger.

The poet was reluctant to shoulder any blame. According to his close friend Frank Parker, Lowell seemed to think "it was just an accident, and he didn't feel responsible particularly. He looked up, there was a dead end. It was not his fault." Blair Clark, a friend of Lowell's since prep school, believes that he had probably taken the big blue Packard without permission: his father "would *never* have let him have his car."

Stafford stayed in the hospital for weeks. As soon as he learned of the crash, Hightower hurried over. "Her face was a mess," he remembers. "My first remark was, 'I'll kill that son of a bitch.' She said, 'Oh, no, you'll do no such thing. It wasn't his fault.' " Hightower arranged his daily hospital visits to avoid running into Lowell, whom he had still not met. Yet according to a later friend, Lowell visited Stafford in the hospital only once before returning to Kenyon College in January.

After more than a month's recuperation, Stafford underwent the first of five facial operations, which stretched through the spring and early summer. Most of the surgical work was done on her nose, which had been mangled in a way that impeded normal breathing. She also had an operation to remove bone fragments from the back of her head. Stafford got in touch with her Boulder friend Howard Higman to ask if he still had the life mask he had made of her. Unwilling to part with the original, Higman made a copy and sent it to Jean. The mask was used by her doctors as a guide in reconstructing her features.

In 1946 Stafford wrote a short story called "The Interior Castle" about her experience in the hospital in 1939. Much anthologized, it is one of Stafford's best pieces of fiction, an excruciating yet somehow detached account of pain and fear. Stafford later claimed that along with "In the Snowfall," "The Interior Castle" was a rare "occasion on which I wrote directly out of my life."

Stafford's protagonist, Pansy Vanneman, is regarded by her doctors as an anomaly because of the passive immobility with which she responds to all treatment, including a spinal tap; they wonder if her reaction is due to shock. Her nose surgeon mourns the damage done to his patient's beauty, while she, oblivious to her looks, is secretly obsessed with the fear of damage to her brain.

The story pivots around Pansy's first operation, a submucous resection, or removal of fragments of gristle and bone from her nose. (Stafford endured just such an operation under local anesthetic about six weeks after the accident.) Her doctor — in real life a man whom Jean considered "vulgar" and a "social climber" — is portrayed in the story as a cheerful sadist: " 'All set?' the surgeon asked her, smiling. 'A little nervous, what? I don't blame you. I've often said I'd rather break a leg than have a submucous resection.' "

During the operation, Pansy's ankles and wrists are strapped to the table.

> He began. The knives ground and carved and curried and scoured the wounds they made; the scissors clipped hard gristle and the scalpels chipped off bone. It was as if a tangle of tiny nerves were being cut dexterously, one by one; the pain writhed spirally and came to her who was a pink bird and sat on the top of a cone. The pain was a pyramid made of a diamond; it was an intense light; it was the hottest fire, the coldest chill, the highest peak, the fastest force, the furthest reach, the newest time. It possessed nothing of her but its one infinitesimal scene: beyond the screen as thin as gossamer, the brain trembled for its life, hearing the knives hunting like wolves outside, sniffing and snapping.

The injuries and operations permanently changed Stafford's looks. Blair Clark felt that "she was badly injured in the pulchritude sense." According to Peter Davison,

> Jean looked very different before the auto accident. She was truly a pretty woman, pug-nosed, freckled, with expressive features. The operations . . . turned her face into something quite different, attractive but somewhat pugilistic, as though its battering combined somehow with the attitude of world-weariness which Jean found it necessary to adopt, for whatever reason.

Anne White, a skilled painter who became Stafford's roommate, observes,

> What the accident did was to broaden her nose. It gave her a sort of lion nose, square-ended. She had a scar across the middle of the bridge. Part of her cheekbone had been broken. Her face looked a little crooked and swollen around the mouth. The whole impression was squarer and more hollowed out under her cheeks. [Months later] she went around with her mouth open. She was not breathing well.

In general, recalls White, the accident gave Stafford "a distinguished, battered look." For the rest of her life her eyes watered uncontrollably. She had also suffered considerable damage to her teeth, and had to make many trips to the dentist throughout the spring of 1939.

There is a cruel irony in the fact that as a small girl Jean had been a terrified passenger in her father's car, often hiding on the floor of the backseat. Perhaps to some extent because of the accident, Stafford would never learn to drive, even though at times it became very inconvenient for her not to be able to operate a car on her own.

It is not easy to determine how well Stafford knew Lowell at the time of their disastrous date in December 1938, since the letters that passed between them have not survived. It is possible that a deep rapport had developed by mail after the summer of 1937, and that for a year and a half Stafford had maintained a second relationship as intense as the one she had with Hightower. But this seems unlikely. In a letter written in 1944 to her CU friend Joe Chay, Stafford claimed that at the time of the accident Lowell still addressed her as "Miss Stafford." This may, however, be merely a retrospective jest about Lowell's stuffy upbringing.

What does seem likely is that the courtship was quite one-sided for the first two years. Lowell's Kenyon friends, including Peter Taylor and John Thompson, were quite aware of the "glorious, talented girl" he had met in Boulder, for he bragged about her openly. After his stormy visit to Cambridge at Thanksgiving 1938, Lowell put his Harvard friend Blair Clark in charge of "keeping an eye" on Jean while he had to be away at Kenyon.

There is no evidence that before December 1938 Stafford confided her feelings about Lowell to anyone, except Evelyn Scott — and even then only guardedly and skeptically. Stafford later told her editor Robert Giroux that Lowell proposed marriage before Christmas 1938 and again in January 1939 and that she rebuffed him both times. Frank Parker says, "With Cal, almost at once, I'd say straight from Boulder on, he thought himself engaged. . . . The engagement was all in Lowell's mind." Blair Clark concurs: "Cal always thought it ought to be marriage right away" (as he had with his first girlfriend, Anne Dick).

At the time of the accident Lowell's parents barely knew that Jean Stafford existed. Quite apart from their outrage over the car crash, they sternly objected to this new relationship. "They disapproved of all Cal's girls," says Clark. "[Lowell's father] went along with whatever Charlotte Lowell said. . . . She would say, 'Of course, Bobby's too young to get married. And anyway, who is this Jean Stafford?' Really snobbish Boston stuff. 'What do we know about her family?' "

According to Clark, Charlotte Lowell "partly blamed Jean for the accident. . . . If Cal had not had this girl, he wouldn't have been in the accident." The relationship signified that he "was breaking out on his own, against them."

At the time of the crash Lowell was twenty-one, two years younger than the woman he was pursuing. He was in his junior year at Kenyon, where he had become the de facto leader of a small group of brainy disciples of John Crowe Ransom who would make an impact on American letters — Peter Taylor, Randall Jarrell, Robie Macauley, John Thompson, and Lowell himself. Thompson recalls the ambitious undergraduate poet:

> [He] had the intelligent habit of lying in bed all day. Around that bed like a tumble-down brick wall were his Greek Homer, his Latin Vergil, his Chaucer, letters from Boston, cast-off socks, his Dante, his Milton. Even in those days before he had published a word we knew he belonged among the peers who surrounded him.
>
> The poems he wrote and rewrote and rewrote in bed then were as awkward as he was, the man of the Kenyon squad who plowed sideways into his own teammates, but strong as a bull, spilling them all over, who never won a game. He aspired to be a Rhodes scholar, and thus had to be an all-around man like Whizzer White. In those days Lowell couldn't tie his own shoe laces. . . .

This bohemian rebel was at the same time strongly tied to his parents in Boston, particularly to his mother. His father, Robert Traill Spence Lowell III, had retired early from an undistinguished naval career, mainly because his wife had refused to live on the military base. He had then taken a job with Lever Brothers, the soap company, and in the words of Ian Hamilton, Lowell's biographer, "when that didn't work out, he declined from job to job. . . ."

Charlotte Lowell had been born a Winslow and was proud to claim descent from a *Mayflower* immigrant. This union of two Boston families of bluest blood had, however, guaranteed neither social comfort nor great wealth. Despite the social cachet of having 170 Marlborough Street as an address, Charlotte Lowell was embarrassed by her husband's ineffectual character and humiliated by the demeaning jobs he was forced to take. Robert Traill Spence Lowell IV, their only child, was related to the poets James Russell Lowell and Amy Lowell. But as the best poet of the three would reflect in 1961, "To my family, James Russell Lowell was the ambassador to England, not a writer. Amy seemed a bit peculiar to them."

In John Thompson's mordant vignette, "Charlotte was a Snow Queen who flirted coldly and shamelessly with her son. [Cal's] father once ordered a half-bottle of wine for five at dinner." Adds Blair Clark, "Old Bob was such a cipher." To his mother, Robert Lowell, the world-famous poet, remained "Bobby" for as long as she lived.

According to Anne White, "The whole first month after the accident, [Lowell] was staying away. It was hard for [Jean] even to get to talk to him." Still, Stafford refused to blame Lowell for her pain and disfigurement. White says, "She was terribly respectful [of him], even when she was talking about how badly he'd behaved."

On the advice of her lawyers, it was decided that Stafford would sue Lowell for insurance money to defray her substantial medical expenses. The lawyers demanded that, in order to avoid the appearance of collusion, Lowell and Stafford not see each other at all. Anne White remembers, "Jean's impression at the beginning was that he was just using the insurance thing as an excuse [not to see her], that he was a little too eager to accept that."

In any event, Lowell returned to Kenyon in January. There he discussed Jean's plight with Frederick Santee, his classics professor. A former child prodigy, Santee had become not only a classical scholar but a medical doctor. Without ever having seen Stafford, Santee persuaded Lowell that she must go to Johns Hopkins, where an expert of Santee's acquaintance would examine her. Lowell put Blair Clark in charge of taking Stafford by train to Baltimore, where he and Santee would meet them.

Upon their arrival, as Clark tells it,

> Santee took Jean to see this specialist. The specialist wanted to do an operation, said that it had been botched in Boston. Jean came to me in tears and terror and said, "Don't let them do it!" . . . I said, "Well, Jean, you've got to tell them you don't want to do it." She wanted me to intervene directly, and I did. I told Cal I just thought there ought to be a pause, that she could not be compelled to have this operation. He was being pressured by this madman Santee.

Clark successfully "stiffened Jean's backbone," averting the new operation. Santee and Lowell went out to the Baltimore train station to see Clark and Stafford off. The tension was palpable: "Jean was furious at everybody." Santee later told Lowell that he could tell by the way Clark walked that he was in love with Stafford, and that the reason Jean would not consent to the operation was that Clark was taking her away from Lowell.

Amazingly, Lowell believed this aspersion. He wrote Stafford a letter revealing Santee's deduction and accusing her of infidelity. Stafford angrily denied the charge, but "she practically broke with him on that issue." Later Lowell wrote Clark "an absolutely crawling letter of apology."

Hightower's disillusionment with Stafford after their painful November had not been essentially altered by the accident; if anything the crash, coupled with her defense of Lowell, only proved to him that he had no real chance with her. Early in 1939 Hightower copied out excerpts from his journal and sent them to her, along with a note saying that he didn't expect to see her again. Stafford's several replies were full of rueful despair.

> I will say nothing, only this: I love you, but my selfishness is so all consuming that I cannot help hurting you. . . . I make myself attractive to men because I am afraid not to, because I still want what I wanted in Boulder and did not get, but the men are damned fools because I'm evil and I know it.

On January 25, awaiting her first operation, she analyzed the ordeal of living with Hightower after that first night when they had made love for the only time:

> I knew as I lay there beside you every night that what you wished was my death so that you could grieve me but no longer desire me. I knew you did not believe in my frigidity — you have so rarely believed me at all. I know you believe nothing I say in this letter and I know you are calling me a bitch and a harlot. But if out of the foul slough of my present life I can offer you anything clean, it is this, that I loved you, that now I persist in thinking of you as my friend, that I did not lie when I said I was frigid. . . . I was afraid of you those nights, sometimes frantic when you touched me. . . . Robert, no aphrodisiac has yet been devised to make me desire[;] to make me submit, yes, but not to desire. All

right, it's whoredom, but I do not revel in it. I want children, I want a house, I want to be a faithful woman. I want those things more than I want my present life of writer. . . .

On emerging from the hospital, Stafford returned to her lonely room in Concord. She spent many hours reading books borrowed from the local library, often sitting in the old cemetery, "hard by Hawthorne's grave." As she had feared, the accident and her arduous recuperation brought work on her new novel nearly to a halt. Stafford had befriended the Atlantic editor Archie Ogden and his wife, and they now pampered her by inviting her to their house for dinners and overnight stays. From New York, Evelyn Scott penned pep talks. But by March Stafford felt that her novel was becoming "progressively lousier." Her efforts to focus on her writing were constantly thwarted by the trips she had to take to Boston to see the dentist, the doctor, the lawyer — and by the persistent pain itself.

In the spring Stafford saw Hightower sporadically (but never in his apartment), and she traded a few letters with him. At the end of his Harvard term he went back to Salida.

Robert Lowell returned to Boston from Kenyon for spring vacation, and apparently saw Stafford on the sly. Ian Hamilton says that the couple became "engaged" at Easter, but it seems likely that this was true only in Lowell's imagination. Just before Lowell's visit, Stafford wrote to Archie Ogden: "I saw the [Ford Madox] Fords in N.Y. and they convinced [me] that Cal Lowell is really pathological and capable of murder, told me such horrible things about him that I am thinking of pressing Stitch [her lawyer] into service to get out an injunction against him. He is to arrive next week. I may have to find a hiding place."

Despite her slow progress, Stafford let Ogden have a look at what she had written, and he passed it on to his colleagues. In early May he had lunch with Jean and — against his own best sense of publishing ethics — showed her the "not altogether favorable" in-house report. Still, he was at pains to reaffirm his belief in the novel.

Amid much maneuvering behind the scenes, the legal forces had been gathering ammunition for the insurance trial of *Stafford vs. Lowell,* which began in July. Stafford's lawyer was Richard "Stitch" Evarts, a distinguished barrister from an old Boston family

who nevertheless, as Jean put it, "looks like a Vermont farmer
and has no time for Boston society." According to Frank Parker,
Evarts was "tough as they make them, hated Lowell, and was
determined to get the best thing" for Stafford. Lowell's lawyer
was a man whom Stafford derided as "very fat and excessively
greasy," with a "Bronx accent." Writing to Hightower, she lam-
pooned the lawyer's line of attack: " 'Still looks like a preddy
cute liddle Irish nose to me. She's a preddy sweet looking gurl
still isn't she, yer honor?' "

The surgeon who had performed Jean's nose operations testified that he had treated her daily from January 16 to May 1 (in
fact he had seen her only about twice a week on the average).
His accumulated bill was $950. Other witnesses included the only
person who had actually seen the accident, the taxi driver who
had taken Stafford to the hospital, her dentist, another doctor, an
intern, an X-ray technician, and some men from the highway
department.

In keeping with the fiction of hostility between Lowell and
Stafford, as Blair Clark remembers, "Jean and Cal were not allowed to talk. And they weren't supposed to meet — that would
have been collusion. They literally didn't talk [to each other] in
the courthouse." Stafford was suing for twenty-five thousand
dollars. She needed money badly. At the end of July she learned
that she had won her suit but that the insurance company had
appealed. There would be a new trial, tentatively scheduled for
October.

To avoid the scandal, Lowell's parents had taken a long vacation in Europe. Charlotte Lowell, who considered the accident
new proof that her son needed to be institutionalized, managed
to wangle an appointment with Carl Jung. If a poem Lowell wrote
years later accurately reflects his mother's meeting with the famous psychologist, Jung told Mrs. Lowell that if she had described her son appropriately, he was "an incurable schizophrenic."

During his parents' absence, Lowell stayed as a guest at the
Harvard Faculty Club. In the middle of the trial he wrote his
mother a letter that was as close to criticism as he dared venture:

About Boston, I gather many people think you have behaved
shabbily about Jean's accident. Such opinion is not my concern
yet I cannot feel the action of my family has in all cases been

ethicilly [*sic*] ideal. I say this not in anger but as a suggestion for a better understanding, an understanding which seemed to be making such strides this winter.

During the summer of 1939 Lowell and Stafford saw each other often. With the second trial still looming, they had to cover their tracks; as a result it is hard now to determine any details of their liaisons. One of the best-kept secrets of Stafford's life is that she rented a room — probably that summer — in a decrepit hotel in Nahant, the then-fading resort town set on an island connected by a jetty to the North Shore, some ten miles northeast of Boston. This interlude would be relatively unimportant had not Stafford's stay in Nahant furnished her with the vividly realized setting for the first half of her novel *Boston Adventure*.

The Nahant residence may have been devised as a secret meeting place for Lowell and Stafford. At the beginning of the summer Jean had moved from her Monument Street room to another house in Concord, where a Mrs. Cole, on learning of Jean's situation from a mutual acquaintance, had generously offered her a free room. Stafford continued to receive her mail at Monument Street. She could meet Lowell neither at Mrs. Cole's house nor at the Harvard Faculty Club, so perhaps Nahant was the clandestine solution.

Between November 1938 and the end of the following summer Stafford's only source of income was her $250 advance from the Atlantic Monthly Press. Even presuming that her doctors, dentist, and lawyer withheld their bills pending settlement of the lawsuit, the obvious question is how Jean could have afforded a summer hotel room in Nahant. And the obvious answer is that Lowell must have been paying for it.

After the first trial ended inconclusively, Stafford decided that she wanted to go out to Mary Lee's ranch in Hayden for a few months. The ranch had become a refuge for her, a place where she could write unimpeded. But Archie Ogden insisted that she finish her novel before leaving Concord; the Atlantic editors had already been understanding in extending the deadline beyond June 1. Hightower wanted Jean to come to Salida, but she curtly refused. In early July she wrote him, "I was 24 yrs. old the other day and I felt right bad about it. . . ." She had returned to signing herself "Bessie."

At the end of the summer Stafford finished a draft of her book and delivered it to Ogden. Around September 1, the momentous date on which Germany invaded Poland, she took the train west to Colorado. Even though the novel she had been immersed in was set in Heidelberg, her letters give little evidence that she was much aware of the political situation in Europe.

By now Hightower was back at Harvard. Stafford seemed to get along best with her close friend when she was farthest away from him. In September and October her letters to him regained their old liveliness. She teased him with the information that the ranch hands recalled his brief visit of the year before: "You are known as old High."

In Hayden Jean came to know both the Dawson Cattle Company ranch (where Mary Lee's husband, Harry Frichtel, was one of four partners raising registered Herefords), and what Harry and Mary Lee always referred to simply as "our ranch," a 312-acre spread about two miles west of town. During her visits Jean spent most of her time indoors, yet she delighted in a voyeuristic way in the raw speech and sweaty toil of the ranch hands. She was uninterested in hiking or hunting, but Mary Lee talked her into a little horseback riding.

Stafford liked to think that she was becoming a "horse fancier," and she bragged to Hightower about learning to ford a river on horseback. With horrified zest she helped Harry skin a heifer and learned "that lambs are castrated by human teeth." She had liked Harry from the moment she had first met him. He seemed to her something of a legendary figure, the real cowboy whom her father's "yarns" had only counterfeited. Slipping into ranch vernacular, she wrote Hightower that "Harry is camping right now on the Divide. . . . They took four pounds of coffee for one week and two quarts of drinking whiskey," and that "Harry is real tolerant of me helping butcher."

In the flush of her new enthusiasm she claimed, "I would like to live right here the rest of my life." Stafford would, of course, have found it intolerable to stay in Hayden for more than a few months at a time. As she had in Oregon during the summer of 1938, she used her Hayden visit to collect "material." Yet while her unhappy stay in Oswego had supplied her with dreary clichés of bourgeois family life, from the ranch she took impressions that would surface six years later in the lyrically rendered landscape and life of *The Mountain Lion*. In that novel the figure of

Uncle Claude, short on book learning but long on integrity and know-how, is based on Harry Frichtel.

On October 5 Archie Ogden wrote to tell Stafford that he had read parts I and II of her manuscript, and that "I want you to know how much I like it. I think there is still quite a lot to do on it, but I won't bore you with the details until you are again in these parts." Eight days later, having received a letter from Jean suggesting that she might not return until December, he sent her a detailed critique of the novel.

In six pages of typed, single-spaced comments, Ogden's critique ranged from queries on word choice to broad complaints about motivation, plot, and character. Yet the letter is a model of a sensitive editor's response to the work of a gifted but erratic young writer. Ogden summed up his advice, "I feel sure that you have the makings of a fine book, and my suggestions are not in any sense carping. I won't be hurt if they are not accepted or if you have an entirely different feeling about the book as a whole."

The manuscript of "The Autumn Festival," as Stafford provisionally titled her book, is among the papers she left to the University of Colorado. The novel is in three sections, the titles of which divide the Heidelberg year: "Herbstfeier" ("Autumn Festival"), "Weihnachten" ("Christmas"), and "Faschings" (roughly "Carnival" — a local Lenten festival culminating in a Mardi Gras–like celebration). Part I opens in Heidelberg but soon wanders into a diffuse flashback that sketches out the background of the protagonist, Gretchen Marburg. Part II returns to Germany in the fall of 1936; it is the best-written and most interesting section of the book. The denouement of Part III is dramatic — indeed melodramatic — and unsatisfying.

If we ignore the ambitious floundering of Part I, the novel has a lean and logical plot. Gretchen Marburg is the American daughter of a German immigrant. In the fall of 1936 she goes with her brother, Karl, to the University of Heidelberg, where their father had studied in his youth. In a beer hall Gretchen meets an intense, handsome Nazi aviator named Rheinhard Rössler. They fall in love and begin a covert affair.

Gretchen gets caught up in the Nazi passion of Rössler and his friends. Meanwhile Karl has joined the Communist party and befriended a Frenchman, a Spaniard, and an American who are essentially spies. At a Nazi rally Gretchen hears a voice disrupting the fervor by singing the "Internationale," and she recognizes the voice as Karl's. She persuades her brother to flee to Paris.

Rössler is called away for training; to Gretchen he admits his conviction that he will die in the Spanish civil war. They meet in Freiburg for a bittersweet two days at Christmas, during which they get engaged and make plans to marry in July. Gretchen's ecstasy is propelled by a reaction against her unhappy childhood; among the Nazis, for the first time, she has a sense of "belonging."

To prove her mettle to Rössler's friends, she betrays her brother's comrades, turning in the Frenchman and the Spaniard and exposing the short-wave-radio sanctum of the American. All three are hauled off by the Gestapo. She even informs on her brother, telling a Nazi officer that it was Karl who had sung the disloyal song at the rally. In the spring Gretchen declines into hedonistic drinking and all-night carousing, but she also begins to question her loyalties. The turning point comes when, visiting the old professor who was her father's mentor, she is caught in a savage raid by brownshirts who suspect the professor's wife of being half Jewish. After all the others have left, a drunken soldier tries to rape Gretchen. She hits him on the head with a decanter, killing him.

In the midst of the *Faschings* ball, Gretchen learns that her fiancé has been killed "on maneuvers" — the Nazi euphemism for Spain. The book ends with her knowing that she will be allowed to escape to Paris to be reunited with Karl.

Whatever its merits as a work of art, "The Autumn Festival" is biographically fascinating. It is the only surviving piece of Stafford's fiction that hinges on politics or history. It also stands as her only serious attempt at a novel or story of suspense; in fact at its best the book has the momentum of a thriller.

In Part III, in her portrayal of Gretchen as she becomes a hard-drinking, jaded libertine who exposes the American's hideout simply because she is bored and wants to amuse her Nazi friends, Stafford conjures up Lucy Cooke. But in a broader, more provocative sense, the novel vividly dramatizes Stafford's own mixed responses to Nazism in 1936–1937. She revered her Jewish professor, Joseph Cohen, and in 1959 she would marry a Jew, but in the late 1930s Stafford was not above slipping into a half-jesting anti-Semitic pose; thus, writing to Hightower about Robert Lowell's "greasy" Jewish lawyer, she opens, "How do I feel about the pogrom in America now, Mr Hitler, well, I will say tomorrow isn't soon enough."

As a whole, "The Autumn Festival" stands head and shoulders above Stafford's Stephens College novel. Some of the writing gives the first clear hint of the magisterial irony Stafford would later perfect. And there is considerable skill in the way Stafford imagines Gretchen's inner surrender to Nazism.

Yet the novel attenuates itself in too many irrelevant minor characters, too much dialogue for dialogue's sake. Stafford's weakness for melodrama spoils the most important effects she tries to build. After he and Gretchen listen to Hitler on the radio, moments before their final parting, Rössler says,

> "I watched your face today when we were listening to the speech and you were as much a part of the fatherland as if you had always lived here."
>
> "More!" she cried and took his hand, "Because I lived so long where there is nothing to be part of! . . . ."
>
> Their hearts beat wildly against their chests. "Don't ever stop believing in the fatherland," he said, "bear me children for the fatherland, and for Hitler!"
>
> "I will never stop believing. It will never hurt me."

All things considered, especially in view of the timeliness of its subject, it is not surprising that Ogden took "The Autumn Festival" seriously. To his Atlantic associates he wrote, "This is not a great book. In places it is terribly overwritten. The Nazi material is authentic and, I think, well done. . . ." He concluded, "I recommend publication on the basis of this book, which stands on its own feet, and on the basis of the author's promise of even better things to come."

His colleagues, however, were less generous. The verdict the staff of the Atlantic Monthly Press delivered to the author in the fall of 1939 is not on record. Perhaps it was outright rejection; perhaps the editors urged her to try one more revision. In any event "The Autumn Festival," never to be published, found its way into one of Stafford's cardboard boxes, and her career drifted away from Archie Ogden and the Atlantic Monthly Press.

While at the ranch, Stafford heard from Stitch Evarts that the second insurance trial had finally been scheduled for early November. On her way east she stopped to visit Lowell at Kenyon College. At last the schoolmates to whom he had talked about

Jean for almost two years got to meet her. "Shining she was," John Thompson would write thirty-eight years later, remembering his first impression. "She was a real knockout," he elaborates.

> We were callow youths. She thought she was a callow youth, but not compared to us. Here she was with her white gloves. She was much more sophisticated than any of us, including Cal, except possibly Peter [Taylor], who was a Memphis society boy. She'd been in Germany, and she knew a lot more about contemporary writing than we did. I remember she had all these strange books that we'd never heard of, like Isherwood's *Mr. Norris Changes Trains* in an English edition.

At the time, along with white gloves, Stafford's favorite apparel included a velvet cape and a pair of once-smelly huaraches she had bought in Mexico during her trip with Marjorie several years earlier. Peter Taylor had prepared himself to be intimidated. "Cal made things difficult," he recalls. "He would build you up and build you up to the other person, telling them how marvelous you were, and then telling you how marvelous they were. When you met, you felt, This other marvelous person is so witty, so gifted, and I'm just nothing. It made talking more difficult. I think I was rather silent on that visit."

At his first sight of Stafford on the train platform, Taylor noticed her long stride and big steps — a mannerism he would come to know as "a sort of self-conscious thing she did." Taylor was well aware of the car accident. "I didn't think she was beautiful when I first met her," he says. "But I had an idea she'd been beautiful."

In Taylor's view, Stafford at that time had a way of putting on airs. She sprinkled her speech with German and French quotations and alluded to "Proust and people like that that I hadn't read much of." Almost four decades later Lowell captured the Stafford of 1939:

> Towmahss Mahnn: *that's how you said it . . .*
> "*That's how Mann must say it,*" I thought.
>
> *I can go on imagining you*
> *in your Heidelberry braids and Bavarian*
> *peasant aprons you wore three or four years*
> *after your master's at twenty-one.*

Taylor remembers one of Stafford's tricks for controlling the conversation. "When she couldn't hold the floor, when she ran out of something to say, she would say, 'Uhhh-uhhh-uhhh,' so nobody else could break in." She had mastered what would be a lifelong talent for turning her past into anecdotes — telling Taylor, for instance, that she had run away from Iowa because she had both a Mahoney and an O'Mahoney in one of the sections she was teaching; she was unable to remember which was which, and it drove her crazy.

Thompson remembers Stafford as "always fleeing" Lowell. Taylor, who roomed with Lowell in Douglass House (off limits to women guests), says, "She'd come up to our room, and Cal would sort of smooch and neck there in the room. There was nothing more to it than that, but it was embarrassing for me and it was embarrassing for Jean. She would say, 'Oh, Cal, stop.'"

Taylor was also vaguely aware of Hightower. "Jean never wanted any of the rest of us to meet him," he recalls. "She always talked about Hightower from the very beginning, but it was sort of a joke — Hightower, this Japanese or Chinese scholar."

Once she was back in Massachusetts, Stafford found an apartment in Cambridge to share with two other women. Bunny Cole was the daughter of the woman who had taken Jean in in Concord; Anne White (then Anne Cleveland) had been Bunny's roommate in New York City. That fall White was taking art courses at Harvard, while Cole had a secretarial job. Hightower had rented another apartment, with a toilet but no bathtub, about five blocks away. He came over to the women's apartment whenever he wanted to take a bath.

In Anne White's memory, Stafford was not a friendly roommate. "She was very self-involved at the moment, she had too many problems, the book and the relationship [with Lowell] and the accident." Even so, the writer and the artist had long conversations. "We used to talk about our brothers," White says. "She loved [Dick], and at that point there were not very many people she expressed simple love for."

Bunny Cole was an attractive woman, but Anne White, in Hightower's view, was "the ugly duckling of the family, [although] a very talented artist, highly intelligent." White was a perceptive observer of Stafford's suitors. Hightower seemed "the only friend she had, really." Yet "their relationship was kind of an odd one. He was more like a confidante than a boyfriend, a woman confidante. She had known him a long time, so that in a way, when they were together they were like sisters." White knew that Stafford and Hightower had been lovers, but she had the impression that the brief sexual affair had taken place years before, in Boulder. Lowell, on the other hand, reminded her of "Heathcliff played by Boris Karloff. In those days, he was very shy. . . . When he arrived to pick her up, he just kind of stood there until she was ready to go."

Stafford picked up a short-term job working for the Basic English Institute in Cambridge. There she got to know the illustrious English critic I. A. Richards and the celebrated English poet William Empson, both of whom were involved with the institute.

At last the insurance suit reached a resolution. At the original trial the auditor had awarded Stafford $4,200 of the $25,000 she sought, but the insurance company had appealed the decision. She later agreed to settle for $3,600, but the company still balked. In the end she received $4,000, though it was some time before she actually got the money.

Meanwhile, despite her disappointment in her dealings with the Atlantic Monthly Press, Stafford had settled into her writing again. According to White, each morning Stafford "used to sit down and read Proust for an hour or so in order to get the rhythm of her writing. . . . She was very disciplined about it. She'd get up, have coffee, read her Proust, and then work all morning on the typewriter." She would let no one else read what she was writing. It may be that in November 1939 Stafford was attempting one last revision of "The Autumn Festival," but there is reason to think that she was starting the book that would become *Boston Adventure*. If so, it was her sixth major effort to write a novel in six years.

White also noticed her roommate's drinking habits. "Sometimes she'd stop [writing] and have coffee, and after a while it got to be one glass of sherry in the middle of the morning." After Stafford stopped writing, around noon, "she could keep [the sherry drinking] up all day." White, who later judged herself naive about alcohol at the time, "assumed it was because she was having so much pain." Stafford was also "chain-smoking, and chain-coffeeing, too. Everything except food."

During November and early December Stafford saw a good deal of Hightower, often lunching in his apartment. On December 19, however, she mailed him the following letter:

I am going to write this instead of say it because it will be much less painful for both of us and if, when you have read it, you don't want to see me again, all you have to do is reply to me by mail. I am going to say it very simply like this: I am engaged to marry Cal Lowell. I will marry him next summer. You said it would happen, you said it in your letter and I did not believe it. Then I hated him but he does what I have always needed to have done to me and that is that he dominates me.

"I felt the bottom was falling out of things," Hightower remembers. "Not [because] she was marrying Lowell, but [because] she was marrying. She was my only friend, really, of that kind." Stafford's letter went on to say that Lowell was in Cambridge and would stay through January 4. Wanting Hightower to meet her fiancé, she invited him almost formally "to dinner Wednesday night about six-thirty."

Stafford added, "And when you come, Robert, try to bring good-will. I will explain nothing to you. . . . I know you are not in love with me now but there may be a scar still. For God's sake, let's leave the scars healed. I have no fewer than you." Good sport to the end, Hightower went to dinner, met Lowell, and liked him.

Looking back, Hightower contemplates Lowell's appeal for Stafford. "He represented a lot of things that were important to her — stability, family money (though he didn't have any right then himself), a major writer. We both knew it from the poems he was writing then. That was what put an end to my poetry writing. I could tell there was a real poet."

Lowell had timidly tried to prepare his parents for the blow. In the fall, from Kenyon, he had written his mother, "Jean is on her brother-in-law[']s ranch. Perhaps you would like to write her but that had better wait until after the trial." At Kenyon Lowell heard rumors that his parents were trying to use intermediaries to persuade Stafford to give up their son, lest he "go insane" if he married her.

The Lowells opposed Stafford to the end, even while they were forced to admit her to their drawing room. To her friends,

Charlotte Lowell referred to Jean as a "hick." Introducing her
future daughter-in-law at gatherings at 170 Marlborough Street,
she would say, "Tell us, Jean dear, where *is* it you come from?"
The contempt was mutual. As Stafford later recalled, "[Char-
lotte] ran her house like a battleship. She, actually, in the mornings after she had had her breakfast, would put on a pair of white
gloves and go downstairs and go over the furniture to see if the
maids were doing a good job." Charlotte proudly told Jean that
during the first two years of his life, "Bobby" had never been
touched by another person except a trained nurse, and had been
kept in a "germ-free" nursery.

Hightower recalls a dinner party on Marlborough Street to
which he, Jean, Cal, Bunny Cole, and William Empson were
invited:

> Mrs. Lowell was horrified with Empson because he was uncouth.
> He had a pair of overshoes which he never took off, and a suit
> that he obviously slept in, and he was talking about Wittgenstein
> and telling stories that had us practically on the floor. Mrs. Lowell
> didn't think it was a bit funny. . . . She talked only to Bunny, as
> being the only presentable, well-brought-up person there.

Shortly after revealing to Hightower that she was engaged,
Stafford suggested that he ought to "do something about Bunny
Cole." Hightower found Cole attractive, but at first he had not
taken her seriously. The push was all he needed: he began dating
her. One morning Lowell and Stafford dropped by Hightower's
apartment and found him still in bed. Cole had spent the night
there but was gone; the woman's dressing gown on the chair,
however, did not escape Stafford's notice.

Lowell returned to Kenyon after Christmas, entering the spring
term of his senior year. Gradually the chill between Stafford and
Hightower thawed. Even though it had been her idea in the first
place, Stafford now came to resent Hightower's attentions to Cole.
Jean started referring to her as "BR," for "Bunny Rabbit." At
last a snide message from Jean — "A little girl who never harmed
a fly told me all last night" — let him know that Bunny had
confessed her new affair.

Stafford and Lowell laid plans to marry quietly and privately
in New York City around the first of April, but instead of feeling joy at the decision, Stafford lapsed into an agitated, cranky

mood of crisis. She began to leave cryptic, angry notes for High-tower. "I was here and I want to know *just* what's up"; "damn *you*, call me tonight." She sent a telegram from her apartment to his: "COME HERE AS SOON AS POSSIBLE."

During the last month before the wedding, it became more and more imperative for Stafford to talk to Hightower. As he recalls it, during this brief period the two became closer than they had ever been: "I've never felt quite as at one with another person." It was then, he remembers, that Jean confessed the truth about her gonorrhea.

Six days before the wedding Stafford sent Hightower a frantic letter, full of oblique references to a conversation they had had the previous evening. She had apparently quarreled with Lowell:

> You and I have made our beds and have to lie in them and there is no possible way out. Last night if we had broken away, we would have been ordering our caskets in so doing. This has been largely my fault. I should never, as I have said before, [have] articulated possibilities. I am really and truly in love now [i.e., with Lowell].

Stafford was desperate to see Hightower once more before the wedding. But she wrote, "The next time you and I see each other, it had best not be alone. . . . Cal suspected something last night and he must not do so again."

On March 30 Stafford and Lowell arrived in New York and checked into the Biltmore Hotel. Stafford had not even told her family she was getting married. Lowell had pointedly avoided inviting his own parents, who may have been trying up to the last minute to thwart the marriage; as Stafford later described the train trip to New York, "We expected interruption at both railroad stations. . . ." Perhaps to avoid detection, on March 31 Stafford and Lowell moved from the Biltmore to the Hotel Albert.

The couple had dinner with Blair Clark, Robert Frost ("we talked about farms"), and Donald Hays and Dorothy Grabill, Jean's old friends from the Cooke circle in Boulder. She wrote to Hightower, "I wanted you to be at dinner but figured you were stopped by Blair. It was a hideous meal of irritations, recriminations and unspeakable fatigue."

The next day Lowell and Stafford went out separately to visit New York friends. In exasperation she wrote Hightower,

Cal got back unfortunately before I did and was furious — and justly and unjustly and oh God, Ma, I'm insane. Hideously this — there is a bottle of rum in my room + I will sit up till 4 AM with it + so forth. He should not have left me tonight and yet at this moment we are so irritated we hate each other. . . . Our lies — yours and mine — have to remain forever. . . .

P. S. He just came in and said you've got to stop drinking and I mean even 1 drink and I was panic-stricken for fear he wd take my rum away. It was very definite, very true and yet I shall perhaps not marry him + if I do not I shall be invisible for the rest of my natural life.

In a vulnerable moment Stafford admitted to Lowell that she "couldn't speak or read or understand" the German language. As she reported it to Hightower, Lowell's reaction was extreme: "He was completely stopped in his tracks + revolted. What wd. he do if he knew me?" On the eve of their marriage, as these letters make clear, Robert Lowell knew Stafford far less well than Robert Hightower did.

In Jean's penultimate letter to Hightower before the wedding, there is a puzzling passage. It reads, "The Wasserman[n] reports haven't come. We can't get a license without them so we won't be married until Tuesday. This is a very frightening business. . . ."

If Stafford had contracted syphilis in 1936, as seems very possible, and if it had not been cured, a Wassermann test in 1940 ought to have detected it even in a dormant stage. Syphilis was common enough in the late 1930s that 5 percent of American adults were thought to have it. The blood tests of the day, however, were unreliable, and more likely to give false negatives than false positives. Proof of syphilis did not prevent a couple from marrying; rather, it was intended to allow the doctor to guide the newlyweds' sexual activity into a precautionary mode. Stafford's openness in mentioning the tests to Hightower suggests that he still had no idea that she had ever had syphilis, as opposed to gonorrhea. Did Lowell suspect? Why were the results of the tests delayed? Did Stafford "pass" her test?

On April 2, 1940, Stafford and Lowell were married in the old church called St. Mark's in the Bouwerie, on Tenth Street in Greenwich Village. Allen Tate, "looking very like a banker" in his blue suit, gave Stafford away, while Blair Clark served as

Lowell's best man. Tate's wife, Caroline Gordon, may have been there, but Clark can remember no other guests, nor was there much of a party afterward.

The day before, Stafford had written a postcard to Hightower. On April 2 she scrawled at the bottom, after her signature, "It is 4:10. At 5 it will be over. *Terrified*. Happy."

Two hours later, before mailing the card, she added a last PS, written sideways in the margin: "6:05 It's done."

X

The Blind Alley

THE ONLY HONEYMOON Stafford and Lowell allowed themselves was a train ride to Ohio. They parted in Cleveland,
and Cal boarded a bus for Gambier. He still needed to finish the
last two months of his senior year at Kenyon, where, as John
Crowe Ransom had reassured Lowell's parents, "Jean will not be
welcome." The separation was fine with Stafford. She continued
west by train to Colorado, to spend the two months on the ranch
in Hayden, where she could plunge back into her writing.

From the train station in Chicago, less than forty-eight hours
after her wedding, Stafford wrote Hightower in a subdued mood:
"I am beginning to see what comfort there is in being married.
He will, I think, make me an honest woman. I am curiously
agonized at his tenderness for you. . . . Poor Cal! What a life he
will have with me."

Lowell's parents had taken the marriage hard. Charlotte Lowell complained to her Boston society friends that the haste of the
wedding "made it look like a forced marriage." Cal's cousin A.
Lawrence Lowell, the former president of Harvard, wrote the
bridegroom a scathing letter implying that he had seriously com-
promised his academic future. Lowell's parents may have even
cut off financial support to their only child.

Stafford felt irked as well by the "tepid tolerance" of her own
family. Writing to Hightower, she caricatured her mother's response to the marriage: " 'We were rather surprised, but it's O.K.
Yesterday I invested in a new corset. . . .' "

On the ranch Stafford felt less comfortable than she had the previous fall. A "possessiveness" she had not noticed before (presumably Mary Lee's) irritated her. One day she came across some old business papers that seemed to give new dimensions to her father's catastrophic stock-market loss of 1921. The papers suggested that in 1920 John Stafford's net worth had been almost three hundred thousand dollars. "What a miserable discovery this was!" Jean wrote Hightower. "I knew he had money but I did not know that he was actually rich."

For a few weeks Stafford worked on a long story about Lucy Cooke. On a stopover in Boulder she had visited Lucy's grave, finding it nearly covered by weeds. "I had the feeling that that was the first time anyone had gone there. . . . She is forgotten as anything but a story and a story so automatic that it has neither horror nor tragedy in it." In May Stafford applied again for a Houghton Mifflin literary fellowship, with, as she told Hightower, "a brand new novel that you haven't even heard of yet." This may be Stafford's earliest allusion on record to the manuscript that would become *Boston Adventure*.

The newlywed couple had no concrete plans beyond Lowell's graduation. He was hoping to stay on in Gambier as a full-time editor on the *Kenyon Review,* a post for which Ransom was championing him. An alternative scheme was for Stafford to work as a secretary for the *Review* while Lowell taught two Latin classes. At various times in April and May Lowell and Stafford seriously contemplated wintering over in some cabins in Mexico and living on a farm in Duchess County, New York. The most bizarre of Stafford's pipe dreams had her and Lowell accompanying Hightower to Peking, China, where the language scholar had a traveling fellowship starting in the fall. "It would have been insane," says Hightower in retrospect.

Despite the brave front she had tried to present to Hightower, Stafford's doubts about her marriage grew. To the ever-maternal Evelyn Scott, she confessed her qualms. Scott wrote back, "I don't think the marriage sounds dismal. . . . We don't have to marry our mothers-in-laws [sic], really." Already Jean was tossing out such nicknames as Harpy Charlotte and Charlotte Hideous for Lowell's interfering mother.

At the end of April a piece of news from Cambridge sent Stafford into a tailspin. Hightower had announced that he was planning to marry Bunny Cole. Jean's first letter in response was venemous and panic-stricken. "I would rather see you dead than married to her," she wrote. Her own betrothal had already taught her some gloomy truths: "I, being married, can tell you what marriage is. Even with respect, with awe of a superior mind and a shining talent — there is claustrophobia."

The brunt of Stafford's argument was a deprecation of Cole. "She wants the Ritz Roof to dance on, she only *thinks* she wants your scheme for [a] simple life. She is hypnotized by sleeping with you but the equipment of any other man would do as well." Almost hysterically, Stafford ordered Hightower to flee Bunny, to "leave without a trace," to go to China without her. She still imagined it possible for Lowell, Hightower, and herself to sail for China together, "if you were to go without that baggage." She sermonized, "I am a bitch, yes, but I am not the fool that you are. I will be ruthless in saving you from your imbecility."

Even today Hightower is persuaded that Stafford's attack on Cole was more than mere jealousy, that it was in some sense disinterested. "She was the one who encouraged me to seduce Bunny," he says. "But she thought it would be a terrible mistake [to marry her], that Bunny was a shallow, frivolous girl."

Stafford's letters from the ranch in late April and May constituted a determined assault on her unsuspecting ex-roommate. Bunny had "a mind like a squirrel-cage," "an irresponsible morality based upon the sonorous but wordless roar of protestant conformity" — "and, oh, Ma, God preserve you, she wants to write." Bunny "is at fault . . . because she has no merit. Ornament, sex, domesticity. Let me destroy them. . . . Sex is not at all remarkable. It may be observed in swine and high-school girls." If Hightower went ahead and married Cole, Stafford claimed, she would never see him again.

Although she could not yet voice unambiguous disloyalty to Lowell, she lamented that she had "married a stranger." Vaguely she flattered Hightower that somehow "there is a place for you in our lives." Yet she promised him that no matter what happened, "throughout my life that relationship [with you] will be transcendent over all others."

Privately Hightower wavered, though he kept all hints of Stafford's crusade from Cole's ears. "Jean made it very difficult," he reflects, "but I was committed by this time. I would have backed out, I suppose, as many men back out of an engagement, if I'd been able to, but I didn't see that I could, and I wasn't going to do it because of Jean."

By early May Stafford was determined that if she could not prevent Hightower's marriage, she must at least arrange a secret liaison with him, if only for a few hours, in which she would divulge "a plan for the rest of our lives." Hightower's intention was to finish the spring term at Harvard, marry Cole, and drive across the country, stopping in Salida for a month before heading on to Los Angeles and then sailing for China. Stafford expected to rejoin Lowell in Ohio at about the same time, as soon as he finished at Kenyon. Somewhere en route she and Hightower might cross paths, going in opposite directions. As early as May 10 she devoted a whole page of a letter to the almost ludicrous cloak-and-dagger logistics of a clandestine meeting in a hotel near the Denver train station.

Besides the secret plan, Stafford promised a confession:

There is a lie I have got sometime to clear up, because it is not a lie and yet you thought it was and until recently, I did myself . . . and I will tell you that there is nothing so hideous as my discovery of this truth and if I ever kill myself, this will be the reason of it . . . but I shall have to be drunk to tell you [ellipses Stafford's].

In subsequent letters she alluded again to this mystery:

I nurse an angry wound of which I've hinted . . . [her ellipses] a lie, told out of bewilderment, which was the truth. . . . My aged wound is not healed now by marriage and will never be healed . . . [her ellipses] wound, though figurative, is not used carelessly and the vocabulary of medical science if not its efficiency obtains. I do not conceal it well, but you will not see it yet. It is of no importance and I shall be a writer and I hope shall not live long.

These cryptic phrases may refer to the "frigidity" Stafford had claimed on the November night in 1938 when she had gone to bed with Hightower for the first and only time. But they also sound like a reference to a venereal disease. Hightower's firm recollection is that Stafford had already confessed her gonorrhea, in the weeks just before her wedding. It may be that his memory is off by a matter of two months, and Stafford's confession came only after these letters. On the other hand, perhaps there was more to tell — about a lingering case of syphilis, for example, which might well make Stafford expect not to live long.

Oblivious to this epistolary drama, Lowell finished up brilliantly at Kenyon. On June 9, 1940, he graduated, as he bragged to his mother, "summa cum laude, phi beta kappa, highest honors in classics, first man in my class and valedictorian." His valedictory address was a muddled if passionate attack on his own prep school, St. Mark's, and on other kindred intellectual nurseries for the American aristocracy.

At the last minute Lowell's plans to stay at Kenyon had fallen through. John Crowe Ransom dashed off a letter to colleagues at Louisiana State University, urging that Lowell be given a graduate fellowship there. Ransom let it drop that Stafford was not only a good writer but an accomplished typist, hinting that she might be well qualified for a job on the *Southern Review*. From LSU his old friend Cleanth Brooks telegraphed Ransom, "PLEASE ADVISE BY WESTERN UNION IF MRS. LOWELL KNOWS SHORTHAND."

Years later, when she could treat it as a joke, Stafford said that she had learned about the change of plans when Lowell sent her a telegram that read, "HAVE JOB. COME AT ONCE." "What I didn't understand," she intoned, "was that the job he had was for *me*. . . ."

In early June Hightower married Bunny Cole in Concord; the next day the couple started driving west. In a flurry of last-minute letters, Stafford had made haphazard arrangements to meet Hightower for a few hours in assorted hotels in, variously, Cleveland, Chicago, Omaha, and Denver. His final understanding was to look for her in Cleveland. He had finally admitted to his fiancée that Jean was bent on seeing him for a last tête-à-tête before they went to China. Bunny magnanimously gave her blessing, agreeing to spend the time in Cleveland with a college friend.

"My feelings were," says Hightower, "I'd have preferred to spend the time with Bunny. I wasn't feeling very good about Jean at the time." In Cleveland he inquired at the designated hotel. There was no sign of Stafford. "So I figured, OK, that's it." Hightower and his bride drove on across the Midwest.

In Omaha, Bunny had another college friend whom we stayed with. Then, at one or two A.M., the phone rang. "I guess it's for you," [said Bunny's friend]. It was Jean. She was calling from the railroad station.

"You get down here right now."

"I'll see you in the morning, Jean."

"You come right now!"

Cursing her with every step, I went right now. There she was. We drove around for two hours looking for a drink in the middle of the night. In Omaha, Nebraska, there isn't a drink in the middle of the night.

Hightower had no idea how Stafford had found him, or how she had guessed the timing of his visit. As two hours passed, Jean unburdened herself.

Her marriage was a terrible mistake. She was frigid. She thought she'd been lying to me. [But it was] true, she was. She couldn't live with him. Let's go to China together, let's get out of here together.

I said no. Oh, she was nasty. "What do you think of your mother-in-law?" . . . Mrs. Cole had taken Jean in, for Christ's sake, and fed her for months. . . .

She wanted to escape, and I was the only escape she knew. It had very little to do with me, I realize now.

I put her on the train, and went back to my wife and her friend and her friend's family, and what they thought about it, I just put out of my mind. And we continued to China.

Only a few hours after this desperate meeting, Stafford wrote Hightower a rueful but philosophical letter from the train station in Chicago. "My feeling is one of disappointment, very bitter disappointment. . . . I feel exiled and it breaks my heart to think that I'm extraneous to your life. . . ." She was through attacking his marriage. "I was of course envious that you had married without sordidness, with, on the contrary, public approval. . . ."

Before going to China, Hightower lent Stafford his record collection and all the books of his that she wanted. From the letters she wrote in May 1940 it is clear that she was still writing regularly in her journal. After that June, however, the journal is never mentioned again. Hightower believes that Stafford destroyed all her diaries when she began living with Lowell, for fear that he would read them and learn the secrets of her past. "I suppose I was the only person she could have left them with," he says, "and I wasn't in the country."

From Kenyon Stafford traveled with Lowell and Peter Taylor to the latter's home in Memphis. As the train pulled into the station, past the town's slums, "Cal was very disapproving and very critical: 'All this will have to go.' He was speaking like an Old Testament prophet." Cal and Jean stayed with Taylor's family for a few days. After a party a woman friend of Taylor's told him, " 'Peter, that marriage won't last. He's so very attractive, and she's not.' "

During the 1930s, the Louisiana governor Huey Long had built LSU into a university that aimed to compete with the best in the country. The leading lights of the English department were Cleanth Brooks, who had come in 1932, and Robert Penn Warren, who had arrived two years later. In 1935, with two other colleagues, Brooks and Warren had launched the *Southern Review*. Despite a circulation that never climbed above fifteen hundred, by the time of Lowell and Stafford's arrival in Baton Rouge the *Review* was widely regarded as the leading American magazine for serious fiction, poetry, and criticism.

Lowell's glowing recommendation from John Crowe Ransom had paved his way at LSU. But it was clear that his surname counted, too, in the minds of his southern-agrarian overseers. "He's a strong man," wrote Ransom to Brooks, "the last of the line of Lowells bearing the name, due to give a good account of himself before he is done. He is a bit slow and thorough, but he has enormous critical sense."

Stafford herself had deeply impressed Ransom when he read her writing at the 1937 writers' conference in Boulder. She may also have come to the attention of Warren in Boulder, where he had taught at the 1935 and 1936 conferences. Nonetheless, in 1940 it was Stafford's promise as a secretary, not as a writer, that made her welcome in Baton Rouge.

The Warrens, who had just bought a country house, sublet their apartment in town to Lowell and Stafford. It was the first time either had been in the Deep South, and they were both shocked by the lushness of the Louisiana summer. Lowell later recalled "the moisture mossing in the green seminar room" and "rats as long as my forearm." Stafford joked about cockroaches "as big as a calf," and set baited cardboard-cylinder traps for them.

Stafford set to work at once in the office of the *Southern Review*. Its quarters included a storeroom with no fan, its windows shut to keep rain from destroying the paper. "I remember the scorched smell there and I remember how, after going in to fetch paper or an early issue, I felt as if I were groping up out of deep anaesthesia; my hair was wet, my eyes were blind[e]d with sweat, I panted like a done-for hound. . . ."

The office, she wrote Peter Taylor, "looks like a hogsty with an accumulation of years of manuscripts (there are some here, really, that were sent in 1938). . . ." Stafford tried to balance the *Review*'s books, something that had never been done before. She was daunted by the editorial arrogance of Brooks, Warren, and their cohort Charles W. Pipkin. "Letters from contributors are rec'd with shrieks of laughter," she wrote Hightower, "mss. are sneered at, rejection slips go out furiously. The Atlantic Monthly looks like a bunch of kind old ladies."

Brooks was extremely pleased with Stafford's efforts: to Peter De Vries he later reported, " 'She worked hard, faithfully, exactly, as a secretary, and never gave airs.' " Lowell did token labor in the office, wrapping back issues, but was "not terribly handy" at it. He also read manuscripts, working himself up into a fury at the ineptitude of the writing. Stafford was apprehensive about the classes her husband would have to teach in the fall as part of his fellowship duties. "There are college boys living all around us," she wrote Hightower. "And by college boys I mean the genuine kind, the kind that wear funny clothes and at stated intervals hang pins on sorority girls. . . . Cal will be teaching these boys next year and Cal has never seen one of them before. They are as new to him as the Spanish moss. . . ."

Stafford's typing was first-rate, but she had to learn shorthand to round out her skills as a stenographer. The approach of her twenty-fifth birthday depressed her, as did every July 1 for the next four decades. "My life seems annually more fogged and my retrogression is steady — now I'm a secretary. And will the next be a telephone operator or will I be the receptionist in a city laundry?"

Her gloom was more than rhetorical. The great future everyone had predicted for Stafford at the writers' conference in 1937 seemed not to be materializing. Her close miss at the Atlantic Monthly Press had led to nothing. As she worked on her sixth serious novel, she could point to only a single publication — a

four-page story in *American Prefaces*. With marriage had come the
tendency of senior men to regard her as a housewife. She was,
in their eyes, "Mrs. Lowell"; indeed she saw herself that way,
and for years would write in the upper left corner of envelopes,
above her return address, "Mrs. Robert T. S. Lowell."

Her husband, on the other hand, quickly became the pet of the
department. Brooks found Lowell a brilliant reader of Milton.
For two hours every afternoon Warren and Lowell read Dante
together in Italian, arguing over nuances and felicities. In the fall
Lowell was Warren's student in a three-hour seminar in sixteenth-
century literature. As the professor later recalled his best pupil:
"[Lowell] was always a naif of one kind or another. And a calculated naif, too. But he had a charm and he had great intelligence and he read widely, and he could be wonderfully good
company." At the time, however, Warren made a prophetic div-
ination: "You talk about a man who was really mad . . . he
was on his way."

As the fall term began, Lowell and Stafford settled into what
from the outside looked like a conventional partnership. They
attended most of the English-department parties, drank recklessly, and went on afternoon field trips with friends. They drove
to St. Francisville to see the Spanish moss hanging from the live
oak in the cemetery; on Sundays they rode the ferry back and
forth across the Mississippi River, playing the slot machines and
listening to boogie tunes on the jukebox. Their teasing could make
them seem long-married. Frank Parker recalls Lowell's wistful
references to his first girlfriend, and Stafford's response: " 'If you
say that Anne Dick looks like Bette Davis one more time, I'll do
you violence!' "

Peter Taylor showed up in August for a visit and, under the
combined ministrations of Brooks, Stafford, and Lowell, was
persuaded to come to LSU for graduate work. Once in Baton
Rouge, he moved in with Jean and Cal. He brought with him a
casual girlfriend who moved in as well. Stafford instantly disliked this "great gauche lummox of a girl." When the four
roommates played bridge, her mind would wander off, forcing
Stafford to scold her back to attention. Once when Stafford had
been drinking heavily, Taylor's girlfriend came home, entered
Jean's bedroom, found a wine bottle, and poured out the contents. "This is what really turned Jean against her," says Taylor.

To Stafford's chagrin, the woman became her assistant on the *Review*.

Taylor and Stafford, however, had been fond of each other from the first and would become the closest of lifelong friends. One evening the three writers were invited to the Warrens' country house for a big party. The Brookses picked them up in their car. As Taylor recalls, "We were scared to death of him, because he was maybe ten years older than we were, and we thought it was great stuff being out with Cleanth Brooks." At the party, Stafford, Lowell, and Taylor got extremely drunk.

> I'd never had that much to drink in my life. We came home in the car, Jean, Cal, and I in the backseat, and we were trying to make conversation with Brooks, who was driving, about Donne and Herbert and all of that.
>
> Jean opened her purse, said, "Well, I think John Donne — " [and threw up into her purse].
>
> We got out of the car. I remember I had on a new gray flannel suit that I was very proud of. Just that much movement, getting out, and I was suddenly sick on the back of their car. I was so humiliated that as they pulled away, I tore off the jacket of my suit and ran after the car, wiping it off.

The Brookses had managed not to notice, but it was years before Taylor could confess his faux pas to them. Stafford had gone inside. "Cal and I came into the apartment, and I could see Jean back in the bathroom, washing dollar bills."

It was perhaps at this same party that, as Stafford told it, "Peter and I got incredibly drunk + exchanged words over the extent of Peter's love for me. . . ." Meanwhile, Taylor's casual girlfriend was sharing with Lowell her suspicion that a romance was developing between Taylor and Stafford. Nothing ever came of it, but according to Stafford, Lowell refused to speak to Taylor for a week after the party.

In the mornings, while Taylor and Lowell lounged around the apartment reading, Stafford would dash off to work before seven-thirty. Neither man could cook, Taylor's one grand culinary effort being a pan of fudge that never hardened, which he and Lowell diluted with hot water to make hot chocolate. Stafford would come home for lunch, finding the men, to her disgust, still in their pajamas. She would fix lunch for them and then hurry back to the office. "We'd usually be dressed by dinner," Taylor says.

In October Frank Parker and Blair Clark arrived for a brief visit on their way to Mexico. They picked up Stafford and Lowell and drove to New Orleans for a night on the town. The two friends took one room in a hotel, Stafford and Lowell another. They had dinner in a fancy restaurant, and there was much to drink.

Parker recalls what happened next. "Jean came down in the middle of the night, in her nightgown, sort of threw herself on our beds, and talked about how awful Cal was, this and that. Then Cal, angry, came down and ordered her upstairs." In their own room, Lowell and Stafford began a quarrel. Lowell swung his fist, hitting her square in the face, breaking the nose that four operations had painfully reconstructed. Says Parker,

> We took her to the hospital. No question her nose was broken, she was bleeding like a stuck pig.
>
> I asked Cal, did he really do it? And he said to me, oh yes, he sort of didn't know what he was doing yet he sort of did. He felt the nose go under his fist.

Clark adds,

> I remember it being just awful and terrifying, because it was such a symbolic reenaction of the accident. Really, for the first time I wondered whether Lowell had some deep, bad strain there that was going to be dangerous. . . . I cannot believe he hauled off and socked her. It must have been partly accidental.

According to Parker, "Cal had a sort of history — it had happened, and it was perfectly dreadful, but I never felt that he felt as remorseful as he should have. . . . I was really shocked."

It is a measure of Stafford's loyalty to her husband that she seems never to have mentioned this terrible incident to any future confidant — although in later years she "would go over it again and again" with Frank Parker. Had the two friends not been present, Lowell's savage act might have escaped recorded notice. Somehow even Peter Taylor, back in Baton Rouge, was kept in the dark about it. In her next letter to Hightower, Stafford mentioned laconically that "I am once more in the hands of a nose surgeon" but did not explain further.

Lowell's school friends were well aware of his propensity for violence. When they were roommates, Taylor had seen Lowell, in an argument about turning out the light, demolish his lamp with his bare hands — "I could see the sparks flying in the dark." And, of course, he and Taylor had fought on the train in 1938 on the way back from New York. His friends also knew that Lowell had no idea of his own strength. Frank Parker had once wrestled with him; as he recalls, "To wrestle Lowell is like getting in a cage with a gorilla. You may never come out. . . . He got me in a headlock, and I realized that if I didn't cry uncle, my head was going to come off. He simply didn't know what he was doing."

Lowell's lack of remorse after the car accident and the fight in New Orleans may have derived from his indulgent upbringing. Remarkably, when Stafford developed a cough in the weeks after her nose had been rebroken, Lowell claimed that its cause was the fact that she "breathed too much."

A year earlier, in telling Hightower about her engagement, Stafford had stressed that although at times she had hated Lowell, "he does what I have always needed to have done to me and that is that he dominates me." Perhaps she accepted his physical abuse as part of her husband's right to dominate. And even as they were quarreling in Louisiana, Lowell and Stafford were developing a certain intimacy.

At Kenyon Lowell had invented a set of imaginary bears. Each of his friends was assigned a bear name; Lowell himself was "Arms of the Law." He loved to recite stories about his creatures. As John Thompson remembers, Lowell "had a funny singsong whine he told these stories in and they were endless. . . . He would tease people with them. They were familiars of some kind — totems that he needed. I don't know where they came from. Arms was like a sheriff — he was always arresting people and scolding people."

In Baton Rouge the Bears were modified into the Wuberts, pronounced "Wu-bear," in the French manner. The inspiration for this renaming was apparently Paul M. Hebert, then acting president of LSU. Stafford eagerly embraced the new fantasy, elaborating myths of her own within its confines. In 1943 she and Lowell sketched out a mock scholarly history of the Wuberts complete with drawings, doggerel, medical reports, and applications for graduate school. The Wuberts became a large clan of domestic beings who lived with Lowell and Stafford. In the mock history Stafford dates their discovery as December 11, 1940, in Baton Rouge. Close friends such as Peter Taylor were privy to the mythology, although Allen Tate "thought it was completely beneath contempt." Lowell also devised the affectionate nickname Eanbeaner for Jean, which she proudly wore in its many variations, including Ean, Bean, and Beaner.

Because he was a poor typist, Lowell expected his wife to type up his poems as soon as he had written them in his peculiar, square, almost juvenile longhand. If on rereading he changed a single word, she had to type the poem over again.

Stafford began to drink seriously in Baton Rouge. A favorite potion was Cuba Libres. She also started downing large quantities of white wine, a drink that made Taylor think "she was so sophisticated. I'd never had a drink of wine in Tennessee while I was growing up." But "Jean was quite a wino by that time. . . . She was really in a pretty bad way with her drinking down there."

As the year wore on, Stafford's unhappiness deepened. In November she wrote Hightower, euphemizing the sources of her anguish, "There is no day without anger and no night with any articulate hope for the next day. I am resentful and despairing; discouragement is quotidian. I have not had, since I have been here, one experience of joy or one hour of solitude. . . ."

By the beginning of 1941 Lowell was well on his way to what would be perhaps the most important shift of mind and heart of his life. He had become seriously interested in Catholicism. Only a year or two before, he had told Taylor, " 'Catholicism is a religion of Irish servant girls.' " Warren thought that Lowell had come to the faith from reading Dante. Frank Parker attributed his interest to an enclave of Catholic poets in Cambridge. In Baton Rouge Lowell began reading the work of such theologians as Etienne Gilson, Jacques Maritain, and Cardinal Newman.

Years earlier Stafford had considered herself a Catholic, having taken instruction in Boulder. By 1937, however, she had completely turned her back on the religion. Her former faith had nothing to do with Lowell's new conviction. In the fall of 1940 Warren had asked the Reverend Maurice Schexnayder, the chaplain of the Catholic student group at LSU, to talk to his seminar about the Reformation. After the class Lowell had followed

Schexnayder into the hall and abruptly asked him for instruction in Catholicism.

Stafford viewed this development with a certain alarm. "Cal is becoming a Catholic," she wrote Hightower in February 1941.

> A real one with all the trimmings, all the fish on Friday and the observance of fasts and confessions and grace before meals and prayers before bed, and while I can stand off and even admire what he is doing, I want to have none of it for myself. It sickens me down to my soul to hear him talk piously and to see in him none of the common Christian virtues as pity and kindness but only the fire-breathing righteousness. . . .

On March 29 Lowell was baptised by Schexnayder in Christ the King Chapel on the LSU campus. At Lowell's insistence, he and Stafford were remarried by Schexnayder so as to rectify their bond within the Church. Shortly after this Lowell spent a week in retreat at a nearby Jesuit monastery.

In a fictionalized but highly autobiographical story Stafford wrote about her marriage many years later, "Theron Maybank," Lowell's alter ego, "immersed in the rhythms of Gerard Manley Hopkins the poet, was explosively ignited by Gerard Manley Hopkins the Jesuit, and, as my mother would have said, he was off on a tear."

In 1941 Lowell set out to convert his own life into a strict fastidiousness on the model of Hopkins's. As Stafford glumly described it,

> Mass at 6:30, grace before and after meals, Benediction at 6:30 PM, the reading of religious books, the rosary before bed. And in addition, confession, talks with the priest, choice of movies according to the Censor, choice of books in the same way, and talk of *nothing* but the existence of God. . . . He wants me to make a retreat now. I cannot do it — we have quarreled for 2 weeks over it.

A rumor circulated on campus that Lowell had turned Stafford out of her bed and made her sleep on a platform of wooden planks as a mortification of the flesh.

In "An Influx of Poets," Stafford's retrospective story, the priest who confirms the narrator's husband has an "austerity" that was "right up Theron's alley, and before I knew what had happened to me, I had been dragged into that alley which was blind." Although her husband at first promises that he will not impose his new faith on her, within weeks she is being remarried in the Church, attending daily Mass, going to benediction, and telling her rosary twice a day. "What had become of the joking lad I'd married? He'd run hellbent for election into that blind alley . . . and yanked me along with him, and there we snarled like hungry, scurvy cats."

The metaphor of the blind alley is all the more striking in view of the scene of the car accident that had smashed up Stafford's face (which incident plays no part in "An Influx of Poets"). One wonders just how conscious Stafford was of this analogy between crash and conversion.

In the spring of 1941, despite her malaise, Stafford tried to see the positive side of her husband's fanaticism. By April she could say to Hightower, "Turnabout as this may sound[,] I believe Cal's Catholicism has been the best thing that has happened." Moreover, so effective was Lowell's domination of her that she made a sincere effort to come back to belief herself. "My ideal notion of the church," she wrote Hightower, ". . . is one of grand dignity, superb intellectual exercise, in short, a composite of ritual and philosophy in which God, the saints and the angels remain timeless — absolutely timeless." After confession, as she forced herself to say the Act of Contrition, "I do not then more than any other time believe but I see and am appalled at the *possibility*. . . ." At certain moments, "I am apprised of sin and no longer believe my history of it is too old for reparation."

At the end of February Stafford was bedridden for two weeks. For over a month she had been having "inexplicable" daily fevers, compounded with a bad cough and pains in her chest. By April she was coughing up blood. A Baton Rouge doctor peering at an X ray thought he found a small spot on Stafford's lungs and diagnosed tuberculosis. It was decided that she should go to the ranch in Hayden for a rest cure.

By the end of June, when Stafford returned from Colorado, she believed she was cured of TB. Then the fevers began again. In dismay, she kept from Lowell any knowledge of the high temperatures she recorded each afternoon. Although eventually Stafford was convinced that the TB diagnosis had been erroneous, in the summer of 1941 she was frightened that the stay in

Hayden had done nothing to abate the deadly disease. At the time she wrote Hightower a cryptic but provocative letter about her illness.

> I could evolve a theory on the facts of "my case" — that I am a coward for not admitting that this is my fault, and a coward for preparing myself so poorly for death, preparing myself for [a] death that I could postpone if I would only submit to treatment, if I would only rest.
>
>   In another year, perhaps I'll be incurable and nothing will be to blame but my foolishness. I can't ask for sympathy and not even for that partial understanding we allow people whose behaviour [sic] is eccentric but not in any way similar to our own — (so that of Lucy I can say, I see why she killed herself, though the "seeing" is done in a part of my mind that is objective, cognizant of the "before the fact" sequences).

This is a very confusing passage. It can just barely be made to read as indicating a conviction on Stafford's part that she had TB. Yet the idea of blaming her own "foolishness," the reference to Lucy (whose health, if "In the Snowfall" can be trusted, Jean knew to have been damaged by gonorrhea), the notion that she can ask for neither sympathy nor understanding — all suggest once again a veiled confession of syphilis. A case of recurring secondary syphilis, four years after Stafford may have caught the disease in Heidelberg, could account for the mysterious fevers. Because Stafford had never actually admitted having syphilis to Hightower, perhaps in this letter her contorted language is a means of avoiding an outright revelation.

That Stafford ever had syphilis remains, of course, a conjecture. The evidence for it amounts to the following: many of the symptoms she reported to Hightower and Berueffy in the spring of 1937 are consistent with the disease; she made a number of subsequent hints about syphilis in letters to Hightower; the arsenic compounds that she was given in 1937 were used to treat cases of syphilis, not gonorrhea; Stafford was forced out of her job at Stephens College on the suspicion that she had syphilis; the results of the Wassermann test for her marriage license were delayed.

In the late 1930s the treatment for syphilis recommended by the best-informed doctors was an arduous series of injections —

thirty shots of an arsenic compound in a vein and forty shots of bismuth in the hip, spaced over a period of seventy weeks. The phrase Stafford used in her letter, "if I would only submit to treatment," may allude to a schedule like this one rather than to the bed rest and high altitude prescribed for tuberculosis. The better doctors of the day used Fournier's five-year rule as a guide to determining whether a syphilitic was cured. This rule called for "no recrudescence during two years following cessation of at least three years of continuous treatment." If Stafford had contracted syphilis in the fall of 1936, by her wedding in April 1940 there would not have been enough time for Fournier's rule to apply. A conscientious physician treating a case of syphilis in 1940 would have counseled both spouses not to have intercourse without a condom, and not to kiss on the lips unless the arsenic treatment was currently being administered.

In 1952, after she was divorced from Lowell, Stafford told her friend Joan Stillman (then Joan Cuyler) that "they had had a glorious affair before they were married, but after he became a Catholic, they never slept together." At some point Stafford told Blair Clark the same thing. Later she told Eve Auchincloss, who became a closer friend than either Stillman or Clark, that she had never slept with Lowell at all, either before or during her marriage to him.

To Wilfrid Sheed, who befriended her in the late 1950s, Stafford claimed that the car accident had caused internal injuries that prevented her from having children. Yet to Lowell Stafford insisted even after they were divorced that she still hoped to have children.

Lowell's fanatical Catholicism may well have given him what he considered a doctrinal reason for eschewing sex. Moreover, at the time he married Stafford, Lowell was quite inexperienced sexually. His fumbling, self-conscious performance the sole time he went to bed with Anne Dick is documented in Ian Hamilton's biography. And Stafford was only his second girlfriend.

From Iowa in the fall of 1938, in her letters to Hightower, Stafford had poured out the passionate feelings of a woman who was reawakening to her own sexuality. "I am built for bed, not for a classroom," she had sworn. When Hightower finally took her to bed, however, she announced, " 'Now, I must tell you, I'm frigid.' "

It is entirely possible that Stafford may have felt sexual at a distance — via the mail — yet been unable to respond in person. Hightower himself sensed that his gentleness was anaphrodisiac to her, that the domineering Fairchilds and Lowells were the only men who could sexually arouse her.

But there is another obvious possibility. If Stafford had had syphilis and could not be certain it was cured, then going to bed with a man was an act freighted with terrible consequences. Perhaps her "frigidity" was an excuse, in which case her persistent worry that Hightower did not believe she was really frigid may have concealed a fear that he knew her more humiliating secret. And if the syphilis was still not cured in 1940, then contriving a way — any way — to avoid sleeping with her husband was nothing less than a moral responsibility.

The whole business is of an interest that transcends mere gossip. In virtually all of Jean Stafford's mature works, the very fact of sexual relations is ignored. Often, when the possibility of sex is even indirectly implied, it is attended by suggestions of shame or disaster. The Stafford her friends knew after 1940 seems to have been a person utterly uninterested in sex. She never flirted, these witnesses maintain; the word *asexual* comes readily to their lips.

What is more, Stafford's rejection of the romantic ecstasies of sexual love has everything to do with her development as a writer. Here, after all, was a disciple of Thomas Wolfe; here was a writer whose "Autumn Festival" had been built upon a Wagnerian exaltation of doomed passion and illicit love. The Stafford who became a first-rate novelist and short-story writer was someone who turned her back on Wolfean or Wagnerian solemnity and bent her talents instead to the development of a comic, ironic view of life, in which romantic love, often as not, reveals itself as an embarrassing delusion.

The personal etiology of this view of sex, however, is a snarled matter. If we can read as autobiographical those scenes from "In the Snowfall" in which the protagonist suffers paternal beatings that are tinged with sexual arousal and revulsion, then there were abundant childhood reasons for Stafford to develop a lifelong disturbance about sexual matters. (Indeed, even if those scenes are imagined, there is enough in the known facts of Stafford's relationship with her father to support such a conclusion.)

Yet the Stafford who became a willing disciple of Lucy Cooke, who went to bed with a fraternity boy in Boulder and a baseball player in Heidelberg, seems to have been an adventurer who at twenty-one was far from set on an asexual path. The traumas of Lucy's tyranny and suicide and of the devastating illness or illnesses Stafford contracted in Germany would have turned almost anyone against sex. And if an infection had also rendered her sterile, here was another heavy blow to her womanhood. It seems all the more poignant, then, that she may have regarded these traumas as secrets she could not confess, as invisible stigmata that she constantly feared others could see.

In her misery, just before heading out to the ranch in April 1941, Stafford sent Hightower one last plea:

> I've *got* to be with you again. I will be getting over t.b. for six weeks. State some plan. You and me, I mean. No ties. Cal would do this for Frank [Parker], I would do it for you. It's *got* to be like that no matter what we sacrifice. . . . I am slowly killing myself and know it and I won't be alive five years. And I am unhappily married. . . .
>
> Ruprecht, it's got to be you and me. Make plans. Send yours by clipper. I imagine maybe Sept or Oct. we'll be together. I've got money — Cal will be drafted. Get rid of your encumbrance. . . .

Even in Peking, for Hightower this letter "came as a threat." He had little confidence in Stafford's feelings, and he was happily married to his "encumbrance." Jean's next letter was a kind of relief: "Ignore, by the way, my last communication written under the influence. I never, of course, mean any of it. I'm actually very happy."

On her way to the ranch in Hayden Stafford made her customary stop in Boulder. For the rest of her life, her visits to the town where she had lived from age ten to age twenty-one served as excuses to debunk the people who had taught and cared for her. Perhaps Stafford thus convinced herself that she had transcended her past. That April her former philosophy teacher Joseph Cohen seemed to her "mighty small potatoes." She dismissed Edward Davison even more rudely. "[He] is now wholly alcoholic. I had drinks with him at his house and he said 'Have you seen my study?,' took me there and kissed me, also hugged me. I felt as unclean as though I had been raped by a nigger."

Stafford found her father in residence at the ranch. It had become John Stafford's regimen to spend every summer in Hayden, living rent-free. As Harry Frichtel summed up his father-in-law many years later, "I had him on and off for a good long time. There was times I could have killed him, but the rest of the time we got along pretty good." John Stafford, who liked to hunt, told Frichtel he had been a champion trapshooter in Missouri. But, says Frichtel, "I don't think he ever killed a deer. He claimed he had, but I think he never got over buck fever. I seen him miss some awful good shots at deer." Nor was the old man much of a fisherman: "He couldn't have caught a sheep in a chute."

On the ranch Jean's father labored incessantly on his great book about government spending, holed up in a converted milk house out back. "He'd write, oh, six–eight hours a day, peck on the typewriter. I don't know how many reams of paper he went through," says Frichtel. "He'd write that book, and then he'd write it over and then he'd write it over and then he'd write it over. The text was always the same. He was just hepped on that one subject."

Jean's meeting with her father filled her with pity and distress. His social behavior seemed to have been reduced to a round of three activities — waxing nostalgic about long-vanished friends; cursing President Roosevelt, the younger generation, and the decline of culture; and sitting in a darkened room, staring at the floor.

As always on the ranch, Jean was able to write. Full of enthusiasm for her new novel, she bragged to Hightower that it was "the first un-autobiographical piece I have done." Regarding it as a "religious" work, she completed a 175-page synopsis and sent it off to Houghton Mifflin. Again she was to be disappointed. In May an editor at the press wrote "complimenting me + offering no cash. . . . The editorial comment was that I was 'almost Proustian.' Guess what famous French novelist I have been reading all winter."

Jean's authorial frenzy was impressive to the denizens of the ranch. Her nephew Robert Frichtel, then eight, remembers a cowhand saying to her, " 'Miss Jean, I just think it's amazing. How do you make all those sentences come out even?' "

On her return to Louisiana, still keeping her daily fevers secret from her husband, Stafford endured another summer of fetid nature and mesmerizing heat. Peter Taylor had left LSU, telling Warren that he had to be a writer, not a graduate student. In his place in their apartment Stafford and Lowell welcomed another member of the Baton Rouge literati. Although she would later grow more liberal on the issue, in 1941, when Jean learned that the man was homosexual, she claimed, "We observe the vicious habit in innumerable people; all his friends are now obvious."

Despite the intellectual and spiritual progress he had made in Baton Rouge, Lowell was not eager to spend another year at LSU. With the help of the Reverend Schexnayder, he landed a job in New York City at Sheed and Ward, a Catholic book publisher. Stafford anticipated the change with an enervated hopefulness: "Thank God anyway we are leaving this death-trap." To Hightower alone she could acknowledge that "the depths of my unhappiness are incalculable." She would move dutifully to New York with her husband, she said, but if things got worse, "I will do an Iowa City disappearing act."

In August a cofounder and editor of the *Southern Review,* Charles W. Pipkin, died of alcoholism at the age of forty-one. Already imbued with some of the sanctimonious Catholicism of her husband, Stafford moralized,

> A more terrible spectacle than his life I cannot imagine unless it would be Lucy's if she had gone on with hers. . . . I had actually seen him not above a week ago and had known, minutely, what his life had been for the last 10 years — impotent intellectually, homosexual, perpetually drunk and [I] considered how this person I had seen, being eased into a car like an old man, the color of leather from jaundice, was perhaps at this moment being judged.

Yet, reflecting no doubt on her own heavy drinking during the year in Louisiana — and with a prescience it is chilling to ponder — Stafford added, "When it was said of him 'It was a terrible state to precede his death,' I experienced again a terror of possibilities. . . ."

XI

Best-Seller

IF THE PERIOD from 1935 through the summer of 1941 had been unremittingly eventful for Stafford, the next three years would seem tranquil, almost placid, by comparison. Having earlier toyed with the idea of running away from it, she now grew reconciled to her marriage. Despite his dogmatic periods, Lowell slowly became Stafford's true confidant, and as this happened their connubial sanctum began to be relatively opaque to outsiders. From 1941 through the beginning of 1945, their best friends drifted into their own entanglements or were removed from close contact with Lowell and Stafford by the war.

Pregnant with her first child, Bunny Hightower came back from China in September 1941; her husband stayed on there. Sensing the inevitability of the war's engulfing the Orient, Robert Hightower planned his escape from Peking for early December, but he was already trapped. Interned by the Japanese, he spent two years out of touch with his wife and infant son.

Hightower came home on the *Gripsholm* in December 1943, as part of a massive prisoner exchange. He remained close to Stafford for the rest of her life, and Jean at last embraced Bunny as a friend whom she no longer had any reason to deprecate. But from 1943 on, the fervor between Stafford and Hightower, the romantic intimacy that had bound these erstwhile soulmates together, was gone. In its place came a rapport based on shared reminiscence, like that of soldiers who had once endured a treacherous campaign together.

In September 1941 Lowell and Stafford found a four-room apartment on West Eleventh Street in Greenwich Village, which they rented for fifty-five dollars a month. To Jean's surprise, New York seemed to be a cheaper place to live than Baton Rouge. The apartment was only three blocks from Lowell's new office.

The publishing house of Sheed and Ward, which was committed to the Catholic Revival (a liberal intellectual movement of the day), had been founded in London in 1927. During the 1930s Frank Sheed and Maisie Ward (Wilfrid's parents) had toured America, speaking in lecture halls and preaching on street corners. In 1940 they had moved to the United States in order to set up a New York branch of the company, which brought out books by American nuns and priests, including Dorothy Day of the *Catholic Worker* and the young Fulton Sheen, who had not yet "succumb[ed] to the bright lights."

Lowell's job at Sheed and Ward involved copyediting and writing jacket blurbs. According to Stafford, he found his colleagues "very pleasant" but "less Catholic and less intellectual than he." "He is really a catch," she bragged, "and I hope they realize it, for he edits mercilessly and from the looks of their proofs, they have lacked just that." At first Jean hoped that Cal's job would bring in enough money to support her while she wrote, but before long she, too, signed on at the publishing house, as Frank Sheed's secretary.

This aggressive, charismatic, and highly intellectual English Catholic found his new assistant delightful: "Frank loved Jean Stafford," is his son's forthright judgment. Lowell, however, garnered a mixed response:

> It seemed Sheed and Ward had recently acquired one of its odd business managers . . . who believed that Lowell was a veritable messiah, someone destined to lead us all out of paths of sin and war. Lowell by chance found this a splendid notion. . . .
>
> Frank retained a blind spot about Lowell almost to the end. He would read a poem of his and snort. "And exactly how does he propose 'fighting the British Lion to his knees?' Where are a lion's knees anyway?"

Lowell insisted that, in addition to her secretarial duties, Stafford must do "Catholic work." She obligingly volunteered to help out at the office of the *Catholic Worker*. On her first day, a seven-block trek "through the kind of slums you do not believe exist when you see them in the movies" unsettled her; then, "The Worker office was full of the kind of camaraderie which frightens me to death and I was immediately put at a long table between a Negro and a Chinese to fold papers, a tiring and filthy job."

In the course of his marriage to Stafford, the only period during which Lowell actually earned his living was the nine months he worked at Sheed and Ward. A small but steady trust-fund income came his way from Boston, but most of the time he lived off the money his wife made — first as a secretary, then as a writer. There is little or no indication that Stafford bridled at this state of affairs. Lowell seemed to take it for granted that his development as a poet exempted him from the normal responsibilities of "providing." The parallel with Jean's father is eerie.

Lowell was by now firmly entrenched in the Church. Says Peter Taylor, "Oh, I remember the pious letters I had from Cal that year." Stafford kept a wry sense of humor about Catholicism when reporting to friends, but for several years she also unapologetically presented herself as a believer. In the mid-1970s, Lowell would recall

> Our days of the great books, scraping and Roman mass —
> your confessions had such a vocabulary
> you were congratulated by the priests —
> I pretended my impatience was concision.

It is thus hard to judge today whether the Catholic charade Stafford's protagonist acts out in "An Influx of Poets" represents Jean's own real but rueful hypocrisy at the time or the retrospective cynicism of one who wished she had not so easily submitted to her husband's zeal for conversion:

I was the lost one, for I did not believe in any of it — not in the Real Presence, not in the Immaculate Conception, not in God — and, to compound my perfidy, I received the Host each Sunday and each day of obligation and did not confess my infidelity. Not to Father Bernard and no longer to Theron [her husband]. In the beginning, I had tried, but he, rapt in his severe belief, had brushed me aside and called my doubt a temporary matter. "But it isn't *doubt!* It's positive repudiation!" I'd cry.

One distinction, however, can be safely made. Lowell's Catholicism during the years from 1941 to 1946 was crucial to his evolution as a poet, and it is impossible to read his work without taking it into account. For Stafford, on the other hand, regardless of whether or not she sincerely believed during those years, Catholicism was all but irrelevant to her writing. Even when she appealed directly to the faith, as when she borrowed the name of Teresa of Avila's work *The Interior Castle* for her short story about her facial operations, she used the title only as a literary metaphor, not as a substantive allusion.

Despite her second setback at Houghton Mifflin, Stafford plugged away at the burgeoning manuscript of her new, "unautobiographical" novel. Before rejecting the book, the Houghton editors had hinted that they thought she had the makings of a best-seller on her hands.

Sometime near the beginning of 1942 an acquaintance of hers who was angling for a job at Harcourt, Brace and Company tipped off the New York house about Stafford's novel-in-progress. The head of the firm, Frank V. Morley, got hold of the unfinished manuscript, which Jean was calling "The Outskirts." After reading it, he handed the work over to a junior editor named Robert Giroux, with the following note attached: " 'It is well written in a way that creeps on relentlessly, giving the interior life of the heroine, Sonie. I found that it kept hold of me; but will it keep hold of a public?' "

Giroux recalls the occasion of his first awareness of Jean Stafford:

> I stuck [the book] in my briefcase with one or two other manuscripts and on my way that weekend to the Morleys in Riverside, Conn., did some reading on the train. I was so enthralled with Sonie and so oblivious to everything else that I rode past my stop and returned to reality only when the conductor yelled "New Haven!"

One evening in early 1942 Giroux went to dinner at Lowell and Stafford's apartment on West Eleventh Street. For the editor it was the beginning of a lifelong, extraordinarily fruitful association with both writers. On April 30, 1942, at the house of Allen Tate and Caroline Gordon in Princeton, New Jersey, Stafford signed a Harcourt, Brace contract for "The Outskirts." To make a ceremony of the signing, Caroline Gordon placed lighted candles on either side of her desk. The terms of the contract were generous: a five-hundred-dollar advance, $250 on signing and $250 on delivery, as well as a two-book option on her future novels. Stafford's deadline was December 1, 1942. At the time, Giroux believed that the book represented Stafford's first attempt at a novel. Despite their close friendship over the subsequent years, he had no inkling until 1984 that Stafford had written any novels before *Boston Adventure.* After all, when she signed the contract, the grateful Mrs. Lowell was only twenty-six.

In July Tate and Gordon invited their protégés to come and live with them in Tennessee, where they had bought a "cottage." Committed though Lowell was to Catholic work, he was tired of copyediting and discouraged about having written so little poetry over the past year. The prospect of a retreat to the country — four writers in one household, with nothing to do but compose immortal works — seemed idyllic. Monteagle, the site of this sanctuary, was a resort compound on a plateau five miles north of Sewanee. Originally a kind of turn-of-the-century chautauqua, the place had become a favorite haunt of many Tennessee writers.

At Monteagle, despite recurring bouts of bronchitis (linked to her endless nasal problems), Stafford made great strides on "The Outskirts." Gordon was working on her novel *The Women on the Porch;* Tate struggled for a while with a sequel to *The Fathers,* his only novel, but abandoned it in favor of a series of sonnets. And in the cool air of Monteagle, Lowell was on fire with poetry. His year's work in Tennessee brought forth the poems that would make up *Land of Unlikeness,* his first book.

Since June 1941 Peter Taylor had been in the army, stationed at Fort Oglethorpe, not far away over the Georgia line. On weekends he would come to Monteagle to visit his four writer friends. He found Lowell's Catholicism unmitigated. Since there was no Catholic church in the vicinity, Lowell and Stafford had to take a bus some twelve miles to worship in Winchester. Each Sunday Stafford made a breakfast that she carried in a paper bag, but Lowell strictly forbade snacking before Mass: according to Taylor, "Cal wouldn't let Jean touch it. Afterwards, they'd sit on a bench waiting for the bus to go back, and eat their breakfast. Jean found it humiliating."

Lowell had tried to volunteer for the navy the previous March but had been rejected because of his poor eyesight. In August he went down to Fort Oglethorpe and offered himself to the army. Having been advised by friends that he would not be able to avoid the draft, he planned instead to make officers' training school. Again his myopia disqualified him.

Stafford continued to feel the fondest affection for Taylor. On one occasion when she had to go to Chattanooga to see the dentist, she met her friend for lunch. The afternoon vanished in round after round of drinks. As Taylor remembers, "Jean was staggering so that the man came and said I would have to take her out. And I said, 'How dare you. This is my crippled sister.' And stared him down."

In the spring of 1943 Taylor met a young woman named Eleanor Ross, who had been Tate's and Gordon's student. It was love at first sight; six weeks later, having shared only a few weekends together, the two were married, with Stafford as maid of honor, Lowell as best man, and Tate once again giving the bride away. It was Stafford's predilection to be possessive of the men she admired and enjoyed. She had denigrated Bunny Cole behind her back; now, even before Taylor's wedding, Jean and Eleanor traded "catty words." In the end a breach was averted, and Stafford accepted Eleanor Taylor as fully as she had come to accept Bunny Hightower.

One measure of Lowell's influence upon Stafford is the extent to which she took up his male friends as her own. After 1941 Stafford stayed close to none of the heretofore important men in her own life, with the exception of Hightower, and even that friendship attenuated greatly. Left behind were Howard Higman, Goodrich Walton, Andrew Cooke, Robert Berueffy, Joe Chay, and the like — not to mention the professors she had once worshiped, who now became the objects of her derision.

On the other hand Peter Taylor, Frank Parker, Blair Clark, and John Thompson — perhaps Lowell's four best friends in the world up to 1942 — became devoted cronies of Stafford's, and these bonds long survived Lowell and Stafford's divorce. She later reinforced this tendency with Randall Jarrell, Delmore Schwartz, and John Berryman.

The time at Monteagle was as beneficial to Stafford's writing as it was to Lowell's. She had recently published her first piece of criticism, a review of Kenneth Patchen's *The Journal of Albion Moonlight* for the *Kenyon Review*. With the spur of a real contract

from Harcourt, Brace — no mere option this time — through the
fall and winter of 1942–1943 she whipped out the pages of her
ambitious book. Robert Giroux had gone into the navy, so his
colleague Lambert Davis took over as Stafford's editor. On February 1 she mailed a gigantic manuscript of almost 250,000 words
to New York.

Anticipating the book's publication, Davis wrote Stafford to
get her thoughts about what name should appear on the cover.
It says much about the conventions of the day that *Boston Adventure* might well have come into the world as the work of one
"J. S. Lowell"; for as Davis wrote the author, "The 'Jean' has
troubled me a little, though I frankly don't know just how important it is. Certainly you should retain the 'Lowell.' . . ."

On March 16 Harcourt, Brace sent Stafford a check for $250,
the second half of her advance. Despite this gesture of formal
acceptance, Davis's editorial response a week later was a discour-
aging one; no doubt Stafford had a familiar sinking feeling as she
received his report. "I am sure," Davis wrote, "that your first
reaction to it will be that I am simply looking for another book
by another writer." The central difficulty of the book, in his eyes,
was that it did not seem credible that the impoverished, poorly
educated protagonist, Sonie Marburg, could become the "master
of a polished and intricate prose style." Although Davis thought
this "a pretty serious defect," he reassured Stafford that she needn't
write an entirely new book.

The logical difficulty noted by Davis persisted as a problem in
the final, published version of *Boston Adventure,* and reviewers
duly complained about it. It had arisen from the unfortunate conjunction of Stafford's decision to narrate the novel in the first
person and her choosing to adopt a style that was "a *conscious*
imitation of Proust." In March 1943, however, Stafford swallowed her medicine and began a thorough revision of her manuscript. In appreciation of her tractability, Davis sent her another
hundred dollars as an advance against royalties, adding a cheerful
vote of confidence that she would remain "a Harcourt Brace author for your career."

Hoping to get a further boost on the massive revision, Stafford
applied to Yaddo, the eccentric writers' colony in Saratoga Springs,
New York. She was accepted, and by mid-July she had moved
north from Monteagle.

Yaddo proved to be more of a distraction than a help. Stafford was awed by the "Florentine" luxury of the place, and she delighted in the lovely grounds and the good meals. She shared a bathroom with Carson McCullers, "who is by no means the consumptive dipsomaniac I'd heard she was, but she is strange." Stafford also met Langston Hughes and renewed her acquaintance with Katherine Anne Porter, with whom she had downed gin and tonics in Baton Rouge. She spent many hours drinking and chatting with her literary stablemates. Much of the talk was of politics and race relations. Under Lowell's influence, Stafford had drifted considerably to the right in the previous two years, as she now discerned when others at Yaddo attacked her Catholicism and gossiped about her possible racial prejudice. Feeling miffed and defensive, Stafford dismissed her critics as "half baked communists."

Her health was precarious throughout the summer. The low fevers of the year before had returned, again baffling her doctors. She was told in July that she was suffering from nervous exhaustion, having lost thirteen pounds in a month. Although Lowell could at times seem too self-centered to heed his wife's ailments, in August he wrote his mother to ask for money to get Jean "thoroughly diagnosed":

> Jean has been having these fevers on and off for three years. No one has been able to cure her or tell her what the matter is. I worry about this night and day. . . . I don't [know] how I can overemphasi[z]e the importance to us of Jean's recovery. Our whole lives depend on it.

Stafford may have had a minor nervous breakdown in July — or so she claimed, at least, to Peter and Eleanor Taylor. She often exaggerated her mental disarray to humorous effect in her letters; after suffering a collapse of some sort at Yaddo, however, she seemed to be genuinely mortified. Despite such tribulations, by the beginning of September she had finished the revision of her novel.

The Monteagle idyll had come to an end with Tate's acceptance of the post of Consultant in Poetry to the Library of Congress. Lowell, meanwhile, was scheduled for induction, just as his friends had warned, on September 8. During the previous year the two poets had engaged in long discussions about the war. Even though he was forty-two, Tate was beset by what his biographer calls "war jitters" and feared that he was about to be drafted. In his mind, one of the greatest horrors of the conflict was the Allies' destruction of European culture.

The evolution of Lowell's own views on war was a curious one. His father had spent most of his career in the navy, and as a child Lowell had listened with rapt fascination whenever he got together with old Annapolis classmates to rehash legendary sea battles. In 1937, during the Spanish civil war, Lowell had sided with Franco; in the face of the vehement Loyalist sympathies of Frank Parker, however, he had sneered, " 'Well, you know, you can't tell, they're both scum. A plague on both their houses.' " In 1940 Lowell had written his grandmother, "If war comes and they want me, I'll gladly go. . . . " In 1942 he had attempted to enlist in the navy and the army but had been turned down by both.

As September 8, 1943, approached, Lowell wrestled with his conscience. The result was a remarkable "Declaration of Personal Responsibility," which he sent to President Roosevelt on September 7. Lowell addressed the President almost as a personal acquaintance: "I very much regret that I must refuse the opportunity you offer me in your communication of August 6, 1943, for service in the Armed Forces."

The gist of Lowell's opposition to the war was none of the traditional bases of conscientious objection — not a refusal to take human life, nor a Christian belief that war was evil. Instead, Lowell told the President that the latter's insistence on unconditional surrender would mean "the permanent destruction of Germany and Japan." (Here Tate's convictions may have cast a shadow.) But the real folly of American policy, wrote Lowell, was that "it will leave China and Europe, the two natural power centers of the future, to the mercy of the USSR, a totalitarian tyranny committed to world revolution and total global domination through propaganda and violence."

To Lowell's friends, his stance seemed at best bizarre. Peter Taylor had joined the army despite his pacifist inclinations; Blair Clark served in Britanny during the Allied invasion of France; Frank Parker was captured in Europe and held in a German prison camp. As Parker says, reflecting on Lowell's manifesto, "What we didn't get over, what I had great difficulty with, was — I approve of conscientious objectors, but someone who objects to the war because he thinks Russia is the enemy and not Germany in 1943, to me it seemed much too far out."

Lowell's action was deeply quixotic. As the results of his attempts to enlist indicate, if he had simply gone to his induction hearing on September 8, he would almost surely have been classified 4-F for his bad eyesight. Nor was he content to protest privately; he and Stafford prepared 110 copies of his declaration and sent them to friends, relatives, and press bureaus. The newspapers picked up the story, making much of Lowell's Boston Brahmin lineage.

In October Lowell was arraigned in district court in New York. He claimed to Judge Samuel Mandelbaum that he was not a conscientious objector; rather, his "conscience revolted at the bombing of whole cities and nations." The judge begged him to reconsider, saying, "You are one of a distinguished family and this will mar your family traditions." Lowell stuck to his guns; the judge sentenced him to a year and a day in a federal prison, the legal minimum (many other COs were sentenced to three years).

Lowell spent a few days in New York's West Street Jail, then served five months in the federal penitentiary at Danbury, Connecticut. Of this period of enforced separation, Stafford said to her friend Eileen Simpson three years later, " 'You won't believe this, but Cal is crazy. That made it easier for him.' "

Stafford rented an apartment on Stuyvesant Square in New York City. While her husband was doing time, she struggled to make ends meet. She was receiving the hundred dollars a month due Lowell from his trust fund, half of which went for rent. Charlotte Lowell treated her daughter-in-law almost as if she were to blame for "Bobby's" predicament. On October 31 she sent Stafford a nagging letter ordering her to find and read a recent book on the legal rights of conscientious objectors, so that the Lowell family might decide whether or not to "employ" its author. The letter ends querulously: "But we cannot afford to make any more mistakes. If we had only known how Bobby felt before he sent that declaration all of this trouble could have been avoided."

Ten days later Charlotte sent Jean an even more condescending letter. The phrasing of its exhortations helps to make it clear why Stafford thought of this meddling woman as "Charlotte Hideous."

I am glad to hear you say that you can, and are willing to support yourself while Bobby is in prison. I have just heard of a woman whoes husband was recently sent to prison for 3 years, after first losing her entire fortune. Although this woman, having always had a great deal of money of her own, was completely untrained to work, she obtained a job in New York, suported herself, and her children, for 3 years, and when her husband was released from prison, she had managed to save quite a sum of money with which to help him to get started; Such conduct is certainly both admirable and heroic. The kind of woman I should try to be were I in your place.

We think that Bobby has been extremely generous in wishing you to have all of the income from his trust fund while he is in prison. this is all the money that he has in the world, and he will be completely penniless when he is released from prison, if you care to impose upon his generosity.

I hope, Jean, for your own sake, as well as for Bobby's that you will see in the present situation an opportunity for, courage, selfdevelopment, and integrity of purpose. [Spelling and punctuation as in original.]

Stafford made trips to Danbury to see her husband as often as she was permitted, which was never more than twice a month. The visits, at least one of which was conducted over a telephone, with a pane of glass between the two of them, deeply depressed her. Yet Lowell's absence made her care more about him. In November she wrote the Taylors, "He is the most attractive and lovable man I know. . . . And I cannot tell you how glad I am that I am married to him and how sick down to my bones it makes me that he isn't in this room and won't be for ages."

At a cocktail party hosted by Philip Rahv of the *Partisan Review,* Stafford suffered an acute humiliation. The philosopher Sidney Hook came up to her and said, " 'Your husband is a heretic. He cannot be a conscientious objector and a Catholic for he is going against the dictates of the Pope.' " Hook's wife persisted throughout the evening in baiting her, until Jean at last burst into tears. "Mrs. Hook gave me a handkerchief, but everyone else sort of turned away in horror."

During the fall and winter Stafford tried to control her drinking, going on the wagon for as long as three weeks at a stretch.

In December she saw Robert and Bunny Hightower, just after his return from his ordeal in China. During a couple of evenings the three spent together, Jean drank prodigious quantities of rum and Coke; it was the relatively abstemious Bunny who passed out cold.

Over the course of the year, in addition to revising her novel, Stafford had finished three good short stories, which appeared in 1944 in *Harper's Bazaar,* the *Kenyon Review,* and *Partisan Review*. They were her first published stories since the cameo "And Lots of Solid Color," which *American Prefaces* had brought out in 1939.

At the end of October Lambert Davis reported to his colleagues (and to Stafford) on her revised novel. While observing that Yaddo had not been "a happy working arrangement" for the young writer, he was pleased to find that "JL [Jean Lowell] has wrought wonders with the manuscript since the first draft was returned to her in April." Nearly all of the editors' previous complaints had been answered. Yet there were still problems: the ending seemed melodramatic, and there remained sentences "that don't hold together grammatically. Even more important, there are sentences which by their over-elaboration give the reader the effect of pretentiousness."

Davis asked Stafford to make one more revision, toning down the ending, simplifying the style, and perhaps weeding out discursive passages. Harcourt, Brace sweetened the pill with a check for three hundred dollars and gave her a new deadline of January 1944. Stafford was bored with her own book by now, yet she toiled away, tailoring her changes in accordance with Davis's suggestions and cutting some fifty thousand words from the text. At last she sent the manuscript back to Harcourt, Brace, and this time the editors were entirely satisfied with it.

On March 15 Lowell was paroled from Danbury. More than one of his fellow COs thought he was being treated with extreme leniency because he was a Lowell. Upon his release from prison he was assigned to mop floors in the nurses' dormitory of a hospital in Bridgeport, Connecticut. Stafford searched the coast for a nearby residence, settling on a house on Long Island Sound, in the town of Black Rock (the locale announced in the titles of Lowell's poems "Colloquy in Black Rock" and "Christmas in Black Rock"). The house was "large, shapeless and built of yellow stone"; although it faced an inlet, it was downwind both from a mud flat that reeked at low tide and from an equally smelly town dump.

Five months in prison had done nothing to dampen Lowell's Catholic ardor; Stafford suspected that he had been quite content in "the pleasurable monasticism of the penitentiary." Now he talked of becoming a soapbox preacher for the Catholic Evidence Guild, somewhat along the lines of his former boss Frank Sheed. Unlike Sheed, however, Lowell was serenely indifferent to the need of making a living; God would take care of them, he told his dubious wife.

Stafford herself felt ambivalent about the Church. Perhaps in a conscious effort to overcome that ambivalence, in June she went with Lowell to a weekend retreat at a Benedictine monastery. "I have never had a more exciting experience than listening to conventual mass," she wrote the agnostic Hightower.

The reunited couple committed to paper their joint fantasy of the Wuberts. It is hard to tell whether they had hopes of publishing this miscellany or whether it was a mere in-joke to be shared with Peter Taylor and a few other conspirators. Stafford began a pseudoscholarly history of the beasts, who had now been in existence for three and a half years. "Thirty two berts and their friends now live with us in Connecticut," she wrote. The Wuberts were immortal, as were their visitors, a pair of large black pregnant male cats called Filth and Fabbage. "A male and a female [Wubert] always travel together, the female carrying an enema bag which is used at intervals by both berts during the day." There were True Wus and corrupt Wus. One winter in New York Bigless Bert (a nickname for Jean) became a Catholic. The unfinished chapter devoted to this development is called "New York: The Conbert."

Over the previous several years Lowell and Stafford had spent a good deal of time visiting his parents in Boston. Charlotte Lowell's condescension toward Jean was alleviated not a whit by the latter's looming success as a writer; after *Boston Adventure* came out, in fact, Stafford felt "more thoroughly, more icily, more deeply disliked than ever" at 170 Marlborough Street — "though it is generally admitted that it's a damned good thing Bobby married someone who makes money writing."

Later, after his mother's death, Lowell insisted that her Bostonian hauteur really sprang from insecurity:

She did not have the self-assurance for wide human experience; she needed to feel liked, admired, surrounded by the approved and familiar. Her haughtiness and chilliness came from apprehension. She would start talking like a *grande dame* and then stand back rigid and faltering, as if she feared being crushed by her own massively intimidating offensive.

But there was more to Charlotte's dismissal of Jean than this. At its core was a refusal to give up her only child to another woman, a tendency that would persist even after Lowell had divorced Stafford and remarried. In 1950, for instance, she would write to her thirty-three-year-old son, "We feel very flat and lonely now that you have left us and it makes me sad to pass your little room and see it so empty." The only spouse she approved of was someone's "dear little wife" or "sweet little wife"; as far as Charlotte was concerned, this woman had best confine her ambitions to the home.

It would not be exaggerating to say that Stafford hated Mrs. Lowell, or that she dreaded the Boston visits. Yet just as she had taken notes in her parents' home in Oregon, so at the Lowell family gatherings Stafford collected sharp-edged impressions of the inner workings of Boston society. These gleanings had laid the foundation for the second half of *Boston Adventure*.

Despite his own rebellious instincts, Lowell was never long parted from his parents; they had visited him in Danbury, and he had earlier made regular trips home from as far away as Louisiana. Lowell never met any member of Stafford's family, however, nor is there any indication that he offered to. According to Blair Clark, this was more Stafford's doing than Lowell's. "Jean always talked in the most negative ways about her family," he says. Lowell, Clark insists, was not the snob his mother was, and would have been interested in Jean's family. That he never met her parents, sisters, or brother was due to "some hang-up of hers."

With Allen Tate's help, Lowell had arranged for publication of his book *Land of Unlikeness* by the tiny Cummington Press in western Massachusetts, which produced hand-set editions. Because of Lowell's stint in Danbury and his habit of rewriting his poems even when they were in galley proofs, the book was delayed a full year. It finally appeared on September 18, 1944 —

three days before the publication of *Boston Adventure*. Stafford told Paul and Dorothy Thompson, "I can't tell you how glad I am his book came out first."

Having made rigorous demands of Stafford in order to shape *Boston Adventure* into the best possible book, the staff of Harcourt, Brace now put its finest efforts into promoting it. As Houghton Mifflin had, the New York publisher saw the potential for a best-seller. Lambert Davis had sent Stafford further infusions of cash — a hundred dollars in January, three hundred more in March, another five hundred in August, and five hundred a week after publication — so that she received $2,300 all told, or $1,800 more than her contract called for. (This generosity seems to have encouraged what would become Stafford's lifelong habit of borrowing heavily against future royalties.)

The title of the novel, which Stafford did not invent and never really liked, turned out to be a canny choice. Lambert Davis finally decided to let the author's name appear on the cover as "Jean Stafford." Several magazines fought over the right to excerpt the novel, with *Harper's Bazaar* and *Partisan Review* prevailing. A thousand sets of bound galleys were sent out to reviewers. Rave blurbs were extracted from Allen Tate, Philip Rahv, Louis Bromfield, Christopher Morley, and Howard Mumford Jones. The editor Donald Friede aggressively peddled the book to "the audible media." A remarkably large first printing of twenty-two thousand copies was run off. In June a Harcourt, Brace editor wrote Stafford, "There is a constantly growing excitement about your book, not only here but elsewhere and I am afraid if you don't look out you are going to be famous." A month before publication, the Book League selected *Boston Adventure* for its members, earning Stafford a quick extra six thousand dollars and "the satisfaction of 200,000 readers."

For almost a decade Stafford had fantasized about the kind of success she now stood on the brink of. Yet as the book's publication date neared, she reacted with something like gloom. Her mail was full of letters from old acquaintances who had been moved to write by the advance reviews and publicity. Stafford cringed at these well-wishers as if they were assaulting her. She ordered Harcourt, Brace not to give out her address. Whether or not in jest, she wrote Hightower that on September 21, the date when *Boston Adventure* would be officially launched, she planned to be in a convent on Long Island. She added, "I don't, as I say, want to be around when the book comes out."

This was no coy show of false modesty. Stafford knew she had better books in her than *Boston Adventure*. It is to her lasting credit that she sensed that the fanfares suddenly blaring from all sides had no more to do with her real merit as a writer than had her failure to publish a novel before 1944. Indeed she went so far as to attribute all the fuss to a historical accident: "The success of this book is both ludicrous and disgusting. It would never, never have happened at any other point in the history of publishing, but books, all books, are selling like mad and Harcourt Brace, of course, have spent a terrific pile on me."

At two hundred thousand words, *Boston Adventure* is by far the longest piece of writing Stafford ever accomplished. In many respects it is also the most ambitious fiction she ever attempted. In 1944 the novel was an anachronism — deliberately old-fashioned in both style and plot, a throwback to the leisurely Victorian novels of education that Stafford had been reading since adolescence.

The story is easily summarized. Book One, called "Hotel Barstow," introduces Sonie Marburg, the pauper daughter of a German shoemaker and a Russian chambermaid, who grows up in the North Shore, Massachusetts, village of Chichester (based on Nahant). Sonie works summers at the Hotel Barstow, where she eavesdrops on the conversations of Boston dowagers and fantasizes about the life of the rich and wellborn on Beacon Hill, which she can see across the water from the hotel, topped by the gold dome of the State House.

Sonie's father abandons his family and is never heard from again. Her epileptic brother dies after a seizure that leaves him helpless overnight in a snowstorm. Her mother goes crazy, eventually having to be institutionalized. Sonie is rescued from her predicament by Miss Lucy Pride, who has noticed the girl at the Barstow and has taken an interest in her. Miss Pride offers Sonie a job as her secretary, to take down the memoirs she has always planned to write.

In Book Two, called "Pinckney Street," Sonie is installed in Miss Pride's house on Louisburg Square, in the heart of Beacon Hill. Initially gauche and timid, she slowly blooms into the society she has always envied from afar. That envy is now focused on Hopestill Mather, Miss Pride's beautiful niece, who becomes engaged to Philip McAllister, a young doctor who has shown an interest in Sonie. Near the end of the book Sonie divines Hopestill's secret, which is that she must marry Philip because she is pregnant. By deliberately getting thrown from a horse, Hopestill induces a miscarriage, but the trauma costs her her life. The novel ends with Sonie pondering a future moment when Miss Pride's death will liberate her from her servitude on Pinckney Street.

In some respects it is astonishing that *Boston Adventure* became a best-seller. The book makes for slow reading: not only is Stafford's style Proustian, it is Jamesian as well, and some of its paragraphs are steeped in a stiff, awkward formality, which, coupled with that tendency toward imitation, betrays Stafford's apprentice standing. Particularly in Book Two, chapters go by in which very little happens, and pages are devoted to the banal conversation of stuffed shirts at parties. The novel is simply too long. Frank Morley's characterization in his note to Robert Giroux is wonderfully apt: the writing indeed "creeps on relentlessly." And an early stricture of Lambert Davis's is equally to the point: Sonie, he complained, is "a curiously passive creature."

On the other hand the novel does develop a powerful and complex landscape — that of Sonie's inner life. At its best, this interior richness, mirrored by the sometimes masterly opulence of Stafford's language, seizes the reader's imagination. *Boston Adventure* is the sort of novel that inspires diametrically opposite reactions. Some who start the book find themselves unable to plow through it; others are just as unable to put it down.

The tragedies of Sonie's childhood in Chichester are handled in a lugubrious but effective manner, more reminiscent of the great Russian novels than of the work of Proust or James. Perhaps the plainest clue to why *Boston Adventure* found so many readers is that in its second half it purports to unveil the most snobbish and exclusive social set in American life (a review in *Newsweek,* for example, hailed the exposé as "delicious").

Here, in a passage in which Sonie contemplates Hopestill's attraction, is a sample of the novel's prose:

Hopestill still lay before the fire in her strategic immobility. It was strategic because she appeared transfixed by an invisible pinion to the floor as if, like the possum or the dung-beetle playing dead, she would come to life at once upon my departure. Her eyes, apparently shut, took in each motion it was necessary for me to make to unpin the flowers from her shoulder and, glancing at the bits of shining eyeball, visible through her long, sparse auburn lashes and seeing once in that brief space of my perusal, the gold-flecked iris that enshrined the eye's soul, I knew myself to be in the presence of desperation so rarefied at this climax reared up by the signal at the outer door that it resembled lethargy. And simultaneously, I knew that no one else would see what I had seen and that she would go scot-free.

Stafford had bragged to Hightower that *Boston Adventure* was the first nonautobiographical work she had written. In a literal sense this claim may be true, but in another sense the novel has a strong psychologically autobiographical bent. In Sonie's loss of her father and brother and in Mrs. Marburg's decline into madness, Stafford dramatizes the alienation she herself felt as a child and as an adolescent. There seems to be an element even of wishful self-orphaning: only by losing her family can Sonie redefine herself in a headier milieu. In the short stories Stafford wrote throughout the 1940s and 1950s, orphaned or half-orphaned protagonists (as she recognized) abound.

Hopestill Mather, of course, conjures up Lucy Cooke, and Stafford explicitly admitted that Lucy had been her model. Furthermore, Sonie's transplantation from country poverty and provincialism to the pinnacle of Beacon Hill society — which in strictly realistic terms defies plausibility — goes to the heart of what may be the central concern of all of Stafford's fiction. This is an exploration of what happens to the "hick" who, by dint of sheer intellectual ambition, invades the glamorous cosmopolitan elite, only to discover her contempt for the artifice and hypocrisy upon which the world she has always hungered for is necessarily built. This may indeed have been the pivotal tension of Stafford's own life. It lay behind her pride in being a "Barbarian" at CU, even as she desperately envied the Pi Phis. It is the same tension that she inflicted upon herself by marrying Robert Lowell, who squired her into parlors full of Charlotte Lowells, those pitiable snobs whom Stafford could not pity because her own yearning for social ease was so acute.

The crucial interpretive question about *Boston Adventure,* then,

is to what extent its second half ("Pinckney Street") aims at satire. It was widely read as such. The *Newsweek* reviewer wrote,
"The irony is not vicious, but it has its moments of devastation
and of high wit." A defensive *Boston Globe* critic repudiated the
novel's accuracy, sneering at the book as a "highly stylized and
romanticized literary adventure." In a sense the *Globe* reviewer
was right, for Stafford's Beacon Hill owes more to her imagination (and to her reading of Victorian and Edwardian novels) than
to firsthand observation. Moreover, at a distance of four decades
it becomes clear that *Boston Adventure* teeters between satire and
enthusiasm, just as Stafford herself did. A part of her was endlessly dazzled by what went on inside those drawing rooms on
Louisburg Square.

Three years later, for the *Junior Bazaar,* Stafford wrote a
shamelessly gushy piece called "Notes on Boston," in which she
reminisced about the very walks and teas that had given her her
"material" for the novel. In the article she rhapsodized about the
smell of her gardenia corsage as she walked up Beacon Hill on
Christmas Eve; about the carolers in Louisburg Square; about
slumming gaily in restaurants on the "wrong" side of the Hill;
about watching the Harvard oarsmen on the Charles and looking
down on the flower beds in the Public Garden from the roof of
the Ritz-Carlton. These effusions cannot be dismissed as a cyni-
cal journalistic sellout; the same ambivalence informs *Boston Adventure,* in which fools and dandies flaunt furniture and paintings
that Sonie Marburg — and Jean Stafford — would have given
anything to own.

The critical reception of *Boston Adventure* was mixed. *Newsweek* called the novel "richly imaginative" and "incisive"; *Time*
was cooler, complaining that the characters are "only technically
alive, and never have any particular depth." Francis Hackett in
the *New York Times* remarked, "Not only is Jean Stafford determined to write literature at any cost, but she is also determined
to give us tons of whipped cream on it." *The New Yorker* was
more generous: "A first novel which will probably invite plenty
of comparison with Proust, and which should stand up under it
amazingly well."

The general public had few reservations. By April 1945 the
book was in its fifth printing. In addition to the Book League's
selection of *Boston Adventure,* the Armed Service Editions had

printed a condensed version. These mass editions earned Stafford little money (three cents per copy from the Book League and half a penny from the ASE), but by May 1945 Harcourt, Brace had sold some 35,000 copies, the Book League 199,000, and the ASE another 144,000. The total sales of *Boston Adventure* thus approached four hundred thousand copies within the first seven months after its publication.

The only other novels published in 1944 that matched the success of Stafford's were Lillian Smith's *Strange Fruit,* about race relations in the South, and Kathleen Winsor's lusty Restoration saga, *Forever Amber.* Both, ironically, were banned in Boston — Smith's for its language, Winsor's for the "questionable morals" of its heroine. *Boston Adventure* outsold Charles Jackson's *The Lost Weekend,* John Hersey's *A Bell for Adano,* and all 6,814 other books — nonfiction as well as fiction — that came out in the United States that year.

Stafford was approached with contracts for play adaptations; she gave (and hated) live radio interviews; and *Life* magazine interviewed her. She was the runner-up to the historical novelist Elizabeth Goudge in an MGM novel contest that paid $125,000 to the winner. *Boston Adventure* made most of the critics' lists of the best books of 1944. *Mademoiselle* gave her a Merit Award as one of the ten outstanding women of the year — as she wrote Joe Chay, "Champagne flowed (at 11 in the morning) in the chic, whimsical offices."

By June 1945 Stafford had earned $20,698.27 from her first published book. She was not wealthy, but for the first time since she was six years old, she could bask in comparative luxury, freed from all immediate cares about money. And her editor's hunch of the previous summer had come true. Jean Stafford was famous.

XII

A Country Love Story

"IN MY FATHER'S OPENLY BIASED VIEW," wrote Wilfrid Sheed in 1979, "Jean made a great mistake in becoming a success before her husband did. Her first novel *Boston Adventure* was a best seller, while Lowell was still fighting his way up through the coteries; and, knowing Lowell's vanity (awesome) and his satanic verbal cleverness, I can imagine he made Jean pay for this a bit."

Lowell's *Land of Unlikeness* got fairly good reviews in *Accent, Poetry,* and *Partisan Review,* as well as a penetrating critique by R. P. Blackmur in the *Kenyon Review.* These notices amounted to a surprising éclat for a book published in an edition of 250 copies, but *Accent* and *Poetry* were indeed the coteries. When Stafford was drinking champagne in the *Mademoiselle* offices with Lauren Bacall (a fellow honoree), Lowell was better known as a draft dodger than as a poet.

In the fall of 1944 fate contrived to prevent Stafford from relishing her triumph. Only a few days after her publication date, she sprained her ankle so badly that she was bedridden, then restricted to crutches. She had incurred the injury, she wrote Joe Chay, "rushing to a train in New York last week after hunting for an 'essential' job for my husband which would not interfere with his principles."

The sprained ankle coincided with an arduous move to new living quarters. The Barn, as it was nicknamed, was a "wonderful house deep in the country" in Westport, Connecticut; the writers had "nine acres, five bedrooms, four bathrooms, two kittens and the handsomest pig-sty in Fairfield County." Just as she had done all the work of hunting for a new place to rent, so Jean took on almost all the labor involved in moving — "Cal has every blessed time managed to be inaccessible both at the packing and the unpacking." The house in Black Rock had to be vacated on September 20, the day before *Boston Adventure* appeared.

Then, in the first week of October, Stafford received a numbing letter from her father. Her brother, Dick, had been killed in a jeep accident in France on September 18. At least, John Stafford wrote, Dick's death had been instantaneous. Eight months earlier, with Carmen, his wife of about two years, Dick had visited Jean in Connecticut. Having joined the army, he was on his way to the European front. "It was astonishing to see him," Stafford wrote the Hightowers just after the visit. "He looks six years younger than I and has a real western accent. I got on very well with him and feel awfully bad that he will be going overseas soon." Jean had seen Dick once more in July, on his last furlough before he sailed for France.

Dick's death came in one of those many absurd military accidents that have nothing to do with combat. The 95th Division field artillery unit of which he was a member was hurrying to join Patton's Third Army; Dick was supervising the movement of a truck column when his jeep crashed.

As soon as she could move around on her sprained ankle, Jean traveled to Oregon to visit her grieving parents. Writing to her sister Mary Lee, she voiced a religious sentiment that sounds entirely sincere: "I am hoping that even though Dick wasn't a Catholic our dear friend Father Dougherty will say a requiem mass for him and I am writing to him today. I am so glad, in this terrible thing, to be a Catholic. And you must believe, as we have all got to believe, that he is just somewhere else. . . ."

Well before Dick's death, Jean had dedicated *Boston Adventure* to Frank Parker, who had been captured by the Germans and was feared dead. On his return to the States Parker discovered the dedication, to his amazement. "It was an honor I didn't deserve. I didn't know what to say. In fact, I didn't say anything to her until years later." Parker feels strongly that Stafford made the dedication to him "because she disapproved of Cal's conscientious objection, and because her brother was fighting in Europe. . . . She had a sort of bitter feeling that Cal should have been."

Her sister Marjorie remembers Jean's visit that fall to Oregon:

> Jean's image at that time was that of a modest teacher or perhaps a female member of the military. . . . Everything about her appearance was somber. Her two-piece suit and her coat were navy blue, I believe she wore a navy beret over her golden locks and her purse was a sober navy blue reticule with no nonsense about it. She rose early every morning to attend the first mass of the day. . . . Her evenings were spent in the company of Mary Lee and me and bottles of fortified wine from the local Piggly Wiggly store.

Jean found her parents "old and broken and [I] felt extremely tender towards them, a revelation that I regret has come too late." Dick's death had intensified John Stafford's bitterness. For the rest of his life he cursed Roosevelt for involving the United States in the war. As soon as the fighting was over he dropped the carpentry job he had been forced to take in the Portland shipyards. For several years he had been writing treatises on what he called his "hell ray" — a kind of magical device for disposing of one's enemies. Immediately after the atomic bomb was dropped on Hiroshima and Nagasaki, Jean heard from her father. "He is probably one of the very few people in the world who greeted it with absolutely unmixed enthusiasm, says that 'this is my long-cherished dream of a hell ray come to life . . . ,' " she wrote Robert Hightower.

Lowell's parole stint mopping floors in Bridgeport had not freed him from his military obligation. He could still be inducted, and if he again refused to serve, he could be sentenced to an even longer imprisonment. To forestall this possibility, Lowell applied to the army medical corps in June 1944. Eventually he was reclassified in "limited service which is really the equivalent of 4-F save in the case of a great catastrophe like the bombing of New York." In a desultory fashion he poked about (or had his wife poke about) for job possibilities; at one point, thinking that he might like to teach classics at St. John's College in Annapolis, he entreated Stafford to make a trip by herself to Maryland to scout for a house. In the end Lowell took no job; instead, as Stafford complained to Hightower, he worked on his poetry while "becoming a Tory on my money."

From the beginning of October on, Stafford was convinced that her "nerves" were "bad." Albert Erskine, whom Lowell and Stafford had met in Baton Rouge, moved into the cavernous "Barn" in Westport with his wife. "The house is so big that there's plenty of space for everyone," wrote Stafford. "It's a comfortable place, a little too much like a men's club to be altogether attractive."

For Christmas Stafford and Lowell invited a number of guests to polish off the fourteen-pound turkey that Mary Lee and Harry had sent from Hayden. The feast seemed to Stafford a failure: "There were undercurrents that ruined all the season's joy, and all the drinking was too steady and determined. And as a result we couldn't face New Year's. . . ." It may be an indication of the difficulty Lowell and Stafford had in living together that they chose so often to share their home with others — with Peter Taylor in Baton Rouge; with Allen Tate and Caroline Gordon in Monteagle; with the Erskines in Westport. Since the first months of her marriage Stafford had complained about a lack of solitude. "I think," she wrote Joe Chay just after Christmas 1944, "I shall only be happy in isolation much more complete than this." Yet not long before, she had begged Chay to visit, claiming, "I truly mean this: we like nothing better than guests who come early in the fall and stay until late in the spring."

In February Stafford started teaching a course in short-story writing at Queens College. Every Tuesday afternoon she commuted tediously from Westport in to Grand Central Station and then back out to Queens by subway and bus, reversing the trip after her class. She got no more pleasure out of teaching in 1945 than she had in 1937. Her fourteen students were "inert"; she taught "extremely badly."

All through the spring and summer of 1945, acclamations came Stafford's way. There was talk of a Broadway play based on *Boston Adventure,* with Judith Anderson playing Miss Pride. An English edition was in the works, and Harcourt, Brace was negotiating for French and Dutch translation rights. Despite Stafford's having borrowed against her royalties, the money continued to roll in. In April she won a Guggenheim grant worth two thousand dollars and an award from the American Academy of Arts and Letters that paid her another thousand. In the *Saturday Review of Literature*'s annual Pulitzer Prize poll, Stafford's novel tied with John Hersey's *A Bell for Adano* for first place. (In the end, Hersey's book won the Pulitzer.)

None of this seems to have done much to cheer Stafford. Teaching at Queens College became an ordeal for her. Again she tried to quit drinking, which "makes New York even more difficult. But if I weren't on the wagon I'd be worse off because I have filthy nerves." As she would for the rest of her life, in times of unhappiness Stafford now became obsessed with cleaning the house: "The place is so big," she wrote Mary Lee, "and has so many crannies and is so foully dirty. . . . [I] propose to spend the entire week scrubbing." By May she was fed up with Westport; the town, she had decided, was "fashionable, vulgar, anti-semitic, expensive, second-rate, bourgeois, politically naive. . . ."

Boston Adventure may have come out under the name Jean Stafford, but the woman who had written it continued to head her return address "Mrs. Robert T. S. Lowell." She had applied for the Guggenheim as Mrs. Jean Stafford Lowell, and the year before, she had gone so far as to publish her story "The Lippia Lawn" in the *Kenyon Review* as the work of one "Phoebe Lowell." There was plenty of precedent in 1944 for a married woman writer's retaining her maiden nom de plume: Jean's older friend Caroline Gordon had never succumbed to being cast as Mrs. Allen Tate. For all Stafford's independence of spirit, she appears to have had a hard time denying her marital fealty in a byline.

Most writers would have been pleased, in the summer of 1945, with the fruits of Stafford's last twelve months, but her own judgment was, "I have largely wasted the year and am ashamed of myself." She had been struggling to get started on a new novel. In February she confided to Joe Chay, "My new [book] is proceeding at a snail's pace and I'm not yet certain whether I want to write it at all: I'm sick of the way I write." Such inauspicious glimmerings were, however, the heralds of Stafford's finest novel, *The Mountain Lion*.

It is not surprising that the writing came painfully and slowly, for Stafford was in the throes of the most important artistic advance of her career. She was indeed "sick of the way I write." After the middle of 1945 the stylized, old-fashioned, wan-humored

prose of *Boston Adventure* was banished for good. In its place came
a supple, lively style, full of concrete diction and startling colloquial juxtapositions, in its own way as well wrought syntacti-
cally as the earlier Proustian cadences but with all the labor of
the craft disguised.

Anxious to gratify Stafford's every whim, her editors at Harcourt, Brace suggested publishing a collection of her short stories. As *The Mountain Lion* began to take shape at the length of a
novella (in terms of saleability, a publisher's nightmare), there
was talk of bringing it out as the anchor piece in the story collection.

At the beginning of May 1945 the Barn was sold by its own-
ers, and Stafford and Lowell were given two months to vacate.
It had long been Stafford's fantasy to own a house of her own,
and she and Lowell had mused about moving far away from both
Boston and New York. Westport had not been nearly so "deep
in the country" as they had hoped. The dream of a refuge in the
wilderness, where the only obligation was to write, became a
practical plan, with the Maine seacoast as its locale.

In early summer Stafford and Lowell traveled all the way to
Eastport, on the New Brunswick border, and started working
their way down the coast. From a "horrid little cottage" that
they rented in Boothbay Harbor, they scouted for a homestead.
In August Stafford found what at once seemed to be the perfect
place. It was an 1820 house — "a real one, not a summer cottage" — in the tiny town of Damariscotta Mills, some fifteen
miles inland from Boothbay Harbor. She bought it outright. The
white clapboard house with green shutters had three bedrooms,
a dining room as well as a living room, an upstairs study, a ga-
bled attic, and a barn. It stood on three acres of land, surrounded
by elms and oaks, above the shore of the fourteen-mile-long Damariscotta Lake. There were plumbing and electricity but no
central heating — just four fireplaces, only one of which worked
at first. Most important, as Jean wrote Hightower, "We are within
a brief walk of the oldest Catholic church north of southern
Maryland."

The writers moved in at the end of August and, under Stafford's direction, immediately put a platoon of local craftsmen to
work sprucing the place up. The latter painted the walls and
woodwork, laid tile, assembled a stove, made bookcases, put in

an oil burner, tested the well, cleaned the chimneys, and puttied the windows. Lowell was less enthusiastic than his wife: "Half-way through each house improvement, he always says, 'Don't you think it would be better if we left it the way it is.' "

Since college Stafford had moved from one rented apartment or house to the next; even the home of her adolescence had been a boardinghouse. To possess her own dwelling — and to reno-vate and decorate it as she pleased — was to fulfill a deep-seated wish. "The house is too wonderful to be believed . . . ," she wrote Peter Taylor. "I have never been so happy anywhere in my life."

The couple's plan was to stay in Damariscotta Mills only until mid-October, when they would leave for Tennessee. They would live there until February, then move to Cambridge and stay with Delmore Schwartz, who would try to wangle a teaching job at Harvard for Lowell. During the winter the craftsmen would con-tinue their work on the house in Maine. Somewhat grandly, Stafford envisioned having two places to live, one in Cambridge and one in Damariscotta Mills, until they could move perma-nently to Maine — "that will be some years hence, I imagine, since we will be awhile getting used to the isolation."

As it turned out, however, Stafford and Lowell never did get to Tennessee. They stayed on in Maine into January and, with the exception of occasional trips to Boston and New York, lived for five months in a far greater solitude than either had ever be-fore attempted.

The site of Damariscotta Mills has an ancient magnificence. The town overlooks the Damariscotta River, which is actually a tidal estuary that meanders for sixteen miles from its head in Great Salt Bay down to its ocean mouth, west of Pemaquid Point. Be-hind the town, dammed by a barrier of granite bedrock, stretches the island-spangled lake, whose surface lies fifty feet above sea level. The lake's outlet stream, around which the town is clus-tered, is a major alewife run.

The Indians knew this as a place of limitless plenty. White set-tlers came in 1638; by 1750 Damariscotta Mills was a wealthy village, and in the early nineteenth century twenty-nine different shipyards lined the shores of Great Salt Bay and the Upper Da-mariscotta River. Entrepreneurs dammed the stream that flows out of the lake, turning the waterpower loose in half a dozen mills. The tall evergreens to the north were felled, rafted down the lake, sawed into boards in the mills, and shipped to Europe. There were paddle-wheel steamers for tourists who wanted to putter from cove to cove on the lake, and the town boasted a posh hotel.

By the time Lowell and Stafford came to Damariscotta Mills, the village had reverted to its sleepiest state in centuries. The Rockland branch of the Maine Central railroad still delivered passengers to a tiny depot, and one or two mills still creaked away, but all twenty-nine of the shipyards were gone, along with the hotel and the paddle-wheelers. There was not even a café or a drugstore in town; the only business was a cluttered general store. On Saturday nights the picturesque old clapboard building that hung over the lakefront turned into a dance hall.

In her walks around the town Stafford quickly acquainted herself with its ingrown society. In the general store, "the men who sat by the stove and whittled had the countenances and the clothes and the politics of cracker-barrel philosophers, but I never heard one of them utter an epigram." She watched men fishing for smelt in the river; in the winter they huddled in tar-paper shacks and angled through holes in the ice. She gazed at the children who swam in the lake in September and skated on it three months later. Her neighbors invited her in for tea, curious and pleased to have a newcomer in their midst.

Her zeal for refurbishing the house became an obsession. "If we stayed here," she wrote the Hightowers in October, "I would never write another line and I am afraid it will be many years before I can trust myself to do anything here besides think up new expensive jobs for the carpenter." Her "nesting and neatening" got on Lowell's nerves; to escape, he went bird-watching.

For half an hour at a time Stafford would do nothing but stand at the windows of her beloved house and look out. In her haunting short story "A Country Love Story," she captures the snugness of her haven: "In the blue evenings they read at ease, hearing no sound but that of the night birds — the loons on the lake and the owls in the tops of the trees. When the days began to cool and shorten, a cricket came to bless their house, nightly singing behind the kitchen stove."

St. Patrick's was up the road, literally a three-minute walk away. An exquisite, small Federal-style church of red brick with white wooden trim, it had been built in 1808. The diminutive cemetery beside the church held the remains of the town's early Irish Catholic settlers. Stafford and Lowell invariably attended Mass at St. Patrick's. The priest, they learned, was an unhappy man: sentenced to this lonely outpost for some offense against his Church, he longed for the city, hated the world and his parishioners, and, rumor had it, had never unpacked his books in all his twelve years in Damariscotta Mills.

Stafford had a novelist's curiosity about her neighbors. Next door lived the aged Mrs. Cabot, with her daughter, an Anglican nun "who appears to have endless holidays from her convent." Mrs. Cabot wrote illegible notes that her daughter delivered and Jean puzzled over: "One of them is about eggs but the others so far remain entirely mysterious." Across the street was the house of Mrs. Booth, the widow of an Episcopal bishop who had left her penniless. She had six children, who were well educated and compulsively gregarious. Beside Stafford's house to the east stood an imposing Federal-style mansion named Kavanagh, after one of the town's early-nineteenth-century lumber barons. Stafford and Lowell often saw its reclusive inhabitant, a lineal descendant of James Kavanagh, rocking in a wicker chair on the front lawn, but they never met her.

The obligatory social visits came to weigh on Stafford's spirit. Lowell inevitably barricaded himself in the upstairs study and refused to deal with the neighbors, while Jean trudged off to teas alone. Her deft short story "Polite Conversation" chronicles these ordeals by boredom.

Nancy Booth, one of the six children of the bishop's widow, was a college student in 1945. The model for the girl who "gurgled like a stomach" in "Polite Conversation," she remembers Stafford sitting on the stool in her mother's kitchen, turning anecdotes about the townspeople into hilarious stories. Several times Stafford accused Mrs. Booth of deliberately misplacing her drink.

Even in the refuge of her own house Stafford was not safe from the neighborly Booths. As she later wrote,

> I remember (with rage) one morning hearing such a furious and lengthy knocking at my locked front door that I concluded someone had come to tell me my house was on fire. I opened the door to find a teen-aged lad from across the road, at home for the

summer holiday from St. Mark's[,] who said to me, "I knew you were at home because I heard your typewriter. May I come in and bother you for a while?"

In a claustrophobic space gerrymandered between the kitchen and the parlor, Stafford set up her own study. Directly above her desk was the underside of the staircase. She liked the location, however, because it gave her the view she wanted — out of as many windows as possible, "so that she could keep an eye on the comings and goings of her neighbors."

In spite of her preoccupation with linoleum and wallpaper, Stafford accomplished some extraordinary writing in Damariscotta Mills. She finished two short stories, one of them — "The Interior Castle," based on her car accident — being the earliest absolutely first-rate story to come from her pen. (Published in *Partisan Review,* it was later anthologized in five different collections, including *The Best American Short Stories, 1947.*) Throughout the fall she made good progress on *The Mountain Lion.* In some sense, Dick's death may have helped to reinvigorate her writing: in shaping the new novella, she had chosen to write directly from her own life again, and to investigate the intimate bond that had tied her to her brother in childhood.

On November 9, 1945, Stafford sat before her typewriter in the grips of an old passion. It was the tenth anniversary of Lucy Cooke's suicide. In a mood that mixed curiosity and loathing, she wrote a one-page note to herself, outlining her idea for a novel based on the episode. It was at this time that Stafford claimed as her motive the "desire to defecate this memory from my spirit." The outline became the germ of her last and most serious attempt to deal with Lucy, the three-and-a-half-year effort that produced the unfinished novel "In the Snowfall."

By December her editors at Harcourt, Brace had read a draft of *The Mountain Lion.* Their enthusiasm for it was so great that they decided to publish the story separately, as a short novel, instead of as the lead piece in a collection of stories. "It shows you in better control of your imagery," Lambert Davis wrote Stafford, "less inclined towards some of those baroque effects we talked about in connection with the first book." On January 17, 1946, Stafford signed a contract for *The Mountain Lion.* She got a two-thousand-dollar advance, payable in four installments, against a generous royalty rate of a straight 15 percent (instead of the usual graduated royalty schedule, which began at 10 percent and worked its way up to 15 percent only after a certain numbers of copies were sold). Her delivery date was April 1.

It is interesting to note that although Stafford was then in the midst of transforming her prose style and realigning her fictional sights, she seems never to have changed the ritual or the process by which she set about putting words on paper. Whenever she tried out a new pen or a new typewriter, or just wanted to get started anew, she wrote out the same incantation: "This is the day when no man living may 'scape away." (The line is from the fifteenth-century play *Everyman*, where it is spoken by Good Deeds — a role Stafford had played in a CU production.)

The surviving drafts of all of Stafford's work from the age of twenty-two until her death point to a remarkable and uniform practice. There are no longhand drafts. (It is possible that she wrote such drafts and then destroyed them, but this seems unlikely, since very few longhand worksheets of any kind have survived. Hightower thinks that at one time Stafford's diaries — which she apparently destroyed before she married Lowell — may have served such a purpose, however.) It seems probable, then, that in general Stafford composed directly on the typewriter.

More surprisingly, Stafford's rough copy almost never shows signs of any extensive revision. Most writers scratch out and scribble over wantonly, but when Stafford rejected a paragraph or even a sentence, she seems to have retyped the whole page from the top. Because she sometimes kept her variant sheets, we occasionally find as many as twenty discrete typed versions of the same page, some differing from others by only a word or a phrase. Her drafts are in this sense exceptionally "clean." It seems likely that just as in conversation Stafford "always planned her way from the beginning of a sentence to the end," so in her written prose all the work of constructing was done in her head.

The Maine winter came early by Stafford's standards. Having loved snow since childhood, she welcomed its advent and marveled at its artistry. The southern rooms of the house got so much warmth from the sun "that they were like solaria." At night,

We read ceaselessly and everything. There was a great deal of nocturnal industry in our house, but presently the racket did not interfere with our concentration and we seldom looked up from our books. The mice and the rats (nothing smaller could have set up such a commotion) worked tirelessly and monotonously in the walls — restoring and remodeling; sometimes there was a scuffle followed by a chase, and at other times someone seemed to be pouring acorns down a tinnily reverberating chute. Now and then there was a thin, terrified scream.

Things were not good between Lowell and Stafford. He had retreated far inside his fortress of poetry and Catholicism; for days on end he hardly communicated with his wife. She laid out cards for solitaire or watched the birds migrating south — "one of the many games she played with and against herself in order to diminish the oppressive knowledge of her solitude and, even more, the depletion of what had formerly been called her 'vitality.' " The sterile closeness of the town was intensified by the fact that Lowell and Stafford did not have a car. Stafford was drinking more and more heavily — no mean trick in Damariscotta Mills, for the nearest liquor store was in Bath, twenty miles away, and in order to stock up on rum she had to hire the sheriff to drive her there and back. On top of the drinking, she had begun to suffer seriously from insomnia.

To ease her loneliness, Stafford had bought a cat, which eventually gave birth to a litter of kittens. Lowell was indifferent to the pets, but cats had furnished one of the deepest pleasures in Stafford's life ever since her childhood. Her affection, mixed with unsentimental observation, emerges in a vignette of "Pretty Baby" and her newborn kittens in "An Influx of Poets":

> I went into the house and saw her carrying the runt of the litter, all black, across the carpet from the nest she had made for them behind the sofa to the basket beside the fireplace, where they properly belonged. The other three were there already, and I wondered if she had taken the runt last because she liked him least or because she feared his fat siblings would smother him. They were still blind and she was still proud, cossetting them with her milk and her bright, abrasive tongue and the constant purr into which, now and again, she interjected a little yelp of self-esteem.

Several friends came north to visit that fall, including Delmore Schwartz and Frank Parker, who was newly returned from his German imprisonment. In late November, when Lowell was away,

Caroline Gordon arrived in Damariscotta Mills. She and Allen Tate had been quarreling about an affair she suspected him of having, many of the details of which he had in fact confided to Lowell. The women's tête-à-tête degenerated into a duel. As Jean wrote her sister Mary Lee,

> Caroline all day long had been interrogating me about Allen and about the girl and she got out of me a great deal that I had never intended to tell her. At dinner she began abusing me and saying that I had been a busybody and that since I had told her these awful things, there was no hope of a reconciliation and before that there had been and that I had thereby ruined the lives of two of the most valuable artists the world has ever known. . . . She went on, screaming recriminations at me and suddenly she threw a glass of water in my face. I was on the point of telling her to leave my house forever, but I said nothing and then she said, "I'm going to break every goddamned thing in the goddamned house" and she began throwing everything she could lay her hands on — dishes, glasses, pitchers, bottles of mayonnaise, peanut butter, the sugar-bowl, a jar of maple syrup.

Stafford ran next door to Mrs. Cabot's house, and her daughter called the sheriff. Gordon exiled herself to Mrs. Booth's house, while Stafford stayed up all night, terrified of a further attack. The scene caused a scandal in the town. Stafford's old friendship with Gordon and Tate did not survive this rupture: Tate haughtily told Peter Taylor, " 'We don't call the sheriff on our friends,' " and seven years later Stafford still said of Tate, "He's a very bad man."

In December the temperature plunged below zero. Unused to the trials of extreme cold, Stafford and Lowell one morning "got up to find icicles hanging from all the bathroom taps and great tumors and hideous fractures in the pipes." For two weeks they had no plumbing, and their only water came from the well outside. The local plumber worked heroically, but by the end of January the writers had decided it was time to go to Cambridge and move in with Delmore Schwartz.

The prodigy of his generation, acclaimed alike for his prose, poetry, and criticism, Schwartz had been teaching at Harvard since 1940. At thirty-two, he was two years older than Stafford and four years Lowell's senior. Even then, however, he had entered

the long decline that would mark him as perhaps the most tragically self-destructive American writer of his time, the inspiration
for Saul Bellow's rueful novel *Humboldt's Gift*. Although he had
once been fond of saying "Jews don't drink," by 1946 Schwartz
had become an alcoholic. Three years earlier he had separated
from his wife, the critic Gertrude Buckman. While he could be
loyal and generous in the extreme to such friends as Lowell and
John Berryman, he could also nurse jealousies and grievances with
bitter dedication, and he was fated to lose many of his friends to
his own suspicion.

In December Schwartz had written Lowell inviting him and
Stafford to come "whenever you like and stay as long as you
like. The longer you stay, the longer I will like it." Apparently
the visit to Cambridge, besides allowing Schwartz to try to fi-
nagle a teaching job for Lowell, was a trial run at a semiperma-
nent living arrangement, a chance to see if the three writers could
make "a harmonious ménage together."

Stafford and Lowell arrived at Schwartz's apartment at 20 El-
lery Street on January 30. At first the trio got along splendidly.
Schwartz regularly made lunch, and Stafford fixed dinner and
scrubbed the bathtub in vain, while Lowell was in charge of
tending the furnace. "In mid-morning," Schwartz wrote Elizabeth Pollet, who later became his second wife, "the household
resembles either a literary movement or a school for typists. The
only unpleasantness is that Jean gets most of the mail."

Lowell and Schwartz sometimes stayed up all night, drinking
gin and waxing elegiac, establishing a poets' brotherhood that
Lowell later evoked in a famous poem:

> *We couldn't even keep the furnace lit!*
> *Even when we had disconnected it,*
> *the antiquated*
> *refrigerator gurgled mustard gas*
> *through your mustard-yellow house*
> . . . .
> *We drank and eyed*
> *the chicken-hearted shadows of the world.*
> *Underseas fellows, nobly mad,*
> *we talked away our friends. "Let Joyce and Freud,*
> *the Masters of Joy,*
> *be our guests here," you said.*

One evening the three writers traded reminiscences of their college days. Stafford began to talk about Lucy Cooke; it is possible that she had never told Lowell the details of her extraordinary story before. When she was finished, both poets "said that I must write it down, that it was obviously my next novel and that it was, so to speak, ready-made. I should write it, they said, just as I had told it to them." If Stafford had been wavering on the brink of starting work on "In the Snowfall," Lowell and Schwartz pushed her over the edge.

According to Schwartz's biographer, James Atlas, the ménage turned sour after Lowell invited Schwartz to his parents' house on Marlborough Street for dinner: "Delmore was intimidated by the servants, heirlooms, and a certain reserve on the part of the Lowells. The elder Lowell's attitude toward Delmore can be guessed from his habit of telling his literary son that he 'talked like a Jew.' " In "An Influx of Poets," Stafford has the Robert Lowell character say of the Delmore Schwartz character, " 'I would never have a Jew as a close friend.' "

When Frank Parker and his wife had visited Damariscotta Mills the previous fall, while Schwartz was in residence, Parker's wife had concluded that there was something romantic going on between Schwartz and Stafford. Worse, she had told Lowell as much, creating a general row. As Parker recalls, "Jean said to Cal, 'Why don't you put them [the Parkers] out the door at once?' Frankly, I don't think anything of the sort was happening. . . . Cal was furious."

Now, a few months later, Schwartz began to tease Lowell with hints that Stafford was interested in another man (presumably him). It did not take much goading to provoke Lowell to violence; at last he swung his fist at Schwartz, and Stafford had to break up the fight. Yet Lowell was also quick to make up; on March 26, just after Lowell and Stafford had left his apartment, Schwartz bragged to Elizabeth Pollet, "Both are so devoted to me now that I am ashamed." On subsequent trips, Lowell routinely stopped to see his friend when passing through Boston.

From Cambridge Lowell headed off to another Catholic retreat, this time among Trappist monks, where he observed a vow of silence. Stafford returned alone to Maine. With no one but a talkative carpenter to disturb her labors, she quickly finished the final draft of The Mountain Lion and sent it off to Harcourt, Brace. Robert Giroux, back from the navy, had become her editor once

again; delighted with the book, he cabled, "NEW ENDING TER-
RIFIC." Giroux had also signed Lowell to a contract for the book
of poetry that would become *Lord Weary's Castle*.

It is one of the eternal mysteries of art that superlative work
can be accomplished in the most vexing of circumstances. By the
spring of 1946 both Jean Stafford and her marriage were in trouble. She later claimed that she knew from May on that she was
"ill." For months before that, she was preoccupied with a "terror
of losing my mind." One night in Maine Lowell went to bed
early, leaving Stafford downstairs with her insomnia. She sat in
front of the fireplace, burning old letters, listening to a loon calling from the lake. "I knew," she wrote later, "that something
was coming, I could smell it like the air before a hurricane and I
thought, 'I can't take it.' "

An irreversible estrangement was creeping over the couple. In
"An Influx of Poets" the protagonist ruminates, "I had often
thought that when I was out of his sight I was literally out of his
mind, that he never imagined me as I might be in a train or a
strange hotel, as I always imagined him when he was away from
home." This rings true of Lowell, as does a complementary picture in "A Country Love Story." In that story, during a year in
Maine the husband withdraws more and more into his work.
"Finally, it seemed to her that love, the very center of their being,
was choked off, overgrown, invisible. . . . She felt the cold old
house somehow enveloping her as if it were their common enemy, maliciously bent on bringing them to disaster."

Stafford's drinking had become a truly serious problem. Blair
Clark remembers a winter visit to Damariscotta Mills: "Jean was
drinking like hell. They had a couple of quarrels while I was
there. . . . I really for the first time saw her as a drunk. She
was hardly drawing a sober breath. And clearly miserable. Cal
was wild, I thought." The tenor of their fights over Jean's drinking is captured in "An Influx of Poets":

> "What the bleeding hell?" I'd yell at him. "You drink as much as
> I do. You drink more!" and he'd reply, "A difference of upbring-
> ing, dear — no more than that. I learned to drink at home in the
> drawing room, so I know how. No fault of yours — just bad
> luck. You don't drink well, dear. Not well at all."

The accents of the husband's condescension do not really sound
like Lowell's, but there is no doubt that Lowell, armed with the

zeal of his Catholic conviction, could and did presume to dictate morality to others. At some point that year, having heard that one of his close friends was carrying on an extramarital affair, Lowell summoned him to Maine, harangued him about his behavior, and sent him home like a truant.

The rumor that Stafford was involved with Delmore Schwartz was almost certainly without basis. All of Lowell's closest friends report that Jean seemed completely uninterested in having affairs. "She always did strike me as sort of sexless," says Blair Clark. "She was a beautiful woman," adds Frank Parker; "Sometimes I thought she was unaware of her charms. When she comes down in her nightgown, this beautiful woman, and perches on your bed [as had happened in the New Orleans hotel room in 1940], you don't know what to think. . . . She had no interest, for example, in me as a man."

Lowell told a subsequent lover of his that Stafford was so bashful that she got dressed and undressed inside a closet: she would never take off her clothes in front of him. Even Lowell found it hard to square this modesty with the fact that Jean had posed nude for life-drawing classes in Boulder.

Many years later, according to Frank Parker, Lowell's second wife, Elizabeth Hardwick, told Parker

> something that I thought was very wise, about Jean: [that] Cal had a way of making his girlfriends his mother, and that Jean understood this from the start and fought it all the way. Elizabeth Hardwick gave Jean full marks for understanding and dealing with the problem. . . .
>
> I think that's it. It's a losing fight. He was making [Jean] into a mother and could therefore repudiate her — she didn't understand him, like his mother, and so on. . . . And he had to have someone else — whom at once he tried to make into his mother, as usual.

Their troubles of the spring climaxed in an event that is impossible to date precisely, and whose details remain shadowy. Stafford later described it to Blair Clark and Frank Parker; Lowell may never have told anyone about it. Parker's version is this:

> [Jean] said she was dreaming of this German lover, the one who was killed in Spain, and Cal was making love to her, and she repeated her German lover's name, and Cal in a perfect frenzy

tried to strangle her. . . . She woke, and was aware that she'd
been calling the name of her German lover, because Cal was telling her that that's what she was doing. And he was strangling
her. But he stopped. I said, "My god, Jean, weren't you afraid?"
She said, "Not really."

However private and potentially mortifying this terrible incident may have been, both Stafford and Lowell chose to write
about it. Jean's original working title for "A Country Love Story"
was "When the House Is Finished, Death Comes." In a fully
finished draft found among Stafford's papers, the wife, estranged
by her husband's self-absorption, begins to fantasize about an
imaginary lover. One night in her sleep she blurts out, " 'Oh, I
love you too!' " Her husband confronts her:

"Who? Who do you love?"
For a moment she was embarrassed for she did not know his
name and then the timbre of his voice re-echoed, assertively, and
she woke and saw her husband's dark head bending toward her,
his mouth like a knife to kill her with. "Who is it you love? Who
did you think I was?"
"You!" she cried, covering the lament of her disappointment
urgently. "I love you! I love you! Oh, believe me, James!"
"You won't tell me then?" He spoke quietly and looked very
solemnly into her eyes. "You were mad to do this to me, May.
You were insane to drive me this way." He knelt above her on
the bed and putting his hands upon her throat, he began dispas-
sionately to strangle her. He whispered, "You bitch, you bitch,
you bitch, to torture me. Who is he? Who did you take me for?"
At first she made no struggle at all and she was not afraid but
was only conscious of the blocking pain which was hindering her
from the relief of real madness. She slid her legs sideways out
of the bed and then she grasped his right wrist and dug her nails
into its flat surface and presently he let her go. He said, "It's not
worth it." And he lay back wearily as if he had finished a hard
assignment.

Whether to protect Lowell or because the real event seemed
too melodramatic for fiction (or for some other reason), Stafford
removed the strangling entirely from the version of "A Country
Love Story" that came out in *The New Yorker* in 1950. Lowell,

however, preserved the incident in his long poem *The Mills of the Kavanaughs,* published in 1951. A variant manuscript of *Mills* introduces into the strangling scene a sexual content that is absent from the published version, but which dovetails with Frank Parker's memory of what Stafford told him: the husband's assault follows what seems to be a thwarted act of rape.

In this morass of remembered account and fictional and poetic appropriation, it is impossible to discern the cold truth about what happened that night in Damariscotta Mills. Despite the absence of any real basis for his suspicions, Lowell had regularly exhibited a wild jealousy (toward, in turn, Blair Clark, Peter Taylor, and Delmore Schwartz) at the merest hint of another man's interest in Stafford. If in Maine she took a fantasy lover, or dreamed about one and spoke in her sleep, Lowell may well have been driven over the easily crossed line that separated him from physical violence.

The notion of Lowell trying to rape his wife in her sleep seems at odds with the sexless relationship that Stafford later claimed had obtained at least since 1941. Yet Peter Taylor, who visited them in the summer of 1946, remembers someone telling him that in Maine Lowell tried to inflict sex on Stafford against her will: "I knew that Cal wanted to have children, and that Jean didn't. Cal tried to force the issue."

In June the "influx of poets" to Damariscotta Mills began — a three-month parade of guests, many of whom stayed, at their hosts' insistence, far longer than they had originally planned. The visitors included Peter Taylor, Blair Clark and his wife, Frank Parker and his wife, Robert Hightower, Delmore Schwartz, R. P. Blackmur and his wife, John Berryman and Eileen Simpson (his wife), Richard Eberhart and a friend, Philip and Natalie Rahv, and Robert Giroux. Not all of the guests were "poets": there were also former neighbors from Westport, the couple's former landlord from Boothbay Harbor (with his wife and his wife's parents), and even Lowell's godfather.

The prospect of having a country house to share with friends had been a large part of Stafford's original joy in owning and refurbishing the place. By June both she and Lowell must have been hoping that the presence of others would dilute their caged antagonism. Still, Stafford was already dreading the guests. "In some ways," she wrote her sister Mary Lee just before the first

visitors arrived, "the problem is not terribly complex. I am suffering from years and years of accumulated fatigue, not only from
working hard but from spreading myself too thin and knowing
too many people. Being a writer and being married to a writer
is a back-breaking job and now my back is broken."

In the company of his writer friends Lowell expanded into
tireless soirées of talk and recitation; for him, staying up half the
night with his cronies, comparing favorite poems or gossiping
about Yeats and Eliot, was the very stuff of being geniuses together. Stafford's view, as she sardonically revived it in "An Influx of Poets," was something other:

> At night, after supper, they'd read from their own works until
> four o'clock in the morning, drinking Cuba Libres. They never
> listened to one another; they were preoccupied with waiting for
> their turn. And I'd have to stay up and clear out the living room
> after they went soddenly to bed — sodden but not too far gone
> to lose [retain?] their conceit. And then all day I'd cook and wash
> the dishes and chop the ice and weed the garden and type my
> husband's poems and quarrel with him.

Eileen Simpson has left a memorable portrait of Stafford as she
seemed that July.

> Had I not been told of the accident I would not have guessed that
> her face had been so badly damaged. Nine healing years [actually
> seven and a half] had passed since then. Besides, it was her eyes,
> rather than her nose, or the darns [from the stitches], that struck
> me. They seemed to be bathed in an excess of fluid, so that they
> looked permanently welled-up, giving the impression that she had
> been crying or might do so at any moment. It may have been
> this, as well as her expression in repose, that made her look sad.
> The sadness vanished as she talked, when, depending on what she
> was saying, she looked sly, shrewd, or mischievous, as she twisted
> her mouth and blew out her cheeks with suppressed glee at the
> wickedly funny things she said.

Lowell, who had stopped drinking, surprised Simpson with
his movie-actor good looks and his "appealing gawkiness" as he
loped up the stairs two at a time with his guests' suitcases in
hand. A weekend visit stretched into two weeks. Lowell and
Berryman compared "three greatest lines" from their favorite

John Stafford, classics major and future western hack writer. A portrait of Jean's father at nineteen, when he was a student at Amity College, Iowa. *(Courtesy Marjorie Pinkham.)*

John Stafford late in life, still trying to write his great book. *(Courtesy Marjorie Pinkham.)*

Ethel McKillop Stafford, Jean's mother: "Big, bountiful, bulbous, optimistic. . . . She was always offering food." *(Courtesy Marjorie Pinkham.)*

The "Big House" in Covina, California, where Jean Stafford was born in 1915. *(Courtesy Marjorie Pinkham.)*

Jean as a young girl, playing with the family cat, Budge, in the side yard in Covina. *(Courtesy Marjorie Pinkham.)*

The four Stafford children, with Jean, the youngest, in front. *Left to right, rear:* Marjorie, Mary Lee, Dick. *(Courtesy Marjorie Pinkham.)*

Dick and Jean on the family bicycle. More than fifty years later, Stafford kept this photo on her bulletin board, "and sometimes when my eye falls on it, I go rather funny in the head at the spectacle of such joy." *(Courtesy University of Colorado Special Collections.)*

Dick, Ethel, and Marjorie, camped beside the black Reo during the family's momentous journey from California to Colorado in 1921. *(Courtesy Marjorie Pinkham.)*

At about age twelve, Jean surprised her father in his basement "yarn factory" by paying him a visit dressed in his suit, complete with blackthorn walking stick. *(Photograph by John Stafford; Courtesy Marjorie Pinkham.)*

Jean's brother, Dick, an outdoorsman and forest ranger, and perhaps the only person she ever loved unequivocally. *(Courtesy Robert Frichtel.)*

Jean at sixteen, in Boulder, Colorado. *(Courtesy Marjorie Pinkham.)*

A studio portrait of Jean taken during her college years at the University of Colorado. *(Courtesy University of Colorado Special Collections.)*

Stafford shocked her classmates at the university by posing nude for life-drawing classes. This study was made by Howard Higman, who had dated Jean in high school. *(Photograph by Bill Warren; Courtesy Howard Higman.)*

Andrew and Lucy Cooke, the law-student couple in Boulder who introduced Stafford to the
bohemian life. *(Courtesy Andrew Cooke.)*

Stafford's 1936 passport photo, taken just before she departed
for Germany at the age of twenty-one. *(Courtesy University of
Colorado Special Collections and Oliver Jensen.)*

Soulmates: Stafford and Robert Hightower, perhaps in Paris, 1937. *(Courtesy University of Colorado Special Collections.)*

Peter Taylor, *left,* and Robert Lowell with Stafford in Louisiana, around 1940. When he saw this photograph again thirty years after it was taken, Taylor remarked, "Jean looks like the keeper of two nuts." *(Courtesy Blair Clark.)*

The house in Damariscotta Mills, Maine, that Stafford bought for Lowell and herself with her earnings from *Boston Adventure:* "*my* house, (my very own, my first and very own)." *(Photograph by the author.)*

Stafford and Lowell in Damariscotta Mills, 1946, estrangement written in their faces. *(By permission of the Houghton Library, Harvard University.)*

Stafford and Oliver Jensen, her second husband, on their honeymoon in
Ocho Rios, Jamaica, in 1950. *(Courtesy Oliver Jensen.)*

Stafford in Port-au-Prince, Haiti, where she and Jensen stopped
briefly on their way to Jamaica. *(Photograph by Oliver Jensen.)*

Jean, *left,* and Mary Lee in Connecticut in the early 1950s, on one of the few occasions when Jean allowed either of her sisters to visit her. According to a Westport friend, "Mary Lee was *far* from a bumpkin." *(Photograph by Oliver Jensen.)*

Next to a bust of the Venus de Milo in the Westport home she shared with Jensen. *(Photograph by Oliver Jensen.)*

Stafford with A. J. Liebling, her third husband, who "made her deliriously happy," in the backyard of their house in The Springs, East Hampton, Long Island. *(Photograph by Therese Mitchell; Courtesy University of Colorado Special Collections.)*

Stafford with Elephi, one of her favorite cats and the protagonist of her only children's book, around 1961. *(Photograph by Janet Malcolm.)*

With her needlepoint — a serious hobby and a handy distraction from writing. *(Photograph by Janet Malcolm.)*

Stafford in one of her many outrageous outfits during the East Hampton years. *(Courtesy University of Colorado Special Collections.)*

"No matter how boozed up she was, she always planned her way from the beginning of a sentence to the end." *(Courtesy University of Colorado Special Collections.)*

poems (a game of Lowell's), ranked themselves against coevals ranging from Dylan Thomas to Elizabeth Bishop, and talked about such mentors as Allen Tate and John Crowe Ransom.

Simpson noticed several telling details about Stafford's domestic habits. Each night before going to bed Jean set the table for breakfast — a habit, she confessed, left over from the days when she had helped her mother in their boardinghouse home. On her desk she kept not only Fowler's *Modern English Usage* and the Merck Manual, but also the Boston Social Register. On learning that Simpson had been an orphan, Stafford pumped her for particulars. As Simpson shrewdly deduced, "She had desperately wanted to be an orphan."

For Simpson and Berryman the serene summer days in Damariscotta Mills composed a halcyon vacation. In the afternoons they walked with Lowell to see the mills, or swam in the lake. A lifelong aquaphobia, however, kept Stafford from even going onto the lake in a boat. According to Simpson, "Jean, who knew the name of every tree, bush, flower and weed, ventured out infrequently, preferring to observe nature through the window."

Stafford could be wryly amusing about Lowell, lampooning his foibles in his presence:

Jean claimed that Cal was the world's champion reviser, sometimes with startling results. "A poem which had begun with the title, 'To Jean: On her Confirmation' . . ."

"Don't listen. She lies. She lies." Cal tried to shout her down.

". . . finished by being called, 'To a Whore at the Brooklyn Navy Yard.' "

But in her more private moments with the sympathetic Simpson, Stafford let the strain show. Lowell's self-righteous teetotalism was hard to bear. " 'I fell in love with Caligula and am living with Calvin. He's become a fanatic. During Lent he starved himself,' " Stafford told Simpson. She tried to make light of her drinking, excusing her frequent trips to Bath with the sheriff by saying, " 'It gives me the wimwams to be in a house that's bone dry.' " But she had started hiding a bottle of sherry behind the cookbooks in her kitchen as insurance against Lowell's efforts to control her habit, and she admitted that on visits to neighbors' houses for tea she sneaked nips from a flask she kept in an oversized pocketbook bought for that very purpose.

Simpson also became aware of Stafford's desperate insomnia. As the visit lengthened, Jean's "somber mood was growing more obvious every day." She wore the same outfit day in and day out — a pair of houndstooth-checked slacks and a baggy black sweater. Simpson was surprised that Stafford "disguis[ed] her model's figure as effectively as if she was wearing a habit. She let her ash-blond hair hang limp, or covered it with a pointed hat. . . . What vanity Jean had was for her house." Simpson and Berryman concluded that Jean and Cal "had been too much alone."

A splotchy snapshot taken that summer in Maine (photographer unknown) is a kind of accidental masterpiece: the impasse between Lowell and Stafford seems to cry out from its image. It looks as though the two of them are walking single-file through a field; the photographer, first in line, has turned around suddenly to shoot his candid photo. Both Lowell and Stafford squint into the sun; she averts her face, mouth twisted, as if begging the camera to leave her alone. A frown rumples her forehead; her hair is braided into severe columns. The overexposed white of her blouse burns out the dark background around it, giving her a ghostly unreality in the outdoors. Behind her, upright, handsome, fit, and frightening, the sleeves of his dark lumberjack shirt rolled up to his elbows, Lowell looms like a nemesis.

By August, in spite of their unflagging efforts to entertain their guests, Lowell and Stafford had come close to the end of their tether. Jean wrote Mary Lee,

> It is quite impossible to determine what we shall do. We know only that we cannot live together next winter, but whether we shall yet make permanent arrangements, I don't know. . . . I have been too long under to[o] beastly a strain and it has been hideous to conceal from all our visitors what is going on. . . . I feel conspired against and have reached the conclusion at last which I should have done long ago, that I *cannot make any plans* [emphasis Stafford's].

On almost the same day, Lowell uncharacteristically confided by mail to Peter Taylor,

> I don't care for confessions, but I suppose I must tell you that everything is chaos between us. Jean is driving like a cyclone and we both have had about all we can stand and more. Right now I

think I'll go to New York sometime in September. . . . Jean has a lot of plans, none of them too good, including going to Hollywood. Anyway, we have got to *leave each other alone* and the future to time [emphasis Lowell's].

One of the last guests of the summer was Gertrude Buckman, Delmore Schwartz's ex-wife and a friend of Stafford's since 1944. As Minnie Zumwalt, the "pretty, small, dark, *zaftig* girl," the "little minx" who is by turns a sharp-tongued literary critic and "adoring as a daft maiden when she was in the presence of a poet," Buckman serves as the villainess of "An Influx of Poets." In that trenchant but bitter story, Minnie arrives like a grand dame, landing on the lake in a Piper Cub float plane. Cora, the narrator, who has been away in Boston consulting a doctor about her headaches, returns to Maine to find her husband and Minnie "sitting in the garden in the perishing day like a Watteau summer idyll, already so advanced in their lore (infatuation acquires its history and literature in minutes) that they were beyond the need of language. . . ."

In fact Buckman did arrive in a float plane, but she was hardly accustomed to such pleasures. A friend had bought her the flight as an advance birthday present; it was the first time she had flown in any sort of airplane. It was Stafford, not Lowell, who had invited her to Damariscotta Mills. The women had first met when Lowell was in Danbury prison, shortly after Buckman's divorce from Schwartz. They had liked each other at once; Stafford had gotten Buckman a job condensing *Boston Adventure* for the Armed Services Edition.

Buckman had been aware even then of Stafford's drinking problem. In New York she had once run into her friend on her way to early Mass, "absolutely reeking of alcohol." On another occasion Buckman, Stafford, and Harold Shapiro had gone out to dinner, and Jean had gotten so drunk that the other two had had to help her home and up the stairs. "She was in such a state," recalls Buckman, "that Harold and I said, let's get whatever liquor is in the house and get it out of here. We looked around everywhere and took away what we found. I remember Jean cackling as we started to go, 'Ha, ha, I've got a bottle hidden where nobody can find it.' "

Stafford was indeed in Boston when Buckman arrived in

Damariscotta Mills. "Cal said, 'Her excuse was, she went to the dentist, but she's in love with Delmore, and she's probably seeing him.' It came as a new idea to me. I didn't know whether to believe it or not."

In Stafford's short story Minnie and Theron (Lowell's alter ego) take picnics out on the lake in order to get away from Cora, who meekly makes sandwiches for them. Minnie is portrayed as a giggly, baby-talking vixen who flirts with Theron in front of his wife: " 'But Cora doesn't know how I got here! I flew down from Castine in a *wee* plane, like a kite exactly. With such a sweet boy, and the plane is still on that *tiny* island. The moon will be full — it's summertime! Say that you want a picnic, sweetie!' "

If one had no other evidence to go on than "An Influx of Poets," it would be easy to conclude that Buckman and Lowell began an affair in Damariscotta Mills, right under Stafford's nose, and that the affair was the chief cause of the dissolution of their marriage. But according to Buckman, "We never so much as touched hands. We used to go to the market to get food, and we used to go out in the rowboat together, and once we brought home a lot of water lilies and put them in the bathtub, and the bathtub became full of little black insects." She insists that Lowell and she did not become lovers until months after he and Stafford had separated.

Yet a strong mutual attraction between the two of them did make itself manifest in Maine. As Buckman recalls,

> It was happening imperceptibly and rather frighteningly, because I had never felt that feeling toward anyone. At the same time, it was very evident that he was feeling the same thing. Whether it was two floundering souls seeking each other's sympathy, I don't know, because it was a very difficult situation, with thunder-clouds always hanging over one, because she stayed in the kitchen all through the night drinking, not sleeping. You couldn't talk to her. He in a way was sublimely removed from all that. One didn't feel that he felt very much for her. . . . There was just a kind of ugliness there.

Buckman avers that when she realized what was happening, she decided to leave, but Stafford objected. "I remember that scene in the middle of the night. I said I couldn't stay, it was just too painful. She followed me and pleaded with me on the stairs, please, please, not to go off. . . . She begged me to [stay]." "An

Influx of Poets" confirms this claim and goes even further: as Cora reflects, "I helped in every way to make the match, which was already a fait accompli and which, when I discovered that it was, was to hurtle me off the brink on which I had hovered so long into a chasm."

It is of relatively minor moment whether it was in Maine or afterward that Lowell and Buckman technically became lovers. The affair in which Stafford so perversely and yet so characteristically collaborated had a far more devastating impact on her than she could have foreseen. As for Lowell, who only months before had summoned one of his best friends to Maine for a dressing-down about an extramarital dalliance, he seems in August to have pursued Buckman with no thought of any moral inconsistency, nor any qualms about the effect his action might have on Stafford.

In September Lowell and Stafford closed the house and rode south together on the train. Their marriage was in tatters. Whether or not the ending of "An Influx of Poets" is accurate as to the precise details of that doleful parting, Stafford's story surely renders her internal experience in September 1946. As the train nears Wiscasset, Theron, carrying on a well-married charade for the sake of the other passengers, suggests to Cora, " 'You look worn out. Don't you want a drink?' "

I nodded, accepting his signal, and gathered together my purse and scarf and book (I had not understood a printed word for months) and, matching my manners to his for the sake of those total strangers, I said, "You needn't come. I know you want to work."

"You're a dear," he said and picked his briefcase up off the floor, opening it to show a Loeb "Confessions of St. Augustine," distended with sheets of onionskin on which for a year or so he had made fine notes, cryptic and self-centered, in black ink, which, however, dried as purple, giving the pages a schoolish look. "I'll join you when I've finished Monica's death."

Liar, I thought. Swindler. Ten minutes before the North Station you'll come into the club car, where you'll find me drunk; the sight of you will drive me wild, for I will know what you have been doing, with your eyes so piously attentive to the Latin of your little book. You will have been dreaming, mooning, delighting yourself with thoughts of your reunion with Minnie, your playmate, this very night. (He had dismissed me with that word. "I don't want a wife," he had said, "I want a playmate.")

I could not help myself. I said, "Where will you have din-din tonight with your playmate?"

My question enraged us both, and I got up before he could answer. As I left the car, I looked back; apparently deep among the Manichees, he was thinking of his doll-sized, doll-dressed doll with her bisque-doll skin.

In the club car Cora takes a phenobarbital with her drink and in her mind looks back a last time on the house in Maine.

We had killed Pretty Baby, and killed her kittens. Theron himself had put them in a gunnysack and weighted it with stones and had rowed halfway out to Loon Islet and dropped them among the perch and pickerel.

He beached the boat. I was waiting for him on the front stoop; I had already locked the door. The idling of the motor in the waiting taxi was the only sound that broke the silence of that absolutely azure and absolutely golden early autumn day.

XIII

Luna Park

S TAFFORD AND LOWELL rode the train together to New York
City, arriving at dusk. In the middle of Penn Station they
said goodbye to each other. Stafford, in a "towering rage," took
a room at the New Weston Hotel, at Madison Avenue and Fiftieth Street. Lowell rented a dingy apartment on the Lower East
Side, in a tenement shared by pimps and prostitutes; during his
tenure there he caught first crabs and then influenza.

According to Gertrude Buckman, Lowell showed up at her
apartment on East Nineteenth Street one day. "He said, 'May I
come to see you?' I said, 'You and Jean are welcome here, but I
won't see you alone.'" Lowell insisted that he was separated from
his wife, but Buckman fended him off. "I was very happy and
feeling romantic about him," she reflects, "but I don't think either
of us was sexually needful of each other. He said he loved me,
but he was so childlike." Before long, though, Buckman had
given Lowell a key to her apartment. She nursed him back to
health when he had the flu, and they became lovers.

Shortly after arriving in New York, Lowell and Stafford had
made a halfhearted attempt at a reconciliation; it had lasted only
twelve hours. Now, however, he could no longer hide his feelings for Buckman, and so all three principals agreed to meet at
her apartment. The confrontation was a predictable disaster; Stafford was convinced that the new lovers were "hurling your insults at me in your planned counterpoint."

Meanwhile, Stafford had begun to see a psychotherapist.

Although in retrospect this seems the obvious thing for a person in her mental condition to have done, in 1946 it was by no means an easy step for her to take. Lowell and his brother poets liked to flirt with the notion that madness was allied to genius, but none of them had yet succumbed to therapy. Eventually Delmore Schwartz spent his last decade in a state of paranoid, psychotic penury; John Berryman became an alcoholic and committed suicide; and Lowell himself, finally diagnosed as manic depressive, was institutionalized for many months. But as Frank Parker ruefully recalls, the members of Lowell and Stafford's intellectually sophisticated circle were slow to recognize the signs of a crack-up in their friends: "We seem to have been awfully stupid about that. We should have known better."

Stafford herself had read Freud sympathetically since college. In September 1946, however, as she faced her own need for psychiatric aid, she wrote her sister Mary Lee, "I am full of self-hatred and disgust for I have always scorned people who could not help themselves to become adjusted, but my heart breaks for all of them now: I understand fully what 'nervous breakdown' means."

Parker met Stafford several times for lunch or to talk. She went to his apartment but refused to go inside: "I guess she didn't want to talk to my wife," he says. They sat together on his front steps, and Parker held her hand while she poured out her unhappiness in near-hysterical monologues: "One minute her hatred of Cal, next minute she loved him. I really couldn't follow it. . . . She tried to get me to intercede, but I knew it was impossible with Cal. And also, she might turn around the next day and say, 'Why are you doing this? You know I really hate him.' "

Stafford had been seeing a well-known psychoanalyst named Gregory Zilboorg. According to Jean, Zilboorg told her "that I was in mortal terror of killing myself" and that *Boston Adventure* was " 'the product of one of the most tormented minds in a woman of my age' that he had ever seen." On one occasion that fall when Lowell visited Stafford, he apparently spoke to Zilboorg on the phone. In an accusatory letter she wrote Lowell months later, Stafford caricatured his manipulation: ". . . when you turned from the telephone you said, 'He said that I should leave you alone and that is what I have been saying all along: now will you go away and stop trying to spoil things for me with Gertrude?' "

Stafford was also seeing Mary Jane Sherfey, a young psychiatrist affiliated with New York Hospital who would be her regular therapist for many years. Lowell took it upon himself to visit Sherfey, and he tried to show her a letter Stafford had written him. When Stafford found out about this, she interpreted his act as sheer malevolence: "In showing my letter to my doctor and in asking her, in effect, to agree with you that it was the product of a deranged mind, you sought to absolve yourself of guilt with the assistance of a medical opinion: tell me, please, you said, that none of this was my fault, that my wife was insane and that I behaved as any man would have done under the circumstances."

In October Zilboorg recommended that Stafford enter a sanatorium in Detroit. "I have trusted my doctor blindly, like a child," she later confessed, "and indeed she seems to have complied with Zilboorg's advice immediately, taking the next train to Michigan. But the moment she signed herself in, Stafford began to panic. "They had not told me that there would be bars on the windows, that there would be no doors on the rooms, that people would be strange and wild-eyed." She stayed only eight hours, managing with extreme difficulty to sign herself out. "I knew somehow . . . that if I let the night fall, I would be there for good."

Stafford bought a train ticket for Chicago, where, flat broke, she found the Harcourt, Brace branch office; after phoning Robert Giroux for authorization, the staff was willing to advance her some money. She continued on to Denver, where she spent five days with Mary Lee. The desperate visit did Stafford little good:

> [Mary Lee] could not understand why I would not come home with her and I commenced to hate her because she judged me morally: "Quit drinking for my sake," she would say until I wanted to scream at her. She said that I was selfish and no matter how hard I tried, I could not make her see . . . that I *hated* to drink, that it made me unspeakably miserable but that I could not help it because I did not know why I was compelled to destroy myself.

By the time Jean reached Chicago on the return journey, she was nearing a breakdown. She stood on a street corner and thought, " 'I cannot go any farther. I must hand myself over to a policeman and tell him that I am no longer responsible, that the state must now take care of me.' " At the Chicago train station she "did a pitiful thing."

I had not been able to read anything for weeks and so, in the station, when I still had some hours to wait, I bought a dollar edition of Boston Adventure and I tried to read it. I went into the women's room and tried to read it there and when I could not, the tears poured out and in a perfect rage I threw it in the trash container.

When Stafford returned to New York, Zilboorg either refused or was unable to see her. For several weeks Jean ricocheted through a maze of plans and dodges. She fled New York, staying incognito at inns in Norwalk and Westport, Connecticut. She consulted priests, one of whom "said all I needed to do was to see Cal and patch things up. . . . He suggested that I become a nun." She took an assignment from *Harper's Bazaar* to write a series of dispatches from Ireland; she planned to sail in early December. To Mary Lee she confessed that, ashamed to tell her parents the truth, she had written them that she had suffered "a small nervous breakdown," not mentioning her separation from Lowell.

Robert Giroux put her in touch with Henry Murray, a psychotherapist and Melville scholar who knew and admired Stafford's work. Because he was moving to Boston, however, Murray was able to schedule only one appointment with Stafford, during which he walked with her in Central Park. She wrote Mary Lee in a momentary transport:

> My marvelous new man — I wish he were our father — does not tell me I am going to kill myself: he makes me see reasons for living. He was so lovely: he did not always look at his watch. He talked to me for over three hours and took me to the park. When we came back + were crossing the street he put his arm around me and said he hoped I wd. regard him as an old friend because he had been haunted by B. A.

Fifteen minutes after parting from Murray, Stafford picked up her mail and read a letter from Lowell in which he asked for a divorce. "Although I had known it was coming, I was stunned utterly." She had heard rumors that Lowell had abandoned his Catholicism, which helped explain why he might now have no qualms about divorcing her. Stafford herself had to wrestle an orthodox conscience: she had already made fruitless inquiries at the chancery of her archdiocese, hoping there might be some chance of an annulment, and now she wrote Mary Lee, "If Cal goes through with the divorce, I can never marry again unless I choose to spend the rest of my life in a state of mortal sin which I certainly do not choose."

Stafford had taken a "gruesome little room" in a Greenwich Village hotel. Her insomnia was worse than ever, she was eating almost nothing, and every evening she drank at the hotel bar until it closed, at which point she went upstairs and guzzled applejack for the rest of the night. She stopped doing her laundry, then found it too much trouble even to bathe. She had had two brief meetings with Lowell. "When I saw him," she wrote her sister,

> he did not ask me one word about how I was feeling, he did not once say he was sorry for anything. He said he had never felt better in his life and he looked like someone who sleeps well every night with a perfectly clear conscience. In my hysterical frenzy I felt such hatred for him that I really wished the world would be rid of him and of all his kind, all the Olympian Bostonians.

A friend named Cecile Starr took charge of Stafford for a few weeks, trying to get her to eat and sleep, but this respite only postponed the inevitable. In spite of her precarious condition, Stafford still planned to go to Ireland; she made travel arrangements and got a passport. Everyone she talked to, however (except the priests), was urging her to go into a hospital. Lowell's demand for a divorce was the proverbial backbreaking straw, especially when he began, through his lawyer, to resort to blackmail to force her to agree. Stafford had let Lowell cosign the title to the house in Maine, even though she alone had paid for it; now he refused to make over the title unless she agreed to the divorce. Furthermore, according to Stafford, Lowell was insisting that they divorce in New York, where the only admissable grounds was adultery — and as she wrote Mary Lee, "It was I, you see, who was to be the defendant in the adultery suit."

At last, around November 26, Stafford faced up to her utter debilitation and consented to be admitted to the Payne Whitney Clinic at New York Hospital. Except for a few brief furloughs, she would be confined to the institution for two weeks short of a full year.

Her reaction on entering the clinic was a barely contained dread:

I knew the doors would be locked and that they would take
everything away from me, that there would be no more whiskey,
that I could not get out once I had signed myself in, that the pain
of the analysis was going to be excruciating. That first night, I lay
perfectly motionless in my bed, fighting off the terror by repeat-
ing what Father Dougherty had told me, "I must resign myself."
I could hear the really disordered patients on the floor above
screaming, beating their heads on the floor. . . .

In time, though, Stafford developed her usual wry humor about
Payne Whitney and found it not at all oppressive, especially after
she was moved to a floor with a more lenient regimen. After
three weeks there she wrote Mary Lee,

Here, one's top bureau drawer is unlocked (but the bottom ones
and the closet are still locked) and it is possible to get your fingernail file from the office at any time, not just on Sunday. Here you
can have as many cigarettes as you want but you still can't have
matches nor smoke in your room. A nurse does not stand in your
room with you while you bathe and your pen and pencil are not
taken away promptly at five. . . .
    The first thing we do in the morning is to go out to a small
courtyard where we walk round and round as fast as the mischief
for half an hour. A high grille separates us from the free world
and you feel that at any moment passersby will toss us peanuts.

Stafford nicknamed the exercise yard Luna Park. The staff had
planted tulip bulbs in its small garden, "and from time to time I
saw them being dug up and chewed by a psychotic adolescent
girl from one of the very sick floors." At Recreational Therapy
Jean eschewed badminton and Ping-Pong: "Thus far I have only
played a few ineffectual games of pool and the rest of the time
have played gin rummy with other people who feel as I do. . . .
I am convinced that if I had had the proper attitude toward physical education in my youth, I would not be in the booby hatch
now."
    In Luna Park the women were allowed to mingle with the
men, who included, Stafford gleefully noted, the Portuguese ambassador, an ex-editor at Fortune, "and fairies in various stages of
decay." One night the hospital organized

a most gruesome dance in the gymnasium where all the crazy men met up with all the crazy women and danced to the music of a sedate four-piece orchestra. Some of the ladies' husbands came and it all did seem most sad and touchingly sincere. I left as soon as ever I could, having remembered, the moment I got there, that this was the sort of thing that more than anything else required very ample liquor.

Although she could unflinchingly describe such scenes to Mary Lee, Jean's shame at being institutionalized was still strong enough to dictate lying to her parents; she wrote them that she had been hospitalized for anemia.

Eileen Simpson and John Berryman visited Stafford and found her looking far better than she had the previous summer, thanks to a balanced diet and no alcohol. Her psychiatrist had prodded her to pay more attention to her appearance, so she wore skirts and blouses: " 'For dinner,' " she told her visitors, " 'I put on pearls — like a Smith College girl.' " Simpson thought Stafford seemed "relieved" and "comforted" to be in Payne Whitney.

There was in fact something about being in the "booby hatch" that was deeply congenial to Stafford's spirit. Her long stay in 1946–1947 was the first in a marathon series of hospitalizations that stretched over the rest of her life. Most of these sprang from bona fide medical exigencies, but she also derived a soothing psychological balm from these sabbaticals, even as she complained about her treatment at the hands of her nurses and doctors.

Early during her Payne Whitney stint she wrote Lowell, "It would be, right now, easy for me to enter the Red Room and shut the door tightly and forever." The Red Room had become one of the two or three most important private symbols in her life. Its meaning is adumbrated in *Boston Adventure,* where Sonie sees a German translation of a famous seventeenth-century Chinese novel, *Der Traum den Rote Kammer* ("The Dream of the Red Chamber.") The title sparks what can only be called a mystical vision — one that Stafford seems to have shared with her protagonist.

The Red Room is an unchanging, "rather shabby," old-fashioned, darkly furnished parlor; every particular is vivid and specific, from the cats sleeping on the windowsills to the unironed white tablecloth. All the windows are red, the color of an autumnal sunset. In the center of the room, atop the table, stands a bottle of red wine with no label. Sonie says, "I cannot say how long the 'vision' of this red room lasted, but while it did, I experienced a happiness, a removal from the world which was not an escape so much as a practiced unworldliness." Later she decides that "the red room would be my refuge."

For Stafford the Red Room came to be both a purely mental symbol of an ideal retreat from the world and a retrievable inner arcadia, a tantalizingly familiar sanctum she had never known in real life, but which she "knew" in intimate detail. Only Stafford's best friends were aware of the Red Room's existence. (Frank Parker thought that in all probability Jean had never read the Chinese novel; the title alone, spied perhaps somewhere in Heidelberg, had worked all the magic.) As Stafford aged, an enforced stay in the hospital — though always an inadequate facsimile — came to seem the nearest thing to the Red Room that she could ever actually enter.

Yet if entering Payne Whitney came as something of a relief to Stafford after the ragged weeks preceding, she had only begun to feel the pain that the failure of her marriage was to cause her. Both she and Lowell had been writing Peter Taylor about the breakup. In his loyalty Taylor tried to intercede impartially. "The thought of taking sides with either of you has not even occurred to me," he wrote Lowell; "I feel like a parent whose two favorite children have had a bitter quarrel and are making a complete break, and that's a pretty terrible feeling." To Stafford he counseled, "Thank goodness you are in a hospital and are really taking care of yourself. . . . You must not let yourself be completely consumed by bitterness, Jean."

Taylor had heard rumors (as had Stafford), that Lowell was thinking of marrying Gertrude Buckman, but he could not believe them. While he thought a separation was a good idea, he begged both parties to hold off on a divorce. In December he proposed a moratorium: "I am asking you both to take matters out of the hands of your lawyers for the time being and to agree to a postponement of the divorce for one year — till January 1, 1948. I ask that you agree not to communicate with each other during that interval, except through me, and that you make a deliberate effort to avoid accidental meetings." He wrote long, empathic letters to each combatant; he understood the tortures of the previous year but could not accept their giving up on the marriage.

This all but heroic act of friendship backfired. Both Lowell and Stafford rejected Taylor's proposal, even as each tried to cadge from him inside information about the other's true thoughts. Both deflected their antagonism toward each other into an irritation at him. On January 2, 1947, Taylor withdrew his offer to act as an intermediary. By doing so, he managed to save his friendship with each.

In her isolation, freed from the normal demands of daily life, Stafford brooded over what she saw as Lowell's betrayal. Her feelings ranged from bitter denunciation to all-forgiving love. She poured out her sorrows in a series of letters to Lowell that were so unguarded, so deeply felt, and yet so articulate that it is painful to read them forty years later. The letters Lowell sent her in Payne Whitney have not survived, but the poet was never one for epistolary self-revelation, and Jean's own letters complain about the paucity and coldness of his. For days on end she waited like a teenager for the phone to ring, for him to visit or send flowers. A few years later Stafford told Joan Stillman that Lowell had come to see her only once during her year in Payne Whitney, and then "he spent the whole visit telling her about Gertrude Buckman's many virtues."

Stafford's escalating success as a writer seemed insignificant to her in the throes of her loss:

> I know this, Cal, and the knowledge eats me like an inward animal: there is nothing worse for a woman than to be deprived of her womanliness. For me, there is nothing worse than the knowledge that my life holds nothing for me but being a writer. . . .
> In your letter you say that you hope I will be recognized as the best novelist of my generation. I want you to know now and know completely that that would mean to me absolutely *nothing*. It could not happen and even if it could, it would not make the days here less long nor would my loss of you be made up for.

Lowell's second book of poetry, *Lord Weary's Castle,* had been published in December and was beginning to make waves. Thus her husband's wish for her success rang patronizing in Stafford's ears. "I have never, as you well enough know, regarded my writing as being as important as yours," she wrote. "But now, while this is still true, I regard myself as being as important as a *writer* as you. I am, I mean, as valuable a human being whose vocation happens to be writing."

Gertrude Buckman's theft of her husband haunted Stafford's hours.

> Gertrude, the clever quicksilver, the heartless fey, the no-woman, the bedeviller. She laughed at me over the telephone and I shall never forget: a melodious laugh of triumph, of double triumph: she had got you, she had laid my life in ruins. I remember the laugh here nights on end.

(Buckman denies that such a phone call took place.)

"She is a child," Stafford wrote on another bad day, "and if she wishes to eat the last piece of candy in the box, she will consult only her desire."

Yet Stafford's sarcasm must have been easier for Lowell to read then the abject pleading it alternated with:

> I have continued to wait for you as I shall wait for you all my life, not because I am possessive, not because I am a coward, but because I love you and because I desire you and desire to be married to you and because even if you never come back, there will forever be my hope that you will.

In January 1947 Stafford learned that her mother was dying of cancer. A doctor had removed a lump from Ethel Stafford's jaw and discovered a widespread melanoma. The information came to Jean as a double threat. She felt obligated to make a deathbed visit to Oregon, yet she temporized with melodramatic excuses to Mary Lee, her only confidante within the family: "How will Dad ever be able to understand this illness of mine and how will Mother if she knows finally that she is going to die? . . . If I came now, sick with my grief over Cal and all the ruin of my life, I would start to drink again and this time I would succeed in what I was trying to do before, I would, that is, drink myself to death." She wrote her mother a letter that in her own eyes was "hopelessly inadequate." She begged Lowell, "I wonder if you could not divorce me until my mother dies."

Her wardens at Payne Whitney agreed to grant her an emergency leave, and in early February Stafford flew to Oregon. She was too late, however: her mother had died just before Jean had left the hospital. The brief visit was devoted instead to consoling her father. Marjorie's amused description of her sister's appearance that February misses the fact that her camouflage must have served, for Jean, as a frantic contradiction of her inner state:

> Jean's image had undergone a remarkable transformation. She had shed her drab clothing and accessories and had taken on the habiliments of a glamorous movie star. She wore an attractive series of dresses with color, a smart coat, black fishnet stockings with clocks, makeup and high heels. Her pretty flaxen hair was cut and styled in a most fetching and becoming do.

Stafford managed not to drink at all in Oregon, even though she felt "nearly overpowered with the desire." Any hope she had of coming to an understanding with her father vanished quickly; the visit turned into an ordeal by tedium. While still in Oregon, Stafford wrote a remarkable note to herself, which penetrates to the heart of her feelings about her family.

> My father has never been more stunningly boring. His larger-than-life-size conception of his role in Mother's illness maddens me in the terrible and familiar way and I feel a perfect bitch because I am unable to make allowances for his grief and his loneliness. . . . In his egomaniacal hatred of doctors . . . he would not give her the medicines that had been ordered because he said it had been evident to him that they were what affected her kidneys. Nor would he give her any sleeping tablets; instead, if she awakened and complained, he would rub her back with Musterole. I did not know that Musterole existed any longer save in my memory and when he said it, everything came back borne on the smell of that dreadful panacea.

To Jean's dismay and contempt, Marjorie teasingly revived her childhood taunts, telling her she had grown fat and would have to wear rubber underwear and take reducing pills, claiming she had been adopted and would soon be kidnapped: "I responded inwardly in the childhood way and wanted to pull her hair. Her face is dead and unintelligent and craven."

Mary Lee had kept Jean's shameful secret. "There has been no mention of Cal but it is clear that they suspect nothing. He simply does not exist for them nor has he ever done. It is assumed

by my father and by Margie that I will come out here to live."
John Stafford had been building a study for Jean in the house: "it
was to be a surprise for me, he said, a much more comfortable
place for me to work than in Maine."

Although her father lived for another nineteen years, Jean saw
him only once more after this. Marjorie lastingly suspected that
Jean felt guilty for not having gotten to Oregon in time to see
her mother before she died. Yet shortly after her trip west, Jean
had reported a quite different reaction to Lowell: "A very wonderful thing happened to me: I absolved myself of my guilt toward
my mother who, no matter what else she was, was the one who
gave me sweetness, the sweetness that will always be in me now
that I understand why it was my father tried to curdle it permanently."

Stafford's joy on the publication of *Boston Adventure* had been
canceled by the news of her brother's death. Now her mother
had died just a month before the publication of *The Mountain
Lion,* and to make matters worse, as the new novel hit the book-
stores its author was back behind the locked doors of the "booby
hatch." There were no publishing parties, no radio interviews,
no glasses of champagne at *Mademoiselle*.

The Mountain Lion is a work of some sixty-five thousand
words — barely a third the length of *Boston Adventure*. The book's
dedication reads, "To Cal and to Dick"; the epigram is from
Proverbs: "A friend loveth at all times, and a brother is born for
adversity." Stafford had finished the novel ten months earlier, in
April 1946, shortly before the "influx of poets" to Damariscotta
Mills and possibly at about the time of Lowell's attempt to strangle her.

The novel is in two parts. Chapters One through Three take
place in Covina, California, in a house and neighborhood modeled exactly on those of Stafford's first six years. Chapters Four
through Nine move the story to the mountains of Colorado; the
locale is a cattle ranch patterned, down to the hopvines on the
west window, on Harry and Mary Lee's ranch in Hayden.

The protagonist, Molly Fawcett, is probably the most memorable fictional character of Stafford's oeuvre, as well as (with Joyce
Bartholomew of "In the Snowfall") one of the two most deeply
autobiographical. In the California chapters Molly is eight years
old; in Colorado she is twelve. Her closest companion is her
brother, Ralph, two years her senior. Their much older sisters,

Leah and Rachel, are would-be debutantes. Ralph is based directly on Stafford's brother, Dick; Leah and Rachel represent what Stafford saw as the affected, pretentious sides of Mary Lee and Marjorie. Many episodes and anecdotes, from Molly's poem "Gravel" to Ralph's disgust at his sister's wearing his Boy Scout shirt, are taken straight from life.

The novel's binding tension lies in the conflict between the two ancestral strains of the Fawcett family — a deft dramatization of Jean's own preference for the forthright Staffords over the effete and huffy McKillops. Grandpa Kenyon (based on Jean's fantasy of her Grandpa Stafford) is a plain-talking, hard-drinking cattleman whose visits are the high points of Ralph and Molly's life. The children's father is dead — a narrative gambit that was, Stafford admitted to Lowell, an evasion of the challenge of dealing with her own father. Bereft of him, Mrs. Fawcett rules the roost with timorous hypochondria and Presbyterian piety.

After Grandpa Kenyon dies suddenly during a visit, Ralph and Molly are packed off to live with their uncle Claude (based on Harry Frichtel) on the Colorado ranch. Against the invigorating background of the Rocky Mountains, immersed in the laconic world of cowhands and ranch work, Ralph and Molly struggle to become adolescents. Molly is a vivid transmogrification of Jean's image of herself: she is round-shouldered, bespectacled, gawky, too tall, and scrawny. Brainy and alienated, an aspiring writer who finds secret groves in the mountains in which to ruminate and compose, Molly longs for other existences: "When she was not unhappy, she was bored." As children, Ralph and Molly form a deep alliance against their "superior" older sisters and the stifling regime of their mother. Most fundamentally, *The Mountain Lion* is about what happens to that alliance as Ralph and Molly come of age.

To tell this story, Stafford shucked off the mannerisms of *Boston Adventure* and discovered a tone and diction almost entirely new for her. The extent of this stylistic transformation can best be gauged by a side-by-side comparison of passages from the two novels.

Here is young Sonie Marburg in *Boston Adventure,* trying to imagine a utopian life in the company of Miss Pride:

> But tonight, in this cold nakedness, I was cheated out of my solace for I could not, with my eyes, burn a way to her in Boston.

The uproar in me was brought on partly by the discrepancy between the placid vagary that was holding my mother's attention
downstairs and my own tempestuous one upstairs, for, although
they were equally profitless, mine had a kind of direction, and it
seemed consistent with my bad luck that she was happy while I
was so miserable, that she could sustain herself indefinitely on fol-
lies and unreal pageants and old woes.

And here is young Molly Fawcett in *The Mountain Lion,* imagining a utopian existence in solitary confinement:

If she ever got fat, she thought, or ever said anything fat, she
would lock herself in a bathroom and stay there until she died.
Often she thought how comfortably you could live in a bathroom. You could put a piece of beaver board on top of the tub
and use it as a bed. In the daytime you could have a cretonne
spread on it so that it would look like a divan. You could use the
you-know-what as a chair and the lavatory as a table. You wouldn't
have to have anything else but some canned corn and marshmal-
lows, and if you got tired of those, you could let a basket out of
the window with a slip of paper saying, "Send up some hot tamales" or some hard-boiled eggs or whatever you particularly
wanted at the time.

Style is the most private of stratagems. The calculations and
experiments that may have lain behind this wholesale reworking
of Stafford's prose, during her fits of craft in Black Rock, Westport, and Damariscotta Mills from 1944 to 1946, remain secrets
between Stafford and her typewriter. In terms of her favorite
writers, the exemplar passed from Proust and James to Mark
Twain.

The transformation, however, is more than a matter of simple
mimicry. When asked about the startling change in prose style
from her first published novel to her second, Stafford tended to
minimize the shift. But her philosophical attitude toward life —
in fictional terms, her tone — had undergone its own revision.
She had discovered an irony appropriate to her surest subject,
childhood and adolescence. As Stafford claimed in a seemingly
offhand interview in 1952, " 'My theory about children is my
theory about writing. The most important thing in writing is
irony, and we find irony most clearly in children. The very in-

nocence of a child is irony. Irony, I feel, is a very high form of morality.' "

It was not as if Stafford had never before tried to write ironically. Her Stephens novel had been awash in facile satire. The great stride forward that *The Mountain Lion* embodies is rather a matter of her having learned (as Twain may have taught her) that the most solemn human predicaments are most effectively rendered not in a melodramatic plot (as in her Heidelberg novel), nor even in the sort of quasi-omniscient periphrases of Sonie's voice in *Boston Adventure,* but in a plain American prose whose tone itself bridges the gap between the protagonist's earnest attack on the world and the author's rich and distant understanding. In that tension — the gulf that separates Molly Fawcett from Jean Stafford — lies all the pleasure and wisdom of a great novel.

As many reviewers noted, the bond between Ralph and Molly verges on the "unnatural." The eight-year-old girl remarks that "today she did not cry: Ralph was too gay, she knew, to comfort her and that was the only pleasure in crying, to be embraced by him and breathe in his acrid smell of leather braces and serge and to feel, shuddering, the touch of his warty hands on her face." When Grandpa Kenyon dies, Ralph and Molly lie on the floor beside his coffin, sobbing in one another's arms.

On the ranch, however, now that Ralph is fourteen, he begins to pull away from his clinging sister. Simply put, Ralph is on the threshold of puberty. For him a sexual interest in other girls is linked with a wish that "Molly had never been born"; daydreaming about his older sister Leah, who he learns is engaged, Ralph feels "a terrified guilt as though he had despoiled [her]." Molly, at twelve, cannot countenance her own coming-of-age. When Ralph tells her about the birth of a calf, Molly sticks her fingers in her ears and screams, " 'You're a dirty liar!' " — "savagely refusing the knowledge of such things."

The turning point of the novel is a powerfully ambiguous scene in which Molly and Ralph are taking a train up to the ranch. As the train enters a tunnel (Stafford, of course, knew her Freud), Ralph's crisis peaks:

> He urged the train to make haste. Once out in the bright green meadows of the valley he thought he would be safe from the thoughts that swarmed about him like a dream of reptiles. As long as Molly was here beside him, though, he could hang on.

And then he knew he had been wrong, that he was not safe; he was weakening and ready to fall, and now he actually slumped down in the seat so that his shoulders were on a level with Molly's and he said, in the lowest voice, "Molly, tell me all the dirty words you know."

He heard himself almost with relief. Before there was time for Molly to move away or to utter a cry, they had emerged into the light which streamed like glory through the dirty window panes. The sun was high and the fields shimmered. Round them, for miles, as far as the eye could see, were the violet mountains, clean-lined, clear of haze. The eye could not detect a single impurity in all the scene.

Ralph's childhood and his sister's expired at that moment of the train's entrance into the surcharged valley. It was a paradox, for now they should be going into a tunnel with no end, now that they had heard the devil speak.

After the tunnel episode, Molly and Ralph are enemies. Ralph thinks that his sister is going crazy, and her behavior does in fact become very strange. While she was writing *The Mountain Lion,* Stafford was beginning to fear that she was losing her own sanity. In the spring of 1947 she wrote Lowell, "Gradually I became Molly. I was so much Molly that finally I had to write her book. . . . All the self-mutilations came back; for I had mutilated myself constantly when I was a little girl in order to gain pity and love." The psychological similarities between the author and her protagonist are telling: Molly, an aquaphobe, must perform an elaborate ritual before she can take a bath, which she does with a bathing suit on; according to Lowell, Stafford at that time could dress and undress only in a closet. Molly dreams of spending the rest of her life in the bathroom; Stafford dreamed of hiding in her Red Room.

The denouement of the novel comes when Ralph, hunting the elusive mountain lion with Uncle Claude (a deed linked in Ralph's mind with becoming a man) fires at it in a clearing but accidentally kills Molly, who has slipped off alone to her secret grove. In naturalistic terms the ending is preposterous, a deus ex machina of a type for which Stafford had an unfortunate weakness (in her Heidelberg novel the death of the German pilot on maneuvers resolves the love story; in *Boston Adventure* Hopestill

Mather's death resolves Sonie's rivalry with her). In symbolic terms, though, the killing seems almost inevitable.

The Mountain Lion was published around March 1, 1947. Confined to Payne Whitney, Stafford could not even browse the newsstands for reviews; she had to wait for Robert Giroux to send or bring them to her. The notices themselves were, however, extremely gratifying. *The New Yorker* called the book "a second novel that is hard to match these days for subtlety and understanding." Robert Fitzgerald, in the *Nation,* observed that Ralph and Molly "suffer from the burden and scariness of being themselves and from the hopelessness of their being inseparable, and beneath the local and satiric pleasure of the story this is put so strongly that, though you read it with amusement, you will feel it aching in you like a tooth for days." Howard Mumford Jones, who had championed *Boston Adventure,* found *The Mountain Lion* fully its equal and said so in the *New York Times Book Review.* The English poet John Betjeman, commenting in the *London Daily Herald,* declared, "It is written with the merciless detachment of a woman picking characters to pieces. Like gossip, it fascinates. Like life, its end is mysterious."

The only major magazine to pan the book was *Time,* whose critic complained of "dank symbolism" and "desperately contrived coincidence." In its inimitable fashion, *Time* adapted the latter stricture in a one-word caption under a photo of Stafford: "Desperate."

Many reviewers commented on the disturbing relationship between Molly and Ralph. The less sophisticated warned their readers, as *Parents Magazine* saw fit to, that *The Mountain Lion* ought not "to be left on the living-room table where the young people in the family may pick [it] up." Howard Mumford Jones, on the other hand, praised as the novel's great strength its "theme ·of family feud, of deep-buried feelings of incest and guilt, of dark ambivalences of brother-sister, child-mother relationships."

With her second book Stafford began to win recognition as one of the important novelists of her generation. In a *Life* roundup in June, John Chamberlain called Stafford the "most brilliant of the new fiction writers." Four months later, surveying the rat race of American letters from the other side of the Atlantic, the all-knowing critic Cyril Connolly said, "Last year's authors (most of the names that have just reached England) are pushed aside and this year's — the novelist Jean Stafford, her poet husband Robert Lowell or the dark horse, Truman Capote — are invariably mentioned."

Despite this acclaim, *The Mountain Lion* was no best-seller. At the last minute, because of a "slump in the book trade," Harcourt, Brace had drastically cut the first printing from thirty thousand copies to ten thousand. The book clubs did not clamor for the novel. The press sent *The Mountain Lion* to thirteen film companies, all of which rejected it.

In the February 22 issue of the *Nation,* Lowell had published a poem called "Her Dead Brother." When Stafford discovered the poem, she flew into a rage. At once she wrote Lowell,

> "Her Dead Brother" appearing in the Nation a week before the publication of my book with its dedication, with its theme of latent incest, at a time when you have left me and I am in the hospital[,] seems to me an act of so deep dishonor that it passes beyond dishonor and approaches madness. And I am trembling in the presence of your hate.

The casual reader of the poem would be hard put to understand Stafford's fury, for in it Lowell characteristically veils in myth and obscure allusion a woman's apostrophe to her late brother. The tone is elegiac, nostalgic, and abstract. Yet the third stanza hints at some dark childhood event:

> *Then you were grown; I left you on your own.*
> *We will forget that August twenty-third,*
> *When Mother motored with the maids to Stowe,*
> *And the pale summer shades were drawn — so low*
> *No one could see us; no, nor catch your hissing word,*
> *As false as Cressid!*

And the poem's epigrammatic peroration in the last stanza announces, "O Brother, a New England town is death/ And incest — and I saw it whole."

The incestuous tensions implicit in *The Mountain Lion,* combined with "Her Dead Brother" and Stafford's violent reaction to the poem, suggest a hypothesis about Jean's childhood relationship with her brother that, though intriguing, must remain purely speculative. It later became Lowell's penchant to turn the confidences of his lovers and wives directly into poetry; the most egregious example of this nasty habit was his publishing, in *The Dolphin* in 1972, several poems whose lines were taken verbatim from anguished letters from his estranged second wife, Elizabeth Hardwick. It seems reasonable to suspect that Stafford may have told Lowell a secret about something that had gone on in childhood between her and Dick; her outrage, then, may have come from seeing that secret betrayed in the pages of the *Nation*.

A manuscript version of "Her Dead Brother" is slightly more explicit:

> *Can you forget that August afternoon*
> *When Mother motored with the girls to Stowe*
> *And the white summer shades were drawn — so low*
> *No one could see us and you came to me*
> *Touching and a[l]most touching there alone!*

Lowell's use of "the girls" here instead of "the maids" hints at Jean's older sisters; the former, however, would have been confusing in simple narrative terms.

Possibly, then, Stafford may have confided to Lowell about an episode in childhood involving a sexual embrace with Dick that had occurred when their parents and two older sisters had gone off somewhere. In fact, several manuscript drafts of Lowell's *Mills of the Kavanaughs,* in the stanza dealing with the husband's attempt to strangle his wife, imply that the lover she dreams of is actually her brother; and some of these drafts even give him the name Richard. One version has the wife speaking within her dream:

> *I, a girl of ten,*
> *I pushed you with my finger. Why not peep*
> *And spy it? I would wake you. Now was then,*
> *One child's bed held us.*

The whole business is fuzzy and potentially misleading. In *The Mountain Lion,* after all, Stafford chose to write scenes that were laden with incestuous guilt and tension; it takes no great leap of intuition to wonder whether Molly and Ralph might be based on the author and her brother. Stafford had further underlined the incest theme by naming the older sisters Rachel and Leah, after the sisters in Genesis who both marry Jacob, their uncle. Why, then, did she express such anger at Lowell's rather more indirect corroboration of that theme — was it because the specific scene he painted in "Her Dead Brother" was too close to the truth?

There is, it must be emphasized, not a shred of documentary evidence that anything even suggestive of incest occurred between Dick and Jean as children. (Marjorie, when asked about the possibility, said, "I just can't believe that there was anything like that. But she had a lot of things that she didn't tell me.") Yet on the other hand, on the basis of the documentary evidence alone, it is also hard to explain the unqualified loyalty and love that Stafford felt all her adult life toward her brother. Dick emerges from the record as an uncomplicated outdoorsman who did not seem to keep close contact with Jean after he went away to college; even Stafford's closest confidant, Robert Hightower, knew next to nothing about him. Jean's devotion to Dick was of a sort she never felt for any other human being; it was the antithesis of the lifelong vexation she felt for the other four members of her immediate family.

In the end, the question cannot be resolved by biography. If it is not a purely imagined fiction, *The Mountain Lion* stands as the only real source for further understanding.

Throughout the spring, summer, and early fall of 1947 Stafford remained at Payne Whitney. Her forays outside were far between and closely monitored. *Life* photographed her in front of the lion cage at the Bronx Zoo. She lunched with her agent, Marian Ives — an ordeal without cocktails. The Harcourt, Brace staff orchestrated "a carefully planned re-entry into the world" with belated get-togethers to celebrate the publication of *The Mountain Lion*. Rebelling mildly against her regimen, Stafford went to a cocktail party given by her friend Cecile Starr without telling her doctors. She handled it well enough until Caroline Gordon showed up, causing Stafford to go "to pieces." In the late spring she took a trip to Maine "to dismantle our house" preparatory to selling it. It was a melancholy visit: everything reminded her of her marriage, and insomnia reclaimed her.

The professional veil of confidentiality prevents us from knowing much about Stafford's psychotherapeutic treatment at Payne Whitney. Perhaps the single most important thing her doctors accomplished was to get her to stop drinking for a whole year. Even on her trips to Oregon and Maine she managed not to drink. Her therapist, Mary Jane Sherfey, warmly congratulated her for her restraint in this, but Sherfey's superior tried (unsuccessfully) to get Stafford to stop smoking as well.

Although at times Stafford could face up to the possibility that she had no control over her drinking, more often she denied it, especially in her letters to Lowell: "I, unlike you, always knew that my drinking was a symptom and not a cause and certainly it was instantaneously proved when I came into the hospital for I suffered nothing at all from the very first. I was not, as I daresay you believed, an alcoholic. . . ."

The clinical understanding of alcoholism in 1947 was not, perhaps, equal to the task of lastingly addressing Stafford's dependency. Now, forty years later, research has illuminated the genetic component of the affliction. The pattern evidenced on Stafford's maternal side — an alcoholic grandfather, a teetotaling mother — would today be seen as a classic indicator. While her doctors at Payne Whitney were able to keep Stafford off the bottle as long as she was inside its walls, Sherfey's approach in the years following Jean's hospitalization seems to have amounted to pleading, in a supportive way, that she not drink. There is no evidence that during the span of Stafford's life any doctor ever urged her to attend Alcoholics Anonymous.

As the weeks in "the bin" dragged on, Stafford wrote letter after letter to her husband. She castigated him for thinking he could turn his back on the Church so easily. In April Lowell was showered with honors: on the strength of *Lord Weary's Castle,* he won a Guggenheim Fellowship and a grant from the American Academy of Arts and Letters (just as Stafford had two years before); he also won the Pulitzer Prize for poetry. In June he was offered the post of Consultant in Poetry at the Library of Congress. Suddenly Lowell was as famous as his wife.

Lowell had indeed told everybody that he was planning to marry Gertrude Buckman; Stafford's dismay was deepened by her knowledge that the news was " 'all over town.' " Lowell apparently promised Buckman that the pair could spend August in the house in Damariscotta Mills; Buckman wrote him saccharine love letters, clucking her tongue over Stafford's resistance to the divorce. Charlotte Lowell, needless to say, was not sorry to see her son cast off the "hick" from Colorado.

For months Stafford refused to resign herself to the inevitable

divorce. At some point in the spring she had a reunion of sorts
with Lowell in Greenwich Village. "There was not a chance of
that interview going right," she sighed afterward. Yet in the wake
of their meeting, one morning in Payne Whitney she sat down
and typed out a nine-page single-spaced letter to her husband. It
is an astounding document: in effect a kind of apologia for her
life and her current condition, it may be the most deeply felt
letter Stafford ever wrote.

The mood that gave birth to the letter was one of unbidden
euphoria. For the first time in a year and a half, she claimed, she
had "awakened with delight in my life." The letter closes with a
heartbreaking assertion of her love:

> I cannot help, with all this lovely love of mine, wishing that we
> could live our lives together and feeling that we have a chance
> that no one we have ever known has had. . . .
>
> Realize, when I say "I love you" that my very blood itself runs
> in this calm and gentle joy. Believe me, dearest, when I tell you
> that it is no mood, it is a transformation, it is a glory and it has
> *never* happened to me before in all my life. . . . You saw it in the
> letter and Cecile [Starr] saw it in my face and the doctors saw it
> in the return of my health and I hope, good Wu, that it simply
> knocked your eyes out when you saw it; I hope it simply streamed
> like glory off that page.

Yet the pages sandwiched between the euphoric opening and
closing not only testify to a most acute unhappiness but also take
Lowell bitterly to task. They outline, as well, Stafford's understanding of the Freudian interpretation her doctors had helped
her form of her plight. The crux of it is this:

> I had become your mother just as you had become my father and
> both of us by now [in Maine] were so far gone that we were
> blindly and savagely attacking those people, not one an-
> other. . . .
>
> My resemblance to your mother and your resemblance to my
> father were of the most superficial kinds, but I have very little
> doubt that these very resemblances had much to do with our mar-
> rying. It is possible to look upon it two ways: we were burdened
> with subconscious guilt in having failed to love them (even though
> they were to blame because they had not loved us) and we were

determined to make up for this failure by acquit[t]ing ourselves with the people who seemed most similar to them. Or, if it was not guilt, it was the desire to avenge ourselves for the unforgivable wrongs that had been done to us when we were children. . . .

[After the success of *Boston Adventure*,] when you cautioned me to be prudent in my spending, I whipped around as if you had insulted me; I thought that you were trying to deprive me of all pleasure just as my father had done when I was a child and out of defiance of my father, I spent the money wildly and I began to drink more and more, still paying *him* back, and it was now convenient for me to force your eccentricities to become *his* eccentricities, and finally you were to blame for everything. And this was perfectly true: you *were* but what I did not know was that you were no longer you, the terribly wonderful and tender man I had fallen in love with, but you were my father, and I hated you deeply.

Not dissuaded, Lowell continued to demand a divorce. Once Stafford realized that she could not change his mind, their dealings deteriorated into a full year's worth of vicious niggling — over the furnishings of the house in Maine, over the terms of the alimony, over which state they should get the divorce in and which of them should seek it. Newly rich himself, Lowell offered Stafford five thousand dollars in alimony, spread over ten years. She wrote back acidly, "To be rather blunt about it, forty dollars a month, paid over a period of ten years is not quite the same thing as what you got in six." Yet shortly thereafter, Stafford theatrically offered to drop all claims for alimony.

It was not long before Lowell lost interest in Buckman. When she tried to visit him in Washington, where he had moved to take up his Library of Congress job, he failed to return her calls and avoided meeting her. He never accounted to her for this change of heart; instead, he tried to brush her off with passive negligence. She was deeply hurt. Reflecting on the affair thirty-eight years later, Buckman says, "He was to the end of his life, I'd say, emotionally undeveloped and irresponsible. . . . We never had much fun together."

Lowell had begun another affair, with a Washington society woman to whom he quickly got engaged. After six months he dropped her. Shortly after that he announced his plans to marry the poet Elizabeth Bishop — even though the two of them were never lovers; he never told Bishop of his ambition; and she was predominantly a lesbian.

Not until October did Stafford feel ready to leave Payne Whitney. She took out a classified ad in the *New York Times,* presenting herself as a novelist looking for someone to share an apartment with. (She got a crank response that she kept for the rest of her life in a file headed "Outrages to Writers": "If your'e [*sic*] a female novelist, unless your'e the exception to the rule, your'e so God-damned ugly that I sure as hell wouldn't live with you.")

Around November 10 Stafford moved from Payne Whitney to an apartment (sans roommate) on West Seventy-fifth Street, just off Central Park. She arranged to have her furniture shipped down from Maine. *The Mountain Lion* had sold so poorly that she felt "awfully broke." At last she was reconciled to the divorce. The future seemed riddled with uncertainty, but she was ready to go on being a writer. In a subdued mood she wrote to Lowell, putting a brave face on things, "Terribly slowly and terribly wonderfully, I am growing up."

XIV

Rebound

THE ONLY SHORT STORIES Stafford published in 1947 were written before she entered Payne Whitney. "The Hope Chest," published in *Harper's,* is a tour de force, the internal monologue of a misanthropic octogenarian spinster. Despite its modest compass, it was the first of Stafford's stories to win an O. Henry Award. "A Slight Maneuver," which came out in *Mademoiselle,* uses Carlsbad Caverns (which Stafford had visited with Marjorie — and disliked — one summer in the early 1930s) as the backdrop for a tale of a romance going sour.

Still, in the midst of her ordeal of convalescence in Payne Whitney, Stafford did manage to do some writing. A pair of articles appeared late in 1947. For *Vogue* she wrote an oddly impersonal essay about her insomnia, in which a self-consciously "poetic" prose wards off the confessional. The other piece, the smarmy "Notes on Boston" for the *Junior Bazaar* (illustrated with photos from a debutante's coming-out party), is an outright embarrassment.

It was with these two unremarkable nonfiction pieces that Stafford began her career as a journalist. With the exception of a pair of book reviews and her high-school pieces in the *Prep Owl,* everything Stafford had published (and almost everything she had written) before 1947 was fiction. Stafford may have looked on the *Vogue* and *Junior Bazaar* articles as mere hackwork by which to earn cash. If so, they ironically prefigure the writing of the last two decades of her life, when she could no longer produce novels and short stories and survived only because of her skill as a journalist.

These first two pieces required no reporting; Stafford could have whipped them up from memory and reflection. In the middle of the summer, however, *Life* gave her her first real assignment in the field — a report on the social life of Newport, Rhode Island. She took a leave from Payne Whitney and plunged into the stuffy decadence of millionaires' "cottages" and dowagers' hotels. The essay that resulted was too leisurely and intellectual for *Life,* which rejected it.

Shortly after her release in November, Stafford got up the nerve to read a paper at a Bard College conference on the novel, in upstate New York. All her life, healthy or ill, on or off the bottle, Stafford dreaded performing in public. At Bard her nervousness was exacerbated by the fear that her listeners would know that she had only just gotten out of the "loony bin." Delivering her lecture, she

> nearly died of terror (for no humane reason Mary McCarthy and Bowd[en] Broadwater [McCarthy's then husband] came on and sat in the front row grinning like cats). . . . Her one comment on my lecture, delivered with all her ignited ice, was "Your speech had a great deal of charm." I wanted, at most, to reply that I was glad, that to be a charming woman was my principal ambition.

Nonetheless, John Crowe Ransom commandeered the essay for the *Kenyon Review,* praising it as " 'belletristic if not academic.' " Stafford herself thought the lecture "awfully bad" but consented to its publication. In this case Ransom and McCarthy were right. "The Psychological Novel," perhaps the only attempt Stafford ever made at writing systematic literary criticism, is a penetrating, wise, and indubitably charming essay.

On her emergence from the hospital, Stafford was in bad financial shape. It is not clear how she paid for a full year of treatment by prestigious therapists at Payne Whitney. She may have mortgaged the house in Maine, and she certainly spent all the money she had earned from *Boston Adventure* and *The Mountain Lion.* As she moved into her Upper West Side apartment, she reported to Lowell that she was $1,290 in debt.

On November 28 Stafford signed a contract with Harcourt, Brace for a new novel, which she had already tentatively entitled

"In the Snowfall." She asked for, and got, a four-thousand-dollar advance, to be allocated in quarterly payments through the following September. (These terms were unusual in that the publisher agreed to pay the full advance before delivery of the manuscript.) Two weeks later Stafford fired Marian Ives, the agent who had represented her for almost three years, and, remarkably enough, persuaded her to return her commission on the "Snowfall" contract.

On December 11 Stafford sold her first story to *The New Yorker.* There were a few other magazines, including the *Saturday Evening Post,* that paid more for fiction, but none that it was more flattering to be published by. Yet from the start it was *The New Yorker* that wooed Stafford, not vice versa. At the time of this initial sale, she signed a "first reader" agreement. This gave the magazine the right of first refusal on all "fiction, humor, reminiscence, and casual essays" for a full year; in exchange, *The New Yorker* paid 25 percent more than its usual rate for each piece it accepted.

The complicated and avuncular relationships that the staff of *The New Yorker* entered into with its writers are the stuff of legend. By the time Stafford came on board, the magazine was paying a minimum of eighteen cents a word for the first two thousand words, and nine cents a word thereafter. Thus a sixty-seven-hundred-word story like "A Summer Day," Stafford's first for *The New Yorker,* earned a base fee of some $780; the first-reader agreement boosted this to $975. Moreover, the per-word rate was a minimum; the magazine routinely paid more "according to our estimate of the value *to us* of the manuscript." On top of that, there was a bonus each year for signing the first-reader agreement (by 1955, for Stafford, the bonus had reached twelve hundred dollars); a clause that added another 25 percent per piece if the magazine bought six pieces within a twelve-month period; and an automatic cost-of-living increase calibrated to the index of the United States Department of Labor.

From the sale of that first story onward, Stafford had Katharine White as her editor at *The New Yorker.* The wife of E. B. White and later a skillful writer of essays about gardening, Katharine White had been on the staff since the magazine's founding by Harold Ross in 1925. She was twenty-two years older than Stafford, but the two women became the closest of friends. White was an editor of high acumen who brought out the best in contributors; in turn, she found Stafford a "remarkable reviser."

In the first eight months after she signed the agreement, Stafford sold four stories to *The New Yorker,* and White sent her a pat-on-the-back note urging her to shoot for the six-piece bonus. The first story the magazine published was not "A Summer Day," however, but "Children Are Bored on Sunday." One of the best short stories Stafford ever wrote, it appeared in the February 21, 1948, issue. Peter Davison, who as a nine-year-old had shyly admired the precocious college girl smoking her cigarette in his parents' living room in Boulder, was a Harvard senior that winter. He has a vivid memory of reading "Children Are Bored on Sunday" the week it came out and saying to himself, "My God, that's the way people should write." The story "seemed to me the *locus classicus* of the difficulties of having been brought up in Colorado."

The story has a deceptively simple structure. Emma, coming off a vaguely explained year "in hiding," wanders through the Metropolitan Museum of Art. In front of her favorite Botticelli she sees Alfred Eisenburg, with whom she once flirted "for seven or eight minutes" and who was the last friend she ran into before her year's withdrawal. The plot does little more than follow Emma through her deliberate avoidance of him until, as she is leaving the museum, just as she has half wished all along, he bumps into her and asks her out for a drink. Eisenburg knows of her "collapse" and is sympathetic; Emma has heard that he, too, has been through a dreadful year, one of divorce and professional failure.

The story's subterranean current is a lucid exposition of Emma's inner terrors; in this respect it is a profoundly autobiographical work. In part, "Children Are Bored on Sunday" represents a meditation on the inadequacy Stafford felt in the cocktail-party company of the "Olympians" — the world of New York intellectuals ranging from the Rahvs to Sidney Hook to Mary McCarthy to Robert Lowell himself.

The story also marks the first occasion on which Stafford wrote about her drinking. As Emma recalls the desperate weeks that led to her going into seclusion, the details mirror Stafford's own crack-up in the fall of 1946:

In September, it had been her custom to spend several hours of each day walking in a straight line, stopping only for traffic lights and outlaw taxicabs, in the hope that she would be tired enough to sleep at night. At five o'clock — and gradually it became more often four o'clock and then half past three — she would go into a bar, where, while she drank, she seemed to be reading information offered by the *Sun* on "Where to Dine." Actually she had ceased to dine long since; every few days, with effort, she inserted thin wafers of food into her repelled mouth, flushing the frightful stuff down with enormous drafts of magical, purifying, fulfilling applejack diluted with tepid water from the tap.

Now, months later, only half out of hiding, Emma responds to Alfred Eisenburg's invitation:

He needed a drink after an afternoon like this — didn't she? Oh, Lord, yes, she did, and she did not question what he meant by "an afternoon like this" but said that she would be delighted to go, even though they would have to walk on eggs all the way from the Museum to the place where the bottle was, the peace pipe on Lexington. . . . To her own heart, which was shaped exactly like a valentine, there came a winglike palpitation, a delicate exigency, and all the fragrance of all the flowery springtime love affairs that ever were seemed waiting for them in the whisky bottle. To mingle their pain, their handshake had promised them, was to produce a separate entity, like a child that could shift for itself, and they scrambled hastily toward this profound and pastoral experience.

The New Yorker snatched up the Newport essay that *Life* had commissioned and then rejected, publishing it in August 1948. The editor Brendan Gill wrote Stafford, "Practically everybody here is in transports of jealous despair over the wonders of your Newport piece. What a job!"

To prepare Stafford for her return to the real world, her caretakers at Payne Whitney had tried to graft new habits onto her old, self-destructive regimen. She was "ordered" to go regularly to a gymnasium for exercise, she went on long walks all over Manhattan, and at one point she contemplated taking swimming lessons. Mary Jane Sherfey continued to see her in therapy three time a week; Stafford's finances precluded the daily sessions necessary for the true psychoanalysis that both she and Sherfey desired.

Stafford may also have been urged to develop "hobbies," for

in her first months out of Payne Whitney she spent a great deal
of time in the Hayden Planetarium and the Central Park Zoo,
"looking at a chimpanzee named Joe who smoked cigars." She
also started a kind of tutorial in biology with a professor at Columbia University. Stafford claimed that part of the incentive for
this was the hope that hanging around a college scene would help
her recapture the feeling of the University of Colorado, the setting for "In the Snowfall." Her Columbia professor, a geneticist,
ran what he called "the mouse room," where he was "breeding
mice with tails like bolts of lightning and mice that danced in
circles clockwise and mice that danced in circles counterclockwise." Stafford had her own desk and microscope, and she attended Tuesday colloquia on tobacco viruses and kindred subjects.

Above all, her doctors entreated Stafford not to touch alcohol.
It was a futile hope: almost at once, she began to have episodes
of drinking, and her insomnia (which in 1947 medical science had
not yet firmly linked to alcohol) returned in full force. Her health
that winter was very poor: she caught pneumonia, had persistent
fits of coughing (one of these, which occurred while she was still
in Payne Whitney, had been stopped only by two injections of
adrenaline), had to have a cyst removed from her arm, and was
told that her chronic sinus problems would require another operation on her nose.

When she had hastily rented the West Seventy-fifth Street
apartment, Stafford had not realized that it was directly above a
music school for children. "Within minutes of the departure of
the moving van," she later wrote, "the fiddles started being used
like buzz saws and the pianos started getting walloped and the
horns began neighing and nickering, and some persevering delin-
quent of ten began, without success, to learn the piccolo obligato
from 'Stars and Stripes Forever.' " Stafford fled to the New York
Society Library to pore over her notes. "In the Snowfall" was
not coming easily. For an article published in December in the
New York World-Telegram, Stafford posed at her typewriter for
an Alfred Stieglitz photo but told her interviewer, " 'I don't work
very long at a time. I can't. . . . It's so easy in New York to fall
into the habit of going to parties. You go to one cocktail party
and then find yourself making a date for another. And having
lunch with someone every day.' "

But the truth was that Stafford was lonely in her new apartment, all of whose windows faced brick walls. She was delighted to find that one of her neighbors was Sax Rohmer, the English novelist who had invented Fu Manchu. They met when taking out their garbage, and began to talk shop; Rohmer invited Stafford over for champagne. The amazingly successful detective writer turned out to belong to a circle of "Tories as doctrinaire as Iowa Republicans." When Stafford asked his opinion of such other thriller writers as Simenon, Agatha Christie, and Graham Greene, Rohmer claimed never to have heard of them. He read only his own works, he said, and liked to gain a nodding acquaintance with foreign languages by reading his books in translation. Stafford was charmed by this "mild, clean little old man" who, because his apartment faced the street, passed on daily weather reports to her in her viewless cell.

In early 1948 honors continued to come Stafford's way. She won her second Guggenheim Fellowship and, on April 3, was given an "award of achievement" by President Truman at the Women's National Press Club in Washington. Among her fellow recipients were Rebecca West, Ingrid Bergman, and Margaret Chase Smith. The dinner, she wrote Mary Lee,

> was really a triumph in a way for me because I didn't get nervous and for the first time in my life I was able to eat soup in the presence of more than four people. . . . After the dinner, we stood in a receiving line and shook hands with all 600 [guests] and Ingrid Bergman and I who stood side by side exchange[d] a few amiably bitter words about it. She was otherwise not very rewarding except to look at. She is painfully shy and is, as a result, a monologist and not an interesting one but a sincere one. I liked Rebecca West and talked a good deal with her.

While she was in Washington Stafford called up Lowell. After more than two years of almost continuous warfare, they had reached a kind of truce. "We are good friends now," Jean wrote Mary Lee, "and feel no bitterness toward each other but only toward our bungling lawyers." Having investigated and rejected Maine, New York, and Nevada as venues for divorce, Stafford and Lowell had at last decided that she would seek the decree in the Virgin Islands. The lawyers had hammered out a financial settlement: Stafford got a one-time lump sum of sixty-five hundred dollars, out of which she had to pay her own legal fees.

To get the divorce, Stafford was required to be in residence in the Virgin Islands for six weeks. At the end of April she flew to St. Thomas. The finality of the action seems to have triggered a new crisis; before she left New York Stafford increased the frequency of her visits to Sherfey to one a day, and on her arrival in the Virgins she must have sent a desperate communication to her therapist, for Sherfey telegraphed back, "PULL YOURSELF TOGETHER AND TAKE IT EASY SAY NO TO EVERYBODY LIVE YOUR LIFE NOT THEIRS NOTHING MORE IMPORTANT I EXPECT YOU TO DO IT KEEP WRITING AS EVER."

Stafford's dependency on her therapist required frequent letters of reassurance. In one Sherfey advised,

> First, there is absolutely no harm in taking phenobarbital with dibenamine. It may make you quite sleepy tho' — which added to the tropical torpor may complete your lethargy. . . . Now, alcohol + dibenamine is another story — in fact, alcohol + Jean Lowell is another story; but since we've been thru that before, I won't dwell on it now.

With glib affection, Sherfey closed, "Remember transferences work both ways, and I sincerely want you back all in one piece. . . . P.S. Stop Drinking — ."

Stafford stayed at the ramshackle Hotel 1829 in St. Thomas. The place was full of holidaymakers and other divorcées-to-be, whose doleful but sympathetic company threw her for a loop. To Lowell, she wrote wistfully:

> I am the only divorcee-to-be on the island who is married to a civilized man; or, alas, perhaps I should state it another way and should say I am the only one whose husband wants to get rid of her as soon as possible. But seeing them all, I cannot help feeling that in spite of all my hideous behavior in the first year of our separation, we have behaved better on the whole than most people do.
>
> I want us both to marry again, don't you? We'll be so much wiser and so much calmer. It is my ambition to live the rest of my life at a low pitch.

In the Virgin Islands Stafford made one pair of lasting friends, Nancy and Robert Gibney: "They fish and swim and they are probably the happiest people I've ever seen." The Gibneys were homesteading on a tiny island off St. John that Stafford visited for a weekend. The boat trip there unnerved her, and on the island, as Nancy Gibney later recalled, "for two days and nights she concealed her panic." On making it safely back to St. Thomas, Stafford stepped out of the boat and was greeted by an acquaintance who asked, " 'How was it?' " Stafford's answer was, " 'Where's the bourbon?' "

As the unhappy holiday drew to a close, Stafford was debilitated by illness. One night she cried through dinner, thinking about the loss of her husband. On June 14 she was officially divorced, after eight years, two months, and twelve days of marriage. Since the financial settlement had already been accomplished, Stafford made only one further legal request: she asked for the return of her maiden name.

Stafford had feared publicity about the breakup, but for the most part she was spared the innuendos of the press. In August a tabloid called the *American Weekly* ran a story entitled "Lost Love of a Rebellious Lowell." Dominating the one-page morality play was a photo of a watery-eyed Stafford, over the caption, "Jean Stafford Crawled Out of the Wreckage of a Car Into Romance and Out of Romance Into a Wrecked Marriage." The sanctimonious but essentially accurate piece concluded, "Books, books, books — from their youth, Lowell and Miss Stafford read them, and wanted to write them, and never came across one to chart a true course of love."

Early in 1948, before her trip to the Virgin Islands, Stafford had become involved with a man whose identity remains shadowy; the "love affair," as Stafford guardedly called it, lasted a full year. On April 10 she had written Mary Lee,

> Another reason that I have been so neglectful lately is that I am in love and I am not having a very good time of it, because I am in love with someone who is terrified of being in love with me. I have never known any man in all my life more gentle nor any with whom I more love to share experience nor any with whom I was more at peace. But I have matured enough to feel sure that though nothing may come of it, I shall weather my disappointment. Please don't mention it to anyone.

Several years later Stafford identified this person to her second husband, Oliver Jensen, as Jamie Caffery, a resident of Washington, D.C., and a young relative of Jefferson Caffery, then the

United States ambassador to France. Jensen, who had met Jamie
Caffery, recalls him as "a little bit of a fellow . . . sort of a
pipsqueak" and as a hanger-on in Stafford's circle who was a
serious drinker. Eileen Simpson was aware of Caffery as a "friend
and playmate" who helped Jean shop for a dress to wear to the
Press Club gala. Caffery was widely regarded to be a homosexual.

All these details may actually jibe. If Caffery were homosexual, that might explain his being "terrified of being in love" with
Stafford, as well as his wanting to keep the affair secret. It is also
unclear just what Stafford meant by "affair"; that appraisal may
well have been motivated by a competitive instinct aroused by
Lowell's very public liaison with Gertrude Buckman. On April
15, 1949, Stafford wrote Mary Lee that a "terminating note" had
come from her lover, and that "the affair ended in complete honesty."

It is entirely possible that this half-secret romance involved no
sex. If it is true that Stafford and Lowell were never lovers, as
she later claimed to Eve Auchincloss, then it is also possible that
by 1948 it had been almost ten years since Stafford had made
love with anyone (the last time having been her one-night stand
with Hightower in November 1938).

In May, from St. Thomas, Stafford had written to Lowell
complaining that she had been sick for ten days "with my
Louisiana-Monteagle disease," on top of a reaction to typhoid
shots. "I can barely move for all my intr[a]venous medicaments
of penicillin and adrenalin[e] and B-complex and typhoid and the
beastly fever goes on and on the way it used to do in that base
fashion." A few months earlier she had had penicillin injections
at New York Hospital — to treat her "virus pneumonia," she
had told Lowell.

If the "Louisiana-Monteagle disease" was in fact secondary syphilis, as seems fairly likely, it is conceivable that Stafford could
still have been having flare-ups in 1947–1948. Penicillin had been
generally available only since the end of the war. The drug was
not effective against viral pneumonia, but it was a miracle cure
for syphilis. During Stafford's yearlong hospitalization at Payne
Whitney, her perspicacious doctors may have uncovered the syphilis and at last cured it with the penicillin treatments that she
mentioned for the first time in 1947. If she had succeeded in
keeping the nature of her complaint a secret from Lowell

throughout their marriage, that would account for the red herrings in her letters to him, the subterfuge about why she was having the treatments.

Another letter to Lowell, which itself may have been a red herring, once more raises the related but separate question of whether her gonorrhea had made Stafford sterile. In 1948, not long after leaving Payne Whitney, she wrote Lowell, asking him to join her in hoping "that I will soon be loved and married so that I can have a child before it is too late." This remark surely implies that Lowell believed his wife to be capable of procreation. Yet only two years later Oliver Jensen found Stafford unalterably opposed to the idea of having children. Late in life she would write, "I love children, but I chose to have none because I knew I would be an abominable mother — by turns indulgent and cold." One obvious explanation for all of these contradictory statements (and others, such as her claim to Wilfrid Sheed that her injuries in the car accident had precluded childbearing) is that Stafford may have wanted to camouflage the possibility that she was sterile by pretending that the choice of whether or not to have children was for her simply a moral and intellectual one.

The year and a half following Stafford's divorce was a relatively tranquil period for her. She continued in therapy with Mary Jane Sherfey, who regularly read her stories and novels, sometimes even in manuscript. At some point her therapist asked Stafford, "What is your feeling about me?" The question provoked Stafford to write a three-page essay by way of reply. (Whether this was Sherfey's "assignment" or simply Stafford's habitually literary response is not clear.) The essay contains some interesting perceptions:

> The direct question, "What is your feeling about me?" reduces me to helpless embarrassment and I cannot be articulate. I think this is partly because I have never been able to demonstrate love except when I have been drunk and the love I have shown then has been trumped up out of the bottle. When I finally knew that I did not love him, I for the first time in my marriage began to tell Cal how much I did.

Stafford mentions also "my feeling toward all doctors, a feeling of almost craven humility that I feel toward only one other group of people, that is, composers."

Stafford had been planning a long writing trip in Europe for

the spring of 1949. At the end of February, however, she began
to hear from old friends that Lowell was headed for a breakdown
of his own, and she postponed her trip abroad.

It was not until some years later that Lowell was diagnosed as
manic depressive and treated with lithium. From late February
through early April 1949, nonetheless, he went through what
sounds like an extreme and extended manic episode, which ended
in forced hospitalization. The details are both tragic and pathetic.

In February, at Yaddo, Lowell became obsessed with the notion that the colony's kindly director, Elizabeth Ames, was at the
center of a Communist plot. Through sheer will, he rallied several other guests to his cause and forced a meeting of the Yaddo
board, at which he denounced Ames in vicious terms and demanded that she be fired immediately. (A counter-rally by Yaddo
veterans, including John Cheever and Alfred Kazin, saved Ames,
but the scandal severely damaged the institution.)

Next Lowell underwent a mystical reconversion to Catholicism, complete with delusions of messianic grandeur. In Chicago
to visit Allen Tate, he started to lose control. He caused a scene
in a restaurant, played a "joke" on his host by giving Caroline
Gordon a list of all of her husband's lovers, and finally had to be
arrested when he raised the window and shouted obscenities into
the night. Tate got Lowell released, then dispatched him by train
to Peter Taylor, who was teaching in Indiana.

In Bloomington Lowell went over the edge. He fled through
the town streets in the middle of the night, got into a serious
fistfight with a policeman, and ended up in a straitjacket in the
police station. By early April Lowell was in a padded cell in a
Massachusetts hospital, where he later had shock treatments.

Stafford was deeply dismayed by the news of Lowell's collapse. Lowell had written her in the midst of his manic spree to
claim that their marriage was still valid. Now it seemed incum-
bent upon her to sort the business out for herself in therapy; "I
am going to stay here where Dr Sherfey is," she wrote Mary
Lee, "and finally liberate myself from my guilt over that poor
boy." Stafford's analysis was that Lowell suffered from "a religious mania combined with his savage hatred of women. . . .
We were both so sick when we married that we didn't have a
prayer."

Stafford also had another reason for putting off the trip to Europe: "In the Snowfall" was not coming together, and she felt honor-bound to finish the book before sailing for London. She had led her editor, Robert Giroux, to believe that the novel was all but completed. But in early July she confessed to Mary Lee,

> My book will not be finished before I go, and I do not know if I shall ever finish it. I have abandoned it now and am breaking the bad news to my publisher this afternoon. Part of it is New York and part of it is the general disorder and loneliness of these last three years. I mean to make a fundamental change in my life when I return, but where I shall go and what I shall do, I don't know. Don't mention the book, not even to me. It is my Achilles' heel and I want, so far as possible, to forget about it. Too many people have talked about it to me too often, I have been badgered by too many questions of "When will it be done?" "What is it about?" And I cannot work that way.

The failure had deeply discouraged her: "I am in despair half the time and my insomnia has returned in full force. There are times when I feel that it is psychiatry that has destroyed my gift, but perhaps the gift isn't gone yet, I don't know."

To Stafford's delight, however, her summer trip to Great Britain, France, and Germany turned out to be "just this side of rapture." On assignment for *The New Yorker,* she traveled through ravaged German cities. The essay she wrote, which was published in December 1949 as a "Letter from Germany," is a superb piece of reporting: read almost forty years later, it conjures up the bitter postwar ironies of the Allied occupation as effectively as the best fiction. The piece is singularly free of nostalgia, even though Stafford must have been flooded with memories as she walked through Heidelberg. Although the place was off-limits to Americans, she stopped for a meal at the hotel where she had lived in 1936:

> The Haarlass is largely unchanged, but it is shabbier now; the waiters' alpaca jackets are threadbare at the elbows, and the checkered cloths on the tables in the park cafe are limp and dirty. I observed that, after all these years, the only change in the menu was the prices, which were doubled or tripled; there was an ample choice, and the cold specialty of the house was still *Schwedenplatte,* an antipasto that I remembered well, for it had been dominated

by cold eel, fished out of the river by a cretinous boy, who now
has grown into a cretinous man.

In September she went to Edinburgh for the International Festival of Music and Drama, where she successfully impersonated
a critic of classical music, dance, and theater. The smooth "Letter
from Edinburgh" that ensued gives evidence of just how effi-
cient a journalist Stafford could be when her spirit was up to it.
She composed the comprehensive essay as the last festival events
were winding down and cabled it to New York on September 8,
in time for *The New Yorker* to publish it in its issue of September 17.

Stafford's original reason for going to Europe was to rent a
cottage in the west of Ireland where she could work without
distraction. Shortly after being discharged from Payne Whitney,
Stafford had written Lowell:

> The greatest joy since my release has been my meeting, several
> times, with Graham Greene who looks very much like me and is
> the nicest man I have met in ages and ages. . . . Greene says he
> thinks I might be awfully happy in Dublin and he proposes that I
> come to England next summer and he will take a cottage for me
> in some romantic sounding place in Ireland where, he says, there
> will be nothing at all in front of me but America on the other side
> of the ocean.

By spring 1948 Greene had located a specific cottage and had
promised to "get me well introduced to 'the best pub-keepers,
ex gun-men, poker-playing priests and an attractive young doctor.' " Sherfey was dubious, but Stafford tried to reassure her: "I
pointed out to her that the Irish are statistically the maddest people in the world and must, therefore, have plenty of psychiatrists
but she came back with the statement that they are also statistically the hardest drinking." Stafford had gone ahead and rented
the cottage for the summer of 1948, but she had been forced to
postpone the trip because of the divorce.

In the summer of 1949 Stafford covered her tracks so well that
while we know she went to Ireland, we know almost nothing
beyond that. Her affection for Graham Greene had not dimmed
since the year before; she had written of him in loving terms in
the essay inspired by Sherfey's "What is your feeling about me?"

Years later Stafford told her friend Berton Roueché that she had
had an affair with Greene. If this was true, the most likely time
for the liaison to have happened was during the summer of 1949,
in Great Britain. Greene himself denies the claim. Responding to
it thirty-eight years later, he writes, "I liked Jean Stafford very
much and also her work but I am afraid there was never an affair
with her."

Stafford also later told several people, including her friends Joan
Stillman, Eve Auchincloss, and Joseph Mitchell, that at about
this time she had had an abortion, an event that may have been
linked to her September visit to Scotland. Whether or not this
was the truth — and if it was, what connection such an abortion
may have had with a relationship between Stafford and Graham
Greene, Jamie Caffery, or someone else — remains uncertain. Like
Stafford's hopeful note to Lowell about wanting to have a child
"before it is too late," a retrospective "admission" of an abortion
could have served as a smokescreen to cover her possible infer-
tility.

In 1949 Stafford published three short stories in *The New Yorker,*
based respectively on her year in Heidelberg ("The Cavalier"),
on Damariscotta Mills ("Polite Conversation"), and on her brief
experience of the Virgin Islands ("A Modest Proposal" — originally published as "Pax Vobiscum"). This last story brought a
protest from the NAACP because of a (bigoted) character's use
of the work *nigger*. Katharine White reassured Jean that the magazine would stand behind her; she and Harold Ross had begun to
regard Stafford as one of their favorite and most reliable writers.

In the fall Stafford wrote Lowell,

> I find *no* advantages in not being married, not one. I think it is
> infinitely *more* complicated besides being the most miserable lonely
> nightmare I've ever known. What fun is it for a girl to meet Dr
> Cohn [an aged mentor] on Tuesday at the Plaza and the rest of
> the time to see fairies and get passed at by the husbands of one's
> friends?

It did not take Stafford long to rectify this situation. At a party
in the late fall she met Oliver Jensen, a tall, well-built, appealing
editor and writer for *Life*. Jensen, instantly smitten by the well-
known novelist, started asking her out. At first the two seemed
to have certain things in common. *Life* had run a satiric piece on

Stephens College; it was, Jensen recalls, "a point of sympathy between us." Like Stafford, Jensen had recently been divorced. He was a year older than she. He had worked at *Life* for a decade, less three and a half years of naval service during the war, an experience that had led to his writing a minor best-seller of 1945, *Carrier War*.

Jensen had money and liked to spend it. According to a friend of Stafford's, "He took her out to dinner every night at 21, bought her flowers. . . . He was like a movie star, and she was temporarily dazzled."

The editor's courtship of the writer was interrupted by a month's sojourn in France and Italy, where he visited assorted literati; everywhere Jensen went, he asked people what they knew and thought about Jean Stafford. When he returned to the States after New Year's, Jensen found that Stafford had gone off to Yaddo for a brief stay. She wrote girlish, flirtatious letters inviting him to visit. He went to Saratoga Springs; like college kids, they "snuck out of the place" and "had a jolly time." Although he had known her for only a few months, Jensen proposed marriage, and Stafford accepted.

On January 28, 1950, they were married at Christ Church Methodist in Manhattan. A number of her friends immediately foresaw disaster. As they left the wedding reception, Harold Ross told Katharine and E. B. White, " 'It will not last.' "

Only a few months earlier, straight out of the hospital in Massachusetts, Lowell had married Elizabeth Hardwick; now Stafford was quick to write him with the news of her own marriage. Whether or not Stafford was acting on the rebound, the impulsive plunge was not really characteristic of her; when Hightower had begged her to leap, she had only dithered. According to her friend Katinka De Vries, "She always said she married Oliver because he took her to 21." Joseph Mitchell remembers Stafford saying, "He was the football player who didn't ask her to the dances at CU."

In later years Stafford joked that she had "only been married twenty minutes" to Jensen; once, when discussing her three marriages on a TV talk show, she claimed to have forgotten the name of her second husband. Jensen himself, while later conceding that the marriage had been "foolish" and "impetuous," had a simpler reason for embarking on it: "I was very much in love with her."

The pair honeymooned in Haiti and Jamaica. Stafford was on

assignment for *Mademoiselle,* for which she tossed off a second-rate article that was devoid of personal details. Once back in the States, the newlyweds set to work house-hunting in Westport, the town Stafford had disdained as "vulgar," "anti-semitic," and "bourgeois" on leaving it in 1945. For thirty-five thousand dollars Jensen purchased an 1810 Joseph Adams Colonial house, a virtual mansion on four acres, with a separate garage and a barn. "It was the house of her dreams," says Joan Stillman, "and she made it terribly attractive."

As she had in her first "dream house," in Damariscotta Mills, Stafford reveled in domesticity. She cooked for her husband (who commuted daily to the *Life* offices in Manhattan), refurbished the old house, threw dinner parties, and set about making friends among the local gentry. The nouveau country wife lived for Westport gossip: "She used to telephone about five times a day," says Stillman.

Stafford's spirits during the first half year of her life with Jensen were higher than they had been at any time since 1945. Peter De Vries, her Westport neighbor and *New Yorker* comrade, claims that the happiest he ever saw Jean was one evening after she returned from a panel discussion in New York where she had been assailed from the audience by a succession of heavy-handed Viennese psychiatrists. Over cocktails at the De Vries house, Stafford was reduced to hysterics as Jensen brilliantly parodied the learned doctors.

Stafford had "arrived in my life," as Jensen puts it, "with a complete baggage of amusing foibles and fancies and artful devices." These included her nicknames from the Lowell period, such as Beaner and Eanbean. She began calling her husband Pode, a play on Toad of Toad Hall in *The Wind in the Willows.* In a girlish hand Stafford wrote valentines and notes to Jensen, sometimes mailing them to him at *Life:*

Dear Pode
  How are you? Please bring the purr machine when you come to visit me as I have no cat.
  Sincerely yours,
    Beaner

Another was addressed to "My Own Bear" and had hearts dotting the I's:

If you want me to hug you hard when she is not looking come to
my house. Please knock loud as I am hibernating — except for
you (!!!!!)
    Loads of love,
      Honey

For one of the few times in her life, Stafford was happy being
someone's lover. Jensen heard the version of Stafford's life history that she wanted him to believe. The illnesses with which
she had come back from Heidelberg in 1937 were "European
typhus" and scurvy. Stafford was candid about Lowell's propensity for violence. She described what she called "the accident"
(the car crash in 1938) and "the incident" (Lowell's attempt to
strangle her in 1946) but omitted mention of his breaking her
nose in New Orleans in 1940. The "incident," she maintained,
had come not on her waking from a dream of another lover but
after an all-night argument sparked by her telling Lowell that she
could no longer take holy communion. (In a letter to Jensen written
nine days before their marriage, Stafford says, "I hope that violence is not one of your interests because I don't like to be an
invalid.")

    According to Joan Stillman, in 1950 Stafford was still in love
with Lowell and talked about him all the time. She also "used to
call with symptoms. 'I've got something on my hand. It's getting all red.' " Says Jensen, "She was always checking in at the
hospital for a cough or a cold or a mysterious breaking out." As
is the case for every other period of Stafford's life, it is hard in
this instance to disentangle her hypochondria from her genuine
medical complaints. In 1950–1951 she had a second tonsillectomy
and yet another nose operation. The latter, some friends thought,
once again appreciably damaged her looks.

    As some of Stafford's closest friends had predicted, tensions
between her and Jensen began to cloud the marriage. Discrepancies in upbringing, politics, and religion began to matter. Jensen
was a Yale graduate, the son of a New England professor and a
very proper Englishwoman — a lineage that seemed to make
Stafford feel defensive about her own plain-folks western background. He tended to wax critical of Catholicism — particularly
of the Irish Catholic influence in New England. By instinct Jensen was a Republican. He was also a sportsman and a habitually

active person. Stafford, however, "had no athletic abilities. She couldn't dance worth a damn — I tried, I like to dance."

At least as important as these other differences was Jensen's lack of sympathy with psychiatry. As he puts it, "I believe in the Blessed Censor — your mind gradually forgetting unpleasantness. But the basis of psychiatry is to drag it all out of you again. . . . Is it not better, I think, to rise above it?" To Jensen's mind, Stafford's visits to Sherfey did her no good: "She'd come back thinking about all the things that bothered her again."

Equally harmful, in Jensen's view, were Jean's friendships with the "weird crowd" from her Lowell period. "I mean a Schwartz, or a Tate," he explains. "I know they were literary figures to some people. To me they were troublemakers who stirred her up."

In turn, Stafford "used to put down and disparage everything to do with *Time, Life,* and *Fortune,*" says Jensen. Her scorn had much to do with Jensen's decision, during the first year of their marriage, to quit his job at *Life* and turn his back on its "fat, comfortable payroll." Teaming up with his friend Joseph Thorndike, the former managing editor of *Life,* Jensen started Picture Press, a small firm devoted to publishing high-quality photography books. He also wrote a popular book called *The Revolt of American Women.* Next Thorndike and Jensen produced segments for the TV show "Omnibus"; then, in 1954, along with another ex-colleague, the two friends launched the extraordinarily successful magazine *American Heritage.* Its cousin *Horizon* appeared in 1958.

Stafford and Jensen also clashed over the question of children. "I had hoped with Jean that perhaps we might have one," he says. "It seemed to me that would have straightened her out no end. But that's a sentimental idea — it probably wouldn't have at all." Although she had told Lowell that she wanted a child, Stafford maintained to Jensen that she had no interest in being a mother.

Jensen was aware of the power Lowell still wielded over Stafford's feelings. "She was no longer *in love* with Lowell," he says today, "but he filled a very large part of her consciousness all the time. . . . Anybody marrying her in these circumstances would probably never fully engross her attention or thoughts."

Their most serious disagreement, however, was over Stafford's drinking. Jensen was and is a relatively abstemious man, who seldom requires a second drink — "because one's enough." When he married Stafford, he had no idea of her dependence on alcohol. "She really was on her best behavior in the brief courtship," he says. "She didn't drink too much, and she was very sweet and demure. . . . I felt that I was in a sense a big sensible fellow coming into her life and could straighten everything out."

Soon enough Jensen discovered his wife's propensity. "She would have one drink," he reflects, "and right away the whole mechanism of alcoholism was triggered. She'd get fuzzy on one drink and she would be dying for another. . . . Her voice was always good and sharp. Her mind was affected to the point that it slowed her speech, and that made her even more effective as a storyteller. There was a look in her eye, an unsteadiness of the hand." As their quarrels about drinking intensified, Jensen resorted to hiding the liquor; he even called both Sherfey and Stafford's medical doctor for help in understanding the problem.

During the span of her marriage to Jensen, Stafford published six short stories in *The New Yorker.* One was "A Country Love Story," her muted but powerful version of the imaginary-lover incident in Damariscotta Mills. The story won her her third O. Henry Award and was thereafter often reprinted in anthologies. Another widely admired story was "The Echo and the Nemesis," in which Stafford mingled memories of Heidelberg with the tale of a struggle between two women student friends, one a compulsive eater. Martha Foley chose this latter for her 1951 anthology of best stories — the fourth time in seven years that she had included Stafford's work.

Yet according to Jensen, Stafford was having trouble producing these stories. "She couldn't get them finished," he says. "They didn't seem to come out. . . . Her method was, she would do two-three-four pages, then throw them out. Do the three or four pages again a little differently, throw them out." Just as Stafford had sneered at *Life,* so Jensen shared a common prejudice against *New Yorker* short stories, which he was not shy to pronounce: "I said, the way to write a *New Yorker* story is, you write the short story, and you cut off the first third and the last third, and they publish the remainder."

In July 1950, for the first time, *The New Yorker* rejected one of Stafford's stories. Katharine White's apologetic note does not identify it; it may have been "Old Flaming Youth," which *Harper's Bazaar* published that December. During the second half of the year White had to turn down two more Stafford stories — "Life Is No Abyss" and "The Connoisseurs," which eventually appeared in *Sewanee Review* and *Harper's Bazaar,* respectively.

Most vexing of all to Stafford was her continuing difficulty with "In the Snowfall." Beset with guilt about taking so long to finish a book for which she had received the full advance two years earlier, she continued to mislead her editors at Harcourt, Brace. Finally, in December 1950, she abandoned the novel for good. In an essay called "Truth and the Novelist," written only a few months later, Stafford declared that one day "the reason why I could not write the novel dawned on me."

> It was ever so simple: I hated my material. The years I had elected to write about had not been happy ones for me nor for any of my characters and we emerged, in my merciless pages, unappealing to a degree in our melancholy; humorless, morbid, self-seeking, unworthy of any but the dreary fates I meted out to us.

Whatever pertinence there is in this harsh self-criticism, it does not tell the whole truth. In the same essay Stafford claimed that on coming to her realization of what was wrong with "In the Snowfall," she at once burned the whole manuscript. This is an outright lie: among the papers Stafford left to the University of Colorado are hundreds of pages of the various drafts of that work. They make it clear (as some of the passages quoted in earlier chapters of this book should demonstrate) that there was an immense potential for a very good novel in the material Stafford struggled with. Joyce Bartholomew, far from coming across as the humorless melancholic Stafford dismisses, instead looms as one of Stafford's most fully realized characters — a vulnerable, idealistic, shy, ambitious college girl in whom credulity clashes with a hunger for sophistication, haughty bookishness with a lust for experience. It is, quite simply, a loss for literature that Stafford could not finish "In the Snowfall."

There may be a psychological explanation for Stafford's failure. The novel's structural problem seems to lie in a tug-of-war that is taking place between two equally ambitious themes. On the one hand Stafford set out to tell the story of Lucy Cooke; on the other, the novel promises a Victorian scope in its attempt to

define Joyce as the heroine of her own escape from her family —
in particular from her vindictive, violent, half-crazy father. Along
with his daughter Joyce, Fulke Bartholomew takes on a vivid
reality in the half-finished chapters of "In the Snowfall" — as
does Maisie Perrine, the moribund hedonist who is based on Lucy
Cooke.

Perhaps, then, Stafford cold not in the end sort out what the
book was really "about" — whether the focus was Joyce and her
father, or Joyce and Maisie. Moreover, she does not seem to have
been able to face putting Maisie's suicide on paper, writing instead all around the edges of it. Nor, finally, was Stafford ever
able to publish any fiction that penetrated the mystery of her
relationship with her father — even though she worked at such
an understanding for the rest of her life. She had hinted on earlier
occasions that her father's very existence imperiled her ambitions as a writer. As far as the creative good of his own daughter was concerned, John Stafford may have simply lived too
long.

A week after she gave up on "In the Snowfall," Stafford started
on another novel, which eventually became *The Catherine Wheel*.
At once she felt liberated by the decision to write an *un*autobiographical book. Robert Giroux, her patient editor at Harcourt,
Brace, wrote the working title of the new novel into her 1947
contract for "In the Snowfall."

During August 1951 Stafford took a brief, dutiful train trip to
Colorado, where she visited her father and Mary Lee on the ranch
in Hayden. With her usual witty grumpiness, she wrote Jensen
about the trials of travel and the ordeal of family.

> I cannot wait to get home — indeed, I am almost wild — and I
> think maybe at last I shall be able to convey to Dr. S[herfey] and
> to you exactly what the blight has been that has twisted and hal-
> lucinated me all my life and perhaps you, Oliver, will finally un-
> derstand my unnatural feeling toward my father — seeing him
> again, I am amazed that all of us did not commit suicide in our
> cradles.

John Stafford, still struggling to break into print at seventy-
seven, had grown to be a burden to his daughters. Harry and
Mary Lee took care of him on the ranch every summer; in the
winter he lived with Marjorie in Oregon. Jean was terrified at

the prospect of having to assume her third of the caretaking. The arrangement caused serious friction among the sisters. Harry Frichtel says, "I'd keep the old man in the summer and then [Marjorie]'d keep him in the winter, and he'd pay her [rent] and then she'd want me to pay her too in the winter, and I told her to go to hell." Marjorie did indeed ask for regular payments from Mary Lee and Jean to help support their father, whereas Mary Lee and Harry put him up free of charge. According to Marjorie, Jean contributed money only at the very end of John Stafford's life, when he had to be put in a nursing home.

For years Jean had been inventing excuses to postpone and prevent her sisters' visits back east. In 1949, for instance, when Mary Lee had wanted to come to New York, Jean had capped a litany of evasive complaints with the intimidating news that one could not get a hotel room in the city for less than ten dollars a day. Much later, when Marjorie finally confronted her about her excuses, Jean "became angry and said she had no intention of jeopardizing the 'edifice' she had erected with her writing and that was the end of that."

In contrast to Lowell, however, Jensen was eager to meet Jean's family. He corresponded warmly with her father and Mary Lee and helped engineer a visit to Westport by the latter, which Jean was powerless to forestall. Mary Lee and Jensen got along extremely well. Jean's Westport friend Joan Stillman found her sister "very attractive, sort of classy. I was amazed, because Jean always described her family as sort of these bumpkins. Mary Lee was *far* from a bumpkin."

As her father and sisters had begun to recognize, by 1952 Stafford was a genuine celebrity. She had longed since childhood for the very career that was now securely hers, as a published novelist with a loyal readership. Yet the fame that attended that career meant little to her. In 1944 Paul Thompson had marveled that in the midst of the great fuss over *Boston Adventure,* Stafford preferred to dwell on the negative reviews and the crank letters her novel had elicited. There was no affectation in her avowal to Mary Lee in 1948:

It is hard to convey, without sounding hypocritical or grotesquely eccentric, how little I like the small fame I have acquired. I feel what I have always felt, "If only they knew what I'm really like, if only they knew what a fraud I am, they would not flatter me in this way."

In 1952 Stafford was chosen to be a member of the National Book Award jury for fiction, along with Budd Schulberg, Brendan Gill, Robert Gorham Davis, and Lloyd Morris. This quintet gave the prize to James Jones's *From Here to Eternity*. Around the same time, Stafford joined the Cosmopolitan Club, an elite social organization on the Upper East Side for professional women. One of her chief motives for belonging was that membership assured her of a room to rent for her visits to Manhattan.

In the summer of 1952 Stafford returned to the writers' conference in Boulder. Fifteen years earlier, as the conference's twenty-two-year-old secretary, she had met Robert Lowell; now, at thirty-seven, she was to be its star attraction, delivering the lecture that was its centerpiece, as Ford Madox Ford had done in 1937 and Thomas Wolfe in 1935.

Stafford combined the conference with a weekend visit to Hayden. Marjorie, who was visiting Mary Lee, remembers that

> On this occasion Jean again looked like the fresh, virginal coed I had remembered from Boulder days. She had gained a bit of weight and looked bloomingly healthy. Her clothing this time was unremarkable but fitting and flattering and immaculate looking. I remember particularly how sweet and pretty she looked in a nice red and white printed cotton dress. She was shy as could be and when friends of Mary Lee came calling she would hide in a closet or bum a ride to the mesa with Harry.

Stafford refused to let any of her family come to Boulder to hear her lecture. The rejection badly hurt Mary Lee's feelings. Says Harry Frichtel today, with measured bitterness, "Jean didn't want to disgrace her friends by her sister being around, I guess."

The truth, however, was that Stafford dreaded the whole conference, particularly the public performance that the lecture required. On arriving in Boulder, she was lionized. The local paper proudly declared, "Jean Stafford is recognized as one of the outstanding writers of this generation. In England she generally is regarded as our foremost young American writer."

Not all her reunions were pleasant ones. Goodrich Walton, Jean's high-school boyfriend, took her out to dinner. As he recalls,

I was stupid enough to tell her that all the characters and all the crap she wrote had tea for blood. I couldn't understand her writing about the old maids in Boston. I unloaded on her about how gutless her writing was in *The New Yorker* and *Mademoiselle*. She was very unhappy with what I said. . . . Her feeling was, "Who in the hell is this guy to be critical of my work? What's he written?" I realized what a great talent she had, but my criticism to her was, "Who the hell cared about these characters?"

Walton and Stafford parted on unfriendly terms. They never saw each other again.

Just as Ford Madox Ford, Evelyn Scott, Howard Mumford Jones, and John Crowe Ransom had been asked to do for her work in the 1930s, Stafford was required to read and criticize the manuscripts of dozens of aspiring writers. She regarded this task as a nightmare. She claimed to have forty-five novel manuscripts to read; they included "two pornographic novels which could easily have caused their authors to be arrested" and another called " 'Appy Roads." Living on campus, Stafford was beset by "children who howl" — the offspring of summer students lodging in the same dorm.

To get through the conference, she had gone on the wagon, but as usual her resolve broke down under the strain of back-to-back cocktail parties. On July 22 she delivered her lecture. For it she had written a delightful and mordant essay called "An Etiquette for Writers," in which she mingled anecdotes of the writer's life, reminiscences of CU, and a frank confession of her ambivalence about returning to the scene of her adolescence. Paul Thompson reported in his diary, "Jean's talk was tremendous: it was sincere and moving and couched in her own brilliant prose. She looked beautiful, and the audience took her to its heart." Jane Fitz-Randolph, Stafford's CU friend and herself now a professional writer, had a different impression:

The night she gave her evening lecture, she said right at the beginning that her editors had learned long ago that they should never send her to be a speaker anywhere, because instead of making people want to buy her books, she completely turned them off. . . . When it came time for questions and answers, she took about two questions and then she simply said, "I'm sorry, I am no good at this, I cannot answer any more questions," and she walked off the stage.

Throughout her marriage to Jensen Stafford's health had remained almost continuously poor. The operation on her nose was "too hideous to describe," she wrote Mary Lee; it was performed by "a handsome lady doctor whom I could hardly dislike more. 'Is it really pain or is it only apprehension?' she asks when she is drilling directly into my skull. . . ." Some of Stafford's physical harm had been caused by her drinking. In March 1951, during a stay at New York Hospital, Stafford learned that "I have a 'damaged' liver, a disorder that seems somehow shameful and the righting of which will be almost interminable and very boring."

In September 1951 she began an extended treatment of largedosage cortisone shots. They were prescribed by her doctor in accordance with "a whole new theory" he and his colleagues had developed about drinking problems; the theory, as Stafford understood it, held that "there is an actual chemical need for alcohol, and that there is, in addition, a need for alcohol as an anaesthetic for the pains that have a physical origin but one that can't be pinned down or cut out or even permanently alleviated." To Mary Lee, Stafford crowed, "Can you imagine how this diminishes my guilt?"

Within its first year, Stafford's second marriage had started to founder. Peter De Vries remembers her dropping by his office one day to announce, "Marriage is an unnatural condition. You don't know how lucky you are." Says Blair Clark, "She started complaining to me about [Jensen] right away. There was one incident in which she claimed he had tried to break her wrist." Stafford was sporting a bandage on her wrist at the time. Says Jensen, "That's simply not true. I've never hit a woman."

The quarrels became epidemic. Jensen recalls, "The battles always got going — she liked to bait me about my politics and religion, or my very proper English mother." In private moments of contrition Stafford would despise herself for picking fights, for "my incurable habit of continuing what is intolerable long after it has reached its logical conclusion." Nonetheless, their basic incompatibility stared both partners in the face. Behind his back, Stafford made cruel fun of Jensen's business style:

> He is in his proper element: he is Operating. Talking into two telephones at once, going to three cocktail parties a day, having

dinner with important people at important clubs. I am sandwiched in: sometimes I get a telephone call late in the afternoon.

Stafford kept making efforts to stay off the bottle. During one
dry spell she turned down a Caribbean sailing cruise with her
husband and a "rich friend" of his. To Mary Lee, Jean reported,

> I refuse to do most things now — I will not go places where I
> know the only way to endure is to drink and this means that I go
> nowhere except to the doctors who are the only people who make
> good sense to me. It is not the drinking that I mind, it is the
> intolerable boredom that I resent — the evenings lasting until one
> or two. So Oliver stays in town [New York City] frequently now
> until all hours and I come out on the earliest possible train and get
> into bed with George Eliot and Silas Marner [the cats] purring at
> my feet. It is not what I would call a full life but I am glad of the
> quiet.

"As we started to break up," Jensen recalls, "she said, it's on
account of you and the marriage that I can't get any work done.
Then she would say, of course that's not true. . . . But it would
flit through her mind and find utterance, and that naturally in-
furiated me, and then we'd have a Mr. and Mrs."

Wilfrid Sheed's memorable summation, derived no doubt from
Stafford's own later view — "At some point, she married Oliver
Jensen, and unmarried him again in haste, as one erases a graffito" — does not do justice to the effort and sorrow on both sides.
For Stafford, the disintegration of the marriage was full of pain.
In an abject mood one night, she left Jensen a note professing
repeatedly that she loved him and admitting, "I am all you say:
a liar, a breaker of promises, an alcoholic, an incompetent, a
[   ]aker, a hypochondriac." The fifth epithet had been made
illegible by Stafford's tearing a small hole in the page.

Jensen did not give up easily. He wrote Mary Jane Sherfey a
long letter begging for counsel, but he could not resist adding a
suggestion that therapy, far from helping Stafford, might have
served instead only to keep her problems "fresh and painful."

By the time of the writers' conference in the summer of 1952,
Stafford knew that a divorce was inevitable; she said as much to
her closest friends in Boulder, Paul and Dorothy Thompson.
Jensen's phone calls to her that August sometimes reduced her
to tears. After one call she told the Thompsons that Jensen had

demanded to talk to the man she was sleeping with in Boulder.
From the conference Stafford wrote her husband long, exhausted
letters that combined the residue of affection with pathetic self-
blame: "I hope with all my heart that some day you will be able
to forgive and forget me."

Once Jean was back in Westport, the marriage spiraled toward
its ineluctable end. One night, drunk, she walked to the railroad
station and took a train to Manhattan, bringing with her no money
and only the clothes she was wearing. When she could find none
of her New York friends at home, she spent the night on a bench
in Grand Central Station. Jensen located her the next day and
drove her back home.

During the fall of 1952, along with her friends Peter and Katinka De Vries and Joan Stillman, Stafford got caught up in Adlai
Stevenson's campaign for the presidency. She donated fifteen
dollars to his cause and then, a day or two after Eisenhower's
landslide victory, wrote Stevenson a passionate letter of "congratulation, rue, and entreaty," avowing, among other things,
that "You opened up before us a world of such splendid possibilities for America that we cannot now commit the sin against
the Holy Ghost, that of despair; you exist as our hope; we, therefore, become responsible." During the campaign Stafford had been
vexed by her intuition that Jensen was going to vote for Eisenhower, a suspicion that he would neither confirm nor deny.

At about the same time, at the beginning of November 1952,
Stafford retreated once more into New York Hospital. She had
been worried about some "tumors" she had, which her gynecol-
ogist assured her were benign and normal in women her age.
Before she left the hospital, however, she did something that
deeply shocked and wounded Jensen. Without telling her husband beforehand, she persuaded her doctor to perform a hysterectomy.

Precisely why Stafford had the operation remains unclear; Jensen himself could never decide whether it sprang from Jean's habitual hypochondria or merely her desire to affirm for good her
choice not to have children. In view of what we know about the
possibility that Stafford was already sterile because of her gonorrhea, it may be that the operation seemed at once to cost her
nothing and to put an end to the need for her to pretend that she
was still toying with the idea of having children.

According to Joan Stillman, the final debacle came on election night. When Jensen came home that evening, he "came into the kitchen, and Jean said, 'Well, now, you tell me. Who did you vote for?' He said, 'Eisenhower.' " Then — so Stafford told Stillman — " 'I said a word I seldom say. I threw down my mop, I ran upstairs and slammed the door.' " In the morning she called Stillman: " 'Come and get me, because I will never spend another night under the same roof as this man.' "

Stafford packed a small bag. Her friend picked her up and drove her to the train station. Without even leaving Jensen an address at which to reach her, Stafford disappeared into New York City.

XV

"Jean Stafford.
Jean Stafford."

UNABLE TO LEARN anything about Stafford's whereabouts, Jensen appealed to Mary Lee, on the assumption that she might have heard from her sister. Instead of demanding information, however, he wrote a long letter that is exemplary in its compassion and perspective.

> This decision has been gathering inside Jean for a long time. For some two years she has threatened divorce as often as once a week. . . . Alcohol, which apparently she will never be able to leave alone permanently, plays a part in this, but not the main one. You must understand the conflicts, knowing Jean so well. Her pessimism, catholic and profound, and her memory, which is photographic only, alas, in respect of unhappy things, hold her in thrall. She believes in disease but not in cures. She is convinced that she cannot live with me and also write. . . . And within her poor unhappy soul the battle rages between Jean Stafford, crusader for literature, art and liberalism, and this straw man she has created. This fictitious Oliver Jensen stands for Philistinism, anti-intellectualism, fascism, bad writing and reaction, and he is cursed out every night in the presence of the genuine Oliver Jensen.

While admitting his bitterness, Jensen anticipated its evaporation, "leaving my genuine admiration and love for Jean, even though I am quite ready to admit that she is too much for me to handle, and I think for any husband." The predominant mood of the letter is concern for Stafford and regret at his own loss: "I don't think I'll ever feel quite the same about anybody as I have about your remarkable, brilliant sister. . . ."

When Stafford finally communicated with her husband, it was through the impersonal voice of her lawyer, who informed Jensen that she was going ahead with a divorce. She would sail for the Virgin Islands around Christmas.

The previous January had seen the publication of *The Catherine Wheel,* Stafford's third novel to reach print. Once she had abandoned work on "In the Snowfall," she had been able to write with a daily efficiency reminiscent of the prolific verve of her early twenties. She wrapped up the novel in seven months, delivering it in the fall of 1951; Harcourt, Brace brought it out barely five months thereafter.

An extravagant Westport bash had toasted the publication of the novel. Both James Thurber and Stafford got so drunk at the party that they fell down the stairs. Thurber, in his inebriated myopia, gave up trying to find an ashtray and flicked his cigarette ashes onto a precious carpet, burning large holes in it. His carelessness outraged Stafford — Thurber had "ruined" her celebration — more than it did the hostess.

The Catherine Wheel is a novel of some seventy-two thousand words — only a little longer than *The Mountain Lion.* The story is set in a northern New England town called Hawthorne, based in most of its particulars on Damariscotta Mills. Its characters, though, are in no important sense autobiographical, and Stafford further distances herself by placing the action in the summer of 1937.

The central themes of the novel concern conscience and betrayal. Katharine Congreve, still a beauty in her early forties, has never married; a Boston society figure, she holds court every summer at Congreve House, her family mansion in Hawthorne, where she is the cynosure of "townies" and summer people alike. Katharine had been raised in the same household as her orphaned cousin, Maeve Maxwell. Twenty years earlier she had set her heart on John Shipley; at the climactic summer party, however, she had watched in numb silence as John fell in love with Maeve instead.

Now John and Maeve, long married, spend each summer traveling in Europe, with their children deposited at Hawthorne, in Katharine's care. Honor and Harriet are silly, pretentious twin sisters in their late teens; Andrew, the only boy, is twelve. The high point of his year is his annual return to Hawthorne, where he resumes his intense palship with Victor Smithwick, a local Tom Sawyer who guides Andrew through the adventures of the country summer.

Stafford narrates her tale from a point of view that alternates between Katharine Congreve and Andrew Shipley. The boy is the novel's great creation: with uncanny authenticity, Stafford imagines her way into the head of a twelve-year-old protagonist of the opposite sex. In the interaction between these two cousins who are a generation apart in age, the author sets up a powerful symmetry of misunderstanding.

For Katharine and Andrew each have a secret. Katharine has begun an affair with John Shipley, who will decide by the end of the summer whether to leave the unsuspecting Maeve and come live with her, or whether to end the affair for the sake of the children. Andrew's summer, meanwhile, has been ruined by the sudden appearance of Charles Smithwick, Victor's older brother, a manly sailor who has seen the world. Now Victor, idolatrous of his sibling, has no time for Andrew Shipley. In despair, Andrew repeatedly prays for Charles Smithwick to die, until his very obsession becomes a voice of evil in his head that he is powerless to quiet — and that he begins to fear Katharine can overhear.

The tension of the novel thus radiates from the psychic rapport between Andrew and Katharine. Each fears that the other has guessed his secret. In reality, neither has any inkling of the other's private torment. The reader knows all, and in this ironic gap of knowledge lies the animating momentum of the story.

In this respect Stafford creates a beautifully balanced plot, which, though edged constantly with humor, threatens at every turn to explode into tragedy. In another sense, however, she paints herself into a corner. No plausible denouement can live up to the richness that the plot promises. Unfortunately, as if she half recognized the dilemma, Stafford resorts to her usual deus ex machina. At a grand summer fireworks party that echoes the one twenty years before, when John fell in love with Maeve, Charles Smithwick's hair catches fire. As Katharine comes to his rescue, her dress is engulfed in flames. The sailor survives; Katharine dies without telling her secret, or guessing Andrew's.

Both *The Mountain Lion* and *The Catherine Wheel* "work" as myth: an ending in which a brother accidentally slays his sister or a fateful fire scourges secret betrayers might ring true in a symbolic world of demigods and enchanted woods. Stafford herself understood these two novels to have symbolic cores. But in works of fiction in which everything else proceeds according to naturalistic conventions, these resolutions seem engineered and gimcrack. Nowhere in Stafford's oeuvre is the artifice more detrimental to the achievement than in *The Catherine Wheel*.

The style of the novel, especially in the chapters written from Katharine's point of view, to some extent harks back to *Boston Adventure;* there is less of Mark Twain here, and more of Henry James. Yet here Stafford is utterly in control, and her prose can be breathtaking in its cadences, its tightrope play between the abstract and the concrete. Here are the two opening paragraphs:

> Between the marriage elms at the foot of the broad lawn, there hung a scarlet canvas hammock where Andrew Shipley squandered the changeless afternoons of early June. Books lay in heaps beneath him on the grass, but he seldom read; he had lost the craft of losing himself and threads of adventure snarled in his mind; the simplest words looked strange. His kite was stuck in the top of a tree and black ants moved militantly over his pole and tackle box. He was waiting.
>
> He waited, in the larger chambers of his being, for the world to right itself and to become as it had been in all the other summers here, at Congreve House in Hawthorne, far north, when he had gathered the full, free days like honey and had kept his hoard against the famine of the formal city winter when he was trammeled and smothered by school and a pedagogical governess and parents whom he barely knew and certainly did not understand.

(The last sentence, for example, is eighty-one words long, without so much as a semicolon; yet it reads with an easy coherence. When attempting such virtuosity in *Boston Adventure,* Stafford had often lost her way.)

The Catherine Wheel is not so good a novel as *The Mountain Lion;* it lacks the unity, the vivid surface, the subtle character development of its predecessor. Yet at the same time it is an extremely interesting performance, a flawed book that has in it the germ of a masterpiece. Almost all of the peripheral details —

the minor characters, the furnishings of personal history, the trial
by gossip in a small Maine town — are handled to perfection.
The prose is consistently dazzling. Moreover, in Katharine Congreve Stafford dramatizes a side of her own psyche that she had
hinted at before only in Lucy Pride of *Boston Adventure* — the
dangerous spinster, the passionate romantic regulated by deco-
rum. Andrew Shipley, in his alienation from his giggling, affected older sisters, is a kind of boy version of Molly Fawcett in
The Mountain Lion — and thus of Jean herself.

Stafford had her doubts about the book. Sending a set of galley
proofs to Mary Lee, she wrote apologetically, ". . . all I ask
you, when you read it, is to remember that this is only the *present*
book and I will write a better one." She admitted to Peter De
Vries that the ending of the novel did not arise inevitably out of
the action preceding it.

The reviews were mixed. One critic after another praised the
writing and the craftsmanship but found fault with the story. As
Orville Prescott put it in the *New York Times,* "This technically
brilliant book, almost perfect in the mechanics of its writing, resembles an elaborate seashell found on a tropic beach. Its pattern
of concentric circles and the soft glow of its pastel colors are
beautiful; but the living organism whose protection was the sole
function of the shell is no longer there. 'The Catherine Wheel'
lacks the breath of life." Perhaps the most perceptive review came
from Anthony West in *The New Yorker,* who granted, "As a
story of misunderstanding, and the width that divides children
from their elders, it is excellent." But he went on to argue,

> At other times, the curse of the catalogue, which Flaubert laid
> upon the novel, descends, and the characters are held frozen while
> the oversensitive eye travels slowly over the materials of their
> clothing, the furniture, the bric-a-brac, the curtains, the wallpa-
> per, and the creepers tapping at the windows. Inevitably such
> writing does much to cloud the virtues of what is in its essentials
> a direct and moving story.

In the week of February 3, *The Catherine Wheel* made its way
into thirteenth place on the *New York Times* best-seller list. (Ahead
of it, among other rivals, were James Jones's *From Here to Eternity,* Graham Greene's *The End of the Affair,* and Herman Wouk's
The Caine Mutiny.) After three months in print, *The Catherine*

Wheel had sold 12,002 copies, earning Stafford $5,283.47, or nearly thirteen hundred dollars over her advance. This profit did not straighten out her finances, however. At the time, she stood $1,986 in the red on *Boston Adventure,* having borrowed against its future sales; and in the previous two years she had also been advanced two thousand dollars against a "general royalty account" — that is, for books as yet unwritten.

Thirty-six years old when *The Catherine Wheel* appeared, Stafford looked forward to a career as a novelist of major importance. She had already written three good books (one of them arguably great), in three quite dissimilar styles. Were she to fulfill the potential that critics had repeatedly proclaimed for her, she might well become recognized, as Lowell had predicted, as "the best novelist of [her] generation."

Stafford lived for twenty-seven more years, but she never completed another novel. The reasons are convoluted and murky; the loss is obvious. If we imagine the careers of some of Stafford's rough contemporaries cut off after three published novels, we would know Gore Vidal only for *Williwaw, In a Yellow Wood,* and *The City and the Pillar;* Vladimir Nabokov only for *Mary, King, Queen, Knave,* and *The Defense;* and Graham Greene only for *The Man Within, The Name of Action,* and *Rumour at Nightfall.*

From the end of December 1952 until mid-February 1953, Stafford put in the six weeks' residence in the Virgin Islands necessary for a divorce. She stayed with her friends from her trip in 1948, Nancy and Robert Gibney, who by now had their own small estate on the island of St. John. Little more than a month after her hysterectomy, Stafford was drinking and taking phenobarbital and sleeping pills. A jet-set doctor named André Kling, who was visiting the Gibneys at the same time, was appalled by her condition; he told his hostess, " 'Nancy, you must not allow this woman to stay in this house. She is like a raging fire — a bomb set to explode. . . . She suffers from every ill she has mentioned and possibly several more. She should never have left the hospital.' "

As if her hysterectomy had made her nostalgic for the children she would never have, Jean played for hours with the Gibneys' one-year-old son — "my first experience with a baby," she subsequently said. Despite her ailments, during her stay on St. John Stafford wrote "In the Zoo," one of her best short stories.

Thanks in large part to Jensen's magnanimity, their divorce, which became final on February 20, 1953, was as amicable as her severance from Lowell had been bitter. As Jensen reflects today, "After a while I thought, maybe this is just as well. . . . There were never two people less suited." Stafford asked for no alimony. From the Virgin Islands she wrote subdued, friendly letters to her soon-to-be ex-husband. In the months following, the two had some squabbles about belongings and taxes, but Jensen bent over backward to be fair. (Even so, in a letter she sent Joan Stillman in June 1953, Stafford reported "a harrowing lunch with Oliver who made a noisy nagging scene . . . Graham Greene was not left out of it and he said that I had led him down the garden path.")

Jensen moved back to Manhattan and sold the house in Westport. "I wish I could erase the last year," he wrote Stafford in April. "And I miss you. Please do write me. . . ." A year after their divorce, aware that Stafford was having financial troubles, Jensen sent her a check for five hundred dollars. "Please accept it," he wrote, "looking at it any way you wish — a contribution or your just due or help from someone who wishes we were still friends." A few days before marrying him, Stafford had written to Jensen, "I can't owe money ever to anyone." Now, four years later, in a letter shot through with rueful humility, she accepted his gift.

Outwardly, the years from 1953 to 1956 were remarkably uneventful for Stafford. Instead of moving back to Manhattan, she took a small second-floor apartment in Westport. The place was quite a comedown from the Colonial mansion where she had lived with Jensen: in her apartment she had only a plain hospital bed, a bed tray for meals, her desk, and a clutter of papers. Visiting her, her friend the poet Howard Moss saw two typewriters. The big one, Stafford told him, was for her novel, the small one for short stories.

During these years of living alone, Stafford vacillated between extremes of sociability and solitude. As Jensen had noticed, "Jean was secretly gregarious. She loved company, she loved conversation. . . . If she was having a lot of visitors, she wanted to be a hermit. And if she was a hermit, she was dying for visitors." This duality had in a sense been characteristic of Stafford since her childhood. When she was in her late thirties, however, a tendency toward real reclusiveness began to emerge in her, together with its complement — a calcifying dismissal of former friends who she imagined had done her some wrong.

As it would for the rest of her life, Stafford's ambivalence in these years centered on the frequent parties to which she was invited. In an antisocial moment, she wrote to Blair Clark and his wife, Holly:

> I now have a list of reasons why I can't accept an invitation:
>
> > My nephew is coming to visit me.
> > I am going to visit my nephew in Korea.
> > I have unilateral atrophy of the tongue
> > I am going to the dentist that night
> > I am going to the alienist that night
> > I am going to the fortune teller that night
> > I have gonorrhea
> > George Eliot has gonorrhea
> > I am blind
> > I hate you
> > I like Ike
> > I am too old and too distinguished

(It is fascinating to see that almost twenty years after she contracted gonorrhea, she still teased at the truth this way to good friends who had no way of knowing she was making a veiled confession.)

Stafford still corresponded irregularly with Lowell. Her letters to him from the mid-1950s strive toward the wisdom of the battle-weary:

> My dear, please never castigate yourself for what you call blindness — how blind we both were, how green we were, how countless were our individual torments we didn't know the names of. All we can do is forgive ourselves and now be good friends — how I would cherish that!

She also tried to be a good sport about Lowell's second marriage: "And I'd love to see Elizabeth too if she'd not feel we'd be shy."

In 1951 Lowell had published *The Mills of the Kavanaughs,* much of which is based on their year in Damariscotta Mills. This difficult six-hundred-line poem baffled critics and friends alike. In densely woven, rhymed stanzas of iambic pentameter, Lowell mingles the myths of Persephone, Ceres, and Apollo and Daphne with Dante's *Inferno;* with the Abnaki, Catholic, and Colonial history of Maine; and with a myth concocted out of his own life. In biographical terms, what is extraordinary about the poem is the fact that Lowell, who seemed to be utterly indifferent to Stafford's feelings during their marriage, could later imagine the whole experience of that marriage from her point of view. In an odd way Lowell seems to have had a remarkable capacity for empathy, without a trace of the compassion that usually accompanies it.

The Mills of the Kavanaughs is thus full of elegiac reminders of the love Lowell and Stafford had once shared, which Stafford's short stories about Damariscotta Mills are too battle-scarred to accommodate. When Stafford read the poem, it seemed to her excruciatingly rich and personal — and not the least bit obscure. As she said to Joan Stillman, " 'There wasn't a line in it that I didn't recognize and know what it meant.' "

It may be no exaggeration to say that in the years after Stafford's divorce from Jensen, her closest friends were her cats. For an obscure publication called *What's New,* she wrote one of her most delightful pieces, an extended paean to George Eliot. Beneath the essay's tone of ironic seriousness, the details of Stafford's love are visible.

There were almost certainly no romances in Stafford's life from 1953 to 1956, even though a number of men courted her. One of these was Alan Campbell, who had been Dorothy Parker's husband: "As he was taking me home he said he would like to marry me if I weren't so much like Dottie. Indeed! I slept scarcely a wink as a result. . . ." Stafford dismissed several other suitors with a show of spinsterly hauteur:

> There is the most awful man who calls himself Dr. Pick who has taken a shine to me and calls me on the telephone in a German voice. And I *think* that a Hungarian photographer has invited me to misbehave in Lenox, Massachusetts. For the time being I will stick to my needlepoint.

Stafford never saw her father again, but all through the 1950s he wrote her bluff, rambling letters. After her divorce from Jensen, he pleaded, "Jean, why the Sam Hill don't you jump a plane some day and come out here for at least a few days. . . . You and I could have a good visit, reminiscent of our great summer at Mrs Meyer's house in El Dora [*sic*]." John Stafford continued to write with a near-maniacal doggedness. In 1953 he sent off a novel to Random House; its hero was an archaeologist. By the next year he had finished a twenty-five-thousand-word manuscript that elucidated his long-sought invention, the hell ray. In ten months he wrote and submitted for publication thirty short articles on the same topic; all, of course, were rejected by the magazines. "How the Hell," he complained to Jean, "does an original thinker go about it in these days to get his conclusions into the field of controversy?"

His other great project, the book on the government's deficit spending, which he had now been laboring over for thirty-odd years, was equally unpublishable. "He had loads of loose sheets," Marjorie remembers. "He couldn't get anybody to listen." Eventually John Stafford's long obsession did bear meager fruit: one brief, all-but-incomprehensible pamphlet that, having at last swallowed his pride, he paid for and published himself toward the end of his life.

In the 1950s Jean Stafford came into her own as a short-story writer. For eight years running she published an average of three stories a year, mostly in *The New Yorker*. A few of the tales venture into territory Stafford had not previously explored. These include "Beatrice Trueblood's Story," about a woman who becomes totally deaf on the eve of her marriage, and "Maggie Meriwether's Rich Experience," which details the mortification of a well-bred young lady who has studied French for years but on her first trip to Paris finds herself (as Stafford had in Heidelberg) unable to understand the language.

During these years Stafford's stories won *seven* O. Henry awards, including first prize in 1955 for "In the Zoo"; four of them were also selected for inclusion in Martha Foley's annual anthology, *The Best American Short Stories*.

The crowning achievement of this period — in fact the zenith of Stafford's career as a writer of short fiction — is a group of seven stories set in Adams, Stafford's mythical equivalent of Boulder. They commence with "The Healthiest Girl in Town," published in 1951. Next come "The Violet Rock," "In the Zoo,"

"Bad Characters," "A Reading Problem," and "The Scarlet Letter," which appeared in 1959. The seventh story, "Treasures of Use and Beauty," was never published; it is, however, the equal of the others.

Stafford does not seem to have conceived the stories as a set; they are not her Nick Adams series. In four of the seven, the protagonist is named Emily Vanderpool (in "The Violet Rock," Tess Vanderpool). All of the tales are told in the first person. In each, the protagonist is clearly Jean Stafford, yet none of the stories is as directly autobiographical as *The Mountain Lion* (not to mention "In the Snowfall"). Most of the stories posit an orphaned or half-orphaned young girl who ranges in age from eight to about thirteen. The parental figures suggest only indirectly a tyranny like John Stafford's; usually the father is deceased.

Although all of the stories are richly comic, they share serious themes: the protagonist struggles against the dead hand of convention and propriety, embodied in her guardians; against the manipulations of her craftier sisters and playmates, who get her into trouble; and against her own "bad character," which foretells the disturbances of adulthood. The great success of the stories springs from a number of virtues. Never had Stafford realized and reinvented a town and its inmates more acutely than she now did Boulder: all of her childhood jaunts to the dump, to the top of the mesa, to the hobo shantytown of the "Jungle" came back to her, allowing her to flesh out a Colorado town that is like nothing in the history books.

Stafford's newfound command of the first person liberated the voice that tells the stories. (Both *The Mountain Lion* and most of the drafts of "In the Snowfall" had been rendered in the third person.) By the 1950s, apparently, Stafford was psychologically far enough removed from the pain and anger she had felt as a child that she was able to rediscover her youth as comedy. The speaker in each of these stories sounds authentically ten or twelve years old, never lapsing into the coyness of the *faux naif* or of the studiedly precocious. All seven tales are sturdily crafted, with old-fashioned plots. Yet the tendency that mars Stafford's novels, her weakness for the melodramatic ending that ties up all the loose ends, never threatens to invade these stories. As events, their denouements are as quiet and quotidian as they are stunning and, in terms of character, just.

Another feature of the Adams stories is the menagerie of eccentrics who cross paths with the narrators. Whether Stafford resuscitated these hobos, traveling evangelists, and juvenile delinquents from her childhood or from imagination alone, she knew exactly how they spoke. Here is the unforgettable Mrs. Mulgrew in "Treasures of Use and Beauty" — the proprietor of a seedy diner who comes to take care of Emily and her sister during an epidemic:

"I'm making French fries [Mrs. Mulgrew tells Emily]. The thing to do in the case of sickness is two things, keep them warm and don't let the night air in and second, give them what tastes good. Now you take your so-called invalid food, your custards and your mollycoddled eggs and your mashed potatoes and how are they going to keep their strength up with those kind of mush? There isn't hardly anything in the world more disappointing than a plate of milk-toast — your sick person takes one look at that milk-toast and says, 'I'd ruther not eat bite one of anything than eat that holy mess.' Believe me, I've ridden herd on enough sick kids and sick hands to know what you want when you're puny is hot tamales, fried ham, doughnuts, chow-chow, chili — things with some gumption to them. Boys from the frat houses will come crawling into the store so laid up from needled beer that they're half way to the last roundup and I say, 'Here, Joe College, have a hot dog with plenty of mustard and a slice of Bermuda engern and a side order of sauerkraut and that'll settle your stomach,' and it does, every time. They ought to hire me at the san — I'd have those lungers up packing their grips to go back East poco pronto just by giving them some decent grub."

Along with the Adams tales, Stafford wrote at least nine other first-rate stories during the 1950s: "A Country Love Story," "The Echo and the Nemesis," "Cops and Robbers," "The Liberation," "Beatrice Trueblood's Story," "Maggie Meriwether's Rich Experience," "The End of a Career," "My Blithe, Sad Bird," and "A Reasonable Facsimile." No American writer produced a finer body of short fiction during that decade.

The money Stafford received from the sale of three short stories a year, however, even from *The New Yorker,* was hardly enough for her to live on, so she also turned out occasional magazine articles during the 1950s. She wrote about winter in New

England for *Holiday,* and about divorce for *Harper's Bazaar* (again, as in her insomnia piece for *Vogue,* with a self-protective impersonality). She produced forgettable essays called "It's Good to Be Back," "The Art of Accepting Oneself," and "New York Is a Daisy."

After firing Marian Ives in 1947, Stafford operated without an agent for nine years. Harcourt, Brace had published her three novels and for the most part had made an exemplary effort to market them. Yet by the fall of 1952, less than a year after the publication of *The Catherine Wheel,* Stafford was seriously at odds with the firm.

It is hard to determine exactly what Harcourt, Brace did to alienate her. Peter Davison suggests that the simple fact that Lowell had the same publisher may have loomed large in her mind. On the eve of Stafford's departure for the Virgin Islands in December 1952, Robert Giroux had driven her to her ship, and had brought along a new contract. She signed it but then had second thoughts and wired Giroux from the boat "demanding that he scrap" the agreement. From St. John she wrote Jensen that her falling-out with Harcourt, Brace was "a narrative that has been unfolding for eleven years and I see no immediate prospect of a happy ending." "Eleven years" would take Stafford back to the earliest days — to all appearances amicable ones — of her acquaintance with Giroux.

In the absence of more telling details, and in view of Stafford's subsequent behavior toward her publishers, the sad truth seems to be that by early 1953 she was already making an irreversible transition. The energetic, tractable young writer who had been willing to revise *Boston Adventure* massively, in accordance with her editors' strictures, was becoming the difficult, suspicious, well-known author who all too easily blamed her publishers for her own creative problems.

In May 1953 Harcourt, Brace brought out a collection of ten of Stafford's stories, called *Children Are Bored on Sunday,* for which she received a two-thousand-dollar advance. The book was widely reviewed, in accents ranging from the mildly positive to the wildly enthusiastic; even *Time* was relatively generous. But the last straw for Stafford in her dealings with her publisher came only a few months later, in a squabble over the handling of the British rights to the collection. Stafford fired Harcourt, Brace as she had fired Marian Ives.

Even without an agent, the momentarily unsigned novelist drew a crowd. Viking, Random House, and Farrar, Straus and Young all wooed her, the latter offering a ten-thousand-dollar advance on her next novel. On October 23, 1953, Stafford signed with Random House, in large part because Albert Erskine, her old friend from Louisiana and Connecticut, would be her editor there. The contract was for a novel and a book of short stories; Stafford got a seven-thousand-dollar advance, with a thousand on signing and the remainder in monthly installments of four hundred dollars each. The novel was to be delivered by May 1, 1955.

In 1954 Stafford agreed to contribute a novella to a collection of four to be published by Ballantine. By disguising her central tale as a flashback enfolded within a flimsy contemporary envelope, Stafford was able to rescue from her files some pages from "The Autumn Festival," her novel about Germany. The resulting novella, "A Winter's Tale," still holds the kernel of the love story between the American student in Heidelberg and the doomed Nazi aviator. Stafford had "refurbished the dull thing," she wrote Jensen, as a favor to the collection's editor, who was a friend; nonetheless, "I thought I could do it in a couple of weeks and it took me the better part of six tortured months." Despite Stafford's low opinion of it, "A Winter's Tale" is a skillful, wistful work.

The novel for Random House, however, was not getting off the ground. The May 1955 deadline came and went without Albert Erskine's ever having seen a single page. In an undated letter to Erskine (written, apparently, in early 1956), Stafford tries to make gloomy fun of her failure, but her raillery bespeaks a deeper woe:

> I'd call and tell you all this but I am too ashamed. The novel just isn't ready and just won't be ready — at this point I think, ever, and I would just as soon you sent the policemen now. It's partly the fault of hepatitis and partly the fault of poverty, so that I keep having to leave the book and write a story, but it's mainly indolence, stupidity and a fundamental lack of talent. I care hideously about my failure to deliver for myself but I care even more hideously that I've let you down. . . .
> If you want to decapitate me, call me and let me know when.

At the beginning of 1956 Stafford finally got herself another agent; James Oliver Brown had been recommended by her friend and fellow novelist Louis Auchincloss. Brown began to push Stafford's work vigorously. He acted as agent not only for her novels, but for her short stories (except at *The New Yorker)* and articles as well. For a year and a half he kept a number of TV, movie, and Broadway producers competing for the right to adapt Stafford's story "The End of a Career," a mordant account of the dotage of a once-great beauty. He wangled the sale of a one-year film option on the story, getting a thousand dollars for it; but Stafford's lack of success with screen and stage persisted, and the project never reached fruition. Brown also roused film and stage interest in "A Winter's Tale," "The Bleeding Heart," and, once again, *Boston Adventure.*

With magazines like *Holiday,* the agent assumed for his client the ugly job of complaining about low fees. By the time Brown began representing her, Stafford was in bad financial shape. A typical note from her instructed him, *"Sell* today to anybody for anything. I'm in a mess with doctor's mistakes." Brown had the wit to convert her penury into something of a virtue; dunning a Hollywood agent for a thousand-dollar option, he claimed, "Jean is in the peculiar position of being probably the top woman writer in America, making the least money and I think we have got to swallow our pride and get little driblets of money for her in the meantime."

In December 1956 Farrar, Straus & Cudahy published a book called *Stories,* an anthology that combined Stafford's work with that of John Cheever, Daniel Fuchs, and William Maxwell. The reviews were laudatory; several of them ranked Stafford's five stories as the pick of the litter. From the book itself, however, Stafford earned only five hundred dollars; her agent's cut was a token fifty.

From the start Brown played an avuncular role with his troubled artist. In the fall of 1956 a silly contretemps developed and, thanks to Stafford's oversensitivity, quickly grew into a tempest. *Life* assigned Margaret Bourke-White to photograph Stafford in characteristic postures at her home in Westport. Like a teenager with stage fright, Stafford made fussy objections. She wrote Brown,

Those dumb-bell LIFE people! I don't *have* any hobbies. . . . I am so insanely hostile right at the moment to Westport, Connecticut that I don't want to be associated with it in any way. I am ashamed to death to live here. Oh, well. I suppose they can do me petting my cat.

Brown faithfully relayed Stafford's qualms. Bourke-White came and took some photos; *Life,* however, never used them. In high dudgeon, Stafford demanded payment for her wasted time. A *Life* editor sent a check for two hundred dollars, only to be told that Stafford was demanding twice that. Her prosecution of this perceived slight to her dignity — with Brown loyally pleading her case — stretched over five months and went all the way to the magazine's legal department before it finally withered into an impasse.

At the beginning of 1956 Stafford was forty years old. Her health was as poor as ever. Besides the hepatitis cited in her letter to Erskine (the disease does not appear in the medical history she gave Dr. Thomas Roberts in 1963), she had developed a foot problem — "a tumor inside the foot," as she described the ailment with her usual relish, "cruelly pressing on the nerves which they expected to be the size of a pea but which turned out to be the size of one's thumb." During a nine-day hospital stay, Stafford had the growth surgically removed; three years later she had to have a second operation to correct a related complaint.

For the summer of 1956 she rented a one-room flat in Belgrave Square in London. One of her motives may have been sheer avoidance of the novel that she could not get written; another was the urge to sail out in search of adventures to give her something new to write about. For the rest of her life Stafford maintained that every trip she took turned into a travel nightmare exceeded in its miseries only by the next journey. Her Atlantic crossing on the *Mauretania* in June was "a monstrous, a really cruel bore"; by the time she arrived in London she had bronchitis. The flat, rented sight unseen, was a disaster:

> The only place I've ever been that was worse was an army billet in Nurnberg. The service does not exist, the porters are fiends, the light is much too dim for a bat, *and* now they have started building something on a bomb site just beyond my wall and I am told that the pneumatic drills will go on for several years.

To add to her distress, she lay in bed day after day and accomplished no writing. "I'd forgotten," she wrote Joan Stillman, "that after the age of twenty-two, the search for experience is narrowing and harrowing."

From London Stafford traveled to Heidelberg, "in an abortive attempt," she later admitted, "to get something for a new story." Once again she visited the Haarlass, sending Hightower a nostalgic postcard. Drinking at her usual pace, she sedated her days with Miltown and her nights with chloral hydrate. "It does not seem at all possible," she wrote her New York friend Ann Honeycutt, "that I spent one year of my life in this place. It is ravishingly beautiful and I am in a quiet and, for comfort, almost American hotel." But as far as her writing was concerned, Heidelberg gave her nothing of use.

In spite of its inconvenience, the London summer turned out to be pivotal for Stafford. By chance she met Eve Auchincloss (distantly related to Louis), a *Harper's Bazaar* editor who was also visiting London. During the course of their first evening together, the women "got good and plastered" and developed an "instant friendship" that lasted for two decades. For much of that time Auchincloss was probably Stafford's best friend. The editor also did more than any other person to keep Stafford in print after 1957.

In her most motherly mode, Katharine White had arranged for Stafford to meet various writers in London, including the *New Yorker* columnist Mollie Panter-Downes and the English novelist Elizabeth Taylor. White also pushed Stafford to meet A. J. Liebling, who had written for *The New Yorker* since 1935 and had been living abroad for a year and a half. "We found him the best sort of companion," White wrote Stafford.

> He is a strange man; often it is next to impossible to get into conversation with him some people think. But he smiles like a Buddha and when he does talk, it is very good indeed. He is a gourmet, who knows the best and least obvious places to eat, and he takes a gusty delight in the English music-hall humors and entertainments. I am very fond of him + I've written him a note to look you up.

Stafford happened to be in *The New Yorker*'s London office one day when Liebling telephoned. He asked to speak to her, then invited her to tea at his hotel. Each knew, and was deeply impressed by, the other's writing. At their first meeting Stafford

was "awfully, awfully timid. . . . I'd been reading him for years."
For his part, Liebling considered Stafford — and had commended her to his friends as — the best living writer of English.

In July 1956 "Joe" Liebling, as his friends called him, was fifty-
one. He was bald-headed, bespectacled, and, at five-foot-nine-
and-a-half and 243 pounds, enormously fat. At the tag end of a
disastrous second marriage, separated from his wife, he had been
"lunging" at women all summer. But instead of lunging at Stafford, he wooed her — taking her to the racetrack in a hired Rolls
Royce, squiring her around the low-life bars of the city, and ordering custom-made suits for her. He also arranged, despite the
fact that London was booked solid, for her to leave her noisy
Belgrave Square flat and move into a room in Duke's Hotel, where
he was staying. Liebling was the perfect distraction for Stafford's
unproductive summer; she luxuriated in his doting company.

Stafford returned to America on the *Queen Mary* at the beginning of October. It took her only a few months to make her
getaway from Westport. It was the town's "galloping contem-
poraneity," she wrote, "that made me retreat, exhausted, to the
stately, old-fashioned ways of life in New York." By the end of
January 1957 she was installed in an apartment on East Eightieth
Street, just off Fifth Avenue.

After her European summer, the pinch of poverty seemed
sharper than ever. According to Ann Honeycutt, Stafford was
"always so poor and so broke, and she was a real poor-mouth,
so she could get very pathetic and people would give her money."
In June, after a friendly drink with her ex-husband Oliver Jensen,
she wrote him an apologetic plea:

> The other night, you may remember, you said you hoped that if
> I were in need I would let you know. Well, I *am* in need, in des-
> perate need and, not to be dramatic but to be realistic, you could,
> if you wanted (and could) just now save my life. This has been a
> worrisome and barren year, the worst I have had in a very long
> time.

Jensen immediately sent her a check.

There were new pleasures for Stafford in New York. With
Joseph Mitchell she went botanizing in Central Park, the Bronx
Botanical Garden, and the Moravian cemetery on Staten Island.
(Identifying plants and flowers was by now Stafford's only

outdoor pursuit.) She saw a good deal of Eve Auchincloss, who
gave her assignments for *Harper's Bazaar.*

Auchincloss paints an incisive portrait of Stafford during this
period.

> She had a sort of squarish, shapeless body. At forty-one, she wasn't
> beautiful. Her head was often cocked to one side, with her eye-
> brows drawn up in a pleading sort of expression. She had very
> big hands and feet. Her hands were slightly shaky, as she would
> guide a cigarette to her lips. Her hair was lusterless, permanented
> in a funny frizz. It sat on top of her head as if it might easily be
> blown off.
>
> Her voice was low and slow, and it got slower over the years.
> Jean always searched for the perfect word or phrase. She would
> keep you a little in suspense, then deliver the goods. She was *very*
> funny. No matter how boozed up she was, she always planned
> her way from the beginning of a sentence to the end.

A. J. Liebling had stayed on in London, but he wrote Stafford
often, puncturing his newsy dispatches with outbursts of self-
conscious flirtation: "I seem to have held a very great lady in my
arms at all those race meetings. It was a very great honor!" In
January 1957 he made a two-week visit to New York, staying at
the Fifth Avenue Hotel. During that brief time Liebling and Stafford were all but inseparable.

By May 1957 Stafford's novel was two years overdue. She had
insisted on not talking about her work while it was in progress;
thus Albert Erskine and his colleagues at Random House had
very little idea of what the novel was about or how much work
she had done on it. Even to her closest friends, Stafford dropped
only vague hints. Sometimes she alluded to her "Westport novel";
on other occasions she implied that she was writing a book about
her father.

To Stafford's great dismay, not only was the novel going badly,
but she was also finding it harder and harder to write short stories. In December 1955, while lunching with Katharine White,
Stafford had complained that she had no ideas. By way of a response, her editor told her a gruesome story from her own childhood, about two family maids who had drowned on a summer
outing, and encouraged Stafford to borrow the incident. Jean duly
appropriated it and produced "The Mountain Day," which *The*

New Yorker published in 1956. As White later noted, "It is not one of her good stories but writing it did help her get out of a writing block."

White's colleagues were less and less enthusiastic about the stories Stafford submitted. In 1953 *The New Yorker* had rejected "Rocks and Reefs"; the next year it had turned down "The Matchmakers," despite a rewrite. Stafford was able to place the latter at *Mademoiselle* (in her *Collected Stories*, the tale is called "Caveat Emptor"), but "Rocks and Reefs" never saw print. It was fatally flawed, in White's view, by "the increasingly misanthropic tone, the unrelieved bitterness in which the whole story (or you, the author) seems to slash away at every thing and every person. . . ."

It caused White considerable anguish to have to turn down her friend's stories, and she always tried to soften the blow with reassurance and encouragement. In October 1957 White retired as *The New Yorker*'s fiction editor. Her painful last duty vis à vis Stafford was rejecting "The Children's Game" after the author had twice revised it. James Oliver Brown did his best to market the story elsewhere. In succession, *McCall's, Ladies Home Journal,* and *Good Housekeeping* returned it. With her characteristic self-deprecation, Stafford wrote her agent, "If I weren't so bloody broke, I'd withdraw it and try to do it better another time. . . ." On Brown's last try, the *Saturday Evening Post* accepted the story.

After White's retirement, Stafford published only two more stories in *The New Yorker*. (Between 1958 and her death in 1979, in fact, she managed to publish only seven more stories anywhere, one of them a throwaway young-adult piece for *Boy's Life*.) At about the same juncture, Stafford's good friend Peter Taylor, whose work *The New Yorker* had also published regularly, began to find that the magazine would no longer buy his stories either. "Jean wanted to form a rejectee club from *The New Yorker*," Taylor jokes today. He attributes their common vicissitude after 1957 to a change in taste that came with the new generation of *New Yorker* editors.

Taylor may indeed have been a victim of fickle literary fashion. Nonetheless, his own integrity dictated that he simply continue to write as he always had, and three decades later the world rewarded him: in 1987 Taylor claimed both the Pulitzer Prize for fiction and the Ritz Hemingway Prize, which had never before been won by an American. In Stafford's case, more tragically, the loss of *The New Yorker* as a steady market for her stories coincided with a drastic depletion of her powers as a fiction writer.

A whole collection of hypotheses can be advanced to explain this creative diminution. Perhaps Stafford simply ran out of "things to say." Perhaps journalism, and the need to pay the bills, distracted her. Perhaps the novel she could not disgorge in turn choked off the supply of short fiction she had in her.

It would be blinking at the facts, however, not to consider the role alcohol must have played in Stafford's decline. By 1957 she was drinking more seriously than ever. And as had been true on and off for at least fifteen years, she often combined nonstop imbibing with going days without eating. A loss of appetite is, of course, one of the common side effects of alcoholism. But given what we know about Stafford's deep ambivalence toward food ever since childhood — as evidenced by her mother labeling her a "problem feeder," by the rage she had felt when teased by her sisters about her imaginary fatness, by her vivid dislike of everything but "raw potatoes and cabbage cores" — it may be germane to consider the possibility that she had a tendency toward anorexia.

Under the exhortations of Mary Jane Sherfey and a host of other doctors and therapists, Stafford had often tried to go on the wagon. In 1952, during one of these dry periods, she wrote a series of cold vignettes about the ordeals of socializing without booze:

> The C——s' drinking habits are among the most depressing I know. . . . [They drink] bad vermouth and cheap wine by the gallon. . . . They offered me the vermouth and the sauterne. D. said I had a will of steel; a few drinks later he suggested that I had stopped drinking in order to sit in judgment on my friends. There were no signs of dinner.

Sobriety never held a lasting grip on Stafford. She was not conspicuously shamed by her drinking; she could, in fact, be jaunty about it, telling Frank Parker in the early 1950s, for instance, " 'It's gotten so that my bathwater smells of Old Fashioned.' "

Joseph Mitchell speculates, "I think she was so miserable at not being able to write that she drank. . . . Then she would drink to get over the hangover. I think when she got stalled in the middle of a story, her worst kind of drinking would start."

A standing joke between Stafford and Mitchell was her nick-naming him Preacher.

> Jean would call me with a terrible hangover, and I'd been through so many of them myself that I'd learned how to talk her out of it. Jean would say, "I'll never speak to a human being again." I'd tell her how everybody had been through this, and I'd kind of mini-mize her guilt. . . .
>
> She'd say, "Preacher, can you do anything for me? I've got a Guinness Book of Records hangover."

In her twenties, Stafford had been able to drink sherry all day and still turn out four thousand words of *Boston Adventure*. At forty-one, she was no longer so resilient. The true depths of her drinking problem were revealed only to a few close friends, one of whom was Mitchell:

> I would get a telephone call from her, over in Grand Central. She would be having auditory hallucinations from her hangover. She'd be standing in that huge open space, hearing voices that said, "Jean Stafford. Jean Stafford." She'd call and ask, would I come and get her? I'd say, try to tell me where the telephone booth is. So I would come over, and she'd be shaking. I would usually get her up to the Cosmopolitan Club, and we'd have lunch, and she would gradually get command of herself.

Eve Auchincloss witnessed an even more disturbing scene:

> She called me very early one morning, and that was peculiar, be-cause Jean wasn't awake early in the morning. She asked me to come up [to her apartment on East Eightieth]. I found the living-room floor covered with bottles. She was in the bedroom. She talked kind of rationally — she had some plausible explanation for the bottles — but she was telling me that there were animals and slimy things crawling on the walls. She was having an attack of the d.t.'s. I stayed until the doctor came.

By 1957 Jean Stafford needed to be rescued. It was Liebling who threw her a life preserver.

XVI

Reporter's Moll

By THE TIME Stafford met him in 1956, A. J. Liebling was a legendary figure in American journalism. During his twenty-two years of writing for *The New Yorker,* he had appropriated certain subjects as his own. His profiles of urban low-life figures — free-lance Broadway promoters operating out of phone booths, carnival hucksters, and grandiloquent con men like Colonel Stingo, whom Liebling made famous — were the envy of a generation of magazine writers. No one ever chronicled the boxing scene with greater insight. His impassioned critiques of his own profession, appearing under *The New Yorker* rubric "The Wayward Press" (a department invented by Robert Benchley), did much to elevate the standards and ethics of reporting in this country. Though not a food writer per se, Liebling celebrated the joys of haute cuisine and gluttony alike. He had a lifelong love affair with France and seized any excuse to visit and write about that country. During World War II, at great personal risk, he had covered the fall of Paris, the Normandy invasion, and finally the Paris liberation for *The New Yorker.*

Born in Manhattan, Liebling had spent most of his life there. The son of a furrier, he was raised in a liberal, nominally Jewish family. When he got kicked out of Dartmouth for cutting chapel too often, he talked his father into subsidizing a blissful year in France. Thereafter he knuckled down to a series of jobs as a newspaper reporter. In New York he worked for the *Times,* the *World,* and the *World-Telegram* before hooking up with Harold Ross's *The New Yorker* in 1935.

Liebling was as prolific as he was eloquent. <u>Almost nothing</u> he ever <u>wrote for *The New Yorker* was turned down</u>. Without irony, his biographer, Raymond Sokolov, cites as proof of the decline of Liebling's powers the fact that in the last three years of his life he wrote only sixty-two articles. His coworker Brendan Gill noted that Liebling's confidence in his own writing was "unbounded": "More than once, I would encounter him seated at his type-writer, staring at a sentence on the sheet of paper in front of him and chuckling — bouncing, joggling — with satisfaction."

The brilliant reporter had, however, been unlucky in love. At the age of twenty-nine he married a beautiful but uneducated movie-theater cashier. She turned out to be schizophrenic and alcoholic, and Liebling had to hospitalize her several times. He divorced her in 1949 but continued unstintingly to write her and send her money. Sokolov believes that Liebling's first wife re-mained the true love of his life, and in her own befuddled way she returned his love. When she heard of Liebling's death, she tried to attend his memorial service but failed to locate the fu-neral chapel. Five months later she was found drowned in a river, her handbag and a half-empty bottle of wine abandoned on an adjacent dock.

Liebling's second wife, Lucille Spectorsky, also a beauty, was a twice-divorced high-school dropout and sometime model. The marriage turned bad almost at once, as Lucille showed her true colors. Writes Sokolov:

> She held Liebling in thrall, played on his physical passion for her, milked him for the furs and dresses he, with his compulsion to put women on gilded pedestals, could never refuse her. She also milked him for all his growing fame as a *New Yorker* writer was worth. Because of him, her life turned into a literary salon. But then she tired of him.

In 1955, to take advantage of a twenty-thousand-dollar tax break for writers living abroad, Liebling moved to London. At the last minute Lucille backed out, using the move to force a separation. On her own in Nevada, she continued to live off her husband's earnings. During the 1950s Liebling earned as much as sixty thousand dollars a year, but he was always broke. His chronic indebtedness was partly a consequence of his prodigal generosity; besides supporting Lucille and sending money to his first wife, he paid for his stepdaughter, Susan Spectorsky, to go to Radcliffe for four years, then gave her a year abroad at his expense in the country of her choice.

Despite a certain naïveté about romance, Liebling was experienced with women. During his separations he had conducted a number of affairs, and in Paris, even as a youth, he had unblushingly made weekly resort to prostitutes. When he began to court Stafford, in his early fifties, he was not well. A lifelong penchant for overeating lay at the root of all of Liebling's medical complaints. By 1956 he was suffering badly from gout and kidney stones and was beginning to show signs of serious kidney, liver, and heart trouble as well. He made radical attempts to diet but always quickly failed.

For Stafford, Liebling's attractions were manifold. Intellectually he was the equal of Robert Lowell, though two more different minds could hardly be imagined. He treated her like a queen, buying her a mink stole and picking her up in a hired Rolls Royce — the antithesis of Lowell's behavior toward her. Temperamentally Stafford and Liebling were attuned. He was a strong liberal who had spoken out fierily against fascism and the red-baiting of the McCarthy era. (Lowell, one recalls, had supported Franco and seen Communist plots everywhere.) Liebling had also participated in the same great reoccupation of Europe that had cost Stafford's brother his life.

Jean's new friend, moreover, was sympathetic to psychoanalysis, having himself sought the counsel of several therapists over the years. Liebling deeply admired Stafford's prose and did everything he could to encourage her to write. Perhaps most important of all, he relished good wine and strong drink; there would be few complaints about her alcohol intake from Joe Liebling's corner.

In romantic terms, Liebling's Achilles' heel was his obesity. Some of Stafford's best friends found him so unattractive that it was hard for them to countenance her interest in the man. "He was so ugly, and fat, and greasy-looking. I couldn't get over anybody being in the same bed with that greaseball," says Ann Honeycutt, who had been James Thurber's mistress. Liebling was, in Eve Auchincloss's view, "obscenely fat"; he "wore his pants below the belly."

In her mildly perverse way, Stafford agreed with her friends. "Not the least of Joe's attractions for her was that he was not good-looking," remembers Eileen Simpson. "He was 'positively ugly,' [Jean] said with girlish delight."

After his two-week visit to New York in January 1957, Liebling returned to London. During the next few months he traveled through the Near East, turning out pieces for *The New Yorker* on the Arab-Israeli conflict. By mail, he courted Stafford more fiercely than ever. Determined to divorce Lucille, he was able to win from her at first only a legal separation. As early as December 1956 he had already unambiguously declared his passion for Stafford:

> I want you to write because you're a great woman, and I love what you write, and because you'll never be happy — for more than one afternoon or one night at a time — unless you do yourself justice. I'll not give you up, and I'll combine things to have you together with me as soon as possible, and I'll make love to you as much as I want, which is certainly as much as you'll want, and we'll see wonderful things together and mortise our minds like the rest of us.

[handwritten marginal note: best writing in book]

Katharine White, delighted at the match she had made, exhorted Stafford to join Liebling once more in London. In September 1957 Jean crossed the Atlantic, to be met by her suitor at Southampton. Liebling's chivalry delighted her: they drove all the way to London in a chauffeured Rolls, pausing during the "supremely sunny, rose-smelling day" for a picnic of caviar, cheese, and red wine. Later, "I longed for my first taste of flattish, warmish English lager so we stopped at a pub called The Catherine Wheel."

At Duke's Hotel Stafford took a separate room. The fall — an extremely happy but unproductive time for her — passed in a dizzy round of racetrack afternoons and dressy evening dinners. Stafford spent six days in Belgium at an international congress of poets,

> all speaking unheard-of languages such as Frisian and Estonian and the worst of all, French. This was held in a gambling casino and I went along for the laughs and the material. Also I learned roulette and got so good the last night that one of the croupier's impassive stares broke into a look of rage.

Somehow Stafford managed to break a finger on the plane to Brussels. The casino, but not the congregation of poets, served as the setting for her story "The Children's Game."

In November the couple returned to New York. Stafford kept her apartment on East Eightieth Street as her official domicile for another two months, but in the meantime she moved into the Fifth Avenue Hotel, just north of Washington Square, with Liebling. Throughout 1958 he maintained a suite on the sixteenth floor while she had a pair of rooms on the sixth.

Sokolov assumes that Stafford kept separate quarters both in London and in New York as a "thin fiction of chastity" while Liebling was trying to pry a divorce out of the recalcitrant Lucille. It may well be, however, that it was Jean's need for autonomy and privacy that dictated this arrangement, more than her instinct for discretion. It is not clear how physically amorous the relationship was. To Oliver Jensen (to whom, of course, it would have been politic for Stafford to minimize the affair) she said "something like, she found it comfortable to be with this nice, friendly, jolly, old, fat, and brilliant writer. She indicated it was a comfortable arrangement, rather than a romance."

Even after Liebling's divorce came through, he and Stafford took their time tying the knot. "We kept getting too busy to get married," Stafford later explained to Sokolov. The wedding took place on April 3, 1959, in a routine civil ceremony at New York City Hall. In lieu of a reception, the newlyweds repaired to Tim Costello's, Liebling's favorite bar, where they held "a sort of open house in the saloon's upstairs room." Mr. and Mrs. Abbott Joseph Liebling moved into a roomy and luxurious apartment at 43 Fifth Avenue — by far the fanciest place in New York City that Jean had ever inhabited.

Marriage gave Stafford a host of new distractions from her work. With the aid of a black maid who also cooked, the Lieblings threw frequent dinner parties. They spent summer weeks in the country. Liebling bought season tickets to the Metropolitan Opera, on the theory that "it would make them feel grown up." He took her to a bar near Stillman's Gym and introduced her to prizefighters and trainers. As Stafford later told Sokolov, "His pleasure in everything was so contagious you couldn't help having a good time."

Instead of pursuing her own muse, Stafford fed Liebling ideas. Although he had already published ten books, Liebling was seized with the conviction that his work was ephemeral. The books had for the most part been woven-together collections of magazine pieces; as a youth, however, Liebling had planned to write immortal novels, and now he longed to find a subject suitable for a full-length book of nonfiction.

Stafford suggested Earl Long, the governor of Louisiana, who had just begun to show bizarre signs of mental aberration. The match was perfect: the flamboyant, reckless governor (Huey Long's younger brother) was the apotheosis of all of Liebling's low-life eccentrics. In the summer of 1959 the master reporter cornered and charmed the governor in the midst of his campaign for re-election; Stafford gladly tagged along. The book that resulted, _The Earl of Louisiana,_ is considered by many to be Liebling's masterpiece.

In late August Stafford, Liebling, and Susan Spectorsky sailed for England on the _Media,_ Spectorsky on her way to the post-graduate sabbatical in Egypt that her doting stepfather was financing. Liebling planned to cover the upcoming British election for the London paper the _Observer,_ and Stafford was on her own assignment — the most bizarre of her career. As she later described its genesis,

> On a winter night, I dreamed these words: "Look anywhere and you will find roots. Samothrace. Gadopolis." It was then revealed to me, through an intelligence existing outside me in the upper air, rather like a disembodied history professor, that my Scotch ancestors had arrived at the Isle of Arran in the Firth of Clyde only in the seventeenth century and that they had come there by a circuitous route from Samothrace. There was the further proposition, parenthetical and ambiguous as if the hour were nearly up and the professor had begun to nod, that these ambitious travelers had not been indigenous to Samothrace but had only paused there for some centuries en route to Britain from their native Turkey. My spectral informant trailed off then without documenting this arresting footnote and I woke up to see fine snow falling among the finials of the First Presbyterian Church across Fifth Avenue. . . . I memorized the dream for re-ex[am]ination in the morning and then went back to sleep.

Stafford had long been interested in dreams: she had read Freud's work on the subject, and since 1940 in Baton Rouge she had made a habit of writing down sketchy synopses of her own most interesting dreams. But this was the first (and only) time in her life that she acted upon a dream as if it were genuinely prophetic and revelatory.

While Liebling covered the election, Stafford traveled to the Isle of Arran. As background for her quest she had corresponded assiduously with her sisters and with her Missouri cousins on her mother's side, searching her family's living memory for details of the McKillops' ancestry. She had apparently talked *The New Yorker* into paying for the trip, on the promise of an essay about her adventures.

On Arran itself she got nowhere. The hotel she stayed in was full of other Americans pursuing, as she scornfully put it, the "tartan mania" — a curiosity really no different from her own. Discouraged, she returned to the mainland and visited the library of Brodick Castle. Here she discovered only that there had been McKillops on Arran since at least 1766 and that the Duke of Hamilton had dispossessed them in 1843 to make way for sheep. She seized on the fact that the name McKillop was a Gaelicism for "Philip's son," convinced that it pointed to a Greek link; she had previously toyed with the fancy that she was descended from Alexander the Great.

Her research, however, only confirmed that the McKillops had been peasants. Trying to invigorate her dry data, she wrote, "Mainly I see a huddle of hayseeds fighting for their places nearest the fire, anatomizing the characters of their neighbors and the factors and the lairds, growling for more dried goat meat and bannocks, and more than likely complaining that they were no better off than they had been in Samothrace." The ironic tone is deceptive: Stafford still clung to a belief in the literal truth of her dream.

So hungry had she been for affirmation that, seeing a little girl on Arran tying her shoelace, she had had a sudden intuition "that my acquaintance with her antedated today and had other dimensions besides the visual." She bragged to Liebling that she looked so much like the Arran natives that "when she got off the boat, they thought she had just been shopping in Glasgow — they hadn't noticed that she was away."

Despite her meager results, Stafford was full of enthusiasm. "If I don't get a story out of this," she wrote her agent, "I'm not and never have been a writer." As soon as he had finished cov-

ering the election, the ever-indulgent Liebling flew with his wife
to Athens; from there they made their way to Samothrace.

On the island itself she found nothing to confirm her dream.
If the levelheaded Liebling regarded the whole journey as a wild-
goose chase, he kept his feelings to himself. To James Oliver
Brown, who had become his agent as well as Jean's, he wrote,
"She should have some great New Yorker pieces, and perhaps a
book, out of her Arran-Samothrace adventures."

It is tempting to see the Samothrace business as a self-conscious
bagatelle Stafford concocted to avoid the demands of the novel
she was unable to face. Yet her notes and letters betray an utter
sincerity about the quest. In psychological terms it seems poignant that, after decades of erecting a self-protective "edifice"
against her family, she should suddenly awaken to such a need
to discover everything she could about her ancestral origins.

During the years of her marriage to Liebling, as Stafford later
told Sokolov,

> I was *extremely* unproductive. It was a source of woe to Joe.
> I could never figure out why it happened. Perhaps it's too sim-
> ple an explanation, but I was happy for the first time in my life.
> He thought that if I wasn't writing, it meant I was unhappy
> with him.

interest

This *is* too simple an explanation. Stafford in fact did try to
write, sometimes with great diligence, during the Liebling years.
Yet many of her efforts, for one reason or another, went awry.

Liebling's affluence had saved Stafford from her financial dol-
drums. Thanks to her good reputation and to her agent's able
promotion, after 1957 there was a steady flow of inquiries and
assignments. The BBC showed interest in airing a radio dramatization of *The Mountain Lion;* the producers of Alfred Hitch-
cock's TV show wanted to render her story "The Warlock" (she
turned them down). In 1959 *Horizon,* which was edited by Oliver
Jensen's former partner, Joseph Thorndike, hired her to interview the aged Isak Dinesen. Stafford received the baroness at the
Cosmopolitan Club, where, if the bar tabs she submitted to the
magazine are any indication, one or both of the women got completely smashed. Dinesen annoyed Stafford by confusing her with
Shirley Jackson, the author of the famous short story "The Lottery." Even so, the profile Stafford wrote is uncharacteristically

star-struck: ". . . I can imagine that she once moved through all her landscapes with a lithe and watchful speed, her great, dark, prompt eyes missing nothing."

Holiday asked Stafford to expound on "New England Summer," as a companion piece to her 1954 essay on winter. Despite an offer of fifteen hundred dollars plus expenses, she said no. *Harper's Bazaar* persuaded her to write on whiskey, *Redbook* on Christmas in Colorado. For *Mademoiselle* she wrote a beguiling memoir of the 1930s, called "Souvenirs of Survival." In 1960 her editor at *Horizon,* still enchanted with her work, appointed her that magazine's film critic. She turned out six columns for five hundred dollars each, only four of which were published. As always, there are memorable sentences in these reviews, but when confronted with such major works as *Hiroshima, Mon Amour* and *Pather Panchali,* Stafford was out of her depth. She knew no vocabulary for film criticism; instead she compared movies to desserts: "Like baklava, *Hiroshima* is filling; unlike baklava, it did not satisfy me."

Evidently swayed by Stafford's new credentials, *Harper's Bazaar* sent her to Reno to report from the set of John Huston's movie *The Misfits.* She wrote Hightower:

> I was flown out (splendidly) and put up (shabbily) by the concern involved in perpetrating this appalling matter, and a good thing, too, because if I'd had to pay a cent I'd have sued like a shot. I was there for six days and returned with a lifetime of squalid memories.

The magazine paid for her essay but never published it; she gave a different version of the piece to *Horizon,* which also never ran it. By early 1961 Thorndike had realized that Stafford was not a film critic; he eased her out of the job and installed John Simon in her place.

Even as she was turning down lucrative offers from *Holiday,* Stafford was writing book reviews, for as little as $125, for such magazines as the *Reporter* and the *Griffin.* One of these efforts, which appears to have been written "on spec," was a savage attack on a first novel called *The Fume of Poppies,* by Jonathan Kozol, a syrupy tale of first love at Harvard and on the Continent. Stafford seized upon Kozol's unfortunate predilection for talking about food and love in the same breath, ridiculing the novel's self-satisfied couple in a piece entitled "The Eat Generation." The review is the first pure example of Stafford's effort in a genre of which she would become a master: the invective. Swiftian though the mockery is, it so definitively tramples the unimportant object of its scorn — nothing more than a mediocre first novel — that Stafford found it all but impossible to place the essay. The *Atlantic Monthly, Harper's, Saturday Review,* and *Mademoiselle* all rejected it before it was finally taken by the *Reporter.*

To make quick cash, Stafford gave talks at universities, even though she hated speaking in public as much as ever. Yet at the same time she turned down chances for much larger paychecks. One feeler came from a surprising source: Gertrude Buckman, now an editor at Harcourt, Brace and World, who suggested that Stafford "do for American eccentrics what Edith Sitwell did for English." In 1961 the State Department invited Stafford to go to Pakistan and India for several months, presumably as part of a cultural program under the new Kennedy administration; she stayed home.

During the four and a half years of her marriage to Liebling, Stafford published only one short story: "The Scarlet Letter," one of the Adams tales, which came out in *Mademoiselle* after being rejected by seven other magazines. It is extremely hard to date Stafford's manuscripts, but there is good evidence that between 1958 and 1963 she wrote a few additional stories and gave up on several others short of completion. Two of Stafford's most interesting failures are titled "Bobette" and "Venus." The first, set in a catty social milieu very like Westport, hinges on the disruptive impact of Bobette, a brainless femme fatale whom one of the regulars brings as his date. Out of envy and malice, the others tease and bait her, to no effect. "Venus" is based on the unexpected visit paid by a former college classmate from Colorado to a New York protagonist (essentially Stafford). The protagonist has no recollection of Marjean, who now lives in Tulsa; Marjean, however, has forgotten nothing from her college days.

On the evidence of these manuscripts, it would appear that in the late 1950s Stafford was developing a new skill in her short fiction. The most impressive thing in "Bobette," "Venus," and "Treasures of Use and Beauty" is Stafford's perfect ear for the idiosyncratic patois of a trio of eccentric female antagonists — Bobette, Marjean, and Mrs. Mulgrew. Marjean's idioms are pure midwestern college girl, circa 1935, and it is a dazzling feat that Stafford was able to retrieve them intact from her auditory memory:

> "Who was Art White? Tell me something, how long did it take you to get this la-di-da New York accent? Keep the drinks coming, honey, and I'll tell you about Art White. All about Art White. I got news for you, I'm tight, I'm crocko, pie-eyed, fried to the gills, period, end of quote."

Yet this very virtuosity threatens to take over the stories, attenuating their plots. In other cases there are simply too many minor characters. The dramatic tension of Stafford's best stories from a decade before, such as "Children Are Bored on Sunday," is here too often diffused in chat.

This is not, however, an adequate explanation of Stafford's troubles with the short story after 1957. The much-rejected "Scarlet Letter," the unpublished "Venus" (turned down by *Good Housekeeping* and the *Saturday Evening Post*), and the likewise unpublished "Treasures of Use and Beauty" (which may be the story alluded to by Katharine White as twice rejected by *The New Yorker*) are the equal of all but the very best of Stafford's earlier tales. All three are quite superior to many stories of hers that *The New Yorker* was happy to publish in the early 1950s.

A good part of the blame for Stafford's decline as a commercially successful short-story writer can be attributed to changing literary fashion. "Venus," for example, is startlingly similar to J. D. Salinger's powerful story "Uncle Wiggily in Connecticut." But Salinger's laconic prose seemed more au courant in the late 1950s than did Stafford's elegant periods. During the 1960s American fiction would be shaped by the confessional intimacy of Philip Roth and John Updike, by the technical experiments of Donald Barthelme and John Barth, by the social consciousness of Bernard Malamud and Saul Bellow. Placed beside the work of such innovators, Stafford's writing began to seem old-fashioned.

It was a characterization she consciously embraced. Speaking at the University of North Carolina in 1960, Stafford inveighed against the idea of creation as personal catharsis: "I hate writing that seems to have been undertaken for the purpose of therapy, and I do not believe that it is possible to get rid of a grief or a guilt or an ugly memory by writing of it." Flying in the face of the notions of the day, she laid down her manifesto:

> The life of a writer is an unceasing and daring pilgrimage and no one who is timid of adventure or of risk should undertake the hardships of the odyssey. It is not an aimless ramble like those engaged in by Mr. Kerouac's maudlin hoboes, but it is a journey with a mission — the search for an original grail of excellence and price. It is, in Henry James's phrase, "the act of life."

Yet if, intellectually speaking, Stafford had the courage to resist the trends and tides of her craft, she did not have the steadfast self-confidence of a Peter Taylor. After 1963 she seems to have made little effort to write short stories at all.

Many who were close to Stafford between 1959 and 1963 feel that those years with Liebling were the most joyful of her life. In E. B. White's view, "The greatest thing Joe Liebling ever did was to marry Jean Stafford. He made her deliriously happy. . . ." Eve Auchincloss recalls, "He had his love affair with France, boxing, horse racing. These things appealed to the tomboy in her." Wilfrid Sheed anatomizes the partnership most memorably:

> Liebling, with his wise-cracking Grand Manner, seems to have opened windows for her and let out some terrors. He was the kind of guy who hired a taxi all the way from eastern Long Island to Manhattan during some paltry train strike: strictly a caviar man, and a funny one. And she was fine for him, with her earthy laugh, her quick-take for the bizarre, and her noble, toughened countenance. A reporter's moll, a kid you could take anywhere.

Liebling's pride in Stafford's excellence as a writer was prodigal. The consummate reporter told his friends that Jean would make a good reporter herself, with her talent for drawing people out. Howard Moss, the poetry editor of *The New Yorker,* bumped into Liebling one day in the elevator at the magazine's offices. Moss, who had just read a manuscript of Stafford's, told Liebling how good he thought it was.

> "I know," he said, "I wish you'd tell her."
> "I *have,*" I said. And added, "I wish I could write prose like *that*. . . ."
> Joe, about to get off at his floor, turned to me and said, "I wish *I* could. . . ."

After the summer of 1960, however, the marriage was not as
close as it had been. "As time went on," writes Sokolov, who
had the benefit of Stafford's testimony, "their lives ran increasingly on separate tracks. Jean was not eager to see many of Joe's
old friends. . . . She tired of racing. And she began to re-ally
herself with some of the literary figures she had known before
her marriage to Liebling." Eve Auchincloss remembers, "Liebling would come home, find Jean with me drinking, and look
disgusted. Jean said he hated intellectuals. I couldn't figure out
why he thought I was one."

Just as she was embarking on the marriage, Stafford had urged
Robert Hightower to visit, insisting, "Joe is understanding of
past associations and is flatteringly unjealous, and if you'll give
me a little warning, I shall arrange to have a long evening free."
Yet when Hightower did call on her, he left feeling frustrated at
Jean's evasion of any personal discussion. Eventually Stafford revised her appraisal of her husband's magnanimity: "Quite often
he does object to friends who antedate him. . . ." On another
occasion, Hightower and Stafford drank all evening and had
Chinese food delivered to her apartment. Around midnight Liebling came home from his office at *The New Yorker,* "cold sober,
tired after a day's work, and not pleased to find me sitting with
my shoes off in the living room. Jean didn't manage this very
well." Blair Clark detected a kindred resentment vis à vis Stafford's first husband: "Liebling always considered that Lowell was
his big rival. He was very jealous of the memory of Lowell."

With or without Stafford, Liebling began to spend more of his
time at his country retreat in The Springs, a tiny settlement near
East Hampton, Long Island. He had bought the two-story, white
clapboard house in 1952, under pressure from his second wife,
Lucille, who liked to fancy herself the mistress of a country estate. Gradually Liebling came to love the house and the thirty-
one acres of land that came with it. One of his favorite self-
indulgences was to lie on his back in the field behind the house,
savoring his property.

Like Stafford, Liebling had never learned to drive. In The
Springs they were dependent on the local taxi and on friends
who picked them up for parties and shopping expeditions. By
1962 the couple was feeling the pressure of money problems. A
steep hike in rent forced them to abandon their beloved Fifth

Avenue apartment and take a much smaller and less comfortable place on West Tenth Street. "Neither of them was happy there," says Janet Malcolm, then a new friend.

For all his own love of drink, Liebling began to be disturbed by the proportions of Stafford's imbibing. Eve Auchincloss thinks that Liebling disapproved of her partly because he believed that, as one of Jean's drinking partners, she encouraged his wife's self-destructive tendencies. For her part, Stafford grew more and more upset about Liebling's eating. One of the ironies of this reversed Jack-Sprat-and-wife situation was the fact that, according to a number of friends, Stafford was a good cook, even though she had almost no interest in food. In the country Liebling again tried to diet, once more failing miserably.

Says Janet Malcolm, "He was not an epicure. He just ate. He'd go to a French restaurant and eat a great meal, then, on his way back to the office, have a Boston cream pie." Raymond Sokolov piquantly analyzes Liebling's lifelong love of food:

> At the center of this vision of ideal manhood was the refusal to obey the bourgeois principle of delayed gratification. In other words, Liebling had raised self-indulgence (as he defined self-indulgence) to the level of a first principle. To eat and overeat was, for Liebling, more than a crude gorge; gluttony was a badge of freedom. His belly was the outward and visible sign of an inward and manly grace.

By the end of 1962, however, Liebling's obesity had become life-threatening.

In and around East Hampton, Stafford began to cultivate her own society. One group with which she felt particularly comfortable comprised the homosexual literati of the area (even in college Stafford had found homosexual intellectuals congenial). Liebling, on the other hand, was annoyed by the "fags who were buzzing around" his wife.

In Blair Clark's view, Stafford and Liebling had "a very strange relationship. . . . She told me he was a melancholic. He would lie in his bed, she'd cradle his head in her arms, and he would weep." Stafford also claimed to Clark that "she didn't write because he felt that she was so much better a writer than he that if she was writing, he couldn't." This sounds like another disingenuous excuse for Stafford's block, but even so, it hints at a struggle between the two writers that was largely invisible from the outside.

Stafford's health was little better than Liebling's. At the age of forty-seven, she had developed, as she wryly put it, "the acne [I] should have got at 17." She attributed this skin condition, for which she took twice-weekly injections, to smoking and drinking combined with a hormone imbalance linked to her hysterectomy.

In October 1963 Stafford first saw Dr. Thomas Roberts, who would be her personal physician for the rest of her life. On a medical-history form, she answered yes to many questions, including, "Do you bruise easily?," "Does your hair fall out easily?," "Do you perspire excessively?," "Do you have to sleep propped up in bed?," "Do you worry very much?," and "Do people often annoy or irritate you?" She acknowledged "frequent or severe sore throats," "hot weather bothers," "lumps or nodules in breasts," "chronic cough," "night sweats," "bronchial trouble," "wheeze or whistle in chest on breathing," "pain or tight feeling in chest on exertion," "heart palpitation," "loss of appetite," "eat[ing] at irregular hours," "pain in stomach," and "nausea and vomiting"; she often was "constipated" and "nervous," "tire[d] easily," and found it "difficult to make up mind." Yet she answered no to a query about whether she had ever had a nervous breakdown.

On the same questionnaire Stafford admitted to sleeping seven to eight hours a day and working three to five; to smoking two packs of cigarettes a day; to drinking two cups of coffee daily and "about 8 ounces" of alcohol. Her blood pressure was a reasonable 140/80, but her pulse was 100. A "deep non-productive cough" was the chief complaint that had first brought her to Roberts.

Despite the reawakened interest in her family prompted by her dream about Samothrace, Stafford continued to keep her sisters at arm's length. Having promised a visit to Mary Lee, she backed out with her usual litany of excuses — illnesses and deadlines. When Mary Lee expressed her disappointment, Jean wrote back, "God damn it, if I had the money, I would come out in spite of the deadlines but there will be *no money* until I have met the deadlines and when I say no money, I mean no money at all. What do you want me to do? Hitch hike?"

When Stafford got drunk, she often pulled out a ouija board and tried to communicate with the dead. Joseph Mitchell, Howard Moss, Dick Cavett, and other friends witnessed Stafford's inevitable efforts to get through to her brother. Says Mitchell, "I can hear her hitting the floor with her heels, in a frenzy: 'Speak! Speak!' " But Moss reports that "these sessions never lasted long. Joe Liebling didn't like Jean using the ouija board, and when we heard his key in the door, the board was hastily put away." At one séance, however, Cavett watched as "Jean shot from her chair, knocking it over, and lurched sideways against the wall. She let out a Medea-like wail, followed by a heart-breaking, 'My . . . brother Dick . . . *hates* being dead!' [Cavett's ellipses and italics]"

By May 1962 Stafford's novel for Random House was seven years overdue. Her editor, Albert Erskine, had still not seen a word of it. Guilt about her procrastination must have afflicted Stafford constantly, yet she kept up the pretense that the book was coming along well. In 1960 she had allowed the *Griffin* to publish a biographical note claiming that she was "writing a sequel to her first novel, *Boston Adventure,* for publication next spring by Random House." Turning down magazine assignments, she wrote James Oliver Brown (who was thereby also losing potential income) that she needed the freedom to put all her energy into her novel.

Meanwhile, over the years Stafford pondered a series of more or less frivolous book projects as stopgaps and divertissements. Typical of these was her proposal to Brown, in 1958, that she and Eve Auchincloss write a book on manners. (Auchincloss indicates that the scheme was never a serious one; nor, she says, was a joint pipe dream of a children's book about a girl named Polly who grows up in Colorado.)

Without even having secured a contract for it, Stafford put in months — perhaps years — of work on her Arran-Samothrace lark. She let Howard Moss read some forty pages of manuscript; "it was," he recalls, "some of the most extraordinary prose I'd ever read." He begged her to publish the piece, even if she never finished it. In the files left behind after Stafford's death, there is a box full of clippings, family letters, notes, and the incipient Samothrace manuscript, which consists of about a hundred pages of typed drafts, most of them — as was Stafford's wont —

variants of one another. She saved fifteen different versions of
her opening paragraph, yet none of the variants goes beyond page
twenty-eight.

There *is* some extraordinary writing among these fugitive drafts,
but it is hard to imagine how it might have all added up to a
book. The pages she completed deal only with Arran. In the absence of a single scrap of evidence that the McKillops had ever
had anything to do with Samothrace, perhaps Stafford was forced
to face the quixotic nature of her whole enterprise.

In 1961, without informing Random House, Stafford had signed
a contract with Farrar, Straus & Cudahy (to which firm her old
friend and editor Robert Giroux had migrated) for a children's
book. She received a mere thousand-dollar advance and a royalty
of 5 percent on the first twenty thousand copies. Stafford cast
her cat Elephi as the book's protagonist. The work proceeded
smoothly, and *Elephi, the Cat with the High* I.Q. was published
in September 1962.

This brief concoction is an utter delight. Elephi lives at 43 Fifth
Avenue in New York with a couple named Moneypenny, whom
he knows as Mr. and Mrs. Cuckoo. The story turns on the conceit that the cat is really in charge: "Earlier, Elephi had sat on
top of a chest of drawers supervising Madella, who ran the vacuum cleaner, as she got ready to go home." It is the book's
achievement that it conveys the life of an apartment-bound pet
from his point of view:

> Then he went into the bathroom and arranged himself in the wash
> basin for a nap (it was exactly the right shape for the Curled Cat
> position — paws tucked in, tip of tail touching tip of nose) but he
> found that he wasn't sleepy.
>
> So he made a tour of the dining room where he found his own
> personal walnut. He played hockey with it until it hid.

Elephi's habit is watching cars — which he assumes are sen-
tient beings — through the window. During an ice storm he sees
a small Fiat abandoned by its college-girl owner. He takes pity
on "Whitey" and manages to manipulate the building's super into
having the car brought up on the freight elevator and put inside
the apartment. Elephi and Whitey converse sympathetically in a
language both are at a loss to identify, until at last the college
girl reclaims her Fiat.

This almost perfect children's book displays Stafford's ear at its best — the super, the cops, Mr. and Mrs. Cuckoo, and the flighty college girl all speak in their own rich idioms, while Elephi and Whitey, though fully anthropomorphized, never descend to being merely cute. In the end, as children who read it can immediately grasp, the tale is about loneliness.

Stafford got a sprinkling of favorable reviews for *Elephi,* as well as a sheaf of fervent fan letters:

> Dear Mrs. Stafford,
> I am in third grade. I would like to ask you a question. Did you write another volume of Elephi? If you didn't please hurry up and write another one. . . .

Nevertheless, the book sold fewer than three thousand copies; because Stafford had ordered fifty-six of those for herself, she ended up $645 in the red. She complained to James Oliver Brown that her publisher wasn't pushing the book.

Stafford came close to signing a contract for an *Elephi* sequel, but she was not able to get the advance she wanted. For another thousand dollars and a 5-percent royalty, she put together a children's book for Macmillan by retelling four tales from *The Arabian Nights.* Brown, as loyal as ever, was nonetheless disturbed by such hackwork deals. "If there is a week's work involved here, OK," he wrote her. "If it is major it is a pity to accept this."

Yet Stafford was beginning to feel she could not afford to turn her back on any easy money. In 1962 she traveled to Ohio State University, as she complained to Ann Honeycutt, "to read a story for $100 to a class of bonehead youths. (All youths are boneheaded.) It will cost about that much to store the cat." There were unmistakable signs in the air that she was now coasting on a reputation she had earned years before. A woman from some "tupenny-hapenny college on Long Island" invited her to give a lecture; as Stafford told it,

> She said that she could raise an honorarium of $10 and she thought it was a good idea because she had read in the Times literary supplement, in an article about the reading habits of college students[,] that "an astonishing majority have never heard of Jean

Stafford, et al." and she felt that it was time for a "Jean Stafford revival."

Along with Herbert Gold and Lewis Gannett, in 1962 Stafford served on the jury for the National Book Award in fiction. To be considered for the award, a book had to be nominated by its publisher; the favorites that year included Joseph Heller's *Catch-22*, J. D. Salinger's *Franny and Zooey*, and Bernard Malamud's *A New Life*.

Liebling had earlier come across a review of an obscure first novel by a man named Walker Percy. Liebling read *The Moviegoer* partly because he knew it was set in New Orleans, which he knew well from his Earl Long days; he loved the book and commended it to Stafford. The novel had sold fewer than five thousand copies in ten months, and its publisher, Alfred A. Knopf, had not nominated it for the NBA. Stafford also thought *The Moviegoer* splendid, and said so to her fellow jurors, as did Herbert Gold, quite independently. In the end, bending the nomination rules, the jury unanimously chose it for the award.

The day after the awards ceremony, Liebling gave a seminar at Columbia Journalism School in which he mentioned his discovery of Percy. Gay Talese, reporting for the *New York Times,* somewhat distorted Liebling's remarks, claiming that he had "conveyed his preference" to Stafford, who "apparently . . . convinced the other two fiction judges on the merits of the novel." A former Knopf editor was quoted as saying that Alfred A. Knopf himself didn't even like the book. A tempest in a teapot ensued.

Liebling, Stafford, Gold, Gannett, and Knopf wrote letters to various publications to set the record straight; Talese made a partial apology. Nonetheless, the controversy became a minor legend, to be rehashed acrimoniously from time to time, as it was in 1971 in *Harper's* by Alfred Kazin. Today, of course, no one needs to apologize for early on having praised Walker Percy, whose career got a crucial boost from the prescience of the 1962 jury.

Sooner or later Stafford had to face up to the mess she was in with Random House. Her seven-thousand-dollar advance had been spent years ago. On May 31, 1962 — eight and a half years after signing her contract — Stafford wrote a letter that shocked Albert Erskine:

For a long time and for a number of reasons, I have wanted to be released from my agreement with Random House, and I hope that as a friend you will understand them.

The only one that needs to be stated is that, in spite of all our making a joke of it, I have an eccentric but ineradicable sense of being still your not very competent secretary, subject to scolding and I hate being scolded. . . . Nor can I help feeling very strongly that this has contributed to my block.

Stafford went on to voice a gratuitous complaint about Random House's handling of a reprint of *The Mountain Lion*.

Barely suppressing his outrage, Erskine wrote back,

Since becoming your "editor" — nearly nine years ago — I have not seen one sentence on which to make any editorial comment, good or bad, so there has been no "scolding" about that. And none about the nondelivery of any manuscript, which I have more and more tried to avoid mentioning at all, beyond periodic expressions of interest (but never concern or even impatience).

He went on to say, however, that if that was really the way she felt about it, he would step aside and let another Random House editor work with her, and would even promise not to read anything she wrote until it was published.

Stafford refused the offer. She had already decided to dump Random House and move to Farrar, Straus & Cudahy. One of the heads of Random, Bennett Cerf, called his old friend James Oliver Brown to try to avert the crisis. "They are 'sick about it,' " Brown wrote Stafford. "They want to persuade you to stay and promise that Albert will be completely out of the picture." Cerf and his partner, Donald Klopfer, pleaded for a chance to meet face-to-face with Stafford to iron things out.

But Stafford had already managed to convince Brown that "the break must be made": Robert Giroux would be the right editor for her. When he and Cerf at last resigned themselves to losing Stafford, Klopfer not unreasonably demanded the return of the seven-thousand-dollar advance, plus 5 percent interest. Brown candidly admitted to Klopfer, "I have no idea how far she is into a novel. I suspect she has notes, but I'm not even sure of that." He asked Klopfer not to charge interest, and in the end, Klopfer relented.

It is hard to judge whether Stafford really believed that Erskine's "scolding" had contributed to her block; by 1962 a kind of paranoia about editors was fast becoming an aspect of her hypochondriacal stance toward the whole world. It does seem evident, however, that the staff of Random House (like that of Harcourt, Brace before it) had consistently treated Stafford with all the support and esteem an author could ask for. Says Berton Roueché, who had Albert Erskine as his first editor, "I can't imagine quarreling with him. . . . He was a real editor . . . most helpful, gentle, sweet-natured, very much concerned with the writers he worked with."

By May Brown and Giroux had hammered out a new three-book contract for Stafford. Farrar, Straus & Cudahy (soon to be renamed Farrar, Straus & Giroux) agreed to give Stafford a twelve-thousand-dollar advance, of which seven thousand would buy off Random House and five thousand would go directly to her. The deadline for the novel was now January 15, 1965. Her new publisher would also bring out a book of her short stories, to be called *Bad Characters,* in 1964.

Although Brown had championed his client throughout the painful realignment, he privately confided to her his worries about her "mortgaging" against her advances:

> You have to work hard to get something which will earn $7,000 in the dim future and a further $5,000 which we may get from Roger [Straus]. This is a lot of money. We take it now and if the novel gets written I think we shall be OK. . . . Otherwise you are going to have a very bad period later on.

Giroux had other qualms. As Brown told Stafford, "Robert is very worried about the Greek-Scotland book (this is very much off the record . . .). They want a novel and it is a novel for which they are gambling."

Meanwhile, Stafford had confided to a few close friends that things were not going well with her marriage. "They really didn't have anything profoundly in common," says Eve Auchincloss today. By 1963, Liebling had sunk into a lasting depression, and the once-prolific reporter was finding it a struggle to finish articles. The year before, he had published his last book, a deft, nostalgic memoir of his early days in France called *Between Meals: An Appetite for Paris.* With Stafford, in July and August 1963 he toured Normandy and the Loire by chauffeured car. In the Allied cemetery on Normandy beach Stafford searched for her brother's grave but could not find it. During their voyage Liebling's depression deepened. Stafford later said, "My surmise is that he knew he would never see France again."

Back in the United States, Liebling soldiered on at *The New Yorker*. One November day when he was on a lunch break with his colleague Philip Hamburger, a disturbing incident occurred. "One of those New York grotesques appeared, half-crippled, half spastic," Hamburger recalls. "Joe took one look and began to cry. I could see something was wrong. He was on the edge."

Despite their marital difficulties, Stafford took Liebling's decline very hard. Shortly before Christmas he came down with a bad case of viral pneumonia. On December 20 Dr. Roberts examined Stafford and noted her "marked anxiety, sleeplessness, depression resulting from anxiety re husband[']s serious illness." Her drinking had also escalated. Aware that she was taking tranquilizers, Roberts added a familiar and futile prescription: *"Rx: no alc."*

On December 21 Liebling was admitted to Doctors Hospital. Stafford tried to keep up her Christmas social rounds; Dick Cavett, who saw her at a bash that week, later judged that "Jean's eyebrow-raising presence at the party indicated not so much a lack of concern and devotion as a highly developed penchant for seeking escape." On December 27 Liebling suffered congestive heart failure as well as renal collapse, and plunged into a coma. Stafford rode in the ambulance with her husband to the intensive-care unit of Mt. Sinai Hospital. She was not, however, with him when he died the next day. According to Sokolov, "His last words were not set down or even precisely understood. They were in French." At the time of his death, Liebling was only fifty-nine.

Eve Auchincloss came over to Stafford's West Tenth Street apartment and stayed through the night with her. As Wilfrid Sheed subsequently observed, "Liebling's death left Jean well and truly stranded. She had, with her gifts, made another wonderful world for herself, like a child on a lonely afternoon[,] and now it too was gone."

XVII

The Widow Liebling

TWO DAYS AFTER LIEBLING'S DEATH, his friends paid tribute to him at a memorial service in a Manhattan funeral chapel. Stafford, who had organized the service, took her husband's ashes to The Springs, where she had them inurned in a plot in Green River Cemetery, a few feet from the large boulder that marks the grave of the painter Jackson Pollock. Stafford had a black slate headstone designed for her husband in Newport. At its top is carved a fleur-de-lis, emblematic of Liebling's passion for France.

The house in The Springs, with its thirty-one acres, was the principal asset left Stafford by her husband. Liebling had died owing money both to *The New Yorker* and to his book publishers. " 'By the time everything was straightened out,' " Stafford jocularly told Joan Stillman, " 'he left me exactly sixteen dollars and forty-two cents.' " On Liebling's death, Stafford began receiving his royalties as well as her own. Even though his most recent books were selling well, Stafford never realized much cash from this arrangement, on account of Liebling's indebtedness.

According to Katherine Roueché, her friend in East Hampton, "Jean said terrible things about *The New Yorker*. . . . [She claimed] they never gave her any money." Yet the magazine wiped Liebling's debts off the record and, seven years after she had last published a story in its pages, continued to carry Stafford on its excellent medical-insurance plan. The coverage would become a godsend for her.

Skillful though her handling of Liebling's funeral had been,

Stafford plunged into despair after his death. She essentially stopped
eating and went on a two-week drinking binge. On January 11,
1964, her doctor admitted her to New York Hospital. He recorded her chief medical complaint as "drinking, run-down, and
depressed." In the cool prose appropriate for a medical summary, Thomas Roberts described his patient as a "48 year old,
white female, who has been a chronic imbiber of alcohol for many,
many years. . . ." The doctor also diagnosed possible cirrhosis
of the liver, chronic bronchitis, chronic malnutrition, reactive
depression, and fibrocystic disease in her left breast. It was Stafford's nineteenth medical admission to New York Hospital.

She stayed there for sixteen days, managing to eat well as she
"dried out." To her worried sister Mary Lee she characteristically wrote, "I am incommunicado in a hospital and am in touch
only with the lawyers. . . . I implore you not to try to track me
down. . . . Tell the Oregon people [i.e., her father and Mar-
jorie] that I have gone away for a bit — say to friends in Vermont." When she was discharged, Roberts put her on antabuse,
a medication that discourages drinking by causing violent sickness when mixed with alcohol. He also prescribed small doses of
Librium as a tranquilizer, chloral hydrate to help her sleep, and
Elavil to alleviate her depression.

Roberts kept close tabs on Stafford throughout February. On
the nineteenth he noted, "More distraught. . . . Trying to do
many things at once, including moving. Not eating well — but
taking antabuse + not drinking." At the end of March Stafford
had surgery to remove a tumor from the ball of her foot and a
calcium deposit from her wrist.

The moving alluded to by Roberts involved Stafford's giving
up the "costly tenement" on West Tenth Street that had been her
last residence with Liebling. Yet even as she packed up, Stafford
had no firm idea of where to go next. After March 1 she used
the Cosmopolitan Club as her mailing address while she stayed
at Ann Honeycutt's apartment on East Sixtieth Street.

On April 5 Stafford was having lunch at the Cosmopolitan
Club when suddenly a pain that stretched from her abdomen to
her upper back "seized me like a bear." The spasm lasted a full
half minute. Although she felt nauseous and faint, Stafford did
not lose consciousness. A doctor who happened to be present
called an ambulance that took Stafford to the emergency room at

New York Hospital. There she was given a narcotic injection; it caused her to vomit, so the attending physician added an anti-emetic shot.

Stafford had suffered a heart attack. For ten days she was closely guarded, her heart regulated by a pacemaker. In the midst of this assault it was discovered that she had an arhythmia, which was diagnosed as potentially dangerous ventricular tachycardia. While in the hospital she also developed a gallbladder problem, but the doctors decided it was too risky to try to correct it so soon after her heart attack.

Stafford stayed in the hospital for five weeks. On her discharge she was saddled with an elaborate medical regime. The drugs she was to take included anticoagulants, painkillers, an antiarhythmic medication, and a barbiturate; she was to go on a low-fat, low-salt diet; she was to do everything she could to quit smoking and drinking; and, as Roberts urged, "you should insofar as is possible avoid nervous strains and stresses."

By June Stafford had moved to The Springs. The house Liebling had left her, at 929 Fireplace Road, was the home in which she would spend the last fifteen years of her life. A two-story, unpainted clapboard saltbox, it had once served as a farmhouse; out back stood a former pigpen and a cottage. The short, curving driveway was lined with junipers; a grand acacia dominated the front yard, and a gnarled apple tree, only one limb of which still put forth blossoms, grew in back. Near the kitchen porch a rusty hand pump conjured up backcountry self-sufficiency.

For a single woman who did not drive, however, it was an awkward place to live. There were no businesses or services within walking distance for Stafford. To buy groceries or a cup of coffee in East Hampton, she had to call up Schaefer's Taxi or cadge a ride from a friend.

Liebling had used the house "as sort of a shack"; shelves of boxing books and walls hung with horse-racing prints were his only concession to decor. Stafford kept her husband's memorabilia on display and built her own nest around them. To her neighbor Eleanor Hempstead, it seemed "a very unhandy house." Entering by the back door — the only one in use — one had to walk through the kitchen and the dining room to reach the parlor, where Stafford entertained guests. The sole bathroom was on the second floor. Stafford took over the upstairs room that had been Liebling's study and made it her own; she turned a downstairs bedroom into a second study. Upstairs, on a Facit typewriter, she worked only on fiction; downstairs, with an Olympia, she plied her journalism. In time the house to which Stafford had moved so dubiously grew to be an extension of herself — the realization of that writer's refuge of which the house in Damariscotta Mills had been her first approximation.

The original settlers in The Springs had been farmers and fishermen, harvesting salt hay, clams, and scallops; an old local name for the indigenes was "Bonackers," after the clam-rich Accabonac Harbor (within sight of Stafford's front windows). The western-born writer delighted in getting to know the true Bonackers and in unearthing specimens of their rich local patois.

She also made friends among the famous in and around East Hampton, including the television host Dick Cavett and his actress wife, Carrie Nye; Craig Claiborne, the expert on cuisine; and Alger Hiss, the pivotal figure in the notorious espionage case of the late 1940s. There were also her fellow *New Yorker* hands Howard Moss, Berton Roueché, and the cartoonist Saul Steinberg. In addition, Stafford inherited some of Liebling's cronies, among them Jean Riboud, a hero of the French Resistance who had made a fortune as the head of Schlumberger, Ltd., and Riboud's equally cultivated compatriots Pierre and Charlotte Guedenet.

Stafford also made friends among East Hampton's tradespeople, and Jeannette Rattray, publisher of the *Star,* the local newspaper, became one of her true colleagues. Jean went out of her way, too, to befriend her neighbors — principally Eleanor Hempstead, Barbara Hale, and, later, Jean Hoffman — and she developed a strong loyalty to her cleaning lady, Josephine Monsell, who was as pure a Bonacker as The Springs could boast. Stafford renovated both the ex-pigpen and the cottage in back and rented them out to a series of relatively impecunious lodgers. These ranged from local folks to the writers Wilfrid Sheed and Craig Nova.

At her best Stafford could be a generous and influential friend. As a young writer struggling to make his mark, Sheed had met Stafford at a lunch in New York in the late 1950s, where they had talked about his writing. (As a boy of nine, Sheed had met her at his father's publishing firm in 1941, but he had retained no memory of her from that time.) Two days after the lunch he had gotten letters from a pair of publishers asking to see his work. "That was the real Jean for years and years," he recalls, "helping every young writer in sight for the love of it. . . ." When Stafford had friends over for dinner, she often brought out a special bottle of wine from Liebling's splendid collection in the cellar. Playing the country yokel, she liked to refer to the sophisticated Eleanor Hempstead as "Neighbor Hempstead," and to herself as "the Widow Liebling."

By 1964 Stafford's most distinctive social trait was her verbal style. Alger Hiss remembers,

> One of her gifts was that if she had an experience that seemed to her worth recounting, she would describe it without permitting interruption. And if later in the week you saw Jean again, and it was an occasion when she happened to tell the same story, not a word had been changed. It was as if she were reciting from memory a polished, finished story. This must have been the way she perceived events.

Her closest friends recognized a paradox in Stafford's oft-proclaimed love of the country. As Eleanor Hempstead puts it,

> Jean never took advantage of anything that had to do with the country. She never took a walk, didn't drive a car. . . . She had a garden, but she had Kenny Miller [one of her backyard boarders] plant it for her. She'd go out and pick a few cherry tomatoes. Or she'd sit under the apple tree and have drinks on a Sunday afternoon. But Jean never went to the beach, she never swam, she never rode a bicycle. Jean was always in her house, unless she was going out to dinner or something.

Fixing up the house became Stafford's abiding pursuit. Some Audubon bird charts that she had once hung in Maine now took their places on the walls beside Liebling's racing posters. She also put up a photo of her father; her copy of the life mask Howard Higman had made from her face; a picture of Elephi; a framed photocopy of the *New York Times* from July 1, 1915 (the date of her birth); a poster advertising Moxie, the soft drink of her childhood; a bumper sticker that read, "Eat More Possum"; a Victorian magazine print warning against the "Fruits of Intemperance"; many drawings by Saul Steinberg; and a favorite apothegm from Thomas De Quincey: "If once a man indulges himself in murder, very soon he comes to think little of robbery, and from robbing he next comes to drinking and Sabbath-breaking, and from that to incivility and procrastination."

Ornamentation was not enough; Stafford "embarked on a long series of renovations, mostly of the interior." She added a downstairs bathroom, redid the kitchen, and converted an upstairs bedroom into a third study. Yet in the eyes of Eve Auchincloss, a frequent guest,

> God, she could be bourgeois. In the country, she kept all her window shades pulled to half-mast. When she was still in bed in the morning I'd pull them up — there was the bay sparkling in the morning sunlight. But when she got up she'd pull them halfway down again. Aesthetically, she hardly had a clue. She had plastic roses on each clip of her shower curtain. She simply had no eye. Yet as a writer, what an eye she had for detail, for people.

For some years after Liebling's death Stafford regularly visited his grave, bringing bittersweet and holly in the autumn, roses and daisies in the summer. She continued to use interchangeable sets of personal cards and letterhead stationery that identified her alternatively as "Miss Jean Stafford" and "Mrs. Abbott Joseph Liebling."

Stafford's health remained precarious throughout the year following her heart attack. Between August 1964 and March 1965 she had three stays in the hospital. Despite Thomas Roberts's injunction, Stafford had gone on smoking at least two packs a day after her heart attack. She had stayed on the wagon for several months, but by December she was drinking heavily once more. Her weight dropped to 114 pounds despite the abundance of calories in the alcohol she was consuming. Roberts found no evidence of liver damage, but he judged that Stafford was suffering from arteriosclerotic heart disease on top of her other complaints. A tantalizing and distressing note records a visit she made to his office in December 1964:

> She has, however, been depressed + has been drinking some[,] acute difficulties being set off by meeting w. R. Lowell resulting in "a re-hash of all the things which led to the divorce" and some physical violence. Has been drinking only wine.

Three weeks later, just after Christmas, Roberts noted: "Drinking a great deal. Twitching fingers + toes."

Stafford published two short stories in 1964 — her first in five years — but neither was new work. "The Ordeal of Conrad Pardee" came out in *Ladies Home Journal,* four years after *The New Yorker* had rejected it. It is Stafford at far from her best — a long-winded Edwardian fable of social climbing whose plot pivots on a contrived slip of the tongue. "The Tea Time of Stout-hearted Ladies" — salvaged from her dead novel "In the Snowfall" — appeared in the *Kenyon Review.* A much better story, it recaptures Stafford's boredom as a college student listening to her mother and the neighbor lady exchange boardinghouse gossip.

It was no longer only fiction that eluded Stafford's typewriter; she had all but ground to a halt as a journalist as well. Since her perfunctory piece on whiskey in *Harper's Bazaar* in 1961, she had published not a single article. All of 1964 and most of 1965 passed without a completed assignment, even though she still received offers. *Town & Country* suggested a "pro-Christmas" Boston piece for a measly two hundred dollars. James Oliver Brown wrote her, "Just write NO on this and shoot it back"; Stafford circled "pro" and added, "Ha! Ha! No." *Venture,* a hardcover travel magazine published by *Look,* offered fifteen hundred dollars for a Newport reflection. Stafford admitted to being tempted, but she declined, telling her agent, "The summer — indeed, the whole past year — has been a mess and I've got nothing done and I'm terribly anxious to be about my proper business of writing fiction."

Apparently with little more incentive than the desperate need for money, in 1964 Stafford accepted a job writing a regular book column for *Vogue.* She had written the odd book review in the past and had served her brief stint as *Horizon*'s movie critic, but from 1964 through 1976 her book reviews would become Stafford's chief (and for months at a time, her only) source of income. Her three consistent outlets during those thirteen years were *Vogue,* the *New York Review of Books,* and the *Washington Post Book World.*

From first to last, Stafford's method was by and large a uniform one. The bulk of the review would be taken up with recounting the plot of the book — "usually," says Eve Auchincloss (who commissioned her reviews for *Book World* and the

New York Review), "better than the writer did." There is thus a disappointing scarcity of critical judgment or of personal asides among these dozens of short pieces. Yet the writing in them is frequently vivid and delightful, and it is obvious that each book, good or bad, fully engaged Stafford's attention. From the manuscript evidence, these reviews, which earned her as little as a hundred dollars each, were never easily dashed off; it was Stafford's modus operandi to take copious notes and to put her copy through a perfectionist's series of drafts.

The best writing in these perforce fugitive pieces often comes in the form of one- or two-sentence epigrams, sparked when Stafford's sympathetic paraphrase lapses into critical insight. In the stories in a Mavis Gallant collection, Stafford observes, "subterranean hatreds smolder and grudges, as old as the hills, are fed like boa constrictors in zoos." Jean-Paul Sartre's *The Words* occasions the *pensée*, "And like all child writers, he plagiarized coldbloodedly." Despite her growing penchant for invective, Stafford often declined to write about a book if she discovered that she didn't like it; most of her reviews are positive. Yet not surprisingly, the most memorable of her pieces in the genre are those in which she lambastes a book that ought to have been better.

In a few of her reviews Stafford seems to have been settling old grudges. Appraising Andrew Turnbull's biography of Thomas Wolfe, she goes after the writer himself for being a racist, an anti-Semite, and a Germanophile, and for being "infuriating and pathetic . . . deformed by self-absorption and self-indulgence." "Like most romantics," Stafford sneers, "he believed himself to be unique, and he believed, moreover, that the Philistines were after him, personally, in full cry." In its excess of indignation, this lucid put-down smacks of an exorcism of Stafford's own youthful enthrallment by Wolfe.

More than a few times Stafford reviewed books written by friends; almost always she gave them raves. All the more puzzling, then, is her vicious attack on Graham Greene's *May We Borrow Your Husband?*, in which she scolds her former friend (and according to her own account, ex-lover) in the accents of a Boston bluestocking:

> Since one is not at every turn assailed and affronted by his particularly noxious brand of prurience, one can with great pleasure rediscover the Greene of earlier years. . . .

In this book Greene has mercifully left out his complicated obsession with the Roman Church and, while Americans are still
abominable, he dwells upon them a little less than usual.

Even so, says Stafford, one American character is "rigged out in
every predictable cliché imaginable."

During these years Stafford claimed to interviewers that she
wrote at least four hours every day. The book reviews cannot
have taken up all that time. There was always the novel, of which
Robert Giroux had seen no more than had Albert Erskine. Unless she destroyed all such aids, Stafford does not seem to have
been the kind of writer who made diagrams, outlines, or extensive notes for her stories and articles. In her later years she kept
neither a diary nor a working notebook. Yet on scraps of paper
and in notepads, she assembled vast collections of verbal ephem-
era. Many of these are lists of overheard phrases, like found objects plucked from the wasteland of language about her. In different inks and at different times, she added to each list whenever
a new item swam into her ken. An example:

> hooligans
> Gorgeous George
> Confucius say
> oldtimers
> scapegrace
> greenhorn
> lead pipe cinch
> coin of the realm

Yet this detritus seems to have had little connection with Stafford's serious writing: Gorgeous George never did work his way
into a story.

In East Hampton Stafford fielded hints that the larger world
had begun to see her work as all but a relic of the past. Scholars
announced that they wished to appropriate her for dissertations;
critics summed up her achievement. (The wisest of these assess-
ments — with no whiff of the postmortem — came in Louis Auchincloss's excellent 1965 study of nine women novelists, *Pioneers
& Caretakers*.) The libraries of Congress, Cornell, and the University of Wyoming requested her papers (she had already donated several manuscripts to the University of Colorado).

In 1964 Stafford sought, and was greatly relieved to get, a year's appointment at Wesleyan University as a Fellow of the Center for Advanced Studies. She was in residence there during the academic year of 1964–1965, "being paid vast sums of money," as she later crowed, "for doing absolutely nothing." With no teaching duties, she was free to while away her time in "brilliant conversation over drinks with my colleagues." These included such scholars as Moses Hadas, René Dubos, Herbert Read, and Paul Horgan. Her favorite crony was the crotchety and dazzling writer-critic Edmund Wilson.

Stafford had hoped to commute for a few days each week between her house in Long Island and the Wesleyan campus in Middletown, Connecticut, but the logistics proved insuperable. She anticipated that her year in academe would force her "to work as I have not done for many years." In actuality Wesleyan provided yet another long distraction — and wreaked havoc on Stafford's sobriety as well. She played host to an afternoon salon, fortifying her visitors with strong drink; Wilson was her daily companion. In Joseph Mitchell's view, Stafford retained a "deep awe" for the academic world, yet "at the same time, she was always afraid she'd be shown up — that her French wasn't any good, her German was not fluent. . . . I think she was afraid of professors."

In March 1965 a lucky meeting with an editor served to rescue Stafford from her drift toward obscurity. Barbara Lawrence at *McCall's* offered her twenty-five hundred dollars to go to Texas to interview the mother of Lee Harvey Oswald, President Kennedy's assassin. For once Stafford took the bait.

In May, again on the wagon, she spent three days in Dallas interviewing Marguerite Oswald. In one sense sobriety made the ordeal (every step of which Stafford dreaded) all the more intolerable; in another, it probably allowed her to see the job through. Using a tape recorder for the first time in her life, Stafford gathered nine hours of rambling pontification and paranoia from the assassin's mother, an unsophisticated, delusional woman who seemed befuddled by the limelight into which she had been thrust.

Stafford later declared, "What I wanted to do was report exactly what I heard and saw, not what I felt. . . . It seemed to me . . . that I had presented the case of Mrs. Oswald without slant or analysis, and that the irony derived from the facts rather than from any commentary." As far as it goes, this is a reasonable description of "The Strange World of Marguerite Oswald," which *McCall's* published in October 1965. Indeed, the real weakness of Stafford's essay is that it *is* so reticent of interpretation, allowing Mrs. Oswald's peculiar rant to go on uninterrupted for pages. Yet in this pathetic creature Stafford had discovered her ultimate verbal eccentric, the living paradigm of her fictional Bobettes and Marjeans and Mrs. Mulgrews. Mesmerized, Stafford handed over the microphone to Mrs. Oswald:

> "Lee purely loved animals! With his very first pay he bought a bird and a cage, and I have a picture of it. He bought this bird with a cage that had a planter for ivy, and he took care of that bird and he made the ivy grow. Now, you see, there could be many nice things written about this boy. But, oh, no, no, this boy is supposed to be the assassin of a President of the United States, so he has to be a louse. Sometimes I am very sad."

Stafford's fascination with that voice survived the assignment; back in The Springs, she held parties at which she played the Oswald tapes for her friends.

Barbara Lawrence's hunch had been a canny one. No other nonfiction piece that Stafford wrote ever came close to provoking the furor and interest that the *McCall's* article did. Along with scattered encomiums, Stafford received a good deal of hate mail. Recognizing a hot property, Farrar, Straus & Giroux rushed an expanded version of the piece into print as a slim book called *A Mother in History*. Within three months of publication the book had sold ten thousand copies in hardback. Although their criticisms were more thoughtful than those of the readers of *McCall's,* the book reviewers swung to equally distant extremes. The antipodes ranged from *Newsweek*'s rave, "a masterpiece of character study and a gem of personal journalism," to Godfrey Hodgson's blast in the English paper the *Observer*:

> Miss Stafford carries detachment to the brink of contempt and sometimes beyond it, punctuating the torrent of Mrs. Oswald's naive self-revelation with cruel little touches of the whip. . . . This is a book about two women, and of the two, I find Miss Stafford, with her knowing New York superiority and her lack of human sympathy, quite as chilling as the other.

All the uproar, however, served to put Stafford back on the map as an active writer. Assignment offers flooded in. *Cosmopolitan* wanted Stafford to report on "wives of soldiers going off to Vietnam someplace in a camp"; the *Saturday Evening Post* fancied an essay on "The Loveless"; *Esquire* longed for her views on "The Art of Weekending"; and *McCall's* was ready for almost anything she might suggest. Stafford got teaching offers, and book ideas came out of the woodwork: J. B. Lippincott proposed that she write on hypochondria; Putnam's thought Stafford ideal for a biography of Edna St. Vincent Millay; and the agent for Edith Wharton's estate wanted to put her to work on an authorized Wharton biography. To all of these Stafford said no. James Oliver Brown dutifully explained to the various editors that her novel had to come first.

For *McCall's* Stafford agreed to write about Kenneth, the famous hairdresser. After one appointment at his salon, however, she gave up on the piece. The months stretched on; throughout the rest of 1965 and all of 1966 and 1967, Stafford published no stories and only a single magazine article. Her profile of the interior designer Ward Bennett, which appeared in *Art in America* in 1966, shows Stafford at her feeblest — bland and uncritical, drooling over the furnishings of a rich man's house.

The causes of this two-year barrenness — Stafford's most unproductive spell since she had begun writing — are not entirely clear. The Oswald opus, which had involved a prodigious amount of work, had proved that she was still capable, at least when she was not drinking, of producing a focused and formidable piece of prose. Financially she was able to coast for a while on her Oswald earnings.

Although she suffered no further physical setbacks as debilitating as her heart attack, Stafford's health during the latter part of the 1960s continued to be a litany of arcane aggravations. She had an excisional biopsy on a tumor in her right breast in 1964, which showed no malignancy, and further surgery on her foot the next year for Morton's neuroma. In 1967 she suffered from "peripheral neuritis" caused (she thought) by eating fresh produce that had been sprayed with insecticide. Spinal problems several months later (she told the Thompsons that in a few years she would not be able to move her head) were followed in 1969 by harrowing root-canal work that stemmed ultimately from the 1938 car accident.

Because Stafford narrated her ailments with a morbid zest, her friends tended to become blasé about them; says Ann Honeycutt, "She was always having brain tumors and breast cancer." But Stafford's longstanding defense against despair was to try to be funny about her bodily decrepitude. In 1966 she claimed that she was "jack-knifed in a bolt-upright sitting position" in an electrically powered hospital bed when she had the misfortune to be caught in the big blackout that affected New York.

Thomas Roberts's notes on Stafford's visits to him during the middle and late 1960s are a catalogue of woes:

> 9/8/65: Upset + depressed — estate taxes are "a mess."

> 2/2/66: Awoke last night w. vomiting + diarrhea.

> 3/4/66: Very upset re having to stop smoking.

> 3/17/67: In for discussion recent sleep-walking + 2 fires set by cigarettes in bedrooms.

> 5/6/68: Has been drinking.

Roberts's efforts to get Stafford to quit smoking and drinking after her heart attack were doomed to failure. By 1965 her alcohol intake had reached sixteen ounces a day, or twice what she had admitted to Roberts when he had first seen her, and by the late 1960s she was smoking three packs a day. One day the doctor, who had moved to East Hampton in 1966, stopped by Stafford's house to pick her up on the way to a social outing. She made him wait a few minutes while she finished a piece that had to go into that day's mail. "She would type a phrase or two," Roberts recalls, "reach over and take a puff, then type another few lines. You got the feeling standing there that *this* was dependent on *that*. I remember saying to myself, 'You'll never get that woman to stop smoking.'

"She was an addictive personality," Roberts adds, "and not only addicted to alcohol, but she would abuse other medication. Yet if I had played the tough doctor and said, 'I'll never give you any of that,' she would have simply gone elsewhere." Instead, Roberts tried to warn her about her medication and to give her just enough to afford some comfort. Although Stafford took antabuse from time to time, says Roberts, "I think she sort of played with it." It comes as no surprise to her close friend Eleanor Hempstead that Stafford never sought out Alcoholics Anonymous: "You have to be a joiner to be in A.A."

Nonetheless, Stafford was no cheerful, devil-may-care souse. When Dick Cavett asked her if she thought she could stop drinking, she stared out the window, then said in a matter-of-fact way, " 'I loathe alcohol. It is my enemy. And my seducer.' " Says Berton Roueché, "I think of Jean and Jackson Pollock in the same way. He was a violent drunk [as Stafford was not]. But he had the same problem with his painting. The more he drank, the less he could paint. I think, the same with Jean."

In the spring of 1967 Stafford's troubles reached a critical juncture. She came very close to committing herself to Payne Whitney, as she had in 1946, for psychological rehabilitation. Since she was no longer seeing Mary Jane Sherfey, Roberts recommended an excellent Manhattan psychiatrist to her. After two visits she wrote the man an anguished note:

> Although I feel most desperately in need of help and solace, I cannot seem to plot a modus operandi whereby I can get it: I cannot afford to come to New York to stay and a weekly trip in is, at the moment, impossibly difficult — I am simply too ill physically to manage.

The psychiatrist took Stafford seriously. It was his judgment that she suffered from an acute and chronic — possibly life-long — depression; he also perceived her as having an integral masochism, which was oddly contradicted by the air of vitality that penetrated her depression. In the short run there was little he could do but endorse Roberts's prescription of 150 mgs. a day of Elavil, an antidepressant. Stafford weathered her crisis and stayed out of what she called "the insane asylum."

In 1964 Stafford's father turned ninety. He had become completely dependent on Marjorie, with whom he lived. John Stafford still wrote Jean regularly, never failing to thank her for the checks she sent him. She found it harder than ever to write back. "Each time I contemplate a letter," she confessed to Mary Lee, "I feel so sick and sad that I find something else to do. That so preposterous a life should be so endlessly prolonged is an unfathomable mystery."

Finally, at the insistence of Mary Lee and Harry, John Stafford consented to enter a nursing home. Despite his advanced age, Marjorie was convinced that "his death was hastened by his incarceration." Just as she had failed in her attempts to persuade Jean to visit their father in his declining years, so Marjorie also failed to extort a pilgrimage to his deathbed. John Stafford expired in January 1966, in his ninety-second year. When Mary Lee telephoned to tell her of his death, Jean was furious at the fact that her sister had called collect.

With the disappearance of Liebling from her life, Stafford swore to her friends, " 'There'll never be another man on the premises, ever.' " Despite the ravages that her living habits had wrought upon her looks, quite a few men still found her attractive. She welcomed the attentions of a few — in particular Jean Riboud, whose avuncular solicitude bore no trace of the romantic, and Stephen Goodyear, a psychiatrist with whom she drank and socialized. Her closest friends, however, judged Stafford to be utterly uninterested in sex. "I never believed she had any real interest in men," recalls Eve Auchincloss. "I think Jean was a puritan underneath," says Ann Honeycutt.

None of her friends from this era knew, of course, anything about the toll that her venereal disease had taken on Stafford. By then, one senses, she was only too glad to have done with physical love for good. Whether or not this stance may in fact have reflected an aversion deeply implanted in Stafford from childhood onward — her flings at CU and in Germany being, in that case, disastrous aberrations that others talked her into — remains one of the crucial yet insoluble puzzles of her life.

Stafford's easy friendship with the male homosexuals of East Hampton earned her an epithet then in local use: "fag hag." John Thompson recalls, "They were crazy about her. . . . They were no threat to her, she was no threat to them. They liked her gossip."

In spite of everything that had happened, Stafford still carried an ambivalent torch for Robert Lowell. On the same occasion when she told Auchincloss that she and Lowell had never made love, Stafford added in the next breath, " 'And then when he married Lizzie Hardwick, he began screwing like a jackrabbit.' " A favorite put-down of her first husband dated from the Liebling years: "She thought it was hilariously funny to call Lowell 'the Cassius Clay of literature.' " Peter Taylor remembers Stafford telling him more than once, " 'I had a telephone call from that boob, trying to make up to me.' " She instructed Blair Clark, " 'Tell him not to telephone me.' " When Clark next saw his old friend, Lowell protested, " 'She asked me to telephone all the time.' "

July 1, 1965, was Stafford's fiftieth birthday. As she settled into the hermitage of her East Hampton life, she began to construct a kind of persona with which to face the world; half-consciously, she portrayed herself as a local eccentric. The tales she told on herself got better with each recounting.

With an odd kind of loyalty, Stafford imposed her mythologizing upon her friends as well as upon herself. As Thomas Roberts puts it, "It was almost as if, being admitted to her inner circle, you had to be fabulous in some way. And if you were not, then she would invent something to make you more interesting than you really might be." Stafford also wrote mock-heroic poems to Eleanor Hempstead's cats.

Her knack for keeping her friends in mutually exclusive coteries intensified in East Hampton. She had her own priorities; Eve Auchincloss was annoyed that Stafford often contrived ways to dismiss her if someone more "important" — usually a man such as Jean Riboud or Peter Taylor — was about to arrive. Says Eleanor Hempstead, "She was interested in men because of what they did or what they wrote, and she didn't want to bother with the women they were attached to"; here, Hempstead thinks, lay a clue to Stafford's interest in homosexual men. When Randall Jarrell was killed by a car while walking beside a highway, Stafford wrote several moving letters of sympathy to his wife, Mary. Yet not long after, she derided "the Widow Jarrell" in a letter to Ann Honeycutt:

> She's the one who wrote and asked me if I had a bench for contemplation beside Joe's grave and who goes around the country singing her husband's poems and accompanying herself on the piano — won't even let the poor devil rest in his grave although I'm sure that to anyone attuned, the racket of his tossing bones must drown out her soprano.

(This vignette seems to be largely Stafford's invention.)

Going to parties became Stafford's favorite pastime. Her skills as a raconteur were so polished that she could always count on having a circle of admirers around her, rapt with admiration. "She could be vastly entertaining," says Thomas Roberts, "although she could sometimes go on in a monotonous harangue if she'd been drinking too much."

"I'm afraid Jean got to be sometimes a little imperious," says Joseph Mitchell. At one party,

> There was a man who didn't know who she was. He kept on talking while she was trying to tell a story. She turned on him and said, "I demand absolute silence." He said, "Madam, you sure do impose harsh conditions." She became so indignant that she got up [and said], "I must go home immediately."

Stafford's escort drove her home.

Several of Jean's newer friends were shocked, on visiting her during one of her hospital stays, to descry her comfort and even her joy in her surroundings. If the hospital approximated Jean's Red Room, it could also serve, as her doctor noted, as her stage. At New York Hospital her visitors were not her only audience; by now the nurses and doctors knew her so well that she was flooded with attention each time she returned.

The metaphor of performance is an intrinsic one. "I think Jean wanted to be somebody else all the time," says Ann Honeycutt. "She thought it would have been wonderful to have been born in the South." Once, after an afternoon spent in the company of Eudora Welty, Peter Taylor, and Joseph Mitchell (all southern-born), Stafford "decided from now on she was going to be a southerner. She was damned tired of Yankees."

It is Howard Moss's powerful insight to link Stafford's "predilection for masks and disguises" to the car accident that had smashed up her face. Stafford came to Moss's house once for drinks, wandered into the kitchen, and emerged wearing a Halloween mask with a big red nose. (According to her friend Barbara Hale, Stafford always thought the scar on her nose had spoiled her looks.) On another occasion Stafford surprised Moss by coming to her door dressed as a cocktail waitress. She had a huge collection of hats, capes, and costumes. It was not always easy to tell whether Stafford wore what she did in order to be deliberately outlandish or, as Eve Auchincloss believes, as the unfortunate result of a complete lack of taste.

There is good evidence for the latter. Dorothea Straus saw

Stafford at one academic gathering, "clad in a black leather jumpsuit that left her still girlish shoulders and back naked, in startling contrast" to the tweedy dress around her. "Her costume seemed to be making a statement; it looked less seductive than lonely." In East Hampton, Jean once dressed for a party at Dick Cavett's in black leotards and a baseball cap; "she looked awful," says John Thompson, who urged her to change when she asked his opinion.

The tenants who rented Stafford's backyard buildings did so at their own peril: most of them sooner or later incurred her wrath. One of the first was a young Wesleyan student who got free summer lodging in exchange for yard work and driving. "The next thing you know, she didn't want him in the house," testifies Eleanor Hempstead. "He drank up all the orange juice and didn't get more." Wilfrid Sheed recalls Stafford's teasing reference to him and his wife, Miriam Ungerer, as her "share-croppers." "On off nights, she'd phone us to say 'I am drunk as a *billy* goat,' which meant that at least she'd like to be, and come on over." Yet Stafford fell out with Ungerer, too, because of her propensity for borrowing things.

Stafford's tenants Kenny and Arlene Miller were Bonackers; he was hired as caretaker and handyman, she as cook. Eventually Stafford sacked the couple, ostensibly because of Arlene Miller's meager culinary talents. Hempstead grants, "Arlene was no Craig Claiborne." But typically, according to Hempstead, Arlene would bring dinner over to Stafford's house at seven o'clock and put it in the oven to keep it warm; only after her drinking guests had departed, usually at around ten, would Stafford go into the kitchen and eat the desiccated remains.

Stafford admitted to one interviewer that her bouts of obsessive cleaning — "I even go into the corners with Q-tips" — were "rituals of depression": " 'But they're better than staring-into-space depressions.' " In a newspaper essay she listed her domestic amusements; they included solving double-crostics, worrying over her five cesspools, listening to "my cats purring in their sleep," and "giv[ing] presents to my house," such as a new cedar closet.

By the late 1960s Stafford was showing signs of real reclusiveness. She began to entertain no more than once a week, never having more than six guests at a time because "there's no drinking space." When Stafford had taken over the house, it had had three bedrooms. In 1970, after a fire caused by her smoking burned a huge hole in the carpet, she turned her bedroom into a sitting room and moved into one of the guest bedrooms. Eventually she converted the other guest room into a study, giving herself a pretext for lamenting, when friends wanted to visit, that there was no possibility of their staying overnight.

To a reporter, she said only half jokingly, "I find the best days are those on which the phone never rings and no one comes to the door. I can imagine myself becoming a recluse." Stafford claimed that she downed only coffee for breakfast and a Hershey bar for lunch. "When you'd come to visit her," says Eve Auchincloss, "she'd make a thing of cooking a meal. But I had the feeling she didn't do much eating most of the time." Stafford had installed an upstairs refrigerator "for milk and orange juice"; she maintained that she stowed her novel manuscript in it (because it was fireproof) when she left The Springs.

The half-secret of Stafford's reclusion, however — as well as, ultimately, in medical terms, a cause of it — was her drinking, which had become truly excessive. In her own house, Thomas Roberts often saw her mix milk and bourbon: "I think part of it was, 'I'm not really drinking.' " When Auchincloss stayed overnight, she says, "I'd get up at seven-thirty or whatever and make myself some breakfast, and a couple of hours later Jean would appear, and she would reek of booze. I assumed she'd had a couple in bed before she got up." Auchincloss remembers opening the downstairs refrigerator to "the smell of rot — as if it hadn't been opened for weeks."

As if to reinforce her isolation, in the late 1960s Stafford began to barricade herself behind a set of impish fences, concocted as fey conceits but nonetheless answering to a real need. She got an unlisted phone number, with an answering service as double protection. Later she used an answering machine, whose lordly message, always on, went something like, "We are at work and cannot be disturbed. . . ." On her back door she posted several signs. One, in capitals, read:

THE WORD "HOPEFULLY" MUST NOT
BE MISUSED ON THESE PREMISES
VIOLATORS WILL BE HUMILIATED

Another announced:

NOTICE NOTICE NOTICE NOTICE NOTICE NOTICE

We are at work and must not be disturbed.

If your business is urgent, please telephone.

This does not apply to delivery men or service people.

It is a warning against time-wasting droppers-in and to
everyone with a petition for or against any cause whatsoever.

Stafford was proud of these caveats, even though, as Sheed
complained, they verged on the tacky and "seemed to contain a
touch more aggression than humor." Besides underscoring Stafford's pose as the private dowager, these messages and signs may
also have served to fortify both her own sense that she was grappling day after day with a major work of fiction and the pretense
that she was holding off the clamorous attentions of a multitude.
In truth, however, by that point there must have been precious
few time-wasting droppers-in coming down her backcountry road
to disturb her solitude.

As another dodge to fend off unwelcome contact, Stafford invented an imaginary secretary named Henrietta Stackpole, after
a character in Henry James. She even had a "Henrietta Stackpole" signature stamp made for signing letters. Stackpole answered her employer's mail on the frequent occasions when "Miss
Stafford is in Teheran shopping for her winter wardrobe." In
part this device amounted to a running in-joke between Jean and
her best friends; the huffy letters Stackpole penned were not all
that different in spirit from the country-bumpkin epistles Stafford had exchanged with Hightower.

But Henrietta Stackpole also served a more crucial role as
dummy for the ventriloquism of Stafford's crankiness. In 1969
James Oliver Brown sent Stafford a first novel called *Coming Together,* written by one of his clients, an "attractive," modern young
woman named Alice Denham. Brown hoped that Stafford would
recommend Denham for a Guggenheim Fellowship. It was
Stackpole, however, who replied:

During Miss Stafford's prolonged sojourn in Iran, I am handling
her correspondence and I take it upon myself to tell you, in no
uncertain terms[,] that Miss S. is not in the habit of reading books
about fucking with the photograph of the author in her birthday

suit on the front cover. After a lifetime of working closely with
Miss Stafford, I have come to adopt all her opinions and I think I
may safely say that she would undergo (as I did) a most grievous
curdling of the blood if she were to read the passages particularly
recommended by Miss Alice Denham.

During 1968, 1969, and 1970 Stafford was only slightly more
productive as a writer than she had been in the dark period just
before. In 1968 *The New Yorker* published "The Philosophy Lesson," the twenty-third story of hers to appear in the magazine —
though the first in eleven years. From her semiretirement in Maine
Katharine White wrote to congratulate Stafford, unaware that the
story was twenty years old: like "The Tea Time of Stouthearted
Ladies," it had been dredged up out of the manuscript of "In the
Snowfall." The piece follows the thoughts in its protagonist's
head as she poses nude for her college life-drawing class. Old
work or no, Stafford was elated by its publication: as a friend
recalls, "She said then, 'I'm not going to do anything any more
but write short stories for *The New Yorker*.' "

For *Boy's Life* Stafford penned a ghost story about Mountain
Jim Nugent, a Colorado gold-rush hell-raiser who had been a
hero of her adolescence. For *Vogue* she wrote about the founder
of the Hampton Day School in a piece as soft and spineless as
her profile of Ward Bennett.

In 1968 Consolidated Edison accidentally billed Stafford $409.28
for a month's worth of cooking gas. When her letters of protest
got lost in the bureaucratic shuffle, she was outraged. Refusing
to take this fairly common snafu in stride, Stafford sat down and
wrote a fifteen-page letter to the president of Con Ed. Fancying
her diatribe a worthwhile piece of journalism, she copyrighted
the manuscript; six years later a much-truncated version was
published in the *New York Times*.

The original letter is a strange document. After a preliminary
outburst, Stafford wanders off into divagations about her daily
routine. It is the kind of aimless harangue she might have delivered at a party when she had had too much to drink; indeed this
is the first piece of Stafford's surviving prose that sounds as if it
actually *was* written while she was drunk. The bulk of the letter
is a tedious recitation of Stafford's evenings with illustrious friends
(ostensibly offered as proof that she could not have been at home

squandering gas). The name-dropping and boasting reveal a side of Stafford that she had previously kept well hidden:

> On consulting my engagement book for the days in question, I find that on April 28th I dined at Le Pavilion (dreadfully over-rated) with M. Jean Riboud, the distinguished president of Schlumberger, Ltd and went with him to the opening of the Royal Ballet. (The dancing engaged us — up to a point — but oh, Good God, that opera house. Those chandeliers — lighted, of course, by Con Ed — could be, were they flesh and blood, haled into court and charged with criminal vulgarity.) On the 29th, I dined at Gino's (excellent food but much too noisy) with Stephen Greene, the celebrated painter . . . and his wife, Sigrid di Lima, one of America's most gifted novelists. On the 30th and the 1st, I dined with slightly less luminous friends.

The letter goes on in this vein for another twelve pages.

If Stafford did other writing in the 1950s and 1960s that was as slack and shameless as this, at least she had the good sense to suppress it on rereading. Although Stafford may be considered an alcoholic writer, she must also be credited with having had enough self-critical wisdom throughout her career to know her good stuff from her bad. Even in her later essays and book reviews, there is almost no trace of the kind of boozy self-parody or garrulous holding-forth indulged in by many great writers, including Faulkner, Hemingway, and Fitzgerald. Instead, alcohol seems to have taken a different toll on Stafford, altogether blocking her fiction writing.

The Con Ed piece reveals another foible. No matter how uninterested Stafford was in her own fame, she was girlishly impressed, as some of her East Hampton cronies perceived, by the fame of her friends; this was one reason she sought the company of a Dick Cavett or a Craig Claiborne on eastern Long Island. Her neighbor Jean Hoffman remembers that Stafford framed and mounted in her bathroom a congratulatory telegram she received from Senator Jacob Javits. Apparently unembarrassed by the name-dropping in her Con Ed piece, she sent a copy to each of the friends she had bragged about therein.

During the 1960s Stafford resisted a number of offers of college writer-in-residence jobs. Despite her cushy deal at Wesleyan, she had been both unhappy and unproductive there. Peter

Taylor, who had survived as a writer by padding his income
with money he earned in a long string of brief teaching sojourns,
made it his practice to recommend Stafford everywhere he went.
In the fall of 1967, no doubt facing yet another financial bind,
Stafford accepted a two-year contract at Columbia University as
Adjunct Professor in the School of Arts.

She rented an apartment on East Eighty-seventh Street —
"small, viewless, uninspired but adequate" — and began commuting to Manhattan on Wednesday evenings for her Thursday
class in creative writing. Although she taught only graduate students, she found them "cretinous." At fifty-two, she felt out of
touch with the youngsters in her charge:

> I didn't know what most of my students were talking about: nor
> did they understand what *I* was talking about when I told them
> that while "a structure may be constructed" is not a mellifluous
> statement it is, nonetheless, linguistically correct; but, said I, it is
> not possible to structure a construct. I think they found me friv-
> olous.

At Columbia Stafford ran head-on into a new generation of students, who demanded "relevance" in their studies:

> "I have nothing to say about 'A Rose for Emily,' " said Y one
> day. "I read two paragraphs, and it didn't turn me on. I don't dig
> Faulkner." And a few weeks later, X said, "Of course I didn't
> read *Heart of Darkness*. Do you seriously think I'd read anything
> by a pig who wrote a book titled *The Nigger of the Narcissus*?"

In the spring of 1968, in the middle of her second term at
Columbia, Stafford witnessed the battle between students and
administration that shut the university down; she was teaching
her class on the very day the police moved in onto Morningside
Campus. Her reaction was dismay and contempt: the subversive
elements, she insisted, were outsiders, "mobs who had never
matriculated in anything but reform schools."

Stafford debated long and hard about returning to Columbia
for a second year; in the end she quit after the fall term of 1968.
The rhetoric of the student revolutionaries had impressed her not
one whit. She liked to tell a story on her friend Dwight Macdon-
ald, who, when she had run into him one day on the train, had
"commenced to applaud the S.D.S."

D.M. These kids have exciting ideas. They have wonderful ideas.

J.S. Oh what a lucky meeting! I have read about these ideas but I cannot understand them. Do explain. What *are* the ideas?

D.M. It's too early to tell.

With her distrust of cant, of intellectual fashions, and of the kind of student political fervor she had seen in Heidelberg in 1936, Stafford turned a cold shoulder to the reform movements of the late 1960s. Despite her liberal instincts, she never let herself be seduced by the millenarian hopes and utopian promises that beguiled so many of her liberal-minded friends. In the face of the SDS, of sexual liberation, of the women's movement, of experimental art, she proclaimed herself a staunch reactionary.

But Stafford was no mere curmudgeon, hankering for the old-fashioned or opposing change on principle. With respect to women's liberation, for instance, she made a clear distinction between what she saw as the valid grievances of her sex and the facile revisionism that she thought dominated the movement itself. In retrospect, we can admire her for seeing through much of the shallow optimism that disguised the intolerant programs of certain self-styled emancipators of the human spirit. And in all of this she found a new set of subjects to write on. In a series of witty declarations and reports, Stafford became what she had long been on the verge of being — a satirist. One of her pronouncements was that the women's movement had

attracted hordes of Dumb Doras and Xanthippes and common scolds, and they raised such a hue and cry at the beginning that you couldn't hear the woodwinds for the crashes of the trees. *Timber!* yelled the battle-axes, and Portia's plea was muffled.

In a *New York Times* essay called "Women as Chattels, Men as Chumps," Stafford groaned at the "teratoid coinage" of the word *sexism,* ridiculed the idea that rape was a political crime, and proposed that feminists agitate against alimony as being a form of reverse prejudice. In the same piece, however, she also pledged her support in fighting for equal pay, equal opportunity, and legal abortion for women.

Pondering student protest, Stafford later confessed a certain sympathy with the outbursts after Kent State. Yet she declared that mass protests tended to be "no more than the manifestations

of the Old Nick, that barbaric ape within us all whom civiliza-
tion has tried to teach us to suppress." She applauded civil-rights
demonstrators and the march on Washington; "What I fear is the
lunatic fringe which inevitably follows the convoy. . . ."

The promises of the sexual liberationists left her cold: "If sex
became 'just a natural part of everyday life,' where was the fun,
where were the play, the thrilling doubts, the mystery, the de-
lectable danger?" She posited Charles Manson as the dark side of
the dream of the commune; in a long piece for *McCall's* in 1970,
she mused with great originality on the horrors of the Manson
murders.

The distillation of Stafford's satiric response to the late 1960s
came when an assignment took her to a place in Detroit called
the American Behavior Science Training Laboratories, where she
was to report firsthand on a "sensitivity training session." Predictably offended by the goings-on, Stafford left after two days
of what was supposed to be a week-long encounter group. She
later described the opening session:

> At the first meeting a throbbing silence lasted for twenty minutes
> until our trainer whose name, let's say, was Boo Ann saw some
> dandy behavior for the group to interpret, and she came over to
> my chair and took the needlepoint I was working on out of my
> hands and went back to her own chair. . . . She addressed a
> trainee . . . who was labelled Inez and said, "How are you relat-
> ing to Jean's bringing her needlepoint to the confrontation?" Inez,
> who was plainly as out of step as I, said she wished she had
> brought her own. I immediately "related" to Inez with warm under-
> standing.
>
> But luckily for Boo Ann my egregious want of esprit de corps
> was just what was needed to start a brisk free-for-all and these
> women t-kayoed both me and Inez and then let each other have
> it. . . . Mildred said to Myrtle, "You turn me off — you've got
> a weight problem," and Myrtle in retaliation said, "Whoever did
> your nose-job must have used a nutcracker." This was just the
> ticket for Boo Ann.

"My (Ugh!) Sensitivity Training" and articles like it signaled
the emergence of Stafford as a satiric polemicist at serious odds
with the fads of the times; Stafford the fiction writer, on the
other hand, was nowhere to be seen. In 1968 Farrar, Straus &

Giroux had decided to publish her *Collected Stories;* on June 27 of that year she had signed a new contract for both her long-awaited novel and that collection. She got an advance of twenty-five hundred dollars for the latter. Surveying the forty-five stories she had published, Stafford selected thirty. On the whole her choices were judicious ones, though she included a few of her less impressive early stories (such as "The Darkening Moon" and "Between the Porch and the Altar") and neglected some of her better late ones (notably two of the Adams stories, "The Violet Rock" and "The Scarlet Letter"). Instead of arranging the tales chronologically, she grouped them by geography, adapting rubrics ("The Innocents Abroad," "The Bostonians, and Other Manifestations of the American Scene," "Cowboys and Indians, and Magic Mountains," and "Manhattan Island") from Henry James and Mark Twain — "to whose dislocation and whose sense of place I feel allied," as she stated in the book's preface.

The Collected Stories of Jean Stafford appeared in March 1969. It was more widely reviewed than any of her previous books, and most of the notices were extremely favorable. By gathering the work of a quarter-century between the covers of a single volume, Farrar, Straus & Giroux had made manifest Stafford's standing as one of the best American short-story writers of her time. In a front-page essay in the *New York Times Book Review,* Guy Davenport hailed Stafford's "awesome integrity" and declared the book "an event in our literature." Elizabeth Janeway, in a long *Atlantic Monthly* review, praised the dialogue: "There is no one else writing today whose people speak more truly, and more surprisingly."

If there was a thread of demurral running through the nearly universal praise for the collection, it had to do with what Joyce Carol Oates in *Book World* called "an undertone of something brutal, something really alarming" in the stories. To read thirty of Stafford's tales at once was to be struck, as one was not in any single story, by "the icy privacy" of her characters, by "shattered dreams and people imprisoned," by "the trapped psyche, the captive mind." Collectively the reviewers seemed uncertain of whether to praise or to shrink back from Stafford's "obsessive themes and images" in stories that "deal with the 'warped' management of life." Today it is easier to see that Stafford's relentless probing of unhappiness and loss — an act that, in her own life, sprang from an instinct for survival — forms one of her chief contributions to American fiction.

On her 1968 contract, the title of Stafford's unfinished novel appears for the first time as "The Parliament of Women" — an allusion to Chaucer, perhaps an amalgam of *The Parliament of Fowls* and *The Legend of Good Women*. As in other title-borrowings of Stafford's ("A Winter's Tale," for instance, which has nothing to do with Shakespeare), the nod to the previous work seems to have been merely a superficial one. The ever-patient Robert Giroux had already waited six years without seeing any part of the novel; at this point Stafford had supposedly been at work on it for fifteen years, since she had first signed with Random House. Using the new contract as an opportunity to nudge her, Giroux imposed a revised deadline of June 15, 1969.

Stafford gave both her publisher and inquiring reporters cause to believe that she was almost finished. In a January 1969 essay on contemporary novelists, *Time* trumpeted the news that

> Jean Stafford . . . who has also siphoned off much energy into intricate short stories, has finished her first novel in 17 years. Titled *A Parliament of Women,* it is set in the author's native Colorado, and one of the main characters will be based on her father.

But as June 1969 came and went, Giroux could only twiddle his thumbs.

Despite the acclamation for her *Collected Stories,* Stafford marked the beginning of the 1970s with a new surge of apathy. Elected a member of the National Institute of Arts and Letters, she got embarrassingly drunk at her induction in January. She checked into a hospital, convinced that she had breast cancer (she did not). In March she wrote Eve Auchincloss, "I am in a hysterical depression and have started washing the house." She suffered the first (recorded) instance of what would become a long series of household accidents when she tripped over one of her cats and fell down the stairs.

There were other aggravations. For two weeks in January Stafford was a visiting writer at Penn State; this time the students were "loutish" as well as "cretinous." She was baffled by her invitation: "None of them [her students] had ever heard of me and certainly had not read me, but this was understandable enough since neither had their teachers." In her class the students asked such questions as, " 'How do you write a New Yorker story?' " Stafford shivered through temperatures of fifteen below in her room at the Nittany Lion Inn, sleeping beneath a mountain of blankets in "panty-hose, a pullover under my nightgown and my wrapper on top."

Because the article had to go to press while she was at Penn State, Stafford was obliged to use the telephone to call in galley corrections and to discuss changes on her Charles Manson piece for *McCall's*. When it came out in March, she flew into a rage over cuts she did not think she had authorized. One of James Oliver Brown's duties was to explain to magazine editors that a condition of Stafford's taking any assignment was "that her material will have no rewriting, that proofs will be submitted to her, and that she will have an absolute veto over changes"; now Stafford wrote a blistering letter to Shana Alexander, her editor at *McCall's,* in which she claimed that the excisions had mutilated her style. She closed with a haughty PS: "Finally, considering that I was asked to put the article through my typewriter twice, I was meagerly paid." *McCall's* had in fact given Stafford thirty-five hundred dollars for the article, more than she had ever received before for a magazine assignment.

The year 1970, however, held one major triumph. On May 4, Berton and Katherine Roueché were visiting Stafford's house when the telephone rang. It was Eve Auchincloss in New York; she had just seen an item that had come across the news wire. Stafford's *Collected Stories* had won the Pulitzer Prize for fiction.

XVIII

The Recluse about Town

STAFFORD WON THE Pulitzer on the same day that the shoot-
ings at Kent State occurred, when four protesting students
were killed by the National Guard. In terms of citizen involve-
ment, May 1970 may have marked the apogee of the political
fervor of the late 1960s. The image of the engagé writer was
reflected by Norman Mailer at the Democratic Convention, by
Gore Vidal vilifying Nixon on TV talk shows. No one was more
surprised than Stafford that someone "as unscatological and un-
polemic as I" should have won the prize. The *New York Times*
editorial hailing the Pulitzer winners focused on Seymour Hersh's
coverage of the My Lai massacre and on a *Newsday* series on
political corruption; with polite condescension, the author of the
essay added, "And if Jean Stafford's stories are more traditional
than adventuresome, they are surely among the best of their kind
being written today."

Stafford was deluged with telegrams and letters of congratulation (cabled Peter De Vries, "SUPPOSE NOW YOU'LL BE IMPOSSI-
BLE"). Somewhat coyly, she wrote Mary Lee, "For a few days
my privacy was outrageously invaded by telephone calls but now
everything has quieted down." New York and Long Island
newspapers interviewed her. To a local reporter she claimed,
"Everybody thinks I was out dancing in the street and drinking
champagne the night I won but I was watching an old Bette
Davis film on the telly." (Her artless inquisitor asked Stafford
what her favorite piece of her own writing was — a question no

one seems to have posed before. Stafford named *The Mountain Lion* among her novels, "In the Zoo" among her short stories.)

The thousand dollars that came with the Pulitzer meant only that "I'll be able to pay my land taxes without borrowing money. . . ." Farrar, Straus & Giroux rejoiced for their author: in one week, they gloated, 1,069 paperback copies of *The Collected Stories* were sold. Stafford's book had also been nominated for the National Book Award for fiction; in the end Joyce Carol Oates won for *Them*. Despite Stafford's show of indifference, close friends such as the Rouechés saw that the burst of recognition seemed to give her a new lease on literary life.

Only two weeks after her hour in the sun, however, Stafford wrote Eve Auchincloss "in a state of boundless gloom" because of taxes: "I must work like the devil and I'm too frightened and woebegone to concentrate." Just what she was working on remains uncertain. During the year after she won the Pulitzer, Stafford turned out book reviews apace for *Vogue* and *Book World* and the *New York Review of Books,* but she published not a single article or short story.

There was no shortage of offers. Among them were an assignment to do a profile of Mrs. Andrew Wyeth for *McCall's* and an all-purpose feeler from *Cosmopolitan.* Dodd, Mead wanted Stafford to write a biography of James Thurber. Viking offered four thousand dollars for a commonplace book (a personal collection of favorite passages and quotations) along the lines of W. H. Auden's *A Certain World.* Even though Stafford gave Auden's book a glowing review, she turned down this attractive offer — in part for fear of offending Robert Giroux. The only journalistic assignment Stafford took during the remainder of 1970 was to write an introduction for a book called *The American Coast,* for which she was paid twenty-five hundred dollars. In this essay she extolled the joys of walking dogs along Long Island beaches, even though, as Berton Roueché good-humoredly points out, "Jean never walked on the beach in her life, and she never had a dog."

The book reviews Stafford wrote during the period from 1970 to 1972 seem mechanically tailored to her usual formula. Even when the excuse for a personal reflection lay close at hand, she resisted the temptation. Yet if an author got under her skin, she could wax venomous. Anne Morrow Lindbergh had become a fairly close friend of Stafford's in the late 1940s; in 1970 Stafford nonetheless attacked Charles Lindbergh, as revealed by his war diaries, as an anti-Semitic admirer of Hitler and a prolix braggart, "as American as cherry pie and the atomic bomb."

Stafford made the occasional public appearance — as at a Manhattan symposium on the short story, where she joined Peter Taylor, Wallace Stegner, John Barth, Mark Schorer, and Kay Boyle but said very little. She turned down a stint at the Iowa Writers' Workshop, perhaps because she was swayed by bad memories of her 1938 sojourn in Iowa City. Although other writers had plumped for her novels with generous dust-jacket quotes, Stafford herself refused to write cover blurbs. She could devote hours, however, to crafting letters of outrage and indignation. One such riposte was inspired by the naive suggestion of an editor at Houghton Mifflin, which was anthologizing Stafford's story "Bad Characters," that she change the phrase "dago red" to "cheap red wine":

> "Derogatory ethnic terms" is pure hogwash, and I intend to devote the rest of my life (which will be about 10 more days) to preaching against the infusion of hogwash into the veins of the living language. *Cheap red wine* is not the same as *dago red*. I am one of the most unprejudiced women I have ever known (except against people I don't like) and one of the most intransigently vigilant of the colloquial.

In the wake of her Pulitzer Stafford seems to have puttered ineffectually over several short stories. Both James Oliver Brown and Robert Giroux remained mystified as to the status of "The Parliament of Women." Whatever doubts they had as to the chances of Stafford finishing her novel, they did not reveal them. She, meanwhile, continued to tease the world with hints of its impending completion. " 'It's sort of roughly about my father,' " she told a *New York Post* reporter, as she gave her a tour of her upstairs (fiction) study. In July 1972, apparently to reaffirm their faith in her work, Farrar, Straus & Giroux gave Stafford an additional three thousand dollars toward "The Parliament of Women," even though it was seven years overdue. It was now nineteen years since Random House had first signed up the book.

As usual, Stafford had no trouble finding distractions from her writing. Most of August and September 1970 was taken up with the famous balloon escapade. Three young adventurers, a jet-set

American couple and a British pilot, chose the field just south of Stafford's house as a launching pad for their attempt to cross the Atlantic — at the time a feat that had never been performed in a balloon. During the weeks of preparation and then the wait for ideal launching conditions, Stafford befriended the balloonists — "though they are mad, they are as nice as pie." The threesome became the nightly drinking companions of her parlor, and she outfitted them with a paperback library for the journey (Hardy, Flaubert, and the like).

Stafford shared the widespread conviction that the three were in over their heads: she maintained that until she suggested it, they had not thought to take along mittens, goggles, or wool socks. The citizens of East Hampton were scandalized to learn that the aeronauts had stayed up all night drinking brandy at Stafford's house before their morning takeoff on September 20. The flight had been planned for the two men only; at the last minute (influenced by brandy?), Pam Anderson jumped into the gondola to join her husband.

Thirty hours later the party radioed that they were going down in a storm over the ocean east of Newfoundland. Despite an extensive search, no trace of the crew or the balloon was ever found. The media had a field day clucking over the crew's inexperience and poor judgment, but the fact is that transatlantic crossings by balloon were and still are extremely hazardous ventures. Even Stafford's brandy probably had nothing to do with the team's demise.

Stafford was lastingly beguiled by the drama of the event. She collected a mass of materials on ballooning, and some acquaintances understood her to be contemplating a book about the attempt. According to Thomas Roberts, "The tragic outcome of it all, she accepted as the natural end of the story."

In March 1971 Stafford was to be a guest speaker in a lecture series at Barnard College. As she wrote her five essays she was "certain that every sentence I utter will be greeted with a Bronx cheer followed by a rotten egg in my face." Once more she was "austerely on the wagon" — and "while this has brought on a great sense of well being, it has also produced great ferocity which, coupled with despair, is an unhandy parlay."

According to Peter Taylor, some of her Barnard students, recognizing how she hated the classroom, begged her never to

perform in one again. Yet her lectures charmed and impressed a
wide audience — and for good reason. The texts of these unpublished essays show Stafford at her expository best, mixing her
stubborn old-fashionedness with a sharp wit and a lightly-worn
wisdom.

On youth:

> The helmets and the masks, the arms and armor that we take on
> later protect and socialize us; they disguise us, and with such cum-
> bersome paraphernalia our route is necessarily roundabout but the
> bylanes offer charming glades and surprising Edens. I look back
> upon the years of my own young life with certain admiration and
> with certain embarrassment and with no desire whatever to live
> them over again.

On children:

> Children should be treated with respect and treated as children,
> not as men and women of small stature and not as inferiors, sub-
> jected to gush and mush and baby talk or shouted at in pidgin
> English as if they were foreign or deaf.

At the end of her last lecture, Stafford disarmed the same audience she had initially feared:

> I feel far less acerb. I can't pretend I want to stay on — In truth,
> I can't wait to get home back to my own bed and my own cat
> and my own work and to see if there are any signs of buds on the
> lilac bushes. But I have liked being here, and I hope that you will
> be as kind to yourselves as you have been to me.

There were other distractions besides balloonists and Barnard
students. Stafford served on several awards committees, including, for three years running, one for the National Academy of
Arts and Letters. She took such work seriously, even while she
gossiped wickedly about the action behind the scenes:

> The meetings themselves are rather good fun because there's scarcely
> anything meaner in this world than a batch of writers getting to-
> gether to cut up other writers. Last year, to our considerable re-
> lief, we lost Loren Eis[e]ley (I asked Joe Mitchell who he was and
> Joe said, "Oh, he writes about science kind of the way Anne
> Lindbergh does."), but he was replaced by Kurt Vonnegut who

keeps saying "Gee!" and recommending the funky serious one-act plays wrought by Black albino paraplegics. I dearly love Henry Steele Commager (he and I agree on just about everything) but I do not like a pig-eyed woman poet who sniffles into Kleenex and whose large woman housemate comes to pick her up in a peanut-butter colored Volkswagen truck: they always try to get me into it, so I hang onto Mr. Commager as tight as I can, feeling as I do, that it would be discomforting for a woman at my time of life to be gang-banged by two strapping tomboys, one of them afflicted with chronic catarrh. . . .

For thirty-five years Stafford had been making an art of the personal letter; there is scarcely a note from her hand that is not memorably phrased, and even her long letters rarely commit the sin of tediousness. By the 1970s a great deal of Stafford's creative effort was being deflected away from other writing and into her correspondence. Her letters of complaint were frequently deft and penetrating. Objecting to a Tiffany & Co. attempt to use her Ward Bennett profile without payment, she wrote, "My work is no more in the public domain than are your star sapphires."

At the same time, Stafford was turning out some first-rate public work. Despite her brouhaha with Shana Alexander, she continued to write for *McCall's*. Out of an unpromising assignment (along with other writers, Stafford was to propose year-end reasons for optimism), she concocted a thoughtful essay called "Intimations of Hope." In "What Does Martha Mitchell Know?," she speculated provocatively about the muzzling of the outspoken wife of the Attorney General.

Starting in 1969, for seven straight years Stafford wrote the Christmas roundup review of children's books for *The New Yorker*. This assignment became the bane of her existence, and the floors of her several studies began to be piled high with children's books by midsummer; she had to wade through hundreds each year in order to review dozens. Recognizing the difficulty of the task, the magazine paid her well — fifty-five hundred dollars by 1974. "She was always late," says Berton Roueché; Stafford would turn in copy and "they'd have to assemble it." If so, thanks may be due for the genius of some unacknowledged editor; the chaos never showed.

Stafford's Christmas roundups became a minor legend of

journalism. As with her work for *Vogue* and *Book World,* most of her commentary in these annual reviews was positive. On anything by Maurice Sendak or William Steig or E. B. White, she lavished praise. What many readers remember, however, are her brilliant attacks on dross. A Britannica effort called the *Young People's Encyclopedia*

> has the ability to lower the I.Q. of a user to the vanishing point, to extirpate curiosity permanently, and, through massive doses of debatable information, woolly abstractions, misleading metaphors, patronizing jargon, and moralizing fiddlesticks, to whisk the victim from puling nonage to addled dotage.

Stafford particularly despised books aimed at "young adults":

> I cannot believe that all people between the ages of fifteen and seventeen are as prurient, mendacious, self-serving, and chicken or, to turn the coin over, as judicious, civic-minded, and priggish as they are made out to be by the perpetrators of these unwholesome tracts. The improbable characters who shuffle and snuffle and sneak through these pages are so preoccupied with palaver about sex that they have no time to daydream about love; they are so reliant on the term "generation gap" to explain and excuse all melancholy and indolence and irascibility (what was known as "growing pains" before the generation-gap syndrome sprang into being) that they are unable to grow into a personality — or, to stick to the current lingo, "a life style."

In 1972 the University of Colorado gave Stafford an honorary Litt.D. degree. Her bronchial troubles had grown so serious that at first her doctor thought she could not travel to Boulder, with its thin air; finally he relented. Robert Giroux accompanied her to Colorado, where she visited the Rare Books Room in Norlin Library (destined to be the depository of her papers), gave a speech, and received her honors. Stafford had not been to Boulder for twenty years. She was pleased that the new campus buildings harmonized with the old, but she remarked that "The street people were among the worst I've seen anywhere and the vast swarming size of the town was flabbergasting." Her respiratory distress was so acute that she "could not even walk from the edge of the campus across the bridge over the pond to look at Macky and Old Main."

Mary Lee had set her heart on coming to Boulder for the ceremony, but Jean managed to dissuade her, making excuses about Mary Lee's own health and insisting that she had no time to see her. For the past twenty years Mary Lee had been Jean's favored sister, while Marjorie had been exiled to partial estrangement; now the tides began to turn, with the Boulder trip in 1972 a pivotal event. Late at night, in her cups, Stafford would call either sister and wax nostalgic for hours; but if one of them tried to plan a visit, Stafford's arsenal of evasions came into play. As Harry Frichtel puts it, "She'd get Mary Lee all built up, and then she'd kick her in the face like that." He remembers,

> She called up one night when Mary Lee was gone. I talked to her, and I was mad anyway about the way she treated her, so I just told her she couldn't hurt me any no matter what she did, but I was getting damned tired of her hurting Mary Lee, and I hung up, and that made her madder. . . . She called my youngest son and told him that I'd lied to her, that Mary Lee was home and I wouldn't let her talk. . . . I never did talk to Jean after that.

In 1969 Stafford had permitted a visit by Robert Frichtel, Mary Lee's son and her favorite nephew. After a hunting accident in 1947 in which Robert had nearly lost his hand, Stafford had pledged to pay his way through Princeton. (Nothing came of the promise.) In the 1970s she told Robert that he was to be her sole heir; she wanted him, she said, either to keep the house in The Springs for himself or to turn it into a Liebling museum.

Jean's other nephews, however, understood that they were not welcome in The Springs; nor did Mary Lee or Marjorie ever visit her there. Stafford's profound love-hate struggle with her sisters baffled her closest eastern friends. Blair Clark recalls, "I would say to her, 'Jean, what about the sisters?' 'You wouldn't last five minutes,' she'd say." Says Eve Auchincloss, "Jean would read me excerpts from their letters, and I couldn't see what she was in such a snit about."

Over the years there had been pretexts for temporary annoyance. Before Stafford's last trip to France with Liebling, Mary Lee had been too busy to look up the precise location of Dick's grave in Normandy; when Jean was unable to find her brother's headstone, she was furious with her sister. Both Mary Lee and Marjorie had asked Jean to try to help them get manuscripts of

their own published; she had carried out the charade, to the predictable polite rejections. Later Stafford "wined and dined" Lowell to get him to sign some rare first editions of his early books
so that Marjorie and Mary Lee (to whom Jean had given them in
the 1940s) could sell them for a profit. Mary Lee got two thousand dollars for *Land of Unlikeness;* Jean took 50 percent as her
commission.

A subtler but deeper antagonism was related to Jean's sisters'
solicitude about her health. By Marjorie's account, all three sisters were hypochondriacs who loved to trade news of each other's afflictions; but at the threat of being taken care of, Jean invariably lapsed into a funk. In 1964, for instance, she wrote Mary
Lee, "I wish, as I have wished all my life, that you would stop
worrying when you don't hear from me. It is not as if I were on
my own in Southern Rhodesia."

Stafford's excuse about having no guest rooms was too flimsy
to fend off her sisters. When they continued to propose visits to
The Springs, she had to be more blunt: "I cannot bear to sleep
in anyone else's house and I cannot bear to have anyone sleep in
mine." It may be that Stafford was ashamed of her drinking,
which neither sister had seen at anything like its worst. When,
after her sister's death, Marjorie learned some of the details of
Jean's alcoholism, her first reaction was, "My mother would just
die if she knew it. And Dad would be crushed."

By the 1970s Stafford was regularly pitting one sister against
the other, and her spleen occasionally spilled over. After Mary
Lee suffered a major injury to her head from some botched dental work, Jean wrote Marjorie,

> When I called the other night — called *her* — I wanted to kill her.
> She profusely thanked me. As pleased as punch she said, "Harry
> doesn't understand why everybody's so worried." There was a
> simper in her voice. She is *so* fortunate to have this new tragedy
> in her life. She has a whole cornucopia of suffering to gorge on.
> Let's call her up and say "Fuck off."

In a similar dudgeon, Jean attacked Marjorie, writing her,

> For a long time I have known that nobody kin to me except Mary
> Lee and Lois [their cousin] ever *reads* me, but only takes pleasure
> in seeing my name in the paper. . . . Because you enjoy collect-

ing injustices perpetrated against others as well as against yourself, I am sure you would welcome news of the disasters, minor and serious, that have plagued me since I last wrote. . . .

This letter will enrage you. But since you thrive on rage, I am probably doing you a service.

If simple hatred had been the sum of Jean's feelings for her sisters, the obvious course would have been for her to break with them for good. But there was always the other side of the coin, the aching nostalgia for the past that fueled Stafford's late-night, drunken phone calls. The ultimate explanation of her fierce, unresolved tangles with her sisters lies perhaps beyond the reach of biography, in the psychological wilderness of early childhood.

Stafford's health grew steadily worse during the 1970s. Thomas Roberts was pleased to report that her cardiac condition was stable several years after her heart attack. But her bronchitis had become intermittently severe, and in 1966 she had suffered a thrombosis in the right arm — both ailments related directly to smoking. A respiratory specialist who saw her in 1972 suspected that asthma and allergies had combined with cigarettes to exacerbate her woes. Among Stafford's other troubles were back problems, a spinal ailment that forced her to wear a cervical collar, a recurrence of the neuroma in her foot, a skin cancer on her cheek, and an early cataract in one eye. Roberts's notes continued to record her distress:

5/26/71 — Very weak legs. Unsteady. Afraid to cross streets, etc.

10/16/73 — . . . Had episode of near hallucination in Boston.

6/20/74 — Not drinking (except for in N.Y.). Aches all over. Principal problem hip.

Stafford's domestic accidents did not help matters. She fell down the attic stairs, broke a rib coughing, and fell hard against a filing cabinet, gashing her head. Drink may have contributed to some of these mishaps. Stafford kept making attempts at sobriety; " 'I'd never realized how *dull* 7-Up is,' " she told Wilfrid Sheed during one ride on the wagon. When she was not drinking, Stafford found it almost impossible to face company, though she could still tell an alcoholic story on herself; one was about the night when, as Jean was being chauffeured home with another lady from one of Craig Claiborne's richer feasts, both women opened their purses simultaneously and threw up into them.

Josephine Monsell, the cleaning lady who came to Stafford's house each Saturday from nine to noon, had to wake her up and get her out of bed. Usually Stafford had taken care to remove any signs of her drinking, but on two occasions "it was really bad" — she staggered downstairs, the smell of booze wafting about her, then went back to bed again. Monsell guessed that Stafford had been up all night drinking by herself. One morning Margaret Simmons, a young staffer on *The New Yorker,* dropped by to help out with the children's books; she found Stafford passed out cold on the floor.

Quitting smoking was even more impossible for Stafford than not drinking. Monsell, who saw her habit at first hand, calls it "terrible. One right after another, as fast as she could light them." Stafford tried snuff as a substitute, but soon she was partaking of both that *and* tobacco. She played herself a "stop smoking" record; she even went to a Manhattan hypnotist for help, but she knew after her second appointment that the treatment was futile.

During the 1970s Stafford ventured from home far less often than she had in the 1960s. For *Esquire* she wrote a brief against travel, called "Why I Don't Get Around Much Anymore." In another essay she claimed that during the annual influx of summer people to Long Island, "I stay in the house with the doors locked and the blinds drawn, snarling."

Yet Stafford enjoyed her own celebrity in East Hampton. With her neighbor Jean Hoffman she lunched at Bobby Vann's restaurant, often in the company of Wilfrid Sheed, Alden Whitman, James Jones, or Willie Morris. The local bookstore became her salon, with a circle of acolytes dazzled by her conversation. In 1973 she was the commencement speaker at Southampton College, which gave her her second honorary degree. Despite her terror of performing in public, she gave a number of readings at the East Hampton Guild Hall. In her low, leisurely, gravelly voice, she paced her sentences with consummate control. "She read the stories exquisitely even when she wasn't well," says Alger Hiss.

Decades earlier, alluding to New York City, Harold Ross had nicknamed Stafford "the recluse about town." At no time was the oxymoron more apt than in East Hampton in the early 1970s.

Stafford had begun to worry constantly about money. Jean Riboud took on an informal role as her financial adviser, fruitlessly proposing scheme after scheme for real-estate and investment deals. She sold some of her and Liebling's first editions of classic books, then regretted the loss: " 'I always thought I didn't give a damn about old books. Seeing them go, I realized that there's nothing I love more.' "

Despite her disdain for mass culture, Stafford had become a regular watcher of television. The Watergate hearings galvanized her, and she rejoiced at each stage of Nixon's disintegration. Howard Moss recalls that when the TV set was off, a stitched sampler that read "God Bless America" lay draped over the screen. According to Josephine Monsell, Stafford often spent all day in her bathrobe. Her cooking dwindled to TV dinners warmed on a hot plate in her bedroom.

If Stafford had spent a decade constructing herself as a character about East Hampton, in the mid-1970s she began to be more difficult than eccentric. The lasting loyalty of many of her friends derived in part from how generous and entertaining Stafford could be when she was in her good moods. Monsell still bursts out laughing when she recalls the time she and Stafford — at Jean's instigation — dressed up in Halloween costumes to put a fright into Monsell's husband when he picked her up after a house-cleaning stint.

"She could be mean to people," says John Thompson, "but she really wasn't. She was very frightened and actually quite sentimental. She needed somebody to take care of her." Jean Hoffman maintains, "I was enormously fond of her. I felt that her foibles were naughty-little-girl foibles, and partly illness, and perhaps terrible loneliness." Ninety percent of their dealings with Stafford, insist the Rouechés, were happy ones. "It's hard to remember simple pleasure. She had her silly side, but we really enjoyed our friendship."

Yet around this time, deliberately or not, Stafford began to alienate some of her best friends. Her late-night phone calls took their toll. In the wee hours, seized by fears about her health, she often appealed to Thomas Roberts. "She drove him crazy," says Ann Honeycutt, "always calling him at three in the morning. My God, he was good to her." Stafford was sometimes so drunk during these conversations that her friends could not understand what she was saying. Eve Auchincloss was burdened with lengthy calls at the office. "She would go on for about an hour, and I just didn't have the guts to say, 'Jean, I have to go.' It was all complaining. In the last few years, when the phone rang and it was Jean, my heart would sink, and I would feel furious and helpless."

Stafford's tendency toward spite and resentment became a fixed attitude. She liked to brag that she sent back mail she didn't want by writing on the envelope, "Not Acceptable to Addressee, Return to Sender." In 1974 she confessed to Auchincloss, "I am growing meaner by the hour and I bitterly regret that I did not prick this sac of simon-pure venom long ago. I knew perfectly well that it was there, ripe for the pricking." Stafford became excessively touchy about personal criticism. "It meant a lot to Jean that Mrs. Monsell was always cheerful and uncritical," says Stafford's friend Pierre Guedenet of her cleaning lady. Eleanor Hempstead testifies, "I never told Jean what to do, ever. I knew that was the kiss of death."

Although it was usually she who had caused the estrangement, Stafford felt abandoned when she didn't hear from one of her friends. "She would forget you for a time and then be hurt and surprised that she had been temporarily forgotten," writes Howard Moss. According to Jean Hoffman, "She would say, 'Nobody ever comes to see me.' Then you'd see a car in the drive, or you'd call up and she'd have somebody there, or you'd hear somebody had been there twenty minutes before you had."

The social posturing that had once amused her friends now often seemed merely peevish. As Moss puts it,

A certain amount of complaining, of being the great-lady-offended had become habitual. Something on the order of "And do you know who had the *nerve* to invite me to dinner last Wednesday?" And so on. But then it would turn out that she had *gone* to dinner, so that the point of the complaint seemed muddled.

Going out at all became more and more of an ordeal for her. Wilfrid Sheed observes, "To live in the country without locomotion is to invalid yourself, whatever the motive — and as Dr. Johnson said, it is very difficult for an invalid not to become a scoundrel."

At parties Stafford was often a tyrannical monologuist. Says

Barbara Hale, "She'd talk a blue streak — nobody could stop her, nobody could interrupt her. She'd just get on some subject and rant." Eleanor Hempstead agrees: "Jean could come over and ruin any dinner party for you." Jean Hoffman remembers Stafford saying, " 'I don't want to come to dinner, but I'll come over and have a drink.' And then she would come and sit, and sit, and sit. I'd say, 'Well, come on, stay for dinner.' No, she wouldn't. Five hours later you were ready to scream."

Imagining insults and offenses, Stafford sometimes savaged her friends behind their backs. A classic instance involved Craig Claiborne. In Claiborne's menu journals (the guest books he kept for fancy dinners), Stafford scribed such encomiums as, "The best meal I've ever eaten." Of an occasion when Stafford came to his house for a special Chinese dinner prepared by his friend Virginia Lee and himself, Claiborne recalled "with particular pleasure the relish she took in sharing a Mongolian Hot Pot with me and my other guests."

Here, however, is Stafford's private report on a kindred repast:

Not long ago I had a scandalously bad meal at Craig Claiborne's and haven't accepted any invitation anywhere since then. (Not that I get any. I am currently the most disliked woman in East Hampton, and I can't tell you how I am rejoicing in my position.) He is writing a Chinese cook-book with a rich, excruciatingly snobbish and voluble Chinawoman. . . . Mme. Lee does not drink, C. C. had told me, so I figured the cocktail hour would be brief and the food would . . . be on the table quickly and I'd be home and in bed by 10 o'clock. But they had lunched heartily and Mme. rejoiced to have the drinks prolonged so that she could tell her intricate life story in pidgin English. . . . I had two gimlets . . . and was invited then to watch the final preparations of the meal. So I was given a *third* stein of vodka and lime-juice . . . and obliged to *stand* at the counter between the kitchen and the "dining area," watching this fat old Chink chop-chop and clip-clop from stove to sink with woks and tomahawks. Finish the meal! She *began* it as soon as she had me captive. She chopped and fried and chatted and bragged and scolded and sauteed and blended for a good hour and the results were appalling — chicken wings (the size, however, of hummingbird wings) fried to such desiccation I felt I was eating toasted toothpicks, accompanied by soup on the side (about

the consistency and similar in taste to Campbells veg.); this was
followed by some great collops of beef, very stringy and gristly
so that when I got home, drunk as I was, I had to spend a long
time with dental floss. The vegetables were, so far as I could judge,
French cut frozen beans and watercress braised. They had made
tons of this matter.

By now, of course, Stafford was seldom interested in food, and
complaining about dinner parties had become one of her stock
forms of calumny.

In her cups, Stafford could turn even on her most loyal friends,
as she did in a post-midnight telephone call to Paul and Dorothy
Thompson in 1974, when she rehashed imagined differences that
dated back to her student days. John Thompson (no relation)
often drove thirty miles to check up on Stafford in The Springs;
sometimes he had to crawl through the window when, passed
out from drink, she did not answer his knock. Although at times
she was grateful for Thompson's concern, Stafford would complain to Peter Taylor, " 'That fool has been here again.' "

Stafford's long relationship with Eve Auchincloss, meanwhile,
succumbed to "a mutual wearying of the whole friendship." The
last time the women actually saw each other was at a dinner in
Washington in the mid-1970s. "She looked like a battered, bruised,
drunken old woman," recalls Auchincloss. As the dinner went
on, Stafford's monologue proceeded in a softer and softer voice,
until Auchincloss had to crane her neck across the table to hear
her. "I thought she was enjoying her power. It was torture."
After dinner Stafford invited her friend back to her hotel for a
few more drinks. "I was very happy to turn my back on her,"
recalls Auchincloss.

In January 1975 Stafford fired James Oliver Brown, after he
had served as her agent for nineteen years. Brown had contracted
hepatitis a few months before and had missed work, but an assistant had carried on smoothly in his absence. In her terminating
letter Stafford voiced concern about Brown's "withdrawal from
the world" but laid the blame mostly on herself: "I am so unproductive . . . that I can't think I will ever bring to you anything but small, unprofitable nuisances. The novel is still miles
and years in the future." Brown responded with courtly magnanimity. No agent had ever more faithfully served an author.

After a brief interval Stafford transferred her allegiance to Timothy Seldes of Russell & Volkening, whom she had met socially on Long Island. Louis Auchincloss, another of Brown's clients and a good friend of Jean's, had tried to intervene, but Stafford was having none of it. She paraded Brown's failings before Auchincloss:

> He appears to believe that I have committed a misdemeanor, that my departure from his stable is unique in the annals of literary business and that it is his right, indeed, his *duty* to punish me. . . . My wildest nightmares have been only a patch on his actual performance. The performance is that of a dog in the manger, and unless a miracle comes to pass, I shall be subjected to the snarling and the gnashing of teeth until the end of my days. The peevishness, the irascibility, the paranoia have not suddenly surfaced with his recent illness: they have been there all along and I have been the victim of them many times before.

These wild charges border on the truly delusional. They sound, indeed, like what psychiatry calls projection — "peevishness," "irascibility," and "paranoia" aptly sum up Stafford's mental traits in the mid-1970s, not those of the mild-mannered Brown. What Stafford gained by jettisoning her agent is hard to discern. Perhaps, like Stafford's firing of Albert Erskine and Random House in 1962, this new dismissal served to deflect her anguish about the novel she could not finish. If her own guilt had convinced her that Erskine was peering over her shoulder, so her two decades' worth of hollow promises to Brown about her progress on the novel may have transmogrified him, in her mind, into a disapproving authority.

The solitude of Stafford's house slowly became a cocoon of despair. With Howard Moss and other cronies, she made many plans for outings, then canceled them. Her neighbors and Josephine Monsell noticed that Stafford sometimes went two weeks without leaving her house. Beset by "night terrors," she stayed sleepless through the nocturnal winter dark, then napped in the daytime, "dreaming the abstract dreams I hate the most." Her bodily ailments had become relentless aggravations, and she was in more or less constant physical pain. As Joseph Mitchell emphasizes, "She was a very brave woman, who put up with a lot of disappointment and agony." In her listless bad humor she "retired" Henrietta Stackpole, giving Mitchell the signature stamp. During stays at the Cosmopolitan Club in New York she twice set mattresses on fire; the club finally refused to let her stay overnight, and Roger Straus had to secure guest privileges for her at the Lotus Club.

Stafford's sixtieth birthday, in 1975, was a hard one for her: as she described it, "I was furious: old enough to be infirm but not old enough to get into the movies half price. It is the only birthday that has ever disturbed me. . . ." In an unpublished sketch for a story, she recorded the constant pain in her hip and knee that accompanied her bad dreams, adding, "She woke then to the freshly mutilating knowledge that she had been a widow for ten years. . . . I am alone, she thought, and I am growing old."

Each year the approach of Christmas occasioned a heavy gloom in Stafford. She could rationalize wittily about the commercialism of "Bing Crosby Day" and the obligatory extortion of gifts, but her sorrow was more fundamental. As Wilfrid Sheed perceived:

> I realized what this season could do to the lost child, the child in the stories, for whom Christmas may have promised many things.
>
> She told me once that she had had a dream eight nights in a row of coming down to family breakfast in Colorado. The sun, if I remember right, was shining and everyone was smiling at her, and "If I have that dream again, I'll go ab-so-lutely crazy."

Marjorie insists that Jean did not hate Christmas as a child. One wonders what part the car accident with Lowell, which occurred only a few days before Christmas 1938, may have played in her subsequent melancholy during the holiday season.

One of the most remarkable documents from Stafford's hand during these years is a 1970 memo from Henrietta Stackpole to Thomas Roberts, "IN RE: Mrs. A. J. Liebling." Behind the joking facade of this tour de force, Stafford reveals a deep understanding of her own psychological predicament:

> In re this referral, we have had nothing but trouble since the party above named entered the kennel. A). She periodically appears to be under the impression that she is 14 or 15 yrs. of age and is therefore immune to the Laws of Deportment: thinks she can stay

up all night long and dance hulas on table tops to the delight (in fact, hopeless boredom) of the drunken company she keeps. . . .

B) Despite massive doses of chloral hydrate, will not sleep. And keeps other inmates awake. Especially Miss Bonacker (Bonnie) whom she tends to hug and kiss all night long. . . .

If she stays away from John Barleycorn, she is, in our opinion, an O.K. kid, and to tell you the honest truth, I think J. B. is basically the root of her problem (he brings on this bloody sonofabitching hula dancing and adorability aforementioned) who, in conjunction with J. Calvin and J. Knox have mucked up this poor woman to a fare-thee-well.

The picture of Stafford hugging and kissing her cat in the middle of a sleepless night is an indelible emblem of her loneliness. And the notion that alcohol and Scottish Presbyterian rigidity lay at the heart of her unhappiness is as canny an insight as has ever been applied to Stafford.

The paradoxes of creativity are perennial. One would expect Stafford's miseries in the mid-1970s to have reduced her writing to a trickle. The truth is that the years from 1973 to 1975 were her most fruitful in a long time. She published nineteen articles during that period, kept up her arduous roundup of children's books for *The New Yorker,* and continued reviewing for *Vogue* and *Book World.* In 1975 she took over Malcolm Muggeridge's book column for *Esquire.* She also contributed the odd review to *McCall's,* the *Saturday Review,* the *Atlantic Monthly, Cosmopolitan,* the *New York Times,* and *Newsday.* In terms of having her work in print, she was more consistently in the public eye than she had been at any time since the early 1950s.

What unifies most of these essays and reviews is a fiercely lucid antimodernism. A trio of short pieces for *Vogue* — "Don't Send Me Gladiolus," "On My Mind," and "Some Advice to Hostesses from a Well-Tempered Guest" — lays down a crotchety etiquette for hospital visiting, gift giving, and dinner-party throwing, respectively. For *Esquire,* which had wooed her with compliments, she produced wry indictments of the contemporary world. "Somebody Out There Hates Me" gives readers a peek at Stafford's hate mail; "How to Cook for One While Drunk" (never published) is a hilarious farce based on the author's own domestic habits. Another *Esquire* piece, "Coca-Cola," a paean

to Stafford's favorite soft drink, had its origins in a letter she
wrote to the company in 1971 to complain about its new screw-
top cap.

Nothing roused Stafford's vexation more surely than abuses of
the language. A piece of hers called "Don't Use Ms. with Miss
Stafford, Unless You Mean ms.," written for the *New York Times,*
is still widely remembered. It produced a bag of angry letters
from feminists, many of whom overlooked the point that it was
the needless neologism, not the claims of gender-prejudice, that
Stafford was objecting to. Her articles "Plight of the American
Language" and "At This Point in Time, TV Is Murdering the
English Language," on the other hand, elicited satchelfuls of
sympathetic letters, many offering further examples of solecisms
and cant to add to the motley batch Stafford had sneered at.

Some of Stafford's strictures about the abuse of language,
however, seem picayune, and her wrath disproportionate. Even
when giving books rave reviews, she never failed to rap an author on the knuckles if she had caught him misusing the word
hopefully. It may be that her pose as the stern guardian of lin-
guistic standards sprang from the dismay she had always felt at
her poor grasp of foreign tongues — just as her insistence on old-
fashioned manners and propriety may have camouflaged her fear
that she was eternally a "rube" from the West.

The weakest of Stafford's efforts during these productive years
was a trio of profiles she did for *Vogue,* prose portraits of three
prominent women: Katharine Graham, editor of the *Washington
Post;* her daughter, Lally Weymouth; and the Republican con-
gresswoman from New Jersey, Millicent Fenwick. All three pieces
are shamelessly generous, even gushy. They might be excused as
hackwork for money; *Vogue* plainly wanted "puff pieces." Yet
something more basic goes awry in these effusions; what seems
to emerge is Stafford's suppressed longing for aristocracy, her
inability to shrug at the accoutrements of class.

Many of Stafford's book reviews during these years are still a
delight to read today; as usual, she was at her most entertaining
"lambasting the bejesus out of James A. Michener" for *Centennial,* or taking Susan Brownmiller to task for her polemic about
rape, *Against Our Wills.* In Eve Auchincloss's view, however,
Stafford's reviews were declining steadily in quality. The analysis
grew even thinner, the paraphrase more naked, and she seemed

unable to curb her habit of writing much too long and then turning her copy over to Auchincloss to cut.

Stafford agreed to serve on the jury for the 1975 Pulitzer Prize
in fiction, along with Carlos Baker and Albert Duhamel. Complaining happily about how much work was involved, she traded
long letters with her colleagues as they narrowed down the choices.
Stafford's candid opinions make for juicy reading:

> I have never countenanced, do not now countenance and doubt
> that I ever will countenance Ishmael Reed.

> I do think [Alison Lurie] writes with skill but the general hateful-
> ness of her characters, while gruesomely recognizable is, I feel[,]
> unjust and inhumane.

In the end, with Stafford leading the way, the jury chose a dark
horse every bit as obscure as Walker Percy had been in 1962:
Michael Shaara, for his historical novel about the Civil War, *The
Killer Angels*.

Despite the bright wit and timely satire of much of Stafford's
writing from 1973 to 1975, her journalism began to display a
certain malaise. The satire in these essays sometimes hardens into
fussy disapprobation, the digressions often amount to no more
than Stafford bragging about her friends, and at times she has
little more to say than how awful the world has become. Peter
Taylor's commemorative remark, though overstated, is to the
point: "She wrote numbers of book reviews and articles, of course,
but frequently with tongue in cheek and always seemingly in a
terrible rage, a rage against life that had contrived to place her in
such a ridiculous situation."

Although the ultimate motive for most of the pieces she wrote
in this period was the need for money, Stafford never made more
than about fifteen thousand dollars a year from her writing during the 1970s. She seems to have all but given up the effort to
write short stories. Despite her financial straits, she engaged more
and more in a practice that was profoundly self-defeating for a
writer as dependent as she was on working for her income. This
was writing "on spec." In her files there are a number of drafts
of essays that had not been commissioned and that, one suspects,
it would not have been easy for Stafford to sell.

Even more pointlessly, Stafford frittered away her creative

energy responding to letters that antagonized her. A young stranger addressed her as "Jean" in a fan note, praising her understanding of women and asking for dating tips; a woman wrote to Liebling, unaware that he was dead, to quibble over an article he had written about Germany. Stafford's rejoinders to these non-entities are bursting with bitter passion. Nor did she merely dash them off — they display as much skill in composition, at as great a length, as some of her articles.

In 1974, desperate for cash, Stafford agreed to write book reviews for *Newsday,* the Long Island newspaper, for only fifty dollars each. When the paper was late sending her a check for one of these, she not only blasted the editor in a letter but took *Newsday* to small-claims court. The editor apologized and sent her the fifty dollars, but he no longer welcomed her reviews. Unable to let matters rest there, Stafford threatened a further libel suit and published an elaborate account of the fiasco (intended as humor, it is instead grimly petulant) in the *East Hampton Star.*

Throughout the early 1970s Stafford had still been promising the world her novel. One evening she read an excerpt to Eleanor Hempstead — perhaps the only friend ever granted a look at her long-awaited work. "It was going to be great," says Hempstead. "She kept saying she was working on it. . . . I had a feeling that there was very little done — you know, she was sick all the time." When Alden Whitman interviewed her for the *New York Times,* Stafford claimed that she was " 'glimpsing the end' " of the book and teased at its contents:

> "I'll tell you this much. . . . It is my first autobiographical novel. It's about Mommy and Daddy and Missouri and Colorado and Massachusetts and New York — all places where I've lived.
>
> "A well-known American poet, with whom I was once closely associated, is petrified. And well he should be! I'm cutting up the poets to a fare-thee-well."

After 1973, however, Stafford stopped talking about "The Parliament of Women." The truth about her progress, alas, was that the novel was, as she confessed to James Oliver Brown in 1975, "miles and years in the future."

One day as Stafford rode the "jitney" (a small commercial van) from New York City back to East Hampton, she made the acquaintance of Maria Polushkin, a young author of children's books.

Stafford immediately took a great liking to the woman, and to her husband, Kenneth Robbins, a professional photographer. A friendship quickly developed. "What she enjoyed about us, I think," says Robbins, "was that we'd come and almost pay court. We'd sit and she'd tell us wonderful stories."

After a short time Stafford impulsively offered the couple the gift of an acre of land adjoining her house. Shocked by her generosity, Robbins and Polushkin at first said no, but Stafford relentlessly persisted.

The deed that gave the couple their forty thousand square feet of land (for one dollar) required that they build a house on the property and occupy it within a year. Says Robbins,

> Giving us the land was, as far as I could tell, an act of pure generosity, on the one hand. On the other hand, it couldn't have escaped anybody's consciousness that she was going to feel better and more secure having us nearby. I don't think she considered that a quid pro quo, and I didn't. But it was a responsibility that both of us took pretty seriously.

From Amagansett, where they were living at the time, Robbins and Polushkin drove daily to Fireplace Road to supervise construction of their new house. They also began doing chores for Stafford. "We were there to be supportive," says Robbins. "She didn't tolerate much in the way of caretaking." At first the friendship seemed flawless. "She was very good to the Robbinses, they were very good to her," says Jean Hoffman.

Several townspeople nevertheless warned the couple about Stafford's notorious record of fallings-out. A seemingly joking remark Stafford had made at the inception of the arrangement stuck in their memories: " 'Take it now, because this is something I really want to do, and it would be good for me to do. Someday I will change my mind and throw it up to you.' " The widely noticed transaction did not seem a benign one to all of Stafford's friends. Stafford initiated a rumor that she had discovered some nude photos Robbins had taken of his wife reclining on Stafford's sofa. (Says Robbins, "I did indeed take some nude pictures — *with* Jean's permission. I used one as an invitation to a show, and I sent her a copy.") Stafford also told Josephine Monsell that "they never took care of her. The deal was the land for taking care of her."

In 1975 Stafford went to a specialist in New York to seek help for the pain in her legs, which had persisted for a full year. This physician recorded, "Patient looks 20 years older than her stated age of 59 but denies being any older as I questioned her gently about the age factor." A month later she entered New York Hospital, where she was diagnosed as having angina pectoris as well as degenerative disk disease. She weighed only 107 pounds.

The most debilitating of Stafford's ailments now, though, was her chronic obstructive pulmonary disease — a close cousin to emphysema and the cause of her chronic fatigue and shortness of breath. Her medical regimen upon her discharge from the hospital made it much harder for her to get out of the house. She was supposed to breathe oxygen through a "venti-mask" for six to ten hours each day. Every four hours she had to inhale Bronkosol, a medicine that dilated the bronchi and produced secretions; she also had "blow bottles" to build up her respiratory capacity. She had to keep an oxygen tank beside her bed, as well as a device she called a "pulmonary toilet" — "It is designed to flush out of my lungs the accumulation of rotted detritus that has been building up for 60 years."

Stafford also had to have a nurse come in twice a day to "cup" her ribs — strike her back with a cupped hand while she coughed, to loosen internal secretions. Unable to bear this indignity, she fired a series of nurses; Maria Polushkin ended up doing much of the cupping. On one occasion Stafford called up Eleanor Hempstead, pleading, " 'I want you to come over here. I have this horrible nurse who's down in the kitchen.' " Hempstead arrived to find Stafford in her bedroom. " 'I want you to go downstairs and make me a Bloody Mary,' " she said. The nurse had refused to perform the favor. Hempstead mixed a weak drink and delivered it.

The debilitations of 1975–1976 convinced Stafford that she did not have long to live. She ordered her tombstone from the same engraver in Newport who had made Liebling's. To Thomas Roberts she wrote, "I do now implore you *never* to withhold anything from me. . . . I have premonitions: I have a great deal of work to do before I am gathered to Abraham's scratchy bosom, and I must husband and not waste my time. I will adapt and abide by *any* regime you set for me. . . ." She confided to Wilfrid Sheed, " 'I don't mind dying in four years, but emphysema is such an *uncomfy* way to do it.' "

A hired driver who occasionally took Stafford to New York once observed her crossing Fourteenth Street, one of Manhattan's busiest crosstown thoroughfares. Not looking either way, she waded into the traffic, oblivious to the risk. Eleanor Hempstead says, "I think Jean had a real death wish. She did everything she could to tear herself down." At twenty-two Stafford had half joked about suicide; then it had been a Werther-like pose of bohemian romanticism. Now she claimed, "I am not half in love with easeful death, I am passionately in love and I wish it would step on the gas."

Around 1976 Robert Hightower paid her a visit. He brought his bicycle on the ferry to Sag Harbor, hoping to spend part of his time touring the backcountry roads. Stafford failed to meet the ferry, so Hightower cycled all the way to her house. His old friend's condition was lamentable: Stafford could walk from her back door to her guesthouse but could not negotiate the streets of East Hampton. Hightower says,

> We didn't get very close, was my feeling. . . . She wanted something to kill herself. She wanted some cyanide, and I didn't have any cyanide. I brought her some methadone, which I assured her was just as good as morphine. Hell, she said, she had morphine, she didn't want that stuff, she wanted something quick.

Yet in the summer and fall of 1976 Stafford still continued to work. *Esquire* fired her as its book columnist; her last published review appeared in October. She soldiered away on the children's-books roundup for *The New Yorker* and agreed to serve on the jury for the 1977 Pulitzer Prize in fiction.

In September Stafford endured a visit from Marjorie, who, at age sixty-seven, was heading off on her first trip to Europe with a former college friend named Hazel, and was as excited as a teenager. Stafford restricted the liaison to Manhattan: "We will be — we will *have* to be very quiet for both our sakes. Thank God you don't want to go to the theatre and thank God you don't want to go shopping. What is the point of my introducing you to anybody? I *hate* meeting new people. . . ."

The two sisters dined at the Cosmopolitan Club. Marjorie had hoped at least to see some museums, but "we didn't go any place." Jean looked "very small and thin and she was carrying an oxygen tank to help her breathe, but her color was fresh and healthy";

she took "a very dim view" of Marjorie and Hazel's gallivanting off to Europe.

> She bought us drinks at JFK and I believe we saw her off rather than the other way around. We parted company with our usual admonitions about wooden nickles [sic] and promises to see each other in church or the funny papers. Hazel giggled appreciatively. That was my last sight of my little sister.

Also in September, Stafford received a letter from Robert Lowell. "I have been thinking of you daily since our phone talk in New York," he began, and then he reminisced about Baton Rouge in 1940:

> Peter and I in pajamas sick over taking out Cinina's cat-shit, waiting still in pajamas outrageously for you to return from the office to get our lunch, Christmas with Red [Robert Penn Warren] staring long at a sheep that looked like Cinina [his wife] and saying it reminded [him] of someone he couldn't place. . . .
> Do you see I am trying to thank you for the past?

It was the only letter of Lowell's that Stafford kept.

Around the middle of November Stafford was lying in bed at home when she was suddenly stricken. She managed to push a buzzer that summoned her backyard boarder; he called an ambulance, which took her to Southampton Hospital. The doctors there, observing Stafford's confusion and shortness of breath, assumed the problem had to do with her chronic obstructive pulmonary disease, and immediately placed a tube down her throat to deliver oxygen.

Thomas Roberts came by a couple of days later. "I think that tube came between them and an accurate diagnosis," he says. Eventually "they got a neurologist in who suspected that something had happened to her central nervous system."

Stafford had suffered a left frontal ischemic stroke. Although her life was not in danger and her intelligence had not been damaged, the stroke had caused a "virtually total" aphasia. The author who lived by her words, who made every conversation a work of art, could no longer speak or write the simplest sentence coherently.

XIX

"Some Day I Write"

STAFFORD WAS SOON moved to New York Hospital, where the intern who examined her described her as "an emaciated, elderly female lying in bed in apparently no physical but tremendous psychological distress." A thorough analysis of her aphasia revealed that

> Speech was non-fluent with virtually total arrest. It was halting. There were a few explosively emitted words which were enunciated correctly. There was some slurring. There was no other language besides English. . . . There was extreme frustration with marked transient anger and pleasure. The vocabulary was apparently full comprehension to uncommon words and insight seemed complete.

After three weeks in the hospital Stafford returned home, only three days before Christmas 1976. During the following month she regained some of her speech function, but not nearly enough to converse normally. Thomas Roberts insisted that a nurse spend part of each day with Stafford. He confessed to a colleague, "We have had a devil of a time getting her to accept some help in the house. . . . I think Jean would simply fall apart in a Nursing Home. . . ."

In the desperation of her muteness, Stafford continued to smoke steadily, though not without guilt. She also drank enough to cause her to suffer two inebriated falls inside her house. She still had to observe the tedious regimen for her pulmonary troubles —

eight to ten hours of oxygen through the "venti-mask," inhaling Bronkosol, and cupping — and she took an assortment of pain-killers and sedatives.

Gradually the news of Stafford's tragedy got around. In East Hampton and New York, it spread by word of mouth among her friends. Her few obligations as a writer were taken up by others. Her Pulitzer jury colleagues noted that Stafford had been leaning toward Stanley Elkin's *The Franchiser* but had added that she would " 'agree to anything. . . . What I won't agree to ever again is being a member of a jury if it involves reading novels.' " The children's-books roundup for *The New Yorker* could not be salvaged, though Stafford had written a lead that her editor thought "delightful."

To Stafford's friends around the country, the news of her disaster came slowly and indirectly; the fact that she was not answering her telephone was nothing new. After two phone calls during which she could make no sense of Stafford's words, Dorothy Thompson thought she heard giggling in the background and wondered (to her later mortification) whether Jean was putting on some strange act for friends. She and her husband finally learned the truth only by contacting Robert Giroux. Stafford's sister Marjorie grew worried when she kept getting the answering-machine message ("We are at work . . ."); after the first unintelligible call from her, Marjorie thought her sister might have been merely drunk.

Stafford bent an extraordinary will toward trying to overcome her enormous handicap. If she had a very patient listener, she could usually stammer out an entire sentence, one word at a time, with yawning pauses between. She learned tricks of circumlocution for the times when key nouns and verbs would not come to her. Still, her frustration was monumental: balked, Stafford would pound the table with her fist and make a grunting noise to fill the void created by the precious word that she could not find.

Even her most loyal friends found talking to Stafford excruciating. Over the telephone, says Peter Taylor, "I would have to just chatter away, and she would respond with things, and curse because she couldn't get the right word. I felt exhausted afterward." For Eleanor Hempstead, "It was absolutely horrendous, exhausting, to go and spend one hour doing all the talking. Once in a while a few words — some very explosive thing — would come out." At a loss for speech, Stafford often uttered a kind of staccato, lip-smacking, "abba-ba-ba-ba-bah" sound.

Thomas Roberts's advice to Jean's friends was to visit in pairs: "One person tends to falter after a bit and more than two people results in confusion. I have found it very important to always give her enough time when I make a visit." Brief one-way chats or phone calls only caused Stafford more distress. Advising the Thompsons, Giroux recommended, "It's better to write her than to call, unless you have the patience of Job on the phone. One method in phoning is to have a list of questions she can answer yes or no. She has less trouble with short words — and cuss words! — than with long ones."

But the impeccable stylist often refused to simplify her speech; she would struggle vainly with an ornate sentence rather than resort to telegraphese. Robert Hightower, trying to find out if Stafford was planning a trip to Massachusetts General Hospital, sent her a self-addressed postcard to return:

Shall I telephone you?   yes no
Are you coming to Boston?   yes no
     this month?   yes no   next month?   yes no
Shall I plan to come Nov. 11?   yes no
Name and telephone of intermediary:

She refused to make use of it.

Even one-word answers caused Stafford trouble. Recalls Berton Roueché, "I'd say, 'Jean, would you like a drink?' And she'd say, 'No.' She meant to say yes. Then she'd realize she'd said no, and she'd [make a gasping noise]."

There was a wide disparity among her friends in terms of how well they could understand Stafford's crippled speech. As she cleaned house and listened to Stafford's attempts at conversation, Josephine Monsell usually could not fathom a word, but she recalls, "I laughed whether I knew what she was saying or not." Even Marjorie, who had been hearing her sister's voice for sixty-one years, had a great deal of difficulty comprehending her over the telephone. When he first learned of Stafford's plight, Joseph Mitchell thought of the inhabitants of Dante's hell, each with a punishment appropriate to his nature, for "Jean was overscrupulous about the spoken word." Both Mitchell and Alger Hiss, however, were able to rely on their vast knowledge of Stafford's history, books, friends, and interests to grasp her utterances. Says Mitchell, "I knew key words. I could say, 'Jean, do you mean to say so-and-so did so-and-so?' And she would be delighted that I got it, and for a little while that seemed to keep her on the track."

Her friends varied widely, too, in the extent to which they avoided or sought her out after the stroke. Some very close friends, including Robert Hightower, simply could not face Stafford's situation. "I couldn't talk to her on the phone," says Hightower, still pained by guilt a decade later, "and I didn't go to see her." Also guiltily, Eve Auchincloss remembers learning that in the hospital Stafford had asked a mutual friend, "Does Eve know I'm here?" "In that way," says Auchincloss, "Jean understood I'd abandoned her."

Others, including Dorothy Thompson and Katharine White, kept up a stream of letters full of news and humor and encouragement; or, like Mitchell and Hiss, Eleanor Hempstead and Jean Hoffman, John Thompson and Thomas Roberts, kept making time to visit her even though they dreaded the ordeal.

The damage the stroke caused to Stafford's ability to write can be gauged from the letters she managed to compose on the typewriter. These heartbreaking artifacts have their own odd poetry. The pages themselves show the marks of the intense remedial struggle — letters and words are crossed out, typed or penned over (in some letters there is a surfeit of exclamation marks, from a writer who had always been exceedingly sparing of them). Here, in its entirety, is Stafford's last letter to Mary Lee, telling her about the stroke a full six months after it happened:

> Dear Mary Lee,
> I had a seizure [*bronchosy* is crossed out] at the end of the year — November 9th — and since my speech has gone altogether now I have to write you. My fine labials + lenes are lean, diabled.
> I have been in New York, disabled, at the Rusk clinic, a growth an end: this mean time and I can't and I cannot write.
> Love,
> Jean

Even so simple a business as paying her bills was now a vexing chore for Stafford. John Thompson periodically went through her checkbook with her to ascertain what bills needed to be paid; she could sign the checks by copying a sample of her own signature. Thompson also cooked many dinners for her. "She'd eat," he says, "if you'd give her a couple of drinks and a carton of cigarettes." Trying to fix her own meal on one occasion, she set fire to her kitchen. Eleanor Hempstead and Jean Hoffman had Stafford over to dinner regularly. "I can remember a supper party at Jean Hoffman's," says Alger Hiss, "when Jean Stafford couldn't say a word. I think the proper word would be *ghastly*."

Nevertheless, Stafford continued to value her privacy, perhaps more than ever. She promptly fired the nurses her neighbors hired to take care of her: "She threw them out as fast as we could get them. She didn't want anyone in the house." Marjorie offered to come from Oregon to take care of her sister. Jean responded,

> I had your Valestine's over the inter-com and I was faiy sick I was away. Don't call me *even* until my marble are back.
>
> My marbles and to are to be back once I devote to a month oftrouble.
>
> I would kill you if you did come my aid: having had this far attended my own aid and comfort, so far, I will be cross as button if you do come.
>
> I can stand for three and have days and more night and a va-moose then.
>
> Jean
>
> P.S. I am very crass with uinal. Please rest assuring than I'm not

Many of Stafford's friends realized that now, because of the stroke, her financial situation might be desperate for the rest of her life. Katharine White, Wilfrid Sheed, and others helped set up a special medical fund to which her friends could contribute. Despite the shoddy way in which Stafford had treated him at the end, James Oliver Brown joined Nora Sayre and Robert Giroux to get some money for her from a special fund administered by the American Academy and Institute of Arts and Letters. In August 1977 the fund sent Stafford fifteen hundred dollars, with the door left open for more later. Jean Riboud, who many suspected had been supporting Stafford financially for years, set up a ten-thousand-dollar line of credit with a bank, money that was available to Stafford anytime she needed it.

Determined to regain her writing skills, Stafford took up speech therapy with several different pathologists. Thomas Roberts

privately felt that the quest was a futile one, but he encouraged
it in hopes that the effort would improve her morale. Says Kenneth Robbins, "Her clinging to life had a lot to do with getting
back the ability to write." Stafford may have convinced herself
that the therapy, which she pursued only intermittently, was doing
some good: at one point she told Dorothy Thompson that she
would be back to normal in a year.

It is poignant to peruse the worksheets Stafford's therapists assigned her; the tasks were comparable to those facing first- or
second-graders in school. One pathologist made her write down
the days of the week and the months of the year. Another gave
her phrases to complete: "A glass of _____ " (Stafford filled in
water); "A gallon of _____ " (she supplied *beer*). But she misspelled words like *united* and *arithmetic* — the latter came out
arithe(c)tic. Some friends feel that Stafford's speech did improve;
the testimony of the closest witnesses, however, is that there was
no real progress.

It might have been easier for Stafford to bear her predicament
had the stroke enfeebled her mind as well. But behind the childlike prating of syllables was a fierce adult intelligence. Stafford
took her speech therapy seriously, but her contempt for its practitioners emerges in a letter to Marjorie:

> I thank you will we furious — my speech directress a hundred
> years behind the times. I *must* have a course (such a course of
> therapy!) beside all this! I go to the this City on Sundry night am
> in it Friday — and it is hot, hotter than Tophet.

In 1977 the University of Colorado set up a Stafford archive.
She donated virtually all her manuscripts to it, and Dorothy
Thompson began the considerable job of cataloguing them. As
she sent off her copies of fugitive articles to CU, Stafford struggled to identify the publications they had appeared in. On her
copy of "Mountain Jim," the story she had written for *Boy's
Life,* she wrote "The Amarcicam Boy," even though the magazine's name appears clearly at the foot of the page.

With so little to occupy her days, Stafford drank with abandon. In Kenneth Robbins's view, some of her binges were "almost suicide attempts." Trying to eat dinner from a TV tray in
her bedroom, befuddled by drink, Stafford spilled her food so
often that a permanent stain on the floor remains visible ten years

later. Stafford's relationship with Robbins and his wife, Maria Polushkin, grew touchier after the stroke, even though the couple had moved into the house they had built on the acre she had given them. The final break came after a sordid incident in which they tried to come to her aid.

Drunk, Stafford had fallen down, "cracked her head open," and lain perhaps half the night on the floor. Checking on her in the morning, as he routinely did, Robbins found her in "a horrible mess." Polushkin arrived and told Stafford that she needed to go to the hospital. She refused. Robbins picked up the phone, saying, "I'm calling an ambulance anyway, I'm sorry." Stafford tried to run from the house; Robbins physically restrained her, and Polushkin phoned the police. Stafford never forgave the betrayal; she called Polushkin "Judas" thereafter.

As if the aphasia were not tribulation enough, Stafford's pulmonary disease grew worse as she continued to smoke. She underwent several admissions to New York Hospital and spent some time at the Rusk Clinic, a rehabilitation center in New York. One of the hospital stays was precipitated by another fall: in the cautious words of the medical summary, "The nature of her present problem is unclear because of her aphasia but apparently she was found in hotel on floor with head injury and no witness to state how long she was such." Tired of hospitals, she wrote Marjorie, "I go now to one asylum + another — /and another; and each time, I have to watch steps each time becuse laughter + the part of time."

Stafford's interest in food, never hearty, dwindled to nearly complete indifference. "She was skin and bones," says Eleanor Hempstead. At an East Hampton restaurant with Howard Moss, she deliberated endlessly over her dinner choice. Moss ordered striped bass; Stafford managed to say, " 'I cannot do striped bass.' " The waitress left and returned; Stafford ordered striped bass. When it came, however, she said, " 'This isn't what I ordered. . . . What I really wanted was the finnan haddie' " (not on the menu). Then, according to Moss,

Suddenly she said, "What do you think of friends?" I was surprised, but babbled on about how they might be the most important people in one's life, not the same as lovers, of course, but desperately needed, a second family, essential. . . . Jean said, lighting a cigarette, "Yes, I must give them up. I'm going to give up smoking." And it became clear she meant the word "cigarettes" or "smokes" when she said "friends."

Because of their rarity, as well as the great effort it took for her to get the words out, her friends were forcibly struck when such full, articulate sentences issued from Stafford's lips. Wilfrid Sheed remembers her stammering, " 'I have not been promiscuous with others,' " and, " 'Let's hear it for suicide.' "

Despite all the work she had put into making her house a cozy sanctum, Stafford debated selling it and moving to a smaller domicile; one reason may have been that it was now extremely difficult for her to climb the stairs. For a few weeks, in fact, she moved to New York City, living in a room at the Westbury Hotel, but the relocation was a disaster, and she returned to The Springs.

In December 1977 Stafford solved all her financial problems by selling her thirty acres of land to Sheila Robbins, Kenneth's aunt, for $114,000. Only the sentimental value of the property — of the fields where Liebling had lain on his back admiring the sky and glorying in his soil — had prevented her from selling it sooner.

On September 12, 1977, Robert Lowell died of a heart attack in a taxi in New York City. The news excited and agitated Stafford in the extreme. At his funeral on Beacon Hill in Boston there were six hundred mourners. According to Peter Davison, "Jean insisted she was going to hire a limousine and get herself up in widow's weeds, drive up from Long Island as the first Mrs. Robert Lowell, and arrive at the Church of the Advent. Bob [Giroux] attempted to dissuade her — successfully."

Even after his death, Stafford never made peace with the man whom she had so ambivalently loved and who had so wounded her. On December 8, 1976, Lowell had given a poetry reading at the Ninety-second Street Y in New York. Only seven days earlier, Stafford had been transferred to New York Hospital with her stroke. At the reading Lowell said, "I want to read two poems to Jean Stafford, my first wife, who is very sick now." With nostalgic self-interruptions to explicate their past together, he recited "My Old Flame" and "Jean Stafford, a Letter." Giroux, who had attended the reading, visited Stafford in the hospital the next day. Thinking she might be pleased, he told her about Lowell's tribute. "She lifted her arms to the ceiling and said, 'The son of a bitch!'"

Before the stroke Stafford had started to make systematic annotations on her copy of Lowell's *The Mills of the Kavanaughs.* She had once claimed that every line had a private meaning for her; now, in a spirit of bitter revisionism, she railed at her ex-husband from the margins. In the second line of the poem, Lowell's persona plays solitaire. Stafford wrote, "I taught him all the other kinds besides Canfield + at the end, in the last months in Maine, we did nothing but play solitaire in separate rooms." Glossing the single word *typing,* she raged,

> R. T. S. L. has little sense of history. I was typing for *him.* At the time he wrote this, my only role was his typist. 60 changes of commas per diem.

The most obscure references evoked footnotes: of "tortoise talons," she groused, "that hideous letter opener from Cousin Belle's estate." Where the widow in the poem muses, " 'My husband was a fool/ To run out from the Navy . . . ,' " Stafford wrote,

> Poor old Mr. Bob Lowell, bossed by Charlotte + despised, despised + patronized by his son. He did, I know he did, love me — he thought I was a regular fella + he also thought I was a pretty girl[.]

As a young boy the character based on Lowell himself recites the seed-blowing chant, " *'O dandelion, wish my wish, be true.'* " But Stafford complained: "I taught him this. He saw nothing of the natural world — *nothing!!*"

In the ninth stanza, a lyrical passage suddenly arrested Stafford's fury. "How marvelous this is," she mused in the margin. "It's the kind of writing that reminds me why I married him." With that remark her annotation ended, far short of the autobiographical heart of the poem.

No one was kinder to Stafford after her stroke than *The New Yorker.* She kept getting checks — three hundred dollars here, eleven hundred there — for her first-reader contracts and as benefits from the magazine's "participation plan." In July 1977 Charles McGrath, one of *The New Yorker's* fiction editors, knowing full well what her condition was, wrote her that he had heard a rumor that she had finished a novel, which he would love to see: "It's high time you were in the magazine again." (McGrath admits that the letter was calculated in part to try to cheer Stafford up.)

It may be an indication of Stafford's awareness that she would never be able to write again that she sent the manuscript of "The Parliament of Women" — not one word of which Albert Erskine, Robert Giroux, James Oliver Brown, or her new agent, Timothy Seldes, had ever seen — to McGrath. He pored over the pages with the magazine's chief editor, William Shawn, but neither could see how to use them; McGrath sent the manuscript back. A few months later Giroux was allowed to read the long-guarded document. With the acumen of four decades as a superb fiction editor, Giroux divined how to excerpt the passages that dealt with the last summer in Maine and convert them into a self-contained short story. McGrath and Shawn reconsidered; the pages became "An Influx of Poets," the last story Stafford published in her lifetime, and one of her best.

Because the manuscript of Stafford's last attempt at a novel is among the papers she left behind, we can speculate as to what the book might have been. (As always, it is possible that Stafford destroyed drafts; but in general, at least after the years of her apprenticeship, she seems to have thrown out far less of her writing than she was wont to claim.) The salient facts about the pages left behind are that they are relatively few and that they add up to something far short of a book. It is clear that in the twenty-four years she worked on "The Parliament of Women," Stafford came much less close to finishing a novel than she had in the three and a half years she had devoted to "In the Snowfall."

Moreover, what she left behind of "The Parliament of Women" is a scattered miscellany of scenes, passages, outlines, and fragments; the most imaginative sleuth would be hard put to project a coherent narrative running through these pieces. It looks almost as if Stafford had toyed with four or five different ideas for a novel, never getting far with any of them; in fact, much of the manuscript lies in folders under a different provisional title, "The State of Grace."

Apparently her earliest conception of the book was that it would be a sequel to *Boston Adventure,* picking up the plot shortly before the death of Miss Pride liberates Sonie Marburg from Beacon

Hill. Sonie would then marry Philip McAllister, whose wife, Hopestill, had died in a horse-riding accident at the end of *Boston Adventure*. The story (so far entirely nonautobiographical) would then converge with a highly personal account of the deterioration of Stafford's marriage to Lowell: Philip McAllister would somehow merge with Theron Maybank, the mask Stafford used for Lowell in "An Influx of Poets." A seemingly early outline indicates that the book was to end after Sonie, having spent a year in an asylum rather like Payne Whitney, divorces her husband.

Later Stafford seems to have extended the tale by having Sonie stay married to Philip into the early 1950s. Several scenes set in a social milieu identical to Westport drip with satire about the kind of life Stafford had endured with Oliver Jensen. It was this conception of the book that led Joseph Mitchell to think of it as "her Westport novel."

At some point Stafford ranged far back into her own family history to develop the bulk of several chapters that detail her parents' (particularly her father's) life in Missouri around the turn of the century. Stafford often called up Berton Roueché, who hailed from Missouri, to quiz him on the background of the state; from this effort, apparently, sprang the hints the author dropped to reporters that the book she was writing was about her father. After her death, Robert Giroux published an excerpt from this part of the text in *Shenandoah;* colorful though the writing is, "Woden's Day" wanders and digresses and leaves the reader puzzled.

To complicate matters further, the manuscript has sections that seem to weave Sonie into the Heidelberg of "A Winter's Tale," and other sections evidently borrowed whole from "In the Snowfall."

In what looks like Stafford's last stab at bringing the many threads of her novel together, she opens another version of the narrative with a heart attack modeled exactly on her own in 1964. Seized by a vivid delirium in the hospital, the protagonist sees all sorts of past events and sorrows parade through her mind. This free-associative congeries was intended, one guesses, to give the subsequent chapters (ranging from nineteenth-century Missouri to Westport and beyond) their logic. In this conception, the novel might even have embraced Stafford's marriage to Liebling, for one of the hallucinatory passages describes his dying:

And then he said to me, "Goodbye." He did not say, "Good night."
He said, "Goodbye." I could not read the feeling in his voice. In
order to live out my allotted span of years, I must believe there
was no reproach in it. . . . He never spoke to me again. He spoke
only to Camus and he spoke in French.

Stafford's individual sentences are as well wrought as ever, and
there are sustained passages (the pages that make up "Influx," for
instance) that promise great things. But in overall terms the
manuscript is a mess. It seems enervated by its fragmentary ambitions; much of it has a kind of nervous bravura just this side of
improvisation. For Giroux, as he read the manuscript after fifteen
years of waiting with the highest hopes, it must have been a
colossal disappointment.

Many of Stafford's friends have their own hunches as to why
she could not finish her last novel; none of their explanations is
adequate, but all lend insight. Joseph Mitchell feels that "she didn't
know Westport well enough." Berton Roueché thinks Stafford's
early success had put her under an intolerable pressure to keep
up her reputation. Eve Auchincloss proposes that Stafford "sort
of stopped living her life" after she left Lowell, and that "she
didn't really know too much about grown-ups." Says Peter Taylor, "Life had become too hard for her. The pure energy it takes
to write a story sometimes just wears out a writer. I think she
was just too exhausted to go on with the manufacture and invention of fictional lives." Everyone who knew Stafford grants that
alcohol took a severe toll. Yet Wilfrid Sheed argues, "Jean's undoing, in my view, was nothing as humdrum as booze or tobacco or malnourishment but a deadly streak of passivity of a
kind that sometimes goes with perfectionism and which I think
she loathed in herself. . . ."

It is eerie to contemplate the extent to which Stafford recapi-
tulated her father's failure. He worked for perhaps his last forty
years on his putative magnum opus, the book about the government deficit, and in the end produced only a woolly, self-published
pamphlet. She struggled for the last twenty-four years of her life
with a novel that "was going to be great" but that she never
came close to realizing. And part of what thwarted that effort —
and perhaps "In the Snowfall" as well — may have been the attempt to write about her father.

Arguably the most important person in her life, John Stafford is startlingly absent from his daughter's published fiction. Before her first stories appeared in print, Jean had wished that her father would die so as not to suffer the competitive humiliation of her success. According to Marjorie, her father was not a great fan of Jean's writing: "He didn't like it too much. . . . I think he thought she didn't have enough of a plot to her stories." In 1969 Jean wrote Mary Lee after her final attempt to read her father's novel *When Cattle Kingdom Fell:*

> I am still unable to read that book and I'm not going to try again. What a waste! Obviously he was gifted but he was completely undisciplined and completely lazy and completely self-indulgent and I can't forgive him.

The appearance of "An Influx of Poets" in the November 6, 1978, issue of *The New Yorker* was a powerfully emotional event for Stafford. Says Kenneth Robbins,

> When it came out, there was a real paranoid episode: "Nobody's called. Nobody's written. Nobody cares." We'd be in the house and the phone would ring. We could hear everybody in the world calling to congratulate her [on her answering-machine tape]. But she complained bitterly that she was being ignored. . . . I think there was some totally irrational anger that somehow this event had failed to turn her life around.

John Thompson took Stafford to a party to celebrate the publication of the story. "She couldn't talk, but people made a fuss over her." Joseph Mitchell recalls, "Reading that story was eerie. I could hear her telling it." "Influx" brought Stafford a large number of emotional letters, from friends, strangers, and writers as various as Bernard Malamud, Edward Albee, and V. S. Pritchett; all admired the story, and some were overwhelmed by it.

At the beginning of 1979 Stafford was sixty-three years old. Smoking had worsened her pulmonary disease to the point where breathing was difficult. Weighing less than 105 pounds, she had all but stopped eating. On February 20 she went into New York Hospital for the thirty-fourth time in her life; the following day she suffered a respiratory arrest that had to be relieved with a chest tube. She stayed in the hospital a full month. Says Thomas

Roberts, "She would turn the oxygen off. It would take her maybe fifteen minutes to walk from her room to the solarium, where she would smoke two cigarettes and then laboriously come back, get back into the oxygen, and carry on for a few hours."

On March 20 Stafford was discharged and taken to the Burke Rehabilitation Center in White Plains, New York. After a few days she told Roberts, " 'I can't stand this place any more.' " He responded, " 'Look, Jean, you've got to stand it. You're there to get well. And I hope you don't have to stay very long.' " To Dorothea Straus, who stopped by to see her, Stafford said in her halting voice, " 'Get — me — out — of here — get — me — out — of here.' " When Robert Giroux visited on March 25, she rode in a wheelchair as he walked beside her; out of sight of the nurses, she moved to a bench and lit a cigarette. As Giroux was leaving, she grasped his wrist and embraced him.

On March 26, 1979, Stafford died abruptly of cardiac arrest. Her doctor at Burke had seen her on morning rounds and found no "special problem"; surprised by her sudden death, he concluded that its likely cause was an onset of the ventricular tachycardia Stafford had had for years. Beside her deathbed lay a two-volume edition of Mark Twain and her half-annotated copy of *The Mills of the Kavanaughs*.

When Stafford's will was read, it was learned to universal astonishment that she had left her whole estate (but for a few paintings, some furniture, some silver, and her books) to Josephine Monsell, her cleaning lady. Even more shocking, she had made Monsell (who had never read her writing and who had only a rudimentary schooling) her literary executor. For years afterward her friends speculated about Stafford's motives; most saw it as her way of "thumbing her nose at the world." Over the years Stafford had made out "dozens" of wills. At one point Peter Taylor had been her literary executor; at another, Oliver Jensen. On one occasion, telling Peter De Vries he was to serve in that function, she invited him to steal what he wanted from her leavings. Around 1974 she had drawn up a will that made Robert Giroux her executor.

Stafford had drafted her last will, with Monsell as beneficiary, on November 15, 1978, barely a week after "An Influx of Poets" had appeared. Perhaps the shadow of her last moment in the sun as a writer had after all been disappointment.

Monsell inherited the house at 929 Fireplace Road and about sixty-nine thousand dollars. The money was eaten up in estate taxes, medical bills, and the like. Eight years later, Monsell rents out the house to summer people and closes it up in the winter. She still cleans houses for a living.

According to several sources, Stafford's lawyer refused to postpone the funeral long enough for distant friends to arrive — even though Stafford had been cremated. Peter Taylor got the lawyer on the phone and berated him, to no avail. Given Stafford's skillful handling of Liebling's memorial service, everyone who attended her funeral was shocked to find that no one was in charge of it. The funeral director, taken aback, finally read the Twenty-third Psalm and "gave a fuddled, all-purpose homily about how we would all, 'regardless of our beliefs, meet again in the next world.' " Then he asked the mourners if any of them wished to speak. They looked at each other; no one came forward. Finally Maria Polushkin, who, like Stafford, had always been terrified of speaking in public, uttered three or four valedictory sentences.

Stafford's ashes were lowered into a plot in Green River Cemetery, beside her last husband's. The tombstone, engraved to her own dictation, reads simply

JEAN STAFFORD LIEBLING
1915–1979

Its sole ornament, at the top of the black slate slab, is a snowflake — an emblem, like Liebling's fleur-de-lis, of what she had loved in life and, ultimately, of the privacy of her soul.

As the service ended, Everett Rattray of the *East Hampton Star* mused, "Her funeral is just like her will." Wilfrid Sheed saw the moment in short-story terms: "The survivors traipsed off, not huddled together by loss, but scattered and bemused, and feeling perhaps that the ending was wrong for the story, not one of Stafford's best."

Later Sheed remembered how Stafford had loved to repeat John Thompson's sardonic phrase, "Happy people don't have to have fun" —

but they don't have to write books either or do anything interesting. With all her heartbroken misanthropy, Jean despised such

people and would not have traded one racking cough or shooting
pain for an hour of their lives. She may not have liked what she
got, but in some curious way she got what she wanted, and she
paid for it one hundred cents on the dollar. If you add the pluses
and ignore the minuses, it was a deceptively good life.

One of Stafford's last letters to Marjorie expresses her gratitude for a gift or a letter or a thought of some sort: "A million
thanks for your brilliance! I was away from home what it came
and I determined that it had come on the day shuldered for my
birthday pass." The letter's closing line, however, hints at how
profoundly unfinished Stafford knew her work to be: "Some day
I write the out thing things that really happened to me — by
then I forget."

Epilogue

IF WE APPLY Santayana's touchstone for tragedy — that we are
compelled to say, "Ah, what might have been!" — then it is
hard to escape the conclusion that Jean Stafford's career was a
tragic one. The promise of her three published novels and of "In
the Snowfall" seems all the more clarion in view of the fact that
those works were all completed by the time Stafford was thirty-
six. She wrote excellent short stories for another six years after
that. But in the last two decades of her life Stafford's output of
fiction was all but nonexistent. It seems a particular shame that
she could not meet the challenge of her own designs for her last
novel, of which "An Influx of Poets" is such a tantalizing har-
binger.

It is also difficult not to conclude that Stafford's life was beset
by almost constant unhappiness. For that, a grueling series of
physical ailments was partly to blame, as well as a psychological
makeup that required self-punishment at every turn. But here,
too, we cannot help pondering what might have been. If only
Stafford had married Robert Hightower instead of Robert Lowell; if only she had stopped drinking once and for all; if only she
had exorcised the demons that her father, her sisters, and — at
the end — her best friends came to resemble. A happier Jean
Stafford, however, might have written even less.

The slenderness of her oeuvre, set against the Wolfean ambitions of her youth, plagues the witness to Stafford's life with an
acute sense of loss and waste. Yet in the scheme of things, do we

really need all the twenty-one novels of John Marquand, the twenty-three of Sinclair Lewis? How many of the works of the sober and industrious Joyce Carol Oates (eighteen novels and counting) will last? How many of Ford Madox Ford's thirty-two novels do we still care to read? Some of Stafford's near contemporaries, including J. D. Salinger and Ralph Ellison, have built sturdy reputations on even smaller bodies of work than hers.

At the time of Stafford's death in 1979, hers was no longer a familiar name to most readers under forty; nor is it today. The usual eclipse that greets a writer upon his expiration had in effect begun for Stafford years before. Despite her Pulitzer, after the mid-1960s she was all too often dismissed as old-fashioned, a "writer's writer," a practitioner of filigree arts no longer in demand. Her obituary in the *New York Times* regretted that

> in a time of changing fictional modes, of experimentation in structure and point of view, Miss Stafford held to traditional forms and accepted ways. Readers who looked to Jorge Luis Borges and John Barth for a new way to say old things found her work unengaging and without challenge.

If Stafford's occultation came early, so too, it seems, has come her rediscovery. Her three novels, which had gone fitfully in and out of print during her last two decades, are, along with her *Collected Stories,* all in print and in paperback eight years after her death. Her often brilliant essays and reviews will be gathered in a collection of her nonfiction work to be published in 1989 by Farrar, Straus & Giroux.

A kind of legend clung to Stafford through her grim last years, and in the 1980s younger analysts, surfeited with Barth and Borges and their legions of imitators, began to read for themselves. James Wolcott, one of our best critics, hailed an Ecco Press reissue of *The Catherine Wheel* (in a series called Neglected Books of the 20th Century) as

> a novel so sensuously deft that it makes most writers look as if they were slopping words on the page with their elbows. . . . What I don't understand is how *The Catherine Wheel* came to be neglected in the first place — it beats hollow nearly every novel published by a "name" author in the post–World War II era.

Across the Atlantic, Michael Wood declared, "I haven't heard Jean Stafford's name lately, and none of her books is in print in England . . . but if we are to resurrect only one work it must be the *Collected Stories*. Her prose is exact and witty; there is a quiet gaiety even in some of her excruciating situations." In an Ann Beattie short story, a character "had read Ian Hamilton's biography of Robert Lowell. 'But the best parts were when he quoted from Jean Stafford's book,' she said. 'She really had their numbers down, didn't she? . . .' "

In 1983 Wolcott argued further for "the well-deserved resurrection of Jean Stafford":

> At a time when so many young female novelists are wistful softies, writing about the lunk snoring on the next pillow or the plink of rainfall on summer lawns, the hard-grained determination of Stafford's fiction takes on an even firmer sturdiness. Unlike those sorority sisters of anomie who now gently cough into their fists at *The New Yorker,* Stafford wasn't trying to capture the whiff of a drifting mood but carpentering stories of loss and estrangement that would withstand the stresses of time and shifting fashion.

A pair of such shifting fashions, which Stafford's work will also withstand, has actually contributed to her reemergence, at least in the realm of academic criticism. Thus some scholars have begun to claim for her a certain significance as a western regional writer, attuned to the handicaps of growing up smart in California and Colorado. Other scholars, mining the feminist-despiteherself vein, have saluted Stafford for her "exploration of what it means to be female" and her resentment of "the patriarchal society's iniquities against the vulnerable."

Stafford's writing, however, is essentially neither regional nor feminist. Like her heroes Twain, Proust, and James, she took the human condition as her subject. Her style, which so many other writers envied, is sui generis, with its exquisitely qualified, complexly subordinated sentences spiced so oddly with the vivid colloquialisms she scavenged from her childhood. If in her weakest fictions the style seems to be an end in itself, in her best work all the technical skill serves, in Wolcott's phrase, "to crack the vault of our most protected feelings."

Boston Adventure, for all its stately, accretive tread, remains a remarkably original psychological novel; there are many readers

who still think it Stafford's best. *The Catherine Wheel,* with its potent syzygy between a possessed twelve-year-old boy and a moribund middle-aged woman guarding her clandestine passion, survives the contrivances of its plot. Deceptively laconic, *The Mountain Lion,* by all odds Stafford's finest novel, is an achingly true examination of adolescence. As Louis Auchincloss wrote of its protagonist, "Molly is one of the memorable children of American fiction."

Although no two readers would come up with the same list, it seems unarguable that some ten or a dozen of Stafford's short stories are near masterpieces. In the long run, it may be her stories for which she is remembered. For this enthusiast, the list would have to include "The Interior Castle," "Children Are Bored on Sunday," "A Country Love Story," "The Healthiest Girl in Town," "The Violet Rock," "Cops and Robbers," "In the Zoo," "Bad Characters," "A Reading Problem," and "An Influx of Poets."

Stafford is perhaps her generation's outstanding investigator of abandonment, voluntary exile, and self-estrangement. Her fiction struggles relentlessly with the effort of the "nobody" to expunge her past and define herself; with the attempt of the "hick" to transcend the beau monde; with the wanderer's quest for her own Red Room. Like the orphan Polly Bay in "The Liberation," ambiguously released by her flight from her tyrannical guardians, Stafford's characters wonder what to do next, how to live with their freedom:

> How lonely I have been, she thought. And then, not fully knowing what she meant by it but believing in it faithfully, she said half aloud, "I am not lonely now."

Notes

For the full citation of any work listed here by author and title alone, please see the bibliography.

Page numbers given here for Stafford's three novels and *Collected Stories* refer to current, not first, editions (see the bibliography).

The following abbreviations are used:

BA: Boston Adventure
Berg Collection: Berg Collection, New York Public Library, New York, New York
BL: Butler Library, Columbia University, New York, New York
CS: The Collected Stories of Jean Stafford
CUSC: Jean Stafford Collection, Special Collections, University of Colorado Libraries, Boulder, Colorado
CW: The Catherine Wheel
DR: David Roberts
HL: Houghton Library, Harvard University, Cambridge, Massachusetts
JOB: James Oliver Brown
JS: Jean Stafford
ML: The Mountain Lion

INTRODUCTION

Pages
  3 "Most brilliant . . . material": Chamberlain, "Young U.S. Writers," 76, 82.
  5 "Though you . . . days": Fitzgerald, "The Children," 399–400.

CHAPTER I

Pages

7–8 John Stafford . . . kids: Pinkham, "Jean Stafford's Family," 1–6.

8 "Mother wasn't slim, anyway": Marjorie Pinkham, interview with DR, 1985.

8–9 Three years . . . lippia: Pinkham, "A Look Backward," 78–82.

9 She sat . . . bands: JS, unpublished autobiographical sketch, CUSC.

9 "Our ground-covering . . . upon": JS, unpublished lecture, CUSC.

9–10 The children . . . salts: Pinkham, "A Look Backward," 79.

10–11 In the evening . . . Pickford: Pinkham, "Jean Stafford's Family," 15; Pinkham, "A Look Backward," 84–88.

11 "closed corporation . . . outsider": Nancy Weingartner, interview with DR, 1986.

11 "We told . . . Victrola": Pinkham, "Jean Stafford's Family," 8.

11 "she usually . . . backseat: ibid., 16, 20, 51.

12 Richard Stafford . . . Texas: Pinkham, interview with DR.

12 "One night . . . nail' ": JS, Samothrace manuscript, CUSC.

12 Richard Stafford . . . death: Pinkham, interview with DR.

12 The McKillops . . .. mother: JS, Samothrace manuscript, CUSC; *The United States Biographical Dictionary and Portrait Gallery of Eminent and Self-Made Men: Missouri Volume* (New York: United States Biographical Publishing Company, 1878), 613–614.

12 They were . . . house: Pinkham, "Jean Stafford's Family," 21.

13 John Stafford . . . Missouri: Pinkham, interview with DR; Pinkham, "Jean Stafford's Family," 14–15.

13 At some . . . City: John Stafford obituary, [unidentified newspaper], [n.d.], CUSC.

13 When Richard . . . Rockies: Pinkham, interview with DR; Pinkham, "Jean Stafford's Family," 13; JS, "Some Advice to Hostesses,"296.

13–14 They honeymooned . . . allowances: Pinkham, "Jean Stafford's Family," 4–5.

14 "The last . . . orders": John Stafford, *When Cattle Kingdom Fell* (New York: Dodge & Co., 1910), 1.

14–15 She gathered . . . family: Pinkham, "A Look Backward," 84; Pinkham, "Jean Stafford's Family," 17–18.

15 "the most pleasant person": Weingartner, interview with DR.

15 "Mother herself . . . too": Pinkham, "Jean Stafford's Family," 31–32.

15 "big, bountiful . . . food": Howard Higman, interview with DR, 1984.

15 When a neighboring . . . Reo: Pinkham,"A Look Backward," 85.

15 John Stafford . . . listener": Pinkham, "Jean Stafford's Family," 9; JS, *CS*, xi.

16 "He quoted . . . of": Pinkham, "Jean Stafford's Family," 14–15.

16 "six-shooter . . . often: Pinkham, interview with DR; Pinkham, "Jean Stafford's Family," 8.

Pages

16 "egomaniacal hatred . . . needle: JS, typewritten note, "Thursday," [n.d.], CUSC.

16 Once, when . . . long: Pinkham, "Jean Stafford's Family," 20.

16 "a problem feeder . . . cores: JS, "On My Mind," 200.

17 "I have it . . . joy": JS to Marjorie Pinkham, December 21, [1974], CUSC.

17 According to . . . rubbish": Pinkham, "Jean Stafford's Family," 20–24; Pinkham, "A Look Backward," 90.

17–18 "A brawny . . . now": JS, "Men, Women, Language," 69.

18 In San Diego . . . virtue: Pinkham, "Jean Stafford's Family," 21.

18 It was . . . conceal: JS to Robert Hightower, [n.d.].

18 At the age . . . Santa Claus: JS, "Home for Christmas," 108.

18 One Christmas . . . Boston: JS, "Jean Stafford on Education."

19 Investing the cash . . . humiliation: Pinkham, interview with DR.

CHAPTER II

20 In July . . . bumpers: Pinkham, "Jean Stafford's Family," 27–29.

20 In the tourist . . . harmonicas: JS, "Going West," unpublished essay, CUSC.

20–21 In Arizona . . . Affairs' ": Pinkham, "Jean Stafford's Family," 29–32.

21 "that land . . . here' ": JS, "Disenchantment," typescript, CUSC.

21–22 For if . . . legislature: Carl Abbott, *Colorado: A History of the Centennial State* (Boulder: Colorado Associated University Press, 1976), 219–24, 252–56.

22 "It was . . . day": Pinkham, "Jean Stafford's Family," 33.

22 The town . . . damage: Marshall Sprague, *Colorado: A Bicentennial History* (New York: W. W. Norton and Company, 1976), 153.

22–23 In Pueblo . . . baths": Pinkham, "Jean Stafford's Family," 33–37.

23 Almost forty . . . tyranny: JS, "Treasures of Use and Beauty," unpublished story, CUSC.

23 They played . . . daily: Pinkham, "Jean Stafford's Family," 40.

23 "he had . . . else": Pinkham, interview with DR.

23 "Every time . . . dinner": Pinkham, "Jean Stafford's Family," 43.

23–24 Ethel bore . . . passengers": Pinkham, interview with DR.

24 A diligent . . . dismay: Pinkham, "Jean Stafford's Family," 23, 34–35, 40–41.

24 From the time . . . dictionary: Breit, "Talk with Jean Stafford," 18.

24 "Gravel, gravel . . . head": JS, *ML,* 31.

24–25 By the age . . . men: JS, "Heroes & Villains," 196; Breit, "Talk with Jean Stafford," 18; JS, "An Etiquette for Writers," 3.

25 "I was . . . toes": JS, quoted in Sheed, "The Good Word."

25 Like Mary Lee . . . word: Pinkham, "Jean Stafford's Family," 42, 47.

25 "I had mutilated . . . Laddy": JS to Robert Lowell, "Tuesday," [n.d.], HL.

Pages

25   "The Stafford-McKillop . . . 7": JS to Pinkham, August 27, [year unknown], CUSC.

26   They rationalized . . . college: Pinkham, "Jean Stafford's Family," 43.

26   Meanwhile, Ethel's . . . opened: ibid., 43.

26–27   The small . . . jobs: Phyllis Smith, *A Look at Boulder: From Settlement to City* (Boulder: Pruett Publishing Company, 1981), 12, 17, 29–30, 117, 122, 124, 151, 155, 162–169, 173–176, 179. The Ku Klux Klan verse was published in the *Rocky Mountain American,* April 24, 1925.

27   One longtime . . . gypsies: Anne Riley, "Simple Pleasures," *Sunday Camera Magazine,* February 9, 1986, 18.

27–28   The most notorious . . . name: Smith, *A Look at Boulder,* 109, 116; Laurence T. Paddock, " 'Em Bugtown' Remembered as Boulder 'Character,' " *Boulder Daily Camera,* [n.d.].

28   seven of her best short stories: "The Healthiest Girl in Town," "The Violet Rock," "In the Zoo," "Bad Characters," "A Reading Problem," "The Scarlet Letter," and "Treasures of Use and Beauty."

28   "dreary" Central . . . churches": JS, "In the Zoo," *CS,* 285.

28   the handsome . . . street: JS, "A Reading Problem," *CS,* 324–329; JS, "Treasures of Use and Beauty," CUSC; JS, "Bad Characters," *CS,* 277.

28   "The street . . . evidence": Pinkham, "Jean Stafford's Family," 43.

29   "stupid things": Pinkham, interview with DR.

29   She walked . . . chat: McConahay, " 'Heidelberry Braids' and Yankee *Politesse,*" 219.

29   "wearing her . . . sidewalk": Higman, interview with DR.

29   One of her . . . priest: Pinkham, "Jean Stafford's Family," 61.

29   In a fictionalized . . . belt: JS, "In the Snowfall," unpublished novel, CUSC.

29   "We all thought . . . potatoes": Pinkham, interview with DR.

29   Jean bit . . . herself": Pinkham, "Jean Stafford's Family," 50–51.

30   "that for . . . increased": John Stafford to Oliver Jensen, November 13, 1950, CUSC.

31   As a consequence . . . porch: Pinkham, interview with DR.

31   The children . . . shop: Pinkham, "Jean Stafford's Family," 44.

31   The house . . . carpet: Pinkham, interview with DR.

31   The family . . . Progenitor": Pinkham, "Jean Stafford's Family," 50.

31   On University . . . light: Pinkham, interview with DR.

31–32   " 'Cave Canem . . . laughter": JS, "In the Snowfall," CUSC.

32   "My father . . . ill": JS, unpublished autobiographical note, CUSC.

32   Marjorie says . . . school: Pinkham, "Jean Stafford's Family," 46.

32   Jean herself . . . pencils: JS, "Heroes & Villains," 196; JS, "An Etiquette for Writers," 3–4.

32   "One sweltering . . . apparatus' ": JS, "Along the Border," unpublished story, CUSC.

33   "Miss Lucy . . . hatter' ": JS, "Miss Lucy," unpublished story, CUSC.

Pages

33 Marjorie remembers . . . better": Pinkham, "Jean Stafford's Family," 46–47.

33–34 "serious and . . . else": JS, "Smith Saga," unpublished story, CUSC.

34 "awfully funny . . . observation": Pinkham, "Jean Stafford's Family," 46.

34 Another untitled . . . stones: JS, untitled, unpublished story, CUSC.

34–35 In a third . . . hands' ": JS, untitled, unpublished story, CUSC.

35 In later . . . veins": JS, "An Etiquette for Writers," 4; Stewart, "Author Adds a Pulitzer."

35 Frost indeed . . . 1931: Lawrance Thompson and R. H. Winnick, *Robert Frost: A Biography* (New York: Holt, Rinehart, and Winston, 1981), 340, 342, 344, 354–55, 399.

35–36 "Since Christmas . . . idleness": JS, "Fame is Sweet to the Foolish Man," unpublished story, CUSC.

CHAPTER III

38 Although Jean . . . Colorado Springs: Marjorie says that Jean started first grade in Ivywild (probably in late 1921 or early 1922), and that in the fall of 1925 "Jean must have been in sixth grade." See Pinkham, "Jean Stafford's Family," 34, 44.

38–39 "[Jean] was . . . remarks": Jane Fitz-Randolph, interview with DR, 1986.

39 "She had . . . nose": unnamed source, quoted in McConahay, " 'Heidelberry Braids' and Yankee *Politesse*," 218.

39 "Her head . . . way": Higman, interview with DR.

39 In high school . . . Livy: JS, "Men, Women, Language," 69, 72.

39 "*Cur* do . . . *aures*": JS, "The Crossword Puzzle" 144.

40 "She always . . . saying": Fitz-Randolph, interview with DR.

40 In tenth . . . *Owl*: Goodrich Walton, interview with DR, 1985.

40 "The whole . . . did": Higman, interview with DR.

40–41 "It seems . . . them": JS, "Vox Populi" column, 3.

41 Long before . . . pinkeye: JS, "Enchanted Island," 140.

42 "a titanic . . . vision": ibid., 140.

42 "Sometimes these . . . hard": JS, "Souvenirs of Survival," 90.

42 In 1929 . . . Hayden: Pinkham, "Jean Stafford's Family," 47–48.

43 "I wasn't . . . bathrooms": Pinkham, interview with DR.

43 In 1930 . . . service: Pinkham, "Jean Stafford's Family," 48.

43 John's relationship . . . son: Pinkham, interview with DR.

43 "I had . . . epidemic": JS, "Coca-Cola," 178.

43 Yet in . . . fever: JS, medical history, [ca. October 1963], Thomas Roberts files, New York City.

43 Since early . . . feeding: JS, "On My Mind," 200.

43–44 Ethel believed . . . animals": Pinkham, "Jean Stafford's Family," 59–60.

Pages
   44 "I went . . . door": Higman, interview with DR.
   44 At Lodge . . . fall: Pinkham, "Jean Stafford's Family," 44; JS, "Souvenirs of Survival," 90.
45-46 "We thought . . . you": Higman, interview with DR.
   46 From her . . . photo: JS's copy of the *Odaroloc* (Boulder, Colorado, State Preparatory School yearbook) for 1930, CUSC. *Odaroloc* is *Colorado* spelled backward.
   46 "She was . . . person": Walton, interview with DR.
46-47 "She'd swipe . . . senior": ibid.
   47 In the spring . . . dear": Manitou Springs student to JS, [n.d.], CUSC.
47-48 "You should . . . herself: student to JS, June 9, 1932, CUSC.
   48 "Now listen . . . lover": student to JS, [n.d.], CUSC.
   48 "I would . . . it": Walton, interview with DR.
   49 "yarn factory": John Stafford to Jensen, November 13, 1950, CUSC.
   50 In 1941 . . . behind": JS, "Truth in Fiction," 4561-4563. JS gives almost identical accounts of the genesis of "In the Snowfall" in "Truth and the Novelist," 187-189 (q.v. for dating), and in "Young Writers," 21-23.
51-52 "The offices . . . Ph.D.' ": JS, "In the Snowfall," CUSC.
   52 In verification . . . me": Pinkham, interview with DR.
52-53 Joyce goes . . . them": JS, "In the Snowfall," CUSC.
54-55 "She was . . . want": ibid.
   55 Sometime in . . . labor: Pinkham, interview with DR.
56-57 "Now and . . . life": JS, "In the Snowfall," CUSC.
   57 "[Jean] used . . . child": Pinkham, interview with DR.
   57 "Long before . . . noticed": JS, "In the Snowfall," CUSC.
   58 "Joyce was . . . him": JS, "In the Snowfall," CUSC.
   58 "That did . . . it": Pinkham, interview with DR.
   58 "She wanted . . . rest": JS, "In the Snowfall," CUSC.

CHAPTER IV

   59 The university . . . dollars: William E. Davis, *Glory Colorado!: A History of the University of Colorado, 1858-1963* (Boulder: Pruett Press, 1965), 346-354, 379-381, 413, 420.
59-60 Stafford, however . . . term: JS, "Souvenirs of Survival," 90.
   60 Student life . . . technique": Davis, *Glory Colorado*, 358-363, 411-431.
   60 "gawky, wobbly, sloppy student": JS, "An Etiquette for Writers," 2.
   60 "restless, plunging . . . things": JS to Lowell, "Tuesday," [n.d.], HL.
   61 "vociferously contemptuous": JS, "Souvenirs of Survival," 90.
   61 "after many humiliating failures": JS, "An Etiquette for Writers," 1.
   61 One of . . . hour: Fitz-Randolph, interview with DR.
   61 "mad with excitement": JS to Alex and Marie Warner, July 30, [1974], CUSC.

Pages

61 She took . . . work: Fitz-Randolph, interview with DR.

61 Cohen also . . . infatuation: Pinkham, interview with DR.

61 "Miss McKeehan . . . heart": Peter Davison, interview with DR, 1986.

61 "exactly the . . . mother": Higman, interview with DR.

61–62 "She came . . . Brownings": JS, "Miss McKeehan's Pocketbook," 408.

62 "destitute and . . . unhappy": JS to Warners, July 30, [1974], CUSC.

62 "mad at . . . gloomy": Isaacs, "Searching for Significance."

62 "in some . . . thrilled": JS to Warners, July 30, [1974], CUSC.

62 A former . . . term: Mary Moore, interview with DR, 1984.

62 Peter Davison . . . cigarette: Davison, interview with DR.

62 "a secret writer": Isaacs, "Searching for Significance."

62 " 'Wind through . . . Stafford": "Student Experimental Plays Open Tonight in C.U. Lecture Theater," [unidentified Boulder newspaper], August 16, 1933, CUSC.

63 "It was . . . it: Walton, interview with DR.

63 Her M.A. . . . twelve: JS, "Profane and Divine Love in the English Literature of the Thirteenth Century" (master's thesis, University of Colorado, 1936).

63 "She gave . . . off: Higman, interview with DR.

64 "We'd near . . . see": Anatole Ehrenberg, quoted in McConahay, " 'Heidelberry Braids' and Yankee *Politesse*," 219.

64 "deadly serious . . . seriousness": Walter B. Lovelace, "You Can Go Home Again," *Colorado Alumnus,* October 1952.

64 "terribly smart . . . house: Moore, interview with DR.

64–65 Even though . . . League: JS, "Souvenirs of Survival," 91.

65 "moonstruck by . . . me": JS "An Etiquette for Writers," 5.

65 "we ascended . . . sick": JS, "Souvenirs of Survival," 174–175.

65 According to . . . thing: Walton, interview with DR.

65–66 One summer . . . outcasts: Pinkham, "Jean Stafford's Family," 52–56. The stories are "A Summer Day" (*CS,* 345–359) and the unpublished "Heyjim Littlefield" (copy in possession of Robert Hightower).

66 In her new . . . charcoal: JS, "Souvenirs of Survival," 91, 175.

66 "You were . . . class: Moore, interview with DR.

67 "it amused . . . down": ibid.

67 "Jean Stafford . . . week: Fitz-Randolph, interview with DR.

67 In the spring . . . child: Paul and Dorothy Thompson, interview with DR, 1984.

68 There was . . . him: Walton, interview with DR.

68 "She told . . . them": Moore, interview with DR.

68 Egged on . . . deeply": Edward J. Chay, quoted in McConahay, " 'Heidelberry Braids' and Yankee *Politesse*," 220.

68–69 A disgruntled . . . her": Robert Hightower, interview with DR, 1985. The phrase "Agenbite of Inwit" occurs five times in *Ulysses.* It is an allusion to *Ayenbite of Inwyt,* or "Remorse of Conscience," a moral treatise translated from the French around 1340. Considering the topic

Pages

of Stafford's M.A. thesis, such a work must have been right up her alley. See Weldon Thornton, *Allusions in Ulysses: An Annotated List* (Chapel Hill: University of North Carolina Press, 1961), 21–22.

69–70 The two . . . overbearing": Hightower, interview with DR.

70 "which, maddeningly . . . child": JS, "In the Snowfall," CUSC.

70–72 Now, in . . . love: ibid.

72 "helped me . . . me!": JS to Warners, July 30, [1974], CUSC.

72–76 In the novel . . . fornications": JS, "In the Snowfall," CUSC.

76 Robert Hightower . . . stand: Hightower, interview with DR.

CHAPTER V

78 Born in . . . Europe: Andrew Cooke, interview with DR, 1985.

78 The diary . . . ingenue: Lucy McKee's diary is among the Stafford papers at CUSC.

78 She wanted . . . task: Cooke, interview with DR.

78 "I don't think . . . pretty": Raphael Moses, interview with DR, 1984.

79 "contract her . . . lips": JS, "In the Snowfall," CUSC.

79–81 One of Lucy's . . . effort: Cooke, interview with DR.

81 By her senior . . . traditions: "Girl Student Shot Herself."

82–83 Donald Hays . . . life": Cooke, interview with DR.

83 It may be . . . protégée: JS, "In the Snowfall," CUSC.

83 "She said . . . seduction": Hightower, interview with DR.

83–84 Andrew escaped . . . watch": Cooke, interview with DR.

84 "It was an . . . them": Higman, interview with DR.

84 Dorothy and . . . Cooke: Hightower, Dorothy and Paul Thompson, Walton, Moore, and Fitz-Randolph, interviews with DR.

84–85 At the same . . . again": Cooke, interview with DR.

85 Four years . . . them": Anne White, interview with DR, 1984.

85 "I don't know . . . mine": Cooke, interview with DR.

85 According to . . . lesbian: Moses, interview with DR.

85 "Jean said . . . friend": Hightower, interview with DR.

85–86 "Had Lucy . . . sex": Cooke, interview with DR.

86–87 Gradually Lucy's . . . 'Bang!' ": Cooke, interview with DR.

87 Lucy had . . . him: "Girl Student Shot Herself."

87 "I never . . . insincere": Cooke, interview with DR.

87 With Jean . . . 10:00 P.M.: "Girl Student Shot Herself."

87 "The jail . . . shock": Cooke, interview with DR.

87 The newspaper . . . matter": "Girl Student Shot Herself."

87–88 For a while . . . suspicion: Walton, Paul and Dorothy Thompson, and Cooke, interviews with DR.

88 To this day . . . her": Cooke, interview with DR.

88 On November 12 . . . funeral: "Girl Student Shot Herself."

88 With the . . . again: Cooke, interview with DR.

88 "Yes, you . . . ever": JS to Chay, [postmarked February 27, 1946], CUSC.

Pages

89 "At the time . . . further": JS, typed note, [November 9, 1945], CUSC.

89 "I daresay . . . entourage": JS to Chay, [postmarked July 3, 1948], CUSC

89 "I desire . . . ink": JS, typed note, [November 9, 1945], CUSC.

89 In the novel . . . Adams": JS, "In the Snowfall," CUSC.

90 Joyce's feeling . . . him: ibid.

90 "That's invented . . . him": Hightower, interview with DR.

90–94 By this point . . . girl": JS, "In the Snowfall," CUSC.

94 After Lucy's . . . says: Cooke, interview with DR.

94–95 The insouciance . . . secret: JS, "In the Snowfall," CUSC.

95–96 The possibility . . . sort": Cooke, interview with DR.

96 In the novel . . . bar": JS, "In the Snowfall," CUSC.

96–97 Andrew Cooke . . . Jean: Cooke, interview with DR.

97–98 In the novel . . . excitement": JS, "In the Snowfall," CUSC.

98 Further, Cooke . . . seriously: Cooke, interview with DR.

98–99 Thus in . . . same": JS, "In the Snowfall," CUSC.

99 "She begins . . . begun": ibid.

CHAPTER VI

100 now every . . . gossip: Paul and Dorothy Thompson, Higman, and Fitz-Randolph, interviews with DR.

100–101 *Tomorrow in* . . . it?": JS, *Tomorrow in Vienna,* unpublished script, CUSC.

101 The Thompsons . . . attacks: Paul Thompson, diary, February 16, 22, 23; March 1, 23, 29; May 7, 30, 31; and June 1, 1936.

101 "I don't remember . . . nursing": Pinkham, "Jean Stafford's Family," 25–26.

101 "by banging . . . platonic: Hightower, interview with DR.

102 In the spring . . . accepted: JS, "Souvenirs of Survival," 175; Paul Thompson, diary, April 17, 1936.

102 "My one . . . free' ": Hightower, interview with DR.

102 Her parents . . . attend: *Boulder Daily Camera,* June [n.d.], 1936.

102–103 During a summer . . . wine: Pinkham, "Jean Stafford's Family," 49, 59; Pinkham, interview with DR.

103 Wolfe sat . . . Perkins: David Herbert Donald, *Look Homeward: A Life of Thomas Wolfe* (Boston: Little, Brown and Company, 1987), 332–336.

104 "by excited . . . stories": Foley, "Novels and Short Stories of Jean Stafford," 5.

104 At the beginning . . . Atlantic: Cooke, interview with DR.

104 "The boat . . . over": JS to Mary Lee Frichtel, September 23, 193[6], CUSC.

104 Her ship . . . 1936: JS, passport, CUSC.

104 Hightower had . . . Heidelberg": Hightower, interview with DR.

Pages

104 "Turn right . . . half-sister: Hightower to JS, September 15, 1936.

104 Later, he . . . rooms: Hightower, interview with DR.

104–105 There was . . . heat: JS to Cooke, [postmarked October 1, 1936].

105 "When I . . . nostalgic": JS to Frichtel, September 23, 193[6], CUSC.

105 "I wish . . . lovely": JS to Cooke, [postmarked October 1, 1936].

105–106 By the 1930s . . . anniversary: *Heidelberg and the Universities of America* (New York: The Viking Press, 1936), v, 3–5, 13, 18, 25, 34, 48–51, 57; Waldemar M. Heidtke, *An American Looks at the University of Heidelberg* (Heidelberg: Heidelberger Verlagsanstalt und Drückerie GMBH, 1968), [unpaginated].

106 "The educational . . . boys": JS to Cooke, [postmarked October 1, 1936].

107 After about . . . hotel: Hightower, interview with DR.

107 The two . . . shaved: ibid.; JS, "Letter from Germany," 86–87.

107–108 She browsed . . . Cafe Sö: ibid., 82–86; JS, "My Blithe, Sad Bird," 28; JS, "The Echo and the Nemesis," 45–46; JS, "A Winter's Tale," 229; JS, "The Maiden," 58.

108 "a body . . . drunk": JS to Hightower, March 11, 1937.

108 "barnlike . . . condiments": JS, "The Cavalier," 30.

108 "I may . . . here": JS to Cooke, October 28, 1936.

108 one of . . . Franco: Ignacio Horica to JS, December 8, 1938, CUSC.

108 She criticized . . . arrest: Pinkham, "Jean Stafford's Family," 57.

109 "I was swept . . . so": JS, "Sense and Sensibility," unpublished manuscript of Barnard lecture, CUSC.

109 "She was . . . thing": Walton, interview with DR.

109 "Hightower, however . . . untrue": Hightower, interview with DR.

109–110 "Hoops was . . . Boulder: Hightower, interview with DR.

110 In one instance . . . Lucy: JS to Hightower, [ca. June 1937].

110 Hightower remembers . . . excerpts: Hightower, interview with DR.

110–111 In the fall . . . silver: ibid.

111 Sometime after . . . war: Frank Parker, interview with DR, 1985.

111 He is called . . . Spain: JS, "The Autumn Festival" and "A Winter's Tale," manuscripts, CUSC.

111 The plausibility . . . list: JS, note, [n.d.], CUSC.

111 "I can almost . . . out: Hightower, interview with DR.

111–112 Around the . . . Chopin: Hightower, interview with DR.

112 The steady . . . hay": JS and Hightower, various letters, September 1936–August 1937.

112 According to . . . well behaved": Hightower, interview with DR.

113 "The score . . . Am[erica]": JS to Hightower and Robert Berueffy, [ca. February 1937].

113 In late . . . Pass: JS, passport, CUSC.

113 Trying to . . . Naples: Hightower, interview with DR.

113 In Italy . . . her: Pinkham, "Jean Stafford's Family," 57.

113 "I was . . . word": JS, "Bessie's Debacle," in JS to Hightower, [ca. June 1937].

Pages

113   " 'Why don't . . . ambitions: JS, "Miss McKeehan's Pocketbook,"
       410–411.

113   Her reunion . . . goodbye: Hightower, interview with DR.

113–114 As soon . . . quarter": JS to Hightower and Berueffy, April 11, 1937,
       and [ca. April 1937].

114   Hightower fed . . . hour: Hightower to JS, June 1, 193[7].

114   "I tell . . . impt.": Hightower to JS, May 18, 1937.

114   "I consider . . . Larry": JS to Hightower, [ca. May 1937].

114   "Donald and Dorothy Babbitt": JS to Hightower, [ca. May 1937].

114   "My grief . . . out": JS to Hightower, [ca. May 1937].

115   "I have four . . . prestige": JS to Hightower, [ca. May 1937].

115   "he was . . . publishable' ": ibid.

115   During lunch . . . all: ibid.

115–116 During two . . . breakdown: JS to Hightower, various letters, [ca.
       May 1937].

116   "It's *female* . . . suicide": JS to Hightower and Berueffy, [ca. June
       1937].

116   "She said . . . else": Hightower, interview with DR.

117   To the doctor . . . illness: Thomas Roberts, interview with DR, 1985.

117–118 Many of . . . bore: Dr. David Savitz, telephone conversation with
       DR, 1987; Theodor Rosebury, *Microbes and Morals: The Strange Story
       of Venereal Disease* (New York: The Viking Press, 1971), 7, 183, 214;
       William J. Brown, et al., *Syphilis and Other Venereal Diseases* (Cam-
       bridge, Mass.: Harvard University Press, 1970), 14, 16, 83, 90.

117   Most suggestively . . . compounds: JS to Hightower and Berueffy,
       [ca. June 1937 and ca. July 1937].

118   "Wherever Jean . . . stick": Hightower, interview with DR.

CHAPTER VII

119   "He just . . . once": JS to Hightower and Berueffy, [ca. June 1937].

119–120 From Oregon . . . clichés: JS to Hightower and Berueffy, [ca. July
       1937].

120   "Last night . . . time": JS to Hightower and Berueffy, [ca. July 1937].

120   "the disease . . . head": JS to Hightower and Berueffy, [late July 1937].

120   "trench mouth . . . syphilis": JS to Hightower and Berueffy, [ca.
       June 1937].

120   "I have started . . . syphilis": JS to Hightower and Berueffy, [late
       July 1937].

121   "He was wheezy . . . bandages": Davison, interview with DR.

121   On August 3 . . . remained: Davison, interview with DR; Arthur
       Mizener, *The Saddest Story: A Biography of Ford Madox Ford* (New
       York: World Publishing Company, 1971), 442.

121   "Saw Bishop . . . hell": JS to Hightower and Berueffy, [late July
       1937].

Pages

122 "said one . . . literature": JS to Hightower and Berueffy, [early August 1937].

122 "That was . . . first": JS to Hightower, [postmarked January 3, 1938].

122 "One Saturday . . . by": Davison to William Leary, April 26, 1986.

122 "he chased her around": John Thompson, interview with DR, 1985.

122 "wooed her something fierce": John Thompson, quoted in Hamilton, *Robert Lowell,* 60.

122–123 After St. Mark's . . . Tate: Hamilton, *Robert Lowell,* 30–43.

123 One day . . . University: Lowell, *Collected Prose,* 58–60.

123–124 In July . . . Boulder: Hamilton, *Robert Lowell,* 50–54.

124 "Well, i . . . time": JS to Hightower and Berueffy, [late July 1937].

124 "he wd. . . . mind": JS to Hightower and Berueffy, [late July 1937].

124–125 "I just . . . novelist": JS to Hightower, [postmarked September 21, 1937].

125 Stephens had . . . memorizing": John C. Crighton, *Stephens: A Story of Educational Innovation* (Columbia, Mo.: The American Press, 1970), 299, 330, 409–410.

125 "the object . . . living": "Life at Stephens," *Stephens College Bulletin* 18 (December 1937): [unpaginated].

125 Twelve hundred . . . needs: ibid.

125–126 "Not even . . . me": JS to Hightower, [postmarked September 13, 1937].

126 "Do you know . . . pointers": JS to Hightower, [postmarked September 21, 1937].

126 "the College . . . sound": W. W. Charters, *The Stephens College Program for the Education of Women* (Columbia, Mo.: Stephens College, 1938), 15.

126 The curriculum . . . time": *Stephens College Bulletin: The Catalogue* (Columbia, Mo.: Stephens College, 1937), 73, 76, 107.

126 "(1) letter . . . storytelling": Crighton, *Stephens: A Story,* 271.

126 "a pleasing . . . women": Charters, *The Stephens College Program,* 32–33.

126–127 The college . . . study": ibid., 42.

127 "My advisees . . . fissures": JS to Hightower, [postmarked September 29, 1937].

127 One of the . . . Stafford": JS to Hightower, [postmarked November 23, 1937].

127 "I have . . . Career": JS to Hightower, [postmarked December 1, 1937].

127 "It is going . . . please": JS to Hightower, [postmarked November 13, 1937].

127 Once they . . . presents: JS to Hightower, [postmarked November 19, 1937].

127 "I have . . . bored": ibid.

127 One English . . . classes: JS to Hightower, [postmarked September 29, 1937].

Pages

127–128 Another figure . . . *dear*": JS to Hightower, [postmarked February 9, 1938].

128 Jean described . . . bounces": JS to Hightower, [postmarked September 29, 1937].

128–129 "There wuz . . . nickel": JS to Hightower, [postmarked November 3, 1937].

129 Stafford's health . . . measles: JS to Hightower, [postmarked October 7 and November 13, 1937; February 18, 25, and March 3, 1938].

129 Hightower was . . . smug: Hightower to JS, various letters, 1937–1938.

130 At first . . . abstractions": JS to Hightower, [postmarked February 9, 1938].

130 Hightower was . . . underestimation: Hightower to JS, various letters, 1937–1938.

130 "I won't . . . know": JS to Hightower, [postmarked October 7, 1937].

131 "he is fat . . . dough": JS to Hightower, [postmarked October 7, 1937].

131 "I told . . . did": JS to Hightower, [postmarked January 7, 1938].

131 "I drank . . . year": ibid.

131 "the only . . . it": JS to Hightower, [postmarked January 3, 1938].

132 "I had . . . would": Howard Mumford Jones to JS, quoted in JS to Hightower, [postmarked September 13, 1937].

132 "You are . . . unpublishable": JS to Hightower, [postmarked February 21, 1938].

133 "Eventually of . . . up!"": John Stafford to JS, quoted in JS to Hightower, [postmarked November 19, 1937].

133 "I don't . . . alive": ibid.

133 Despairing of a . . . winner: JS to Hightower, [postmarked May 26, 1938].

133 "I'm sick at heart": JS to Hightower, [postmarked June 23, 1938].

133 "Thus far . . . sure": JS to Hightower, [postmarked March 3, 1938].

134 "Which of . . . keys": JS, "Prologue," enclosed in JS to Hightower, [postmarked December 6, 1937].

134 "A word . . . Dharma": JS, "Magdalene's stream," enclosed in JS to Hightower, [postmarked December 6, 1937].

134 "I ainta . . . what": JS to Hightower, [postmarked February 21, 1938].

134–135 "the most . . . contempt": JS to Hightower, [postmarked February 4, 1938].

135 I have not . . . school": JS to Hightower, [postmarked February 25, 1938].

135 "actively hated . . . people": JS to Hightower, [postmarked March 17, 1938].

135 "i hate . . . more": JS to Hightower, [postmarked March 9, 1938].

135 "they bore . . . stupid": JS to Hightower, [postmarked March 17, 1938].

Pages

135 "the biggest . . . Mississippi": JS to Hightower, [postmarked May 26, 1938].

135 "not have . . . resign": JS to Hightower, [postmarked March 3, 1938].

135 "i want . . . polish": ibid.

135 "Sometimes the . . . me": JS to Hightower, [postmarked June 25, 1938].

136 "I guess . . . years": JS to Hightower, [postmarked May 20, 1938].

136 "I have . . . beer": JS to Hightower, [postmarked March 7, 1938].

136 "I am . . . last": JS to Hightower, [postmarked March 19, 1938].

136 "He shot . . . dies": JS to Hightower, [postmarked May 1, 1938].

137 In March . . . pariah: JS to Hightower, [postmarked March 7, 1938].

137 "frequently summoned . . . blackboard": JS, "What Does Martha Mitchell Know?," 31.

137 "having ordered . . . Flaubert": Mary Darlington Taylor, "Jean Stafford's Novel."

137 In a third . . . composition: Higman, interview with DR.

137–138 On about . . . syphilis: JS to Hightower, [postmarked April 20, 1938].

138 "sick, deathly . . . me": JS to Hightower, [postmarked April 26, 1938].

138 "hatreds that . . . headaches": JS to Hightower, [postmarked April 20, 1938].

138–139 "dirty, smelling . . . newspapers": JS to Hightower, [postmarked April 26, 1938].

139 She took . . . profit": Evelyn Scott to JS, and Creighton Wellman to JS, [ca. May 1938], CUSC.

139 One Saturday . . . before": JS to Hightower, [postmarked April 26, 1938].

139 On June 12 . . . New York: Hightower to JS, [ca. June 8, 1938].

CHAPTER VIII

141 Waiting in the . . . prevailed: JS to Hightower, [postmarked June 28, 1938].

141 The next . . . alone: Hightower, interview with DR.

141–142 At last . . . fingers: Hightower to JS, [postmarked October 7, 1938].

142 In the morning . . . engaged: Hightower, interview with DR.

142 On the first . . . me": JS to Hightower, [postmarked June 23, 1938].

142 One day . . . Salida: Hightower, interview with DR.

142 After she . . . hand: JS to Hightower, [postmarked June 21, 1938] and [ca. June 24, 1938].

142 In their . . . married": Hightower, interview with DR.

142–143 In letters . . . dismay: JS to Hightower, [postmarked June 28, 1938].

143 "If I . . . been": JS to Hightower, [postmarked June 23, 1938].

143 "Paul is . . . yet": JS to Hightower, [postmarked June 21, 1938].

143 "didn't survive . . . before": Hightower, interview with DR.

144 " 'I will . . . Salida": JS to Hightower, [postmarked June 21, 1938].

Pages

144 "Mother has . . . *visit*' ": JS to Hightower, [ca. June 24, 1938].

144 "Aunt Ella . . . complex": JS to Hightower, [postmarked July 31, 1938].

145 "He sits . . . soon": JS to Hightower, [postmarked June 23, 1938].

145 "Of course . . . Tennyson": ibid.

145 "He said . . . *Courtier*": JS to Hightower, [postmarked July 31, 1938].

145 " 'trying to . . . etc." : JS to Hightower, [postmarked July 5, 1938].

145 One day . . . convulsion: JS to Hightower, [postmarked July 21, 1938].

146 "psychopathic. He . . . about": JS to Hightower, [postmarked August 20, 1938].

146 "Your article . . . exist": Joseph Barber, Jr., to JS, July 12, 1938, Atlantic Monthly Press files.

146 Within ten . . . Press: JS to Hightower, [postmarked June 27, July 2, and August 24, 1938].

146 Meanwhile, during . . . fellowship: JS to Hightower, [postmarked July 7, 1938].

146 "I love you, darling": JS to Hightower, [postmarked June 23, 1938].

146 "how I . . . days": JS to Hightower, [ca. June 24, 1938].

146 "I think . . . happen": Scott to JS, [summer 1938], CUSC.

146–147 but in another . . . bond": Scott to JS, July 10, 1938, CUSC.

147 "entirely physical . . . own": JS to Hightower, [postmarked June 28, 1938].

147 "bourgeois respectability . . . Dad": JS to Hightower, [postmarked July 7, 1938].

147 "I would . . . all": JS to Hightower, [postmarked August 12, 1938].

147 "Come marry me": JS to Hightower, [postmarked August 27, 1938].

147 In July . . . Stephens: JS to Hightower, [postmarked July 15, August 1, and August 12, 1938].

147 "I am terrified . . . prelims": JS to Hightower, [postmarked August 4, 1938].

147–148 Although it . . . Bible: JS to Hightower, [postmarked July 5, August 1, and August 4, 1938].

148 "Our first . . . time": Hightower, interview with DR.

148 "I was sick . . . anything": JS to Hightower, [postmarked September 19, 1938].

149 "College is . . . isn't": JS to Hightower, [postmarked September 23, 1938].

149 "I am not . . . laugh": JS to Hightower, [postmarked September 30, 1938].

149 She had . . . desk: JS to Hightower, [postmarked September 30, 1938].

149 "I hate teaching": JS to Hightower, [postmarked October 23, 1938].

149–150 One of these . . . town": A. G. Ogden, "Report on novel by Jean Stafford," [n.d.], Atlantic Monthly Press files.

150–151 The president . . . quick": JS, unpublished Stephens College novel, CUSC.

Pages

151 "I am so . . . pleasure": JS to Hightower, [postmarked September 19, 1938].

151 "And how . . . you?": JS to Hightower, [first of two letters postmarked September 30, 1938].

151–152 "Your remarkably . . . Boston?": JS to Hightower, [second of two letters postmarked September 30, 1938].

152 "implacably jealous . . . again: Hightower to JS, [postmarked ca. October 1–6, 1938].

152 "I have . . . love": JS to Hightower, [postmarked October 3, 1938].

153 "I was . . . them": Hightower, interview with DR.

153 He dreamed . . . street: Hightower to JS, [postmarked October 10 and October 15, 1938].

153 "Oh, God . . . lost": Hightower, interview with DR.

153 "Darling, if . . . immediately: Hightower to JS, [postmarked October 10, 1938].

153 "No, I . . . consummation": JS to Hightower, [postmarked October 15, 1938].

153–154 The McKees . . . novel: JS to Hightower, [postmarked October 18, 1938].

154 His affair . . . more": Hightower to JS, [postmarked October 23, 1938].

154 "Come now . . . 20$": Hightower to JS, [ca. October 25, 1938].

154 In accordance with . . . again: JS to Hightower, [postmarked October 28, 1938].

154 On November . . . later: JS to Hightower, [postmarked March 9, 1938].

154 Herself now . . . eastward: JS, "Miss McKeehan's Pocketbook," 410.

154 She left . . . headed: Paul Thompson, diary, November 23, 1938.

154 Stafford changed . . . November 6: JS to Hightower, [postmarked November 3, 1938].

154 "ARRIVE 1105 . . . JEAN": JS to Hightower, telegram, November 8, 1938.

154–155 That evening . . . torture": Hightower, interview with DR.

155 "ARRIVING TOMORROW . . . CAL": Lowell to JS, telegram, November 20, 1938, collection Hightower.

155 Pressing her . . . love: Hightower, interview with DR.

155 "LOWEL ARRIVING . . . UNSIGNED": [Berueffy] to JS, telegram, November 20, 1938, collection Hightower.

155–156 In Hightower's . . . address: Hightower, interview with DR.

156 At Thanksgiving . . . there: Peter Taylor, interview with DR, 1986.

156 "glorious, talented . . . hair": Peter Taylor, "1939," 328.

156 Taylor recalls . . . Stafford?": Taylor, interview with DR.

156 Stafford, who . . . poet: Hightower, interview with DR.

156 "Darling he . . . him": JS to Hightower, November 23, 1938.

156–157 "I was rather . . . again: Taylor, interview with DR.

157 Stafford had . . . art": Scott to JS, November 12, 1938. Stafford's knack for keeping her friends in separate worlds bedevils even schol-

Pages

ars. Thus McConahay, in " 'Heidelberry Braids' and Yankee *Politesse*," mistakenly assumes that the Scott letters from the summer of 1938 are about Lowell, not Hightower, and contorts "double ménage" to mean Stafford's conflict between art and love. McConahay seems unaware of Hightower's existence, let alone of the fact that Stafford considered marrying Hightower.

157–158 "I would . . . secret: Hightower, interview with DR.

158 On December . . . 1939: Ogden to JS, November 29 and December 9, 1939, Atlantic Monthly Press files.

158 "Jesus Christ . . . center: Hightower, interview with DR.

158 She began . . . together: JS to Hightower, [postmarked January 25, 1939].

158 "I am very . . . you": JS to Hightower, [postmarked December 13, 1938].

158–159 Before she . . . it": Hightower, interview with DR.

159 A few . . . skull: Hamilton, *Robert Lowell,* 62; Hightower, interview with DR; JS, medical history, [ca. October 1963], Thomas Roberts files.

CHAPTER IX

160 The driver . . . hysterical: JS to Hightower, [postmarked July 29, 1939].

160 At least . . . gift: Eberhart, *The Mad Musician,* 144; Ann Honeycutt, interview with DR, 1984; Gertrude Buckman, interview with DR, 1985.

160 On the other . . . drunk: JS to Hightower, [postmarked July 29, 1939].

160 Lowell was . . . endanger: Engle, "Lost Love," 4.

160 According to . . . fault": Parker, interview with DR.

160 "would *never* . . . car": Blair Clark, interview with DR, 1986.

161 "Her face . . . met: Hightower, interview with DR.

161 Yet according . . . January: White, interview with DR.

161 She also . . . head: JS, medical history, [ca. October 1963], Thomas Roberts files; Clark, interview with DR.

161 Stafford got . . . features: Higman, interview with DR.

161 "occasion on . . . life": JS, "Truth and the Novelist," 188.

161 Stafford endured . . . accident: JS, medical history, [ca. October 1963], Thomas Roberts files.

161 in real . . . climber": JS to Hightower, [postmarked July 29, 1939].

161–162 " 'All set? . . . snapping": JS, "The Interior Castle," *CS,* 186, 192.

162 "she was . . . sense": Clark, interview with DR.

162 "Jean looked . . . reason": Davison, interview with DR.

162 "What the . . . look": White, interview with DR.

163 In a letter . . . Stafford": JS to Chay, October 12, 1944, CUSC.

163 After his . . . Kenyon: Clark, interview with DR.

163 Stafford later . . . times: Giroux, "Hard Years and 'Scary Days,' " 28.

Pages

163 "With Cal . . . mind": Parker, interview with DR.

163–164 "Cal always . . . them": Clark, interview with DR.

164 "[He] had . . . laces": Thompson, "Robert Lowell 1917–1977," 14.

164 His father . . . take: Hamilton, *Robert Lowell,* 3–4, 11–13.

165 "To my . . . them": Lowell, *Collected Prose,* 256.

165 "Charlotte was . . . dinner": Thompson, "Robert Lowell 1917–1977," 14.

165 "Old Bob . . . cipher": Clark, interview with DR.

165 "The whole . . . that": White, interview with DR.

165–166 There he . . . apology": Clark, interview with DR.

166 "I will . . . it": JS to Hightower, [postmarked January 10, 1939].

166–167 "I knew . . . writer": JS to Hightower, [postmarked January 25, 1939].

167 "hard by Hawthorne's grave": JS, essay on American places.

167 "progressively lousier": JS to Hightower, [postmarked March 16, 1939].

167 Ian Hamilton . . . Easter: Hamilton, *Robert Lowell,* 64.

167 "I saw the . . . place": JS to Ogden, [n.d.], Atlantic Monthly Press files.

167 Despite her . . . novel: Ogden to JS, May 12, 1939, Atlantic Monthly Press files.

168 "looks like . . . society": JS to Hightower, [postmarked July 29, 1939].

168 "tough as . . . thing": Parker, interview with DR.

168 "very fat . . . department: JS to Hightower, [postmarked July 29, 1939].

168 "Jean and . . . courthouse": Clark, interview with DR.

168 To avoid . . . Jung: Hamilton, *Robert Lowell,* 63.

168 "an incurable schizophrenic": Lowell, *Day by Day,* 122.

168–169 "About Boston . . . winter": Robert Lowell to Charlotte Lowell, July 19, [1939], HL.

169 One of the . . . *Adventure:* Parker, interview with DR.

169 "I was 24 . . . Bessie": JS to Hightower, [postmarked July 5, 1939].

170 "You are . . . High": JS to Hightower, [ca. September 30, 1939].

170 In Hayden . . . riding: Harry Frichtel, interview with DR, 1985.

170 Stafford liked . . . life": JS to Hightower, [postmarked September 17 and 20, 1939] and [ca. September 30, 1939].

171 "I want you . . . parts": Ogden to JS, October 5, 1939, Atlantic Monthly Press files.

171 In six . . . whole": Ogden to JS, October 13, 1939, Atlantic Monthly Press files.

171–173 The manuscript . . . me": JS, "The Autumn Festival," unpublished novel, CUSC.

172–173 "How do I . . . enough": JS to Hightower, [postmarked July 29, 1939].

173 "This is not . . . come": Ogden, "Novel — Jean Stafford," Atlantic Monthly Press files.

174 "Shining she was": Thompson, "Robert Lowell 1917–1977," 14.

Pages

174 "She was a . . . edition": John Thompson, interview with DR.

174 "Cal made . . . of": Taylor, interview with DR.

174 "Towmahss Mahnn . . . *twenty-one*": Lowell, *Day by Day*, 29.

175 "When she . . . crazy: Taylor, interview with DR.

175 "always fleeing": John Thompson, interview with DR.

175 "She'd come . . . scholar": Taylor, interview with DR.

175 Bunny Cole . . . for": White, interview with DR.

175 "the ugly . . . intelligent": Hightower, interview with DR.

175–176 "the only . . . go": White, interview with DR.

176 Stafford picked . . . Cambridge: Mary Darlington Taylor, "Jean Stafford's Novel."

176 There she . . . institute: Hightower, interview with DR.

176 At the original . . . balked: Robert Lowell to Charlotte Lowell, [postmarked October 23, 1939], HL.

176 In the end . . . money: Engle, "Lost Love," 4; Simpson, *Poets in Their Youth*, 126.

176 "used to . . . writing: White, interview with DR.

176 "Sometimes she'd . . . food": ibid.

177 "I am going . . . me": JS to Hightower, [postmarked December 19, 1939].

177 "I felt . . . kind": Hightower, interview with DR.

177 Stafford's letter . . . you": JS to Hightower, [postmarked December 19, 1939].

177 Good sport . . . poet": Hightower, interview with DR.

177 "Jean is . . . trial": Robert Lowell to Charlotte Lowell, [fall 1939], HL.

177 At Kenyon . . . her: Hamilton, *Robert Lowell*, 69.

177–178 To her friends . . . hick": Giroux, "Hard Years and 'Scary Days,' " 28.

178 "Tell us . . . from?": Simpson, *Poets in Their Youth*, 125.

178 "[Charlotte] ran . . . nursery: Stillman, notes of interview with JS, 1.

178 "Mrs. Lowell . . . notice: Hightower, interview with DR.

178 "A little . . . night": JS to Hightower, [ca. February–March 1940].

179 "I was here . . . tonight": JS to Hightower, [ca. January–February 1940].

179 "COME HERE . . . POSSIBLE": JS to Hightower, telegram, December 9, 1939.

179 "I've never . . . gonorrhea: Hightower, interview with DR.

179 Six days . . . again": JS to Hightower, March 27, 1940.

179 On March 30 . . . stations": JS to Hightower, March 30, 1940.

179 Perhaps to avoid . . . Albert: JS to Hightower, March 31, 1940.

179 The couple . . . fatigue": JS to Hightower, March 30, 1940.

180 "Cal got . . . life": JS to Hightower, March 31, 1940.

180 "couldn't speak . . . understand": JS to Hightower, [April 1940].

180 "He was . . . me?": JS to Hightower, March 31, 1940.

180 "The Wasserman[n] . . . business": JS to Hightower, March 30, 1940.

180 Syphilis was . . . mode: William A. Hinton, *Syphilis and Its Treatment* (New York: Macmillan Co., 1936), 153–161.

Pages

180–181 On April 2 . . . afterward: Clark, interview with DR.
   181 "It is 4:10 . . . done": JS to Hightower, April 2, 1940.

CHAPTER X

182 "Jean will not be welcome": John Crowe Ransom, quoted in Merrill Moore to R. T. S. Lowell, June 27, 1939, HL; quoted in Hamilton, *Robert Lowell*, 65.

182 "I am beginning . . . me": JS to Hightower, April 4, 1940.

182 "made it . . . future: JS to Hightower, [postmarked April 21, 1940].

182 Lowell's parents . . . child: Cutrer, *Parnassus on the Mississippi*, 197.

182 "tepid tolerance . . . corset": JS to Hightower, [postmarked April 23, 1940].

183 One day . . . rich": JS to Hightower, [not sent?; ca. May 20, 1940].

183 "I had . . . it": JS to Hightower, [postmarked April 21, 1940].

183 "a brand . . . yet": JS to Hightower, [postmarked May 6, 1940].

183 He was hoping . . . him: Cutrer, *Parnassus on the Mississippi*, 196–197.

183 An alternative . . . New York: JS to Hightower, [ca. May 20, 1940].

183 "It would . . . insane": Hightower, interview with DR.

183 "I don't . . . really": Scott to JS, April 30, 1940, CUSC.

184 "I would . . . imbecility": JS to Hightower, [postmarked April 20(?), 1940].

184 "She was . . . girl": Hightower, interview with DR.

184 "a mind . . . girls": JS to Hightower, [postmarked April 23, 1940].

184 If Hightower . . . again: JS to Hightower, [postmarked April 23, 1940].

184 "married a . . . others": JS to Hightower, [postmarked April 23, 1940].

184–185 "Jean made . . . Jean": Hightower, interview with DR.

185 "a plan . . . lives": JS to Hightower, [postmarked May 10, 1940].

185 "There is . . . you": JS to Hightower, [postmarked April 23, 1940].

185 "I nurse . . . long": JS to Hightower, [postmarked April 27, 1940].

186 "summa cum . . . valedictorian": Robert Lowell to Charlotte Lowell, [June 1940], HL.

186 His valedictory . . . aristocracy: Hamilton, *Robert Lowell*, 68–69.

186 At the last . . . SHORTHAND": Cutrer, *Parnassus on the Mississippi*, 196–197.

186 Years later . . . *me*": Simpson, *Poets in Their Youth*, 126.

186–187 "My feelings . . . China": Hightower, interview with DR.

187 "My feeling . . . approval": JS to Hightower, [postmarked June 6, 1940].

187–188 Before going . . . country": Hightower, interview with DR.

188 "Cal was . . . not' ": Taylor, interview with DR.

188 Despite a . . . criticism: Cutrer, *Parnassus on the Mississippi*, 74.

188 "He's a strong . . . sense": Ransom to Cleanth Brooks, January 15, 1940; quoted in Cutrer, *Parnassus on the Mississippi*, 196.

Pages

188 "the moisture . . . forearm": Lowell, *Day by Day*, 25.

188 "as big as a calf": JS to Peter Taylor, [June 1940]; reproduced in JS, "Some Letters to Peter and Eleanor Taylor," 27.

189 "I remember . . . hound": JS, unpublished essay on Baton Rouge, CUSC.

189 "looks like . . . 1938": JS to Peter Taylor, [June 1940]; reproduced in JS, "Some Letters to Peter and Eleanor Taylor," 27.

189 Stafford tried . . . before: JS, unpublished essay on Baton Rouge, CUSC.

189 "Letters from . . . ladies": JS to Hightower, [postmarked June 21, 1940].

189 " 'She worked . . . airs' ": Peter De Vries, interview with DR, 1985.

189 "not terribly handy": JS to Peter Taylor, [June 1940]; reproduced in JS, "Some Letters to Peter and Eleanor Taylor," 27.

189 He also . . . laundry?": JS to Hightower, [postmarked June 25, 1940].

190 Brooks found . . . literature: Cutrer, *Parnassus on the Mississippi*, 197–199.

190 "[Lowell] was . . . way": Robert Penn Warren, interview with David Farrell; quoted in Cutrer, *Parnassus on the Mississippi*, 199.

190 They drove . . . jukebox: JS, essay on American places.

190 " 'If you say . . . violence!' ": Parker, interview with Patricia Bosworth; quoted in Bosworth, *Diane Arbus: A Biography* (New York: Alfred A. Knopf, 1984), 47.

190 "great gauche . . . girl": JS to Hightower, [postmarked October 31, 1940].

190–191 When the four . . . bills": Taylor, interview with DR.

191 "Peter and . . . me": JS to Hightower, [postmarked October 31, 1940].

191 Meanwhile, Taylor's . . . Stafford: Taylor, interview with DR.

191 Nothing ever . . . party: JS to Hightower, [postmarked October 31, 1940].

191–192 In the mornings . . . says: Taylor, interview with DR.

192 In October . . . fist": Parker, interview with DR.

192 "I remember . . . accidental": Clark, interview with DR.

192 "Cal had . . . shocked": Parker, interview with DR.

192 "would go . . . again": ibid.

192 "I am once . . . surgeon": JS to Hightower, [postmarked October 31, 1940].

193 When they . . . New York: Taylor, interview with DR.

193 "To wrestle . . . doing": Parker, interview with DR.

193 "breathed too much": JS to Hightower, [postmarked October 31, 1940].

193 "had a funny . . . people": John Thompson, interview with Ian Hamilton; quoted in Hamilton, *Robert Lowell*, 56.

193–194 In 1943 . . . Baton Rouge: Lowell and JS, "Wuberts," assorted unpublished manuscripts, CUSC.

194 Close friends . . . contempt": Taylor, interview with DR.

Pages

194 Because he . . . again: Peter De Vries, interview with DR.

194 A favorite . . . Libres: JS, "Coca-Cola," 178.

194 "she was so . . . there": Taylor, interview with DR.

194 "There is . . . solitude": JS to Hightower, [postmarked November 15, 1940].

194 " 'Catholicism is . . . girls' ": Taylor, interview with DR.

194 Warren thought . . . Dante: Robert Penn Warren, interview with David Farrell; quoted in Cutrer, *Parnassus on the Mississippi*, 198.

194 Frank Parker . . . Cambridge: Parker, interview with DR.

194 In Baton Rouge . . . Newman: Hamilton, *Robert Lowell*, 78.

194–195 In the fall . . . Catholicism: Cutrer, *Parnassus on the Mississippi*, 198.

195 "Cal is . . . righteousness": JS to Hightower, [postmarked February 10, 1941].

195 On March 29 . . . monastery: Cutrer, *Parnassus on the Mississippi*, 198–199.

195 "immersed in . . . tear": JS, "An Influx of Poets," 49.

195 "Mass at . . . it": JS to Hightower, [postmarked August 6, 1941].

195 A rumor . . . flesh: Cutrer, *Parnassus on the Mississippi*, 199.

195–196 "austerity . . . cats": JS, "An Influx of Poets," 49.

196 "Turnabout as . . . happened": JS to Hightower, [postmarked April 10, 1941].

196 "My ideal . . . *possibility*": JS to Hightower, [postmarked August 6, 1941].

196 "I am apprised . . . reparation": JS to Hightower, [postmarked April 10, 1941].

196 At the end . . . cure: JS to Hightower, [postmarked March 4 and April 10, 1941].

196–197 By the end . . . sequences": JS to Hightower, [postmarked June 30, 1941].

197–198 In the late . . . administered: Hinton, *Syphilis and Its Treatment*, 153–161.

198 "they had a . . . together": Stillman, notes of interview with JS, 1.

198 At some . . . thing: Clark, interview with DR.

198 Later she . . . him: Eve Auchincloss, interview with DR, 1985.

198 To Wilfrid . . . children: Sheed, "Miss Jean Stafford," 93–94.

198 His fumbling . . . biography: Hamilton, *Robert Lowell*, 38.

200 "I've got . . . encumbrance": JS to Hightower, [postmarked April 17, 1941].

200 Even in . . . encumbrance": Hightower, interview with DR.

200 "Ignore, by . . . happy": JS to Hightower, [postmarked May 1, 1941].

200 "mighty small potatoes": JS to Hightower, [postmarked August 6, 1941].

200–201 "[He] is . . . nigger": JS to Hightower, [postmarked May 12, 1941].

201 "I had him . . . subject": Harry Frichtel, interview with DR.

201 His social . . . floor: JS, unpublished autobiographical note, CUSC.

201 "the first . . . done": JS to Hightower, [postmarked March 4, 1941].

Pages

201 Regarding it . . . Houghton Mifflin: JS to Hightower, [postmarked April 10, 1941].

201 "complimenting me . . . winter": JS to Hightower, [postmarked May 12, 1941].

201 " 'Miss Jean . . . even?' ": Robert Frichtel, interview with DR, 1984.

202 Peter Taylor . . . student: Cutrer, *Parnassus on the Mississippi,* 203.

202 In his place . . . obvious": JS to Hightower, [postmarked August 6, 1941].

202 With the help . . . publisher: Cutrer, *Parnassus on the Mississippi,* 201.

202 "Thank God . . . possibilities": JS to Hightower, [postmarked August 6, 1941].

CHAPTER XI

203 Pregnant with . . . exchange: Hightower, interview with DR.

204 In September . . . Baton Rouge: JS to Hightower, [postmarked September 9, 1941].

204 The publishing . . . lights": Wilfrid Sheed, *Frank and Maisie* (New York: Simon and Schuster, 1985), 64–65, 92–121.

204 Lowell's job . . . that": JS to Hightower, [postmarked September 9, 1941].

204 "Frank loved . . . anyway?' ": Sheed, *Frank and Maisie,* 137–138. The line quoted by Frank Sheed is from the poem "Salem," in Lowell's *Land of Unlikeness.*

204–205 Lowell insisted . . . job": JS to Peter Taylor, [October 1941]; reproduced in JS, "Some Letters to Peter and Eleanor Taylor," 30.

205 "Oh, I . . . year": Taylor, interview with DR.

205 "Our days . . . concision": Lowell, *Day by Day,* 29.

205 "I was . . . cry": JS, "An Influx of Poets," 48–50.

206 Before rejecting . . . hands: JS to Hightower, [postmarked September 9, 1941].

206 Sometime near . . . novel-in-progress: JS to Peter Taylor, [later dated "(October 1941)" by Taylor but probably early 1942]; reproduced in JS, "Some Letters to Peter and Eleanor Taylor," 31–32.

206 The head . . . New Haven!' ": Giroux, "Hard Years and 'Scary Days,' " 29.

206 One evening . . . Street: JS to Peter Taylor, [later dated "(October 1941)" by Taylor but probably early 1942]; reproduced in JS, "Some Letters to Peter and Eleanor Taylor," 31.

206–207 On April 30 . . . desk: Giroux, "Hard Years and 'Scary Days,' " 3.

207 The terms . . . 1942: Harcourt, Brace contract for JS, "The Outskirts," April 30, 1942, CUSC.

207 At the time . . . *Adventure:* Giroux, "Hard Years and 'Scary Days,' " 3.

207–208 Since June . . . away: Taylor, interview with DR.

Pages

208 "catty words": Taylor to JS, May 24, 1943, CUSC.

208 She had . . . *Review:* JS, "Walpurgis Nacht, 1940."

209 Anticipating the . . . Lowell' ": Lambert Davis to JS, November 5, 1942, and February 1, 1943, CUSC.

209 "I am sure . . . book: Davis to JS, March 24, 1943, CUSC.

209 "a *conscious* . . . Proust": JS to Hightower, [postmarked September 9, 1941].

209 "a Harcourt . . . career": Davis to JS, April 2, 1943, CUSC.

209–210 Stafford was . . . Baton Rouge: JS to Eleanor and Peter Taylor, [July 10, 1943]; reproduced in JS, "Some Letters to Peter and Eleanor Taylor," 38–39.

210 Much of . . . communists": JS to Eleanor and Peter Taylor, [July 1943]; reproduced in JS, "Some Letters to Peter and Eleanor Taylor," 42.

210 She was . . . month: JS to Peter Taylor, July 20, 1943; quoted in Hamilton, *Robert Lowell,* 87.

210 "thoroughly diagnosed . . . it": Robert Lowell to Charlotte Lowell, [August 1943], HL.

210 Stafford may . . . novel: JS to Eleanor and Peter Taylor, [July and September 1, 1943]; reproduced in JS, "Some Letters to Peter and Eleanor Taylor," 40, 43.

210–211 During the . . . culture: Radcliffe Squires, *Allen Tate: A Literary Biography* (New York: Pegasus, 1971), 156–157, 174.

211 as a child . . . battles: Lowell, *Collected Prose,* 331–341.

211 In 1937 . . . houses' ": Parker, interview with DR.

211 "If war . . . go": Robert Lowell to Mrs. Arthur Winslow, [n.d.], HL; quoted in Hamilton, *Robert Lowell,* 75.

211 "I very . . . violence": Lowell, *Collected Prose,* 367–370.

211–212 "What we . . . out": Parker, interview with DR.

212 Nor was . . . bureaus: JS to Mary Lee Frichtel, [n.d.], CUSC.

212 He claimed . . . traditions": Engle, "Lost Love," 4.

212 " 'You won't . . . him' ": Simpson, *Poets in Their Youth,* 145.

212 She was receiving . . . rent: Hamilton, *Robert Lowell,* 94.

212–213 On October 31 . . . purpose": Charlotte Lowell to JS, October 31 and November 10, 1943, Blair Clark files.

213 Stafford made . . . her: JS to Eleanor and Peter Taylor, [October 1943]; reproduced in JS, "Some Letters to Peter and Eleanor Taylor," 45.

213 "He is . . . horror": JS to Eleanor and Peter Taylor, [November 1943]; reproduced in JS, "Some Letters to Peter and Eleanor Taylor," 46–47.

213 During the . . . stretch: JS to Robert and Bunny Hightower, [ca. January–February 1944].

214 In December . . . cold: Hightower, interview with DR.

214 Over the course . . . *Review:* JS, "The Darkening Moon," "The Lippia Lawn," and "A Reunion," respectively.

Pages

214 "a happy . . . pretentiousness": Davis, report on JS, *BA,* October 23, 1944, CUSC.

214–215 "large, shapeless . . . dump: JS, "The Home Front," 151.

215 "the pleasurable . . . wife: JS to Peter Taylor, February 11, 1944; quoted in Hamilton, *Robert Lowell,* 96.

215 in June . . . mass": JS to Hightower, [postmarked June 9, 1944].

215 The reunited . . . Conbert": Lowell and JS, "Wuberts," assorted unpublished manuscripts, CUSC.

215 "more thoroughly . . . writing": JS to Cecile Starr, May 5, 1945; quoted in Hamilton, *Robert Lowell,* 101–102.

216 "She did not . . . offensive": Lowell, *Collected Prose,* 330–331.

216 "We feel . . . empty": Charlotte Lowell to Robert Lowell, August 26, [1950], HL.

216 The only . . . home: Charlotte Lowell to Robert Lowell, various letters, HL.

216 "Jean always . . . hers": Clark, interview with DR.

216–217 It finally . . . *Adventure:* JS to Robert and Bunny Hightower, [postmarked October 3, 1944].

217 "I can't . . . first": Paul and Dorothy Thompson, interview with DR.

217 Lambert Davis . . . for: Harcourt, Brace to JS, January 12, 1945, CUSC.

217 The editor . . . famous": "JW" to JS, June 13, 1944, CUSC.

217 A month . . . readers": Davis to JS, August 18, 1944, CUSC.

217–218 Her mail . . . out": JS to Hightower, [postmarked September 8, 1944].

218 "The success . . . me": ibid.

219 "a curiously passive creature": Davis to JS, March 24, 1943, CUSC.

219–220 "Hopestill still . . . scot-free": JS, *BA,* 387.

220 Stafford explicitly . . . model: JS to Chay, [postmarked February 27, 1946], CUSC.

221 "The irony . . . wit": "Miss Pride's Companion," *Newsweek* 24 (September 25, 1944): 102–103.

221 "highly stylized . . . adventure": Mina Curtiss, "Beacon Hill Brahmins," *Boston Globe,* October 11, 1944, 17.

221 Three years . . . Ritz-Carlton: JS, "Notes on Boston."

221 *Newsweek* called . . . incisive": "Miss Pride's Companion," 102–103.

221 *Time* was . . . depth": "Proust on Pinckney Street," *Time* 45 (January 22, 1945): 94, 96, 98.

221 "Not only . . . it": Francis Hackett, "Collision with Boston," *New York Times,* September 23, 1944, 17.

221 "A first . . . well": [Peter De Vries], *The New Yorker* 20 (September 23, 1944): 78.

222 These mass . . . 144,000: Harcourt, Brace, various royalty statements for JS, *BA,* 1944–1945, CUSC.

222 The only . . . year: Alice Hackett, "New Novelists of 1944," *Saturday Review of Literature* 28 (February 17, 1945); *Newsweek* 24 (December 18, 1944).

Pages

222 Stafford was . . . her: Davis to JS, February 5, 1945, CUSC; JS to Chay, December 12, 1944, CUSC.

222 She was . . . winner: JS to Hightower, [postmarked September 8, 1944].

222 "Champagne flowed . . . offices": JS to Chay, December 12, 1944, CUSC.

222 By June . . . book: Harcourt, Brace, royalty statements for JS, *BA*, 1944–1945, CUSC.

CHAPTER XII

223 "In my father's . . . bit": Sheed, "Miss Jean Stafford," 93.

223–224 "rushing to . . . County": JS to Chay, October 12, 1944, CUSC.

224 "Cal has . . . unpacking": JS to Hightower, [postmarked September 13, 1944].

224 Then, in . . . instantaneous: JS to Frichtel, October 8, [1944], CUSC.

224 Eight months . . . soon": JS to Robert and Bunny Hightower, [ca. February 1944].

224 Dick's death . . . crashed: George D. Hendricks to JS, January 27, 1970, CUSC; Pinkham, "Jean Stafford's Family," 60.

224 "I am hoping . . . else": JS to Frichtel, October 8, [1944], CUSC.

224–225 "It was . . . been": Parker, interview with DR.

225 "Jean's image . . . store": Pinkham, "Jean Stafford's Family," 60–61.

225 "old and . . . late": JS to Robert and Bunny Hightower, [postmarked November 27, 1944].

225 Dick's death . . . shipyards: Pinkham, "Jean Stafford's Family," 60.

225 "He is probably . . . life": JS to Robert Hightower, August 22, [1945].

225 "limited service . . . New York": JS to Alfred Kazin, [postmarked November 27, 1944], Berg Collection.

225 In a desultory . . . house: JS to Robert and Bunny Hightower, [postmarked November 27, 1944, and December 28, (1944)].

226 "becoming a . . . money": JS to Robert Hightower, [postmarked September 13, 1944].

226 "The house . . . attractive": JS to Alfred Kazin, [postmarked November 27, 1944], Berg Collection.

226 "There were . . . Year's": JS to Chay, January 1, 194[5], CUSC.

226 "I think . . . this": ibid.

226 "I truly . . . spring": JS to Chay, October 10, 1944, CUSC.

226 Every Tuesday . . . badly": JS to Robert and Bunny Hightower, [postmarked March 21, 1945, and May 2, (1945)].

226 There was . . . Pride: JS to Robert and Bunny Hightower, December 28, [1944].

227 "makes New York . . . nerves": JS to Chay, February 4, [1945], CUSC.

227 "The place . . . scrubbing": JS to Frichtel, [postmarked April 4, 1945], CUSC.

Pages

227 "fashionable, vulgar . . . naive": JS to Robert and Bunny Hightower, May 2, [1945].

227 "I have largely . . . myself": JS to Robert and Bunny Hightower, [postmarked March 21, 1945].

227 "My new . . . write": JS to Chay, February 4, [1945], CUSC.

228 Anxious to . . . collection: Davis to JS, August 13 and 31, 1945, and Harcourt, Brace to JS, August 25, 1945, CUSC.

228 At the beginning . . . vacate: JS to Robert and Bunny Hightower, May 2, [1945].

228 In early . . . coast: JS to Robert Hightower, July 8, [1945].

228 "horrid little . . . homestead: JS to Chay, July 28, [1945], CUSC.

228 "a real . . . Maryland": JS to Hightower, August 20, [1945].

228–229 The latter . . . life": JS to Taylor, [later dated "(September 28, 1943)" by Taylor but actually 1945]; reproduced in JS, "Some Letters to Peter and Eleanor Taylor," 51–55.

229 "that will . . . isolation": JS to Hightower, August 20, [1945].

229–230 White settlers . . . hotel: Harold W. Castner, *The Story of the Great Salt Bay and Vaughn's Pond* (Damariscotta, Me.: Lincoln County News, 1950), 5, 11–20.

230 The Rockland . . . hall: Barbara Pinkham, interview with DR, 1986.

230 In her walks . . . midst: JS, "New England Winter," 38, 40, 42.

230 "If we . . . carpenter": JS to Robert and Bunny Hightower, October 1, [1945].

230 "nesting and neatening": JS, "An Influx of Poets," 51.

230 to escape . . . bird-watching: Lowell to Peter and Eleanor Taylor, May 23, 1946; quoted in Hamilton, *Robert Lowell*, 111.

230 For half . . . out: JS, "New England Winter," 40.

230 "In the blue . . . stove": JS, "A Country Love Story," *CS*, 136.

231 The priest . . . mysterious": JS to Peter Taylor, [later dated "(September 28, 1943)" by Taylor but actually 1945]; reproduced in JS, "Some Letters to Peter and Eleanor Taylor," 54; Buckman, interview with DR.

231 Stafford and . . . her: Simpson, *Poets in Their Youth*, 117.

231 Nancy Booth . . . drink: Nancy Booth, interview with DR, 1986.

231–232 "I remember . . . while?' ": JS, "Manners Are Morals," unpublished essay, CUSC.

232 "so that . . . neighbors": Simpson, *Poets in Their Youth*, 133.

232 She finished . . . pen: The other story was "The Captain's Gift."

232 On November 9 . . . spirit": JS, typescript note, CUSC.

232 Their enthusiasm . . . book": Davis to JS, December 21, 1945, CUSC.

233 On January . . . April 1: Harcourt, Brace contract for JS, *ML*, JOB papers, BL.

233 Whenever she . . . production: JS, *ML*, author's note.

233 twenty discrete . . . phrase: JS, various manuscripts, CUSC.

233 "always planned . . . end": Auchincloss, interview with DR.

233–234 "that they . . . scream": JS, "New England Winter," 38, 40, 44.

Pages

234 "one of . . . vitality' ": JS, "A Personal Story," unpublished story, CUSC.

234 "I went . . . self-esteem": JS, "An Influx of Poets," 47.

234–235 In late . . . town: JS to Frichtel, [postmarked November 27, 1945], CUSC.

235 Tate haughtily . . . friends' ": Taylor, interview with DR.

235 "He's a . . . man": Stillman, notes of interview with JS, 1.

235 "got up . . . pipes": JS, "New England Winter," 40.

235 For two weeks . . . outside: JS to Chay, [postmarked February 27, 1946], CUSC.

235–236 The prodigy . . . suspicion: Atlas, *Delmore Schwartz*, 153, 187, 195, 243, *et passim*.

236 "whenever you . . . it": Delmore Schwartz to Lowell, December 15, 1945; quoted in Schwartz, *Letters*, 223.

236 "a harmonious ménage together": JS to Robert and Bunny Hightower, January 4, [1946].

236 Stafford and . . . mail": Schwartz to Elizabeth Pollet, February 2, 1946 (quoted in Schwartz, *Letters*, 231); Simpson, *Poets in Their Youth*, 119.

236 *"We couldn't . . . said"*: Lowell, *Life Studies*, 51.

237 One evening . . . them": JS, "Truth and the Novelist," 187–188.

237 According to . . . Jew' ": Atlas, *Delmore Schwartz*, 250.

237 " 'I would . . . friend' ": JS, "An Influx of Poets," 56.

237 When Frank . . . furious": Parker, interview with DR.

237 Now, a . . . fight: Atlas, *Delmore Schwartz*, 250–251; Simpson, *Poets in Their Youth*, 143.

237 "Both are . . . ashamed": Schwartz to Elizabeth Pollet, March 26, 1946; quoted in Schwartz, *Letters*, 236.

237 From Cambridge . . . silence: ibid.

238 "NEW ENDING TERRIFIC": Robert Giroux to JS, telegram, May 7, 1946, CUSC.

238 She later . . . ill": JS to Lowell, [n.d.], #1159, HL.

238 "terror of . . . it' ": JS to Lowell, [n.d.], #1171, HL.

238 "I had often . . . home": JS, "An Influx of Poets," 46.

238 "Finally it . . . disaster": JS, "A Country Love Story," *CS*, 138.

238 "Jean was . . . thought": Clark, interview with DR.

238 " 'What the . . . all' ": JS, "An Influx of Poets," 46.

239 At some . . . truant: Clark, interview with DR.

239 "She always . . . sexless": ibid.

239 "She was . . . man": Parker, interview with DR.

239 Lowell told . . . Boulder: Buckman, interview with DR.

239 Many years . . . usual": Parker, interview with DR.

239–240 "[Jean] said . . . really' ": ibid.

240 In a fully . . . assignment": JS, "A Country Love Story," typescript draft, CUSC.

241 A variant . . . rape: Lowell, *The Mills of the Kavanaughs*, manuscript draft, HL.

Pages

241 Yet Peter . . . issue": Taylor, interview with DR.

241 Not all . . . godfather: Hamilton, *Robert Lowell,* 114; JS to Frichtel, [postmarked August 16, 1946], CUSC.

241–242 "In some . . . broken": JS to Frichtel, [postmarked June 13, 1946], CUSC.

242 "At night . . . him": JS, "An Influx of Poets," 43.

242–244 "Had I . . . alone": Simpson, *Poets in Their Youth,* 115–146.

244 A splotchy . . . nemesis: The photograph is among the Lowell papers, HL.

244 "It is quite . . . *plans"*: JS to Frichtel, [postmarked August 16, 1946], CUSC.

244–245 "I don't . . . time": Lowell to Taylor, August 13, 1946; quoted in Hamilton, *Robert Lowell,* 115.

245 "pretty, small . . . language": JS, "An Influx of Poets," 43–44, 47.

245–246 In fact . . . not": Buckman, interview with DR.

246 " 'But Cora . . . sweetie!' ": JS, "An Influx of Poets," 45.

246 "We never . . . [stay]": Buckman, interview with DR.

247 "I helped . . . chasm": JS, "An Influx of Poets," 56.

247–248 " 'You look . . . day": ibid., 58, 60.

CHAPTER XIII

249 Stafford and . . . Street: Stillman, notes of interview with JS, 2.

249 Lowell rented . . . lovers: Buckman, interview with DR.

249 Shortly after . . . hours: Stillman, notes of interview with JS, 2; JS to Lowell, [n.d.], #1155, HL.

249 Now, however . . . counterpoint": JS to Lowell, [n.d.], #1156 and #1157, HL.

250 But as Frank . . . better": Parker, interview with DR.

250 "I am full . . . means": JS to Frichtel, [postmarked September 23, 1946], CUSC.

250 Parker met . . . him' ": Parker, interview with DR.

250 According to Jean . . . seen": JS to Lowell, [n.d.], #1171, HL.

250–251 "when you . . . circumstances": JS to Lowell, [n.d.], #1156, HL.

251–252 In October . . . container": JS to Lowell, [n.d.], #1171, HL.

252 "said all . . . nun": JS to Frichtel, [postmarked November 1, 1946], CUSC.

252 "a small nervous breakdown": JS to Frichtel, [postmarked November 8, 1946], CUSC.

252 Robert Giroux . . . B. A.": JS to Frichtel, [postmarked October 25, 1946], CUSC.

252 Fifteen minutes . . . utterly": JS to Lowell, [n.d.], #1171, HL.

252–253 Stafford herself . . . choose": JS to Frichtel, [postmarked November 8, 1946], CUSC.

253 Stafford had . . . bathe: JS to Lowell, [n.d.], #1171, HL.

Pages

253 "When I . . . Bostonians": JS to Frichtel, [postmarked November 19, 1946], CUSC.

253 Stafford had . . . suit": ibid.

253 Except for . . . year: JS to Robert Hightower, [early 1948].

254 "I knew . . . floor": JS to Lowell, [n.d.], #1171, HL.

254 "Here, one's . . . peanuts": JS to Frichtel, [postmarked December 21, 1946], CUSC.

254 Stafford nicknamed . . . Park: Simpson, *Poets in Their Youth,* 146.

254 The staff . . . floors": JS, untitled, unpublished essay or story, CUSC.

254–255 At Recreational . . . anemia: JS to Frichtel, [postmarked December 21, 1946], CUSC.

255 Eileen Simpson . . . Whitney: Simpson, *Poets in Their Youth,* 150.

255 "It would . . . forever": JS to Lowell, [n.d.], #1155, HL.

255–256 Its meaning . . . refuge": JS, *BA,* 424–425, 434.

256 Frank Parker . . . magic: Parker, interview with DR.

256 "The thought . . . feeling": Taylor to Lowell, November 19, [1946], HL.

256 "Thank goodness . . . Jean": Taylor to JS, December 8, [1946], CUSC.

256 "I am . . . meetings": Taylor to JS, December 28, [1946], CUSC.

256–257 He wrote . . . each: Taylor, interview with DR.

257 A few . . . virtues": Stillman, notes of interview with JS, 5.

257 "I know . . . for": JS to Lowell, [n.d.], #1155, HL.

257–258 "I have . . . writing": JS to Lowell, [n.d.], #1156, HL.

258 "Gertrude, the . . . end": JS to Lowell, [n.d.], #1157, HL.

258 Buckman denies . . . place: Buckman, interview with DR.

258 "She is . . .desire": JS to Lowell, [n.d.], #1155, HL.

258 "I have . . . will": ibid.

258 "How will . . . death": JS to Frichtel, [first of two letters postmarked February 3, 1947], CUSC.

258 She wrote . . . inadequate": JS to Frichtel, [second of two letters postmarked February 3, 1947], CUSC.

258 "I wonder . . . dies": JS to Lowell, [n.d.], #1157, HL.

259 "Jean's image . . . do": Pinkham, "Jean Stafford's Family," 61.

259 "nearly overpowered . . . desire": JS to Lowell, [n.d.], #1171, HL.

259–260 "My father . . . Maine": JS, typewritten note, "Thursday," [early February 1947], CUSC.

260 Although her . . . died: Marjorie Pinkham, interview with DR.

260 "A very . . . permanently": JS to Lowell, [n.d.], #1158, HL.

261 "When she . . . bored": JS, *ML,* 209.

261–262 "But tonight . . . woes": JS, *BA,* 117.

262 "If she . . . time": JS, *ML,* 180–181.

262–263 " 'My theory . . . morality' ": Bond, "Fascination with Words."

263 "today she . . . face": JS, *ML,* 11–12.

263 "Molly had . . . born": ibid., 144.

263 "a terrified . . . [her]": ibid., 148.

263 " 'You're a . . . things": ibid., 118–119.

Pages

263–264 "He urged . . . speak": ibid., 158–159.

264 "Gradually I . . . love": JS to Lowell, [n.d.], #1171, HL.

265 "a second . . . understanding": *The New Yorker* 23 (March 8, 1947): 97–98.

265 "suffer from . . . days": Fitzgerald, "The Children," 399–400.

265 Howard Mumford Jones . . . *Review:* Howard Mumford Jones, "A New Jean Stafford," *New York Times Book Review* 52 (March 2, 1947): 5.

265 "It is . . . mysterious": John Betjeman, *London Daily Herald,* March 30, 1948.

265 The only . . . Desperate": "Colorado Adventure," *Time* 49 (March 10, 1947): 100.

265 "to be left . . . up": *Parents Magazine,* August 1948.

265 "theme of . . . relationships": Jones, "A New Jean Stafford," 5.

265 "most brilliant . . . writers": Chamberlain, "Young U.S. Writers," 76, 82.

265–266 "Last year's . . . mentioned": Cyril Connolly, "Introduction," *Horizon* (London) 93–94 (October 1947): 5.

266 At the last . . . thousand: JS to Frichtel, [late December 1946], CUSC.

266 The press . . . it: Annie Laurie Williams to JS, November 29, 1946, CUSC.

266 " 'Her Dead . . . hate": JS to Lowell, [n.d.], #1156, HL.

266 "*Then you* . . . whole": Lowell, *Lord Weary's Castle and The Mills,* 104–105.

266–267 the most . . . Hardwick: Hamilton, *Robert Lowell,* 421–427.

267 "*Can you* . . . *alone!*": Lowell, "Her Dead Brother," manuscript draft, HL.

267 In fact . . . *us*": Lowell, *The Mills of the Kavanaughs,* manuscript drafts, HL.

267 after the . . . uncle: Genesis 29–30.

268 "I just . . . me": Pinkham, interview with DR.

268 *Life* photographed . . . Zoo: Simpson, *Poets in Their Youth,* 152.

268 She lunched . . . cocktails: JS to Frichtel, [postmarked February 2(?), 1947], CUSC.

268 The Harcourt . . . *Lion:* JS to Frichtel, [late March 1947], CUSC.

268 Rebelling mildly . . . pieces": JS to Lowell, [n.d.], #1171, HL.

268 "to dismantle our house": JS to Hightower, [early 1948].

269 Her therapist . . . well: JS to Frichtel, [postmarked February 11, 1947], CUSC.

269 "I, unlike . . . alcoholic": JS to Lowell, [n.d.], #1155, HL.

269 In April . . . Congress: Hamilton, *Robert Lowell,* 124.

269 Lowell had . . . town' ": JS to Frichtel, [late March 1947], CUSC.

269 Lowell apparently . . . Mills: Buckman to Lowell, [n.d.], #288, HL.

270 "There was . . . right": JS to Lowell, [n.d.], #1171, HL.

270–271 For the first . . . deeply": ibid.

271 "To be . . . six": JS to Lowell, [n.d.], #1162, HL.

Pages

271 It was not . . . together": Buckman, interview with DR.

271–272 Lowell had . . . lesbian: Hamilton, *Robert Lowell,* 131–135.

272 She took . . . you": F—— L—— to JS, October 24, 1947, CUSC.

272 She arranged . . . up": JS to Lowell, [n.d.], #1167, HL.

CHAPTER XIV

274 "nearly died . . . ambition": JS to Lowell, [n.d.], #1168, HL.

274 " 'belletristic if . . . bad": JS to Lowell, [n.d.], #1186, HL.

274 As she . . . debt: JS to Lowell, [n.d.], #1168, HL.

274–275 On November . . . September: Harcourt, Brace to JS, November 28, 1947, CUSC.

275 Two weeks . . . contract: Harcourt, Brace to Marian Ives, March 20 and April 12, 1948, Harcourt Brace Jovanovich files.

275 On December . . . *Yorker:* Katharine White to JS, August 18, 1948, CUSC.

275 At the time . . . accepted: R. Hawley Truax to JS, December 10, 1947, CUSC.

275 By the time . . . Labor: ibid.; White to Ives, December 12, 1947, CUSC.

276 "remarkable reviser": Davis, *Onward and Upward,* 154.

276 In the first . . . bonus: White to JS, August 18, 1948, CUSC.

276 Peter Davison . . . write": Davison, interview with DR.

276 "seemed to . . . Colorado": Davison to William Leary, April 26, 1986.

276–277 The story . . . experience": JS, "Children Are Bored on Sunday," *CS,* 373–383.

277 "Practically everybody . . . job!": Brendan Gill to JS, August 24, 1948, CUSC.

277 She was . . . desired: JS to Hightower, [ca. December 1947]; JS to Lowell, [n.d.], #1168, HL.

277–278 Stafford may . . . counterclockwise": JS, "Truth in Fiction," 4562.

278 Stafford had . . . subjects: JS to Lowell, [n.d.], #1185, HL.

278 It was a . . . nose: JS to Lowell, [n.d.], #1167 and #1168, HL.

278 When she . . . notes: JS, "Truth in Fiction," 4557, 4662.

278 For an article . . . day' ": Carol Taylor, "Girls Write Their Different Tickets."

279 But the . . . cell: JS, "Truth in Fiction," 4557–4558; JS, "Mr. Rohmer," 1–3.

279 "was really . . . lawyers": JS to Frichtel, [postmarked April 10, 1948], CUSC.

279–280 The lawyers . . . fees: JS and Lowell, divorce agreement, March 1948, HL.

280 "PULL YOURSELF . . . EVER": Mary Jane Sherfey to JS, telegram, April 28, 1948, CUSC.

Pages

280 "First, there . . . Drinking": Sherfey to JS, May 20, 1948, CUSC.

280 "I am . . . pitch": JS to Lowell, [n.d.], #1190, HL.

280 "They fish . . . seen": JS to Lowell, [n.d.], #1192, HL.

281 "for two . . . bourbon?' ": Flagg, "People to Stay," 68.

281 One night . . . husband: JS to Lowell, [n.d.], #1193, HL.

281 On June 14 . . . name: JS, complaint for divorce action, June 7, 1948; JS and Lowell, divorce decree, June 14, 1948, HL.

281 In August . . . love": Engle, "Lost Love," 4.

281 "Another reason . . . anyone": JS to Frichtel, [postmarked April 10, 1948], CUSC.

281–282 Several years . . . drinker: Oliver Jensen, interview with DR, 1985.

282 Eileen Simpson . . . gala: Simpson, *Poets in Their Youth,* 163–164.

282 On April 15 . . . honesty": JS to Frichtel, April 15, 1949, CUSC.

282 In May . . . Lowell: JS to Lowell, [n.d.], #1193, HL.

283 "that I . . . late": JS to Lowell, [n.d.], #1168, HL.

283 "I love . . . cold": JS, "Sisterhood," unfinished essay, CUSC.

283 "The direct . . . composers": JS, "What is your feeling about me?," typescript, CUSC.

284 It was . . . valid: Hamilton, *Robert Lowell,* 142–161.

284 "I am going . . . boy": JS to Frichtel, [postmarked April 12, 1949], CUSC.

284 "a religious . . . prayer": JS to Frichtel, April 15, 1949, CUSC.

285 "My book . . . way": JS to Frichtel, [postmarked July 5, 1949], CUSC.

285 "I am in . . . know": JS to Frichtel, [postmarked June 10, 1949], CUSC.

285 "just this . . . rapture": JS to Lowell, [n.d.], #1195, HL.

285–286 "The Haarlass . . . man": JS, "Letter from Germany," 86–87.

286 "The greatest . . . ocean": JS to Lowell, [n.d.], #1167, HL.

286 "get me . . . drinking": JS to Lowell, [n.d.], #1186, HL.

287 Years later . . . Greene: Berton Roueché, interview with DR, 1986.

287 "I liked . . . her": Graham Greene to DR, December 2, 1987.

287 Stafford also . . . Scotland: Stillman, Auchincloss, Joseph Mitchell (1985), interviews with DR.

287 "I find . . . friends?": JS to Lowell, [n.d.], #1194, HL.

287–288 At a party . . . *War:* Jensen, interview with DR.

288 "He took . . . dazzled": Stillman, interview with DR.

288 The editor's . . . accepted: Jensen, interview with DR.

288 On January 28 . . . Manhattan: JS and Jensen, marriage certificate, January 28, 1950, CUSC.

288 As they . . . last' ": White, note appended to White to JS, August 29, 1948, CUSC.

288 "She always . . . 21": Katinka De Vries, interview with DR, 1985.

288 "He was . . . CU": Mitchell, interview with DR.

288 "only been . . . minutes": Berton Roueché, interview with DR.

288 once, when . . . her": Jensen, interview with DR.

288–289 Stafford was . . . details: JS, "Enchanted Island."

Pages

289 For thirty-five . . . barn: Jensen, interview with DR.

289 "It was . . . attractive": Stillman, interview with DR.

289 "She used . . . Stillman: ibid.

289 Peter De Vries . . . doctors: Peter De Vries, interview with DR.

289 Stafford had . . . *Willows:* Jensen, interview with DR.

289 "Dear Pode . . . Beaner": JS to Jensen, [n.d.], CUSC.

289–290 "My own . . . Honey": JS to Jensen, [postmarked April 4, 1950], CUSC.

290 Jensen heard . . . communion: Jensen, interview with DR.

290 "I hope . . . invalid": JS to Jensen, January 19, 1950, CUSC.

290 "used to . . . red' ": Stillman, interview with DR.

290 "She was . . . out": Jensen, interview with DR.

290 In 1950–1951 . . . operation: JS, medical history, [ca. October 1963], Thomas Roberts files.

290–292 Jensen was . . . problem: Jensen, interview with DR.

292 Martha Foley . . . work: The others were "The Interior Castle" (1947), "Children Are Bored on Sunday" (1949), and "The Healthiest Girl in Town" (1952).

292 "She couldn't . . . remainder": Jensen, interview with DR.

292–293 In July 1950 . . . December: White to JS, July 28, 1950, CUSC.

293 During the . . . respectively: White to JS, January 19 and August 4, 1951, CUSC.

293 Finally, in . . . manuscript: JS, "Truth and the Novelist," 188–189.

294 A week . . . book: ibid., 189.

294 "I cannot . . . cradles": JS to Jensen, [August 1951], CUSC.

295 "I'd keep . . . hell": Harry Frichtel, interview with DR.

295 According to . . . home: Pinkham, "Jean Stafford's Family," 63.

295 In 1949 . . . day: JS to Mary Lee Frichtel, [postmarked June 10, 1949], CUSC.

295 "became angry . . . that": Pinkham, "Jean Stafford's Family," 62–63.

295 "very attractive . . . bumpkin": Stillman, interview with DR.

295 In 1944 . . . elicited: Paul Thompson, diary, October 29, 1944.

295–296 "It is . . . way' ": JS to Frichtel, [postmarked April 10, 1948], CUSC.

296 "On this . . . Harry": Pinkham, "Jean Stafford's Family," 62.

296 "Jean didn't . . . guess": Harry Frichtel, interview with DR.

296 "Jean Stafford . . . writer": *Boulder Daily Camera,* July 22, 1952.

297 "I was . . . again: Walton, interview with DR.

297 She claimed . . . dorm: JS to Stillman, June 30 and August 19, 1952; JS to Jensen, [postmarked July 24, 1952], CUSC.

297 "Jean's talk . . . heart": Paul Thompson, diary, July 22, 1952.

297–298 "The night . . . stage": Fitz-Randolph, interview with DR.

298 "too hideous . . . boring": JS to Mary Lee Frichtel, [postmarked March 12, 1951], CUSC.

298 In September . . . guilt?": JS to Frichtel, [postmarked September 12, 1951], CUSC.

Pages

298 "Marriage is . . . are": Peter De Vries, interview with DR.

298 "She started . . . time: Clark, interview with DR.

298 "That's simply . . . woman": Jensen to DR, December 7, 1987.

298 "The battles . . . mother": Jensen, interview with DR.

298 "my incurable . . . conclusion": JS to Frichtel, [spring 1952], CUSC.

298–299 "He is . . . afternoon": JS to Frichtel, [postmarked September 23, 1951], CUSC.

299 "I refuse . . . quiet": JS to Frichtel, [postmarked October 29, 1951], CUSC.

299 "As we . . . Mrs.": Jensen, interview with DR.

299 "At some point . . . graffito": Sheed, "Miss Jean Stafford," 94.

299 "I am . . . page: JS to Jensen, [n.d.], CUSC.

299 He wrote . . . painful": Jensen to Sherfey, February 22, 1952, CUSC.

299–300 she said . . . Boulder: Paul Thompson, diary, August 3, 4, and 12, 1952.

300 "I hope . . . me": JS to Jensen, August 9, 1952, CUSC.

300 One night . . . home: Jensen, interview with DR.

300 She donated . . . cause: JS, canceled check, October 17, 1952, CUSC.

300 "congratulation, rue . . . responsible": JS to Adlai Stevenson, [postmarked November 11, 1952], Joan Stillman files.

300 She had . . . hysterectomy: Jensen, interview with DR; Jensen to Frichtel, November 18, 1952, CUSC.

301 When Jensen . . . New York City: Stillman, interview with DR.

CHAPTER XV

302–303 "This decision . . . Christmas: Jensen to Frichtel, November 18, 1952, CUSC.

303 An extravagant . . . hostess: Peter De Vries, Stillman, interviews with DR.

305 "Between the . . . understand": JS, *CW,* 15–16.

306 "all I . . . one": JS to Frichtel, September 23, 1951, CUSC.

306 She admitted . . . it: Peter De Vries, interview with DR.

306 "This technically . . . life": Orville Prescott, *New York Times,* [date unknown].

306 "As a story . . . story": Anthony West, "Books: 'Parsifal' in Modern Dress," *The New Yorker* 27 (January 12, 1952): 81.

306 In the week . . . list: *New York Times,* February 3, 1952.

306–307 After three . . . unwritten: Harcourt, Brace to JS, May 9, 1952, CUSC.

307 She stayed . . . stories: Flagg, "People to Stay," 70–72.

308 February 20, 1953: *New York News,* February 21, 1953.

308 "After a . . . suited": Jensen, interview with DR.

308 "a harrowing . . . path": JS to Stillman, June 20, 1953.

Pages

308 "I wish . . . me": Jensen to JS, April 1, 1953, CUSC.

308 A year . . . friends": Jensen to JS, February 26, [1954], CUSC.

308 "I can't . . . anyone": JS to Jensen, January 17, 1950, CUSC.

308 The place . . . papers: Stillman, interview with DR.

308 Visiting her . . . stories: Moss, "Jean: Some Fragments," 79.

308 "Jean was . . . visitors": Jensen, interview with DR.

309 "I now. . . distinguished": JS to Blair and Holly Clark, [n.d.].

309 "My dear . . . shy": JS to Lowell, [n.d.], #1198, HL.

310 " 'There wasn't . . . meant' ": Stillman, notes of interview with JS, 4.

310 For an obscure . . . visible: JS, "George Eliot."

310 "As he . . . result": JS to Ann Honeycutt, [ca. August 1956], CUSC.

310 "There is . . . needlepoint": JS to Blair and Holly Clark, [n.d.].

311 "Jean, why . . . El Dora": John Stafford to JS, February 1, 1955, CUSC.

311 By the next . . . controversy?": John Stafford to JS, February 1954, CUSC.

311 "He had . . . listen": Pinkham, interview with DR.

313 " 'I'm making . . . grub' ": JS, "Treasures of Use and Beauty," unpublished story, CUSC.

314 Peter Davison . . . mind: Davison, interview with DR.

314 On the eve . . . agreement: JS to Albert Erskine, [January 1953], BL.

314 "a narrative . . . ending": JS to Jensen, [January 1953], CUSC.

314 In May 1953 . . . advance: JS to Harcourt, Brace, March 19, 1953, Harcourt Brace Jovanovich files.

314 But the . . . Ives: JS and Harcourt, Brace, various letters and memos, September–October 1953, Harcourt Brace Jovanovich files.

315 Viking, Random . . . novel: Alexander Lindey to JS, various letters, fall 1953, CUSC.

315 On October 23 . . . 1955: Random House contract with JS, October 23, 1953, JOB files, BL.

315 Stafford had . . . months": JS to Jensen, March 1954, CUSC.

315 "I'd call . . . when": JS to Erskine, [n.d.], BL.

315–316 At the beginning . . . Auchincloss: JOB, interview with DR, 1985.

316 For a year . . . fees: various letters, JOB files, BL.

316 "*Sell* today . . . mistakes": JS to JOB, July 16, 1956, JOB files, BL.

316 "Jean is . . . meantime": JOB to Alvin Manuel, July 2, 1957, JOB files, BL.

316–317 "Those dumb-bell . . . cat": JS to JOB, October 13, [1956], JOB files, BL.

317 Brown faithfully . . . impasse: JOB and *Life,* various letters, 1956–1957, JOB files, BL.

317 "a tumor . . . thumb": JS to Jensen, [spring 1956], CUSC.

317 "a monstrous . . . years": JS to JOB, [July 1956], JOB files, BL.

317–318 "I'd forgotten . . . harrowing": JS to Stillman, June 15, 1956.

Pages

318 "in an . . . story": JS to Hightower, May 29, [1959?].

318 Drinking at . . . hydrate: JS to William Maxwell, July 20, [1956].

318 "It does . . . hotel": JS to Honeycutt, July 16, [1956], CUSC.

318 By chance . . . decades: Auchincloss, interview with DR.

318 "We found . . . up": White to JS, July 29, [1956], CUSC.

318–319 Stafford happened . . . staying: Sokolov, *Wayward Reporter*, 268–278.

319 It was . . . New York": JS, "New York Is a Daisy," 126.

319 "always so . . . money": Honeycutt, interview with DR.

319 "The other . . . time": JS to Jensen, June 25, [1957], CUSC.

319 With Joseph . . . Island: Mitchell, interview with DR.

320 "She had . . . end": Auchincloss, interview with DR.

320 A. J. Liebling . . . inseparable: Sokolov, *Wayward Reporter*, 278, 283.

320 In December 1955 . . . incident: Davis, *Onward and Upward*, 6–8.

321 "It is . . . block": White, note added to White to JS, December 22, 1955, CUSC.

321 In 1953 . . . person": White to JS, May 11, 1953, and December 2, 1954, CUSC.

321 Her painful . . . it: White to JS, September 30, 1957, CUSC.

321 In succession . . . it: JOB files, October 1957–July 1958, BL.

321 "If I . . . time": JS to JOB, October 12, [1957], JOB files, BL.

321 "Jean wanted . . . editors: Taylor, interview with DR.

322 "The C———s' . . . dinner": JS, untitled, unpublished essay, CUSC.

322 " 'It's gotten . . . Fashioned' ": Parker, interview with DR.

322–323 Joseph Mitchell . . . hangover' ": Mitchell, interview with DR.

323 "I would . . . herself": ibid.

323 "She called . . . came": Auchincloss, interview with DR.

CHAPTER XVI

324–326 By the time . . . failed: Sokolov, *Wayward Reporter, passim.*

325 His coworker . . . satisfaction": Brendan Gill, *Here at The New Yorker* (New York: Berkeley Medallion Books, 1975), 344.

325 "She held . . . him": Sokolov, *Wayward Reporter*, 236.

326 buying her a mink stole: Peter De Vries, interview with DR.

326 "He was . . . greaseball": Honeycutt, interview with DR.

326 "obscenely fat . . . belly": Auchincloss, interview with DR.

326–327 "Not the . . . delight": Simpson, *Poets in Their Youth*, 247.

327 "I want . . . us": A. J. Liebling to JS, December 13, 1956; quoted in Sokolov, *Wayward Reporter*, 283.

327 Katharine White . . . London: White to JS, August 8, 1957, CUSC.

327 Liebling's chivalry . . . Wheel": JS to JOB, [received September 16, 1956], JOB files, BL.

327–328 "all speaking . . . Brussels: JS to Honeycutt, September 16, [1957], CUSC.

328 Sokolov assumes . . . Lucille: Sokolov, *Wayward Reporter*, 290.

Pages

328 "something like . . . romance": Jensen, interview with DR.

328 "We kept . . . room": Sokolov, *Wayward Reporter,* 290, 298.

328 With the . . . up": ibid., 298–300.

328 He took . . . trainers: JS to Tom Hightower, [n.d.].

328 "His pleasure . . . time": Sokolov, *Wayward Reporter,* 300.

328–329 Although he . . . *Observer:* ibid., 300–303, 307–308.

329 "On a winter . . . sleep": JS, Samothrace manuscript, CUSC.

329–330 since 1940 . . . dreams: JS, unfinished essay on dreams, CUSC.

330 She had . . . adventures: JS to Robert Hightower, September 21, [1959].

330 On Arran . . . visual": JS, Samothrace manuscript, CUSC.

330 "when she . . . away": Liebling to Joseph and Therese Mitchell, October 1, 1959; quoted in Sokolov, *Wayward Reporter,* 308.

330 "If I . . . writer": JS to JOB, September 22, [1959], JOB files, BL.

331 "She should . . . adventures": Liebling to JOB, [ca. October 30, 1959], courtesy of Joseph Mitchell.

331 "I was . . . him": Sokolov, *Wayward Reporter,* 299.

331 The BBC . . . down: John Van Bibber to JS, [n.d.] and May 15, 1958, JOB files, Butler Library.

331 Stafford received . . . Lottery": JS, bar tabs, March 24 and 29, 1959, and JOB memo, April 1, 1959, JOB files, BL.

331–332 Even so . . . nothing": JS, "Isak Dinesen," 110–113.

332 *Holiday* asked . . . no: JOB memo, January 1961, JOB files, BL.

332 In 1960. . . published: note cards, JOB files.

332 "Like baklava . . . me": JS, "Movies: War and Peace," 121–122.

332 "I was flown . . . memories": JS to Hightower, September 7, [1961].

332 The magazine . . . it: note cards, JOB files.

332 Even as she . . . *Griffin:* ibid.

332–333 One of these . . . essay: JS, "The Eat Generation," 33–34.

333 The *Atlantic* . . . *Reporter:* note cards, JOB files.

333 One feeler . . . English": Buckman to JOB, August 10, 1961, JOB files, BL.

333 In 1961 . . . administration: JOB memo, April 13, 1961, JOB files, BL.

333 The first . . . effect: JS, "Bobette," unpublished story, CUSC.

333 "Venus" is . . . days: JS, "Venus," unpublished story, CUSC.

334 " 'Who was . . . quote' ": ibid.

334 turned down . . . *Post:* JOB memos, March 12 and May 21, 1963, JOB files, BL.

334 which may . . . *Yorker:* White to JS, January 12, 1958, CUSC.

334–335 "I hate . . . life' ": JS, "Young Writers," 16, 23.

335 "The greatest . . . happy": E. B. White to Joan Wintercome, November 28, 1977, CUSC.

335 "He had . . . her": Auchincloss, interview with DR.

335 "Liebling, with . . . anywhere": Sheed, "Miss Jean Stafford," 95.

335 The consummate . . . out: Pierre Guedenet, interview with DR, 1986.

Pages

335 Howard Moss . . . could' ": Moss, "Jean: Some Fragments," 80.

336 "As time went . . . Liebling": Sokolov, *Wayward Reporter*, 310.

336 "Liebling would . . . one": Auchincloss, interview with DR.

336 "Joe is . . . free": JS to Hightower, May 29, [1959?].

336 "Quite often . . . him": JS to Hightower, July 1, [1962?].

336 On another . . . well": Hightower, interview with DR.

336 "Liebling always . . . Lowell": Clark, interview with DR.

336 With or . . . property: Sokolov, *Wayward Reporter*, 237–238, 310.

336–337 By 1962 . . . Street: Sokolov, *Wayward Reporter*, 314.

337 "Neither of . . . there": Janet Malcolm, interview with DR, 1985.

337 Eve Auchincloss . . . tendencies: Auchincloss, interview with DR.

337 One of . . . food: Guedenet, *Alger Hiss* (1986), interviews with DR.

337 "He was . . . pie": Malcolm, interview with DR.

337 "At the center . . . grace": Sokolov, *Wayward Reporter*, 306.

337 "fags who . . . around": Malcolm, interview with DR.

337 "a very . . . couldn't": Clark, interview with DR.

338 "the acne . . . hysterectomy: JS to Honeycutt, July 9, [1962], CUSC.

338 In October 1963 . . . Roberts: JS, medical history, [ca. October 1963], Thomas Roberts files.

338 "God damn . . . hike?": JS to Frichtel, [postmarked September (5?), 1958], CUSC.

339 "I can . . . Speak!' ": Mitchell, interview with DR.

339 "these sessions . . . away": Moss, "Jean: Some Fragments," 81.

339 "Jean shot . . . dead!' ": Cavett, "The Cavett Album — II," 97.

339 In 1960 . . . House": JS, "The Jabberwock Anatomized," 2.

339 Typical of these . . . manners: JOB memo, February 7, 1958, JOB files, BL.

339 Auchincloss indicates . . . Colorado: Auchincloss, interview with DR.

339 She let . . . it: Moss, "Jean: Some Fragments," 80.

339–340 In the files . . . Arran: JS, Samothrace manuscript, CUSC.

340 She received . . . copies: Farrar, Straus & Cudahy contract for JS, *Elephi*, August 4, 1961, JOB files, BL.

340–341 This brief . . . loneliness: JS, *Elephi, passim.*

341 "Dear Mrs. . . . one": Student to JS, April 10, 1967, CUSC.

341 Nevertheless, the . . . red: JOB to JS, March 29, 1963, CUSC.

341 She complained . . . book: JOB memo, November 21, 1962, JOB files, BL.

341 Stafford came . . . wanted: JS and Farrar, Straus & Cudahy, various letters, 1962, JOB files, BL.

341 For another . . . *Nights:* Macmillan contract for JS, *Arabian Nights*, March 1, 1962, JOB files, BL.

341 "If there . . . this": JOB to JS, January 4, 1962, JOB files, BL.

341–342 In 1962 . . . revival' ": JS to Honeycutt, [postmarked February 27, 1962], CUSC.

342 Liebling had . . . award: A. J. Liebling, "A Small Argument," *Show*, August 1962.

Pages

342 Gay Talese . . . book: [Gay Talese], "Story of a Novel: How It Won Prize," *New York Times,* March 15, 1962: 25.

342 Liebling, Stafford . . . apology: Hallowell Bowser, "A Season of Discontent," *Saturday Review* 45 (October 6, 1962): 22–23.

342 as it was . . . Kazin: Alfred Kazin, "The Pilgrimage of Walker Percy," *Harper's* 242 (June 1971): 81–86.

343 "For a . . . Lion: JS to Erskine, May 31, [1962], BL.

343 "Since becoming . . . published: Erskine to JS, June 7, 1962, BL.

343 "They are . . . her: JOB to JS, August 15, 1962, JOB files, BL.

343 When he . . . interest: Donald Klopfer to JS, June 18, 1962, JOB files, BL.

343 "I have . . . relented: JOB to Klopfer, June 21, 1962, JOB files, BL.

344 "I can't . . . with": Berton Roueché, interview with DR.

344 By May . . . 1964: Farrar, Straus & Cudahy contract with JS, May 1, 1963, JOB files, BL.

344 "You have . . . gambling": JOB to JS, June 27, 1962, JOB files, BL.

344 Meanwhile, Stafford . . . today: Auchincloss, interview with DR.

344–345 By 1963 . . . car: Sokolov, *Wayward Reporter,* 319.

345 In the Allied . . . it: Pinkham, interview with DR.

345 During their . . . edge": Sokolov, *Wayward Reporter,* 319–320.

345 On December 20 . . . alc.": Roberts, notes on JS, December 20, 1963, Thomas Roberts files.

345 Stafford tried . . . escape": Cavett, "The Cavett Album — II," 96.

345 On December 27 . . . French": Sokolov, *Wayward Reporter,* 320.

345 Eve Auchincloss . . . her: Auchincloss, interview with DR.

345 "Liebling's death . . . gone": Sheed, "Miss Jean Stafford," 95.

CHAPTER XVII

346 Two days . . . chapel: Sokolov, *Wayward Reporter,* 321–323.

346 Stafford had . . . Newport: JS, "East Hampton," 13.

346 " 'By the . . . cents' ": Stillman, interview with DR.

346 "Jean said . . . plan: Katherine Roueché, interview with DR, 1986.

347 She essentially . . . out": Roberts, medical summary on JS, January 26, 1964, Thomas Roberts files.

347 "I am incommunicado . . . Vermont": JS to Frichtel, January 14, [1964], CUSC.

347 When she . . . depression: Roberts, notes on JS, February 5, 1964, Thomas Roberts files.

347 "More distraught . . . drinking": Roberts, notes on JS, February 19, 1964, Thomas Roberts files.

347 At the end . . . wrist: JS to Hightower, December 14, [1964].

347 The moving . . . Street: JS to Hightower, February 7, [1964].

347 when suddenly . . . consciousness: JS to Hightower, December 14, [1964].

Pages

347–348 A doctor . . . Hospital: Roberts, interview with DR.

348 There she . . . attack: Roberts, medical summary on JS, May 9, 1964, Thomas Roberts files.

348 For ten . . . pacemaker: JS to Hightower, December 14, [1964].

348 In the midst . . . attack: Roberts, medical summary on JS, May 9, 1964, Thomas Roberts files.

348 On her discharge . . . stresses": Roberts to JS, June 1, 1964.

348 "as sort of a shack": John Thompson, interview with DR.

348–349 To her neighbor . . . study: Eleanor Hempstead, interview with DR, 1985.

349 Upstairs, on . . . journalism: Whitman, "Jean Stafford and Her Secretary," 78.

349–350 As a young . . . it": Sheed, "Miss Jean Stafford," 98.

350 When Stafford . . . cellar: Roberts, interview with DR.

350 "One of . . . events": Hiss, interview with DR.

350 "Jean never . . . something": Hempstead, interview with DR.

350–351 She also . . . procrastination": Honeycutt, Auchincloss, interviews with DR.

351 "embarked on . . . interior": Moss, "Jean: Some Fragments," 81.

351 "God, she . . . people": Auchincloss, interview with DR.

351 For some . . . summer: JS to Mary Jarrell, January 12, [1966?], Berg Collection.

351 She continued . . . Liebling": Mitchell, interview with DR.

351 Between August . . . hospital: Roberts to Charlotte Goodman, March 20, 1985; Roberts, medical summary on JS, March 19, 1965, Thomas Roberts files.

351–352 Stafford had . . . toes": Roberts, notes on JS, October 14 and December 4 and 29, 1964, Thomas Roberts files; Roberts, interview with DR.

352 four years . . . it: note cards, JOB files.

352 *Town & Country* . . . No": JOB to JS (and JS, note to JOB), September 21, 1965, JOB files, BL.

352 *Venture,* a . . . fiction": JOB to JS, August 7, 1964; JS to JOB, August 15, [1964], JOB files, BL.

352–353 "usually," says . . . did": Auchincloss, interview with DR.

353 "subterranean hatreds . . . zoos": JS, review of *My Heart Is Broken,* 56.

353 "And like . . . cold-bloodedly": JS, review of *The Words,* 98.

353 Despite her . . . it: JS to Auchincloss, various letters, 1967–1975.

353 Appraising Andrew . . . Wolfe: JS, "Wolfe Hunting," 17–20.

353–354 All the . . . imaginable": JS, review of *May We Borrow Your Husband?,* 78.

354 "hooligans . . . realm": JS, note, CUSC.

354 The libraries . . . Colorado: Liebling file, CUSC.

355 In 1964 . . . Studies: JS to JOB, July 7, [1964], JOB files, BL.

355 She was . . . Wilson: JS to The President, Con Edison, July 20, 1968, JOB files, BL.

Pages

355 Stafford had . . . years": JS to Frichtel, [postmarked August 25, 1964], CUSC.

355 She played . . . companion: Roberts, notes on JS, April 28, 1965, Thomas Roberts files.

355 In Joseph Mitchell's . . . professors": Mitchell, interview with DR.

355 In March 1965 . . . assassin: JOB to JS, March 16, 1965, JOB files, BL.

355 again on the wagon: Berton Roueché, interview with DR.

355–356 "What I . . . commentary": JS, "Truth in Fiction," 4564–4565.

356 " 'Lee purely . . . sad' ": JS, *A Mother in History,* 23.

356 Stafford's fascination . . . friends: Roberts, Guedenet, interviews with DR.

356 Within three . . . hardback: Farrar, Straus & Giroux contract for JS, *A Mother in History,* October 21, 1965; JOB to JS, April 26 and June 3, 1966, JOB files, BL.

356 "a masterpiece . . . journalism": "Mama Oswald," *Newsweek* 67 (February 28, 1966): 92A–94.

356 "Miss Stafford . . . other": Godfrey Hodgson, "Mrs. O. and Miss S.," *Observer* (London), September 11, 1966, 26.

357 *Cosmopolitan* wanted . . . camp": JOB to JS, November 29, 1965, JOB files, BL.

357 the *Saturday* . . . Loveless": JOB to Thomas B. Congden, July 29, 1966, JOB files, BL.

357 *Esquire* longed . . . Weekending": JOB, note, [ca. February 25, 1966], JOB files, BL.

357 Stafford got . . . offers: JOB to John R. Humphreys, March 1, 1966, JOB files, BL.

357 J. B. Lippincott . . . hypochondria: Tay Hohoff to JOB, December 7, 1965, JOB files, BL.

357 Putnam's thought . . . first: JOB to JS, December 1, 1965, and September 21, 1966, JOB files, BL.

357 For *McCall's* . . . piece: JOB to *McCall's,* October 8 and 11, 1965, JOB files, BL.

357 Her profile . . . house: JS, "Portrait: Ward Bennett," 44–47.

357 She had . . . malignancy: Roberts, medical summary on JS, December 10, 1964, Thomas Roberts files.

357 further surgery . . . neuroma: Roberts, notes on JS, November 24, 1965, Thomas Roberts files.

357 In 1967 . . . insecticide: JS to Auchincloss, [n.d.]; JS to JOB, September 7, 1965, JOB files, BL.

357 Spinal problems . . . head: Paul Thompson, diary, November 13, 1967.

357 were followed . . . accident: JS to Hightower, April 5, 1969; JS to Bunny Hightower, [n.d.].

358 "She was . . . cancer": Honeycutt, interview with DR.

358 "jack-knifed in . . . York: JS, "The Snows of Yesteryear," unpublished manuscript of Barnard lecture, CUSC.

Pages

358 "9/8/65 . . . drinking": Roberts, notes on JS, Thomas Roberts files.

358 By 1965 . . . her: Roberts, medical summary on JS, March 19, 1965, Thomas Roberts files.

358 and by the . . . day: Roberts, notes on JS, March 31, 1969, Thomas Roberts files.

358–359 One day . . . it": Roberts, interview with DR.

359 It comes . . . A.A.": Hempstead, interview with DR.

359 When Dick . . . seducer' ": Cavett, "The Cavett Album — II," 100.

359 "I think . . . Jean": Berton Roueché, interview with DR.

359 "Although I . . . manage": JS to Jacques Quen, March 7, 1967, Thomas Roberts files.

359 The psychiatrist . . . antidepressant: Quen to Roberts, March 8 and 16, 1967, Thomas Roberts files.

359 "the insane asylum": JOB to JS, April 20, 1967, JOB files, BL.

359 "Each time . . . mystery": JS to Frichtel, [postmarked August 25, 1964], CUSC.

359–360 Finally, at the . . . year: Pinkham, "Jean Stafford's Family," 62–64.

360 When Mary Lee . . . collect: Barbara Hale, interview with DR, 1986.

360 " 'There'll never . . . ever' ": Stillman, interview with DR.

360 "I never . . . men": Auchincloss, interview with DR.

360 "I think . . . underneath": Honeycutt, interview with DR.

360 Stafford's easy . . . hag": Roberts, interview with DR.

360 "They were . . . gossip": John Thompson, interview with DR.

360 " 'And then . . . literature' ": Auchincloss, interview with DR.

361 " 'I had . . . me' ": Taylor, interview with DR.

361 " 'Tell him . . . time' ": Clark, interview with DR.

361 "It was . . . be": Roberts, interview with DR.

361 Eve Auchincloss . . . arrive: Auchincloss, interview with DR.

361 "She was . . . men: Hempstead, interview with DR.

361 When Randall . . . Mary: JS to Mary Jarrell, October 17, 1965, and January 12, [1966?], Berg Collection.

361 Yet not . . . soprano": JS to Honeycutt, [n.d.], CUSC.

362 "She could . . . much": Roberts, interview with DR.

362 "I'm afraid . . . home: Mitchell, interview with DR.

362 Several of Jean's . . . surroundings: Berton Roueché, Malcolm, interviews with DR.

362 it could . . . stage: Roberts, interview with DR.

362 At New York . . . returned: Jean Hoffman, interview with DR, 1986.

362 "I think . . . South": Honeycutt, interview with DR.

362 Once, after . . . Yankees": Mitchell, interview with DR.

362 It is Howard . . . nose: Moss, "Jean: Some Fragments," 78.

362 According to . . . looks: Hale, interview with DR.

362 On another occasion . . . waitress: Moss, "Jean: Some Fragments," 78.

362 or, as Eve . . . taste: Auchincloss, interview with DR.

363 "clad in . . . lonely": Straus, "Jean Stafford," 86.

363 In East Hampton . . . opinion: John Thompson, interview with DR.

Pages

363 One of . . . more": Hempstead, interview with DR.

363 Wilfrid Sheed . . . over": Sheed, "Miss Jean Stafford," 95.

363 Yet Stafford . . . remains: Hempstead, interview with DR.

363 Stafford admitted . . . depressions' ": Eckman, "Adding a Pulitzer," 21.

363 In a newspaper . . . closet: JS, "East Hampton," 13.

363 She began . . . space": JS to Bunny Hightower, [n.d.].

364 In 1970 . . . overnight: Liebling file, CUSC; Hempstead, interview with DR.

364 "I find . . . recluse": Stewart, "Author Adds a Pulitzer."

364 Stafford claimed . . . lunch: Eckman, "Adding a Pulitzer," 21.

364 "When you'd . . . time": Auchincloss, interview with DR.

364 Stafford had . . . Springs: Eckman, "Adding a Pulitzer," 13.

364 In her own . . . drinking' ": Roberts, interview with DR.

364 "I'd get . . . weeks": Auchincloss, interview with DR.

364 She got . . . protection: Higman, interview with DR.

364 Later she . . . disturbed": Sheed, "Miss Jean Stafford," 97; Straus, "Jean Stafford," 86; Auchincloss, interview with DR.

364–365 "THE WORD . . . whatsoever": JS to Frichtel, [postmarked November 28, 1969], CUSC.

365 Stafford was . . . humor": Sheed, "Miss Jean Stafford," 97–98.

365 She even . . . letters: The stamp is now in the possession of Joseph Mitchell.

365 "Miss Stafford . . . wardrobe": JS to JOB, carbon enclosed in JS to Honeycutt, [n.d.], CUSC.

365–366 In 1969 . . . Denham": JS to JOB, carbon enclosed in JS to Honeycutt, [postmarked February 1, 1970], CUSC.

366 From her . . . old: White to JS, August 20, 1968, CUSC.

366 "She said . . . *Yorker*' ": Katherine Roueché, interview with DR.

366 For *Boy's Life* . . . adolescence: JS, "Mountain Jim."

366 For *Vogue* . . . Bennett: JS, "To School with Joy."

366–367 In 1968 . . . pages: JS to The President, Con Edison, July 20, 1968, JOB files, BL; JS, "Once upon a time," 31.

367 Her neighbor . . . Javits: Hoffman, interview with DR.

367–368 Peter Taylor . . . went: Taylor, interview with DR.

368 She rented . . . writing: JS to JOB, [ca. June 28, 1967], JOB files, BL; JS to Robert Hightower, October 12, [1967].

368 "cretinous": JS to Mary Elizabeth O'Rourke, February 12, 1969, CUSC.

368 "I didn't . . . frivolous": JS to Howard Mumford Jones, March 3, [year unknown], HL.

368 " 'I have . . . *Narcissus*?' ": JS, "Intimations of Hope," 118.

368 she was . . . Campus: JS to The President, Con Edison, July 20, 1968, JOB files, BL.

368 "mobs who . . . schools": JS, "Intimations of Hope," 118.

368–369 She liked . . . tell": JS to Jones, March 3, [year unknown], HL.

369 "attracted hordes . . . muffled": JS, "Intimations of Hope," 77.

Pages

369 In a *New* . . . women: JS, "Topics: Women as Chattels, Men as Chumps."

369 Pondering student . . . State: Stewart, "Author Adds a Pulitzer."

369–370 Yet she . . . suppress": JS, "The Good Life Is Indeed Now," 30.

370 She applauded . . . danger?": JS, "Sense and Sensibility," unpublished manuscript of Barnard lecture, CUSC.

370 She posited . . . murders: JS, "Love Among the Rattlesnakes."

370 "At the first . . . Ann": JS, "Sense and Sensibility," CUSC.

371 on June 27 . . . latter: Farrar, Straus & Giroux contract for JS, *CS,* June 27, 1968, JOB files, BL.

371 "to whose . . . allied": JS, *CS,* xii.

371 In a front-page . . . literature": Guy Davenport, *New York Times Book Review* 74 (February 16, 1969): 40.

371 "There is . . . surprisingly": Elizabeth Janeway, "The Worlds of Jean Stafford," *Atlantic Monthly* 223 (March 1969): 138.

371 "an undertone . . . alarming": Joyce Carol Oates, *Washington Post Book World,* February 9, 1969, 6.

371 "the icy privacy": Margot Hentoff, *Vogue* 154 (July 1969): 56.

371 "shattered dreams . . . imprisoned": Marion Simon, "American Exiles," *National Observer* 8 (March 10, 1969): 23.

371 "the trapped . . . mind": Thomas Lask, "Points East and West," *New York Times,* February 14, 1969, 37.

371 "obsessive themes . . . life": Irving Malin, *Commonweal* 90 (April 25, 1969): 174–175.

372 Stafford gave . . . finished: Roger Straus to JS, February 6, 1970, CUSC.

372 "Jean Stafford . . . father": "The Year of the Novel," *Time* 93 (January 3, 1969): 66.

372 Elected a . . . January: National Institute of Arts and Letters to JS, January 29, 1970, CUSC; Berton Roueché, interview with DR.

372 She checked . . . not: JS to Honeycutt, January 31, [1970], CUSC.

372 "I am in . . . stairs: JS to Auchincloss, March 28, [1970].

372 this time . . . cretinous": JS to Hempstead, February 9, 1970.

372–373 "None of them . . . story?' " JS, "On Writing," unpublished manuscript of Barnard lecture, CUSC.

373 Stafford shivered . . . top": JS to Honeycutt, [postmarked January 11, 1970], CUSC.

373 One of James . . . changes": JOB to George Walsh, December 6, 1968, JOB files, BL.

373 now Stafford . . . paid": JS to Shana Alexander, March 1, 1970, JOB files, BL.

373 *McCall's* had . . . article: note cards, JOB files.

373 On May 4 . . . fiction: Berton Roueché, Auchincloss, interviews with DR; Eckman, "Adding a Pulitzer," 21.

CHAPTER XVIII

Pages

374 "as unscatological . . . I": Pinkham, "Jean Stafford's Family," 70.

374 The *New* . . . today": *New York Times,* May 6, 1970.

374 "SUPPOSE NOW . . . IMPOSSIBLE": Peter De Vries to JS, telegram, [ca. May 5, 1970], CUSC.

374 "For a . . . down": JS to Frichtel, [postmarked May 12, 1970], CUSC.

374–375 "Everybody thinks . . . stories: Lewis, "An Interview.'

375 "that I'll . . . money": JS to Frichtel, [postmarked May 12, 1970], CUSC.

375 Farrar, Straus . . . sold: Farrar, Straus & Giroux to JS, [n.d.], CUSC.

375 Despite Stafford's . . . life: Berton Roueché, interview with DR.

375 "in a state . . . concentrate": JS to Auchincloss, May 17, 1970.

375 Among them . . . *Cosmopolitan:* JOB to JS, May 27, 1971, and JS to JOB, March 28, [1972], JOB files, BL.

375 Dodd, Mead . . . Thurber: JOB to JS, May 26, 1970, JOB files, BL.

375 Viking offered . . . Giroux: JS to JOB, June 29, [1970], JOB files, BL; JOB to JS, July 8, 1970, JOB files, BL; JOB to Giroux, July 8, 1970, JOB files, BL; JS, review of *A Certain World,* 34.

375 The only . . . beaches: JOB to JS, December 1970, JOB files, BL; JS, introduction to *The American Coast,* 15–27.

375 as Berton . . . dog": Berton Roueché, interview with DR.

375–376 in 1970 . . . bomb": JS, "Gooney Bird," 14–17.

376 Stafford made . . . little: *New York Times,* November 21, 1970.

376 She turned . . . City: Lawrence Lafore to JS, November 11, 1970, and JS to Lafore, February 8 and March 28, [1971], CUSC.

376 Although other . . . blurbs: JS to Auchincloss, April 6, [year unknown].

376 One such . . . colloquial": JS to Anne Sullivan, March 21, 1971, JOB files, BL.

376 " 'It's sort . . . study: Eckman, "Adding a Pulitzer," 21.

376 In July 1972 . . . Women": note cards, JOB files.

376–377 Most of . . . demise: various clippings, "Hot-air balloons," CUSC; Aurthur, "Hitting the Boiling Point," 94–96.

377 "though they . . . pie": JS to Jensen, August 4, 1970, CUSC.

377 The threesome . . . like: Hempstead, Berton Roueché, interviews with DR.

377 she maintained . . . socks: Thomas Molyneux, "Peter," *Shenandoah* 27 (Winter 1977): 59.

377 The citizens . . . 20: Berton Roueché, interview with DR.

377 some acquaintances . . . attempt: Aurthur, "Hitting the Boiling Point," 95.

377 "The tragic . . . story": Roberts, interview with DR.

377 "certain that . . . parlay": JS to Auchincloss, [early 1971].

377–378 According to . . . again: Peter Taylor, "A Commemorative Tribute," 57.

Pages

378 "the helmets . . . again": JS, "Sense and Sensibility," CUSC.

378 "Children should . . . deaf": JS, "Teaching of Writing," unpublished manuscript of Barnard lecture, CUSC.

378 "I feel . . . me": JS, "The Snows of Yesteryear," unpublished manuscript of Barnard lecture, CUSC.

378–379 "The meetings . . . catarrh": JS to Cavett, [n.d.], quoted in Cavett, "The Cavett Album — II," 99.

379 Objecting to . . . sapphires": JS to Public Relations, Tiffany & Co., September 7, 1972, JOB files, BL.

379 "She was . . . it": Berton Roueché, interview with DR.

380 A Britannica . . . dotage": JS, "Christmas Books for Children" (1970), 203.

380 "I cannot . . . style' ": JS, "Christmas Books for Children" (1969), 204.

380 Her bronchial ⋮ . . honors: Paul Thompson, diary, January 2–May 27, 1972.

380 She was . . . Main": JS to Frichtel, [postmarked June 30, 1972], CUSC.

381 Mary Lee . . . her: JS to Frichtel, [postmarked May 1, 1972], CUSC.

381 "She'd get . . . that": Harry Frichtel, interview with DR.

381 In 1969 . . . museum: Robert Frichtel, interview with DR.

381 "I would . . . say": Clark, interview with DR.

381 "Jean would . . . about": Auchincloss, interview with DR.

381–382 Before Stafford's . . . commission: Pinkham, interview with DR; Pinkham, "Jean Stafford's Family," 66.

382 By Marjorie's . . . afflictions: Pinkham, interview with DR.

382 "I wish . . . Rhodesia": JS to Mary Lee Frichtel, [postmarked August 25, 1964], CUSC.

382 "I cannot . . . mine": JS to Pinkham, [n.d.], CUSC.

382 "My mother . . . crushed": Pinkham, interview with DR.

382 "When I . . . off' ": JS to Pinkham, September 16, [1976], CUSC.

382–383 "For a . . . service": JS to Pinkham, August 27, [year unknown], CUSC.

383 Thomas Roberts . . . smoking: Roberts to Stephen Sigler, January 27, 1972, Thomas Roberts files.

383 A respiratory . . . woes: George A. Falk to Roberts, November 24, 1972, Thomas Roberts files.

383 Among Stafford's . . . eye: White to JS, December 18, 1971, CUSC; Dorothy Thompson to JS, June 6, 1971, CUSC; JS to Auchincloss [early 1974]; JS to Moss, [n.d.], Berg Collection; Roberts, notes on JS, November 22, 1972, Thomas Roberts files.

383 "5/26/71 . . . hip": Roberts, notes on JS, Thomas Roberts files.

383 She fell . . . head: Dorothy Thompson to JS, July 4, 1971, CUSC; JS to Auchincloss, September 25, [year unknown]; Mitchell, interview with DR.

383 " 'I'd never . . . is' ": Sheed, "Miss Jean Stafford," 96.

383–384 though she . . . them: Mitchell, interview with DR.

Pages

384 Josephine Monsell . . . herself: Josephine Monsell, interview with DR, 1984.

384 One morning . . . floor: Margaret Simmons, interview with DR, 1987.

384 "terrible. One . . . them": Monsell, interview with DR.

384 Stafford tried . . . tobacco: JS to Auchincloss, [n.d.].

394 She played . . . record: JS to Hightower, February 24, [year unknown].

384 she even . . . futile: Mitchell, interview with DR.

384 "I stay . . . snarling": JS, "My View."

384 With her . . . Morris: Hoffman, interview with DR.

384 The local . . . conversation: Jim Devine, interview with DR, 1986.

384 "She read . . . well": Hiss, interview with DR.

384 Decades earlier . . . town": Berton Roueché, interview with DR.

385 " 'I always . . . more' ": Cavett, "The Cavett Album — II," 103.

385 Howard Moss . . . screen: Moss, "Jean: Some Fragments," 80.

385 According to Josephine . . . bedroom: Monsell, interview with DR.

385 Monsell still . . . stint: ibid.

385 "She could . . . her": John Thompson, interview with DR.

385 "I was . . . loneliness": Hoffman, interview with DR.

385 Ninety percent . . . friendship": Berton and Katherine Roueché, interview with DR.

385 "She drove . . . her": Honeycutt, interview with DR.

385–386 Stafford was . . . saying: Taylor, interview with DR.

386 Eve Auchincloss . . . helpless": Auchincloss, interview with DR.

386 She liked . . . pricking": JS to Auchincloss, [August 1974].

386 "It meant . . . uncritical": Guedenet, interview with DR.

386 "I never . . . death": Hempstead, interview with DR.

386 "She would forget . . . forgotten": Moss, "Jean: Some Fragments," 83.

386 "She would say . . . had": Hoffman, interview with DR.

386 "A certain . . . muddled": Moss, "Jean: Some Fragments," 83.

386 "To live . . . scoundrel": Sheed, "Miss Jean Stafford," 98.

387 "She'd talk . . . rant": Hale, interview with DR.

387 "Jean could . . . you": Hempstead, interview with DR.

387 "I don't . . . scream": Hoffman, interview with DR.

387 In Claiborne's . . . guests": Claiborne, *Memorable Meals*, 79–87.

387–388 "Not long . . . matter": JS to Auchincloss, [n.d.].

388 In her cups . . . days: Paul Thompson, diary, November 17, 1974.

388 John Thompson . . . again' ": John Thompson, Taylor, interviews with DR.

388 Stafford's long . . . Auchincloss: Auchincloss, interview with DR.

388 In January 1975 . . . future": JS to JOB, January 16, 1975, JOB files, BL.

389 After a . . . Island: Timothy Seldes, interview with DR, 1987.

389 Louis Auchincloss . . . before": JS to Louis Auchincloss, March 19, 1975, CUSC.

Pages

389 With Howard Moss . . . them: Moss, "Jean: Some Fragments," 77, 79.

389 Her neighbors . . . house: Monsell, Hiss, and Hempstead, interviews with DR.

389 Beset by . . . most": JS to Eve Auchincloss, January 29, [year unknown].

389–390 "She was . . . Club: Mitchell, interview with DR.

390 "I was furious . . . me": JS to Jensen, December 13, [1975], CUSC.

390 In an unpublished . . . old": JS, untitled, unpublished manuscript, CUSC.

390 Each year . . . fundamental: JS to Pinkham, January 4, 1974, October 26, [year unknown], CUSC.

390 "I realized . . . crazy' ": Sheed, "Miss Jean Stafford," 96.

390 Marjorie insists . . . child: Pinkham, interview with DR.

390–391 One of . . . fare-thee-well": JS to Roberts, December 12, 1970, CUSC.

391 "How to . . . habits: JS, "How to Cook for One," unpublished manuscript, CUSC.

391–392 Another *Esquire* . . . cap: JS to Coca-Cola Co., August 8, 1971, CUSC.

392 It produced . . . to: various letters to JS, 1973–1974, CUSC.

392 Her articles . . . at: ibid.

392 The weakest . . . women: JS, "Katharine Graham," "Modern Romanticism," "Millicent Fenwick."

392 "lambasting the . . . *Centennial:* JS to Warners, July 30, [1974], CUSC.

392 taking Susan . . . *Wills:* JS, "Brownmiller on Rape," 50, 52.

392–393 In Eve Auchincloss's . . . cut: Auchincloss, interview with DR.

393 Complaining . . . *Angels:* JS to Albert Duhamel and Carlos Baker, October 16 and 25, November 26, and December 16, 1974, CUSC.

393 "She wrote . . . situation": Peter Taylor, "A Commemorative Tribute," 58.

393 Although . . . 1970s: Duane Whelan, interview with DR, 1986.

394 A young . . . tips: correspondent to JS, [n.d.], CUSC.

394 a woman . . . Germany: [?] to Liebling, [n.d.], CUSC.

394 In 1974 . . . *Star:* "Springs Author Zaps Media," 6.

394 One evening . . . time": Hempstead, interview with DR.

394 When Alden . . . fare-thee-well": Whitman, "Jean Stafford and Her Secretary," 78.

394–395 One day . . . persisted: Kenneth Robbins, interview with DR, 1986.

395 The deed . . . year: JS, legal agreement with Robbinses, March 24, 1976, CUSC.

395 "Giving us . . . caretaking": Robbins, interview with DR.

395 "She was . . . her": Hoffman, interview with DR.

395 Several townspeople . . . you' ": Robbins, interview with DR.

395 Stafford initiated . . . her": John Thompson, Monsell, interviews with DR.

395 "I did . . . copy": Robbins, telephone conversation with DR, December 4, 1987.

Pages

396 In 1975 . . . factor": Rolla D. Campbell, medical summary on JS, April 1, 1975, Thomas Roberts files.

396 A month . . . disease: Roberts, medical summary on JS, May 15, 1975, Thomas Roberts files.

396 She weighed . . . pounds: Paul Thompson diary, October 11, 1975.

396 The most . . . bed: Roberts to JS, August 18, 1976, Thomas Roberts files; Roberts, interview with DR.

396 "pulmonary toilet . . . years": JS to Jensen, December 13, [1975], CUSC.

396 Stafford also . . . secretions: Roberts, interview with DR.

396 Unable to bear . . . cupping: Robbins, interview with DR.

396 On one occasion . . . it: Hempstead, interview with DR.

396 She ordered . . . Liebling's: Paul Thompson, diary, October 11, 1975.

396 "I do now . . . me": JS to Roberts, October 9, 1975.

396 " 'I don't . . . it' ": Sheed, "Miss Jean Stafford," 96.

397 A hired . . . risk: Arnold Hoffman, interview with DR, 1986.

397 "I think . . . down": Hempstead, interview with DR.

397 "I am . . . gas": JS to Auchincloss, [n.d.]

397 Around 1976 . . . quick": Hightower, interview with DR.

397 *Esquire* fired . . . columnist: White to JS, August 20, 1976, CUSC.

397 "We will . . . people": JS to Pinkham, September 16, [1976], CUSC.

397 The two . . . place": Pinkham, interview with DR.

397–398 Jean looked . . . sister": Pinkham, "Jean Stafford's Family," 67–68.

398 "I have . . . past?": Lowell to JS, September 4, 1976, CUSC.

398 Around the . . . Hospital: Monsell, interview with DR.

398 The doctors . . . system": Roberts, interview with DR.

398 Stafford had . . . aphasia: medical summary on JS, New York Hospital, December 22, 1976, Thomas Roberts files.

CHAPTER XIX

399 the intern . . . complete": medical summary on JS, New York Hospital, December 22, 1976, Thomas Roberts files.

399–400 During the . . . sedatives: Roberts to Norman M. Gerber, February 2, 1977, Thomas Roberts files.

400 Her Pulitzer . . . novels' ": Herman Kogan to [?], December 13, 1976, CUSC.

400 The children's-books . . . delightful": White to JS, December 10, 1976, CUSC.

400 After two . . . Giroux: Paul Thompson, diary, February 27, March 2 and 5, 1977.

400 Stafford's sister . . . drunk: Pinkham, "Jean Stafford's Family," 68.

400 If she . . . find: Roberts, Guedenet, interviews with DR.

Pages

400 "I would . . . afterward": Taylor, interview with DR.

400–401 "It was . . . sound: Hempstead, interview with DR.

401 "One person . . . visit": Roberts to Sonia Keahon, September 28, 1978.

401 "It's better . . . ones": Giroux to Dorothy Thompson, March 3, 1977.

401 "Shall I . . . intermediary": Hightower to JS, October 14, 1977.

401 "I'd say . . . noise]": Berton Roueché, interview with DR.

401 As she . . . not": Monsell, interview with DR.

401 Even Marjorie . . . telephone: Pinkham, "Jean Stafford's Family," 68.

401 When he . . . word": Mitchell, interview with DR.

401–402 Both Mitchell . . . track": ibid.; Hiss, interview with DR.

402 Some very . . . her": Hempstead, Hightower, interviews with DR.

402 Also guiltily . . . her": Auchincloss, interview with DR.

402 "Dear Mary Lee . . . Jean": JS to Frichtel, [postmarked May 9, 1977], CUSC.

402–403 John Thompson . . . kitchen: John Thompson, Robbins, interviews with DR.

403 "I can . . . *ghastly*": Hiss, interview with DR.

403 "She threw . . . house": Jean Hoffman, interview with DR.

403 "I had . . . not": JS to Pinkham, [postmarked July 10, 1977], CUSC.

403 Katharine White . . . contribute: White to Sheed, February 26, 1977, Bryn Mawr College Library, courtesy of Linda Davis; White to JS, July 13, 1977, CUSC.

403 Despite the . . . Letters: JOB to Giroux, January 31, 1977, JOB files, BL.

403 In August 1977 . . . later: American Academy and Institute of Arts and Letters to JS, August 29, 1977, CUSC.

403 Jean Riboud . . . it: Jean Riboud to JS, November 9, 1978, CUSC.

403–404 Thomas Roberts . . . morale: Roberts, interview with DR.

404 "Her clinging . . . write": Robbins, interview with DR.

404 Stafford may . . . year: Paul Thompson, diary, January 25, 1979.

404 One pathologist . . . *arithe(c)tic*: JS, "Speech and language therapy," CUSC.

404 "I thank . . . Tophet": JS to Pinkham, [postmarked April 11, 1977], CUSC.

404 On her copy . . . page: copy of JS, "Mountain Jim," CUSC.

404 In Kenneth . . . attempts": Robbins, interview with DR.

404–405 Trying to eat . . . later: Monsell, interview with DR.

405 Stafford's relationship . . . thereafter: Robbins, interview with DR.

405 One of the . . . such": medical summary on JS, New York Hospital, February 12, 1978, Thomas Roberts files.

405 "I go . . . time": JS to Pinkham, [postmarked February 24, 1977], CUSC.

405 "She was . . . bones": Hempstead, interview with DR.

Pages

405–406 At an East . . . friends' ": Moss, "Jean: Some Fragments," 83–84.

406 Wilfrid Sheed . . . suicide' ": Sheed, "Miss Jean Stafford," 98.

406 Despite all . . . Springs: Hiss, John Thompson, interviews with DR.

406 In December . . . $114,000: Whelan, interview with DR.

406 On September 12 . . . mourners: Hamilton, *Robert Lowell,* 473.

406 "Jean insisted . . . successfully": Davison, interview with DR.

406 On December 8 . . . Letter": Robert Lowell, "Robert Lowell: A Reading," tape (Caedmon CDL 51569).

406–407 Giroux, who . . . bitch!' ": Mitchell, interview with DR.

407 In the second . . . poem: JS's copy, Lowell, *The Mills of the Kavanaughs,* courtesy of Joseph Mitchell.

407 She kept . . . plan": Milton Greenstein to JS, July 21, 1975; William Maxwell to JS, December 14, 1977, CUSC.

407–408 In July 1977 . . . up: Charles McGrath to JS, July 13, 1977, CUSC; Charles McGrath, interview with DR, 1987.

408 He pored . . . best: McGrath, interview with DR.

408–409 The salient . . . century: JS, "The Parliament of Women" and "The State of Grace," unpublished manuscripts, CUSC.

409 Stafford often . . . state: Berton Rouéché, interview with DR.

409–410 To complicate . . . improvisation: JS, "The Parliament of Women" and "The State of Grace," CUSC.

410 "she didn't . . . enough": Mitchell, interview with DR.

410 Berton Rouéché . . . reputation: Berton Rouéché, interview with DR.

410 Eve Auchincloss . . . grown-ups": Auchincloss, interview with DR.

410 "Life had . . . lives": Taylor, interview with DR.

410 "Jean's undoing . . . herself": Sheed, "Miss Jean Stafford," 97.

411 "He didn't . . . stories": Pinkham, interview with DR.

411 "I am . . . him": JS to Frichtel, [postmarked August 19, 1969], CUSC.

411 "When it . . . around": Robbins, interview with DR.

411 John Thompson . . . her": John Thompson, interview with DR.

411 "Reading that . . . it": Mitchell, interview with DR.

411 "Influx" brought . . . it: various letters to JS, November–December 1978, CUSC.

411 Weighing less . . . eating: medical summary on JS, Burke Rehabilitation Hospital, March 26, 1979, Thomas Roberts files.

411 On February 20 . . . month: medical summary on JS, New York Hospital, March 20, 1979, Thomas Roberts files.

412 "She would . . . long' ": Roberts, interview with DR.

412 " 'Get — me . . . here' ": Straus, "Jean Stafford," 90.

412 When Robert . . . him: Giroux, "Hard Years and 'Scary Days,' " 29.

412 On March 26 . . . years: Charles P. Bredin to Roberts, May 4, 1979.

412 Beside her . . . *Kavanaughs:* Mitchell, interview with DR.

412 When Stafford's . . . executor: JS, Last Will and Testament, November 15, 1978, CUSC.

412 "thumbing her . . . world": Hiss, interview with DR.

Pages

412 Over the . . . wills: Pinkham, interview with DR.

412 At one . . . Jensen: Alexander Lindey to JS, January 3, 1955, CUSC.

412 On one occasion . . . leavings: Peter De Vries, interview with DR.

412 Around 1974 . . . executor: Giroux to DR, November 30, 1987.

413 Monsell inherited . . . living: Monsell, interview with DR.

413 According to . . . avail: Taylor, Hoffman, interviews with DR.

413 The funeral . . . sentences: Hoffman, Berton Roueché, Robbins, and Isabel Johnson (1986), interviews with DR; Sheed, "Miss Jean Stafford," 92.

413 As the service . . . will": Berton Roueché, interview with DR.

413–414 Wilfrid Sheed . . . life": Sheed, "Miss Jean Stafford," 92, 99.

414 "A million . . . forget": JS to Pinkham, [postmarked April 11, 1977], CUSC.

EPILOGUE

416 "in a time . . . challenge": Lask, "Jean Stafford, 63, Writer, Dead," B12.

416 "a novel . . . era": Wolcott, "Dissecting Our Decline," 136.

417 "I haven't . . . situations": Wood, "Neglected Fictions."

417 "had read . . . she?' ": Ann Beattie, "Logic," *Fiction Network* no. 3 (Fall 1984): 4.

417 "At a time . . . fashion": Wolcott, "Blowing Smoke into the Zeitgeist," 59.

417 Thus some . . . Colorado: e.g., Sid Jenson, "The Noble Wicked West of Jean Stafford," *Western American Literature* 7 (Winter 1973): 261–270; William Leary, "Native Daughter: Jean Stafford's California," *Western American Literature* 21 (Fall 1986): 195–205; Mary Ellen Williams Walsh, "The Young Girl in the West: Disenchantment in Jean Stafford's Short Fiction," in *Women and Western American Literature,* edited by Helen Winter Stauffer and Susan J. Rosowski (Troy, New York: Whitson Publishing Company, 1982), 230–243.

417 Other scholars . . . vulnerable": see Mary Davidson McConahay, "Colorado's 'Voice of Flaming Insight': Jean Stafford Reconsidered" (Ph.D. dissertation, University of Colorado, 1986); McConahay, " 'Heidelberry Braids' and Yankee *Politesse,*" 213–236; Gelfant, "Reconsideration," 22–25; Elizabeth Janeway, "Women's Literature," in *Harvard Guide to Contemporary American Writing,* edited by Daniel Hoffman (Cambridge, Mass.: Harvard University Press, 1979), 345, 352, 354.

417 "exploration of . . . female": Walsh, *Jean Stafford,* [unpaginated].

417 "the patriarchal . . . vulnerable": Maureen Ann Ryan, "Innocence and Irony: The Fiction of Jean Stafford" (Ph.D. dissertation, Temple University, 1984).

Pages

417 "to crack . . . feelings": Wolcott, "Blowing Smoke into the Zeit-geist," 59.

418 "Molly is . . . fiction": Auchincloss, *Pioneers & Caretakers,* 157.

418 "How lonely . . . now' ": JS, "The Liberation," *CS,* 322.

Acknowledgments

To MANUFACTURE A NOVEL, a memoir, or a book of verses, the author can simply sit down in his study, turn off the telephone, and write. Very few biographies, however, have emerged without the aid and good will of a host of accomplices. In my case, dozens of sympathizers who had nothing to gain but my gratitude lined the crooked path of my three-year journey toward an understanding of Jean Stafford, holding lanterns and whispering directions. They cannot, of course, be held responsible for the book I have written, but whatever there is of truth in it is owed mainly to them.

My greatest debt is to two people who pushed hard to persuade me to attempt a biography and kept my spirits up during the many dark moments that ensued. One is Eve Auchincloss, who was perhaps Jean Stafford's best friend in the late 1950s and 1960s. Eve had been my editor at the *Washington Post Book World* and *Connoisseur*. Throughout my biographical labors, she managed with extraordinary grace to juggle her roles as one of my chief sources of information, as a coach barking pep talks at regular intervals, and as a vigilant reader of the work in progress. My agent, Max Gartenberg, a gentleman of the old school of belles lettres, kept nudging me toward Stafford when I was all too content to churn out what he called "ephemeral journalism"; he attended my labors with an exquisite balance of enthusiasm and caution.

Three others read the book while I was writing it. Sharon

Roberts had a sharp eye for purple prose and maundering pedantry alike; she was required, as well, to put up with the author during the months when drudgery turned to obsession. Jon Krakauer and Judi Wineland were ready with vibrant responses to each chapter, and both had the courage not to hide their alarm when I launched my first expedition in a badly leaking boat.

In my efforts to locate documents and ransack memories, there were inevitably dead ends. Some who had known Stafford declined to talk to me. A collector who had purchased an important cache of letters from Stafford to one of her best friends managed to thwart my efforts to read those letters, in spite of the seller's explicit wish that they be available to scholars. In a posthumous proviso, E. B. White put a ten-year moratorium on anyone's reading the letters Stafford had written to his wife, who had been Stafford's editor at *The New Yorker* — this despite Katharine White's evident intention to make the letters accessible by leaving them to the Bryn Mawr Library.

Yet I was happily surprised by the willingness of so many to hunt down old papers and to tell me what they remembered. My single most valuable source was Robert Hightower, a subtle scholar and a wry, yet passionate, man. He not only let me interview him dry, but also lent me the 591-page, forty-two-year correspondence between Stafford and him — the most remarkable epistolary record I have ever read.

Each of my sources made some unique contribution. I must inadequately thank them here, in crass alphabetical order. They are James Oliver Brown, Gertrude Buckman, Blair Clark, Andrew Cooke, Susanna Cuyler, Linda Davis, Peter Davison, Jim Devine, Peter and Katinka De Vries, Jane Fitz-Randolph, Harry Frichtel, Robert Frichtel, Pierre and Charlotte Guedenet, Barbara Hale, Eleanor Hempstead, Howard Higman, Alger Hiss, Jean and Arnold Hoffman, Ann Honeycutt, Oliver Jensen, Isabel Johnson, Charles McGrath, Janet Malcolm, Joseph Mitchell, Josephine Monsell, Mary Moore, Raphael Moses, Mary Elizabeth O'Rourke, Frank Parker, Marjorie Pinkham, Kenneth Robbins, Thomas Roberts, Berton and Katherine Roueché, Timothy Seldes, Margaret Simmons, Joan Stillman, Peter Taylor, John Thompson, Paul and Dorothy Thompson, Goodrich Walton, Nancy Weingartner, Duane Whelan, and Anne White.

My first editor at Little, Brown, Ann Sleeper, cared beyond

the call of duty about Jean Stafford and about my book. I was distressed to see her leave the firm while I was still wading in midstream, but I came to be equally delighted with her successor, Jennifer Josephy, who admirably combined firmness and indulgence as she beckoned from the far bank. My thanks also go to Roger Donald at Little, Brown for his stewardship, to Sarah Pence for her attention to detail, and to Dorothy Straight for her vigilant and sensitive copyediting.

At the Rare Books Room in the University of Colorado's Norlin Library, where Stafford's papers are kept, Nora Quinlan and Sonia Jacobs gave me a tremendous amount of help during the many months I spent in research. The staffs of Harvard's Houghton Library and Columbia's Butler Library were also generous with their assistance.

Josephine Monsell, Stafford's executor, granted me permission to quote from many important letters and unpublished works; Timothy Seldes, the agent for the estate, was equally helpful. Farrar, Straus & Giroux, the Atlantic Monthly Press, and Harcourt Brace Jovanovich granted me access to correspondence and allowed me to reprint passages. Ande Zellman at the *Boston Globe* and Chris Jerome at *New England Monthly* backed up their own enthusiasm for my Stafford efforts with collateral assignments. Dr. David Savitz gave me expert medical advice. I retain a lasting gratitude also to Allan Kallman of Gnomon Copy in Cambridge, Massachusetts, who was in a meaningful sense my first "publisher," and to Jonathan Toner of Radio Shack in Cambridge, who spent an unpaid weekend rescuing forty pages of manuscript that had vanished in a wilderness of scrambled bytes inside my word processor.

Selected Bibliography

For the serious student, Wanda Avila's *Jean Stafford: A Comprehensive Bibliography* (New York: Garland Publishing, Inc., 1983) is indispensable. The volume offers capsule summaries of 220 publications by Stafford and of 428 critical works about her. The book is, however, far from comprehensive, for it leaves out quite a few of Stafford's essays and reviews; it also contains a number of errors.

The following bibliography gives all of Stafford's published books and short stories; a selected list of her articles and reviews; and a selected list of critical and background works. All of the publications referred to in the text are given here. In the case of Stafford's three novels and her *Collected Stories,* the first listing gives the original publication; the second, the current edition.

WORKS BY STAFFORD

Novels:

Boston Adventure. New York: Harcourt, Brace and Company, 1944; New York: Harcourt Brace Jovanovich, 1983.

The Catherine Wheel. New York: Harcourt, Brace and Company, 1952; New York: The Ecco Press, 1981.

The Mountain Lion. New York: Harcourt, Brace and Company, 1947; New York: E. P. Dutton, 1983.

Novella:

"A Winter's Tale." In *New Short Novels,* edited by Mary Louise Aswell. New York: Ballantine, 1954.

Short-Story Collections:

Bad Characters. New York: Farrar, Straus & Co., 1964.

Children Are Bored on Sunday. New York: Harcourt, Brace and Company, 1953.

The Collected Stories of Jean Stafford. New York: Farrar, Straus & Giroux, 1969; New York: E. P. Dutton, 1984.

Selected Stories of Jean Stafford. New York: New American Library, 1966.

Stories (with John Cheever, Daniel Fuchs, and William Maxwell). New York: Farrar, Straus & Cudahy, 1956.

Other:

Arabian Nights: The Lion and the Carpenter and Other Tales from the Arabian Nights, Retold. New York: Macmillan Co., 1962.

Elephi, the Cat with the High I.Q. New York: Farrar, Straus & Cudahy, 1962.

A Mother in History. New York: Farrar, Straus & Giroux, 1966.

Short Stories:

(The notation *CS* indicates a story's appearance in *The Collected Short Stories of Jean Stafford,* with corresponding page numbers.)

"And Lots of Solid Color." *American Prefaces* 5 (November 1939): 22–25.

"Bad Characters." *The New Yorker* 30 (December 4, 1954): 42–51; *CS:* 263–282.

"Beatrice Trueblood's Story." *The New Yorker* 31 (February 26, 1955): 24–32; *CS:* 385–405.

"Between the Porch and the Altar." *Harper's* 190 (June 1945): 654–657; *CS:* 407–413.

"The Bleeding Heart." *Partisan Review* 15 (September 1948): 974–996; *CS:* 147–170.

"The Captain's Gift." *Sewanee Review* 54 (April 1946): 206–215; *CS:* 437–445.

"The Cavalier." *The New Yorker* 24 (February 12, 1949): 28–36.

"Caveat Emptor." *Mademoiselle* 43 (May 1956); *CS:* 75–90.

"Children Are Bored on Sunday." *The New Yorker* 23 (February 21, 1948): 23–26; *CS:* 373–383.

"The Children's Game." *Saturday Evening Post* 231 (October 4, 1958); *CS:* 19–33.

"The Connoisseurs." *Harper's Bazaar* 86 (October 1952).

"Cops and Robbers." *The New Yorker* 28 (January 24, 1953): 28–34; *CS:* 423–435.

"A Country Love Story." *The New Yorker* 26 (May 6, 1950): 26–31; *CS:* 133–145.

"The Darkening Moon." *Harper's Bazaar* 78 (January 1944); *CS:* 251–262.

"The Echo and the Nemesis." *The New Yorker* 26 (December 16, 1950): 28–35; *CS:* 35–53.

"The End of a Career." *The New Yorker* 31 (January 21, 1956): 35–42; *CS:* 447–463.

"The Healthiest Girl in Town." *The New Yorker* 27 (April 7, 1951): 32–40; *CS:* 197–217.

"The Home Front." *Partisan Review* 12 (Spring 1945): 149–169.

"The Hope Chest." *Harper's* 194 (January 1947): 62–65; *CS:* 113–119.

"I Love Someone." *Colorado Quarterly* 1 (Summer 1952): 78–85; *CS:* 415–422.

"In the Zoo." *The New Yorker* 29 (September 19, 1953): 24–32; *CS:* 283–303.

"An Influx of Poets." *The New Yorker* 54 (November 6, 1978): 43–60.

"The Interior Castle." *Partisan Review* 13 (November–December 1946): 519–532; *CS:* 179–193.

"The Liberation." *The New Yorker* 29 (May 30, 1953): 22–30; *CS:* 305–322.

"Life Is No Abyss." *Sewanee Review* 60 (July 1952): 465–487; *CS:* 93–112.

"The Lippia Lawn." *Kenyon Review* 6 (Spring 1944): 237–245; *CS:* 171–178.

"Maggie Meriwether's Rich Experience." *The New Yorker* 31 (February 26, 1955): 24–32; *CS:* 3–17.

"The Maiden." *The New Yorker* 26 (July 29, 1950): 21–25; *CS:* 55–64.

"A Modest Proposal." *The New Yorker* 25 (July 23, 1949): 21–24; *CS:* 65–74.

"The Mountain Day." *The New Yorker* 32 (August 18, 1956): 24–32; *CS:* 323–344.

"Mountain Jim." *Boy's Life,* February 1968.

"My Blithe, Sad Bird." *The New Yorker* 33 (April 6, 1957): 25–38.

"Old Flaming Youth." *Harper's Bazaar* 84 (December 1950).

"The Ordeal of Conrad Pardee." *Ladies' Home Journal* 81 (July 1964).

"The Philosophy Lesson." *The New Yorker* 54 (November 16, 1968): 59–63; *CS:* 361–369.

"Polite Conversation." *The New Yorker* 25 (August 20, 1949): 24–28; *CS:* 121–132.

"A Reading Problem." *The New Yorker* 31 (June 30, 1956): 24–32; *CS:* 323–344.

"A Reasonable Facsimile." *The New Yorker* 33 (August 3, 1957): 20–30.

"A Reunion." *Partisan Review* 11 (Fall 1944): 423–427.

"The Scarlet Letter." *Mademoiselle* 49 (July 1959).

"A Slight Maneuver." *Mademoiselle* 24 (February 1947).

"A Summer Day." *The New Yorker* 24 (September 11, 1948): 29–35; *CS:* 345–359.

"The Tea Time of Stouthearted Ladies." *Kenyon Review* 26 (Winter 1964): 116–128; *CS:* 219–230.

"The Violet Rock." *The New Yorker* 28 (April 26, 1952): 34–42.

"The Warlock." *The New Yorker* 31 (December 24, 1955).

"Woden's Day." *Shenandoah* 30 (Autumn 1979): 6–26.

Articles and Reviews:

"The Art of Accepting Oneself." *Vogue* 119 (February 1, 1952).

"At This Point in Time, TV Is Murdering the English Language." *New York Times,* September 15, 1974, section 2.

"Brownmiller on Rape: A Scare Worse Than Death." *Esquire* 84 (November 1975).

"Children's Books for Christmas." *The New Yorker* 45 (December 13, 1969): 191–212; 47 (December 4, 1971): 177–214; 50 (December 2, 1974): 170–204; 51 (December 1, 1975): 162–188.

"Christmas Books for Children." *The New Yorker* 46 (December 5, 1970): 200–220; 48 (December 2, 1972): 190–212; 49 (December 3, 1973): 194–220.

"Coca-Cola." *Esquire* 84 (December 1975).

"The Crossword Puzzle Has Gone to Hell!" *Esquire* 82 (December 1974): 144–145.

"Divorce: Journey Through Crisis." *Harper's Bazaar* 92 (November 1958).

"Don't Send Me Gladiolus." *Vogue* 161 (March 1973): 146.

"Don't Use Ms. with Miss Stafford, Unless You Mean ms." *New York Times,* September 21, 1973, 36.

"East Hampton from the Catbird Seat." *New York Times,* December 26, 1971, section 1A.

"The Eat Generation." *Reporter* 20 (February 19, 1959): 33–34.

"Enchanted Island." *Mademoiselle* 29 (May 1950).

Essay on American places. *Newsday,* May 13, 1973.

"An Etiquette for Writers." Lecture given at the University of Colorado, Boulder, 1952.

"George Eliot: A Medical Study." *What's New,* Christmas 1957.

". . . The Good Life Is Indeed Now." *McCall's* 97 (January 1970): 30.

"Gooney Bird." *New York Review of Books* 15 (October 8, 1970): 14–17.

"Heroes and Villains: Who Was Famous and Why." *McCall's* 103 (April 1976).

"Home for Christmas." *Mademoiselle* 32 (December 1951).

"Intimations of Hope." *McCall's* 99 (December 1971).

Introduction to *The American Coast* (New York: Charles Scribner's Sons, 1971), 15–27.

"Isak Dinesen: Master Teller of Tales." *Horizon* 2 (September 1959): 110–113.

"It's Good to Be Back." *Mademoiselle* 34 (July 1952).

"The Jabberwock Anatomized." *Griffin,* June 1960, 2–11.

"Jean Stafford on Education." *East Hampton Star,* June 14, 1973, section 2.

"Katharine Graham." *Vogue* 162 (December 1973).

"Letter from Edinburgh." *The New Yorker* 25 (September 17, 1949): 83–88.

"Letter from Germany." *The New Yorker* 25 (December 3, 1949): 69–81.

"Love Among the Rattlesnakes." *McCall's* 97 (March 1970).

"Men, Women, Language, Science and Other Dichotomies." *Confrontation,* Fall 1973, 69–74.

"Millicent Fenwick Makes an Adroit Politician." *Vogue* 165 (June 1975).

"Miss McKeehan's Pocketbook." *Colorado Quarterly* 24 (Spring 1976): 407–411.

"Modern Romanticism: Lally Weymouth." *Vogue* 163 (June 1974).

"Movies: War and Peace in Two Foreign Films." *Horizon* 3 (November 1960): 121–122.

" 'My Sleep Grew Shy of Me.' " *Vogue* 110 (October 15, 1947).

"My (Ugh!) Sensitivity Training." *Horizon* 12 (Spring 1970): 112.

"My View: Jean Stafford." *Newsday,* [n.d.].

"New England Winter." *Holiday* 15 (February 1954): 34–36.

"New York Is a Daisy." *Harper's Bazaar* 92 (December 1958).

"Notes on Boston." *Junior Bazaar,* December 1947.

"Once upon a time, Con Edison made a big mistake in Jean Stafford's gas bill. Well, she's a writer and relishes a good fight. But wait, let her tell it in her own words." *New York Times,* June 8, 1974, 31.

"On My Mind." *Vogue* 162 (November 1973).

"Plight of the American Language." *Saturday Review World* 1 (December 4, 1973): 14–18.

"The Polyglot Mr. Rohmer." *Rohmer Review* 14 (July 1976): 1–3.

"Portrait: Ward Bennett." *Art in America* 54 (November–December 1966): 44–47.

"Profiles: American Town." *The New Yorker* 24 (August 28, 1948).

"The Psychological Novel." *Kenyon Review* 10 (Spring 1948): 214–227.

Review of *A Certain World* by W. H. Auden. *Vogue* 156 (August 15, 1970): 34.

Review of *May We Borrow Your Husband?* by Graham Greene. *Vogue* 149 (June 1967): 78.

Review of *My Heart Is Broken* by Mavis Gallant. *Vogue* 143 (April 15, 1964): 56.

Review of *The Words* by Jean-Paul Sartre. *Vogue* 144 (October 15, 1964): 98.

"Some Advice to Hostesses from a Well-Tempered Guest." *Vogue* 164 (September 1974): 296–298.

"Somebody Out There Hates Me." *Esquire* 82 (August 1974): 108–109.

"Some Letters to Peter and Eleanor Taylor." *Shenandoah* 30 (Autumn 1979): 27–55.

"Souvenirs of Survival." *Mademoiselle* 50 (February 1960).

"The Strange World of Marguerite Oswald." *McCall's* 93 (October 1965).

"Suffering Summering Houseguests." *Vogue* 158 (August 15, 1971): 112.

"Topics: Women as Chattels, Men as Chumps." *New York Times,* May 9, 1970, 24.

"To School with Joy." *Vogue* 151 (May 1968).

"Truth and the Novelist." *Harper's Bazaar* 85 (August 1951).

"Truth in Fiction." *Library Journal* 91 (October 1, 1966): 4557–4565.

"Vox Populi" column. *Prep Owl* (Boulder, Colorado, State Preparatory School student newspaper), April 24, 1931, 3.

"Walpurgis Nacht, 1940." *Kenyon Review* 4 (Winter 1942): 106–108.

"What Does Martha Mitchell Know?" *McCall's* 100 (October 1972).

"Why I Don't Get Around Much Anymore." *Esquire* 83 (March 1975).

"Wolfe Hunting." *New York Review of Books* 19 (May 9, 1968): 17–20.

"Young Writers." *Analects* 1 (October 1960): 16–24.

WORKS ABOUT OR REFERRING TO STAFFORD

Atlas, James. *Delmore Schwartz: The Life of an American Poet.* New York: Avon Books, 1978.

Auchincloss, Louis. *Pioneers and Caretakers.* Boston: G. K. Hall & Co., 1985.

Aurthur, Robert Alan. "Hitting the Boiling Point, Freakwise, at East Hampton." *Esquire* 77 (June 1972).

Baker, Nina Brown. "Jean Stafford." *Wilson Library Bulletin* 25 (April 1951): 578.

Bond, Alice Dixon. "Fascination with Words Started Jean Stafford on Writing Career." *Boston Sunday Herald,* January 27, 1952.

Breit, Harvey. "Talk with Jean Stafford." *New York Times Book Review* 57 (January 20, 1952): 18.

Carroll, Walter. " 'Flummoxed' Author Finds Lot of Writer Excruciating." *Syracuse Post-Standard,* February 23, 1966.

Cavett, Dick, and Christopher Porterfield. "The Cavett Album — II." In *Eye on Cavett.* New York: Arbor House, 1983.

Chamberlain, John. "Young U.S. Writers." *Life* 22 (June 2, 1947): 75–82.

Claiborne, Craig. *Craig Claiborne's Memorable Meals.* New York: E. P. Dutton, 1985.

Cutrer, Thomas W. *Parnassus on the Mississippi: The Southern Review and the Baton Rouge Literary Community, 1935–1942.* Baton Rouge: Louisiana State University Press, 1984.

Davis, Linda. *Onward and Upward: A Biography of Katharine S. White.* New York: Harper & Row, 1987.

Eberhart, Richard. *The Mad Musician.* In *Collected Verse Plays of Richard Eberhart.* Chapel Hill: University of North Carolina Press, 1962.

Eckman, Fern Marja. "Adding a Pulitzer to the Collection." *New York Post,* May 9, 1970, magazine section.

Engle, William. "Lost Love of a Rebellious Lowell." *American Weekly,* August 22, 1948, 4.

Fitzgerald, Robert. "The Children." *The Nation* 164 (April 5, 1947): 399–400.

Flagg, Nancy. "People to Stay." *Shenandoah* 30 (Autumn 1979): 65–76.

Foley, Martha. "Novels and Short Stories of Jean Stafford." *Book Find News* [n.d.].

Gelfant, Blanche. "Reconsiderations: *The Mountain Lion,* by Jean Stafford." *New Republic* 172 (May 10, 1975): 22–25.

"Girl Student Shot Herself Late Saturday." *Boulder Daily Camera,* November 11, 1935.

Giroux, Robert. "Hard Years and 'Scary Days': Remembering Jean Stafford." *New York Times Book Review* 89 (June 10, 1984).

Hamilton, Ian. *Robert Lowell: A Biography.* New York: Random House, 1982.

Isaacs, Stan. "Searching for Significance in Some Years at 17." *Newsday,* December 14, 1972.

Lask, Thomas. "Jean Stafford, 63, Writer, Dead; 'Collected Stories' Won Pulitzer." *New York Times,* March 28, 1979, section B.

Lewis, Sue. "An Interview with One of Our Local Pulitzer Prize Winners." [Newspaper uncertain; ca. May 1970].

Lowell, Robert. *Collected Prose.* Edited by Robert Giroux. New York: Farrar, Straus & Giroux, 1987.

———. *Day by Day.* New York: Farrar, Straus & Giroux, 1977.

————. *Land of Unlikeness*. Cummington, Mass.: Cummington Press, 1944.

————. *Life Studies*. New York: Vintage Books, 1956.

————. *Lord Weary's Castle and The Mills of the Kavanaughs*. New York: Harcourt, Brace & World, 1951.

McConahay, Mary Davidson. " 'Heidelberry Braids' and Yankee *Politesse:* Jean Stafford and Robert Lowell Reconsidered." *Virginia Quarterly Review* 62 (Spring 1986): 213–236.

Moss, Howard. "Jean: Some Fragments." *Shenandoah* 30 (Autumn 1979): 77–84.

Oates, Joyce Carol. "The Interior Castle: The Art of Jean Stafford's Short Fiction." *Shenandoah* 30 (Autumn 1979): 61–64.

Pinkham, Marjorie Stafford. "A Look Backward at Covina and West Covina." *Mt. San Antonio Historian* 16 (Spring 1980): 78–89.

————. "Jean Stafford's Family." Typescript, 1984. A condensed version appeared as "Jean" in *Antaeus* 52 (Spring 1984): 7–32.

Roberts, David. "Beautiful and Damned." *Boston Globe Magazine,* December 18, 1983.

————. "The Failed Escape." *New England Monthly* 4 (August 1987): 64–67.

Schaffner, V. "Springs Author Zaps Media." *East Hampton Star,* August 15, 1974, section 2.

Schwartz, Delmore. *Letters of Delmore Schwartz*. Edited by Robert Phillips. Princeton, N.J.: Ontario Review Press, 1984.

Sheed, Wilfrid. "The Good Word." *New York Times Book Review* 78 (March 4, 1973).

————. "Miss Jean Stafford." *Shenandoah* 30 (Autumn 1979): 92–99.

Simpson, Eileen. *Poets in Their Youth*. New York: Random House, 1982.

Sokolov, Raymond. *Wayward Reporter: The Life of A. J. Liebling*. New York: Harper & Row, 1980.

Stern, Linda. "Jean Stafford on Writing, Language, Women's Lib. . . ." *Barnard Bulletin,* March 10, 1971, 7.

Stewart, Phyllis. "Author Adds a Pulitzer to Collection." *Long Island Press,* May 31, 1970.

Stillman, Joan [Joan Cuyler]. Notes of interview with JS, October 16–17, 1952. Typescript.

Straus, Dorothea. "Jean Stafford." *Shenandoah* 30 (Autumn 1979): 85–91.

Taylor, Carol. "Girls Write Their Different Tickets." *New York World-Telegram,* December 5, 1947.

Taylor, Mary Darlington. "Jean Stafford's Novel — 'A Superb Literary Accomplishment.' " *Bridgeport Sunday Post,* January 13, 1952.

Taylor, Peter. "A Commemorative Tribute to Jean Stafford." *Shenandoah* 30 (Autumn 1979): 56–60.

————. "1939." In *The Collected Stories of Peter Taylor*. New York: Penguin Books, 1986.

Thompson, John. "Robert Lowell 1917–1977." *New York Review of Books* 24 (October 27, 1977): 14–15.

Vidal, Gore. "Ladders to Heaven: Novelists and Critics of the 1940's." In *Rocking the Boat*. Boston: Little, Brown and Company, 1962.

Walsh, Mary Ellen Williams. *Jean Stafford*. Boston: Twayne Publishers, 1985.

Whitman, Alden. "Jean Stafford and Her Secretary 'Harvey' Reigning in Hamptons." *New York Times,* August 26, 1973, 78.

Wolcott, James. "Blowing Smoke into the Zeitgeist." *Harper's* 266 (June 1983): 57–59.

———. "Dissecting Our Decline." *Esquire* 97 (March 1982): 136.

Wood, Michael. "Neglected Fictions." *Times Literary Supplement,* October 18, 1985, 1186.

Index